W9-ACQ-098

# UNDERSTANDING MASS COMMUNICATION

UNIVERSITY OF NEW HAVEN LIBRARY

# UNDERSTANDING MASS COMMUNICATION

## *A Liberal Arts Perspective*

### SIXTH EDITION

**Melvin L. DeFleur**

Boston University

**Everette E. Dennis**

Fordham University

**Houghton Mifflin Company**    BOSTON    NEW YORK

Sponsoring Editor: George T. Hoffman
Editorial Assistant: Kara Maltzahn
Packaging Services Supervisor: Charline Lake
Senior Production/Design Coordinator: Sarah Ambrose
Senior Manufacturing Coordinator: Marie Barnes
Marketing Manager: Pamela J. Laskey

Cover design: Linda Wade, Wade Design
Cover image: Linda Wade, Wade Design

For permission to use copyrighted materials, grateful acknowledgment is made to the copyright holders listed on page 588, which is hereby considered an extension of this copyright page.

Copyright © 1998 by Houghton Mifflin Company. All rights reserved.

No part of this work may be reproduced or transmitted in any form or by any means, electronic or mechanical, including photocopying and recording, or by any information storage or retrieval system without the prior written permission of Houghton Mifflin Company unless such copying is expressly permitted by federal copyright law. Address inquiries to College Permissions, Houghton Mifflin Company, 222 Berkeley Street, Boston, MA 02116-3764.

Printed in the U.S.A.

Library of Congress Catalog Card Number: 97-72459

ISBN: 0-395-87112-3

123456789–QH–01 00 99 98 97

# ▼ Brief Contents

# ▼ Contents

## Part One ▼ *Print Media* 29

## PART THREE ▼ *Media Industries and Audiences* 235

## PART FOUR ▼ *Media Influences and Issues 425*

# PREFACE

This sixth edition of *Understanding Mass Communication* has been significantly changed from previous editions. New chapters have been added, existing ones have been extensively modified, and those retained from the fifth edition have been updated in terms of their data about the media and their references to published works. Important new features have been added to the book to make it easier for the student to understand the nature and functions of contemporary mass media and the influences that they have on us as individuals and as a society.

## Focus of the Book

*Understanding Mass Communication* amply covers the nuts and bolts of daily media content and how it is processed and delivered to a variety of audiences who selectively attend. Considerable attention is given to the ways in which professional communicators function within each media setting. However, *Understanding Mass Communication* differs from many of its competitors in that it is organized around three broad questions that go well beyond what a beginner's survey needs to include. These questions place each of the media within a broad *liberal arts perspective*. That perspective draws on concepts and conclusions derived from many disciplines that have helped us to understand the process and effects of mass communications. The three broad questions to which the book is addressed are

1. *How have our American mass media come to be organized in the way that they have*? What demographic, economic, political, and technological factors have shaped our nation's privately owned, profit-oriented mass media in such a way that they attract wide audiences mainly by presenting popular culture and entertainment?

2. *How do American mass media actually function*? How do professional communicators in each of the major media decide on the content that they select, modify it, and present it in various ways, using a variety of technologies so as to reach specific kinds of audiences?

3. *What effect does this flow of information from media to audiences have on us, both individually and collectively*? Does it have only minor influences on our thoughts and behavior as individuals and modify our culture and society in only limited ways? Or, is mass communication a powerful force that shapes both individual conduct and our nation's history?

## New to the Sixth Edition

This edition of *Understanding Mass Communication* has new chapters and distinctive features that are not found in earlier versions of this text or in similar books. Specifically, two completely new chapters have been added. Chapter 8, "The New Media," is organized around the great changes and convergences in our media system brought on by the digital transition, the widespread adoption of computers by Americans, and the rapid growth of the Internet with its World Wide Web. Chapter 14, "International Media," discusses the global reach of contemporary media and the changes that they bring throughout the world.

An important feature retained and expanded from the fifth edition is "Explaining Media Effects." These boxed inserts provide brief introductions to sixteen different *theories of mass communication*. Each is stated in the form of five basic propositions. The explanation and background of each theory is presented at a level that can be readily understood by beginning students. These theories address a question that such students often ask but to which they seldom receive clear answers: namely, how do mass media function and how does their content influence us, both as individuals and as a society? The theories show students that, as a result of scholarly analyses and massive amounts of research, we can now explain many aspects of how the media process and deliver content, how people respond to what the media provide, and what kinds of influences the media have on them. Each theory deals with a separate kind of process or effect. Each is also integrated into relevant issues discussed in the body of the text.

An important feature called "Trends in Media Use" has been retained and upgraded. Each trend includes a brief explanation to aid in interpretation of the charted numerical information. These trends and their accompanying charts show how Americans have increasingly or decreasingly used a particular medium over the years. The overall lesson presented by these materials is that we live in a complex and ever-changing media environment and that it is very unlikely that the specific technologies we have in our homes at present will be the same as those we will use in the future.

Chapter summaries are provided at the end of each chapter in the form of bulleted lists. These serve as aids to students in identifying the major points made.

The sixth edition continues to include a series of boxed inserts entitled "Media and the Liberal Arts." These brief essays explain significant issues that link the media to the traditional arts, sciences, and humanities. The overall lesson provided by this feature is that mass communication is not just a professional field to be studied only by those who will enter its labor force to pursue occupational careers. It is a field whose development and contemporary issues are intimately linked to major aspects of American history and closely intertwined with a host of topics that are central to the classical and liberal traditions at the heart of American higher education.

## Acknowledgments

The authors would like to acknowledge the contribution of Paul Anderson, not only in the instructor's manual he prepared, but also for the many suggestions he has offered concerning ways to improve our book. An important contribution was made by Margaret DeFleur, who permitted us to use a number of the theories she developed for her forthcoming book. Thanks also to the following people for suggestions and critiques that have been incorporated into the sixth edition: Michael Elasmar, Edward Downes, Philip Napioli, John Schulz, Brent Baker, Shaila Sayed Afzal, Charles Barber, Carrie Klein, Cate Dolan, Dirk Smillie, Larry Norman, and Deborah Rogers.

We also want to thank the following prerevision reviewers:

Mario J. Acerra
*Northampton Community College*

Janice M. Long
*University of Cincinnati*

John Doolittle
*American University*

Jacob Matovu
*Appalachian State University*

Margaret J. Haefner
*Illinois State University*

Paul Bowers
*Buena Vista University*

## To The Student

This book has been prepared by its two authors as a tool for you. Our goal has been to help you understand the increasingly important part played by mass communications in our society as part of your personal intellectual development. We sincerely hope that you find the book interesting and that it serves you well. If it does not, we will have to share part of the blame. For that reason, if you find any parts of this book to be difficult to understand, if we have failed to touch on matters that you feel are important, or if we have dwelled too long on issues that do not deserve such extensive treatment, we would like to hear from you. In fact, we would be delighted if you would offer any suggestions as to how we can make this book better. To that end, after you have finished any chapter or the whole book, we invite you to write or send us an e-mail message and offer any kind of criticism or comments that you feel are important. You will have our full attention!

Melvin L. DeFleur,
College of Communication
Boston University
640 Commonwealth Avenue
Boston, MA 02215
e-mail: defleur@bu.edu

Everette E. Dennis,
Graduate School of Business
Fordham University at Lincoln Center
113 West 60th Street
New York, NY 10023
e-mail: edennis@bschool.bnet.fordham.edu

# UNDERSTANDING MASS COMMUNICATION

# Introduction

## The Nature of Mass Communication

*U*sing technology of breathtaking sophistication, today's mass media reach audiences whose numbers stagger the imagination. More than one billion people viewed the last World Cup soccer championship game on TV—more than have ever seen one of Shakespeare's plays performed on a stage since they were first written in the late 1500s. About sixty million Americans will read a newspaper today. A popular first-run movie will be seen by tens of millions. With such massive numbers attending to the media, it is little wonder that many thoughtful people are concerned about how readers, listeners, and viewers are influenced by what they see and hear.

For many in those audiences—clearly the majority—the mass media are mainly a source of entertainment. People turn to television for their favorite game show, the newspaper for the sports pages, the radio for popular music, a paperback novel for relaxation, their computer for on-line interests, or the movies for an action adventure. Generally, recreational users of the media do not worry much about the effects of mass communication on society, or even on their own behavior. If they criticize the media, it is with complaints that they cannot find enough of their favorite type of TV program, they did not like the last movie they saw, or they are bored by the news.

A more thoughtful segment of the public realizes how deeply embedded the media are in modern life and is concerned about how their content influences us both individually and collectively. Are those influences beneficial, harmless, or hazardous? Moreover, how does one tell? These people want to understand how our media operate, what influences they have on both children and adults, and how much control we actually have over their content. They are concerned about such issues as violence, sexual depictions, and vulgar language—and how such content will affect their children. Obviously, these complex questions have no quick and easy answers. Nevertheless, enough information is available from media researchers, scholars, and other sources that we can gain some perspective on the functioning and influences of the mass media in American society. Indeed, providing information for understanding our contemporary mass media, how they were shaped by the American society, how they function today, and how their content influences audiences is a major goal of this book.

## ▼ *Mass Communication In Contemporary Society*

Any attempt at understanding mass communication in modern life must begin with the recognition that our media are an essential part of our society and of our personal daily lives. There is simply no way we can get along

# EXPLAINING MEDIA EFFECTS
## *Media Information Dependency Theory*

People in contemporary urban-industrial societies, such as ours, make heavy use of the content of our mass media. They read newspapers, magazines and books; they go to the movies, watch television, rent films for their VCRs, and listen to the radio. In part, they do this because they enjoy media content. However, people in modern society have come to rely on mass communications for all kinds of information that they would find difficult to obtain from other sources. They turn to the media (far more often than to neighbors, friends, and family) for entertainment. They do so when they want to find out the latest news, or how to interpret it. They also turn to the media to find out where they can purchase things they need at the best prices, to locate suitable housing, to obtain many kinds of services, to seek employment, or sometimes to find someone to date or even marry.

A major reason for this *media information dependency* is that we live in a society in which networks of interpersonal ties are not as deeply established as they once were in preindustrial societies. Although in contemporary "mass" societies we do retain family ties and networks of friendships, we receive only a limited amount of information through them. Moreover, they are

not as extensive and open as was the case in the older traditional societies, where people lived together in small communities generation after generation without mass media.

In modern life, people of many diverse backgrounds live in physical proximity to each other, but with extensive differences based on ethnicity, race, education, income, religion, and other characteristics. Such social and cultural differences pose many barriers to interpersonal communication. This tends to inhibit the free flow of information between people and leads them to turn to other sources to get the information they need. As a consequence, in large part it is the mass media today that fill these needs, creating a condition of dependency on mass communications. This explanation of the relationship between the content of the mass media, the nature of society and the communications behavior of audiences is called **media information dependency theory,** and its major propositions can be summed up in the following terms:[2]

**1.** People in all societies *need information* in order to make numerous decisions about such matters as food, shelter, employment, transportation, political issues, entertainment, and other aspects of daily life.

**2.** In traditional societies, people tend to pursue similar ways of life and are linked to *word-of-mouth* networks of extended families, deeply-established friendships, long-term neighbors and other social ties from which they obtain information they need.

**3.** In urban-industrial societies, populations are composed of unlike people brought together through internal migrations and external immigrations. They are *greatly differentiated* by race, ethnicity, occupational specialization, and complex economic classes.

**4.** Because of their far greater social differentiation, people in urban-industrial societies have *fewer* effective word-of-mouth channels based on deeply-established networks of social ties through which they can obtain the information needed in daily life.

**5.** Therefore, people in urban-industrial societies become *dependent* on mass communications for information needed to make many kinds of decisions as the mass media provide them with a flow of information, advice, and role models through news, advertising, and entertainment content, which they use as a basis for many decisions.

without them, other than by returning to a way of life such as people led before the industrial revolution. Any discussion of the mass media, then, begins with the recognition that we are very *dependent* on their presence and their content.[1]

Dependence on the media is both social and personal. At the *societal* level, the media play an indispensable part in all of our social institutions—economic, political, educational, religious, and family. They provide jobs for millions of workers in the media industries and indirectly they enable additional millions of family wage-earners to earn a living in media-dependent activities. For example, virtually every business or industry of any size selling goods or services is dependent on the media for their advertising. Whether one likes advertising or not, large numbers of people are directly employed in its labor force. Moreover, without advertising people would never know what products exist and goods and services would not sell. The same dependency is true of public relations—that professional activity would be impossibly restricted without mass media. Whatever the popular view of public relations is, it is essential in a society that must have trust in the for-profit and nonprofit groups that produce the products and services people require and use every day. Similarly, industries such as spectator sports and popular entertainment are uniquely media dependent. For example, the popular music industry is deeply dependent on radio, movies, and television. Without them, neither the performers nor the recording business could survive.

Mass communication has also become a central part of American politics. Candidates gain exposure for themselves and their ideas through the media. In fact, electing a president these days would be dreadfully cumbersome if candidates had no other means of campaigning than traveling around the country making speeches from tree stumps and railroad platforms, as they did before electronic media were available.

The list could go on and on: Even educational and religious groups make extensive use of the media. Families depend on media for recreation and diversion. The popular culture that the media present is consumed on a daily basis as viewing television, going to the movies, and reading print media remain a central part of modern family life. In a less visible way, as large profit-making industries in their own right, the media provide investment opportunities for many Americans, either through direct stock ownership or indirect participation in retirement fund portfolios.

Media dependency extends to a more *personal* level because we make heavy use of mass-communicated information in our day-to-day existence as individuals. We listen to the radio as a background for many kinds of work and recreation. We look to the newspaper for all kinds of consumer information, from the best buys at the supermarket and the used-car lot to stock market quotations and job openings. During the day millions of us follow the latest adventures in a favorite soap opera. As we drive to work or do chores at home, we catch the latest tunes and news bulletins on the radio. At night we may surf the Internet for information. Books and magazines bring us specialized information needed for school, hobbies, or in-depth understanding of public affairs. Thus, individuals use the mass media day-in and day-out to gratify the need for entertainment or enlightenment, as well as for other practical purposes.

There is, however, another, darker side to this dependency. The effects of the media may be *bad*, claim some critics. They warn us that mass communication

Much of the public's fears and concerns about the mass media focuses on their potential influence on children. It is widely assumed by parents and others that television can cause children to become violent and can erode their moral character. Politicians anxious to please the voters are sensitive to such concerns and regularly initiate policies to try to limit what the medium can offer. The First Amendment, however, prevents censorship of the media. (Copyright © Michael Newman/PhotoEdit)

may be doing things to us that we really do not want. Some say that media content makes our children more violent; weakens our moral character; controls our beliefs, attitudes, and opinions; leads us to buy things we do not need; and heavily influences many of the decisions that we think we make independently.

Other media analysts claim the media are forces for *good* in society. They say that the media enrich our lives and bring us all closer together, provide us with satisfying, stress-relieving entertainment, and make us more aware of important public issues and problems. These analysts maintain that the media help us understand social problems, enlighten us politically, improve our aesthetic tastes for good music and theater, and aid in rooting out bad or incompetent behavior of those in government.

Most of us suspect that all these conflicting claims are true, and that the media produce both positive *and* negative effects—not only on us but on our neighbors and friends, and beyond them, on the nation and even the world. We understand that because the media are complex and present many kinds of content, for a variety of purposes, to people in all walks of life, there are bound to be controversies as to their influences and effects.

## ▼ Fundamentals of Human Communication

Language and its use are at the heart of the process by which mass communication takes place. To understand that process more fully, we must first look at how human communication takes place in the *absence* of media—that is, what are the fundamentals of face-to-face human communication? With that analysis as a basis for comparison, we will take a close look at mass communication. This, in turn, will permit a comparison of the two and a fuller understanding of the advantages, limitations, and effects of communicating with our contemporary media.

Human beings communicate in ways that are very different from those of any other species on our planet. Specifically, we communicate with some form of learned and shared verbal and nonverbal language that is part of a culture that has accumulated and grown increasingly complex over time. Other species communicate with signs and signals in ways that have changed little since the dawn of their existence. In spite of romantic ideas about whales, porpoises, and other animals that supposedly "talk," animals do not use languages based on culturally shared systems of symbols, grammar, and meanings. Animals clearly do communicate with each other, sometimes in relatively sophisticated ways. However, they do so with behavioral systems that in most cases are inherited, and in some cases learned, but that are never part of a culture in the true sense. In other words, no matter how one looks at it, in any realistic sense, only human beings communicate with language based on shared cultural rules.[3]

## The Origins of Language

If we count a human generation as about thirty years on average, we need go back only about two thousand grandmothers ago to come to a time when our prehistoric ancestors did not use language as we know it. Early human beings, such as *australopithecus, homo habilis,* and *homo erectus,* clearly did not speak. In fact, they *could not* because the structure of their voice boxes was like that of modern apes and chimpanzees.[4] They could make vocal noises, as do their anthropoid counterparts today, but the human anatomy of the time did not permit them the delicate control over vocal sounds that are required for speech. That anatomical limitation continued even through the more recent era of the Neanderthal *(homo sapiens, neanderthalensis),* who inhabited wide areas of our planet starting about 150 to 125 thousand years ago. The Neanderthal apparently were able to communicate reasonably well, but they had to do so with gestures, body movements, and a limited number of sounds that they were capable of making.

Between about ninety and thirty-five thousand years ago, the Neanderthal were replaced by a very different type of human being. These were the Cro-Magnon *(homo sapiens, sapiens),* our direct ancestors. If dressed in modern clothes, they would be indistinguishable from people today. Because they had the same larynx, voice box, tongue, and lip structures as do modern people, the Cro-Magnon were able to generate and control voice sounds in intricate ways.[5] This made it possible for them to speak and develop language. Thus, the use of complex languages began about forty thousand years ago, give or take a few thousand years. This was a relatively recent development in the several mil-

Although there seems little doubt that our earliest human ancestors, such as the *Australopithecene* family depicted here, were able to communicate, they were undoubtedly limited to nonverbal signs and signals.

lions of years of the evolutionary history of our species.[6] It was the first great communication revolution.

The subsequent development of increasingly efficient and flexible systems for storing, recovering, and disseminating information through the use of various media provided additional revolutions. At first, each step took thousands of years. Few people today are even aware of that long history, or of the great breakthroughs that each step required—first language, then writing, the alphabet, portable media, books, print, newspapers, telegraph, film, radio, television in various forms, computers, and the rest. With those media in place today, human beings can use language and media together to conquer time and distance in ways that would have defied even the wildest imagination of people only a few generations back.

## The Use of Verbal and Nonverbal Symbols

In our current age of mass communication, we still communicate, whether face-to-face or through media, by using verbal and nonverbal *symbols*. A **symbol** is a word, action, or object that "stands for" and arouses standardized internal meanings in people in a given language community. By an established convention (a well-established rule) each symbol—such as "dog," "child," or even complex terms like "carcinogen" and "biodegradable"—is supposed to arouse similar internal meaning experiences in everyone who uses it. In a similar way, actions, such as gestures and facial expressions, can be governed by meaning conventions. The same is true of certain objects, such as a cross, a Star of David, or a wedding ring.

Language also includes rules for putting symbols together in patterns that themselves arouse meanings. The familiar rules of *grammar* establish standard ways for linking and modifying classes of symbols (like verbs, pronouns, and adjectives) to give more precision and flexibility to their use in complex messages. Another common category of rules, called **syntax,** provides for ordering symbols so as to make the meanings clear. For example, syntax determines whether you say "the ball struck the man" or "the man struck the ball." Other familiar rules are those for **pronunciation**—socially accepted ways to make the sounds for words.

## Human Communication: A Basic Linear Model

Although symbols, conventions of meaning, grammar, syntax, and pronunciation are all important, they do not provide a basic perspective on exactly how human beings communicate. To gain a more complete overview of what takes place when people engage in an act of communication, let us first analyze the process in terms of six specific stages (Figure 1.1) that take place in the following order:

1. The act of human communication begins with a "sender" who decides to *initiate* a message that expresses a specific set of intended meanings.
2. That sender *encodes* the intended meanings by selecting specific words and gestures whose conventionalized interpretations the receiver will presumably understand.
3. The message is then *transmitted*—spoken or written so as to cross the space between sender and receiver as a signal of patterned information.
4. The "receiver," the individual to whom the message is directed, attends to and *perceives* the incoming patterned information, identifying it as a specific language message.
5. The receiver then *decodes* the message by constructing his or her own interpretations of the conventionalized meanings of the symbols.
6. As a result of interpreting the message, the receiver is *influenced* in some way. The communication has some effect that can range from trivial to profound.

These actions describe a *basic linear model* of the human communication process. Although it is obvious that such a model greatly oversimplifies the process, its value is that it permits us to understand each of the stages represented. Looked at in this somewhat artificial way, the communicative act begins, goes through the stages one at a time, and then stops—like a tape recorder being turned on and off.

In reality, the human conversations that we engage in with people around us are much more complex. Most face-to-face human conversations are *transac-*

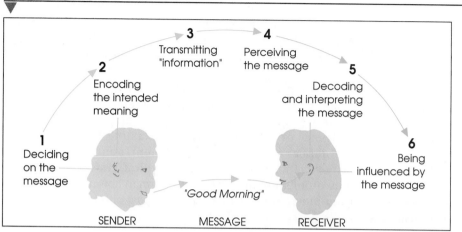

**Figure 1.1**
**A Basic Linear Model of**
**Human Communication**

*tional* in that each party encodes and decodes messages at the same time and is alert to all kinds of cues from the other person.[7] Many factors influence the process. What has already been said plays a key part in what comes next. In addition, the meanings constructed by each party are influenced by the relationship between sender and receiver (friends, boss–worker, parent–child, etc.). Moreover, the sociocultural situation and even the physical surroundings can influence the meanings constructed by both parties (for example, a conversation at a homecoming party versus one at a funeral).

In spite of its simplicity and obvious limitations, the basic linear model is useful for *analyzing* the communication process, breaking it down into its distinct stages so as to understand what happens at each. Also, those stages are at the heart of the complex transactions of any conversation. Both parties can be simultaneously encoding, transmitting, and decoding, and also serving as senders and receivers, initiating and receiving messages. In other words, the six stages previously noted are *embedded* within the complexities of simultaneous transactional communication. Thus, the basic linear model simplifies the task of looking carefully at each stage of the process separately so as to see exactly how people use symbols and conventions of meaning to accomplish the act of human communication.

## Communicating Complex Messages

Thus far we have explained the act of human communication at a very simple level. However, there are three deficiencies in our explanation. First, common sense tells us that most instances of interpersonal communication are far more complex than our linear model suggests. Second, the meanings may not match— that is, one person may fail to understand what another person is saying, even with a simple message, because there are various sources of inaccuracy that are difficult to control. Finally, as we have suggested, communication is a simultaneous back-and-forth, or *interactive*, process. People are not merely passive and linear senders and receivers. They respond to the content of others' meanings, ask for clarification, and indicate agreement. Thus, we need to understand how each person shifts roles to become a sender at one moment and a receiver at another.

In addition, we noted earlier that we normally put words together into sentences, paragraphs, and various constructions using accepted rules of *grammar* and *syntax*. These patterns themselves introduce meanings that go beyond those associated with each of the words used. For example, the pattern "The boy killed the snake" implies a meaning totally different from the pattern "The snake killed the boy," even though the words are identical. However, these patterns pose no serious problem in understanding human communication. We learn the patterns and their associated meanings as part of our language, just as we learn the meanings of each word.

## Communicating Accurately

As just suggested, the meanings intended by communicators and those interpreted by receivers may not be perfectly parallel. In that case, the communication has suffered a loss of *accuracy*. In fact, a perfect match between the meanings of both parties is unlikely, perhaps with the exception of trivial messages. In a common-sense way, then, loss of accuracy can be defined as any reduction in the correspondence between the details of the sender's intended message and those of the receiver's interpreted message.

**The accuracy principle.**   There can be many causes of a loss of accuracy between meanings. It can result from dim light, poor acoustics, disruptive sounds, or any other physical condition that interferes with the transfer of information. Limited accuracy can also result from memory failure, faulty perception, or unfamiliarity with the language. Or, it may happen when the sender and receiver do not share the same cultural rules for the use of language—a common problem in a multicultural society. In other words, inaccuracy can arise from any physical, psychological, social, or cultural condition that reduces similarities between the intended meanings of the sender and the interpreted meanings of the receiver.

If accuracy suffers, from whatever sources, the communication will be less effective in achieving the goals of the communicator. Inaccuracy can be a problem in interpersonal communication, and as will be made clear, it can be devastating in mass communication. This conclusion regarding accuracy and its consequences can be stated more formally as a rather common-sense generalization which we can call the **accuracy principle:**

> The lower the level of correspondence between the intended meanings of the sender and the interpreted meanings of the receiver, the less effective an act of communication will be in achieving either mutual understanding or an intended influence.

Clearly, then, it is important for both the sender and the receiver to strive for accuracy if they are to achieve either goal of understanding or influence. How, though, aside from careful selection of words and thoughtful organization of a message, can communication be made more accurate? Actually, in interpersonal communication there are two very effective ways: One is by the receiver's providing *feedback,* and the other by the sender's engaging in *role-taking.* As we will see, these two ideas have profound implications for understanding the differences between face-to-face and mass communication.

**The feedback principle.**   Usually, interpersonal communication is an ongoing process that goes back and forth between the parties. For example, you start to explain something to a friend and at some point your friend may frown or shrug as you are talking. Seeing this, you sense that he or she may not have understood very well. So, you try to explain that point in a different way or provide a brief example as you continue with your account. Your friend then nods and you conclude that you have made it clear. In such a face-to-face situation, the sender is ever alert to observable verbal and nonverbal signals coming back from the receiver. These cues provide **feedback**—essentially a reverse communication by the receiver back to the communicator that indicates whether the message is getting through. In face-to-face communication, the receiver usually provides both verbal and nonverbal feedback on an ongoing basis to influence the communicator's selection of words, gestures, and meanings. Thus, the two parties alternately become both sender and receiver as the messages of one stimulates feedback from the other.

Television has reshaped American politics. Before TV, only a few Americans saw presidential candidates in motion pictures. Most knew little about their personalities, speaking styles, and mannerisms. Today, voters come to know every feature of a candidate, from his or her facial blemishes, hairstyle, and dental health, to the way in which the individual phrases ideas in speeches, press conferences, and informal interviews. (Reuters/ Corbis-Bettmann)

Feedback may be deliberate or not. In any event, the communicator takes feedback into account to try to increase communication accuracy. This idea is important. Stated simply, feedback leads to greater accuracy in communication. Conversely, without feedback, accuracy is likely to suffer. This can be stated as a second important generalization, which we can call the **feedback principle:**

> If ongoing and immediate feedback is provided by the receiver, accuracy will be increased; that is, the intended meanings of the communicator have a better chance of being similar to those constructed by the receiver.

**The role-taking principle.**    When a sender correctly interprets feedback cues from the intended receiver and adjusts the message in order to increase accuracy, the communicator figuratively places himself or herself in the receiver's shoes. Stated in another way, mentally, the sender tries to *be* the receiver in order to understand how he or she is likely to respond to the message being transmitted. In this process, called **role-taking,** the sender tries to understand how the message looks from the other person's point of view and to modify it where needed to increase accuracy. Thus, role-taking can be defined as the use of feedback by the sender to judge which words and nonverbal cues will work best to arouse the intended meanings in the receiver.

Some people are better at role-taking than others. Also, some situations are better suited for it than others. Role-taking can be most effective in close, personal, and intimate situations where the communicating parties know each other well. It is most limited and ineffective in interpersonal situations where strangers are trying to communicate. These considerations lead to a third generalization, which we can call the **role-taking principle:**

> In communication situations where the sender can engage in sensitive role-taking, accuracy is increased; that is, meanings intended by the sender more closely match those constructed by the receiver.

In summary, what these three principles tell us is that: (1) Face-to-face communication is accurate to the extent that adequate feedback cues are provided by the receiver. (2) Accuracy depends on the extent to which the communicator uses role-taking appropriately to formulate the message in terms that are likely to be well understood by the receiver. These principles governing the relationship between feedback, role-taking, and accuracy in the case of interpersonal communication need to be kept in mind as we turn to an analysis of the nature of mass communication. As we will see, it is with respect to these issues that the two kinds of communication differ considerably.

## ▼ *The Mass Communication Process*

Communicating with media is not new. As Figure 1.2 suggests, human beings have used various technologies to preserve messages in time or to send them over distances for thousands of years. In spite of their speed and audience size,

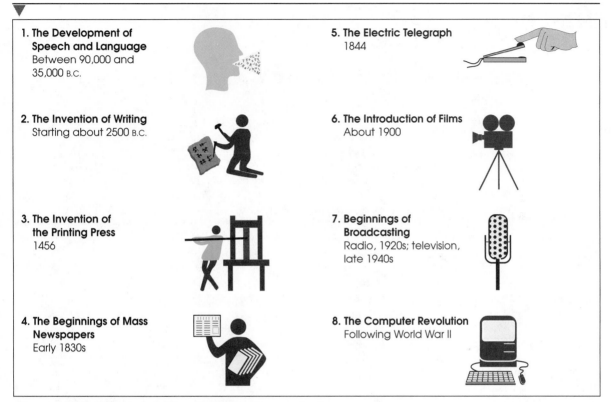

1. **The Development of Speech and Language**
Between 90,000 and 35,000 B.C.

2. **The Invention of Writing**
Starting about 2500 B.C.

3. **The Invention of the Printing Press**
1456

4. **The Beginnings of Mass Newspapers**
Early 1830s

5. **The Electric Telegraph**
1844

6. **The Introduction of Films**
About 1900

7. **Beginnings of Broadcasting**
Radio, 1920s; television, late 1940s

8. **The Computer Revolution**
Following World War II

**Figure 1.2 Significant Transitions in Human Communication**

today's mass media still perform the same functions as their more primitive predecessors. Like the stone walls on which hieroglyphics were carved, the smoke signals of Native Americans, or the jungle drums of earlier times, modern media move *information* across either time or space. Information consists of a patterned physical signal corresponding to a message. Such information should not be confused with the meaning of the message. One example of information is the patterned sound waves we can hear when people speak to us. Both the speaker and the receiving person have to construct their own meanings of those physical signals, using their memories of their shared language. In more complex and contemporary media, information is transmitted as particular patterns of electronic radiations, as in radio, or as in the light waves we use to read, watch television, or view a movie. Only human beings can transform meanings in their heads into such signals, or as receivers, decode them back into a similar internal experience.

Using media that can reach huge audiences more or less simultaneously adds still additional complexities. To help in discussing and clarifying the nature of the mass communication process making use of such media, it will be helpful to develop a formal definition of mass communication. At first glance,

## *Media and the Liberal Arts*

### Consequences of the First Great Communications Revolution
A Linchpin to Cultural Anthropology

When you got up this morning, dressed, ate breakfast, and traveled to school, you probably made use of a host of physical objects and technologies that were first developed by ancient people. Many were innovations that arose during what anthropologists now call the Neolithic period, or the New Stone Age. The people of that time were the beneficiaries of what we have called the first great communications revolution (to the Age of Speech and Language).

The Neolithic era began about 10,000 B.C. and was followed by the Bronze Age, beginning about 3000 B.C., and the Iron Age, which began about 700 B.C. Altogether these were times of extraordinary invention and remarkable cultural achieve-

ment, especially by comparison with the slow pace of earlier human cultural evolution.

The development of human culture quickened following the invention of language by the Cro-Magnon, who were the first human beings with anatomical features that permitted them to make the complex sounds required by speech. Using language enabled people of the Neolithic period not only to talk to each other but also to think and reason in complex ways. They could classify, analyze, generalize, and reach conclusions from premises. This helped them to devise solutions to many practical problems. Furthermore, they could pass on to succeeding generations the solutions they were able to invent.

What this means for us today is that we are still using versions, albeit much improved, or many inventions from the Neolithic period. For example, if this morning you put on cotton or wool clothing and shoes made of leather, you made use of two Neolithic innovations (weaving and leather tanning). If during breakfast you drank from a cup and ate off a plate, you employed objects whose origins are truly ancient (pottery was being made in Japan by 10,000 B.C.).

If you had bacon or sausage with your breakfast, you owe a debt to these early people. They were the first to domesticate animals (by about 7000 B.C.), an event that was part of the great transition from hunting-gathering economies to

this may seem unnecessary. After all, we are already familiar with such media as movies, newspapers, and television. However, when we use film, print, or broadcasting to communicate with large audiences, what is actually happening? Do all the media operate according to the same underlying principles of communication, or is each medium unique in some way? And in what ways are the principles underlying mass communication different from those for a face-to-face conversation between two people? These questions are critical to understanding the nature of mass communication.

We cannot define mass communication in a quick and simple way with just a sentence or two because each medium includes its own special kinds of communicators, technologies, groups, kinds of content, types of audiences, and effects. To develop a good definition of mass communication we must take all these aspects into account and proceed one step at a time, describing each of the major features before pulling them together. In the sections that follow, that is exactly our strategy. We will look at each "stage" in the mass communication process before combining all the stages into an overall basic definition. The first step is to explain how and why mass communication is a *linear process.*

farming and fixed village life. During the early part of the Neolithic period, people in various parts of the world began to plant, harvest, and store food from many kinds of crops. Thus, the wheat from which your toast was made, as well as the butter you spread on it, have Neolithic origins.

Another Neolithic innovation was the metal in the spoon you used to stir your cup of coffee or tea. The technology to make implements of metal (copper) was first developed about 5000 B.C. If you bought a newspaper with a coin on your way to school, you used an object that was developed about 3000 B.C. This list could go on and on. If you traveled to school in any kind of vehicle, you were once again part of a long tradition: the wheel was in use centuries before the birth of Christ.

Perhaps more important than all of these physical artifacts and technologies was the great transformation in social life that occurred when

Neolithic people began to live together in villages, towns, and cities. In time, some individuals became rich and others were forced into slavery. Occupational specialties developed, making the society far more diverse. Leaders rose to organize, coordinate, or control social life. Since productive land was valuable, military groups were organized to capture or hold it, and warfare became common. Increasingly sophisticated weapons came into use: the bronze sword, the two-wheeled chariot, the bow and arrow, body armor, and many others. Religions were devised to explain the origins of human life and the nature of the physical world. Governmental systems became increasingly complex so as to protect citizens, provide public services (such as roads), and, of course, collect taxes.

Thus, the first great communications revolution that took place after human beings learned to use language had enormous consequences

with which we still live today. Still other revolutions followed with the invention of writing and of printing. We are now in the midst of an even more profound alteration of human communication based on incredibly complex technologies that include various types of mass media, electronic systems, satellites, and computers. This revolution will inevitably enrich human life, just as did the complex transitions that occurred during the Neolithic period.

---

*Sources:* Peter J. Wilson, *The Domestication of the Human Species* (New Haven, Conn.: Yale University Press, 1988); Sara Anderson, *The Neolithic and Bronze Ages* (Princeton, N.J.; American School of Classical Studies at Athens, 1971); Robert L. Stigler, *The Old World: Early Man to the Development of Agriculture* (New York: St. Martin's Press, 1974); and Dan Lacy, *From Grunts to Gigabites* (Urbana: University of Illinois Press, 1996).

## The Linear Nature of Mass Communication

Mass communication can be conceptualized within an expanded version of the same linear model that helps explain face-to-face communication. Although each stage is far more complex, as we can see, the basic stages are similar in many ways:

1. Mass communication begins with senders who are "professional communicators." They *decide on the nature and goals of a message* to be presented to an audience via their particular medium. (That message may be a news report, an advertising campaign, a movie, or some other media presentation.)

2. The *intended meanings are encoded* by production specialists (such as a news team, film company, or a magazine staff). The encoding process includes not only the selection of verbal and nonverbal symbols, but also the special effects that are possible with a particular medium (such as sound, graphics, and color).

3. The *message is transmitted* as information through the use of specialized media technologies characteristic of print, film, or broadcasting to disseminate it as widely as possible.

▲

In mass communication, the first three stages of the linear model are much more complex than in the case of face-to-face, interpersonal communication. Professional communicators formulate, encode, and transmit messages of many kinds for a multitude of purposes to a great variety of receivers. (Copyright © 1990 Tom Benton, Impact Visuals)

4. *Large and diverse* (mass) *audiences* of individual receivers attend to the media and *perceive* the incoming information, decoding it into a message of conventionalized verbal and nonverbal symbols.

5. *Individual receivers* selectively *construct interpretations* of the message in such a way that they experience subjective meanings, which are to at least some degree parallel to those intended by the professional communicators.

6. As a result of experiencing these meanings, *receivers are influenced* in some way in their feelings, thoughts, or actions—that is, the communication has some effect.

These six stages provide not only a basic identification of what takes place in the process of mass communication, but also a convenient framework for defining it carefully. After discussing each stage more fully, we can formulate a rather precise definition of mass communication, enabling us to separate it clearly from other forms.

**Stage one: Deciding what to communicate to whom.**    The first stage in the mass communication process occurs when one or more *professional communicators* (senders) decide upon the nature and goals of a message to produce in a form suitable to be transmitted via a particular medium. Such communicators are specialists who make their living working for some part of the communication industry. There are a great many kinds—reporters, film directors, actors, authors, editorial writers, advertising executives, preachers, official spokespersons, and many more. These are people who gather, edit, or design media content—news, entertainment, dramas, advertising messages, public relations messages, political campaigns, and so forth.

**Stage two: Encoding media messages.** Professional communicators depend on a host of specialists to help formulate and produce, that is *encode*, intended meanings in their messages. Creative people—artists, authors, researchers, composers, copy writers, editors, and directors—shape and reshape messages into specific forms for eventual transmission. Technicians handle the mechanical and electronic aspects of the media. Commercial sponsors trying to sell their products supply funds to finance the production efforts. Other auxiliary groups supporting the professional communicators include agencies that prepare commercial advertising, wire services that provide news reports, polling groups that tell communicators how many people they are reaching, and researchers who discover better ways of getting the message across.

▲

Professional communicators include a large number of specialists whose task it is to generate and encode the messages transmitted by the media. In the case of TV news, far more stories flow in than can be used, and the news director has to select each program's agenda and sequence of presentation. This encoding process can affect what people perceive and how they are influenced. (Copyright © M. Schwartz/Image Works)

**Stage three: Transmitting media messages.** One of the major characteristics of mass communications is relatively *rapid dissemination.* Modern media are truly remarkable in their ability to move information across distance and time. Even books, the slowest of the media, are disseminated rapidly by comparison with earlier times. Centuries ago, months or even years of painstaking hand-lettering was required to reproduce a single *manu scriptus*; it took even longer for such a book to get to its ultimate users. Today high-speed presses can run off hundreds of thousands of copies of a book that can be distributed around the country in a matter of days. The same is true of the other media: once a film is produced, copies can be sent to theaters all over the country virtually overnight, to be seen within a few weeks by millions of viewers. Radio, television and computers, being virtually instantaneous, conquer vast distances without delay. As many as a billion people may see a single broadcast showing events occurring "live," (for example, the funeral of Princess Diana).

Besides being rapid, modern mass communication is usually *continuous* rather than sporadic; that is, the messages are sent on a scheduled basis, not on someone's whim. Newspapers appear every day, magazines weekly or monthly; publishers and movie producers provide a continuing flow of books and films to the public.

Although this is completely obvious, information transmission involves the use of *mass media*. We note this because it is important to understand exactly what such a medium is, and what it is not. Consistent with our earlier discussion, the definition of a medium (of any kind) is quite simple:

> A **medium** is any object or device used for communicating a message by moving patterned physical information over distance or preserving it through time.

Long before the age of print, film, broadcasting, and computer networks, people used media that could transmit messages over distance or preserve them through time. Prehistoric people used cave drawings that have lasted for fifteen thousand years or more. Many people used flags, smoke signals, drums, or handwritten manuscripts as media to extend their ability to communicate. Some of these media are still in use. Today, the media of mass communication are usually identified as those of *print, film,* and *broadcasting* (with associated cable and VCR technologies), along with *computer networks* that are now being added at a rapid pace. They depend on sophisticated, elaborate technologies, such as microwave transmission, computerized typesetting equipment, optic cables, high-speed modems, communications satellites, and the like.

Each medium has advantages and limitations that influence how it is used to disseminate information and messages. Print, for example, depends on learned skills of reading and writing. It would be silly to use print to communicate with a child who does not know how to read, or with a person who cannot speak your language. It would also be silly to try to transmit an opera via the newspaper, because television, video, and movies are much better than print at transmitting things like moving images and sounds.

**Stage four: Perceiving media messages.**   The "mass" in the term "mass communication" provides an important key to the way in which media messages are perceived by large and diverse audiences. It came to be part of the name of the process many years ago, and refers to the social nature of audiences rather than to their size. The meaning of the word *mass* grew out of beliefs concerning the nature of modern society that were popular among intellectuals early in this century. They believed that urban-industrial societies were increasingly made up of individuals whose social ties to others were slipping away. Such observers saw that the extended rural family, which included grandparents, aunts, uncles, and cousins, was breaking down as people flocked to the cities. They saw that immigration mixed people with different national origins, ethnic and racial characteristics, and distinctive cultural backgrounds. Concentrating such diverse groups together in cities, they assumed, would result in a society where social bonds between people would be weak, rather than strong as in earlier times. This, they thought, would result in a society composed of people who would maintain psychological distance from each other and *would not communicate readily* on a one-to-one basis.

Essentially, then, this is what was meant by a "mass society": one in which people act as socially isolated individuals rather than as members of families or other kinds of groups.[8] Thus, modern society was thought to be a kind of

The term "mass communication" implies a large and diverse audience. The term derives from the concept of a *mass society.* This refers not just to the idea that large numbers of people are involved, but to the fact that they do not have as many close personal ties to one another as was the case in earlier, more traditional settings. In earlier societies, people were bound closely by ties based on family, long-lasting friendships, and traditional loyalties to rulers. (Copyright © 1993 Ted Soqui, Impact Visuals)

"lonely crowd" made up of diverse people who did not know one another well, were not bound to one another by strong friendships, loyalties, or family ties, and who did not have an open flow of interpersonal communication.[9]

This kind of society, early students of mass communication thought, would form the audiences of receivers for the media that were developing at the beginning of this century. The importance of the "mass" idea is that individuals in such large, socially diverse audiences were thought to be particularly easy to influence—individual by individual—with the use of propaganda and other forms of mass communication content. Because each person was supposedly isolated, the assumption was that effects of mass media messages would not be softened by social influences from other sources, such as networks of friends and family members.

Today we no longer assume that audiences for the mass media are a "lonely crowd" made up of isolated individuals. Research by social scientists over several decades has shown that people in an urban and industrial society still maintain strong relationships with their families, friends, and other groups. They are not psychologically isolated individual receivers at the mercy of every form of propaganda that comes along. What they interpret from the mass media is heavily influenced by the people around them. In other words, the older ideas once attached to the word "mass" just do not accurately describe these audiences.

At the same time, it is very clear that American society is culturally diverse to a great degree. Because of its history of immigration, it is made up of literally hundreds of groups with different national, ethnic, or racial origins. Each brought, and retains to some degree, a somewhat distinct culture. The population is also highly stratified in terms of income, education, power, and prestige.

Different kinds of people have more or less of these characteristics. We can add the influence of age, gender, region, and occupation, and it is clear that receivers in American audiences for mass communications are exceedingly diverse.

This great social, economic, and cultural diversity is the basis of a huge range of tastes and interests in media content. Because of those differing tastes and interests, both attention to and perception of media messages is *highly selective.* What may appeal to and be attended to closely by an affluent resident of Italian-American origin living in a northeastern suburb may be totally ignored by a poor Cajun farmer living in rural Louisiana. Thus, attention to and perception of media messages is closely related to the social, cultural, and psychological characteristics of each individual receiver in the potential audience.

**Stage five: Decoding and interpreting media messages.** We have seen that the essence of human communication is the achievement of more or less parallel sets of meanings between those sending and those attending to the message—which holds true whether the communication is a face-to-face conversation or a television message transmitted to millions of viewers. We stressed that in person-to-person communication the receiver interprets the message by drawing on his or her own stored meanings for verbal and nonverbal symbols. The result is that the meanings constructed by the receiver may or may not be identical to those intended by the sender. That is also precisely the case in mass communication.

In an audience of great diversity it is to be expected that the multitude of receivers will also have a multitude of ways in which to assign meaning to an

▶

In our capitalistic economic system, for the most part the media are supported financially by advertising. Such messages are designed to persuade consumers to make choices desired by the communicator. Although some critics object, there are few alternatives to this arrangement—such as having media operated by government—that would be acceptable to the majority of Americans. (Copyright © B. Daemmrich/Image Works)

incoming mass-communicated message. The very social, cultural, and psychological characteristics that determine patterns of attention and perception will also determine how different kinds of people interpret the meaning of mass-communicated messages. For this reason, one person may be thrilled by a movie that seems dull and boring to another. Some people will find a particular news item exciting and important while others see it as uninteresting and insignificant. Still others will be moved by an advertisement to purchase a product that others regard as objectionable "clutter."

**Stage six: Influencing media audiences.**   The last stage in mass communication is the outcome of the preceding stages: As a result of interpreting the meaning of the message, receivers in the audience are *changed* in some way. The changes may or may not be immediately visible and can range from trivial to profound. Most are minor. But whatever their nature, they constitute precisely what is meant by the "effects" of the media, at least at an individual level. For example, a person may learn some relatively inconsequential new facts by hearing a favorable weather report on the radio. Thus, providing a person with information that he or she did not have is a change brought about by the medium. Or, again at a trivial level, a person may be entertained by reading the comics in the Sunday paper. In this case, causing a person to feel better is also a form of media influence.

Exposure to the content of mass communications can also change individuals in far more significant ways. Under some circumstances it can influence their beliefs, opinions, and attitudes—altering their thinking about public issues or political party preferences. Or, meanings aroused by media messages can alter people's actions—influencing them to buy, donate, dress differently, give up smoking, vote, go on a diet, or bring about many other forms of behavior.

Although significant changes of this kind usually occur in minor stages over a long period of time, these are the kinds of influences that concern critics of the media. Some believe that rock music encourages youngsters to use drugs, engage in sex, or adopt Satanism. Others charge that some television programs stimulate children to defy authority and act aggressively. It is not easy to prove or disprove such claims. At this point, research suggests the public's fears about such influences may be exaggerated. As later chapters show, such influences can occur, but when they do it is through a complex and long-term process.

At a social or *collective* rather than personal level, mass communication can change our culture. One example is language and its shared understandings. The media constantly introduce

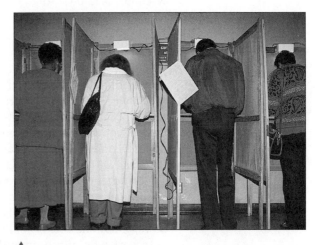

▲
The majority of citizens get most of their information about political candidates and their policies from the mass media. It is clear from decades of research that the media have a strong influence on the beliefs, attitudes, and actions of voters and thereby help shape the outcomes of elections. For that reason, most politicians are deeply sensitive to what the media report about them. (Copyright © J. Sohm/Image Works)

new words and their meanings, or alter the meanings of older words. For example, until about 1992, Americans did not have a shared meaning for the term "ethnic cleansing." However, after the wars in Serbia and Bosnia (in the former Yugoslavia) received wide media coverage, millions of people learned a new term and its meaning as a form of genocide. Other examples from recent decades are nerd, perestroika, AIDS, yuppies, crack, and sound-bite.

Mass communication can also change our feelings about social issues. The American news media's images of tanks and soldiers attacking demonstrating students in Beijing's Tiananmen Square in 1989 evoked widespread outrage toward China's leadership. Thus, the media play a part in swaying public opinion, and by doing so they help modify history. The study of the various kinds of effects of mass communications is a complex field. We will review such influences in detail in later chapters.

**A concise definition.**    Each of the six stages we have described must be part of a succinct definition of mass communication. With these stages in mind, we can define the process in the following terms:

> **Mass communication** is a process in which professional communicators design and use media to disseminate messages widely, rapidly, and continuously to arouse intended meanings in large, diverse, and selectively attending audiences in attempts to influence them in a variety of ways.

With this definition in mind, we must ask which media really are (or are not) mass media. This question is not an idle one because it sets *boundaries* on what needs to be studied under the general heading "mass communication."

## Which Media Are Mass Media?

Is the telephone a mass medium? How about a fax machine, or personal computers linked in a network? What about a large museum? Should we include rock concerts, theatrical performances, church services, or even parades in our study of mass communication? After all, each of these human activities is a form of communication. For our purposes, whether or not they are mass media depends on whether they can carry out the process of mass communication we have just defined.

To be true to our definition, we would have to conclude that talking on the telephone is *not* really mass communication, because the audience is not large and diverse; usually there is only one person at each end of the line. Furthermore, telephone users usually are not "professional communicators." The same is true of a fax machine with phone lines, or even two personal computers when individuals merely exchange messages. (The Internet and the World Wide Web do qualify for some usages.) A museum does not participate in mass communication because it does not provide "rapid dissemination" with "media." Neither does a rock concert qualify, because it does not disseminate messages "over distance"; it is a form of direct communication to audiences.

Similarly, a situation in which live performers and an audience can see each other directly—in a theater or church, at a sports event or parade—is not an example of media communication. Large-scale advertising by direct mail might qualify, except that it is not really "continuous." Thus, our definition turns out to be relatively rigorous. It enables us to set definite boundaries on what can be included and studied as a medium of mass communication. By definition, none of the activities just listed is such a medium, although all of them can arouse meanings and influence people.

Similarly, although people often speak of "the news media," this expression is misleading. As we will see in Chapter 9, news is a special form of content produced by media organizations that present their products to the public through the use of the same mass media that bring us communications about drama, music, and sports. Thus, we will treat the gathering and distribution of news not as a distinct mass medium in itself but as an important *process* dependent on the print and broadcast media.

By exercising the criteria set forth in our definition, then, we can identify precisely what we consider to be mass media in this text. The major mass media are print (including books, magazines, and newspapers), film (principally commercial motion pictures), and broadcasting (mainly radio and television, but also several associated forms such as cable and VCRs). Increasingly, the Internet (and particularly its World Wide Web) are becoming mass media that fit this definition. Although other kinds of media are worth studying, the focus of our attention will be on those that closely fit our definition of mass communication.

# ▼ *Comparing Face-to-Face and Mass Communication*

Having examined the nature of both face-to-face and mass communication, we can now ask how these two processes differ from each other. Our starting point is that mass communication (1) depends on mechanical or electronic media and (2) addresses a large, diverse audience. We can ask, then, do these two characteristics alter the communication process in some fundamental way? Or is mass communication just like any other form of human communication? More simply: What difference does the use of media make?

## The Consequences of Using Any Medium

Human communication, whether with a medium or not, depends on verbal and nonverbal symbols and all the stages discussed in our basic linear model. However, introducing a medium into communication between two people clearly alters the process. One major consequence is the *loss of direct and immediate feedback*. A second is *severe limitation on effective role-taking* because of that loss.

**Lack of immediate feedback.**    As was suggested earlier, when we communicate with another person and have a medium intervening, we cannot perceive the rich nonverbal cues that are available when we converse face-to-face. Even when using the phone in direct interpersonal communication we cannot detect visual, nonverbal messages like a puzzled look, raised eyebrows, a smile—or even subtle tones of voice or small changes of pitch and emphasis that may not come through the system. Exchanges of messages by fax machines or by personal computer using e-mail are even more limited. The fax paper or the computer screen does not show visual, nonverbal signs or signals, and it cannot convey nuances of pronunciation and timing. All these cues help us know how our message is being received in face-to-face interpersonal communication—or indeed, whether it is being received at all.

**Inability to engage in effective role-taking.**    Limitations on simultaneous feedback in virtually all mediated communication reduce our ability to understand how well our message is being understood by the person or persons toward whom it is directed. Because of these limitations, accuracy when using a medium is less attainable than in the direct, face-to-face, interpersonal mode. In addition, communication effectiveness can be reduced—a point that most people understand very well. Each of us has at some time told a friend, "Let's not try to settle this over the telephone. Let's get together and talk it over."

Still, talking on the telephone, typing messages to each other with computers, or sending fax documents is clearly human communication, because each depends on learned patterns of meaning, labeling with language symbols, transmission of information over distance, perception by the receiver, and the construction of reasonably similar meanings by receiver and sender. In short, while communication through virtually any medium follows the same stages as face-to-face communication, using a medium definitely does alter the process.

**Loss of accuracy.**    As the foregoing indicates, the big difference between face-to-face and any form of mediated communication is a loss of accuracy due to limitations on feedback and role-taking. Stated more formally:

1. The use of a medium *reduces the richness of feedback and limits the process of role-taking.*
2. Both of these limitations *increase the possibility of inaccuracy between meanings of senders and receivers.*
3. When meanings between sender and receiver are dissimilar, *accuracy is reduced and mutual understanding is limited.*
4. Decreases in accuracy of communication *reduce the probability the message will influence people.*

These limitations certainly apply to mass communication. Indeed, they are even more important when communication takes place via a medium such as a newspaper, a movie, or television. In mass communication, a large, diverse audience is at the receiving end. There is no realistic way for the communicator to engage in any role-taking during the process of transmitting a message, or for the audience to provide immediate and ongoing feedback while transmission is taking place.

These limitations are well understood by professional communicators. Dan Rather or Tom Brokaw can never place themselves mentally in your personal shoes as you view the evening news and thus be able to understand and predict accurately how you personally will receive and interpret the broadcast. By extension, there is no way that such newscasters can modify their ongoing presentation on the basis of your feedback so as to make you understand more fully. The same situation applies to any professional communicator, whether the medium is a newspaper, a movie, a radio broadcast, and so on.

At the same time, professional communicators know some things about the audience in a collective sense. To provide a kind of *a priori* form of feedback, large communication corporations (for example, the major television networks) conduct extensive research on audience characteristics and behavior. The results of such research provide guidelines concerning the likely tastes and interests of at least the majority of their audience at a particular time. Researchers study many categories of people to give an overall picture.

The information obtained from such research is the basis for certain necessary assumptions about audiences, and it has to replace individual-by-individual role-taking. However, that approach has serious limitations, because assumptions can be inaccurate. That hundreds of magazines, newspapers, films, and television programs have failed over the years despite extensive "market research" testifies to how imperfect such role-taking assumptions can be.

Feedback is similarly limited. Indeed, for all intents and purposes it does not exist. Audience members cannot interrupt what they see as a confusing or infuriating television reporter, or gain immediate access to a newspaper editorial writer. Although mass media often invite letters or phone calls, this kind of reverse flow provides only a delayed trickle of feedback information from the few people who are motivated enough to go to the trouble.

Thus, by comparison with face-to-face communication, mass communication is essentially a *rigidly linear process*. Communicators try to guess how their messages will be received, with only indirect, delayed feedback in the form of advertising revenues, research findings, a few telephone calls, occasional letters, movie reviews, and box-office receipts. This delayed feedback may help them shape future communications, but it provides no basis for altering a message while it is being disseminated. As a consequence, accuracy and influence on any particular member of the audience are significantly limited compared to what can be accomplished in face-to-face communication.

## The Consequences of Large, Diverse Audiences

Mass communication differs from face-to-face communication and from mediated interpersonal communication not only because it involves more complex media but also because the audience is *large and diverse.* Still, whether there is one receiver or there are a million, the basic activities of sender and receiver are the same. Even if the sender is a professional and the audience is immense, the act of communication still depends on messages composed of verbal and nonverbal symbols linked to meanings by cultural conventions, on grammar and syntax, and all the rest. Thus, we can conclude that mass communication is not a process that depends on some exotic or unique principles of communication. It is a special form of mediated communication that is limited in accuracy and influence because simultaneous role-taking and feedback are difficult or impossible.

However, the existence of a large and diverse audience can pose still other significant limitations on the content, accuracy, and influences of the messages transmitted by a mass medium. Inevitably, much mass media content—perhaps most of it—is designed for the tastes and presumed intellectual level of the "average citizen" or, often, for the average member of a specialized category of people who are assumed to share some common taste or interest (for instance, all fishing enthusiasts, football fans, or fashion-conscious men). In forming appropriate message content, assumptions must be made about such audiences. In fact, most professional communicators tend to assume that the majority of people in their audiences

1. have a limited attention span,

2. prefer to be entertained rather than enlightened, and

3. quickly lose interest in any subject that makes intellectual demands.

With no intention of being either critical or elitist, it seems clear that in large part these assumptions are correct. Well-educated people with sophisticated tastes and high intellectual capacity are a relatively minor part of the population. Only about 20 percent have graduated from college. Among that category, not all are either affluent or urbane. Those who are will probably not attend to the majority of content presented by the American mass media. However, this is not really a problem in a profit-oriented media system, because those cultivated citizens who are in short supply constitute a very small segment of purchasing consumers. Therefore, in attempting to maximize profits, professional communicators who prepare media content can safely ignore them. It is much more profitable to reach the much larger numbers of intellectually undemanding receivers, *whose aggregate purchasing power is immense.* In other words, as we will show in later chapters, reaching large numbers of exactly the right kind of people is critically important in the advertising-driven and profit-oriented American system of mass communication. Thus, all of the factors just discussed work together in a kind of system that *encourages media content that is high in entertainment value and low in intellectual demands.*

It is important to understand the conditions and principles that fit together to produce this consequence, because they explain a great deal about why our media function as they do. Furthermore, we can then more readily understand why the media inevitably attract the attention of deeply concerned critics who have generated a long list of charges and complaints that the media are both trivial and harmful in some way.[10]

The fact is that there is indeed much to criticize regarding what the system delivers. From the outset of mass communication, the content of American media has prompted thoughtful people to object to its generally shallow nature. We do not wish to imply that all media content is superficial, or that it caters only to the interests of limited-capacity audiences. There certainly are books, newspaper analyses, magazines, radio programs, and television content for the educated and sophisticated as well as for those of less developed capacities and tastes. Undeniably, however, most media content is of limited aesthetic or intellectual merit. Earlier in this century critics focused on "yellow journalism" and the emphasis on crime in newspapers. Today's low-brow content includes such forms as quiz shows, paperback thrillers, violent portrayals, personal-interest "news," soap operas, quiz games, explicit sexual depictions, popular music, unsophisticated sit-coms, ball games, wrestling, and telemarketing.

The critics want different content. They urge the media to inform, enlighten, and uplift—to provide information in depth as a basis for intelligent political decision making, arts appreciation, and improvement in moral standards. These are commendable goals, which no thoughtful person can seriously dispute. At the same time, the environment in which the media operate makes it very unlikely that these goals will ever be fully achieved—not because greedy people will always control the media, but because our society has defined mass communication as part of the private enterprise system. However, when pressed, few critics of the American media would exchange our system for one such as exists in China, North Korea, or Cuba, where content remains tightly controlled by an authoritarian government.

The remaining chapters of this text address three major areas: First, the many ways in which American society has shaped its media are addressed in some detail in Chapters 2 through 4. The factors to be considered are the development of technology, the influence of a growing population with a multi-cultural composition, a democratic political system, and a profit-oriented economic system in which private ownership is valued. Second, chapters in the first three parts of the book address the unique features of each medium. They discuss how it operates to disseminate its particular kind of information. They also describe its pattern of adoption by the American population. Finally, the third area explores how our media have influenced us. This area has two parts. One looks at influences on us as individuals—modifying our beliefs, attitudes, and behavior at a personal level. The other looks at the influences of our media on changes in our society at a collective level—that is, how our media have brought about changes in our norms, in our political system, or in our general culture. These issues will be discussed in the final part of the book, after examining the first two of the major areas just described.

Finally, these broad questions are addressed within a *liberal arts perspective*. The discussion of the development, functioning, and influences of our mass media draws upon a number of fields, including anthropology, the arts, economics, history, psychology, sociology, and even theater. Thus, it presents a broad rather than a narrow view of mass communication in the United States.

## CHAPTER REVIEW

▼ At both a societal and personal level we are deeply dependent on the content and process of mass communication in contemporary society. They are essential to our economic and political institutions and find important uses in virtually every sphere of our social and personal lives.

▼ Human communication differs sharply from the processes used by other species. It depends on systems of learned and shared verbal and nonverbal symbols, their meanings, and conventionalized rules for their use.

▼ The basic act of human communication can be analyzed in terms of a linear model that includes six major steps: deciding on a message, encoding the message by linking symbols and meanings, transmitting information to span distance, perceiving the incoming information patterns, perceiving the message, and constructing its meanings. As a result, receivers experience some effect.

▼ In face-to-face communication, feedback and role-taking are important principles related to accuracy.

▼ Mass communication is also a linear process in which professional communicators encode and transmit various kinds of messages to present to different segments of the public for a variety of purposes. Through the use of mass media, those messages are disseminated to large and diverse audiences, who attend to the messages in selective ways.

▼ Members of the audience interpret the message selectively, and the meanings they construct may or may not be parallel to those intended by the communicator.

▼ Mass communication and face-to-face communication differ in important ways. Because of feedback and role-taking, interpersonal transactions can be flexible and influential. Mass communication lacks these features and is largely a one-way, relatively inflexible process.

▼ In an advertising-driven and profit-oriented system, media content must be tailored to the majority, whose collective purchasing power is huge, but whose intellectual level and tastes are not sophisticated. This tailoring of content results in many criticisms.

▼ The study of mass communication must include attention to three broad sets of issues: (1) the many ways in which a society's history, values, and economic and political realities have influenced its media; (2) the unique features of each medium in the system that make it different from the other media; and (3) the kinds of influences that media have on us as individuals and on our society and culture.

# Print Media

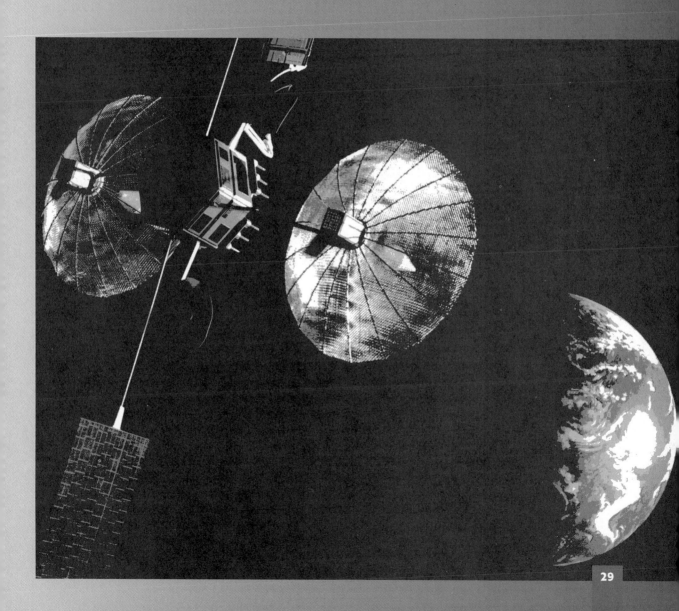

# *Books*

## The Oldest Mass Medium

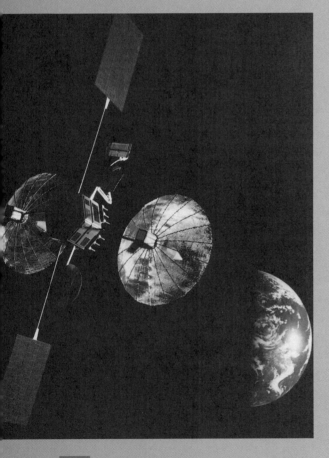

*U*ntil about five thousand years ago, no system for writing had been devised. Although human culture was developing at an ever-increasing pace, no *media* were available that could conquer either time or distance. Except for the occasional use of such artifacts as notched sticks or devices like flags, smoke, or drums, preliterate societies were limited to the capacity of the human voice to conquer distance and to the capability of personal memories to preserve ideas through time.

The lack of writing was a significant handicap. In a society limited to oral communication, skilled storytellers could train new generations in myths and legends to preserve a group's history. However, because an accumulation of ideas could not be permanently stored, societies found it difficult to accumulate either elaborate technologies or a rich cultural heritage. Furthermore, without writing it was very difficult for a tribe or society that had conquered another to establish efficient control over what they had won. Conquerors could not exert close administrative supervision over large populations that were beyond their immediate visual inspection. As a result, of all of these limitations of the oral society, social, political, and economic progress was agonizingly slow.

Writing changed all that. It was the second great communications revolution following the development of speech and language that came about forty or so thousand years earlier. Inventing efficient systems of writing took a long time. The first medium people used extensively was stone, but it was very cumbersome. Stone "documents" could not be moved around easily. Within a few centuries, however, more *portable* media came into use. Ancient societies began to preserve and accumulate ideas in written form using such media as scrolls and tablets. Once it became possible to send information across great distances by using media that were easy to move, the administration of conquered lands became much easier. Larger and larger empires were established, and trade increased contacts between dissimilar peoples. These effects of writing enriched cultures and quickened the pace of social change.

Centuries later, the introduction of *books* with pages bound on one edge increased portability still more. Although early books were much more efficient than scrolls, making even a single copy was a woefully laborious process. Using quill pen and simple ink, a skilled scribe might need a year or more of diligent work to copy one book. Consequently, books were in very limited supply. Few could afford them, and only a tiny segment of the population could read.

The printing press and movable type revolutionized communication and they represent the third great communications revolution. Today we have difficulty realizing what a drastic change printing brought about. By comparison with the dazzling color and moving images of the television or computer screen, a printed book may seem drab and dull. However, in the broad sweep of human history the book was undoubt-edly one of the most influential inventions of all time. Next to language itself, no form of communication played a greater part in shaping human development.

Within a few years of the introduction of printing, millions of copies of books were pouring from the presses of Europe. The rich history of books—from the first primitive tablets to the contemporary book industry—is a vital part of the evolution of human culture. Books remain our most respected medium of communication. With great portability, flexibility, and simplicity, they store and make available for later recovery the most complex and significant knowledge developed by humankind. Even today's fantastic electronic marvels cannot do that as efficiently.

This chapter reviews milestones in the incredibly long history of books, beginning with efforts to develop techniques for storing and recovering information, and reviewing the state of the book industry today. Of great importance in the unfolding story is the evolution of *technology*. Even the earliest media represented advances in technology— for example, the progression from stone to portable media as writing surfaces. Each major communications revolution, from the development of writing to the electronic systems of today, was based on significant solutions to technical problems.

In Europe in the fifteenth century, a few decades before Columbus sailed, a great breakthrough in technology made the printed book a reality. Today, a thriving book publishing industry continues to transmit information to us—from escapist fiction to the complex technicalities of supercomputers and high-energy physics. It seems highly unlikely that books will soon be replaced.

## ▼ *The Transition to Writing*

The first step in understanding our contemporary print media is to examine the origins of writing. The graphic representation of ideas, unlike speaking, requires a *medium*. Thus, the development of writing and the evolution of me-dia are part of the same process. A medium is simply a device for moving physical information (sound, light, radio waves, etc.) through time or space. It can be any object or arrangement of objects used to accomplish those goals so as to enable human beings to transmit, receive, and interpret messages. Media used in writing depend on some physical "representation" of thoughts and ideas, either by "pictures" or other kinds of graphic symbols placed on a surface. Those marks or pictures are associated with culturally agreed-on meanings. The earliest known attempts to represent ideas with pictures—the first step toward the development of writing—were *cave paintings*. Fifteen to twenty thousand years ago, unknown artists painted hundreds of dramatic

One of the first forms of writing was the use of pictographs to stand for actions, ideas, or objects. Such systems were developed independently by the Egyptians, Chinese, Mayans, and others. Thought writing is still common today. The ideograms shown here remind us that we continue to make use of this kind of information storage and retrieval. (Copyright © Peter Vandermark, Stock, Boston)

murals on the walls of caves in what is now Southern Europe. Well-known examples are in Lascaux in France and Altamira in Spain. The paintings show bison, reindeer, wild horses—even extinct animals—and the men who hunted them. The artists' tools were bones, sticks, and primitive brushes used to color their images. The pigments were made of animal fat mixed with charcoal and powdered earth of several bright colors.[1]

As artistic products, the prehistoric paintings are large, vivid, dramatic, and surprisingly contemporary in appearance. Certainly, they show a grasp of the complex principles of pictorial representation equaling that of modern artists. Picasso himself, after seeing the great cave at Altamira, is said to have remarked that artists today have learned nothing (about color and composition) beyond what those prehistoric painters knew. However, for all their artistic merits, as a way of communicating ideas such paintings are extremely limited. Their meaning to the people who made them, and the reasons for which they were done, remain unknown.

Nevertheless, representing something *graphically* was a significant step beyond oral description of the objects and events being portrayed. Even if they were only mnemonic devices, serving loosely as memory stimulators, depictions such as cave paintings could help a storyteller provide a more detailed and accurate account, compared with unaided recall. In fact, this illustrates one major purpose of writing. In all its forms, writing is a tool for preserving ideas that were expressed earlier. In other words (to borrow today's computer jargon) writing is a system for *information storage.* Just as we seek more and more storage capacity in computers, primitive people sought systems of graphic representation of language symbols to free themselves from the limitations and inaccuracies of human memory.

Writing must also serve another purpose. Ideally, it permits people who did not record the ideas originally to recover accurately the meanings and implications of those who did. In this sense (to borrow again from contemporary computer usage), writing is a means of *information exchange.* Thus, the development of picture drawing was not enough. Only the original artist could recall accurately the intended meanings represented. The next step was to *standardize* both the depictions and the rules for interpreting their meaning. That advance took more than ten thousand years!

## From Glyphs to Alphabets

Even before writing was developed, people were using many complex non-verbal communication systems. They communicated with hairstyles, clothing, tattoos, scars, jewelry, crowns, and other objects and ornaments. They used these to signify rank, status, power, marital status, achievement, occupation, family membership, and dozens of additional meanings that were vital to life in their societies. However, it was not until about 4000 B.C. that people began to leave records in the form of codified writing that can be understood today. They left graphic representations on many surfaces—pottery, baskets, sticks, cloth, walls, animal skins, bark, stone, and even leaves. On these media they rendered a rich variety of signs, symbols, drawings, and decorative motifs to convey socially important ideas.

**Representing ideas with written symbols.**    At some unknown point between 5000 and 4000 B.C., people in several areas of the Near East began to use drawings to represent ideas in a somewhat more uniform way.[2] Most were agricultural people, and their early attempts at writing grew out of their need to keep accurate accounts so as to record land ownership, boundaries, crop sales, and the like. Some were traders who needed reliable records of cargoes, profits, and commercial transactions. Generally, these peoples' symbols were pictures of what they knew—birds, the sun, a bundle of grain, a boat, the head of a bull, or parts of the human body. Writing in a technical sense began to emerge when such graphic signs came to represent *standardized meanings* that were agreed upon by conventions among a given people. Thus, for those who understood the rules, a simplified drawing of a human form could mean "a man"; a crudely drawn rising sun might be "one day"; a stylized human foot, "walking"; and a wavy line, "water."

The use of such graphic representations was a form of writing because each symbol was associated with one and only one idea or concept. When strung together they could tell a story. For example, the stylized drawings discussed above might mean "A man walked for a day along a river." Such a system is called **ideographic** or "thought writing." Because it associates specific whole thoughts or meanings with pictures, it is also sometimes called **pictographic writing.** This style of writing links carefully drawn, often highly stylized representations of objects to ideas, rather than to specific sounds. Well-known ideographic systems of writing were those developed independently by the early Egyptians, the Chinese, and the Maya of the New World.

Actually, ideographic writing works quite well given enough ideograms. A separate picture or drawing is needed for each idea or thought that is to be recorded. However, as a society and its culture become more complex, more and more ideas or concepts need to have their own pictures or symbols, which increases the complexity of writing by requiring an increasing number of standardized ideograms. In a complex society, such a system can become very cumbersome indeed.

The number of characters required in a system of ideographic writing can eventually become staggering. The *hieroglyphic* (sacred carving) system used during the early Egyptian dynasties required only about seven hundred different ideograms. Traditional Chinese is based on highly stylized ideograms and conducting routine affairs today requires knowledge of about four thousand characters. Truly literary Chinese scholars may know up to fifty thousand. Thus, "thought language" or ideographic systems can be very difficult to learn and use. Historically, where such systems have been used, the majority of the population remained illiterate. Even powerful rulers were sometimes unable to read and write and, like others, relied on professional scribes. Because of their importance and skill, scribes often enjoyed high status and impressive financial rewards.

**Graphic representation of sound.**   A much simpler system of writing is to link graphic symbols not to ideas or thoughts, but to *sounds.* Here, instead of ideograms, simpler *phonograms* are all that are needed. A **phonogram** is a graphic symbol linked to a specified sound by a convention or rule that prevails among those who speak a particular language. The twenty-six letter

The Egyptians produced a beautiful form of pictographic writing sometime between 5000 and 4000 B.C. Their hieroglyphs were ideograms, with each symbol standing for a separate idea. Later, they introduced phonograms into their system for consonants, but did not provide for vowel sounds. Thus, we cannot pronounce their ancient language today. (The Granger Collection, New York)

▲

Alphabetical writing was first developed by the Sumerians between 3000 and 2500 B.C. They made impressions on clay tablets with a wedge-shaped stick to produce *cuneiform writing.* The tablets could be preserved by baking. Each of the stylized symbols stood for a particular sound, like one of our syllables, rather than for a whole idea, or concept. Combining symbols to form words meant that only a few hundred symbols were needed, rather than thousands of pictograms. By around 500 B.C., the Greeks had refined this system greatly and standardized an alphabet so effectively that only about two dozen letters were needed to represent the sounds of all the words in their language. (The Bettmann Archive)

alphabet that we use every day is the obvious example. It comes to us from ancient sources. Even its name reveals its origins—*alpha* and *beta* are the first two letters of the ancient Greek version.

Alphabets, like books and printing, rank as one of the great human breakthroughs. They made reading and writing—a hideously complex activity with ideographic systems—literally "child's play." All of us, when we first tackled our A,B,Cs as children, learned the consonant and vowel sounds uniquely linked to each of the twenty-six letters. Along with our numbers and numerals, plus a scattering of additional symbols representing punctuation, contractions, and so on, we can transform into spoken words virtually any set of ideas that need to be expressed in our language (or vice versa).

**Origins of our alphabet.** It took over two thousand years after the earliest attempts at writing to develop the alphabet that you are now using to read these passages. We inherited our contemporary alphabet from the Romans. They had refined the one that they obtained from the Etruscans, who in turn, copied most of theirs from the Greeks. But the Greeks did not invent the idea. They refined their alphabet from origins leading back through the Phoenicians, the Assyrians, and the Babylonians, to the Sumerians (who probably did start the process).

Apparently, our phonetic system of writing originated when the Sumerians began to use **cuneiform writing** as a means to make records.[3] The Sumerians were an agricultural people who lived from about 3000 B.C. to around 1700 B.C. in the so-called Fertile Crescent—a region that included parts of Iraq, between the Tigris and Euphrates rivers, plus portions of present-day Israel, Jordan, Syria, Turkey, and Iran. This was the part of the ancient world where the earliest known civilizations developed.

The Sumerians found that a pad of wet clay held in a small flat box made an excellent medium, at least compared to stone. They made little drawings on the surface with a sharpened stick to represent ideas in pictographic form. They soon simplified the pictures into highly stylized forms and those drawings evolved into abstract ideograms that were unrecognizable as representations of actual objects. In part, the reason for this was that the writers sharpened their sticks to a wedge-like shape at the end, and it was hard to draw lifelike pictures with this instrument. Again, technology shaped the medium.

What the Sumerians eventually hit on was the idea of letting a particular *character* (graphic symbol) stand for a sound. In their system, sounds were usually whole syllables, rather than the much simpler sound elements, as in the alphabets that came later. Even though it was complex by comparison with today's alphabets, the Sumerian cuneiform system, using phonograms to represent sounds rather than ideas, was a major breakthrough. It was an innovation that other societies would soon improve upon and simplify.[4]

Beginning about 500 B.C., the Greeks developed a remarkably efficient alphabet (including vowels) out of the many versions that had been developed earlier. Standardizing their alphabet greatly enriched Greek culture. For example, in 403 B.C. Athens passed a law making one version (the Ionian alphabet) *compulsory* in official documents. The simplified alphabet promoted increased literacy, formal education, and learning. Much of Greek culture was passed on to become an important base of contemporary western civilization because they had a written language that could easily be read.

## Portable Media

Phonetic writing with a standardized alphabet was not the only innovation that enabled the Greeks to develop a rich culture. Another factor was that portable media were in wide use by their time. Although the clay tablets of the Sumerians were portable, they were still heavy and bulky. As early as 3000 B.C., the Egyptians had developed **papyrus** (from which, incidentally, we get our modern word "paper"). Actually, papyrus is a tall reed common to marshy areas of the Nile. Its stalks, up to two inches thick, were sliced thin and laid out in two layers at right angles to each other. When pounded together, pressed, and dried, papyrus yielded a paperlike surface suitable for writing with brush or reed pen. The sheets were sometimes joined together at the ends and rolled up on a stick to produce **scrolls,** which were in fact early books.

It was a great technological solution, but because papyrus was controlled by the Egyptians (and later the Romans), it was often difficult to obtain and was in perpetually short supply. As the use of writing spread, alternatives had to be devised. One important writing surface that was used until relatively modern times was **parchment,** which is tanned skin of a sheep or goat. Another was **vellum,** which resembled parchment but was prepared from the skin of a young calf. They were very expensive. A single animal produces only a few pages. However, animal skin surfaces were very durable, which helped some ancient scrolls survive into later centuries.

## ▼ *The Development of Books*

Throughout the time that writing, alphabets, and portable media were being developed, societies themselves were undergoing great changes. Sophisticated urban centers were established; techniques of agriculture were refined;

technologies of war and conquest were developed; and the pace of trade and contact between unlike peoples quickened. Above all, great empires rose as a result of military conquest. An example was the huge Roman Empire, in which virtually the entire known Western world was brought together under a single government administration. Communicating to administer this vast political system was a constant challenge.

## The Need for Lengthy Documents

A variety of forces led to the need for documents for recording lengthy and complex ideas. Hundreds of years before biblical times, thinkers were debating complex and perplexing questions: What is the true nature of reality and how do people know it? What supernatural forces exist and what part do they play in people's lives? What is a just social order? What are those bright bodies in the sky, and why do they move in such regular patterns? How do animals differ from human beings? What happens to us after death?

Human curiosity and intelligence led the search for answers and knowledge about the physical, social, and religious world accumulated. This created the need to record far more than just short messages, such as edicts, land claims, and administrative commands. For example, one of the great problems for all who governed was how to stabilize the social order and make it work more justly. Ancient *codes of law* were required to provide formal guidelines for behavior and to specify punishments for deviance. A classic example is the system of 282 laws developed by the Babylonian king Hammurabi almost four thousand years ago. His laws covered everything from the regulation of commerce and military affairs to the practice of medicine and the treatment of children. In the absence of books, he had his laws carved on huge *stellae*—blocks of basalt eight feet square—that he had set up in the center of each major city in his empire. But it was a terribly cumbersome system. Portable media were far more efficient, and by the time of Christ, the Romans were using books to store their famous legal codes.

The rise of great religious systems created a need to record sacred writings. The Old Testament of Judaism is an outstanding example of a long and complex set of ideas that could not have been passed on accurately in oral form over many generations. Later, Christians began to record the revelations, testimony, and injunctions of their scriptures and Islam followed with the sacred Koran.

## Copying Books by Hand

With alphabetical writing well developed, and with the availability of efficient portable media, such as papyrus, parchment, and vellum, it was not a difficult step for the Romans to move beyond the cumbersome scroll to the bound book with cut pages of uniform size. It was the Romans who developed the book into the form that we know today.[5] They gave us pages with writing on both sides and bound at the edge between boards or covers.

The Romans did far more than just develop the physical nature of the medium. They also produced many innovations that shaped the formats we use in preparing books. For example, they greatly refined the alphabet and originated much of the grammatical structure of sentences we follow today. They brought us the idea of *paragraphs,* and they standardized systems of punctuation, much as we use them now. Their **majuscule** letters, used extensively on their monuments, became our capital letters, just as they are used on the present page. Their smaller **minuscule** letters (refined under the influence of Charlemagne in the eighth century as Carolingian scripts) became the lowercase letters that you see on the present page. (However, the terms *uppercase* and *lowercase* actually came from early printers, who stored majuscule and minuscule type in separate trays—upper and lower cases—for easy access.)

Beginning in A.D. 410, illiterate tribes (the Germanic Visigoths and Vandals) began to invade Rome. Rome was quickly overrun. By 476, the last emperor was deposed and the great empire that had dominated the world for nearly a thousand years came to an inglorious end. The Roman alphabet and the art of book production were all but lost as the Western world entered the so-called Dark Ages, which would last for another seven centuries.

It was within the Christian monasteries that the precious knowledge of alphabetical writing and books was preserved and improved. Using the Roman alphabet and letter forms (sometimes modified in various ways) and the Latin language, diligent monks hand-copied thousands upon thousands of *manu scripti,* a term we still use.[6] Most of the books produced in the monasteries were merely working documents used for practical purposes in churches and schools.

Producing a *manu scriptus* was a demanding and laborious process. Between the fifth century, when Roman civilization was destroyed, and the fifteenth century, when printing began, writing skills were preserved in monasteries and *scriptoria,* where skilled craftsmen copied books letter by letter on parchment or vellum. (The Bettmann Archive)

However, some were exquisite works of art, "illuminated" (decorated) with elaborate letters and drawings. Perhaps the most beautiful book ever made is the extraordinary *Book of Kells,* created by monks around A.D. 800 in a remote monastery in the western part of Ireland. Written and illuminated using precious materials gathered from all parts of the world then known, the *Book of Kells* was prepared as an act of deep religious devotion. It survives intact today as a great national treasure of Ireland, carefully preserved at Trinity College in Dublin.

As Europe slowly emerged from the Dark Ages, interest in books and writing began to grow. It was no longer only monks who were copying books by hand. In many urban centers, commercial establishments called *scriptoria* manufactured and sold books. One factor that encouraged this type of book production was the growing proportion of the population that was literate. During the thirteenth century, universities were established in the major cities in Europe as centers of learning and of the arts. Many books were produced for teaching. The wealthy student could buy books already copied from the official texts by professional scribes; the poor student had to rent textbooks, one chapter at a time, and laboriously copy each page. For the most part, Latin remained the language of the learned. But more and more, as the thirteenth century progressed, some scribes wrote in the local "vulgar" or *vernacular* languages common to the people, such as English, French, German, and Italian.

One of the technologies that would become critically important in the development of print as a medium was the manufacture of *paper.* The Chinese had developed paper and used it extensively as early as the second century.[7] During the middle of the eighth century, Persian soldiers captured a group of Chinese paper makers, who either taught the process to their captors or revealed it under torture (depending on whose version of the story one believes). In any case, the Islamic world had paper long before Europeans, and it was brought to Spain by the Moors in the twelfth century.

The use of paper caught on quickly, and within a century it was being skillfully produced in all parts of Europe. Some paper makers became truly skilled craftsmen, and they made beautiful papers from linen rags. Some of the paper produced in the 1400s and 1500s rivals the best seen today. Most, however, was cruder, but it had two qualities that made it highly attractive—it was cheap (by comparison with sheep and goat skins) and it was available. It would be a long time, however, before parchment and vellum were entirely replaced for the best-quality books.

## ▼ *The Invention and Spread of the Printing Press*

The development of printing technology did not, as we will see, come out of nowhere. Many of the prerequisites—paper and parchment, literacy, the need for lengthy documents, and a sophisticated format system for books—were already a part of Western culture. Nevertheless, the invention of a practical and efficient press marked one of those occasions when the ideas of a single person made a great difference. Furthermore, once it became available, printing with "movable" type was immediately recognized as a truly extraordinary technological advance.

## Gutenberg's Remarkable Machine

Printing as such was not really unknown by Gutenberg's time.[8] The Chinese had begun making inked impressions from elaborately carved wooden blocks shortly after A.D. 175, when they first developed paper. Whole books done in this manner by the Koreans and Japanese during the eighth century survive today. The Koreans had even cast individual letters in metal, although very crudely, more than a century before Gutenberg perfected the process. Block printing, however, was extremely difficult and inefficient. To print from a block, an entire page of characters had to be carved (in reverse) on a single slab of hard wood. Ink was applied to the carved face, and paper or parchment was pressed onto the surface. A roller or brush was passed over the surface, and an impression resulted. The characters did not reproduce very clearly because the wood did not take razor-sharp edges. Also, the process was very laborious. Even if all went well, only a limited number of copies (perhaps a hundred or

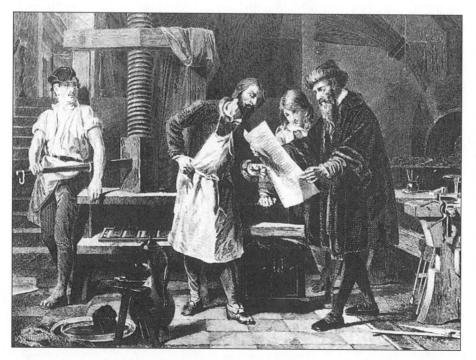

One of the significant transitions in the ability of human beings to communicate came when Johannes Gutenberg developed movable type with individual letters cast in metal. The age of printing began in 1455 when he produced two hundred copies of his famous Bible. He worked many years to perfect his invention and feared that such mechanical reproduction would never be accepted. (Culver Pictures, Inc.)

so) could be printed by this technique before the wood became too worn. In many ways it was almost as easy to copy the work by hand.

While all of these forerunners had been around for a long time, Johannes Gutenberg made a truly significant technological advance. He eventually managed to cast *individual letters* in molten metal in such a way that they would be as clear and sharp as those on this page. The individual letters (movable type) could be set up in lines, one letter at a time, as needed and they could be used over and over without wearing out quickly.

It took Gutenberg about twenty years to develop just the right process for making the letters, arranging them in a suitable press, developing the right inks, and bringing all the components together into a practical system. First, he made hard steel punches with the letters engraved in relief on the end. Then he made little molds by striking the letters individually into suitable pieces of softer brass. With the help of a special metal alloy of his own formula, he was able to cast crisp letters individually and to make many identical castings of each one. He also developed an ink made from lamp black (a soft soot) ground in a linseed oil varnish.[9] These techniques were so simple and practical that they remained in use for hundreds of years.

Gutenberg also worked out a superior system for pressing the blank pages against the inked type. It was essentially a screw-type press, much like those used for centuries for making wine. Even that invention required many years' experimentation to get just the right pressure on the parchment or paper. He experimented with many techniques, toiling to produce beautiful examples of printed copy so that when he was ready, his products would have a market among the rich. But he was filled with doubts. Would people buy what he was going to produce? He was not at all sure that mechanical printing would ever catch on. He feared that many people would still want their books copied by hand.

Unfortunately, just before he was ready to produce his first great book, he ran out of money. To continue his project, he borrowed heavily from his lawyer, Johannes Fust (whose son-in-law Peter Schoffer was the foreman in the print shop). Eventually, in 1455, Gutenberg was ready for his first great success. He designed, set the type for, and printed two hundred copies of all the pages needed for his famous forty-two-line Bible. It was, and still is, one of the world's most beautiful examples of the printer's art.

The work was intended for an elite and wealthy market. He even managed to produce "illuminated" letters complete with colors with his press. But before the copies were ready for binding and final sale, Fust demanded repayment of the loan. Gutenberg did not have the money, so the lawyer took him to court. With his assistant Schoffer testifying against him at the trial, Gutenberg was stripped of his press, type, Bible, and even legal claim to his inventions. The lawyer and his son-in-law took over everything and left Gutenberg financially ruined. The poor man lost his eyesight and remained destitute until, toward the end of his life, a nobleman named Adolph von Nassau took pity on him and made him a member of his court, providing him with a yearly allowance of cloth, grain, and wine. The brilliant inventor, whose work changed the world and enriched the lives of billions of people in later centuries, died in 1468 at age seventy, blind and without any recognition of his timeless contribution to humanity. Even today, little or no mention is made of his contributions in college and university history textbooks (printed by the process he invented).[10]

## The Print Revolution

The number of books available exploded as the printing press quickly spread throughout Europe. During the *incunabula* (the period between 1455 and 1501—not even a half-century) a tidal wave of books printed in popular languages passed into the hands of increasingly eager populations. No one knows how many were published during the period, but estimates range between eight and twenty million copies.[11] (The average press run was only about five hundred copies per book, so these figures represent a very large number of titles.)

Because more and more of these books appeared in the vernacular, printing greatly accelerated developments in science, philosophy, and religion. Knowledge of many topics became available to almost anyone who was literate in a common language and could purchase a book. They were still expensive, but much cheaper than the older *manu scripti*. It is very likely that even before Columbus's departure for the New World (about thirty-six years after Gutenberg's first press run), more books were printed than the accumulated total of all the *manu scripti* that had been copied during the previous thousand years since the fall of Rome. As presses and printing technology were improved during the 1600s and 1700s, and as paper became increasingly available, the number of books printed each year grew sharply.

Printing in the New World began very early. In 1539 (approximately a century before the Pilgrims arrived at Plymouth Rock), Juan Pablo set up a press in Mexico City and printed the first book in the Americas, a religious work entitled *Breve y Mass Compendiosa Doctrina Cristiana*. This book, like many others that followed, was printed under the authority of the Spanish archbishop of Mexico.

The development of education in many countries contributed greatly to the growth in book publishing. More universities were established every year until, by the sixteenth century, they were common in all parts of western Europe. Religious changes (primarily the rise of Protestantism) brought a considerable demand for Bibles and other religious works. In addition, the Renaissance, with its expansion of art, science, philosophy, and literature, contributed to the demand for more and more books. Gutenberg had unleashed a powerful medium indeed.

At first, books were not recognized as a political force. But as soon as those in authority realized that printing could be used to circulate ideas contrary to those of the ruling powers, presses came under strong regulation. In 1529, for example, Henry VIII of England established a list of prohibited books and a system of licensing. In spite of these measures, many documents expressing political opinions were circulated. Still, the Tudors, who controlled the Crown in the mid-1500s, were effective censors of England's presses. This suppression was to last more than a century.[12]

## Book Publishing in North America

Book publishing was slow to start in North America. The early settlers were not avid readers. Nevertheless, book publishing started in New England almost as soon as the Pilgrims arrived. In September of 1620, one hundred and one passengers, along with forty-eight crew members and a number of chickens and pigs, left England on the *Mayflower*. Nearly two months later they landed on Cape Cod, where they spent another eight weeks before moving to the mainland. There they quickly laid out a road up from the shore and began constructing shelters. Within two years they had a small village of simple homes that they had named New Plymouth. The houses they built were small and compactly arranged on each side of the road, each with its own garden plot.

The people in the new community worked hard all day, but had very little to do after sunset, other than talk with their families and friends. There were religious services on the Sabbath and family daily prayers, but the strict codes of the Pilgrims did not permit frivolous activities. Aside from the family Bible, there was nothing to read in most of the houses. Even if there had been, the majority could neither read nor write. Even for the few who could, it was difficult. After dark, tallow candles, crude lamps, and the fireplace provided barely enough light to move around inside. Thus, by comparison with today, the citizens of New Plymouth led a life almost free of any form of communication other than talking.[13]

Within a short time, however, the first printing press in North America was set up at the newly established Harvard College in Cambridge, Massachusetts, where the first book was published in 1640. It was a religious work: the *Whole Booke of Psalmes* (most often called the *Bay Psalm Book*). The college controlled the press until 1662, when the Massachusetts legislature took it over.

In spite of this start, book publishing was slow to develop in the North American colonies, partly because of restrictions imposed by the Crown. But political dissent before the Revolution stimulated all forms of publishing. In the decades following the Revolution, New York, Boston, and Philadelphia became established as centers of a budding publishing industry. Books published early in America's history included religious works, almanacs, and political and social treatises.

Before the 1800s, only a small proportion of the American population was able to read. After the turn of the century, however, the new democratic political system spurred an increasing interest in reading and writing. Public schools were established to teach children to read and write. Democracy required an informed citizenry if it was to survive as its architects had hoped. By the 1840s, a growing audience for books existed in America. In addition to scholarly and religious works, cheap paperback reprints of popular books appeared, and then sensational fiction. By 1855, the United States far surpassed England in the number of books sold. That year saw the first publication of Whitman's *Leaves*

## Examples of Books That Made a Difference

**Adam Smith,** *The Wealth of Nations* **(1776)** This work set forth the basic theory of capitalism that served as a guide for the early Industrial Revolution. Even today, many of his ideas are fundamental to the values guiding business and industry throughout the world.

**Karl Marx,** *Das Kapital* **(1867)** This analysis of history and the relationship between owners and workers provided the philosophical foundations on which were developed huge communist empires in the twentieth century. They had profound influences on millions of people who lived within them and on millions who resisted them.

**Gunnar Myrdal,** *An American Dilemma: The Negro Problem and American Democracy* **(1944)** This respected Swedish scholar's analysis of race relations in the United States accurately identified as the nation's greatest problem its structure of laws and deeply institutionalized beliefs and practices justifying prejudice and discrimination against African-Americans. Myrdal's ideas made important intellectual contributions to the civil rights movement of the 1960s and consequent changes in federal and local laws.

**Rachel Carson,** *Silent Spring* **(1962)** This book provided a wake-up call regarding the impact of pesticides on the environment. It was a powerful message widely credited with stimulating the environmental movement that has been so important in recent decades.

**Betty Friedan,** *The Feminine Mystique,* **(1963)** This book revived the women's movement that flowered during the nineteenth century and then faltered after women won the right to vote in 1918 (with the 19th Amendment to the U.S. Constitution). Friedan decried the stereotyping of women as little more than homemakers and sex objects. Her ideas led to the current trend of reshaping women's roles in society.

*of Grass,* Longfellow's *Hiawatha,* and Bartlett's *Familiar Quotations* (which is now in its fifteenth edition). Probably no other book in American history had as much impact on its time as one published during this period: Harriet Beecher Stowe's antislavery novel *Uncle Tom's Cabin.* Thus, as the nineteenth century progressed, book publishing in the United States became well established as a business, as a shaper of American culture, and as a mass medium.[14]

Books today are still our most respected medium. They allow the slow, thorough development of ideas that serious and complex subjects demand. At the same time, they are also a diverse medium. Everything from Einstein's theory of relativity to hard-core pornography is available in book form. At this point, the future of books seems secure. But so did the future of radio and general circulation magazines in the 1940s. New media continue to appear, and it is not impossible that books may some day be replaced by competing technologies. A long-term decline in reading ability poses another question. College textbooks, for instance, must be easier to read now than they were twenty years ago. Both factors could cause the publishing industry problems in years to come.

# ▼ *Books as a Contemporary Medium*

Because they are so common and familiar, it may be difficult for people today to appreciate the truly remarkable nature of books and to grasp easily the irreplaceable services they provide to individuals and society. The fact that they have not only survived but prospered in the face of increasingly sophisticated competing media is one indicator of their importance. They remain a medium of entertainment, the principal repository of our culture, guides to our technical knowledge, the source of teachings on many subjects, and our basic reference to religious doctrines.

## The Unique Character of Books

Books obviously have distinctive characteristics that set them apart from other media. Certainly, they differ from other print media, such as newspapers and magazines, in that they are bound and covered and are consecutive from beginning to end. Because books (such as the present text) often take a year or more to produce, even after the author gives the finished manuscript to the publisher, they are less timely than newspapers and magazines. Nevertheless, like other mass media, they are encoded by professional communicators and generally transmitted to relatively large and diverse audiences. One obvious difference from several other media is that, like movies, they are not basically supported by advertising. Thus, books have to earn profits for their producers on the basis of their content. Moreover, books are made to last longer than any other medium, and this feature lends itself to in-depth, durable exploration and development of a topic or idea.

These characteristics suit the book for a special role among the mass media. Most books sell only a few thousand copies. Even a national runaway best seller will probably sell no more than ten million copies over its effective life—less than the soap opera audience during a single day of television. Yet the social importance of books can hardly be overestimated. Like opinion magazines, books often persuade the influential, and they can have an impact far beyond their actual sales and readership. In addition to serving as a major channel for transmitting the cultural heritage, they have promoted powerful ideas and inspired changes, even revolutions.

## The Book Publishing Industry

Between the authors of the content of a book and the public who receives its messages lies the publishing company. The publisher's role is threefold: (1) to *select* and help shape what will be published; (2) to *produce* the book as a physical artifact; and (3) to *distribute* the book to receivers—usually retail book stores that sell it for a profit. Whereas authors prepare the actual content of a book,

publishers take the risks involved in investing the money to convert a manuscript into a book and to promote and distribute it to consumers. Because most publishers are private businesses, they have a clear necessity to earn a profit. In recent years, the industry's changing economics have influenced the way publishers carry out their other roles.

Figure 2.1 shows the changes in the output of book publishers in the United States during this century. Clearly, publishing is a growing industry, with more books in publication in recent years than at any time since World War II in our nation's history. There are several reasons for this. During the first half of the century, book publishing took an important turn toward *commercialism*. What it offered the public was determined more and more by a sharp focus on profits. Many kinds of books were found to be profitable, and the number published rose steadily. In the 1920s, the Book-of-the-Month Club and the Literary Guild were founded, expanding the market for novels and other works by reaching those who lived far from bookstores. Following World War II, more and more Americans pursued higher education. Demand for textbooks

## Trends in Media Use

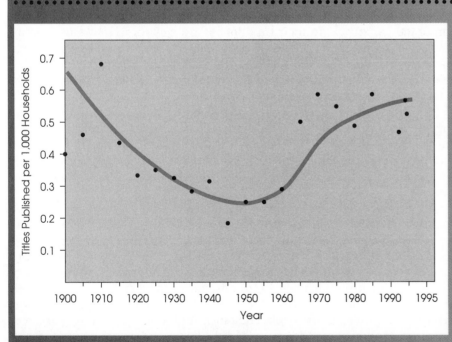

**Figure 2.1**
**Trends in Book Publishing in the United States, 1900–1995**

Early in this century, when radio and television were not available, Americans bought and read more books per capita than at any period since that time. Then, as alternative media became available (and as societal conditions changed with the Great Depression and World War II), book publishing declined sharply. Since 1960, with the coming of the inexpensive paperback, book publishing and consumption have shown a strong upward trend. These data seem to contradict the generalization that Americans no longer read.

The coming of inexpensive paperback books during the 1950s reversed a sharply declining trend in book purchasing by the public. Today, hundreds of thousands of titles are available in paperback and their content includes almost every conceivable topic and subject matter. (Copyright © Rob Crandall, Stock Boston)

soared as returning veterans, helped by the GI Bill, filled colleges and universities. And, with the postwar baby boom more children entered school than ever before. Today, the children of those baby-boomers are overflowing primary and secondary schools, and will soon be attending colleges and universities. Once again, the demand for textbooks will increase significantly.

One of the important innovations in book publishing in the United States was the introduction of the now-familiar small *paperback.* Even during the nineteenth century, following the development of cheap paper and high-speed presses, paperback "dime" novels were widely available and an important part of American publishing. However, until well into the present century, more "serious" books were always published in hardcover form. In Europe, less expensive paperbound books came into wide use well before World War II, but they did not catch on in the United States.

A decline in book sales over four decades was a major factor in the adoption of the paperback. In their traditional hardback form, books became increasingly expensive and sales were not keeping pace with population growth. Then, cheaper printing and binding processes were introduced during the 1950s. Thus, the small paperback format made it possible for all kinds of books to reach much larger audiences than ever before.

The dollars Americans spent for books increased by a whopping seventy-three times from midcentury to the present. For example, total sales went from just over $435 million in 1947 to more than a projected $32 billion in 1998! Even after taking inflation into account, that is a truly significant change. Moreover, the number of places where one could buy books also increased. Books were sold in 8,360 stores in 1957 compared to 25,529 in 1991.[15]

These trends were accompanied by noteworthy changes within the industry. Book publishing had long been something of a dignified "gentlemen's" profession. It had not been the place to find either "big money" or shrewd business practices. Much of the industry had consisted of family-owned enterprises passed on from one generation to the next. To take advantage of the new opportunities for growth, however, publishers needed new resources. They "went public," which means that they sold stock in their companies. That was an important turning point. Banks and other profit-oriented investors began to buy the stock, which increased the demand for a good return on investment. The bottom line, rather than the intellectual satisfaction of publishing important books, became the driving force.

Another trend is a consolidation of ownership. Since the 1960s, many publishers merged or were acquired by communications corporations and conglomerates. As a result of such buyouts and consolidations, publishing firms gained financial resources along with more sophisticated business and marketing skills. However, there was a cost. Many publishers lost autonomy in decision making. More and more, they had to show constant profits for their stockholders and new owners. Publishing was no longer a dignified club, but an objective business. Today, mergers and sales of companies take place at a dizzying pace. Publishing companies are now no different from other businesses, being subject to buyouts, takeovers, and, above all, concern about annual earnings.

These economic changes forced publishers to alter the ways that they acquired, produced, and sold books. Until recent decades, publishers ran their own printing plants, binderies, and bookstores. Now they "outplace" much of what they once did "in-house." They contract with freelancers outside the company to design the book, edit the manuscript, provide photos, draw illustrations, proofread copy, prepare indexes and do many of the other tasks that are part of the process of producing books. The completed manuscript then goes to independent printers and bookbinders who manufacture the finished product.

Critics of publishing's new economic realities most fear the increasing role of *market research* in determining what will be published. Traditionally, publishers produced many meritorious works simply because they valued their high literary or scientific quality. They knew that such books would never yield large profits, but they published them anyway because the firms felt obligated to maintain high standards and to contribute to the accumulation of knowledge. However, as publishing houses passed into the hands of owners interested mainly in profits, they had to adopt a completely businesslike approach, together with modern management techniques.

Today, few book publishers are likely to express interest in noteworthy but unprofitable manuscripts. Instead, they are more likely to consider themselves simply as entrepreneurs, little different in principle from producers of beer, soap, or soup. Their aim is to manufacture a product that they can persuade consumers to buy, regardless of its other qualities. Thus, publishing today looks less like a craft or an intellectual enterprise and more like any other modern industry. Critics fear that neither the meticulous craftsmanship of the traditional publishing industry nor intellectual standards will survive, and that in their place we will soon find only "conformity to the median of popular tastes."[16]

## ▼ *The Publishing Process*

In addition to publishers, the key people in the production and distribution of books are authors, editors, book manufacturers, bookstores, and sales personnel. Naturally, many kinds of specialists and technicians have supporting roles. Since nonemployees now do so much of the work of developing a book, to a great extent contemporary publishers have become orchestrators—hiring and coordinating the work of many outside suppliers.

## Types of Publishers and Types of Books

Like theatrical producers, publishers (to some extent, at least) have styles and reputations. In part, these come from how they organize the publishing process, how they deal with authors, and the physical appearance of their books. In spite of the press for profits, a few publishers are still known for their craftsmanship, producing books of high quality. The majority, however, produce books as quickly and cheaply as possible. A few publish "instant" books shortly after news events. During recent years books came on the market almost overnight on such topics as the Oklahoma City bombing, several airline crashes, and various natural disasters like the San Francisco earthquake. Others focused on events that captured widespread interest, such as the O.J. Simpson trial. Such books take advantage of headlines while they are still freshly in mind.

A more important consideration is content area. Many companies focus on a general topic—for example, science, fiction, fine arts, medicine, law, or religion. There are other bases of specialization among publishers, such as nonfiction, high school texts, and so on. Table 2.1 shows a classification of books according to audience and function. As the pie chart (Figure 2.2) shows, trade books account for the largest share of books sold by publishers. Trade book sales, totalling about $4.4 billion, make up more than one-third of publishers' total book sales—and that share is rising.[17] Included are books published by university presses, although their output is a very small part of the overall

### Table 2.1    Types of Books

| Type | Description |
| --- | --- |
| Trade | Includes literature, biography, and all fiction and nonfiction books for general reading. These books are usually handled by retail bookstores. |
| Textbooks | Includes books for elementary and high schools, colleges, and universities. These books are usually sold through educational institutions or college bookstores, but publishers make their sales pitches to state or local school boards or faculty members. |
| Children's | Sold through bookstores or to schools and libraries. |
| Reference | Includes dictionaries, encyclopedias, atlases, and similar books. These require long and expensive preparation. |
| Technical and Scientific | Includes manuals, original research, and technical reports. |
| Law | Involves the codification of legal materials and constant updating. |
| Medical | Also requires frequent updating. |

Source: Smith, *Guide to Book Publishing*, pp. 128–129. Used by permission of University of Washington Press

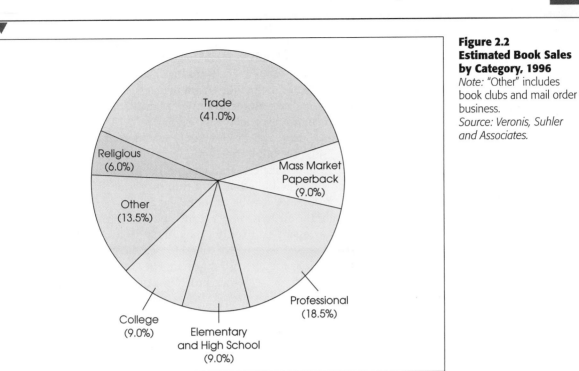

**Figure 2.2**
**Estimated Book Sales**
**by Category, 1996**
*Note:* "Other" includes
book clubs and mail order
business.
*Source: Veronis, Suhler
and Associates.*

Trade
(41.0%)

Religious
(6.0%)

Mass Market
Paperback
(9.0%)

Other
(13.5%)

Professional
(18.5%)

College
(9.0%)

Elementary
and High School
(9.0%)

business. However, university presses, associated with and often subsidized by a particular educational institution, are often far more important than their dollar sales would suggest. Their books are aimed primarily at scholars and scientists. However, in recent years many university presses have become more profit-oriented and have been expanding their lists to include topics of popular interest.

## From Manuscript to Finished Book

Since the time of Plato, whose *Republic* is the earliest surviving book-length work, books have had their first stirrings of life as ideas in the heads of their authors. However, authors are in a very real sense "outsiders" in the publishing world—that is, they are rarely employees of the publisher. However, because publishing is a competitive business, the author represents an important resource. Publishers must have a continuing flow of new manuscripts to process and sell and, therefore, authors are key players in book publishing. Whereas publishers have little trouble finding fiction manuscripts—indeed, the fiction publisher is often inundated—that is not the case for technical works and textbooks.

Beginning novelists may have a difficult time getting their works read by a publisher, but once a work is accepted, and especially if an author has previously produced successful works, things get better. The fiction author often receives a substantial advance (against royalties) from the publisher, ranging from a few thousand dollars (for a beginner) up to several million dollars or more (for a well-known writer). Royalties are some agreed-upon small percentage of the publisher's earnings from selling books to retailers. If the book is successful, a novelist may receive huge additional income from paperback contracts and even movie or television rights.

In the trade book world, authors normally use *literary agents* to represent them. The agent ferrets out book ideas, identifies authors whose works are likely to be of interest to publishers, contacts publishing houses and particular editors who may be interested in what an author is working on, and negotiates a contract with the publisher for the author. The agent receives a percentage (usually 15 percent) of the author's share from a book's earnings.

Either an author, an agent, or an editor may initiate the idea for a trade book. As publishers have increased their use of market research, the editor's role in initiating or reshaping the idea for a book has grown. For example, Time, Inc., sometimes sends prospective readers elaborate brochures describing a proposed book or series of books and eliciting responses. The replies received may lead editors to cancel the project or to change its proposed content, format, and promotion.

On the textbook side, the relationship between publishers and authors is different. Textbook authors are often sought out and asked to undertake a work that the publisher feels will sell. They are offered contracts before writing the book on the basis of a detailed outline and perhaps a draft of a chapter or two. However, textbook authors must be specialists in the field in which they are writing, and publishers carefully screen prospects. The financial incentives are also different. Textbook authors usually command lower advances than novelists or writers of other trade books, but a good textbook can often go through several editions, providing a continuous if modest source of income for both the writer and the publisher.

Clearly, publishers are risk-takers. Editor Dan Lacy, commenting on the "essence of publishing as entrepreneurship," notes, "The publisher pays the costs and assumes the risks of issuing each book, and hence he occupies a highly speculative position."[18] Of course, authors also take a risk. Writing a successful novel or a complex textbook can take years. Although the author may receive advances from the publisher before book publication, almost all the money will come much later from royalties. If the book does well, the author gets paid; if it does not, he or she has toiled a very long time for very little.

Once the publisher receives the author's original manuscript, several kinds of editors work on it. Publishing companies have many specialized editors, often with impressive-sounding titles, who are responsible for such activities as bringing in manuscripts, analyzing and editing them, and preparing the final copy for the typesetter. One kind is an *acquisitions* editor, whose work may be devoted mainly to generating ideas for books and finding able and willing authors. Other editors may evaluate the quality of manuscripts and their sales potential. Some work directly with the author as *developmental* editors to organize the book and help make it the most effective statement of its topic. There are also *copy* editors, whose main task is to check the spelling, syntax, and grammar of a manuscript and check *proofs* (preliminary printed versions of pages). Other specialists develop illustrations and design the print style, cover, and format of the book. As noted earlier, many of these tasks may be done by freelancers on a contract basis.

To set the manuscript into type, publishers hire outside companies called *compositors.* Publishers also buy paper and contract with printers and binders. Sales representatives from the publishing company persuade independent booksellers to carry the company's books, school boards to adopt them, or college and university faculty members to assign them. A few publishers also run their own chains of bookstores.

Thus, the publisher brings together and coordinates a complex team including authors, editors, designers, compositors, printers, and booksellers. Through the various stages of bookmaking, publishers try to control the cost, schedule, and quality of the work. Their role, in publishing executive Dan Lacy's words, is "somewhat analogous to that of a theater producer, or an independent film producer."[19]

## The Publisher as Entrepreneur

Like the other media industries in the United States, the book industry largely pays its own way. One of the few exceptions is the U.S. Government Printing

The retail book industry is undergoing a pattern of change that took place for many other kinds of products in earlier years. Today, the sale of groceries, office supplies, hardware and home improvement products, and even clothing is dominated by supermarkets, superstores, and discounters. Mom-and-pop bookstores and the relatively small establishments in shopping malls are being replaced by elaborate and economically efficient retail outlets owned by large chains and conglomerates. (Copyright © Andrew Brilliant, The Picture Cube)

Office, the nation's largest publisher. It turns out thousands of documents, pamphlets, and books each year, but it does not do so for profit.

The mainstream of American publishing is found in the large publishing houses, many of which are located in New York City. In fact, just 2 percent of the nation's publishers account for about 75 percent of book sales.[20] However, small publishing houses flourish across the country. A publishing company can begin with only one or two people and little equipment, hiring outside suppliers on a book-by-book basis. Unlike the small radio or TV station, the small book publisher needs no federal license, and unlike a small newspaper, the enterprise is not limited to a local audience. Through selective promotion and direct-mail advertising a new firm can command national attention and sales. Book publishers can thus begin with limited capital, publishing only a few titles until they begin to show a profit.

In view of what we have said up to now, it may seem surprising that many books—perhaps most—*never turn a profit!* It is very difficult to forecast whether a book will succeed, so the publishers are forced to gamble. However, publishers survive because the earnings for a good seller can be high enough to pay for other books that lose money or barely break even. Moreover, if a book at least breaks even, it keeps a highly skilled staff in place and working until the really hot seller comes along. If that does happen, they are sorely needed indeed.

A continuing debate centers on the quality of contemporary books. As a profit-oriented industry, often owned by large conglomerates concerned more with the bottom line than anything else, many critics feel that the book industry has lost important qualities that it once had:

> Of late, books and book publishing have come under fire not only as a doomed medium, but as a once-great institution fallen to schlock and profit mongering. Publishing houses have turned into houses of ill repute, the critics sniff, charging that the bottom line and market-oriented decision making has resulted in such a lowering of quality that book publishers, if not doomed by illiteracy and competition, should be nonetheless put out of their low-brow misery.[21]

The contemporary book industry uses a variety of marketing techniques. Included are direct mail, telephone marketing, professional meeting displays, book clubs, and magazine ads. Publishers sometimes offer a reduced rate for buying the book in advance of the publication date. Virtually every promotional device used to market other products has been tried for books. However, traditionally, publishers have tiny advertising budgets compared with other consumer product industries. Perhaps more than other forms of print, books depend on other media. For example, they depend on magazines and newspapers to promote books through reviews and paid advertising. Authors frequently appear as guests on television and radio talk shows, where they promote their books.

The problems of profit making on the trade side of publishing and on the textbook side are quite different. Publishing college textbooks is not a large industry. Total dollar sales were only about one-third the dollar sales of trade books. Moreover, it is an industry with an uncertain future. For example, Table

2.2 shows that the trade side of publishing is thriving. The number of trade books sold each year has *increased* steadily and their prices have kept pace with the general rate of inflation. College texts, however, show a slower pattern of growth. Table 2.3 shows that the number of new college texts sold has increased only gradually. Although there were slight drops in overall college enrollments until about 1992, that trend has now been reversed. Even so, drops due to earlier declining enrollments do not even come close to explaining the significant lag in the number of new textbooks sold in our nation's college bookstores.

Accompanying the slow growth in new college texts sold is a significant rise in the wholesale prices charged by publishers. They have nearly trebled over the last decade and a half, rising far faster than the rate of inflation. How can these glaring differences between trade books and textbooks be explained? The answer is that this trend in textbook costs reflects not publishers' greed but the growth of a highly sophisticated *used-book trade*. This phenomenon poses a serious problem for students who are captive consumers and who suffer the most.

The problem begins when publishers produce new or newly revised textbooks, which instructors adopt for their classes. Textbooks are expensive to produce, and because knowledge in most fields advances regularly, new books and updated versions of ones previously published are constantly required. However, at the end of the semester, bookstores buy up used copies very cheaply from students who bought them new. Students watching their budgets have little choice but to sell at the price offered by the bookstore (there are no alternative buyers). Once the used books are obtained, the bookstore holds them until the beginning of the next semester and then sells them back to the next wave of students. Those books that remain unsold locally are wholesaled at a profit to companies specializing in swift nationwide redistribution of used books. This process is repeated after each semester.

At first glance, the used-book trade looks like it ought to be a boon to students—after all, they do not have to buy new books. They can get a used copy for slightly less. In fact, however, the

**Table 2.2  Trade Books Versus Textbooks: Millions of New Books Sold by Publishers, 1982–1996**

| Year | Trade Books | Textbooks |
|------|-------------|-----------|
| 1982 | 459.2 | 115.2 |
| 1984 | 519.7 | 112.2 |
| 1986 | 562.6 | 111.1 |
| 1988 | 609.7 | 130.2 |
| 1990 | 704.5 | 136.9 |
| 1992 | 760.4 | 136.6 |
| 1994 | 779.0 | 135.2 |
| 1996 | 827.0 | 138.9 |
| 1998* | 885.0 | 138.4 |

*Estimated

Source: Veronis, Suhler and Associates, *Communications Industry Forecast*

**Table 2.3  Retail Prices Charged by Publishers for College Texts, 1982–1986**

| Year | Price |
|------|-------|
| 1982 | $ 8.99 |
| 1984 | 10.42 |
| 1986 | 11.88 |
| 1988 | 13.75 |
| 1990 | 15.13 |
| 1992 | 16.16 |
| 1994 | 17.40 |
| 1995 | 18.97 |
| 1998* | 20.68 |

*Estimated

Source: Veronis, Suhler and Associates, *Communications Industry Forecast*

system is the engine that is relentlessly driving up both new *and* used textbook prices. What happens is that the bookstores price the used copies just below the cost of a new book. This is logical enough; they buy low and sell high—the classic formula for success in a capitalist system. And, because they have no production costs (which are all borne by the publisher), their profits are very high.

An unfortunate consequence of the system is that the costs of both new and used books for the student rise sharply for two reasons: First, publishers have to compensate for their loss of markets by revising books more often so as to create more new products. A few years ago, textbook revisions were on a four- or even five-year cycle. Today, the cycle is only two years on average and it may grow even shorter. Second, each revision creates publisher's costs. Book editing, producing, and marketing is a labor-intensive process, and it cannot be done cheaply by machines as is the case with many consumer products. Thus, publishers have to price all new books high enough to cover their production costs, knowing that used books will eat up their market within a single year, or two at most.

This situation has produced a kind of spiraling escalation that has already made textbooks very expensive, whether new or used. This spiral poses serious problems for *publishers* whose profits shrink, for *authors* who lose their financial incentive for writing them, and above all for *students* who have to pay increasingly high prices for both new and used books.

Tremendous controversy surrounds this situation. No one blames the students for trying to stretch their dollars by selling their books or buying used versions. No one blames bookstores for being efficient capitalists. No one blames publishers for wanting to stay in business. But the present system artificially forces both new and used textbook costs sky-high and likely to go higher. At present, there does not seem to be any viable way of reversing this cycle.

Another factor pressuring textbook costs upward is the unauthorized reproduction of copyright-protected work of authors and publishers using photocopying machines. Whereas individuals are allowed to copy material for personal use under the "fair use" provisions of copyright law, reproducing copies to sell for profit is illegal. One well-known firm (Kinko's) specializing in making such copies has been successfully sued by a coalition of publishers for extensive reproduction of copyrighted material being sold to students.[22]

## The Future of Books

What will be the future of books? All in all, they are reasonably profitable today, and they play a substantial role in American intellectual life and entertainment. However, for some years now pundits have predicted the death of books as they now exist—printed on paper, bound between covers, and sold in bookstores or by other retailers. It would be much more efficient, such futurists maintain, to place books on-line, where they could be accessed via the Internet. This vision includes the idea that libraries with hard copies will disappear, to be replaced by databases of electronic books. Then, students or other kinds of readers could simply call them up and read them on their computer screens. Or, if they prefer hard copy, the pages could be printed out on the home printer.

At present, these changes seem unlikely. Although there certainly is a great deal of textual material on the Internet and its World Wide Web, and for some uses this is highly efficient, there are reasons to doubt that electronic versions of books will soon replace their traditional form. There are a variety of reasons for this conclusion. First, it is difficult to see how publishers could make a profit from people in various parts of the world who would log on to a site where the book would be available. Perhaps that will eventually be accomplished in some way, but current technology is not suitable for this task. Second, given the limitations of the Internet, it would take a very long time to download a book of several hundred pages. Moreover, it is not clear under such a system how adequate protection could be provided for protection of intellectual property. Third, reading a book from a computer screen while scrolling down continuously seems awkward. Printing a book on a home printer would be a Jovian task, at least with present technology. Finally, it is difficult to see how authors would receive payment to write such a book in the first place.

Perhaps at some future point an increasing number of books may be available on-line. This would require some sort of small and inexpensive computer-like device to show pages on a screen that could easily be read and assumes the other problems will be solved. At present, the best guess is that books will survive and remain popular as a traditional paper-based medium for much the same reasons as they have enjoyed since printing began—that is, books in their present form are *portable, permanent,* and *cost-effective.*

First, portability is an attractive attribute—one can carry a book anywhere without need for electronic circuitry or a cord to plug into the wall. Electronic miniaturization may eventually reduce this advantage of books but probably will not eliminate it any time soon. Books also have permanence. Unlike other more transitory media, we can save them on our shelves for decades and refer to them conveniently whenever we want. Books are user-friendly—they require little effort to open and read. One does not need special software or complex technical skills, which is not true of alternative media. As yet it remains difficult to thumb leisurely through an electronic system, which requires expensive machines. Although we have deplored the surge in costs of textbooks, even an expensive text is cheap on a cost-per-word basis compared with buying a computer and associated software to read print on a screen. These features, along with the fact that education is becoming more and more important in our "credential" society, indicates that books appear to be here to stay.

One trend that is having an influence on the book industry is a pattern now developing in retailing. A new wave of "superstores"—bookstores stocking up to one hundred thousand titles or more and owned by large conglomerates—has arrived.[23] These are increasingly replacing small chain-owned stores in malls as well as privately owned neighborhood operations. The superstores do to bookselling what Home Depot, Kmart, MacDonald's, and supermarket chains did to the hardware, general merchandise, fast-food, and grocery industries. The older "mom and pop" bookstore is rapidly becoming a thing of the past, just as are the neighborhood hardware store, the small grocery store, and so on.

Clearly, the book industry remains robust, especially in trade books, even though critics once claimed that the public would tire of all forms of print. It is difficult to make forecasts at a time when all media are in a state of change and realignment. However, a number of scholars and observers of the book publishing industry foresee the following trends ahead:

- Because of escalating production costs, hardcover books may be on the way out, as publishers find it increasingly difficult to compete in today's mass market in both trade and text publishing.

- Highly diversified small publishing houses and university presses with far lower marketing and distribution costs will flourish, while big labor-intensive commercial houses may decline.

- Because of rising costs, direct-mail sales to customers may begin to replace retail marketing in both text and trade publishing.

Overall, the outlook for books is positive. With expanding markets, new retailing, and vigorous publishers, books will remain a powerful force, even in the face of the electronic media. Although we recognize that at some point in the future there may be changes, books will remain popular, will be important, and will continue to be printed on paper for the forseeable future.

## CHAPTER REVIEW

▼ Cave paintings were human beings' first attempts to represent ideas graphically. Such efforts represent a transition from purely oral description to the graphic depiction of ideas.

▼ Ideographic systems based on pictographs began about 4,000 B.C. Improvements came slowly over about two thousand years until phonograms came into use. Eventually writing was greatly simplified when alphabets were invented. Our alphabet is based on early forms standardized by the Greeks and passed on to the Romans.

▼ Solutions to technological problems have always been the basis of more effective media. When portable media replaced stone, longer documents and even libraries of scrolls became possible. The Romans made the first books with letters on both sides of cut and bound pages and end boards or covers. They also developed many of the written

language formats that we still use in books and other printed material.

▼ The skills of writing and manuscript preparation were kept alive during the Dark Ages by the Christian monasteries, but after the twelfth and thirteenth centuries they passed into lay hands as well. Meanwhile, paper had come into use, and the stage was set for print.

▼ A great technological advance came when Johannes Gutenberg developed both a workable press and cast metal type. His invention was enormously important and quickly spread throughout the Western world.

▼ Book publishing came late to North America, but when it caught on books had a powerful influence on the spread of literacy and on popular opinions and ideas.

▼ As a medium, books are slow to produce, but they provide permanent storage of ideas that can be repeatedly referred to at a pace convenient for the user. They remain society's most influential medium—and the major repository of civilization's most significant ideas.

▼ A publishing house processes the content of a book from author's manuscript to finished product. The publishers, who risk capital, hoping to make a return on their investment, fill the role of bringing together individuals with diverse talents to create an end product, somewhat in the manner of a movie or theater producer.

▼ There are many kinds of books and publishing houses. A major division is between textbook and trade publishers. An emerging category is the software publisher.

▼ Publishers are entrepreneurs who use different strategies to make a profit on what they produce. Many books published do not make a profit, and the ones that do have to support those that do not.

▼ Textbook publishers' profits are hurt and the cost of books is forced up by the resale of used books, with only the bookstores benefiting, and by illegal reproduction of copyright-protected material.

▼ Books in their traditional form are likely to survive due to their portability, permanence, and cost-effectiveness. The changes that lie ahead are more likely to be in their production and retailing than in a drastic modification of their form.

## CHAPTER 3

# *Newspapers*

## The First Medium for the Mass Society

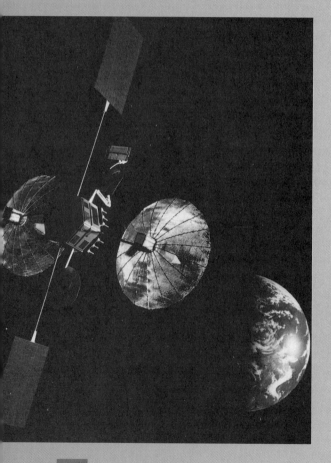

S ince the earliest use of language, people have been interested in gossip and tidings about people in their midst, others outside their group, and events in distant places. For millennia, the only way they exchanged such news was at social gatherings, taverns, and fairs. Their only medium was word-of-mouth information passed on by travelers or roving troubadours. Traditional media for exchanging news were other people and verbal exchanges.

The first *published* news (in the sense of being formally "made public" in writing) came shortly after the birth of Christ. Every day, the Roman Senate posted handwritten information sheets, called *acta diurna populi Romani* (daily transactions of the Roman people), in public places.[1] These announcements provided current reports about the Senate's actions and decisions, along with more general information on political and social life in the capital. Professional scribes made their living by copying these bulletins and delivering them to interested citizens in the city or abroad. For many centuries, however, the delivery of news in written form was confined to private correspondence and newsletters. The clients for such services were mainly diplomatic envoys, the aristocracy, and merchants.

The development of newspapers was first spurred by *technology,* as was the case with each of the mass media. Gutenberg's printing press provided a critical foundation. Four centuries later, the ability to print soared swiftly as steam was linked to a power-driven press. Then in the 1800s came cheaper paper, zinc engraving, the telegraph for news-gathering, the typewriter, photography, the electric press, and typesetting machines. In recent decades computers and satellites have become essential, both to assist in gathering news and in controlling many of the mechanical functions required to produce and distribute a newspaper.

But technology is only part of the story. Various social systems had to be designed to gather news, prepare it for the press, and deliver it to users. Economic solutions were another major factor. Like everything else, operating a newspaper costs money. Ways of paying for the labor, materials and related services had to be invented. Finally, newspapers, like other forms of print, have the potential of shaping people's ideas. That seemed to pose a threat to those in power. Even today, some national leaders control newspaper content in order to maintain existing relationships between rulers and the ruled. For Americans, the regulation of newspapers by government became a significant issue during the eighteenth century. It was one of the issues that led to the American Revolution. Freedom from such control was established in the First Amendment to the new nation's Constitution.

# ▼ *The Development of Newspapers*

Essentially, the story of newspapers begins with Gutenberg's press. Soon after its invention, printed descriptions of important news began to appear. These brief documents were the forerunners of newspapers, and they were sent relatively quickly to distant places. For example, the story of the voyage and discoveries of Columbus spread through Spain in the form of printed copies of his own accounts within a few months of his return. From there, by word of mouth and private correspondence, descriptions of what was found (often grossly exaggerated) traveled relatively swiftly to all the major cities in Europe.

## The First Newspapers

The printing press was used in a variety of ways to provide news, even during its earliest years. In the mid-1500s, leaders in Venice regularly made available to the public printed news sheets about the war in Dalmatia. To receive a copy, Venetians had to pay a *gazetta,* a small coin. (The term "gazette," so frequently used in newspaper titles, comes from that source.) An obscure forerunner of what we would now call a newspaper was apparently printed in Germany in 1609. Not much is known about it. Better known is the *coranto* of the same period. The coranto was a brief printed news sheet whose form originated in Holland. During the early 1600s, corantos were being published periodically for the commercial community in several countries. The oldest surviving example, printed in 1620, is shown on page 63. It could be regarded as the first newspaper in English, although it lacks certain features of a true newspaper as we define them today.

Newspapers of more modern times have several characteristics not found in these earlier publications. Edwin Emery, a distinguished historian of journalism, has defined a newspaper in the following terms. He said that a true newspaper

1. Is published at least weekly
2. Is produced by a mechanical printing process
3. Is available (for a price) to people of all walks of life
4. Prints news of general interest rather than items on specialized topics such as religion or business
5. Is readable by people of ordinary literacy
6. Is timely
7. Is stable over time[2]

By this definition, the first true newspaper was the *Oxford Gazette* (later called the *London Gazette*). First published in 1665 under authority of King Charles II, the *Gazette* appeared twice a week and continued publication well into the twentieth century. This was an "authorized" newspaper, which means that its content was controlled and screened by the Crown.

The new tydings out of Italie are not yet com.

Out of Weenen, the 6 November.

THe French Ambaſſadour hath cauſed the Earle of Dampier to be buried ſtately at Preſburg. In the meane vvhile hath Bethlem Gabor cited all the Hungeriſh States , to com together at Preſburg the 5. of this preſent , to diſcourſe aboute the Crovvning & other cauſes concerning the ſame Kingdom.

The Hungatians continue vvith roveing againſt theſe Lands. In like manner thoſe of Moravia , vvhich are fallen upon the Coſackes yeſter night by Hotleyn, ſet them on fire , and ſlaine many dead , the reſt vvill revenge the ſame.

Heere is certaine nevves com , that the Crabats , as alſo the Lord Budean, are fallen unto Betlem Gabor.

The Emperour ſends the Earle of Altheim, as Ambaſſadour to Crackovv in Polen, to appeare upon the ſame meeting-day.

Novv comes tidings, that Betlem Gabor is at Thurna, there doe gather to gether great ſtore of States.

The Emper. Maj. hath appoynted heere a meeting-day upon the 1. of Decemb. thereupon ſhould appeare the 4. Proclaimed States. The appoynted taxing ſhall bring up a great ſom of money.

Out of Prage , the 5 of November.

Three dayes agone are paſſed by, 2.mile from this Cittie 6000.Hungarians ( choſen out Soldiers) under the General Rediſerens, vvhich are gon to our Head-camp, & the Enimie lieth yet near unto ours by Rackonits , though the crie goeth,that the enimie cauſed all his might to com togither,to com this vvayes againſt Prage, if that comes to paſſe, it ſhall not run off vvithout blovves,the vvhich might be revealed vvith in ſevv dayes.

It coutinues, that in the Satſer Crais are gathered togither 10000 Coutrie-men,moſt high-dutch-men, againſt Meiſlen, & no Bohemians , they vvill help the King,to drive the enimie out of the Land. In like manner ſom certaine 1000 Contrie-men rebel in the LentmaritſcherCrais, but it is feared that thoſe Countrie-men are ſtarred up , through practiſe of the Adverſarie, that the enimie in the meane vvhile might com to Prage. We underſtand, that Bucquoy hath not been in the Camp,but by the Duke of Saxen ſom certaine dayes , therefore vve are to looke to our ſelves,for feare of Trecherie. And it is thought that the Emperour vvill leave Auſtria to the Hungorians, & ſee to effect his intention only uppon Praghe.

Out of Ceulen, the 21. Novemb.

Writing from Marpurg in Heſſen , that the Earle of the ſame Land, doth cauſe the foreſaid Cittie to be ſtrongly fortified , there on doe vvorke many 100 men dayly , and there is muſtered in the Earleſhip Zigenheym not long ſince 1 .Governement of foote-men , & 6.Cornets of horſe-men , the foote-men are ſent to Marpurg & Rijnfels. But the horſe-men are lodged in the Villages about the Cittie , & thereafter are alſo muſtered the Duke of Saxen Lauvvenburgs Governement in Tries-Zigenheym, novv further vvhere they ſhallbe laid & uſed, is yet unknovvn. The ſames Brothers Governement,there quarter is laid by Caſſel , the Souldiers vvhich are taken on about Hamburg, Lubeck,in the Dukeſhip of Holſteen , & Meckelenburg,ſhould alſo be muſtered about Caſſel , & be uſed vvhere neede ſhall require.

Since the laſt vve cannot enquire, that there is any thing of any importance paſſed betvvixt the Marquis Spinola & the Vnited Princes. We underſtand that the foreſaid Spinola vvil lay his Souldiers in Garniſſon vvith the firſt , & deale them unto divers places,on part to Oppenheym, Altzey,Ingelheym & Cruiſinach,the other part at Summeren & Bacharacht , the ſpeech goeth that there ſhalbe layed vvith in Ments a good Company in Garniſſon.

The Biſhop at Halberſtadt, Duke Chriſtiaen at Bruynſvvyck,doth cauſe to be taken on 2000 Muſquetters,to ſend to the Vnited Princes.

Heere is tydings , that betvveen the King of Bohemia & the Emperours ſolke hath beene a great Battel about Prage , but becauſe there is different vvriting & ſpeaking thereuppon , ſo cannot for this time any certainety thereof be vvritten,but muſt vvayte for the next Poſt. As alſo of the Cittie Pilſen , vvhich the Earle of Manſvelt (ſo the ſpeech goeth) ſhould have delivered into the Emperours hands.

From Cadan in Bohemia , 4 mile from Raconits,the 12. November.

From Solts is certaine adviſe that the Emperours folk have made them ſelves vvith all theire might out of theire Camp,& taken their vvay to vvards Praghe, like as they vveare then com to the long mile , but as the King underſtand ſuch , he is broken up vvith his armey,and com to the log mile beforen the enimie, vvhere they have had a very ſtrong Battelle & on both ſides more then 6000 men ſlaine , though moſt on the Kings ſide , alſo hath the enimie gotten of the King ſom peeces of Ordentaunce and vvaggens vvith amunitie,ſo that the King muſt retire back to Praghe , and the enimie to the Weiſſenberg , there he lies yet and roves from thence to the Leut Maritſciter Crais unto Brix,

The oldest known newspaper in English of which a copy survives was printed on November 21, 1620. It lacked a title, suggesting that it was not published regularly in the manner of a true newspaper. However, as you can see, this page provided relatively current reports about events in several European countries.
(The British Library)

The first daily newspaper in English, the *Daily Courant* (from *coranto*), began publication in London on March 11, 1702. A newspaper of high quality and considerable integrity, the *Courant* was not really a "mass" medium, because it maintained a sophisticated literary level and appealed primarily to an affluent and educated elite. However, like the more popular newspapers that would come in the nineteenth century, it recovered some of its costs from advertising.[3]

After the late 1600s, censorship was rarely enforced in England. However, it was a different story in the American colonies. The colonial press was tightly controlled, because insurrection was always regarded as a possibility in such remote colonies. Thus, control of printing presses was relatively constant, and it came from the Crown's governor of each of the colonies. In spite of those efforts, however, colonial governments soon faced lively and independent newspapers.

## The Press in the American Colonies

The growth of newspapers in the American colonies was tied closely to cultural, economic, and political circumstances that existed at the time. Both the population and commerce grew steadily, creating a market for news of shipping and trading as well as a need for a limited amount of advertising. As political tensions over such issues as taxes and control of trade grew, the colonial newspapers often published criticisms of the Crown's policies. One of the more significant of such criticisms appeared in Boston on September 25, 1690—the first (and last) issue of a paper titled *Publick Occurrences Both Forreign and Domestick.*

This four-page paper was the work of Benjamin Harris, a printer who previously fled to Boston from London, where the authorities first jailed him and later seized one of his publications. In it, Harris managed to insult both the Indians, who were allies of the British, and the French king. The governor of Massachusetts banned Harris's paper on the grounds that it was published "without authority" (prior review by the Crown's representatives) and that it contained material disapproved by the government.

While it survived only a single issue, *Publick Occurrences* was important, not only because it was first in time but also because it spoke out against the government. However, because it was not published continuously, it does not really fit our definition of a newspaper. The honor of being the first American paper in that sense should go instead to a dull publication called the *Boston News-Letter,* which first appeared—"published by authority"—in April 1704. John Campbell, the publisher, was also the postmaster of Boston. As postmaster he was able to mail the paper without postal charges. For early colonial papers, a connection with a post office was almost indispensable, because there really was no other way to distribute the paper.

The *Boston News-Letter*'s content consisted mainly of dull treatises on European politics, shipping reports, and some advertising. The result, according to Edwin Emery, was a paper that was "libel-proof, censor-proof, and well-nigh reader-proof."[4] Because of a lack of public interest, the paper never really became a financial success, but it did survive for seventy-two years. Somewhat better was the *Boston Gazette,* which William Brooker began in 1719. It was much like the *Boston News-Letter,* but both its printing and its news information were crisper.

## Establishing Traditions in American Journalism

The manner in which the American press operates today is very different. Newspapers are protected by the First Amendment's provision for freedom of the press and by a body of law developed over two centuries. Those protections are an end product of a long chain of events that started during the colonial period. As the eighteenth century progressed, colonial governors continued to suppress articles that criticized the government. However, their control was gradually subverted by rather bold printers and publishers in a long struggle marked by numerous conflicts and harsh repressions.[5]

**The Press as Watchdog of the Public Interest.**   In 1721, James Franklin—an older brother of Benjamin Franklin—started his own paper, the *New England Courant.* It was something of a departure from the restrictive colonial tradition because it was not "published by authority" and had no connection with a post office. It was aimed at a well-educated and prosperous elite and appealed mainly to those who liked literary essays and controversial political opinions. It also contained shipping reports and information from nearby towns.

The *Courant* was the first newspaper in the colonies to "crusade" on a public issue. During an outbreak of smallpox in Boston, it argued strongly against the newly invented medical procedure of smallpox inoculation. While, from a medical standpoint, its position turned out to be wrong, using the newspaper to "speak out" against a situation seen as harmful to the public began an important tradition that would come to characterize American newspapers. Increasingly newspapers would become "watchdogs of the public interest," a role that they continue vigorously today.

Successful and bumptious, the *Courant* criticized this person, poked fun at that one, and finally attacked the governor himself. As a result, the governor cracked down, and Franklin was thrown in jail for a month. He was ultimately forbidden to publish the *Courant* or any paper "of like nature." Franklin was clever, though, and he got around the restriction by making his brother Benjamin the publisher.

Young Ben Franklin had been apprenticed to his brother at age thirteen and began to gain firsthand experience with printing. He worked as a "printer's devil," setting type for the paper, and did all the other chores of an apprentice. At a tender age he even tried his hand at writing essays, signing his first works "Silence Dogood" and craftily slipping them under the door of the print shop at night. They were cleverly written and when published provoked many replies by other essayists. When his brother was in jail, young Ben operated the print shop and paper. By 1729 he had moved on to take over the *Pennsylvania Gazette* in Philadelphia. Franklin not only made that paper a success but anticipated another tradition that would characterize journalism later—he established a small chain of newspapers.

**Establishing the Principle of Freedom of the Press.**   Of great importance in the unfolding struggle to establish a free press was the conflict over the rights of the press that developed early in the 1700s. This conflict would result in a court trial that pitted John Peter Zenger against William Cosby, governor of New York. Its outcome would help establish the principle of freedom of the press in the colonies. Printer Zenger was persuaded (and funded) by a group of businessmen in New York to establish a newspaper, the *New York Weekly*

*Journal*, because they wanted to have a paper in opposition to the officially authorized *New York Gazette*. Zenger began publication in 1733, and his paper ran articles openly critical of the governor and his policies. That was too much for Governor Cosby, and he had Zenger clapped in jail on a charge of "seditious libel." **Sedition** means promoting disaffection with government—inciting people to revolt against constituted authority. **Libel** means publicizing untruths. However, under British law of the time, it really did not matter whether what the defendant published was true; it was the seditious intent that was the major offense and the central issue of the case.

Zenger was brought to trial before a jury of fellow colonials in 1734. The governor's case seemed airtight. Zenger had, in fact, broken the existing law. However, Andrew Hamilton, a distinguished lawyer, undertook his defense. Hamilton freely admitted that Zenger had published articles criticizing the government. However, he argued with great conviction that the articles were true, and that in spite of what the law said, no one should be punished for printing the truth. Hamilton's argument convinced the jury that they should ignore the judge's instructions and declare Zenger not guilty. They did so, in a stunning upset. The governor was furious. The significance of Zenger's trial was that it established an important principle: the press should be allowed to criticize government. That idea would eventually find its way into the First Amendment to the Constitution, which would be formulated a half-century later.

## Characteristics of the Colonial Press

The colonial papers were small, usually about four pages of a mere ten by fifteen inches each. By 1750, most Americans who could read had access to some kind of newspaper. However, although many newspapers were started during the period, few were successful because they were difficult to support financially, and distribution remained a problem. The majority failed after only a few issues.

The colonial papers were very limited in many ways: Their news was seldom up to date, they were published infrequently, and they were slow to reach their subscribers. The papers were usually delivered by mail, traveling to subscribers by horse and carriage, pack trains, or sailing vessels. Rapid delivery of newspapers would have to wait until the next century. In addition, until 1783, when the *Pennsylvania Evening Post and Advertiser* was started, the colonies had no daily newspaper.

The colonial papers were also limited by existing technology. The hand press used by Benjamin Franklin and others in the late 1700s was little different from the one used by Gutenberg in the mid-1400s. Paper was still made from rags, not wood, and it was both expensive and always in short supply. Compounding the problem, literacy rates were very low by comparison with later centuries. No universal systems of free public education had been established. Schools were available mainly for the children in the larger towns and for the elite who could afford private tutoring or academies. Little schooling was available for the vast majority who lived on farms.

We noted earlier that advertising is an important source of financial support for newspapers. However, there really was a limited need for advertising in colonial times. The great rise in consumerism that we know today had not yet arrived. It was a product of the Industrial Revolution, the advent of easy distribution by improved transportation, and the development of well-coordinated retail systems. Thus, there were not many products to be advertised and few markets could provide a solid financial base for the support of newspapers.

Another factor limiting colonial newspapers was that they restricted their own audiences. Many were *partisan* papers. They consistently argued for only one point of view. When political parties developed at the end of the eighteenth century, each had certain newspapers under its control. Some even subsidized their papers. After the Revolution, the number of *commercial* newspapers increased, but they were also intended for a restricted audience. They recorded commercial transactions and business matters, such as shipping and foreign economic news, which interested merchants but few others.

All the papers, commercial and partisan, were aimed at comparatively well-educated and relatively affluent subscribers, who made up only a small part of society. They were also very expensive, which made them unavailable to the common people. Around the time of the American Revolution, a newspaper might cost six to ten dollars a year, about as much as a worker's salary for one or two weeks. In today's terms, that would be like paying several hundred dollars for a year's subscription. Few people would be willing to pay that much.

In spite of these limitations, the colonial press established valuable traditions of journalism that were to become an important part of the emerging American press. Many papers defied the Crown's authorities, and spoke out on behalf of the public. They showed that the press could be a political force. Writers such as Thomas Paine and Samuel Adams helped build public support for independence. After the Revolution the most famous treatises debating various features of the Constitution (the *Federalist Papers*) were first presented in newspapers. From its colonial beginnings, then, the American press established itself as an important political force—a monitor and critic of government. By any measure, it retains that position today.

## ▼ *Newspapers for the Common People*

By the early nineteenth century, the Industrial Revolution had started. Innovators were beginning to solve the technological and other problems needed to provide widely circulated newspapers for the public. It was a time when all

▶

A technological limitation holding back the development of the mass newspaper was the hand-powered printing press. This engraving shows how newspapers were produced shortly before the introduction of steam-powered presses in 1830. Note the typesetter at the left rear using the upper and lower cases for majuscule and minuscule letters. The compositor in the foreground is arranging the lines of type in a frame. The man near the press is applying ink to a frame of type, and the one in the center is checking a printed page prior to hanging it up to dry.

kinds of new machines were being driven by steam power to accomplish many tasks with astonishing rapidity and uniformity. The printing press was no exception. With the old screw-type press, a well-trained team of two printers working full speed could put out only a few hundred sheets per day at best. By 1830, steam-powered rotary presses were introduced. They were a truly significant improvement in technology. Even the earliest could produce 4,000 sheets per hour printed on both sides.[6]

At first, the new presses benefited only book publishing. However, their existence also meant that newspapers would be able to greatly increase their circulation if the right combination of content, subscribers, and financial support could be found. Both the population and the percentage of people who could read had increased, but existing newspapers were still expensive at six cents a copy. For a working person who made only four or five dollars a week, they remained a luxury. If a daily newspaper wanted to multiply its circulation, it had to overcome this price barrier—recovering its costs in some other way.

## The Emergence of the Penny Press

On September 3, 1833, a strange little newspaper appeared on the streets of New York. Published by Benjamin Day and called the *New York Sun*, its masthead carried the slogan "It Shines for All." That slogan was somewhat misleading. The *Sun* was not designed to appeal to everyone, but specifically to the less sophisticated. Day offered his readers news that was nearest at hand—the incidental happenings of New York life. The *Sun* was filled with human interest items about common people. In its first issue, on page one, Day declared: "The object of this paper is to lay before the public, at a price within the means of everyone, all the news of the day, and at the same time afford an advantageous medium for advertising."

Day began an important newspaper tradition when he hired the very first salaried "reporter," who went to the local courts each morning and wrote lively stories about local happenings, with an emphasis on crime, human interest, accidents, and humorous anecdotes. (The term "reporter" is derived from those who recorded court proceedings.) Another feature of the new paper was that it was sold on the streets by **newsboys** for only a penny. This system of distribution worked well. The newsboys (some of whom apparently were girls who dressed like boys) bought the papers in lots of a hundred for sixty-seven cents. If they sold the whole hundred, they earned thirty-three cents, which was quite a profit for a youngster at the time.

One of the most important features of the *Sun* was that advertising played the central financial role in Day's system. The penny that buyers paid for their copy did not recover the costs of production. The *Sun* made its profit by selling advertising space for a great variety of products and services. This was possible at the time because the new factories were producing a greater variety of goods, and new retail establishments were selling to larger and larger markets.

The paper was an instant success. Soon it was selling more than eight thousand copies per day. From there its sales doubled, and within three years it was

◀

Using enterprising newsboys to distribute papers began in the 1830s. It was part of the innovative systems used by the penny press to reach new and much larger audiences. This form of distribution was relatively rapid compared to delivery by mail, which was the only means available during earlier periods. (Library of Congress)

selling an astonishing thirty thousand copies daily. Other journalists were astounded and they scrambled to imitate Day's model.

Within a few months the *Sun* had competitors and the mass press became a reality. Together, all the competing newspapers who adopted Day's basic formula were known as the **penny press.** Particularly noteworthy was the *New York Herald,* founded in 1835 by the colorful James Gordon Bennett. Bennett imitated Day, but he also added many features that became part of modern newspapers—for example, a financial page, editorial comment, and more serious local, foreign, and national news. Horace Greeley's *Tribune* and Henry Jarvis Raymond's now famous *New York Times* were also started during this period.

The penny papers had very distinctive characteristics that made them completely different from the colonial press. They were vulgar, sensational, and trivial in many respects. Publishers after Bennett, however, began to carry increasing amounts of basic economic and political news as well as editorial viewpoints regarding public matters. As they developed, then, the penny newspapers brought at least some significant firsthand information and ideas to large numbers of people who had not been readers of newspapers up to that time.

## The Impact of Society on the Growth of Newspapers

During the nineteenth century, three great changes took place in American society that had significant influences on the growth of the nation's newspaper industry. One was the rapid expansion of the *population.* The second was the remarkable evolution of *technology,* which increased enormously the ability of journalists to gather, transmit, print, and distribute news. The third was the influence of the *Civil War,* which stimulated a great demand for news and the development of increasingly efficient systems for getting it to newspapers and from there to subscribers.

**Rapid population growth.** The rate of population growth in the United States during the nineteenth century was unprecedented in history. During the two decades preceding the Civil War (1840–1860), millions of people arrived, especially from northern Europe. Most settled in our eastern states and the Great Lakes region. At the same time, steady streams of internal migrants moved westward, settling along a continuously expanding frontier, establishing new towns and cities where newspapers were needed. Even higher levels of immigration, especially from southern and eastern Europe, came during the last half of the century. People were needed to occupy the vast lands that had been acquired from France and Mexico. As these new residents acquired English, they subscribed in ever-increasing numbers to daily newspapers.

**The revolution in technology.** As the nineteenth century progressed, the industrial and mechanical arts flourished at a remarkable pace. Beginning about 1830, ever larger and more elaborate steam-powered rotary presses could print, cut, and fold increasing thousands of finished newspapers per hour. Cheap paper to feed these presses was being made from wood as early as 1867.

In another great advance in technology, the telegraph wires along the rail lines linked major cities and made possible the rapid transmission of news stories to editors' desks. The same day Samuel F. B. Morse sent the historic "What hath God wrought?" from Washington to Baltimore (May 25, 1844), he also sent over the wire the news of a vote in Congress. Soon **wire services** would be established and newspapers in all parts of the country began to receive a flow of stories from the "lightening lines."

The telegraph truly opened a new era. It was the beginning of a fourth great revolution in human communication (following speech, writing, and printing). It ushered in an era of instantaneous communication across great distances. From the dawn of human awareness until the invention of the steam train, communication between two people over a distance had been limited to the speed of a swift runner (about 15 miles per hour), or a galloping horse (about 25 miles per hour) or at most a flying pigeon (perhaps 35 miles per hour over distance). But by the early 1840s, trains had achieved the awesome speed of 45 miles per hour. Many people regarded this as a final limit, and thought that any further increase would be a violation of God's plan for humankind. They warned that people might fly apart if such dangerous speeds were exceeded.

It is difficult today to imagine what people thought when it was announced that a means had been devised to send a message at the mind-boggling speed of *186 thousand miles per second*—more than fifteen times around the world in a mere wink of the eye. It was, in the words of moon astronaut Neil Armstrong, more than a century later, "a giant leap for mankind." As we will see later in the chapter, the telegraph opened a new era in the history of newspapers as associations were formed to transmit news along the new network of wires.

The rapid expansion of the railroads and steamboat lines also promoted the growth of newspapers. Now daily papers printed in the city could be delivered across substantial distances so that people in surrounding communities could receive the news in a timely manner. The ancient dream of conquering both time and distance with an effective medium of communication was becoming a reality.

**The Civil War.**   The great conflict between the North and the South enormously stimulated the development of newspapers. Its battles resulted in terrible slaughter—the worse loss of life our country has ever known. People on both sides of the conflict were desperate for reports of the battles and news about the fate of their loved ones. The hundreds of reporters in the field often devised ingenious methods to get their reports out ahead of their competitors. Faster and faster steam presses across the nation churned out millions of copies daily.

By 1839, photography had been developed. It would be more than three decades before photographs could be printed in newspapers, but the existence of the technology stimulated the beginnings of pictorial journalism as photographers captured the nation's history on their plates. During the Civil War, one of the country's leading photographers, Mathew Brady, persuaded President Lincoln to let him make a photographic record of the battlefields. Brady was

▶

During the Civil War, newspapers sent hundreds of reporters to the fields of action. The reporters lived and traveled with the military forces. The officers in charge wanted favorable publicity. The top photo shows the portable field headquarters of the *New York Herald,* with its staff being briefed on the next engagement. The grim side of the war is shown in Mathew Brady's photo of soldiers killed in battle. Although the printing of photos in newspapers was still a decade away, Brady's 3,500 photos of the conflict became American classics of great significance. (Smithsonian Institution Photo No. 73-5137; Library of Congress)

given unrestricted access to military operations, together with protection by the Secret Service. He and his team made some thirty-five hundred photographs—one of the most remarkable photographic achievements of all time.[7]

By the end of the century, the newspaper was a technologically sophisticated and complex mass medium. Newspaper publishers had at their disposal a rapid telegraphic news-gathering system, cheap paper, linotype, color printing, cartoons, electric presses, and, above all, a corps of skillful journalists. The newspaper had settled into a more or less standard format, much like what we have today. Its features included not only domestic and foreign news but also a financial page, letters to the editor, sports news, society reports, "women's pages," classified sections, and advice to the lovelorn. Newspapers were complex, extremely competitive, and very popular. Furthermore, they had no competition from other media.

## The Era of Yellow Journalism

Because newspapers in the United States were profit-oriented, privately-owned businesses, they were very competitive. It was this competitiveness that led to a brief era of *yellow journalism,* one of the most colorful periods in the history of American newspapers. It came about because the key to financial success in a newspaper, then as now, was to attract as many readers as possible. By showing advertisers that more people would see their messages than in a competing paper, a publisher could sell more ad space at higher prices and enjoy greater revenues. During the last decade of the century, the competition for readers among the large metropolitan papers led to a remarkable period of sensational journalism.

The penny papers took the first steps, with their emphasis on crime, human interest, and humor. Then, by the early 1890s, Joseph Pulitzer succeeded in building the circulation of the New York Sunday *World* to over 300,000. To do this, he combined good reporting with "crusades," an emphasis on disasters and melodramatics, sensational photographs, and comic strips—all to intensify reader interest. Pulitzer also crusaded against corrupt officials, for civil service reform, and for populist causes, such as taxes on luxuries, large incomes, and inheritances. He pioneered the use of color printing of comics in newspapers, which did much to spur the circulation of his Sunday editions.

One popular cartoon in the *World* made history. It featured a bald-headed, toothless, grinning kid, clad in a yellow sacklike garment. The "Yellow Kid," as the character came to be called, appeared in settings that depicted life in the slums of New York and was soon at the center of a controversy when William Randolph Hearst, who founded the *San Francisco Examiner,* set out to master the art of attracting readers. Hearst expanded to the east and purchased the New York *Journal* in 1895, determined to build its flagging circulation to surpass that of Pulitzer's *World.* Hearst simply bought the Yellow Kid cartoonist from his rival with a large salary and added other writing and editorial talent. Then he published more comics, more sensational reports, and more human interest material—all of which led to greater circulation.

As the circulation of Hearst's *Journal* began to rival that of Pulitzer's *World,* the two newspaper barons led their papers further into practices that would significantly influence the style of American journalism of the period. Many smaller papers resisted the trend, but for more than a decade, many large metropolitan newspapers came to be preoccupied with crime, sex, sob stories, exposes of sin, disclosures of corruption in high places (many of which were gross exaggerations), sports, dramatic photographs, misrepresentations of science—indeed, anything that would attract additional readers.

It was said that each issue of Hearst's papers was designed to provoke one reaction from its readers: When they saw the headlines, Hearst wanted them to say, "Gee whiz!" Responsibility to the public seemed to have been abandoned. The new style came to be called **yellow journalism.** Many historians believe the label derived from the Yellow Kid cartoon character because it symbolized the newspapers' mindless intellectual level.

As the nineteenth century came to a close, yellow journalism in the Pulitzer/Hearst tradition died with it. Essentially, newspapers were reaching a saturation penetration of American homes and it was no longer possible to gain large increases in circulation by such tactics. In addition, people tired of that type of newspaper and wanted a more responsible press. However, as we will see, sensational journalism is alive and well in some metropolitan newspapers, especially in the curious tabloids commonly sold in the supermarkets.

# ▼ Trends That Have Shaped Today's Newspapers

As daily newspapers became available to the public, they were not immediately subscribed to by every family in the nation. Like other innovations, the number of people who adopted them was limited at first. Soon, however, the number grew rapidly. Then, after reaching a high point, it leveled off. Thus, over time, their pattern of use of the daily newspaper forms a typical **curve of adoption** of innovation. One of the major trends in the present century, then, is the ever-changing relationship during each decade between the number of subscriptions to a daily newspaper in the nation compared to the number of households in the country at that time.

A second trend that began in the last century is the development of two major *auxiliary services* that supply newspapers with content they do not generate themselves. One such auxiliary is the wire services, mentioned earlier, that bring to local newspapers a daily flow of stories from beyond their community. The second is made up of a number of **syndicates**—commercial groups that contract with publishers to provide a great many of the features that make up the content of today's newspapers.

A third major trend is the changing *pattern of ownership* that has characterized American newspapers in this century. Only a small proportion of our nation's papers remain in the hands of the families who started them. Increasingly, newspapers are owned by *chains*. Some of the chains, in turn, are owned by even larger groups—conglomerates made up of many kinds of businesses and industries. These changes have brought about a significant decline in the number of daily newspapers that publish in the United States. This concentration of ownership has generated a great deal of debate as to whether the nation is being well or poorly served by its contemporary press.

## Newspapers as Cultural Innovation

Scholars who study patterns of social and cultural change in societies have noted that inventions introduced into a society, or items borrowed from other societies, follow a typical pattern as they are taken up—that is, adopted and used.[8] Specifically, when the proportion of the population in a society who

# EXPLAINING MEDIA EFFECTS

## *Adoption of Innovation Theory*

In a changing society, there is a constant flow of new technical products, solutions to problems, interpretations, and other kinds of innovations. They can range from the trivial, such as a new dance step, to the profound, such as a new political philosophy (like communism or democracy). Sometimes the origin of an innovation is well known. Specific persons may invent them at a particular point in time, as when Thomas Edison invented the phonograph on July 18, 1877. At other times the origins of an innovation are lost. For example, it is entirely unclear who first invented the hamburger, although that delicacy has been almost universally adopted by the American population.

Many innovations are adopted by a population after having been invented elsewhere. For example, many in the world eagerly adopted the powered aircraft after Orville and Wilbur Wright first flew one in 1903. Other borrowed innovations are adopted by people in a society by a far less obvious process. For example, the now-popular pizza was virtually unknown in most of the United States before about 1945.

But whether invented or borrowed, every innovation is taken up by people in a particular society in a rather regular process well-described by the theory of the **adoption of innovation.** This theory is important for the study of mass communication for two reasons: First, each of our major mass media was originally an innovation that had yet to be adopted and widely used. Examples are the mass newspaper (which began in New York in the early 1830s), the motion picture (beginning at the turn of the century), home radio (early 1920s), television as a mass medium (post–World War II) and so on. Each spread through the society following a curve of adoption. A second way in which innovation theory is important to the study of mass communication is that the media are often largely responsible for bringing new items to the attention of people who eventually adopt them.

The theory of the adoption of innovation was originally formulated by sociologists, but it is now widely applied to many fields.[9] It can be summarized briefly in the following set of propositions:

**1.** The adoption process begins with an *awareness stage* in which those who will ultimately adopt an innovation learn of its existence (often from the mass media), but lack detailed information about it.

**2.** Awareness is followed by an *interest stage*, during which those who contemplate adoption will devote increasing attention to the innovation and seek additional information about it. The media are often providers of some of this information.

**3.** In an *assessment stage* such individuals use the information obtained to evaluate the applicability of the innovation to their present and expected future situations.

**4.** In a *trial stage* a small number of these individuals acquire and apply the innovation on a small scale to determine its utility for their purposes.

**5.** Therefore, in the final *adoption stage*, a few innovators actually acquire and use the innovation on a full scale. After that, increasing numbers adopt it and the accumulation of users follows a characteristic "S-shaped curve" that starts upward slowly, then rises quickly, and finally levels off.

---

Not all adopters go through all of these stages in acquiring every innovation. In addition, some innovations spread swiftly and are taken up by virtually everyone, while others are adopted more slowly to be used by a smaller final proportion of the population.

begin to use such an innovation is plotted against time, a *curve of adoption* is described. Figure 3.1 shows the adoption curve for newspapers in terms of the proportion of U.S. households who subscribed to a daily paper over succeeding decades.

Subscribing to a daily newspaper by the reading public followed the classic curve of adoption well into this century. In later years, a declining pattern has been evident as subscriptions per household have continued to drop. The classic curve of adoption is an S-shaped pattern that starts slowly, rises swiftly, and then levels off. As Figure 3.1 shows, after a slow start during the nineteenth century, subscriptions to daily newspapers per household did grow sharply during the last decades of the 1800s, reaching a peak early in this century until about the time of World War I.

These major features of the pattern can best be understood in terms of the relationship between newspapers and other mass media in America. By the time of World War I, circulations had grown to a point where many households in the United States were subscribing to both a morning and an afternoon paper. Thus, during the early decades of the new century, newspapers enjoyed a

## *Trends in Media Use*

**Figure 3.1 The Curve of Adoption of Daily Newspapers in the United States, 1850–1996**

Subscriptions to daily newspapers rose at an increasing pace during the last half of the nineteenth century, especially during the era of yellow journalism. Newspaper usage peaked around the time of World War I, when many households subscribed to both a morning and an afternoon paper. It was the medium's golden age. People urgently wanted news, and there were no competing sources. Later, as radio, magazines, and then television began delivering news, subscriptions declined steadily. At present, about two households in three maintain a subscription to a daily newspaper.

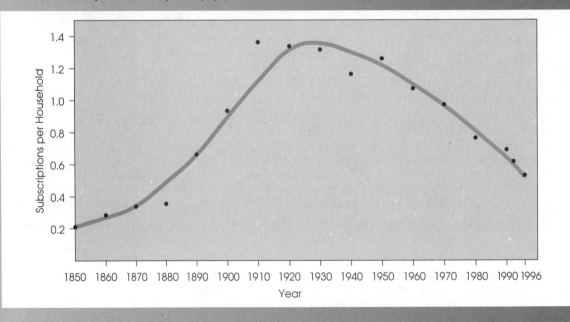

kind of "golden age." However, as the curve of adoption indicates, it would not last. Newer media arrived and newspapers entered a pattern of decline in subscriptions per household—a trend that continues today.

As a consequence of these changes in usage, there has been a corresponding pattern of change in the *number* of daily newspapers published in the United States. Between 1880 and 1900 that number more than doubled, from 850 to 2,226. But, as Figure 3.2 shows, after 1910, when the country had over 2,200 English-language plus nearly 400 foreign-language dailies, the number of papers grew smaller and smaller. Some papers merged; some dailies became weeklies; others suspended publication completely. The U.S. Census reports that the number of daily newspapers declined from 2,042 in 1920 to just over 1500 in 1997.[10]

As Figure 3.1 showed earlier, the golden age of the newspaper was between about 1910 and 1930. Subscriptions per household were about twice what they are today. The great decline was a consequence of several factors. Obviously, as the 1930s began, television was not a reality and radio was neither a serious contender as a news medium nor a strong competitor for the advertising dollars of business and industry. Furthermore, as we pointed out

## Trends in Media Use

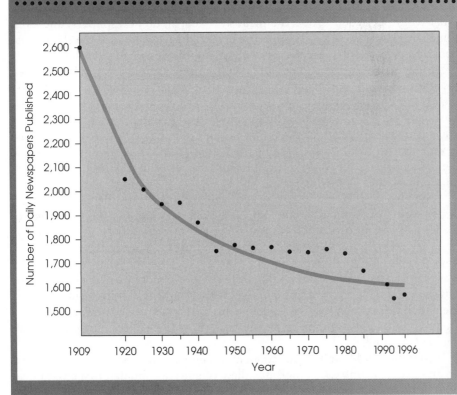

**Figure 3.2
Daily Newspapers
Published in the United
States, 1909–1996**

The number of daily newspapers published in the United States has declined sharply since the early part of this century. During the first decade, the daily paper had no competition as a source for news. As other media began competing, not only for the news audience but also for advertising revenues, a long-term trend of consolidation and concentration of ownership began. Today, many cities have only one newspaper, and most papers are owned by chains. The trend toward concentration of ownership continues as papers merge or are purchased by chain owners.

earlier, the mass newspapers had both impressive technologies and elaborate news-gathering systems. After 1930, however, the costs of news gathering and all other aspects of publishing began increasing. Furthermore, competition for advertising dollars from radio, and eventually television, rose relentlessly. Consequently, papers began to fail financially or were purchased by their rivals to consolidate production and other facilities. These trends have continued up to the present time and are likely to continue.

## The Growth of Wire Services

The second trend influencing newspapers is the growth of two kinds of national organizations that supply them with much of their daily content. These are the *wire services* and various *feature syndicates*. If you doubt the extent to which modern papers depend on these sources, take your local newspaper, clip all the stories that come from wire services and the material provided by feature syndicates, and put the clippings aside. You will probably be left with only stories from your local community, a lot of advertisements, and little more.

Thus, even though most newspapers are still geographically local, they depend on the wire services to bring them regional, national and international news, and on syndicates to provide cartoons, comic strips, columns, crossword puzzles and other familiar features found in the daily paper. The advantages of these services are many. One is lower cost. For example, hiring a full-time comic artist would be well beyond the means of most small newspapers, and even some large ones. But a syndicate can hire such an artist and sell the strip to papers across the country, greatly reducing the amount charged to each.

Today's wire services grew out of an agreement in the early 1840s between several newspapers in New York, Baltimore, and Philadelphia who pooled their resources to provide faster, cheaper, and more comprehensive news of the Mexican War.[11] This temporary but innovative agreement set a precedent in that the newspapers were cooperating rather than competing in covering the news. Then, in 1848, several small papers in upstate New York agreed to share the cost of having a reporter telegraph news stories from Albany, the state capital, to each paper along the wire.

The idea of a wire service worked well and others decided to try it on a larger scale. A few months later, six New York newspapers signed an agreement to share the costs of telegraphing foreign news from Boston, where ships first arrived with the latest dispatches from Europe. This agreement was the forerunner of the modern Associated Press (AP). During its earliest years, AP was mainly an organization linking eastern newspapers. However, as Americans moved westward and railroads grew, the new wire service began to cover the nation rather than just the East. During the Civil War, AP newspapers covered the great battles and troop movements, providing subscribing papers with detailed accounts.[12]

After the Civil War, various cooperating and competing AP groups sprang up around the country. Some groups died; others consolidated in a reorganization of the Associated Press in 1900. The competitive undercurrent, however, pointed up a problem—membership in AP was closely controlled. In some cities rival newspapers had difficulty holding readers because they lacked the advantages of AP membership and its extensive news coverage. These conditions led to the development of competing wire services. Shortly after the turn of the century, Edward Wyllis Scripps, the owner of the Scripps chain of newspapers, founded the United Press Association (UP), which began operation in 1907. William Randolph Hearst formed his own press association, the International News Service (INS), in 1909. From that time until 1958, the United States was served by the three rival services (although AP always outdistanced the other two). In 1958 UP and INS merged into United Press International (UPI), to promote more vigorous competition with AP.[13] This, however, never happened, and UPI's demise has been predicted for years. New to the competition is North American Reuters, the British Service, which has a large client base in the United States. Added to the mix are a number of vigorous supplemental wire services organized to provide a variety of news and feature material.[14] Examples are The New York Times Service, the Washington Post/Los Angeles Times Service, the Copley News Service, the Knight-Ridder News Service, and Gannett News Service.

From their beginnings, the "wires" changed American newspapers. In the early days, sending stories by telegraph was very expensive, and clarity and precision were essential. The correspondent in the field had less time for the flowery language and elongated sentences common to early nineteenth-century newspapers. Before long, reporters and editors began to distinguish between "telegraph" and "newspaper" stories. The concise writing needed for wire stories eventually produced AP's famous lead of "who, what, where, why, and how." Stories transmitted by wire were organized into the **inverted pyramid style,** in which the most important elements were first, the next important second, and so on. Thus, if a local newspaper needed to save space, a story could easily be shortened by dropping less important details from the tail of the inverted pyramid.

Another consequence of the system resulted from the fact that wire stories had to appeal to newspapers in different regions with various political persuasions. This meant limitations on opinionated and controversial interpretations of the news. To achieve this goal, AP pioneered what would later be called the **objective** report.

Thus, almost from the beginning the wire services broadened the content of news—allowing more newspapers to have a wide range of coverage from distant points, narrowing journalistic style, and increasing the level of objectivity in news coverage. Today, stories are not sent by telegraphic wire, but are transmitted via computer networks linked in various ways by telephone line, optical cable, or even satellites.

## The Development and Role of Syndicates

The feature syndicates, like the wire services, trace their origins to the mid- and late nineteenth century. Early on, journalists recognized the importance of entertaining readers as well as informing them. Entrepreneurs among them surmised rightly that they could make a profit by offering newspapers a package of ready-to-print "features" including opinion columns, poetry, cartoons, short stories, and many other kinds of non-news content. They formed companies to provide such material.

The first syndicate was organized by two Wisconsin newspapermen just after the Civil War. By the late nineteenth century, several more offered services to newspapers. By the early 1900s, syndicates offered opinion pieces, political cartoons, and comic strips as well as columns on fashion, personal problems, politics, and other topics. Almost from the beginning, the syndicates played an important role in making the work of particular writers and artists popular among millions of readers.

The earliest syndicates directed their appeals to small papers that could not afford to produce their own material, but eventually they also sold to larger papers. Some syndicates were tied to a particular group of newspapers; others sought clients throughout the country. At first they provided printed pages that had feature material on one side and blank pages on the other so that local papers could fill in local advertising and news. Later, syndicates circulated copy that could be photographed and used by offset presses. Today there are more than three hundred syndicates, ranging from those with billings of more than $100 million per year to small firms that represent one or two writers.

The role of the syndicates is not without its critics. Some are concerned that they exert too great an influence on newspapers.[15] Certainly, the syndicates provide a remarkable variety of entertainment and opinion material for newspapers, including editorial cartoons, serializations of popular books, columns by noted political commentators, comic strips, puzzles and games, movie critics, plus columnists who write about astrology, automobiles, books, bridge, politics, gossip, consumer advice, human relations, music, religion, and television. In addition, some syndicates sell design services, graphics, and even newsstand racks. They promise that their material will bring circulation gains and readership studies indicate that they are sometimes right. For example, "Dear Abby" and "Ann Landers" often head the list of the most-read items in a newspaper, and the comics have always had strong appeal. Newspapers have occasionally fought vicious court battles to retain a particular columnist or cartoonist.[16]

Because relatively little is written about syndicates and all are privately-held companies, even their size and scope remains something of a

Syndicates provide many kinds of content to newspapers on a daily basis. This source relieves local publishers from having to produce such material independently and reduces their costs in the long run. It also results in a certain similarity among American daily newspapers, with the public able to read syndicated material such as Dear Abby whether they are in Boston, Kansas City, or San Francisco. (UPI/Corbis-Bettmann)

mystery. One way to measure the reach of a syndicate is by the number of newspapers or magazines it serves. The top five by this criterion are King Features Syndicate (started in 1914 by William Randolph Hearst), United Media (owned by Scripps-Howard), North American Syndicate (founded by Rupert Murdoch), Tribune Media Services (owned by The Tribune Co.), and Universal Press Syndicate.

## Changing Patterns of Ownership

A third major trend that has shaped today's newspapers is the consolidation of their ownership. This consolidation has taken place because in spite of the fact that newspapers have lost the enviable position they held early in the century as the *only* source of news, and that they now must compete for advertising dollars with other media, they continue to earn a great deal of money. Although information on newspaper profits can be hard to obtain, the data that are available show that newspaper profits are almost *twice* what is being earned per dollar of investment by the nation's five hundred leading corporations![17] Thus, although subscriptions are shrinking, profits remain high.

**The growth of chains.**   The profitability of American papers is due largely to the buying up of individual papers by chains. Like the mom and pop hamburger stand, the independently owned newspaper is very close to extinction. Economic forces—soaring costs in labor, material, and services—have led to a great expansion of chain ownership of newspapers. For example, by 1997 the Gannett Corporation owned 92 daily newspapers as well as 18 television stations and 3 radio stations in 37 states, Guam, and the Virgin Islands. Gannett, which owns *USA Today,* one of the nation's largest newspapers, also owns *Sports Weekly, Sunday Magazine,* a printing company, new media, offset printing firms, and other holdings. Such chains also own other kinds of businesses.

Determining the relative size and scope of a newspaper chain or group is more difficult than it may seem. Some critics are fond of counting the number of newspapers owned, whereas others look more to circulation figures. What is easier to assess is the pattern of change over time. Going back to 1920, during the period when newspapers were enjoying a virtual monopoly on the news industry, there were only 31 chains or newspaper groups in the United States, and each owned on the average fewer than 5 newspapers.[18] By 1960, 109 chains were becoming more common and they controlled an average of 5 newspapers each. By 1986, this number had risen to 127 chains with an average of 9 dailies per chain. Looked at another way, the number of actual papers owned by chains rose from 153 in 1920 to just over 1200 by 1990. Thus, chains own about 75 percent of all of the daily newspapers published in the United States.[19]

The trend will slow in the years ahead because in 1997 only 351 independently owned newspapers were left to be absorbed. Chains are not likely to establish additional papers because they would then be competing either with themselves or with well-established papers that already dominate local markets. However, in the decades ahead, big chains most likely will continue gobbling up smaller ones. A pattern will probably emerge that looks very much like what happened to the fast foods and American automobile manufacturers. In 1920, there were more than a hundred brands of cars being manufactured in the United States. By 1990, only Ford, Chrysler, and General Motors remained. In like manner we may soon see a "Big Three" of chains controlling our nation's newspapers.

**The implications of chain ownership.**  For many critics, this change in newspaper ownership has ominous implications. As Richard McCord points out, those who established the chains often used dubious practices and harsh means.[20] Moreover, chain ownership implies an ability on their part to control the news and thereby (potentially) to shape how readers think about events. Another troublesome factor is that most communications enterprises have in the past been owned by companies that specialize in communications, although other corporations have moved into the field. Media critics warn that in a few years a handful of corporate conglomerates might have a stranglehold on the nation's newspapers.

There are three reasons why control by such "absentee owners" is more alarming than dominance by large communications industries. One is that absentee owners, with far-flung and diverse economic interests, have little commitment to local communities *per se*. Second, they are not likely to be committed to expensive but critical journalistic watchdog traditions. And third, a conglomerate is designed primarily to make profits on "products," and news may come to be defined as only one of many products in a conglomerate's portfolio.

Those who plead the cause of media diversity argue that big media ownership greatly limits the number of independent local voices. They also note that family-owned, locally-controlled papers are often better papers. This view is disputed by William H. Henry III, of Time, Inc. who has written that family-owned newspapers are often marked by nepotism and parochialism.[21] Moreover, both minorities and women benefit from strong equal opportunity programs at group-owned papers.

When all is said and done, however, the big question is whether the trend toward consolidation of newspaper ownership will actually restrict debate and robust discussion of issues in such a way that it will change the *missions* and *quality* of the American press. In the days of William Randolph Hearst, the corporate offices in New York dominated his chain's newspapers. As our account of yellow journalism showed, that *did* change their mission and quality. Today, however, only a few newspaper groups issue direct orders to local editors about editorial policies, although they do firmly control finances and have generally high expectations about local newspaper profits.

Overall, the implications of chain ownership remain an open question. At some point in the future, Americans may find that the papers they read have about as much local autonomy in what they print as does a Kentucky Fried Chicken franchise in what it cooks. On the other hand, as we have seen, the search in the past few decades has not been for ways in which to dominate readers' opinions regarding political or moral positions. Their search instead has focused on ways to maximize profits by giving readers more of what *they* want and think they need. In other words, newspaper content in a profit-oriented economic system is *audience-driven* rather than *owner-driven.* Although that may limit corporate control of news, it may also mean that, in the search for greater returns on investment, the focus on entertainment will increase at the expense of providing information to the public.

## New Roles for Computers

As computers developed from the giant "electronic brains" of the 1940s and 1950s to increasingly smaller and more powerful desktop machines of today, they found their way into newsrooms and other divisions of newspapers. Computers now not only set type, keep track of payrolls, and help manage other business data, they have become a working tool of everyone from reporters to top managers. Dean Brent Baker of the College of Communication at Boston University predicts that computers will play an increasing role in journalism during the years to come. Indeed, as he points out, in many ways that future is already here.[22]

The development of the Internet, with quick access to databases, is an important part of this development. As part of their function in providing in-depth coverage and analysis, many journalists now use computers to access on-line databases as part of their basic tool kit. Huge amounts of data on virtually every conceivable subject are available to them through vendors who assemble and manage databases such as Lexis/Nexis and similar computerized systems. Most newspapers in the country (except the smallest) subscribe to such services. Today, reporters routinely access on-line databases to search for background information that can be helpful in developing stories.

Photo journalists have benefited from new digital technologies. Increasingly the older cameras and wet-development processes are being replaced with digital counterparts that permit sophisticated editing and modifications of pictures. By using computer software, it is relatively easy to create pictures that totally misrepresent reality. It would be no great trick to produce a picture of President Clinton embracing Saddam Hussein on the White House steps. Recent cases of doctoring photographs have raised significant ethical issues for photojournalists. When *Time* magazine produced a picture of O.J. Simpson for their cover, they deliberately darkened the skin tone of his face. Critics felt that this made him look more ominous.

Hundreds of newspapers and magazines now produce on-line counterparts that can be reached via the World Wide Web on the Internet. The degree to which this convergence of electronic and print technologies will have an impact on newspapers is difficult to forecast. It is as likely to increase revenues as it is to reduce them. It remains unclear at this point how to make a solid profit from these on-line services. This situation changes almost daily, and the ultimate nature of the Internet, its content, uses, and financial support may be different in the future than it is at this time.

Another important application of computers to journalism is in what Margaret H. DeFleur and others have called **CAIR** analyses (Computer-Assisted Investigative Reporting).[23] This is essentially the use of computer-based statistical analyses of the electronic records of government or other agencies to develop news stories on their activities. CAIR was developed because few such agencies continue to keep massive files on paper. Almost all have turned to keeping their records in electronic form. This has made it difficult for investigative reporters to monitor the activities of government agencies by using traditional investigative strategies of "leaks" of documents, interviews with whistle-blowers, and so on. Such analyses of an agency's full records of transactions over a period of years can reveal patterns that would never be found by more traditional means. At first, this change hampered the watchdog function of the press. Today, however, CAIR analyses of computerized records routinely expose what has been happening within local, state, or federal agencies. Combining such computer analyses with traditional strategies of investigative reporting, newspapers have learned to monitor government and even private agencies to expose disquieting conditions that could be uncovered in no other way.

# ▼ *The Newspaper as a Contemporary Medium*

The difference is great between the simple colonial newspaper run by a single printer in a tiny shop and the complicated computerized operations of today's major dailies. As we have noted, more than 1500 newspapers now sell some 62.6 million copies every day. To examine this huge medium within a contemporary perspective, this section begins by examining various *types* of newspapers currently published. We then identify the *functions* that these newspapers serve for their readers. Our focus then turns to the *dual identity* that is shaped by both their political and their economic environment of newspapers. And finally, we summarize briefly the way newspaper work is *organized*.

## Types of Newspapers

Contemporary American newspapers come in all types and sizes, but most, past and present, have shared at least one characteristic: they are very *local* in their orientation and coverage. Although most American dailies cover national and international news, community and regional events receive far more space. In contrast, newspapers in many other nations emphasize national news and concerns. The United States does have a few national newspapers—for example, *USA Today,* the *Christian Science Monitor,* and the *Wall Street Journal.* In addition, the *New York Times*, and to some extent, the *Washington Post* are read nationwide, although both depend on their respective cities for most of their readers and each gives special attention to its area. Both carry at least some news of their city on the front page and devote a section to their region. Other large American papers, such as the *Boston Globe* and the *Seattle Times*, are regional papers with a distinctive local stamp.

We can divide almost all of America's thousands of newspapers into two very broad categories—*general-news* papers intended for readers within their area, and *specialized* papers aimed at a particular kind of reader, such as a specific minority group, those of a particular religious faith, or people with a well-focused interest. Both can be further classified in terms of how *often* they publish (daily, weekly, etc.) and their *circulations*—that is, how many people they reach. Using these criteria, most of America's newspapers fall into one of the following categories:

**Metropolitan dailies.**   Newspapers in the nation's largest cities have circulations (copies sold) that usually exceed 250,000 and a potential readership several times larger. Most metropolitan newspapers are printed full size—usually fourteen by twenty-two inches with six or seven columns, and they usually publish seven days a week. Their Sunday edition typically devotes considerable space to books, travel, the arts, personalities, and similar topics. Examples are the *Chicago Tribune* and the *Los Angeles Times*. Such papers reach readers not only in their metropolitan area but also in a large, multistate area. Others, such as the *Kansas City Star*, serve a more limited region around their cities. Still others, like the *Emporia* (Kan.) *Gazette*, have a primarily local readership. All, however, are distributed house-to-house by carriers, on the street in coin boxes or newsstands, and occasionally by mail.

The major metropolitan dailies include news, features, entertainment, sports, and opinion. They rely on the wire services for much of their national and international news, although a few have national staffs (usually based in Washington) and foreign correspondents in important cities around the world. Several have set up special investigative teams, such as the Spotlight Team of the *Boston Globe*, who put together detailed analyses of local or even national issues, problems, or scandals. Much of their content comes from syndicates.

Some metropolitan dailies are **tabloids.** Today, the term refers mainly to a special size—twelve by sixteen inches, with five columns. At one time a tabloid newspapers was one of low quality and sensational content. The big-city tabloids were usually splashy, designed to capture attention and high street sales with large bold headlines. Today the distinctions are less clear because tabloids (in the sense of size and format) include papers that mix sensationalism and professionalism (*New York Post* and *Boston Herald*) as well as the more sedate *Christian Science Monitor*.

Quite another category of tabloids are those displayed and sold at the check-out counter in supermarkets, and that feature unusual or bizarre stories often defying the imagination. Examples are the *National Enquirer*, the *Star*, and the even more extreme *Weekly World News*. Despite their remarkable content, these tabloids earn a great deal of money. The *Enquirer* earns a profit of over $17 million a year, with sales of well over $4 million a week.[24]

**Medium-sized and small dailies.**    Middle-sized newspapers in this category have more modest circulations (50,000–100,000), but are often physically hefty. They may have fewer of their own editorial resources than the major dailies, but they use wire service news and subscribe to syndicates that provide much of their feature material. Small dailies have a circulation under 50,000. They are even more locally focused than medium-sized dailies and sometimes are meant to be read along with a larger nearby regional paper. They are usually small relative to other dailies and use less material from external sources.

**Non-daily newspapers.**    Sometimes called the *community* or *grassroots* press, the weeklies were once exclusively rural or suburban publications. They ranged from suburban papers that featured lifestyle stories (for example, on apartment living or how to fund day-care centers) to small country papers dominated by local events and country correspondence. During the 1980s, an increasing number of new urban weeklies were founded. Some concentrate on their own neighborhood; others are sophisticated, cosmopolitan publications that review such topics as politics and the arts. Urban weeklies like New York's *Village Voice,* Chicago's *Reader,* or San Francisco's *Bay Guardian,* are mainly supplementary reading for people who are already informed about news and public affairs from other media.

**Free-distribution newspapers.**    Papers that were originally called "shoppers" by the commercial press have been published for decades. Beginning in the 1980s, many of these papers took a more aggressive stance in competing with traditional daily and weekly newspapers by adding more news and entertainment material, as well as calendars of local events and various features. Many have been willing to print publicity material for local organizations and groups without much editing. These papers, once dismissed by the mainstream press, have become formidable competitors for advertising. Indeed, a number of conventional papers have begun their own free-distribution papers.

**The ethnic press.**    During those periods of our history when massive numbers of immigrants were pouring into the United States, the foreign-language press was substantial. In colonial times, French papers were common. During the late nineteenth century, German and Scandinavian papers prospered. But as the older immigrant groups assimilated into the general population, foreign-language papers tended to die out.

Today, both foreign-language papers and papers written in English but aimed at a particular ethnic group make up the **ethnic press.** Because of continuing immigration from Mexico and Latin American countries, the number of Spanish papers is increasing. The same is true of papers aimed at Asian immigrants. However, many of the papers serving racial and cultural minorities are now published in English rather than in foreign languages.

The African-American press began in the nineteenth century. Today the United States has several black-oriented newspapers, including the *Baltimore Afro-American*, New York City's *Amsterdam News*, and the *Chicago Defender*. Most of these newspapers emerged because of segregation in the white press, which virtually ignored African-American people and their concerns. For many years it was difficult for blacks to get jobs within the mainstream media. By and large, the press itself took steps to reverse this situation. Many industry and professional newspaper organizations have developed special programs for recruiting and training minorities, although many fall short of their goals. There has also been greater emphasis on reporting on the minority community, although many media critics consider this coverage inconsistent.

**Other specialized papers.** The list of specialized papers can go on and on, including industrial and commercial newspapers, labor newspapers, religious newspapers, and those serving environmental interests, people pursuing unconventional lifestyles, special hobbyists, members of voluntary associations, and of course college students. There are even prison newspapers. Some of these papers are supported not by advertising but by membership fees or an organization's profits.

## Changing Functions and Content

Whatever the size of a newspaper, running it as a business means knowing how to make a profit, which means knowing how to sell the paper to the largest possible audience. A newspaper must derive income to survive. The struggle for existence, in the case of the newspaper, has been a struggle for *circulation*.[25]

To win this struggle, to maintain a flow of income from advertisers, newspaper publishers have had to adjust to the changing demands of their audience; they have done this by fulfilling a variety of needs among their readers and offering them many kinds of content that provide gratifications. The ways in which they do this can be called the *functions* of the newspaper. Even though they change from time to time, at least six major functions can be identified.

**Persuading, informing, and entertaining.** Around the time of the American Revolution, the number of functions served by newspapers was limited. As we have indicated, one major category at the time was the political papers, whose main function was persuading readers (or at least reinforcing the views of those already committed to the paper's point of view). To some extent today's newspapers continue to serve this *persuasion* function by supporting particular political candidates, promoting public policies, endorsing programs, and taking positions in their editorial pages. Some provide favorable or unfavorable news coverage of institutions, candidates, and issues. However, contemporary papers are more restrained and balanced in this function than were their counterparts a century ago.

The second category of early newspapers was the commercial papers, whose main function was providing information about the arrival and departures of ships, the availability of cargoes and goods, insurance matters, and so forth. In modern times the *information* function of the newspaper is especially alive and well, served in part by that portion of the paper actually devoted to news. This can be surprisingly small. After all the other material—such as feature stories, comics, syndicated columns, and advertising—is given space, room remains for important and unimportant news stories. This space—referred to as the **news hole**—makes up only about one-fifth of the paper. Other parts of the paper, such as weather forecasts and stock market reports, also serve this function.

To stay alive financially, contemporary newspapers must also serve an **entertainment function.** For this reason, a large amount of their content has little to do with news. It is designed to amuse and gratify readers. Thus, newspapers offer human interest stories, crossword puzzles, recipes, gardening hints, sports, and advice on everything from medical problems and fashions to how to rear your child.

One might be tempted to criticize newspapers for providing entertainment so as to boost circulations. It is obviously a strategy to generate advertising revenue from which the newspaper makes much of its profit. However, advertising messages are a necessary part of the newspaper's information function. People need a source to find out where in the local community they can apply for a job, lease an automobile, go to a movie, rent an apartment, buy a bed, or get clothing and food at reasonable prices—all of which are provided by various categories of advertising. Thus, advertisements by retail establishments and the classified sections are more than just promotional propaganda. They provide necessary information to consumers for the choices they need to make in daily life. In this sense, they contribute to the economic viability of the local community.

**Providing in-depth coverage and analysis.**   The *in-depth* or *analytic* function is closely related to informing. However, it goes beyond transmitting information by providing background details relevant to the news, explanations of related events, and analyses of their importance and implications. Newspapers are able to do this better than most other media. An increasing emphasis on this function in newspapers occurred when radio began to broadcast news reports. This posed a real threat, because newspapers lost their edge in *timeliness.* Radio (and later television and the Internet) could always get the news out faster. However, broadcast and even on-line formats provide for little more than a summary of the day's events. Consequently, newspapers today place less emphasis on the news "scoop" and more on the details and discussions of the meaning and significance of events.

**Serving as the "official" communicator.**   Increasingly over the years newspapers have worked out a special function as their local government's *medium of public record.* According to *Black's Law Dictionary,* an "official" newspaper is one "designated by a state or municipal legislative body, or agents empowered by them, in which the public acts, resolves, advertisements, and notices are required to be published." For example, the laws of a city or state may require that the government publish (in the sense of making public) notices of candidates filing for elections, auctions of property seized for failure to pay taxes, or building contracts open for bids. When a local government designates a paper as its official newspaper, it pays the paper to print these notices and advertisements as a means of placing them in the public record. Local governments often subsidize selected newspapers to serve as their official communicator in this manner. Sometimes the subsidy has made the difference between survival and bankruptcy. In many cities and towns the official newspaper is simply the community's main daily or weekly, but in large cities it is often a specialized legal or commercial publication.

**Appealing to specialized interests.**   Another change came during the second half of this century when newspapers took on the function of appealing to specific reader interests with whole sections of the paper devoted to particular kinds of content. For example, even the *New York Times,* known for its coverage of hard news in a staid, serious, and reliable style, now includes special sections each week called "Home," "Living," and "Weekend." Other papers appeal to readers' specialized interests with sections on food, personal ads, automobiles, and travel. Today, a typical newspaper might allot 20 percent of its space—about the same as for news—to various kinds of such interest-related sections, plus sports, comics, and so on.

A number of such interest-related topics have been aimed at one group in particular: the youth market—those in their late teens to late twenties. Newspaper executives have been increasingly alarmed by studies showing that fewer and fewer young people are newspaper readers, much less newspaper buyers. The trend suggested a bleak future for newspapers and it did not please advertisers. People in this age group, after all, are among those whom many advertisers most want to reach. As a result, the Newspaper Advertising Council urged newspapers to provide more material of interest that would provide gratifications for young people. The result has been special sections and more coverage of entertainment, such as rock groups and clothing trends.

In an effort to make it easier to serve all of the previously mentioned functions, newspapers have made many changes in format. Older papers had rather dreary formats with as many as nine columns of rather small type. By the 1990s, however, most papers had reduced the number of columns, added white space between them, and cut the size of the page. The result is a newspaper that looks livelier and is easier to read.

## Newspapers' Dual Identity and Built-in Conflict of Interest

Earlier in this chapter, we defined newspapers with a simple list of characteristics. However, not everyone sees newspapers in those terms. In fact, they can seem like different things to different people: Some simply see a profit-oriented business whose main goal is to make money for its owners. Others see an important source of information serving the public as a guardian of democracy. Still others see it as some combination of the two. For example, the United

States Department of Commerce defined newspapers in both business and public service terms:

> Newspaper publishing is the nation's tenth largest industry and its fifth largest industrial employer. The United States Constitution and its interpreters see newspapers as conveyors of information and opinion vital to the operation of government and the maintenance of freedom . . . The millions who read newspapers see them in myriad roles . . . . The newspaper is at once a private enterprise struggling in a highly competitive economy and a quasi-public institution serving the needs of all citizens.[26]

Thus, contemporary newspapers have a *dual identity.* On the one hand, the newspaper is a quasi-public institution charged with being the watchdog of the public interest and often an antagonist of government and other forces in power. This identity is a product of honored traditions of journalism established over more than two hundred years. On the other hand, as a business, the newspaper seeks to make a profit and function as a member of the business community, a major employer, and a member of the chamber of commerce.

This dual identity often brings with it an inherent conflict as business values and those of serious journalists clash. For example, the advertising department and news editors may compete for space, or they may argue over how some stories should be covered. Or, if a publisher sees the paper as only, or primarily, a business, why bother to fund an expensive computer-assisted investigation of a public agency that might reveal a pattern of bribes paid by local merchants to state regulators? Such a scandal is likely to antagonize advertisers and that would mean a loss of revenue. Why not just focus on human interest stories, gossip columns, the comics, and the sports section? These will maintain circulation and bring more advertising dollars. On the other hand, if the publisher does not see the paper as a business, and insists on using it as a means of social reform, it can easily go under financially. Thus, the dual identity of the newspaper can pose a serious dilemma.

## How Newspaper Work Is Organized

Although newspapers range in size from the *New York Times,* with a staff of about six thousand employees, to the country weekly with a staff of three or four, one aspect of their organizational structure is the same in each case: All papers have two basic divisions, the business and editorial operations. Generally, the business side manages the paper's financial affairs and its advertising, which generates income and keeps the paper alive. The editorial side includes reporters, editors, and all the others who acquire and process the information that goes into the paper's news stories and other editorial (nonadvertising) content.

**Overview of departments.**    The larger the paper, the more complex the organization. On the business side, several essential activities are often organized as separate departments. The *advertising* department handles both display advertising from merchants and businesses and the "classified" announcements (such as apartments for rent, used autos for sale, and help wanted). The *production* department is responsible for typesetting (which today is done largely by complex computerized systems) and printing. The *circulation* department is responsible for arranging for home or mail delivery or sale by street vendors. A general *business* department handles such things as accounting, personnel, and building maintenance.

**The editorial staff.** The people who produce the news content of the paper are those who gather, write and edit stories, handle photographs, select what to publish from the wire services and syndicates, and prepare final selections for printing. They are organized into a ranked system of power and prestige. A number of supervisory people have titles that include the term "editor," and this can be confusing. However, each has a different level of authority, is responsible for different parts of the paper, and supervises workers who prepare distinct forms of content.

Heading the entire editorial department is the **editor-in-chief**—sometimes simply called the *editor* or, with the advent of chain ownership, the **executive editor.** The editor works directly for the *publisher* (either the owner or the principal owners' representative), and is responsible for all the paper's content, with the exception of advertising. Reporting to the editor-in-chief is the **editorial page editor** (sometimes called the *associate editor*), who is responsible for the editorial page and the "op ed" page (opposite the editorial page). The editorial page editor reports directly to the editor because newspapers try to separate "opinion" from "news" to the greatest extent possible. Also reporting to the editor is the **managing editor,** who is responsible for the day-to-day operation of the newsroom. The managing editor is a relatively powerful figure who hires and fires staff members and supervises various specialized editors. For example, the **city editor** (or *metropolitan editor* in large papers) works under the direction of the managing editor and is responsible for local news coverage, including assignments for local reporters.

Depending on the size of the paper, other news-gathering sections such as sports, business, entertainment, and features will also have editors supervising them. The number of separate sections working within a newsroom is determined by the size of the paper more than any other factor. Also working for the managing editor is the **news editor,** who is responsible for preparing copy for insertion into the pages. The news editor supervises **copy editors** (who really do "edit" stories and write headlines). The news editor also oversees the design of the pages and decides where stories will be placed. On major stories, the news editor will often consult with the managing editor and other lower-level editors before a decision is made. Finally, the **wire** or **news service editor** selects, edits, and coordinates the national and international news from the wire services, such as the Associated Press (AP). Although smaller papers may not have personnel with all of these specific titles, someone on the newspaper staff must perform each of the activities in order to see that a paper gets produced.

A familiar part of the editorial staff are the **reporters**—journalists who seek out news information and initially write stories. There are basically three kinds of reporters. **General assignment reporters** cover a wide range of news as it happens, regardless of the topic. They also rewrite stories. **Beat reporters** are assigned to particular areas of government, such as the courts, police, and state government. **Specialist reporters** cover fields such as business, science, and urban problems. A special category, about which we have much to say in our discussion of news in Chapter 9 ("The News Process") is **investigative reporters,** whose probes help the press carry out its vital "watchdog" activities.

Larger and more complex newspapers obviously have greater specialization in the reporting and editing functions. For example, large newspapers have specialized business reporters, columnists, and editors, who monitor commercial and industrial events. Some papers have local columnists who write about colorful people or events and reflect the general character of the city. Other columnists might specialize in politics or race relations.

**Other specialists.**   Photo journalists have played a major role in the American press since before the turn of the century. Today, their work is indispensable, as stylized, illustrative photography has become more vital to overall design. Photography came into its own when newspapers began to use more and more color. Earlier, up until about the end of the 1970s, most newspapers (except Sunday editions) were produced in black and white. Spurred by *USA Today's* eye-catching color photography and elaborate graphics, many other papers followed suit during the 1980s and "repackaged" their product. They made greater use of drawings, photos, and color in an effort to make the paper more attractive to readers. As a result, many papers now employ art and design directors who work with editors to design the paper and its special sections. In September 1997, the once-staid *New York Times* was one of the last holdouts to add color to its daily paper.

## ▼ *The Future of the Newspaper*

As we noted, newspapers are slowly declining in terms of the percentage of our population who subscribe to them. They are also declining in terms of the share of the total amount of money spent by the nation's advertisers. Nevertheless, they remain quite profitable for their owners. This is because newspapers command the largest share of American advertising dollars—spent by local businesses who must advertise their goods and services to local customers. Moreover, newspapers remain a personal and local medium, where people find information about events, people, and institutions in their own community. Thus, newspapers continue to serve needs that are difficult for other media to fulfill.[27]

Those who own and control newspapers constantly seek new services to offer their subscribers so as to provide information that fills the needs of people dependent on media as sources for information to use in their daily lives. For example, as Debra Merskin and Mara Huberlie point out, many newspapers now have sections in which people can place ads about themselves and seek compatible people for social relationships.[28] More than a hundred newspapers are now offering free-to-call voice services. Callers can dial a central number and get many kinds of information on stocks, weather, sports, soap opera summaries, election results, and even horoscopes.

Technological advances in communication make the future of the newspaper difficult to predict over the long run. Included are the mushrooming growth of the Internet plus the rapid adoption of multimedia-capable computers by people using them at home. Based on these technologies, a number of changes are taking place in the world of journalism. One important change is the development of a host of sites that provide news available via the Internet's World Wide Web. Some have been developed by newspapers themselves to provide additional systems for accessing news. Good examples are the *New*

With the increasing adoption of computers by the public and the growing capacity of the Internet to transmit information rapidly, the news industry now produces a number of services. Subscribers and others can receive news stories specially tailored to their interests via the World Wide Web. (© Image Works Archives)

*York Times News Service* (http://nytsyn.com/live/news.html) and the on-line service of the *Boston Globe* (http://www.boston.com/).

Specialized news services are already available—systems by which computer software selects for the individual those stories that fit his or her special interests. If one has no interest in either crime or sports, for example, such stories will not appear in the tailored news file. If the person is interested in new Paris fashions, special art exhibits, and political news from Argentina, those stories will be selected from available sources and transmitted to his or her file. Exactly how these systems will fit into the media mix, what their impact on traditional newspapers will be, and how these changes will shape the news labor force, is not yet clear. As Weaver and Wilhoit note:

> Although we don't agree that U.S. newspapers are not long for this world, we do suspect that [recently], there was more growth in news and information jobs in specialized magazines, computerized information services, and various cable television programs than in daily newspapers and other more traditional news media.[29]

A very interesting change is that amateurs can now publish news. By developing a web site and posting stories on an Internet address, virtually anyone can be a journalist. This rankles many professionals who maintain that such news stories lack the quality control provided by traditional standards. A considerable debate surrounds these developments:

> "Since late 1993 or so, journalists have nervously been trying to figure out if they and their traditional news-gathering skills are going to be rendered obsolete by the Internet explosion. These journalists have filled the country's journalism reviews with soul-searching essays and articles exploring the future of journalism in the age of the Web. Some rage against the dying of the light; others welcome the new challenges posed by the amorphous Web."[30]

One can find compelling arguments on both sides of this debate. For example, Alvin Toffler, well-known author of *Future Shock,* is not impressed with the World Wide Web: "All those Web pages that people are rushing to put out there—it's fine for them to experiment and get their knickers wet, but they don't add up to very much."[31] Like many other analysts, Toffler believes that it is entirely too early to make pronouncements about drastic changes in journalism that the new technologies will bring in the immediate future. Even those who prepare and manage news on the Web are not convinced that their product presents a great threat to the traditional printed newspaper. For example, Andrew Hearst, editor of the on-line *E-News,* puts it this way:

> "Though my job as editor of e-news places me squarely in the new media, and I therefore sit in front of a computer most of the day, I'm a big fan of paper . . . Despite all the hype about news on the Web, at this point newspapers and magazines are the most efficient delivery systems for information. [Other media are faster.] But when you have a newspaper in your hands, you can access anything in the paper in seconds, and you can generally figure out how important a story is by the size of the headline and its location on the page."[32]

Other observers and pundits proclaim that the printed newspaper represents the past and that it is doomed to extinction as the technology of the Internet continues to advance. For many, however, that position seems too extreme and they predict that the newspaper will survive in its present form, at least for the foreseeable future.

However, three very different factors will probably continue to reduce both the proportion of Americans who read newspapers and their revenues in the future. First, many newspapers are owned by corporations that also own radio and television stations—that could reduce competitive efforts. Second, there is a finite number of advertising dollars available in our economy, but these revenues are being chased by an increasing number of competitors (newspapers, radio, television, cable, magazines, direct mail, and perhaps phone companies and computer systems in the future). As a consequence, newspapers are getting a smaller slice of the pie. Third, media consultants maintain that consumers will spend only a certain, constant percentage of their income on information and entertainment, no matter how many outlets and services are available. Thus, that revenue pie is also only so large, and as the number of media competitors increases, they will have to cut it into smaller and smaller pieces. Inevitably, these factors will decrease the profitability of newspapers. In spite of these problems, however, it seems clear that newspapers will survive for the foreseeable future. Their long range prospects are less than clear.

## CHAPTER REVIEW

▼ The origins of newspapers lie far back in history. The first newspaper in English that meets contemporary criteria was the *London Gazette,* the official newspaper of the British Crown, which began publication in 1665.

▼ Newspapers were slow in coming to the American colonies. The first to publish more than a single issue was the *Boston News-Letter* of 1704. A succession of small colonial newspapers followed, and a tradition of free expression was slowly established. The dramatic trial of Peter Zenger in 1734 was an important landmark in establishing the concept of a free press.

▼ The colonial papers were small, slow, aimed at affluent and educated readers, and limited in coverage. Some were partisan papers published to express and support a particular political position; others were commercial papers of interest mainly to merchants and traders. Nevertheless, they established important traditions as guardians of the public interest and played a key role in spreading ideas that became important to establishing the new nation.

▼ Newspapers for common people became increasingly possible as the Industrial Revolution brought new technologies, and as immigration, the growth of cities, and increased literacy led to larger potential audiences. In the *New York Sun,* Benjamin Day put together the necessary components of printing technology, advertising support, news content with wide popular appeal, and an effective distribution system. Quickly, the penny papers spread to America's other cities.

▼ A number of changes in American society spurred the growth of newspapers. These were rapid population growth through immigration, increasing literacy, technological changes brought by the steam press, telegraph, trains, and steamboats. Intense competition for readers among competing urban newspapers fostered an era of yellow journalism.

▼ Early in the twentieth century, the newspaper was the nation's only mass medium, and had been adopted by most American households. However, as other media arrived, its number of subscriptions per household declined. That downward trend continues today.

▼ Both wire services and syndicates developed to supply newspapers with news stories from many sources and with non-news features that had great appeal to their readers. This made newspapers increasingly popular, but more and more oriented toward entertainment.

▼ Even before World War II, chains began buying up independently-owned papers. That pattern of ownership now predominates, and less than one-third of all newspapers are now still in the hands of families and other independent owners.

▼ Computers are changing the nature of the way journalists work. Not only are the mechanical and business aspects of papers computerized, but reporters and editors also use computers extensively in gathering and editing their stories. Computers have become vital in searching databases for needed background information, in editing photographs, and in computer-assisted investigative reporting.

▼ There are many types of newspapers, classifiable according to size, the area they cover, the nature of their readership, and the kinds of content they emphasize. These include metropolitan dailies, medium-sized and small dailies, nondaily and free-distribution papers, and ethnic newspapers.

▼ The functions of newspapers began to change with increased emphasis on corporate profits. The older function of informing readers is still there, but entertaining them has assumed new importance. Newspapers increasingly emphasize their tradition of in-depth coverage and interpretation because of competition from radio and television, which get the news out much faster.

▼ Newspaper work is organized around two broad divisions—editorial and business—and within them a number of departments, including advertising, production, and circulation. Within the editorial division is a hierarchy of editors who have specialized assignments and responsibilities for various categories of news. Several kinds of reporters provide surveillance of the environment and develop stories to be processed and published.

▼ Finally, although readership, advertising revenues, and profits may continue their slow decline, there is little doubt that newspapers will be with us in the foreseeable future because they meet needs and serve interests that currently cannot be met in other ways. Whether the growth of news services on the World Wide Web will eventually cause a significant problem for print newspapers is not clear at this time.

# Magazines

## Voices for Many Interests

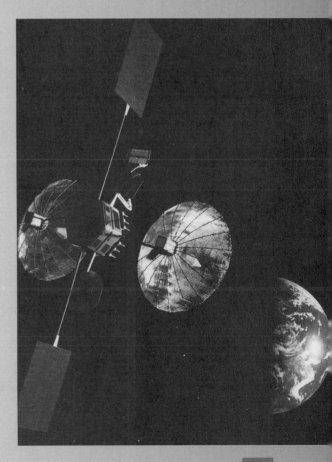

*T*he word "magazine" entered the English language in the late 1500s, but it did not refer to a printed medium. The term comes originally from the Arabic *makhasin,* which means "storehouse." Thus, in ancient times the term magazine referred to a place containing a collection of different items, usually military stores. We still use the word to describe many kinds of military enclosures where explosives are kept. In the 1700s, when the early printed periodicals began to appear, they eventually came to be called magazines because they were in a sense storehouses of writings about various topics.

Obviously, magazines depended on the same technological developments in movable type, presses, printing, and paper as did books and newspapers. However, magazines are not like other print media. Although they have some of the features of books and are published on some regular schedule like newspapers, they are a unique medium in their own right.

Magazines were originally established in London, where they prospered in a great city with many urbane and educated residents. The very different societal conditions prevailing in America all during the eighteenth century held back their development. However, as the nation expanded, became more urban, and developed improved transportation, magazines began to prosper in the United States. By the end of the nineteenth century, they were a serious and respected medium serving millions of readers.

During the early twentieth century, magazines played an important role in exposing unacceptable social conditions and stimulating social reform. Between the two world wars, before television became a household medium, they were one of the major mass media advertising nationally distributed products. After World War II, the growth of television had a significant impact on the magazine industry. Large-circulation general magazines were severely hurt financially, but new kinds of magazines were founded and the industry thrives today.

Magazines have always served specific functions in society that differ from those of either newspapers or books. Furthermore, those who subscribe to and read magazines constitute a distinct segment of U.S. society. Magazines' functions and audiences have a long and colorful history, and although they have changed greatly over time, at least some remain remarkably similar to what they were from their beginnings.

# ▼ *The First Magazines*

The history of the magazine began in London in 1704 with the first issue of a small periodical called *The Review.* In some ways this little publication resembled a newspaper of the time, in that it was printed on about four small pages, and (at first) was published weekly. Yet it was different from the early newspapers because it was much less concerned with news; it focused mainly on articles about domestic affairs and national policy.[1] It was still a time in England when people could be jailed for writing and publishing material contrary to the policies of the Crown. As it happened, the founder of *The Review* had been doing precisely that just before starting his magazine. The founder was the outspoken Daniel Defoe (who later wrote *Robinson Crusoe*), and he wrote the first issue while he was in Newgate Prison. He had been arrested earlier because of his critical writings denouncing certain policies of the Church of England.

Thus, the magazine was born as an instrument of politics. *The Review,* like many of the magazines that would follow it, was a vehicle for political commentary, and was intended to influence its readers' beliefs and opinions. At the same time, it was an instrument of entertainment—at least for sophisticated readers—in that it also contained essays on literature, manners, and morals. Both of these functions were central to this medium from the beginning, and for many magazines, they remain so today.

After his release, Defoe continued to produce *The Review* on a more frequent schedule, about three times a week, until 1712. The significance of Defoe's little publication was that it was almost immediately imitated, and the idea of magazines as a separate kind of print medium began to catch on. By 1709, Richard Steele had begun publication of *The Tatler,* offering a mixture of news, poetry, political analyses, philosophical essays, and even coffee house gossip. Within a short time, Joseph Addison joined Steele and together they produced *The Spectator,* which quickly became a favorite of London's urbane elite, enjoying a circulation of several thousand.

Although these early publications are now seen as the first magazines, they were not called that at the time. The term was not applied to a periodical until 1731, when Edward Cave, a London printer, first published his monthly *Gentlemen's Magazine.* Cave's use of the term was appropriate because his was a kind of printed "storehouse" of reports, articles, and treatises that had already appeared in other journals. In some ways it was an early form of today's *Reader's Digest,* which still serves similar functions. The *Gentlemen's Magazine* was quite successful and eventually reached some 15,000 subscribers, truly a remarkable circulation for the time.

What made these early magazines so different from newspapers of the period was both their content and their authors. The magazines presented material by some of the ablest writers of the time. Their pages contained essays, stories, and entertaining commentaries by such figures as Samuel Johnson,

Alexander Pope, and, as noted, Daniel Defoe, Joseph Addison, and Richard Steele—among the most respected English writers of the eighteenth century.

As the form and substance of the new medium came together by the middle of the 1700s, the functions it was serving in society were unique. The magazine was clearly designed to make a profit. It depended on subscription payments by its readers and, to a limited extent, on advertising revenues. It sought to attract readers with a mixture that was heavy with political commentary, but also included discussions of controversial topics and issues and opinion-shaping essays. Its literary quality was high and its typical reader was a member of the affluent, well-educated elite. It was not a medium for the masses.

By the middle of the century, a number of rival magazines were being published successfully in England, and the concept was spreading to other parts of the world. Thus, by the time of the American Revolution, hundreds of publications that we would recognize as magazines today were being produced in the major cities of Europe.

# ▼ The Development of American Magazines

Magazines were slow to develop in America. Although attempts to produce them started even before the American Revolution, they almost always ended in failure. The central reason for this was that the conditions of society needed to support this kind of medium did not exist in the United States until after the beginning of the nineteenth century. Then, as education, transportation, printing technology, and other conditions improved, many magazines were started, some of which were extraordinarily successful.

## Barriers to Development in the Eighteenth Century

The magazines that had been established in England were impressive models. To some intellectuals it seemed like a great idea to begin the publication of such a periodical in the colonies. In fact, Benjamin Franklin, ever the innovator, tried to get one started in 1741. It had the awesome title of *The General Magazine, and Historical Chronicle, for All the British Plantations in America.* It even had a competitor with an equally awesome title, Andrew Bradford's *The American Magazine, or A Monthly View of the Political State of the British Colonies.* Franklin's effort lasted only six issues; Bradford's failed after only three.[2]

After that, attempts to produce a magazine were sporadic.[3] Several, including *The American Magazine and Historical Chronicle*, and the *Christian History,* also appeared during the 1740s. Neither lasted more than two or three years.

Then, a whole decade went by with no attempt to publish a magazine. Somehow the idea was not working as it had in England.

If Franklin, Bradford, and the others had been able to hire a modern market researcher, he or she would have looked carefully at colonial "demographics," as we say today, to try to determine if there was a realistic market for a magazine. It would not have taken much research to reveal that such projects were doomed before they even started. There were four major conditions that created barriers to the successful establishment of magazines in America and caused their development to lag considerably behind that of their European counterparts: (1) the nature and dispersion of the population, (2) the economics of publishing at the time, (3) the state of transportation and the postal system needed for delivery, and (4) the characteristics of the readers themselves.

**The population factor.** At the time Franklin and Bradford brought out their rival magazines, the population of the entire thirteen colonies was only about one million, and few were village or city dwellers. During the colonial period, people were spread over a huge land area, about twelve hundred miles along the seacoast and a few hundred miles inland. The majority of the colonists lived on farms, often in isolated locations. While there was some commerce, the principal industry was agriculture. There was no manufacturing of the kind that would later draw laborers to factory locations to form industrial cities and there really were only a handful of communities of any appreciable size. By 1790, a half-century later, when the first official U.S. census was taken, only 3.9 million white and black people lived in the entire original thirteen states. And there were only twenty-four "urban places" (having more than twenty-five hundred inhabitants). Only Philadelphia and Boston had populations in excess of twenty-five thousand. Altogether, city dwellers made up only 3.5 percent of the entire American population.[4]

Generally regarded as the first American periodical of its kind, *The General Magazine, and Historical Chronicle* was published by Benjamin Franklin in Philadelphia in 1741. An inexpensive postal system for delivering magazines to subscribers did not exist then, and there were too few educated and affluent colonials to support such a medium. The magazine was an idea whose time had not yet come, and this one lasted for only six issues. (Boston Public Library, Department of Rare Books and Manuscripts)

As a consequence of these population conditions, no accessible market existed for a magazine in eighteenth-century America. If Franklin and Bradford and those who tried later to start magazines had understood how these factors were related to the success of their medium, they probably would not have even taken the trouble.

**Obstacles to magazine delivery.**    Along with sparse and dispersed population, colonial transportation retarded the development of magazines in America. The colonies' primitive roads prevented overland movement of almost anything. It is difficult for us to imagine what it was like to take a trip in early America. Traveling from New York to Boston today requires only minutes by air and just over four hours on the interstate highway by car. By contrast, in the middle of the eighteenth century, it was a rough eight- to ten-day trip by stage coach, and just getting there was an accomplishment. Hauling goods (such as bundles of magazines) by wagon or pack animal was much slower. In many parts of the country, mud or snow made the rude tracks that did exist impassable during long periods of the year. Even near population centers such as Boston and Philadelphia, travel was difficult. In the less-settled areas there were few roads of any kind, and most travelers went by horseback, sailing vessels, or even canoes. In 1790, the steamboat was decades away, and railroads would not link the nation's cities until after the 1840s.

Today, we receive magazines in the mail routinely and reliably. Subscribers seldom think about postage because it is paid by the publisher (and is really quite inexpensive). Getting magazines to subscribers in the eighteenth century was a different matter. As early as 1710, a mail system had been established by the Crown. It was mainly for letters that were carried by postal riders, and it was not available for bulky magazines. By the 1790s, however, the new Congress did allow magazines to be sent by post, but this was not practical because the fee was based on weight. Full letter postage was required, which made mailing heavy magazines prohibitively expensive. A few years later the Congress changed to a system based on the number of pages plus the distance required for delivery. This did not work well either, because magazines became very expensive for people who lived far away. Postage, which had to be paid in advance by the subscriber, added from 20 to 40 percent to the cost of the periodical.

It was not until 1852 that postal rates for magazines could be paid at the point of mailing by the publisher. By that time, roads had been greatly improved, and both steamship lines and railroads were operating on regular schedules to carry the mails quickly, cheaply, and efficiently. The lower costs led most publishers to absorb the postage as part of the subscription price.

**The cost of subscribing.**    A magazine in the early days was a real luxury. It is difficult to try to convert the various coin and money systems of colonial America into today's dollars. However, the first magazines produced by

Franklin and Bradford, for instance, sold for a shilling per issue in the currency of the time, and this was the going rate up until the time of the American Revolution. At that time in New England, a shilling was about half a day's wages for a farm laborer. A year's subscription would equal what a laborer could earn in about four or five days. Added was the cost of delivery, about another day's wages. Today, a laborer working for five or six days at five dollars an hour would make at least two hundred dollars. Few among us would be willing to pay that much for a magazine subscription. For the same reason, few in the eighteenth century were willing to pay the going price.

Magazines were then, and would remain for a substantial period, a medium for the well-to-do. They were just what was needed in European cities like London and Paris. The presence of affluent people made these cities centers not only of commerce and political power, but also of fashion, the arts, and literature—exactly the topics discussed in the magazines. In other words, the elite of the population centers made up a pool of potential subscribers. In contrast, the farmers and laborers of America, thinly scattered over a vast area, were not a potential market.

## Catalysts for Development in the Nineteenth Century

Although virtually every imaginable factor conspired against the development of magazines in America during the 1700s, the situation started to change significantly after the new century began. As noted, transportation improved greatly and changes came about in the postal system. In addition, printing technologies developed quickly, the population grew sharply, people were better educated, cities expanded, and there were great issues about which the population urgently needed detailed information. These were just the conditions needed for a great flowering of magazines.

**Rapid population growth.**    A significant factor in the development of American magazines during the nineteenth century was the same rapid growth in the population that helped the spread of newspapers. The first American census (1790) counted only 3.9 million people. Ten years later the figure had increased to 5.3 million. Then, during only five decades, the population soared to 23.2 million, which represents an increase of over 400 percent. By the end of the nineteenth century, due in large part to massive immigration, it had skyrocketed to 75.9 million. Few nations in history have ever recorded such an astonishing rate of population growth.

Population expansion remained a factor helping to decide the fate of magazines well into the present century. Massive immigration continued into the 1920s before it was slowed by legislation. All during the nineteenth century and into the present one, the birth rate was also high, adding to population growth. The rate finally dropped during the Great Depression of the 1930s but climbed sharply again after World War II when the "baby boom" generation

▶ The proportion of Americans living in cities was very small in 1800. The vast majority lived on and worked on farms. As this drawing shows, even a relatively large city, such as Philadelphia, was more like a small town as we think of them today. The low level of urbanization and the limitations in transportation were major factors in slowing the development of the magazine. (North Wind Picture Archives)

was born. (Our population is now more or less stable with well over 250 million.) The golden age of magazine growth during the nineteenth century would never have occurred without these long-term population trends. As we will see, that population growth also provided the market base for the large-circulation general magazines that characterized the first half of the present century.

**Urbanization.**   Not only did the population grow numerically, it also became more urban; that is, increasing numbers of citizens lived in villages, towns, and cities rather than on farms. In part, this trend toward urban living arose from the spread of transportation networks that made it possible to move farm goods to domestic and foreign market centers. With construction starting in 1815, the great Erie Canal linking lakes, rivers, and a wide ditch between them was dug (without power machinery) across an incredible three hundred miles, connecting Albany on the Hudson River with Buffalo on Lake Erie. By this route, combining horse-drawn barges and Great Lakes steamboats, travelers and goods could journey cheaply along a network from New York City to the new city of Chicago.

As farm products and consumer goods moved over this great transportation system, hundreds of communities sprang up in the Midwest and in northern parts of Pennsylvania, New York, Indiana, and Ohio. Southward links allowed barge traffic to move from Lake Erie down the Miami River into the Ohio and on into the Mississippi. Thus, before mid-century, one could travel by canal barge and paddle-wheel steamboat from New York City to New Orleans by way of the Great Lakes. New York City itself, at the eastern end of the system, grew into a great port for exports and imports. It became the largest and most important city in the United States—and because of that, eventually the center of the nation's mass communication industries.

Between about 1840 and 1880, the railroads, too, had spread to most parts of the country, fostering their own share of towns and cities. The United States was developing into one of the most productive agricultural and industrial powers the world had ever known. Steel mills, factories, and hundreds of other kinds of production facilities were established by the end of the century, drawing more people into concentrated communities. Thus, while all segments of the population were growing, the mix was changing. Increasing proportions lived in towns and cities and earned salaries and wages. During the same period, smaller and smaller proportions were living on farms.

The growth of towns and cities meant more concentrated populations with larger cash incomes and higher levels of education. These were precisely the conditions required for an expanding market for magazines. To give some idea of the shift, in 1790 more than 95 percent of American families lived on farms. By 1820, this figure had dropped to 80 percent. At the time of the Civil War it was about 70 percent. The flow of people from farm to city continued and even accelerated in the present century. By 1920, only half of the nation's families lived on farms. Today it is less than 2 percent. We are truly an urban nation. Over half of us live on only 1 percent of the land mass.

**Increasing education.**   Although sheer numbers and their concentrations are important, the quality of the population is also a factor shaping the market for a product like a magazine. In its early years, the United States was a nation whose citizens for the most part had received little or no formal instruction in reading. Even at the beginning of the nineteenth century, education beyond the rudiments was largely a matter of training the elite. Few ordinary people went to secondary school, and only the wealthy attended college.

Nevertheless, a remarkable and uniquely American idea at the beginning of the nineteenth century was that of education for all citizens (at the time, that meant all white citizens). Here, after all, was a new kind of society, based on assumptions of personal freedom, equality, and participation in the political process. A literate citizenry was essential to the system. Furthermore, as industrialization began, it became increasingly clear that reading, writing, and arithmetic were skills needed to improve a person's chances in life. Free public education was vigorously promoted by reformers and enthusiasts early in the century. The most prominent among them was Horace Mann of Massachusetts, who had by 1834 persuaded his state's legislature that a system of universal and mandatory education was a good idea. Essentially, Mann's concept consisted of three basic principles: (1) *tuition-free* (that is, tax-supported) elementary and secondary schools should be available to all children; (2) teachers should receive *professional training* in special schools devoted to their education; and (3) all children should be *required to attend* school (either public or private) to a minimum age.

In those conservative times, Mann's system was widely regarded as a wild and radical scheme and was vigorously opposed by large numbers of the wealthy and by propertied classes. They feared that universal education would foster too many critics of the prevailing system (which they for the most part controlled). Many religious leaders also fought it, holding that too much book learning would clearly lead to godlessness.

In spite of the controversies, the Massachusetts system for educating all citizens quickly spread to the other states. The Civil War disrupted society greatly, including educational development, but following that conflict increasing proportions of the nation's children were enrolled in free elementary and high schools. Table 4.1 shows the spread of education over more than a century. This great social change had profound implications for the development of magazine markets.

**The great issues.**    As population changes occurred during the 1800s, demands for specialized information played a part in the spread of the modern magazine. Providing that information became its special task. It was a medium that could present positions, details, opinions, and analyses in ways quite different from the newspaper, and in much greater depth. It was from magazines that Americans learned about important trends, controversies, and significant issues affecting their society.

The entire century was marked by extraordinary events, sweeping changes, and truly significant movements in thought, politics, and religion. For example, there was no more important event for Americans during the century than the Civil War, with its accompanying debates over slavery. Works like Stowe's *Uncle Tom's Cabin* were serialized in magazines and reached a reading public far exceeding the number who had access to the book.

Intellectual debates of monumental significance provided unique content for magazines. An example was the explosive issue of Darwin's explanation of the origin of species. Magazines were an important forum in the debate over evolution versus creation. Magazines also delved into topics like financial panics and depressions,

**Table 4.1    The Growth of Education in the United States for Selected Periods from the Civil War Era to Modern Times**

| Period | School Enrollments* (percent) |
|---|---|
| 1869–1870 | 57.0 |
| 1889–1890 | 68.6 |
| 1909–1910 | 74.2 |
| 1929–1930 | 81.7 |
| 1949–1950 | 83.2 |
| 1969–1970 | 86.9 |
| 1977–1978 | 88.7 |
| 1987–1988 | 96.5 |
| 1997 (est.) | 98.0 |

*Percent of population ages 5–17 enrolled in elementary and high school.

Sources: U.S. Bureau of the Census; U.S. Department of Health, Education, and Welfare, Statistics of the School Systems, 1986–1987; U.S. Department of Education, Mini-Digest of Educational Statistics: Enrollments, 1995.

controversial discoveries in medicine, great religious revivals, and the continuously expanding frontier.

During the middle and later part of the century, no issue stirred the population more than the question of the proper place of women in society. Many magazines were aimed directly at women and provided stories and commentary on changes advocated by leaders of the growing women's movement. There was an emotionally charged debate between those who advocated, and those who wanted to prevent, women from voting (women's suffrage). Others believed that women should have the right to obtain credit, to get a mortgage, to initiate a divorce, to wear more comfortable clothing, and even to work outside the home in jobs traditionally reserved for men. Magazines presented views on all aspects of these issues.

## American Magazine Characteristics in the Nineteenth Century

With the catalysts noted above, the United States magazine industry flowered during the nineteenth century. It was a dynamic industry, constantly seeking new formats, new audiences, new appeals, and new ways to increase profits. Although thousands of magazines were started only to die within a short time, some lasted for generations.

**Numbers and circulations of magazines.** The number of magazines published in the United States showed a remarkable pattern of growth over a seventy-five-year period. In 1825 there were fewer than 100 magazines in circulation.[8] By 1850, there were 685 periodicals other than newspapers being regularly published. The Civil War held down magazine growth, but by 1870 the number had risen to 1,200. It then doubled in a single decade to 2,400. By the end of the century, 5,500 magazines were circulating.

During the nineteenth century, magazines were a major medium for informing people about great issues that confronted the population. It was a time of great social change, political controversy, and intellectual ferment. One issue that divided people sharply was Darwin's theory. On one side were those who accepted the evolutionary explanation of the origins of species, including human beings. On the other were those who held that human beings, along with the entire natural world, were created by God as described in scripture. (The Granger Collection)

Paralleling this rapid expansion in the number of magazines published was growth in circulation rates. Actual circulation amounts were not systematically

# Media and the Liberal Arts

## Early Magazines as Media of Literary Expression: A Linchpin to Literature

Long before cheap books became widely available to the public, magazines served as the main medium of literary expression. Some of the first literary magazines, such as *The Spectator* and *The Tatler*, were created in eighteenth-century England as journals of satire and criticism. By virtue of the genius of their founders, these journals raised the discursive essay to an art form, one that still enjoys a popular following in many modern magazines.

By the mid-nineteenth century a relatively new literary form, the novel, had become the most popular form of literature in Europe and the United States. By the 1870s, fiction dominated the content of most American magazines. Indeed, mag-

azines were often the first to publish, in serialized form, many important works that achieved lasting critical importance. For much of the nineteenth century and well into the twentieth, magazines played a major role in raising the cultural awareness of subscribers scattered across a vast country, many of whom lacked access to schools, colleges, books, and libraries.

Even the great muckraking magazines of the period, such as *McClure's* and *Collier's*, routinely included short fiction by writers such as Arthur Conan Doyle, Jack London, Booth Tarkington, O. Henry, Frank Norris, Edith Wharton, Owen Wister, and Zane Grey. Many other magazines of the period were cre-

ated precisely as vehicles for short stories. Magazines such as the *Golden Argosy, Story Teller, Pocket Monthly,* and *Short Stories* were given entirely to short fiction, most of it sentimental tales of romance and adventure now thankfully lost and forgotten. Other magazines of the period—*Black Cat, Gray Goose,* and the *Owl*—sponsored short-story contests, published the winning entries (some of them quite good), and were very successful. Another type of periodical immensely popular during the 1890s was the "dime novel"; it featured a short novel, usually of the action and romance variety.[4-5] Many of these publications were considered somewhat racy by contemporary standards,

recorded during the century, but various figures are available that show a sharply increasing trend. For example, during the late 1700s a magazine would have been lucky to have 1,500 subscribers. Most had fewer. In contrast, the *Country Gentleman* in 1858 had 250,000—apparently the largest audience of the time. By the eve of the Civil War, *Harper's Weekly* had 120,000 subscribers. Other magazines that year were within the same range. *Godey's Lady's Book,* a very popular magazine among women, had 150,000 subscribers.

Within fifteen years circulations had risen sharply. For instance, in 1885 the *Youth's Companion* was the leader with 300,000 subscribers. The more literate *Scribner's Monthly* had a respectable 200,000.

A magazine for every taste and interest.    During the last years of the nineteenth century, magazine publishers came to understand their markets very well. "Every interest had its own journal or journals—all the ideologies and movements, all the arts, all the schools of philosophy and education, all the sciences, all the trades and industries, all the professions and callings, all organizations of importance, all hobbies and recreations."[9] In other words, whereas newspapers provided their readers with a daily cafeteria of many different

and their low price and special appeal to the young often caused them to become the target of censors and urban anti-vice societies.[6]

Nonetheless some of the nation's best narrative talents also published their short stories in magazines. Mark Twain published his comic tale "The Jumping Frog," later rewritten as "The Celebrated Jumping Frog of Calaveras County," In the *Saturday Press* in 1865. Bret Harte published his great stories "The Luck of Roaring Camp" and "Outcasts of Poker Flat" in an 1868 issue of *Overland Monthly;* and the classic American parable "The Lady or the Tiger?" by Frank Stockton first appeared in the November 1882 issue of *Century.* *Scribner's* magazine, one of the great magazines of this period, published by the New York book publisher of the same name, enjoyed a near monopoly of the short fiction and poetry of Robert Louis Stevenson and published other American poets and fiction writers as well, among them Thomas Wolfe, Ernest Hemingway, and Stephen Crane—whose 1897 *Scribner's* story "The Open Boat" is now regarded as an American masterpiece.

Other magazines, such as *Harper's* and *The Atlantic,* published in serial form novels by such popular European writers as Charles Dickens, George Eliot, Victor Hugo, William Thackeray, and Thomas Hardy. These magazines also published the work of then lesser-known American novelists such as William Dean Howells, Henry James, and Bret Harte. Of these, Howells was considered the preeminent writer of the day, though there were other, more popular American novelists at the time. Mark Twain, for example, did not publish his longer work in magazines, though in the mid-1880s *Century* reprinted in serial form both *Tom Sawyer* and *The Adventures of Huckleberry Finn,* both of which in book form were widely banned from library shelves.

The literary tradition in magazine publishing found new voices in the early twentieth century with such publications as *The Saturday Evening Post,* which published some of the early work of William Faulkner and Ben Hecht, among others. In 1936, the *Post* published Stephen Vincent Benet's classic short story "The Devil and Daniel Webster."[7]

The role of the literary magazine declined greatly after newer media came into being and as Americans gained greater access to books and other sources of information during the twentieth century. However, there are still a number of influential magazines devoted to literature, among them *The New Yorker, Harper's,* and *The Atlantic Monthly,* as well as several literary journals.

types of content, magazines zeroed in on specific social categories—on people who shared an interest in a particular subject.

As the century came to a close, the world of magazines was varied indeed. There were a number of religious periodicals. In fact, by 1885 there were some 650 aimed at different groups, from the main denominations to those interested in every obscure religious taste and philosophy. Scores of magazines were devoted to the arts, including music, theater, and literature. Short stories, travel accounts, and virtually every other conceivable subject of interest were served by a periodical. Many of what are now the nation's most prestigious professional and technical journals were started during the last years of the nineteenth century.

Generally, then, by the end of the 1800s, the magazine had become a mature and important medium. For many citizens, magazines supplied the major source of opinions and analyses concerning complex issues and topics that were not covered in depth by newspapers. For other people they offered amusement and trivial entertainment. Some read them to reinforce their religious views or to gain insight into complex political questions. Others subscribed simply as a means of gaining information about a particular hobby. Magazines were as varied as were readers' interests and concerns.

## Trends in Media Use

**Figure 4.1
Increases in the
Number of Magazines
Published in the United
States During the Nine-
teenth Century**

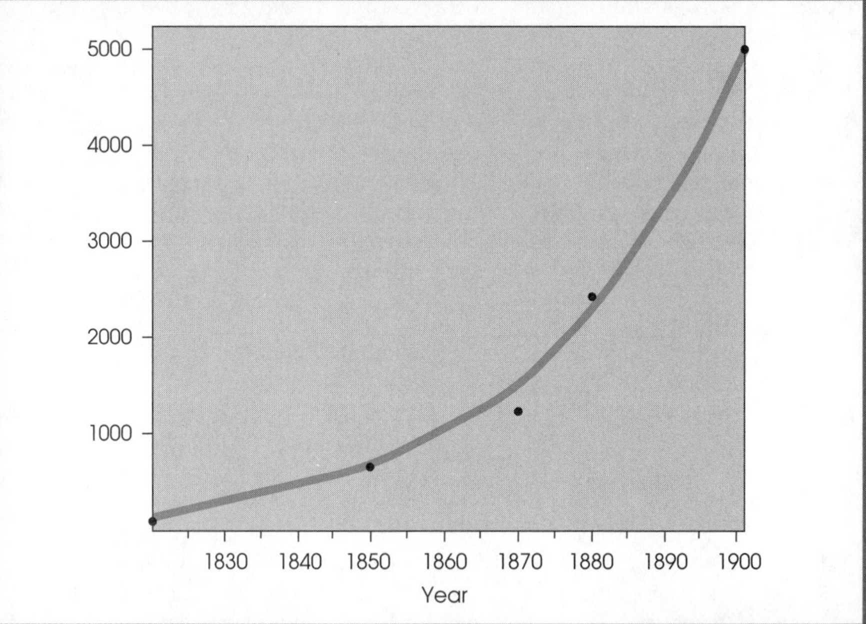

# ▼ Magazines in the First Half of the Twentieth Century

Magazines gained additional respect early in the twentieth century when a number of them became vehicles for exposing political corruption, social problems, and economic exploitation. During the first decade of the new century, prestigious magazines took the lead in pricking the nation's social, moral, and political conscience as their writers, editors, and publishers probed into economic and political life. As we will see, the conditions revealed during this period resulted in many needed reforms and corrective legislation.

Yet ultimately, magazines, like all other American mass media, were produced and distributed for the most part because they made a profit for their owners. It was true that some were started because of some special communication mission—for example, to provide religious information to the faithful. Even so, revenues to support them had to be found. If none were available, they died. Subscriptions were very important, paying a considerable portion of the costs of producing and distributing the magazines. However, as in newspapers, the real profit was in attracting advertisers.

As an advertising medium, the magazines of the nineteenth and early twentieth century were formidable. There were no other widely distributed media for touting wares on the national market. Radio would not arrive as a household medium until the 1920s; television would not be a reality for decades. Newspapers were local, and neither books nor movies used advertising in the same way. In a very real sense, magazines were the national advertiser's only hope. For the cost of the space, a magazine circulated nationwide could guarantee that potential customers all over the country would be exposed to the message.

This advertising function led to the large-circulation general magazines of the first half of the twentieth century. Aimed at a nationwide readership drawn from all walks of life, they truly were magazines in the original meaning of the term. They had something for everyone in every issue—fiction, biography, travel, humor, advice for the homemaker, a sprinkling of political commentary (but not much), and sports. Magazines like *Collier's*, *Cosmopolitan*, *Liberty*, and the *Saturday Evening Post* would come to dominate the industry during the mid-twentieth century.

## The Muckrakers: Magazines as a Force for Social Reform

One of the most important periods in the history of magazines began just before the turn of the century, to last until the end of World War I. It was a time when a limited number of magazines took the lead in what we would now call **investigative reporting.** At the time it was called **muckraking,** a term coined by President Theodore Roosevelt to characterize journalists who, instead of extolling the virtues of America, were determined to expose its dark and seamy side. Roosevelt compared such journalists to the "Man with the Muckrake" in John Bunyan's classic, *Pilgrim's Progress,* in which the central figure would not look up from the filth on the floor even when offered a glittering crown.

Particularly forceful in the muckraking movement were *McClure's*, *The North American Review, Forum,* the *Atlantic Monthly,* and even the *Saturday Evening Post.* These were national publications with a huge combined circulation. A number of their writer-investigators probed political, social, and economic conditions as part of the popular reform movement sweeping the country. Those investigative writers were vigorous, relentless, and thorough. As early as the 1870s, *Harper's Weekly* campaigned to oust New York City's political dictator "Boss" Tweed. Another nineteenth-century magazine, *Arena,* attacked slums, sweatshops, and prostitution, demanding sanitation laws, birth control, and socialized medicine. By the turn of the century, thorough exposés of corruption in the cities and abuses by industry had been published and widely read.

With the new century, the movement to expose unsatisfactory social conditions moved into even higher gear. Perhaps the best-known example of muckraking was a series in *McClure's* by Ida M. Tarbell on the giant Standard Oil

▲
One of the most important magazines of the muckraking era was *McClure's Magazine*. On its staff were both Lincoln Steffens and Ida Tarbell, both of whom left indelible marks on the history of investigative journalism. Steffens's investigations of political corruption in American cities resulted in many reforms, and Tarbell's reporting about the Standard Oil Trust brought her world fame. (Clockwise: State Historical Society of Wisconsin; Culver Pictures, Inc.; Bettmann Archive)

Company. Ida Tarbell was a remarkable woman, whose accomplishments illustrate the best traditions of journalism as the watchdog of society. Samuel S. McClure (who published the magazine of the same name) had confidence in Ida Tarbell because she had already written very good biographies of Napoleon and Lincoln for him. She was an outstanding writer and a thorough researcher. McClure hired her as a staff writer and assigned her to produce a series about Standard Oil, expecting a portrayal of the high achievements and efficiency of American industry in producing and distributing an important product.

As it turned out, he got something very different. Tarbell spent five years preparing and writing seventeen articles about the giant trust. She dug into every public record she could find, interviewed people, and examined letters, court transcripts, and thousands of other documents. She did report that Standard Oil was superbly organized and that it achieved its objectives with great efficiency. However, she also showed in merciless detail how John D. Rockefeller and his corporation had used "bribery, fraud, violence, corruption of public officials and the railroads, and the wrecking of competitors by fair means and foul."[10] The public was outraged, and McClure's circulation soared. Tarbell's series gained worldwide recognition as an example of thorough investigative reporting.

The names of other reform-minded writers like Lincoln Steffens and Ray Stannard Baker also became household words. Steffens produced the widely praised "Shame of the Cities" series, showing how corrupt governments worked in a number of American communities; Baker's "The Right to Work" was a series on the problems of workers and corruption in labor unions. These writers and dozens of others of the muckraking period made a tremendous impression on the public and became the conscience of the nation. Powerful political figures took up their cry for reform, and both federal and state governments acted to correct the political and economic abuses that were exposed.

Eventually, a great many magazines turned to this kind of material. Some did it well, but many churned out poorly researched criticisms of virtually everything about which stories could be written. Eventually the public tired of this tidal wave of criticism, and magazines had to change. The muckraking period ended with World War I, but it may have been the high point in the social and political importance of magazines.

Some magazines tried to push social change in ways other than investigative reports. *Cosmopolitan* actually sent a correspondent to Spain to negotiate the purchase of Cuba during the Spanish-American War. The correspondent was ignored, but his dispatches made good copy. The magazine also sent "goodwill ambassadors" to foreign countries, asking that they be allowed to meet with heads of state. *Cosmopolitan* proposed an international language and an international congress. It even started a national correspondence university, complete with a campus. Like the other schemes, it was a complete failure.

## The Challenge of Television

After interest in muckraking declined, new classes of magazines began to appear. One was

The 1950s were the last decade of the Golden Age of slick magazines with huge national circulations. These colorful periodicals were highly successful because they were virtually the only medium in which products sold across the nation could effectively be advertised. But, by the 1960s, as network television became the medium of choice for many of their advertisers, most ceased publication. (The Granger Collection, New York)

the **newsmagazine,** a term coined by Henry Luce and Briton Hadden in 1923 when they founded *Time*. New concepts arose, too (or more accurately, old concepts were revived), such as the **digest**—a collection of excerpts from other publications. Even today, *Reader's Digest* remains one of the most successful magazines of all time. The *New Yorker* was also founded in the 1920s. In 1936 the picture magazine *Life* was first published and met instant success. In 1945 the black picture magazine *Ebony* was founded. For almost thirty years, from the 1920s into the 1950s, large general-circulation magazines such as *Life, Look, Collier's,* and the *Saturday Evening Post* dominated the market. National circulations reached into the tens of millions. Magazines were far ahead of newspapers and books in the effective, sophisticated use of photographs and graphic design. They were beautifully printed, efficiently distributed, rewarding to read, great as an advertising medium, and enormously profitable for their owners. People loved them and they seemed to be a part of society that would last forever.

Then came television! As this new medium's popularity grew, the general large-circulation magazine found its subscriber pool shrinking and its advertising revenues dwindling. Television was its own kind of "magazine," and was much easier to use. Furthermore, it was free to the user. Those who were marketing products nationally began turning in droves to the networks and TV commercials. Within a few years, the magazine industry had to make major adjustments. As it turned out, most of the big general magazines with the "something for everybody" approach died. For example, *Collier's* and *American* were early casualties, succumbing to economic pressures in the 1950s. In the 1960s many others failed, including the large picture magazines *Life* and *Look*. Some, like *Life,* returned in the 1970s and 1980s, but in their new form they have smaller, more carefully targeted circulations.

There are still a few immensely popular magazines appealing to the general population, including *Reader's Digest* (circulation over 16 million), *TV Guide* (over 14 million), and *National Geographic* (over 9 million). But most magazines today are directed not to a broad heterogeneous audience preferring a "storehouse" of mixed content; rather they aim toward a more defined group with distinct interests. In place of general, large-circulation magazines there are now thousands of more narrowly focused, special-interest magazines. Some enjoy huge circulations, such as *Modern Maturity,* the publication of the American Association of Retired Persons (with a circulation of over 22.6 million). Other very popular magazines include *People, Playboy, Skiing, PC* (for personal computer enthusiasts), and *Better Homes & Gardens.*

Meanwhile, the venerable newsmagazines like *Time, Newsweek,* and *U.S. News and World Report* are experiencing difficulties. Although their circulations have been increasing slightly (18 percent during the past twenty years), the demographic category at which they aim—college-educated readers between the ages of twenty-five and forty-four—has nearly trebled during the same period. Thus, they have lost a large share of their target group during a time when their circulations should have boomed. Whether this type of magazine can survive in today's competitive news and advertising environment remains to be seen.[11]

Regularly published in the United States are thousands of individual magazines that appeal to various categories of readers with specialized interests and tastes. However, as is the case with other media, ownership is becoming increasingly concentrated. Large corporations, such as Times Mirror Magazines, regularly acquire successful magazines started up by others and thus publish a great variety of periodicals. In this way, a single corporation can potentially connect with a huge audience. (The Terry Wild Studio)

## The Growth of Specialty Magazines

As of the late 1990s, there were more than 11,000 periodicals of all kinds in circulation in the United States, and as previously noted, most of them focus on special interests. There is a specialty magazine (in fact, there are often several) for every conceivable interest, hobby, and taste—from tennis, fly fishing, and model trains to wine collecting and wooden boats. There is even one called *Prison Life: Voice of the Convict* for those incarcerated.[12]

Advertisers love specialized magazines because they are so effective in reaching precisely the categories of consumers who buy their kind of product. For example, no maker of expensive hand-crafted bamboo fly rods would advertise those wares on national television, in a newspaper, or on local radio, because most people using those media will not be interested. The product should be brought to the attention of relatively affluent potential buyers of such equipment scattered all over the nation, and perhaps even in foreign countries. Such contacts can be reached by placing an ad in one or more of the magazines devoted to fly-fishing enthusiasts. Subscribers will see the ad, and the magazine will likely be passed on to other fly-fishing enthusiasts. Thus, a single advertisement can reach precisely the targeted potential customers for the product. Furthermore, such advertising is cheap by comparison with other media. It is because of these factors that so many narrowly focused magazines can make a profit today; by this pattern the magazine industry has adapted to and survived the challenge posed by television.

# ▼ *The Magazine as a Contemporary Medium*

After reviewing the history of magazines over more than two centuries, it may seem idle now to ask just what a magazine is and how it differs from a newspaper. Actually, this is a necessary question, because in contemporary publishing it is sometimes difficult to distinguish between the two. Generally, a magazine is published less frequently than a newspaper. It is also manufactured in a different format—usually on better-quality paper, bound rather than merely folded, and with some kind of cover. There are exceptions to all these characteristics, but for the most part they satisfactorily distinguish the form of magazines from that of newspapers. To these differences in form we can add differences in the audiences, content, functions, and influences of contemporary magazines.

We have already seen how magazines usually probe issues and situations more carefully than newspapers; however, with an increasing interest in investigative reporting on the part of today's larger newspapers, that is not always the case. What we do find in magazine content is less concern for the details of daily events and more for interpreting topics in a broad context. Historically, magazines have appealed to a regional or national audience and have been free of the fierce localism of newspapers. Theodore Peterson offered this succinct description of the modern magazine:

> Although the magazine lacked the immediacy of the broadcast media and the newspaper, it nevertheless was timely enough to deal with the flow of events. Its timeliness and continuity set it apart from the book. As a continuing publication, it could provide a form of discussion by carrying responses from its audience, could sustain campaigns for indefinite periods, and could work for cumulative rather than single impact. Yet its available space and the reading habits of its audience enabled it to give fairly lengthy treatment to the subjects it covered. Like the other print media it appealed more to the intellect than to the senses and emotions of its audience. It was not as transient as the broadcast media, nor did it require attention at a given time; it was not as soon discarded as the newspaper; its issues remained in readers' homes for weeks, for months, sometimes even for years. In short, the magazine by its nature met well the requirements for a medium of instruction and interpretation for the leisurely, critical reader.[13]

Magazines today, then, retain their traditional functions. They are a major medium of **surveillance,** often delivering information ahead of the rest of the media. Some magazines, like *Time,* are intended mainly to inform, and others, like *Playboy,* to entertain. However, among the various functions served by magazines in contemporary society, the most notable is still **correlation.** This refers to interpreting society and its parts, projecting trends, and explaining the meaning of the news by bringing together fragmented facts. Other print media also inform and entertain, but it is in performance of the correlation function that magazines stand out. Magazines, in other words, are the great *interpreters.*

The long-held distinction among newspapers, published magazines, and electronic magazines is becoming increasingly blurred. Indeed, when newspapers have made major changes in packaging and presentation, it is often said that they are adopting a "magazine format." Thus, newspapers have become more like magazines, both in marketing methods and in writing style. Even television has been influenced: CBS's *60 Minutes* and its current imitators call themselves "television newsmagazines"; and various stations now produce local "evening magazine" shows.

The distinction in format between printed magazines and other media may become even less clear in the future. With the spreading use of computers capable of connecting to the Internet and the World Wide Web, information providers like Lexis/Nexis, along with such services as America Online, people may eventually be able to create their own specialized magazines without benefit of paper or magazine editors. However, for the foreseeable future, most analysts think, the magazine will continue to exist in its present printed form, because of its portability and its permanence.

## The Magazine as an Industry

To reach specialized audiences, magazine publishers sort potential readers into neat demographic categories with the help of computers; then they refine their products to match those readers' interests. In other words, they target their content and tone to attract specific audiences, thereby appealing, as we have noted, to many advertisers, who like to direct their advertising to probable customers.

For magazines, as for other media, audience ratings and audience surveys are important in determining advertising rates. But as Philip Dougherty has pointed out, there is an interesting twist for magazines:

> If an editor creates a magazine that is so on target that subscribers refuse to part with it, that's bad. If, however, the editor puts out a magazine that means so little to each individual that it gets passed from hand to hand to hand, that's good. Reason: the more the magazine is passed along, the higher the total audience figure will be. In that way, the ad agency rates will look more efficient to agency people, who would be more likely to put the magazine on their . . . schedule [for advertising].[14]

Thus, like all other media that are supported by advertising, a magazine must pay keen attention to its audience in order to survive. In fact, American magazines seem to be in a continual process of birth, adaptation, and death. Because magazine publishers rarely own their own printing presses, the initial investment needed to found a magazine is rather modest, and so starting a magazine is comparatively easy. Maintaining it is much more difficult. Most leading observers agree that many magazines die because the publisher failed to strike a balance between revenue from circulation and revenue from advertising. Some magazines die because the publisher failed to fine-tune the product to meet changing fashions and interest. The most successful magazine publishers produce more than one magazine. If one magazine fails, they still have others to keep their company alive.

**Types of magazines.**    As noted, the American magazine industry today provides a periodical for just about every interest. Magazines also target categories defined by income, age, education, and occupation.

Although there are various ways to categorize magazines, the industry typically speaks of two broad categories: consumer magazines and business magazines. **Consumer magazines** are those readily available to the public by subscription—to be received through the mail—or by direct purchase at newsstands. **Business magazines,** on the other hand, cover particular industries, trades, and professions, and go mainly to persons in those fields.

*Writer's Digest,* a publication with a considerable focus on magazines, classifies them into only four major types: trade journals, such as *Garbage* or *Modern Machine Shop*; sponsored publications, such as *American Legion;* farm publications, like *National Hog Farmer;* and consumer magazines, such as *Vogue* and *Road and Track.* Table 4.2 describes the main types of consumer magazines and the leading business magazines.

Consumer magazines, like *McCall's* and *Ebony,* are also called "slicks," because of their coated paper. Many in this category are mass-circulation magazines, but a subcategory, the secondary consumer magazine, includes broadly circulated magazines that concentrate on a specialized topic or a specific interest—examples are *Private Pilot, Yachting*, and *Gourmet.*

During the 1990s, about seven hundred new consumer magazines were established; reportedly, the number of titles grew by 68 percent. Typically, entrepreneurs who want to start a new magazine develop a business plan charting a course for the magazine and "proving" with statistics (on potential readership and related market research) that there is a niche (market) for the new publication. Then a staff is hired and offices established. Typically, printing is contracted out, as are arrangements for distribution and circulation. Advertising space can be sold either by the magazine staff or by national advertising media representatives. Many new magazines start with high hopes, only to find that no significant niche exists to make the new publication profitable. Often, new magazines that do succeed are quickly sold to large magazine and media companies, whose economies of scale make it profitable to publish many different magazines under the same corporate roof.

The number of new magazines that appear each year has grown sharply in recent times and is now nothing short of phenomenal. The failure rate, however, is equally phenomenal. Industry sources indicate that literally hundreds of new consumer magazines are introduced every year. However, on average, only two in ten of the newcomers are expected to survive for more than ten years. The 1997 edition of *Guide to New Consumer Magazines,* edited by Sam Husni of the University of Mississippi, reported the number of start-ups in 1996 in the categories shown in Table 4.3.

## Table 4.2   Types of Magazines

**Consumer magazines:** Periodicals purchased on newsstands or subscribed to by the general public for home delivery. Examples are *Reader's Digest, Life, Ebony, TV Guide,* and *Sports Illustrated.*

**Trade journals:** Magazines aimed at a particular trade or industry (also called the businesspaper press). Examples are *Editor & Publisher, Modern Machine Shop,* and *Publishers Weekly.*

**Sponsored publications:** Internal publications of particular organizations, unions, and other groups, including college and university magazines, customers' publications, and employee magazines. Examples are *American Legion, Columbia College Today,* and *On-Line.*

**Farm publications:** These magazines are given a category of their own because of their large number and the degree of specialization within the farm press. Examples are *Farm Journal* and *Agribusiness.*

**Newsmagazines:** Serving as national newspapers in America, newsmagazines include *Time,* which was once known for its strong Republican bias but is now more moderate politically; *Newsweek,* a less doctrinaire publication, with a generally liberal bias; and *U.S. News & World Report,* with a strong business orientation.

**City magazines:** Publications such as *New York, San Diego, The Washingtonian,* and *Boston* exemplify city magazines, which tend to concentrate on the activities of a particular city or region. Most major cities (such as Columbus) and many smaller ones (for example, Albuquerque) now have city magazines that investigate public affairs and try to critique the local scene (especially entertainment and restaurants).

**Sex magazines:** These publications have substantial circulations and generate considerable revenues. They take pride in their fiction and nonfiction articles and interviews as well as their suggestive photographs. This group includes such general-interest sex magazines as *Playboy, Playgirl,* and *Penthouse.* Publications such as *Hustler* and *Screw* cater to people with unusual sexual appetites. There are sex magazines for gays and bisexuals as well as for heterosexuals.

**Sports magazines:** Americans are preoccupied with sports of all kinds, and there are scores of magazines to satisfy their interests, ranging from *Sports Illustrated* and *Sport,* which cover a variety of sports, to specialized magazines covering just one sport, such as *Runner's World, Racquetball,* and *Skiing.* A new sports fashion will quickly generate magazines. When racquetball gained enthusiasts in the 1980s, several racquetball magazines appeared. Sports magazines, like sex magazines, once seemed to be intended for men only; but women now make up more and more of the audience for general sports magazines, and some sports magazines are designed especially for women.

**Opinion magazines:** These include some of the oldest and most respected journals in the United States. They range from the venerable *Nation,* which has been publishing since the Civil War, to the *National Review,* a conservative magazine founded in the 1950s by columnist William F. Buckley. Some others are the liberal *New Leader, New Republic,* and *The Nation.*

**Table 4.2   Types of Magazines (continued)**

**Intellectual magazines:** These small-circulation publications are very similar to opinion magazines, but they usually have denser copy and are aimed at a more intellectual audience. Examples include *Commentary, American Scholar,* and *Tikkun.* Both opinion magazines and intellectual magazines pride themselves on "influencing the influential."

**Quality magazines:** Although these magazines are similar to opinion and intellectual magazines, they usually have slightly larger circulations (perhaps as much as 500,000) and reach a more general audience. Some examples are *Atlantic Monthly, Harper's, Men's Health, Gourmet, The Smithsonian,* and *National Geographic.*

**Men's interest magazines:** These publications, such as *True: The Man's Magazine* and *Argosy,* sometimes overlap with sex magazines and sports magazines. *Gentleman's Quarterly* and other similar magazines represent men's new preoccupation with fashion.

**Women's interest magazines:** Some of the most successful magazines in the country, with the highest circulations, are aimed at women. The first American magazine in the nineteenth century to have a circulation of more than 1 million was *Ladies' Home Journal,* which continues today. Other magazines in this class are *Savvy, Better Homes and Gardens, Good Housekeeping,* and *McCall's.* A women's interest magazine that departs from the traditional mold of women's periodicals is *Ms.,* which reflects a moderate feminist viewpoint (*Ms.* led the way for feminist magazines, and today there are several available with varying editorial formulas and viewpoints).

**Humor magazines:** Taking hold in the 1870s with *Puck, The Comic Weekly,* humor magazines have been with us ever since and include *National Lampoon, Mad,* and *Harpoon.* A highly successful humor magazine of the 1980s and 1990s is *Spy.* Related to humor magazines are comic magazines and comic books, forming an industry in themselves. Many of these publications are not humorous at all, but use cartoon-style artwork to present complex plots and characters and diverse views and social commentary.

**Business magazines:** Few subjects are more compelling to the American audience than business. Among leading business magazines are *Business Week,* published by McGraw-Hill; *Fortune,* a Time-Warner publication; and *Forbes,* which uses the whimsical slogan "A Capitalist Tool." *Barron's* is published by Dow-Jones, which also produces the *Wall Street Journal.* Some business magazines offer broad-based news coverage; others are designed to advise their readers on the machinations of the stock market. There are also many specialized business magazines, especially those covering high technology and electronics, such as *Byte* and *Computer World* (in fact, the publishing industry has benefited a great deal from changes in technology; there are many new publications just on computers).

The greatest increase from 1995 to 1996 was in sports (41 percent). For seven of the last nine years, sex was the leading category, with sports a close second. That changed in 1996, with sex dropping to fifth place. Some of the newcomers on the list were established by large publishing companies; others were low-budget projects begun by private individuals.

**Making a profit.** Consumer magazines are the industry's major money makers. According to Veronis, Suhler & Associates (a media forecasting firm), revenues from magazine advertising and circulation totaled $20.8 billion in 1993, and of that amount consumer magazines generated $14.1 billion, whereas business magazines accounted for $6.8 billion. The total was expected to rise to $27.8 billion by 1998.

The vast majority of magazine sales are through mailed subscriptions. In fact, this number rose from 67.6 percent in 1980 to 82 percent in 1996. This statistic is important because about half of the total earnings of consumer magazines comes from subscriptions (and newsstand sales), and the other half

**Table 4.3 New Magazines Started in 1996, by Category**

| | |
|---|---|
| Sports | 111 |
| Epicurean | 58 |
| Special interest | 57 |
| Computers | 53 |
| Sex | 51 |
| Crafts & hobbies | 42 |
| Home | 39 |
| Media personalities | 33 |
| Metropolitan/region | 31 |
| Comics | 31 |
| Average cover price | $4.65 |
| Average total pages | 92 |
| Average total ad pages | 19 |

comes from advertising. For business magazines, the revenue picture is radically different. In 1998, forecasters say, business magazine revenues will reach $8.7 billion, of which approximately 90 percent will come from advertising. Thus, subscriptions are not a significant part of the profit picture in the business magazine. In fact, many business magazines are actually given away free; that is, they have controlled, nonpaying distributions. The magazines using this pattern of distribution can afford to do so because they literally blanket the relevant field or industry, which makes them especially attractive to advertisers. Magazines aimed directly at a given industry tend to be read by a large percentage of people in that field—exactly the people that the advertisers want to reach.

In recent years, magazine starts and failures have paralleled changes in the general economy. As America has moved from an economy based on heavy manufacturing and extractive industries (such as coal, iron, and oil) to one based on information, communication, and services, a corresponding decline has occurred in business publications serving the older industries, with an increase in magazines aimed at covering computer, electronic, and financial services.

Like other media, magazines are creatures of the marketplace. Although they can be a powerful medium for precise, demographically defined advertising, they are also susceptible to fickle consumer demands. As Chapter 10 explains, media advertising is a complex and dynamic process that links together specific forms of advertising content, specific media, and consumer demands for particular products. Thus, when consumer demands change, advertising content in magazines moves up and down in volume, causing the magazine industry to prosper or decline accordingly.

For example, although both the numbers and readership of magazines rose sharply during the 1980s, from about 1985 until the late 1990s, the actual profitability of magazines in the United States grew only slowly. In fact, in this sense, the industry lagged behind the nation's general economic growth. One reason for this lag is that several major industries (computers, cigarette/tobacco, gasoline/fuel, and liquor) reduced their expenditures for advertising. Before the cutback, these industries accounted for 20 percent of total consumer magazine advertising.

Why did those industries reduce their expenditures for advertising? Analysts believe that several factors converged at the same time. One was the decline of the home video game fad. The corresponding decline of public interest in home entertainment computers in effect killed some new computer magazines. A second factor is the same as that affecting the tobacco industry. When the ban against cigarette advertising on television went into effect, the magazine industry hoped to gain advertising revenues displaced from TV. However, public consumption of tobacco products declined—and so did the industry's overall advertising expenditures. A third factor was an increase in gasoline prices and a reduction in miles driven by Americans. With respect to the liquor industry, increasingly health-conscious Americans reduced their consumption of alcohol; and down went magazine advertising revenues from that source (hard spirits cannot be advertised on television). Although there were some countertrends in such products as soaps, cleansers, and pet foods, as well as in real estate and entertainment, these patterns did not balance out the income losses in the other areas.

**Ownership trends.**    Much that was said in chapters 2 and 3 about trends in media ownership also applies to magazines. Today, many are owned by chains. Large corporations and conglomerates regularly buy up successful beginners and incorporate them into their financial empires. The resulting concentration of magazine ownership, whether by multinational firms from abroad or by large media corporations in the United States, appears to be continuing unabated.

## The Influence and Importance of Magazines

As we have shown, magazines differ greatly in their circulations. However, size and importance are not the same; nor can total revenues be equated with power and influence. Under such an evaluation, *TV Guide,* perhaps the nation's most financially successful publication, boasting the largest circulation, would seem more important than a magazine like *Foreign Affairs,* an influential quarterly with a very modest circulation. But whereas millions may read the former and only a few thousand the latter, the smaller magazine may influence a much more powerful audience.

Editor Hendrik Hertzberg addresses the issue of the relative importance and impact of magazines in this earthy comment:

> Browse through any newsstand and you will be obliged to conclude that journals of opinion occupy a laughingly piddling place even in that relative backwater of "the media" known as magazine publishing. General magazines of any kind—that is, magazines read for their own sake rather than as adjuncts to cooking, masturbating, riding dirt bikes, wearing clothes, or collecting guns—take up less and less shelf space; and journals of opinion (never big sellers at the drug store to begin with) are a next-to-invisible subset. Yet, no student of American society and its power relationships would dispute that *The Nation* (circulation 80,000) is somehow more important than *Self* (circulation 1.2 million), *National Review* (circulation 120,000) and *The New Republic* (circulation 96,000) more important than *Weightwatchers* (circulation 950,000).[15]

While Hertzberg's analysis may seem elitist, he has a point. The journals of opinion exert influence far beyond their numbers. They are read by government officials, business leaders, educators, intellectuals, and others who affect public affairs more than does the average person. The opinion magazines set agendas, shape ideas, start trends, and offer labels for virtually everything (like "yuppies" and the "X Generation"). Perhaps more important, they speak to what it is that magazines do better than almost any other medium. Clearly, magazines inform, but compared with the reach of television news or the immediacy and impact of daily newspapers, this function is modest in any overall assessment. The same is true for entertainment, where television and movies are the champions. Even fiction, where magazines were once very important, accounts for little of their content today. In none of these is the magazine a strong contender.

Opinion magazines have limited circulation compared to more popular periodicals, but their influence often goes far beyond mere numbers. Such magazines are often read by people who fill important decision-making roles in society and who seek a more in-depth understanding of important issues, events, and trends. *Foreign Affairs* is one such magazine. (Reprinted by permission of *Foreign Affairs*, July/August 1997, © 1997 by the Council on Foreign Relations, Inc.)

It is in the realm of *opinion* that magazines triumph. They have the luxury of expressing their biases, being openly liberal or conservative, and as grumpy or savage as they choose. Other media, trying to court larger audiences, could never accomplish this. Magazines also can make long investigations and present their findings in equally lengthy form. For example, the *New Yorker*, a widely respected opinion magazine, can have lengthy articles that take up such topics as law and justice in a cerebral and philosophical sense, or it can present articles about the United Nations that severely challenge the moral authority of that institution. The *New Yorker* does this kind of thing in the context of an eighty-year history during which it has earned a high reputation for such analyses. As with other respected opinion magazines, when the *New Yorker* speaks on an issue people listen, and the ideas it presents are picked up and diffused by more popular magazines, newspapers, and even television to audiences far beyond its readership. Thus, a respected opinion magazine can have an influence far beyond what the number of its subscribers would suggest.

## ▼ *The Future of Magazines*

Many of the same challenges faced by newspapers because of the development of multimedia computers and the World Wide Web also confront magazines. Changes are taking place very rapidly in this technological world and it is impossible to predict over the long run how they will influence any of the print media. Many people, however, are not ready to believe that electronic media will displace magazines in print form. Their demise has been predicted many times in the past. As Daly, Henry, and Ryder note:

> On more than one occasion in the past 250 years or so, someone has sounded the death knell for the American magazine. Improvements in the printing press and mail distribution in the late 1880s enabled some magazines to increase their circulations dramatically. That was bad news for one editor who gloomily predicted that magazines wouldn't be worth reading any more because large circulations could only mean mediocrity and conservatism.[16]

Of particular importance for the future are magazines that are on the Internet. New terms have been developed to label magazines that are available on-line. For example, the term **e-zines** has come into use to identify magazines available in this form. These range from highly specialized and crude tracts to truly sophisticated electronic magazines. Web pages are easily found for subscribing to magazines, often at significant discounts. A number of pay-per-read sites provide full-text articles. A good source for finding information about magazines on the World Wide Web is http://www.newslink.org/.

Whatever the relationship between their print and electronic form in the future, the magazine is not only likely to survive as a medium; it may also thrive in the decades ahead. In facing their many challenges over its long history, magazines have survived by adapting to an ever-changing system of mass communication. The great diversity to be found in the industry provides something for everyone, and in a form that is current, portable, permanent, and presented at a level within the readers' capability. That is a formidable formula. So although the medium may have to adapt to a new mix in the media system over time, it seems at this point that Americans will continue to support this voice for their many interests.

## CHAPTER REVIEW

▼ Magazines as we know them today started in London, where there was a concentration of urbane, affluent, and literate people. The earliest magazines were mainly instruments of politics, both in England and in the United States.

▼ It was difficult to establish magazines in the American colonies because people were spread out, literacy was not widespread, and the population was not affluent. In addition, such factors as transportation and mail service were uncertain at best.

▼ During the 1800s societal changes encouraged the growth of magazines in the United States. The population grew, cities became larger, more citizens were educated, the mails became more reliable and less costly, and all forms of transportation improved. In addition, it was a century of great issues.

▼ The magazine flourished early in this century during the era of the "muckrakers." Prestigious magazines took the lead in exposing corruption in business and government and unacceptable social conditions. Magazines played a significant role in the reform movement that characterized the first decade of the 1900s.

▼ New kinds of magazines appeared in the 1920s. One category was the newsmagazine. Another was the large general-circulation magazine containing something for everyone. Such magazines had huge circulations, making them important vehicles for national advertising. They were very successful, and it seemed that they would be a permanent feature of society.

▼ When television arrived it absorbed much of the advertising that had previously gone to the large general magazines, many of which failed in consequence. However, the industry adapted remarkably well by developing a host of specialty magazines aimed at markets with well-defined interests and characteristics.

▼ The magazine as a contemporary medium continues to serve surveillance functions, monitoring what is going on, transmitting the culture, and entertaining the population. Its most notable function, however, is correlation—that is, interpreting the society by bringing together diverse facts, trends, and sequences of events.

▼ The magazine business today is fiercely competitive and very dynamic. An impressive variety of magazines are published. Every year, many are started; however, the majority fail. The two basic types are consumer and business magazines; of the two, the consumer magazine predominates.

▼ Trends in American magazine ownership parallel those in other media; that is, most are owned by chains. Large conglomerates, with many kinds of businesses, buy magazines and add them to their diverse holdings. The consequence of such consolidation of ownership is difficult to predict.

▼ The sheer number of people who subscribe to or even read a magazine is no indicator of either its ability to make a profit or its influence. The most influential periodicals are the opinion magazines. Their circulations are small compared with more popular magazines, but the people who read such magazines tend more than others to occupy positions of power and leadership, where their decisions can markedly influence public affairs.

▼ Although the new computer technologies challenge magazines as well as newspapers, generally, the magazine is likely to survive in its present form. It is a medium that presents material tailored for the interests of specific kinds of people in a manner that they prefer. It is likely that Americans will be reading magazines for a long time to come.

# ▼ PART TWO

# Audio, Visual, and Multimedia

# CHAPTER 5

# *Film*

## Moving Pictures as a Medium

*I*n superficial ways, movies and television are alike. They both have moving images in color and sound. As mass media, however, the similarities end there. We have long had a dynamic, separate industry that makes films. It existed before television was even a dream in the heads of electronic engineers. By the time of World War I, the motion picture was a fully developed form of popular entertainment with audiences in the millions, whereas television existed only crudely in early laboratory experiments. Today, although the motion picture medium has had to change in many ways to adjust to the impact of television, it remains a thriving and vital industry. Above all, the movies have left and continue to leave an indelible stamp on our nation and its culture.

The history of the motion picture is short, spanning just over a century. The events that led to motion pictures, however, go back to much earlier times. The first steps in this story involved solving a series of complex technical problems. A motion picture, after all, is a series of still pictures rapidly projected on a screen in such a way that the viewer perceives smooth motion. To achieve this illusion of motion, problems in optics, chemistry, and even human physiology had to be overcome. Lenses, projectors, cameras, and roll film had to be invented. Only then were "the movies" born.

## ▼ *Magic Shadows on the Wall*

The first problem to be solved was how to focus and project an image. Convex quartz lenses for magnifying and focusing the sun's rays were used as early as 600 B.C. Most of us as children experimented with magnifying glasses that could set a piece of paper on fire by concentrating the rays of the sun. That feature of lenses was understood long ago. In 212 B.C., Archimedes earned fame by frightening the Romans with a lens during the defense of Syracuse. He is said to have mounted on the wall of the city a large "burning glass" that could set fire to the Roman ships. The story may or may not be true, but it indicates that the ancients had begun to grapple with one of the main problems that would later be associated with cameras and projectors—how to use lenses to focus light.

The next major advance came nearly two thousand years later. A German priest, Athanasius Kirscher, conducted experiments on projecting a visual image by passing light through a transparency. In 1645, he put on a "magic lantern show" for his fellow scholars at the Collegio Romano, using slides he had painted himself. His projected images of religious figures could barely be seen, but his show was a sensation. No one had ever seen anything like it. The images on the wall looked like ghosts. In fact, there were dark rumors that he was in league with the devil and was conjuring up spirits through the practice of "black arts."[1]

In the eighteenth century, the public became increasingly aware of the idea of the projected image. Traveling magicians and showmen entertained audiences with shadow plays and projected images of ghostlike figures. By the mid-1800s, improved lanterns with reflecting mirrors and condensing lenses provided fairly reliable sources of light. By the 1870s, the simple oil-burning lantern had been replaced by a powerful light produced by burning hydrogen gas and oxygen through a cylinder of hard lime. That form of illumination was widely used in the theater to spotlight acts and events. (Hence the expression *limelight*). Ultimately, of course, electric lights provided the necessary illumination.

## Developing the Technology

Because movies focus so strongly on popular entertainment, it is easy to think of them in less than serious terms and to overlook the fact that they depend on a highly sophisticated base of scientific knowledge. The technological components in the motion picture are far more complex than those of print, and they were a very long time in coming. However, they all came together by the end of the nineteenth century.

**Photography.**    The science of lenses and projection advanced earlier than that of photography. Until the nineteenth century, people could project images, but no one had been able to capture images to form a still picture. However, advances in chemistry in the late 1700s and early 1800s set the stage for the development of photography. Several experimenters worked to perfect a photographic process. However, it was a French artist and inventor, Louis Daguerre, and a chemist, Joseph Niepce, who arrived at the best method after years of work. Niepce died shortly before success was achieved, but his partner, Daguerre, carried on.

In 1839, Daguerre announced the success of his work and showed examples of his sharp, clear photographs to the public. He called his process the **daguerreotype.** Each picture was made on a polished copper plate that had been coated with gleaming silver. In total darkness, the silver coated plate was exposed to iodine fumes, which formed a thin coating of light-sensitive silver iodide on its surface. When the well-protected plate was placed in a camera and then exposed briefly to a strongly lighted scene, the pattern of light and dark entering the lens of the camera altered the silver iodide. Chemical baths then fixed the image on the plate. Because Daguerre's pictures were much clearer and sharper than those of others (who tried to use paper), his process was rapidly adopted all over the world.[2]

Photography was received enthusiastically in the United States. By the time of the Civil War, there were daguerreotype studios in every city. Everyone wanted their picture taken and photos of their loved ones. It was even common to photograph the recently deceased in their coffins so that the family could retain a final image. Itinerant photographers traveled the back country in wagons to meet the surging demand.

By the 1880s, as chemistry and technology improved, such pioneers as George Eastman transformed photography from an art practiced by trained technicians to a popular hobby. More than anything else, it was Eastman's development and marketing of flexible celluloid roll film and a simple box camera that made popular photography a success.[3] The availability of flexible film also made motion pictures technically feasible. Before they could become a reality, however, the development of photography had to be matched by progress in understanding visual processes and the perception of motion.

**The illusion of motion.**   Motion pictures, of course, do not "move." They consist of a series of still pictures rapidly presented that capture the moving object in progressively different positions. When the stills are run through a projector at the correct speed, the viewer perceives an illusion of smooth motion. At the heart of this illusion is a process called visual lag or **visual persistence**: "The brain will persist in seeing an object when it is no longer before the eye itself."[4] We "see" an image for a fraction of a second after the thing itself has changed or disappeared. If we are presented with one image after the other, the visual persistence of the first image fills in the time lag between the two images, so they seem to be continuous.

The discovery of visual persistence by Dr. Peter Mark Roget in 1824 and its study by eminent scientists of the time led to widespread interest in the phenomenon. Toys and gadgets were produced that were based on visual lag. For example, a simple card with a string attached to each end can be twirled with the fingers. If a figure, say a bird, is drawn on one side of the card and a cage on the other, the bird will seem to be inside the cage when the device is spun. The reason for this is that both the bird and the cage are retained by the human retina for a brief period during the rotation. Today, for the same reason, children who rapidly twirl a Fourth of July "sparkler" see the entire circular pattern made by the moving point of light.

By the middle of the century, the wheel of life (or *phenakistoscope,* as it came to be called) was highly developed. In various versions it consisted of a large disk on which was mounted a series of drawings showing a person or animal in progressively different positions. By rotating the disk and viewing the drawings through an aperture as the "wheel" turned, a person could "see" smooth motion. When elaborated and combined with the photography of things in motion, its principles provided the basis for movies.

**Capturing and projecting motion with film.**   During the closing decades of the nineteenth century, a number of people tried to photograph motion using a series of still cameras. One major advance was the result of a bet. Governor Leland Stanford of California and some of his friends made a large wager over whether a running horse ever had all its feet off the ground at once. To settle the bet, they hired an obscure photographer with an odd name, Eadweard

▶

During the latter half of the 1800s, a variety of devices were developed to take advantage of the principle of visual lag in order to create the illusion of motion. Each inventor gave his apparatus a complex name, such as phenakistascope, mutoscope, or zoetrope. They all worked on the same principle, however— showing the viewer a succession of still drawings that when seen in rapid sequence produced the illusion of motion. Shown is the praxinoscope developed by Émile Reynaud, who astonished Paris with his displays of moving images. (The Bettmann Archive)

Muybridge. Muybridge photographed moving horses by setting up a bank of twenty-four still cameras, each of which was tripped by a thread as the horse galloped by. His photographs showed that a horse did indeed have all four feet off the ground at once.

The photographs created such interest that Muybridge took many more, refining his techniques by photographing people in motion. He eventually traveled to Europe to display his work and found that others had been making similar studies. Interest in the photography of motion became intense, but in 1890 no one had yet taken motion pictures as we do today. Further advances in both cameras and projectors were needed.

During the late 1880s and early 1890s, various crude motion picture cameras were under development, and a number of showmen were entertaining people with moving pictures based on serially projected drawings. Then, during the 1890s, applications of film and viewing procedures virtually exploded. By 1895, greatly impressed French audiences were seeing brief motion pictures projected on a screen by August and Luis Lumiere. Other applications of the new technology soon followed, and several individuals clamored for the title of inventor of the motion picture. But it was William Dickson, assistant to Thomas Alva Edison, who developed the first practical motion picture camera.

Meanwhile, Edison and another assistant, Thomas Armat, developed a reliable projection system. Edison and Armat obtained U.S. patents and began to manufacture their projector, which they called the **Vitascope**. Edison also set up a studio to produce short films—mostly of vaudeville acts. Although it had many shortcomings, the Vitascope worked quite well. Its major flaw was that it projected at a wasteful forty-eight frames per second, whereas sixteen frames easily provide the illusion of smooth motion.

Because Edison, ever the penny pincher, declined to spend $150 to obtain foreign patents, his machines were quickly duplicated and patented in Europe. In fact, numerous improvements soon made Edison's original machines obsolete. Furious patent fights in the courts later threatened to kill the new medium.

Then Edison decided to exhibit his moving pictures in a peep-show device that he called the **Kinetoscope**. For a nickel, a single viewer could turn a crank, look inside the machine, and see a brief film on a small screen. This one-viewer-at-a-time approach, Edison thought, would bring a larger return on investment than projecting to many people at once. Edison's approach did not catch on; instead, in the end the industry developed along the lines of the traditional theater model. The Lumiere brothers and others in Europe had seen clearly that this was the way to exhibit films. By 1896, however, Edison was projecting motion pictures to the public in New York for the first time in America.

In general, by 1900 all the scientific and technological underpinnings of the motion picture were in place, and the new device was now ready for mass use. Millions of people were eager to pay to be entertained. It was now a matter of developing the medium to present content that people wanted to see and to identify ways to maximize profits to be obtained from the movies.

## The Movies Become a Medium

The first few years of the fledgling medium in the new century were marked by experimentation. Many of the early films ran for only a minute or two. Yet just the sight of something moving on the screen could thrill an audience. Inevitably, however, the novelty wore off and patrons wanted something different. In response, the motion-picture makers began to try longer films offering more interesting content. The fledgling medium developed at a rapid pace.

By 1903, both American and European producers were making "one-reelers" that lasted ten to twelve minutes and told a story. One-reel films were produced on every conceivable topic, from prize fights to religious plays, for exhibition at vaudeville halls, saloons, amusement parks, and even opera houses. Some have become classics, such as *A Trip to the Moon* (1902), *Life of an American Fireman* (1903) and *The Great Train Robbery* (1903). Many others have been lost or perhaps were not worth preserving. By 1905, two-reelers were becoming increasingly common, lasting up to twenty-five minutes. These were more interesting for audiences, and as the popularity of the new movies increased, production and distribution of films expanded at an extraordinary pace.

**The nickelodeons.**   The idea of renting films may seem to be of little significance, but it made the local motion picture theater possible as a small business venture. The required investment was modest and the profits could be high. One could rent a film and a vacant store, add some cheap decorations, install folding chairs, buy a projector, piano, and screen, and open the doors for business. In 1905, two entrepreneurs from Pittsburgh, Harry P. Davis and John P. Harris, did just that. They charged five cents for admission and called their theater "The Nickelodeon." In a week they made $1,000, playing to near-capacity houses. At the time, this was the next best thing to owning an Alaska gold mine.

The success of the first nickelodeon greatly impressed the entertainment world, and there was a stampede to set up others in cities across the nation. Within a year one thousand were in operation, and by 1910, ten thousand were showing films. National gross receipts for 1910 have been estimated at $91 million.[5] The motion picture medium was skyrocketing to success.

Most of the early theaters were located in the hearts of industrial cities of the Northeast. Movies were made to order for that time and place. America was a nation of immigrants, most of whom were newly arrived and many of whom lived in the larger urban centers. Many of these people spoke either no English or very little. Because the early movies were silent, language posed no barrier for an immigrant audience. Going to the movies was cheap, so they provided entertainment for people in the bottom strata of society. Because of their near-universal appeal and modest price, the nickelodeons have been called "democracy's theaters." They showed stereotyped plots, overdramatized acting, and slapstick humor—needed for their audiences at the time. Even the illiterate could understand a pie in the face, a lover crawling out of a window as the husband came in the front door, or a mean boss.

The early movies proved to be popular beyond the wildest dreams of their pioneers. In New York City alone, more than a million patrons attended the nickelodeons each week in the early 1900s. Although the nickelodeons were associated with slums and ghettos, movies had become big business, and corporations were quickly formed to produce, distribute, and exhibit films.

**Movies for the middle class.**    Although the nickelodeons brought the motion picture to the urban poor, the industry was anxious to lure other kinds of customers into the theaters—especially the huge mass of middle-class families. However, at first such people viewed movies as vulgar and trivial. The young medium not only bore the stigma of low taste but was associated with the least prestigious elements of society. Even poor immigrant women were afraid to sit in the dark surrounded by strange men.

To shake this image and bring middle-class patrons to the box office, attractive theaters were built in better neighborhoods, and movie "palaces" opened in the business districts. Moviemakers produced longer, more sophisticated films to exhibit in such improved surroundings. While striving for a better product, producers discovered that they could increase attendance by giving prominent roles and media attention to particular actors and actresses. They hired "press agents" to publicize them as artists and important personalities. These early public relations specialists created masculine idols and love goddesses of the "silver screen" that could be adored from afar by unsophisticated fans. Thus the "star" system was born—and gave a tremendous boost to the popularity of motion pictures.

By 1914, an estimated 40 million patrons attended movies every week, including an increasing number of women and children. The movies were being accepted by the middle class. Movie theaters were respectable and the era of the tacky nickelodeon was over. Meanwhile, as Europe entered World War I, Hollywood had been established as the center of American movie making. The film industries in Europe had to close because of the war, leaving production and the world market to American filmmakers. They took swift advantage of the opportunity, and a huge growth in film attendance occurred all over the globe. American films have been popular in the world market ever since.

**The talkies.**   Since the 1890s, inventors tried to combine the phonograph and the motion picture to produce movies with synchronized sound. Few of their contraptions worked well. The sound was either weak and scratchy or poorly coordinated with the action in the film. The public soon tired of such experiments, and moviemakers thought that talking pictures posed insurmountable technical problems.

However, the difficulties were overcome by the mid-1920s. American Telephone & Telegraph (AT&T) used its enormous capital resources to produce a reliable sound system. Based on optical recording of sound incorporated directly into the actual film, it eliminated the problem of people being seen speaking with the sound coming earlier or later. Recently, controversies have arisen over who really invented the key devices, such as the vacuum light tube and the photoelectric cell, making it possible to develop practical sound movies.[6] In any case, by 1926 Warner Brothers had signed an agreement with AT&T and the transition to sound was underway. Warner produced a new feature including sound for the 1927–1928 season. Starring Al Jolson, *The Jazz Singer* actually did not have a full soundtrack. It included only a few songs and a few minutes of dialogue; the rest of the film was silent. It was an enormous success, however, and other talkies followed quickly.

Almost overnight, the silent movie was obsolete; the motion picture with a full soundtrack became the norm. As technical quality, theaters, acting, and other aspects of the medium improved, motion pictures entered their maturity. Within little more than a decade, color would be possible and the movies as we know them would be a reality.

**Portrayals of the fast life.**   The 1920s were a time of great transition. The old Victorian codes of morality simply crumbled following World War I. As the twenties progressed, there was a great emancipation from—some said deterioration of—the old rules. Women had been confined to lengthy dresses stretching from wrist and chin to the ground, tight corsets, and long hair. Prim codes of conduct made demure behavior and even chaperones mandatory for generations. By the mid-1920s, women could smoke, wear short dresses and cosmetics, cut their hair short, and even drink alcohol without being branded as harlots for life. It was a time of fast music, fast cars, "fast bucks," and, many thought, "fast women." These changes shocked an older generation but delighted the "flaming youth" of the twenties.

## Media and the Liberal Arts

### Literary Classics and the Movies  A Linchpin to World Literature

The modern Hollywood blockbuster movie, critics say, is often lacking in any real storytelling vigor. In the blockbuster, narrative is less important than concept, which is usually developed through flashes, crashes, and an ever-louder soundtrack—all of which lead, randomly and unconvincingly, to something resembling an ending.

It wasn't always so. Many of the earliest American movies made for commercial showing were based on classic and popular novels and plays and brought these works to life for moviegoing audiences who otherwise might not have had the opportunity to enjoy them.[7] In 1912, the Famous Players Film Company, the forerunner of what would become Paramount, produced its first feature-length film, *The Count of Monte Cristo,* then one of the most popular and longest-running plays in American theater history. The film starred James O'Neill, who had made fame and fortune in the stage production of the play and whose son, Eugene, would later see his own great works for stage made into classic films.

Movie studios routinely turned to popular books and plays for their stories in the early years of moviemaking, resulting in such early box office triumphs as D. W. Griffith's *Birth of a Nation* and *The Four Horsemen of the Apocalypse,* starring a then unknown Rudolph Valentino.

But in 1923 box office success and critical acclaim alike came for Universal Studios' production of Victor Hugo's novel *The Hunchback of Notre Dame,* starring Lon Chaney in a poignant portrayal of the suffering Quasimodo. In 1924, the newly formed Metro-Goldwyn company made the first film adaptation of Lew Wallace's famed novel *Ben-Hur* for the unheard-of cost of nearly $4 million. That same year the Warner brothers—Samuel, Harry Albert, and Jack—produced *The Sea Beast,* based on Herman Melville's classic *Moby Dick* and starring the eminent stage actor John Barrymore. By the end of the decade a new age in filmmaking would bring Quasimodo, Judah Ben-Hur, and Captain Ahab

---

It is hard to say whether the movies of the time contributed to these changes in social norms or merely portrayed them as they developed. In any case, in its struggle for increased profits, the movie industry began to introduce subject matter that for the times was sexually frank and that portrayed modes of behavior very clearly unacceptable by the standards of the older generation. Within a short time, major religious groups actively opposed portrayals in the movies of easy money, gangsterism, alcohol use, and sexual themes. These were powerful critics, and the industry was forced to take steps to police itself. As we will see in more detail later, in 1930 the industry adopted its first voluntary code for censoring films before exhibition.

**The "golden age."**    During the thirties the movies increasingly tried to appeal to entire families and become their major form of entertainment. In the process, the standards in the motion picture code became about as sinful as a Norman Rockwell painting. By the mid-1930s, for example, the code banned words such as broad, hot, (woman), fairy, pansy, tart, and whore. Bedroom scenes always showed twin beds, a table and lamp in between, and fully clad actors. The code

to the big screen again—the age of sound.[8]

Throughout the 1930s, Hollywood studios turned regularly to classic and popular literature and drama for material. The romantic adventure novels *The Three Musketeers* and *Captains Courageous* were made into popular films in the 1930s. Metro-Goldwyn-Mayer made highly successful films from Charles Dickens's *David Copperfield* and *A Tale of Two Cities*, and in 1938 MGM released *Gone with the Wind*; based on the Civil War epic by Margaret Mitchell, it was the biggest box office success thus far in film history. In 1930, Universal Studios produced one of the great antiwar films of all time, *All Quiet on the Western Front.* Based on the controversial novel by Erich Remarque, the film received that year's Academy Award for best picture.

With some exceptions, Hollywood turned to war as its creative source during the 1940s. Most notable among the exceptions were John Ford's 1940 film adaptation of John Steinbeck's *The Grapes of Wrath,* with a young Henry Fonda as Tom Joad, and John Huston's 1948 production of *Hamlet,* starring Laurence Olivier. *Hamlet* went on to take best picture at the annual Academy Awards, with Olivier winning as best actor.

Hollywood returned to literature and the stage for its inspiration in the 1950s and early 1960s. In 1951, Vivien Leigh and Marion Brando brought Tennessee Williams's *A Streetcar Named Desire* alive on the big screen, and two years later Brando gave a memorable performance as Marc Antony in the film adaptation of Shakespeare's *Julius Caesar.* In 1959, MGM released its highly profitable remake of *Ben-Hur,* starring Charlton Heston, then followed with a hugely successful film adaptation of Boris Pasternak's *Doctor Zhivago* in 1965.

Gregory Peck recreated Captain Ahab in a 1956 remake of *Moby Dick,* and in 1962 won an Academy Award for best actor for his stirring portrayal of Atticus Finch in the film adaptation of Harper Lee's great novel *To Kill a Mockingbird.*[9]

In every decade, screen and video adaptations of literary classics continue to delight audiences. In the late 1990s, modern versions of Shakespeare's *Richard III* starring Ian McKellan and *Romeo and Juliet* starring Leonardo DiCaprio won critical and commercial acclaim while several of Jane Austen's novels including *Emma, Pride and Prejudice,* and *Persuasion* were also seen on the silver screen. Virtually every generation enjoys new versions of Sir Arthur Conan Doyle's *Sherlock Holmes,* and the popular play *Front Page,* depicting Chicago newspaper reporters in the 1920s, has had no less than four film versions.

was rigidly enforced, and by the 1940s the movies had become a wholesome, if bland, form of family entertainment.

It was during this same period—from 1930 to the late 1940s—that American movies in many ways reached their peak. During those two decades movies were the most popular form of mass entertainment in America. In the Depression decade of the thirties, there really was not much else one could enjoy in the way of popular entertainment for so little money. The price of admission for adults was usually less than fifty cents. Children could get in for half price or less. A whole family could go to the movies together, have a snack afterward, and generally have what was regarded as a "swell time" while barely denting the hard-earned family resources. The golden age of movies had arrived, and people loved them. On average between two and three tickets to the movies were sold each week for every household in America.

**The decline.**   Box office receipts held steady until the late 1940s. Movies were especially popular during the war years (1941–1945). By 1946, some ninety million tickets were being sold weekly. Then, with extraordinary rapidity, a new

# Trends in Media Use

**Figure 5.1**
**The Curve of the Adoption of the Motion Picture: Motion Picture Attendance per Household, 1920–1992**

People began to purchase tickets to the early motion picture theaters, such as the nickelodeons, a number of years before systematic data were collected by the U.S. Bureau of the Census and by the motion picture industry. However, beginning in 1922, more systematic estimates became available. As we can see in Figure 5.1, the peak period for paid movie attendance was the golden age, between about 1930 and the end of World War II. After that, television cut into ticket purchases, and the movie industry had to adapt to the new medium.

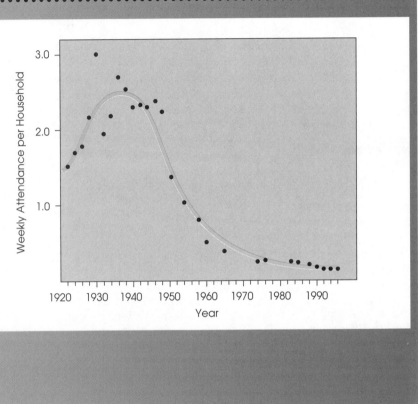

medium arrived and was adopted by the public, in a way that had a devastating impact on motion picture theaters. It would also alter the rigid standards that had been imposed by the industry. With the rise of television, the movies in their traditional form underwent a precipitous decline. By 1960, when television had been widely adopted, only one-fourth as many tickets were being sold to American families as had been the case in 1948 (just before TV arrived).

To try to draw patrons back to the theaters, moviemakers turned to a variety of gimmicks and innovations. They tried increasing the use of color, escalating levels of violence, increasingly explicit sexual portrayals, horror themes, spectacular special effects, space fantasies, and even an occasional three-dimensional (3D) production. None of those efforts really helped. Attendance at motion picture theaters has shown a downward trend ever since the arrival of television. It is clear, then, that on a per capita basis, movie attendance will never again be what it was before television. Movie exhibitors (those who own theaters and show films) continue to be plagued by a number of negative trends. Audiences today do not consist of entire families, as in earlier decades, but mainly of young people for whom going to the movies can be a cheap date or a peer activity. The older neighborhood theaters and drive-ins closed long ago, when TV became popular. Today multitheater cinemas, often located in or near malls, offer young viewers a range of films from which to choose.

In spite of these trends, the movie as a medium is here to stay. Fewer people may pay at the box office but they see movies in other ways. The original social and cultural forces that drove the motion picture to heights of popularity are still in place. The United States is still an urban-industrial society in which people who work all day want to enjoy popular culture during evenings and weekends. In such a society there is an almost insatiable demand for popular entertainment that costs very little and makes few intellectual demands. Movies fill that need very well indeed. When there was no other way to see a movie, people left home, traveled to a theater, and paid at the box office. They had no options. Today, huge numbers of people want to sit back and have movies come to them. Thus, the industry has survived and prospered by producing movies for broadcast and cable television. The rapid growth in movie rentals for home VCR showings has greatly improved the profit picture. Foreign markets add still another dimension.

Before television, both neighborhood and drive-in movie theaters were popular. A drive-in screen could be found in virtually every community and a movie house in every neighborhood. With the decline in movie attendance, however, both types of theaters became relics of the past. Today, many neighborhood theaters have long been boarded up and drive-in theaters have all but vanished. (Copyright © 1994 Ted Curtin, Stock Boston)

## ▼ Film as a Contemporary Medium

Perhaps more than any other medium, the motion picture industry has attracted the popular imagination. Screaming supermarket tabloids, gushing movie magazines, and caustic television commentators pass on the latest Hollywood gossip and speculation to a fascinated public. The pictures themselves, from *The Birth of a Nation* to the latest "blockbuster" churned out by the industry, can be seen by tens of millions. The stars have always been in the public eye. Enthusiastic followers have been fascinated with the smallest details of their lives.

The movies are more than entertainment. They have played a long-term role in shaping our culture. Our nation's standards of female beauty and sexual

▶

Directors who put their personal stamp on a category of movies are called *auteurs.* Starting in the 1930s, film directors such as Eric von Stroheim and Cecil B. De Mille played major roles in creating personal styles. Alfred Hitchcock continued the tradition after World War II. Today, auteur Steven Spielberg produces films such as *Close Encounters of the Third Kind, E.T., Star Wars,* and *Jurassic Park,* with complex special effects. (Copyright © by Universal City Studios, Inc. Courtesy of MCA Publishing Rights, a Division of MCA, Inc.)

attractiveness have for generations been derived in some part from movies. It started early in the century when Lilian Gish began to set the norms. It continued with the "vamps" of the 1920s and great beauties like Greta Garbo and Ingrid Bergman in the 1930s. By mid-century "sex goddesses" such as Marilyn Monroe and Elizabeth Taylor served as models. Today the definition of female sexual attractiveness is set by actresses such as Demi Moore and Michelle Pfeiffer. Similarly, our conceptions of handsome manliness have been influenced by such figures as John Wayne, Clark Gable, and more recently Tom Cruise, Brad Pitt, and Denzel Washington. These standards can have a profound influence on the behavior of millions, in everything from using cosmetics to criteria for selecting a mate.

All the publicity and popularity may do more to hinder than to help our understanding of movies. Behind the gossip and the glamour lie the complex realities of the industry as a mass medium. In addition to being a medium of communication and a social force, motion pictures are both a huge and diversified industry and an intricate art form. As art, film takes in the whole spectrum of forms that the term implies: it is a *performing art,* like the theater and dance; it is *representational,* like a painting; and, like music, it is a *recording* art. Evaluating the artistic merit of films, however, is beyond the scope of this book.

As a social force, film raises issues concerning the medium and industry's presumed influences on morals, manners, beliefs, and behavior. We consider those issues in later chapters. In this section, we are most concerned with film as a contemporary medium of communication with different kinds of content that serve distinctive *functions.* Both the content and the functions are determined by professional communicators—the industry that produces the pictures—and their large and diverse audience.

## The Functions of Films

For the people who make films, the medium provides an avenue for expression and an opportunity to practice a complex craft. It is also a means to wealth for some and simply a livelihood for others. The end product may be frivolous and diverting; it may provide information or training; it may make a social or political statement; it may have important aesthetic qualities. Thus, a particular movie may seek to amuse or *entertain* by providing diversion and enjoyment; to *educate,* as many documentaries do; to *persuade* or influence (as in the case of wartime propaganda films); or (perhaps less frequently) to *enrich* our cultural experiences. Most often, a film will have combined functions: For the audience, the film may be informative, an escape, or an engaging lesson in history, morality, or human relationships. For their producers, films are a source of profit. For directors and actors, films can be a means of supporting artistic values, whereas for writers, films may be a way of raising consciousness about social causes.

Film's function is, of course, partly in the eye of the beholder. For example, most people consider vintage Walt Disney family films to be wholesome entertainment. Others interpret them as rigid ideological statements that praise an unrealistic image of America, showing artificial, antiseptic WASP communities devoid of social problems. It is safe to say, however, that the main function of American films has been, throughout their history, to *entertain.* In this very important respect, movies differ from the print and broadcast media. We refer not to their obvious mechanical aspects, but to the traditional functions inherent in their origins. The origins of magazines and newspapers were related to the functions of providing information and influencing opinion, but films grew from the traditions of both theater and popular amusements. These traditions had far less to do with transmitting information and opinion. Their central focus was always on entertainment. Today, films continue those traditions, and their principal function has always been to take their viewers away from the pressing issues and mundane details of everyday life, rather than to focus their attention on them.

## The Development of Themes and Styles

The early movies looked to the established forms of drama (comedy, tragedy, musical) for their themes. Then and now they often turn to books for ideas and screenplays. Due to the nature of their audiences, the early films relied on the art of *mime.* Soon, however, American films developed their own forms and traditions. In the silent period, Mack Sennett, Charlie Chaplin, Buster Keaton,

Harold Lloyd, and others created their own forms of acting and storytelling; later, directors such as Eric von Stroheim and Cecil B. De Mille added their mark. These, and filmmakers of today such as Spike Lee and Steven Spielberg, who create films with a distinctive style, are known as **auteurs.**

Eventually, film content and style were influenced less as a dramatic form by material from plays or books and more by film's own emerging traditions. The 1930s research of Edgar Dale provides a glimpse at those traditions. Dale analyzed the content of five hundred films that had been released by 1920, another five hundred released between 1921 and 1925, and still another five hundred released between 1926 and 1930. He found that three major themes—crime, sex, and love—accounted for approximately three-fourths of the movies produced during the period.[10] In many ways, these are still the major themes of the industry.

In general, *directors* were the dominating force shaping films until the 1930s. Then, in the 1930s and 1940s, the *studios* became dominant. Several studios came to have recognizable styles. MGM was long known for its richly produced, glossy epics aimed at middlebrow tastes. Paramount was said to give its films a European sensibility. Warner Brothers often shot on location because creating the sets was too expensive, so Warner developed a reputation for realism.[11]

Today these differences in production styles have disappeared as the influence of the major studios has declined. However, even in the heyday of the studios, some individuals—such as directors, actors, or cinematographers—marked their films with their own distinctive stamp. Different members of the filmmaking teams may dominate at any time and in any film. During the 1970s and 1980s, the director once again held sway as the king of film. Today, on the whole, there is a greater awareness of varying directorial styles.

## The Content of American Films

A film's content is almost always shaped by conflicting forces. The audience, technology, economics, and the filmmakers themselves play a part. Producers look carefully at the balance sheet, continually worrying about audience interests. They ask: What is technically and economically possible and efficient, and what does the audience want? The search for efficiency led, for example, to standardized *lengths* for films, although those lengths have changed through the decades. The public wants and expects realistic *locations* or settings for films, whether in jungles, cities, or submarines. People enjoy *special effects* that seem realistic. The public wants and expects *coherent plot structures.* Old Westerns, for example, were usually melodramas with a hero, a villain, a beautiful girl, a sidekick, a handsome horse, and perhaps inaccurately portrayed Indians. The audience had particular expectations of what they would see, and plots usually conformed to those expectations. That principle still prevails.

However, old formulas can become trite. Over time audiences change, in terms of both their characteristics and what they want to see. Anxious to keep track of audience composition and tastes, studios hire the services of groups like the Opinion Research Institute of Princeton, which puts together a profile of moviegoers. Today, for example, about three-fourths of those attending movies are under age thirty; and a very large part of those are teenagers. Slightly more than ten percent are fifty years of age or older.[12] Making movies for the young, therefore, became a more certain way to make money than making them for mature audiences.

Still, the balance sheet is not the only factor that determines the shape of films. Directors, actors, and even producers may also want to put the mark of their own imagination on a film. According to one film historian, the workings of these opposing forces—bottom line versus personal expression—"drove the Hollywood cinema: the clash between the artist's sensibility and the classic mythic structure of the story types that were identified and popular."[13] Out of this clash came a broad range of films and film genres.

**Genres.**    Balanced against the filmmaker's desire for individuality, then, is the need to give the audience a message it will understand and accept—the need for successful dream building. As a result of this need, plots become more or less standardized. Story types, or **genres,** develop—a category of films with the same basic kind of characters, settings, and plots. The gangster film is an example. Another is the war film. Still another is the slapstick comedy. Probably the most popular film genre of all time has been the Western. It was a completely American invention, with brave men and women living the rugged life of the range, or moving across the frontier where they met hardship in battle with the elements, Indians, and the law. (The Republic studio in particular made a large number of early Westerns.)

Musicals were once immensely popular and some studios, such as Warner Brothers, virtually specialized in this genre. It was Warner Brothers that produced Busby Berkeley's elaborate, geometrically choreographed dance films of the 1930s, featuring group dancing with performers forming intricate patterns when photographed from overhead. Many of Berkeley's "dancers" knew nothing (and did not need to know anything) about genuine dance. All they had to do was to move precisely together in a few scenes. He used unusual camera angles and fast-paced editing to create spectacular effects.

Comedies have always attracted wide audiences. They have ranged from dry-witted, British-inspired parlor comedies to screwball films by the Marx Brothers, the Three Stooges, and Laurel and Hardy to those of contemporary comics like Chevy Chase and Jim Carrey. Other genres include horror films, historical romances, and detective thrillers. Occasionally public taste dictates development of a new genre, such as the science fiction thrillers of the 1950s, the teen-horror movies of the 1980s, and action-thrillers in the 1990s. Today, with the use of computer technology, a new cyborg genre is developing.

Public attitudes and social conditions have often influenced (some would say dictated) the treatment of racial and ethnic minorities in film. For many years it was difficult for African- and Hispanic-American actors to get good film roles. They were often depicted in a subservient position that reinforced racial stereotypes. In more recent years, there have been new images for minorities in screen roles. In the early 1970s, several major studios began to distribute films that portrayed the life, achievement, or problems of African-Americans. Some, such as *Shaft* (1971) and *Superfly* (1972), starred heroes achieving victory over the white establishment. Others showed unity among blacks. Still others, such as *Glory* (1989), *Driving Miss Daisy* (1990), and *Waiting to Exhale* (1996), were sympathetic portrayals of the achievements, character, or problems of African-Americans. However, despite their portrayal of African-Americans and their themes, and even though African-Americans such as Spike Lee often wrote, directed, and acted in these films, they were actually owned and distributed by white-run studios. In recent times another ethnic genre appeared featuring comedians such as Eddie Murphy and Richard Pryor. Although such efforts have provided opportunities, black performers and artists still complain, justifiably, that there are not enough roles for them and for members of other racial minorities.

Films depicting women and women's issues have also gone through a number of phases. In the early films, women were usually melodramatic heroines—pretty girls threatened by evil villains and saved by virile heroes. However, by the 1930s and 1940s, actresses such as Bette Davis, Joan Crawford, and Barbara Stanwyck portrayed very strong women. In the 1950s, the "sexy blonde" role, most prominently associated with Marilyn Monroe, brought a different and much weaker image of women. During the 1980s and 1990s, women returned in less demeaning film roles. Indeed, a number of popular films took on clear feminist themes, with actresses playing important roles dealing with issues and problems of special interest to women; examples include *Nine to Five* (1982), *Terms of Endearment* (1983), *Out of Africa* (1987), *Working Girl* (1988), *Beaches* (1989), *Thelma and Louise* (1991), *Prince of Tides* (1991) and *The First Wives Club* (1996). However, female stars are rarely as "bankable" as top male stars, who continue to get higher salaries and multimillion dollar deals.

**Documentaries.**    Although the public overwhelmingly identifies "the movies" (both as an industry and as products for consumption) with the entertainment function, an important category of nonfiction films providing an education function are *documentaries*. The term was first introduced by British filmmaker John Grierson, although his film was not the first of the category. His nonfiction film *The Drifters* (1929) depicted the lives of herring fishermen in the North Sea. In the documentary's purest form, the filmmaker intrudes as little as possible; the director, for example, does not direct actors or set up scenes.

From an intellectual perspective, documentaries can have a lasting importance, far exceeding entertainment films, as records of human culture in particular periods. In our flights of fancy we can imagine what we might see if someone at the time could have made documentaries of the ancient Egyptians building the pyramids, of Gutenberg developing printing, or the first encounters of Columbus with the people of the New World. At some point in the future, some of the documentaries produced in this century will have precisely that value. An example is the World War II documentary series, *Victory at Sea*, which recorded that global conflict for future generations. Another example is the film and video records of the first human beings on the moon. These are priceless records of human struggle and achievement that will have immense value to future generations far beyond the latest film produced for entertainment.

Through the years documentaries have dealt with people at work, the efforts of nations at war, social problems, and other issues. Some are timeless and artful classics that are now intellectual treasures, like Robert Flaherty's *Nanook of the North* (1922), which depicted Eskimo life just before the native culture was transformed into a more contemporary form. Some documentaries take bits and pieces of a process and weld them into a film. For example, Emile de Antonio and Daniel Talbot's award-winning *Point of Order!* (1963) used sequences from the McCarthy hearings that others had filmed. The directors creatively put together the work of other filmmakers and of camera operators not under their direction to produce an outstanding film. Documentaries often carry a powerful message, like Peter Davis's *Hearts and Minds* (1975), which traced the painful relationship between the United States and Vietnam.

By the late 1980s, documentaries began once again to reach audiences. Some were shown in movie theaters; others came via television. An outstanding example was the 1990 four-part documentary, *The Civil War,* based mainly on still pictures from the period. It electrified Americans when it was presented on public television. Nevertheless, there are ample reasons to question whether the documentary is becoming an endangered species. If it is on the wane, that is a loss to us all.

◀

Making a documentary involves not only thorough research of the facts about the subject matter but also all of the creative and communication skills involved in making any other type of film. In some ways, creating a documentary can be more difficult than filming a fictional story. Often, props and re-creations of events need to be prepared when the original scenes cannot be obtained as file footage. (© Remi Benali/The Gamma Liaison Network)

**Public preferences.**    Many factors influence preferences: trends in morality, current fads and recent events, plus various styles and standards. The 1930s fostered stark realism and grim themes of the Great Depression, as well as cheerful musicals that helped the public escape from its troubles. Historical and patriotic themes as well as war films were popular during World War II and after, but so were light comedies. In the 1950s, films seemed to reflect the lighthearted mood of the country. Comedies and Westerns were increasingly popular, and sexual themes were becoming more explicit. In the late 1960s, during a period of dissatisfaction with prevailing standards and styles, some films successfully celebrated the antihero and began to take on controversial social topics. Films from the late 1960s into the 1990s explored such themes as racism, drug use, feminism, and homosexuality. However, there was still time for the nonsense comedy and the lighthearted musical. Recent films have also explored international espionage and organized crime, as well as labor strikes, sports, and the supernatural.

## ▼ *The Movie Industry*

Above all, makers of motion pictures want profit. Art has never really been a prime mover of the industry. Charlie Chaplin, whose "Little Tramp" films are now regarded as art, put it bluntly in 1972: "I went into the business for money and the art grew out of it. If people are disillusioned by that remark, I can't help it. It's the truth."[14] There can be no doubt that filmmaking is a process in which money talks. To sketch a profile of this industry, we will look briefly at its organization—owners, studios, and employees—the source and size of its financial rewards, the number of its theater screens and films, and how many people watch films.

### The Filmmakers

By the late 1920s, the movies were a billion-dollar-a-year industry employing thousands and claiming a lion's share of America's entertainment dollar. Because of its benign weather and abundant sunshine for filming, the early studios of the 1920s chose southern California (specifically Hollywood) as the home for their huge dream factories. They established their studios on back "lots" that could be made into a Western town or a jungle paradise. However, as the industry matured, films were made in many locations. Hollywood became in some ways more of an administrative than a production capital. Nevertheless, it remained a symbol of glamour. As editor Peter Buckley wrote, "Hollywood was synonymous with everything that came out of the U.S. film industry, yet few films were actually made there. . . . Hollywood was a wonderful, fanciful state of mind: the film capital that never really was."[15]

**Owners and studios.**   The glamour myth of Hollywood overstated the geographic concentration of the film industry. From its beginnings, the industry forged financial links with Wall Street as well as artistic and production ties with European countries, and movies were often filmed on remote locations. Nevertheless, concentration of control and ownership was always part of the equation in American film. Major studios, such as the Big Five, have been the dominant force in Hollywood since its early days. The studios organized early and gained tight control over the whole production process, as well as over distribution and exhibition.

Founded by legendary motion picture moguls (such as Samuel Goldwyn and Louis B. Mayer) the studios ran their huge production plants in high gear. If you wanted to work in the movies in the heyday of the 1930s and 1940s, you worked for a studio, which had its own writers, directors, actors, and actresses under contract, as well as its own technicians, equipment, and lots. Through a practice known as **block booking,** each studio forced theater owners to show its bad films if they wanted a chance to show the good ones. The studios even owned their own chains of theaters. Thus, they had an assured outlet for their films—good or bad—whereas other smaller producers found it difficult to have their movies exhibited. In short, the studios had control from idea to camera to box office. It was little wonder that smaller companies had difficulty breaking into the business. Then the federal government stepped in. The courts ruled that major studios must stop block booking and give up their theaters. Because of this decision, filmmaking became a riskier business, and the major studios became less powerful.

In the 1960s various corporations bought up studios and theaters, integrating these holdings with other kinds of investments. Large corporations bought up the old major studios. Gulf & Western bought Paramount. In the early 1990s, Columbia Pictures was purchased by Sony, the Japanese conglomerate. Warner Brothers was bought by Kinney National, which also owned funeral parlors, parking lots, and magazines, among other things. In the 1990s, the whole conglomerate became Time Warner, and Disney bought ABC Television. In the 1970s, the trend toward conglomerate ownership of studios abated in favor of emphasis on independent production companies, which continued through the 1990s. (America has also seen a corresponding rise in the number of cable system channels owned by other types of media companies.)

The mix keeps changing. The top motion picture studios today, such as Sony (Combina-Tri Star), Buena Vista (which owns Disney), MGM, Universal, and 20th-Century Fox, dominate theatrical film distribution. Although the names of these studios have survived for many decades, they are no longer what they once were—the private empires of single movie moguls; they are now publicly held by numerous stockholders.[16] Thus, the movie industry is more diverse and scattered today than it was in the first half of the century, with independent producers making many films. The major studios continue to lead the industry, financing and distributing most films produced by independents as well as producing their own. They collect more than 90 percent of the total income of movie distributors, although they share this income with the independent producers and directors whom they hire for particular services or assignments.

**Making a movie.**   Making movies is a communal process. They are the product not of one person but of many. As a result, according to Professor John L. Fell,

> The substance of any particular production is likely to change appreciably between its early idea stages and the final release print. These changes may be dominated by some individual's vision, ordered by his own evolving understanding of what the movie is, but such a happy circumstance is never altogether the case, . . . even if most of the time someone pretends to be in charge.[17]

Moreover, every film requires the solution of both mechanical and aesthetic problems. The many people who are part of the team making the film must have different skills. Just consider the various unions involved in filmmaking: the Writers Guild of America, the American Cinema Editors, the Directors Guild of America, the Screen Actors Guild, and the International Association of Theatrical and Stage Employees. In other words, films are put together under chaotic conditions with a variety of artistic, technical, and organizational people.

Fell has identified seven stages or elements in the process of filmmaking:

1. *Conceptualization.* The idea for a film may come from any one of various people. Early directors often wrote their own scripts.

2. *Production.* To produce a film means to get the money together, organize all the people involved in the schedule, and continue supervising the process until the film is ready for distribution.

3. *Direction.* Once financial backing is secured and the script is acquired, then the director is chosen.

4. *Performance.* Actors must be chosen and their performances calibrated to the script and to other personnel involved in the film.

5. *Visualization.* The planning and execution of the actual filming involves cinematographers, lighting technicians, and others.

6. *Special effects.* Everything from camera trickery to monsters to stuntmen and stuntwomen comes under this heading.

7. *Editing.* This process involves choosing takes from all the film that has been shot and processing a finished film.

The producer is a key figure in putting all these elements together. In most cases he or she is part of a film studio that has the space, facilities, and personnel to complete the film. It is the producer who carries the responsibility for most of the central decisions, other than technical ones about acting, editing, and so on. The producer initiates the development of a film by acquiring a story or a script, or may merely take an **option** on a story (that is, an agreement giving one the right to purchase at a later date) until he or she sees if the talent and the money are available to produce the film. If financial backing is available and suitable acting talent can be placed under contract, then the producer finds a director and assembles the rest of the filmmaking team. Directors are in charge of the shooting.

**Employees.**  Working for the studios is a host of specialists: electricians, makeup artists, property workers, grips, projectionists, studio teamsters, costumers, craft workers, ornamental plasterers, script supervisors, actors, extras, film editors, writers, composers, musicians, cameramen, sound technicians, directors, art directors, and set directors, not to mention the stars. Almost all the technical workers are unionized. The Bureau of Labor Statistics estimated that in 1991 about 386,200 people were employed in the industry. The total payroll in 1992 was approximately $6.6 billion. Some superstar actors make many millions of dollars per film. (Sylvester Stallone reportedly received $27.5 million plus 35 percent of profits—totalling $63 million—for each of his Rocky and Rambo films.) Jack Nicholson reportedly received between $50 and $60 million for each of the *Batman* movies. Most actors obviously get far less. Recently, the number of those employed in the motion picture industry has steadily increased. As Table 5.1 shows, most of these people are engaged in making films, or advertising and distributing them to exhibitors. Note that the number of people employed in movie theaters has declined steadily, because movie attendance has decreased while theaters have become smaller. Theaters have consolidated into multiscreen establishments, and equipment has been automated.

Wages, of course, are only part of the cost of movies. By one estimate, the stars and other members of the acting cast account for only 20 percent of the costs, whereas sets and physical properties account for 35 percent.[18] The average cost of making a film in 1996 was $34.2 million. Many cost far more. Advertising and other costs were an additional $15.1 million per film on average. The money that the studios take in to balance such costs obviously depends on the number of films they distribute, the size of their audience, and the cost of admission. The industry took in $5.9 billion dollars at the box office in 1996, a new all-time high.[19] However, what accounts for the increase is not more people going to the movies but continuing inflation in the price of admission.

## The Movie Audience

After the film is made, the next step is to distribute it in such a way that a maximum number of people will pay to see it. This boils down largely to renting it to exhibitors who operate theaters. Some are independent, but like newspapers, more and more are owned by chains. Furthermore, during the Reagan administration some of the older antitrust restrictions that kept movie studios from owning their theaters were dropped. As a result, at least four of the major studios now own theaters or shares in companies that do.[20] To understand the

**Table 5.1   Number of Persons Employed in the Motion Picture Industry, 1980–1996**

| Year | Production/ Services | Distribution/ Videotape | Theaters | Total |
|------|------|------|------|------|
| 1980 | 80,811 | 11,000 | 128,511 | 220,322 |
| 1981 | 71,911 | 10,778 | 131,478 | 214,167 |
| 1982 | 76,756 | 10,544 | 125,156 | 211,456 |
| 1983 | 84,200 | 10,367 | 116,166 | 210,733 |
| 1984 | 96,633 | 10,389 | 109,100 | 218,122 |
| 1985 | 101,400 | 11,411 | 108,156 | 220,976 |
| 1986 | 103,044 | 11,300 | 105,010 | 219,356 |
| 1987 | 115,167 | 12,500 | 103,489 | 231,156 |
| 1988 | 114,800 | 131,478* | 107,922 | 354,200 |
| 1989 | 132,592 | 137,750 | 106,658 | 377,000 |
| 1990 | 154,800 | 131,800 | 107,900 | 394,500 |
| 1993 | 171,900 | 141,200 | 104,600 | 417,700 |
| 1994 | 237,400 | 158,800 | 109,900 | 506,100 |
| 1995 | 314,400 | 160,100 | 115,800 | 590,300 |
| 1996 | 240,400 | 172,100 | 112,100 | 524,600 |

*In 1988, the U.S. Department of Commerce added the video distribution sector to this category (which previously had covered motion picture theaters only). This accounts for the sudden increase.

Source: Department of Commerce.

current situation of distribution, we need to look at both the number of films being released and the number of theaters that show them to the public.

**Theaters and the cost of admission.**   In the late 1940s there were just over 20,000 (single-screen) theaters in the United States. By 1996 there were 26,690 (indoor and outdoor) screens. Although that looks like somewhat of an increase, keep in mind that the U.S. population expanded from about 150 million to approximately 263 million during the period, so that the per capita decline in moviegoing has been truly significant. Even the number of seats per theater has declined. Whereas in 1950 the average indoor movie theater had about 750 seats, by the 1990s the average theater had just under 500.

The average weekly attendance at movies reached a peak of more than 90 million in the late 1940s; it was down to just over 18.5 million by 1992. The rate of decline leveled off during the 1990s, but there is little prospect that it will rise significantly again. Clearly television has been the major factor in this precipitous decline, but the increasing price of admission may also have discouraged moviego-ing. The price of attendance to a first-run picture (a single adult ticket) rose from an average of only 23 cents in 1933 to more than $7.50 in most mid-sized and larger U.S. cities at a typical mall theater. In metropolitan areas admissions are even higher. For example, to attend a first-run picture in a major movie theater in New York City, the average price of admission in January 1997 was $8.50.

Overall, Americans are now spending more money on movies than ever before. However, in real terms the industry is attracting a much smaller part of the family entertainment dollar than before. For example, in 1943 Americans spent more than 25 percent of their recreational expenditures on movies. By 1996, this figure had dropped to less than 5 percent.

Who pays at the box office?    As indicated earlier, movie theaters draw a youthful audience and appeal less to those who are older (see Table 5.2). The youthful vitality of the theater audience and its relative stability in makeup are an important force in keeping the industry alive and well. Most mass commu-nication industries see young audiences as very desirable, because it is that portion of the population that in the future will buy goods and services and participate in the political process. For about twenty years, starting in about 1970, due to a declining number of births earlier, the young movie audience was slowly shrinking. By the mid 1990s, however, the number of teenagers in the population started an upward trend. Today, with the nation's grade schools and even high schools crammed with rising numbers of students, the young movie audience will increase steadily in the years ahead.

How often do people pay to see a movie in a theater? Not very frequently, according to national studies, but those who do go attend and pay quite often. So-called frequent moviegoers make up only about a fifth of the public over age twelve, but this group accounts for the lion's share (over 80 percent) of all movie admissions. Although detailed data on the social characteristics of moviegoers are not easily obtained, research that is available indicates the following: Single peo-ple continue to be more frequent moviegoers than those who are married. In fact, about twice as many single people compared to those who are married *frequently* go to the movies. At the other end of the attendance scale, at least a third of married people say they *never* go to the movies, somewhat more than the number of sin-gle people. More males than females describe themselves as frequent moviegoers. Finally, movie attendance tends to increase with higher educational levels among adults, suggesting that the moviegoing audience tends to be better edu-cated than those who do not go.[21]

**Table 5.2   Movie Admissions by Age Group**

| Age Group | Percentage of Population | Percentage of Total Yearly Admissions |
|---|---|---|
| 12–20 | 16 | 27 |
| 21–29 | 17 | 22 |
| 30–39 | 21 | 19 |
| 40–49 | 15 | 15 |
| 50–59 | 11 | 7 |
| 60 and over | 21 | 8 |

Source: Motion Picture Association of America, Inc., 1994.

# ▼ *Cleaning Up the Movies*

As the movie industry grew massively earlier in the century, much of the public feared that films were having both powerful and harmful effects. A number of people believed the new medium was negatively influencing children and teaching them unwholesome ideas. Many civic and religious leaders concluded that the movies would bring a general deterioration of moral norms and harmful political changes to American life. These concerns pressured the industry to "clean up" its product, and efforts to suppress certain kinds of content in the movies have continued. Most of the criticism now centers on films with "mature" themes—by which people usually mean those that deal with sex.

## Sex and the Movies

During the 1920s, when the first strong pressures arose to censor films, the industry responded by cleaning up its own house. The Motion Picture Producers and Distributors Association appointed a former postmaster general, Will H. Hays, to head their organization. Part of Hays's charge was to develop a system of self-regulation and to create a better public image for the movies. Hays and his group cooperated with religious, civic, and women's groups who had set up motion picture councils. During this early period Hays's office was a buffer between the film industry and the public. Hays finally developed a tough self-censorship code, which all producers in the association had to follow. Without code approval, a film could not be shown in American theaters. Film producers who tried to defy this dictum were subjected to costly legal battles. The code restricted depictions of sex in particular. From the mid-1930s until the rise of television threatened the industry, movies avoided direct treatment of sexual themes and sexual behavior.

Meanwhile, a number of local governments screened and censored films. Even through the 1960s, Chicago gave this assignment to its police department, which called on a group of citizens to screen controversial films. Among the private groups most active in efforts to censor films was the Catholic Legion of Decency, which was established in 1934. It developed a list of recommended and nonrecommended films, and it promoted the list to both Catholics and the general public. The ratings carried a special moral force and occasionally were reinforced by bishops who warned Catholics to stay away from certain films.

Eventually, the Legion of Decency was replaced by the Catholic Church's Office for Film and Broadcasting, which published regular newsletters and film guides. A group within the U.S. Catholic Conference continues to promote this system, publishing ratings in Catholic diocesan newspapers as advisories for Catholic parents. The ratings and their assessments are as follows:

A-1: Morally unobjectionable for general patronage

A-2: Morally unobjectionable for adults and adolescents

A-3: Morally unobjectionable for adults

A-4: For adults with reservations

A-5: Morally objectionable in part for all

C: Condemned

Efforts like those of the Legion of Decency and other critical groups stimulated creation of a set of guidelines that Hays developed for the industry, the Motion Picture Production Code. Although the code was not tough enough for groups such as the Legion of Decency, others regarded it as harsh, repressive, and too legalistic. Some film historians think the code hindered the development of American motion pictures.

By the late 1960s, the production code had been modified greatly. Numerous legal actions had broken efforts to apply rigid censorship. The industry entered a new era of self-regulation by establishing a movie classification system. Instead of barring certain films from theaters, the new system required that the public be warned of what to expect in a film. The result, which has been modified four times since it was adopted in 1968, is the following:

G: All ages admitted, general audiences

PG: Parental guidance suggested, for mature audiences

PG-13: Parents are strongly cautioned to give special guidance to children under thirteen

R: Restricted, children under seventeen must be accompanied by a parent or other adult

NC-17: No one under seventeen admitted (until fall 1990 this category was rated X)

The classification does not indicate quality; it is only a guide for parents considering what motion pictures their children should see. The industry, through the Motion Picture Association of America, in effect puts its seal of approval on the first four categories of films and denies it to the fifth. This system won public support and stilled some criticism, but some film producers feel that the system is too restrictive. There has been no active move to overturn it, however. Interestingly, there are less than half as many G- and PG-rated films as there are films with PG-13, R, NC-17, or X ratings.

Efforts to suppress a particular motion picture can backfire. Perhaps no film in recent times has aroused such an outcry as *The Last Temptation of Christ* (1988), a low-budget movie that became something of a financial success at the box office largely as a result of the furor. Various church groups and other critical people threatened and carried out boycotts and protest demonstrations. These efforts were thoroughly covered by both national and local television news, and

▶

In our mass society, many categories of people with differing values, interests, and preferences exist. Almost any film not suitable for general family entertainment will be seen as objectionable by one group or another. However, some movies provoke especially vigorous outcries because of their themes or content. A recent example that deeply offended many Christian groups was *The Last Temptation of Christ.* Many theaters showing the film were picketed by demonstrators who deemed it blasphemous. (AP/Wide World Photos)

of course by newspapers. The publicity brought crowds of curious viewers to the theaters to see what all the fuss was about. Some observers have speculated that if the film had been ignored, it would quickly have died as a dud.

## Violence and Vulgarity

As television became a highly competitive medium for motion pictures, the industry turned away from the earlier production and review code developed by Will Hays. The problem was rapidly declining ticket sales at the box office. The box in the living room was displacing the silver screen downtown, in the neighborhood and at the drive-in theater (which declined from 3,720 in 1971 to a mere 826 by 1996). Even before VCRs and cable, people increasingly preferred to watch free entertainment on their TV receiver rather than travel to a theater and pay to get in.

To meet this competition from network television, the movies began to alter their content. Once again, as they had done during the 1920s, they turned to depictions that went beyond the more conservative norms of the traditional segment of the public. Aside from the sexual portrayals previously discussed, which were always the most controversial, the producers also began to incorporate an increasing level of violence and vulgarity into their films.

In some ways, this was successful and in some ways it was not. It clearly altered the composition of the audience but it also may have reduced its size. There was limited success in that after about the mid-1960s, the rate of decline in box office ticket sales slowed down. Fast action drama, packed with violence and with the actors using vulgar language, was a clear change from the older sanitized movies that had been governed by the Hays code. Increasingly, the industry began producing fast-paced films in which macho heroes shot it out, had brutal fistfights, and raced through the streets in spectacular crash-filled car chases. New genres, such as horror, surf and beach epics, and more sophisticated special effects monsters also proved to be popular. However, with these changes in content, a transformation of the audience was underway in which the movies changed from a form of family entertainment that mom, pop, and the kids all attended together into one made up of younger, single people. In particular, themes of violence and vulgarity were just right for younger audiences, but they were not appealing to older married people and unsuitable for their children. Thus, while the loss of ticket sales slowed, the movies effectively shut out the more conservative majority of older, married people.

A very interesting pattern can be seen when looking back at the history of the relationship between audiences, their moral norms and the content of the movies. During the period just before and after World War I, the content of the films did not transgress general norms concerning either sexual depictions, violence, or vulgarity. As the country entered the changing period of the 1920s, as noted earlier, movies increasingly challenged those norms. The Hays code temporarily halted that and reversed the trend. Challenged by television, however, movies once more began to cross the line in terms of what many people wanted to see on the screen. In more recent years, further competition came to the industry from cable TV and from VCRs. Again, seeking increased audiences and profits, movies seemed to many to transgress traditional norms regarding sex, violence, and vulgarity. The result was a pattern of pressing forward to the limits of such norms, to draw back when public outcries become too shrill, and wait until people adapted to the new standards being set. When outcries become fewer, the industry pressed on once again until it encountered resistance. Because of this cycle, the public gradually became *desensitized* to content of the movies that at one time would have caused a serious problem for the industry.

This "creeping cycle of desensitization" expressed as a theory (see the boxed insert) is not unique to motion pictures and can apply to other media as well. What it explains is that when movies get sexier, more vulgar, and increasingly violent, one need not assume that these changes are simply due to immoral decisions made by bad and greedy people who are in charge of the movie industry. Such people may not be saints or leaders in a movement to purify the popular culture of America, but their decisions are largely products of the economic system in which our media are embedded. Their choice can be stark—make money for their investors (highly approved) or go bankrupt (highly disapproved)! With no political system of censorship to restrain them,

# EXPLAINING MEDIA EFFECTS
## *The Creeping Cycle of Desensitization Theory*

As one looks at the movie industry from the 1920s to the present, it is clear that the industry has survived not only because it has found alternative markets for the industry's products, but also because, compared to the wholesome films of the 1930s and 1940s, it has increasingly incorporated sexual themes, violence, and vulgar language into their content.

To illustrate how greatly public tolerance has changed, we can note that in the late 1940s movie, *The Outlaw,* Jane Russell's display of much of the upper part of her prominent bosom brought howls of protest from a large segment of the public. Even the word "damn" uttered by Clark Gable in 1939's *Gone with the Wind* raised many eyebrows. Today, however, frontal female nudity and open sexual coupling are routinely depicted in films. Movies currently show savage beatings, deadly car bombings, rape, torture, and wholesale shootings. Actors now routinely use four-letter words that would have shocked movie audiences little more than a generation back. Although politicians sometimes decry these patterns, the outcry from the general public is largely muted. Why have both the movies and the public changed so much?

A theory that can explain these changes has been called the "creeping cycle of desensitization."[22] It refers to the increasing failure of traditional moral norms of soceity to hold back the depiction of ever-increasing levels of violence, explicit sexual behavior, and vulgar language in our movies (and other media). Contributing factors are the lack of content control due to the protections of the First Amendment and the failure of critics to crack down effectively. The cycle of desensitization started in the 1920s when movies became increasingly explicit, showing women in undergarments, young people using alcohol, and violent behavior by gangsters. These transgressions of the moral norms brought about the movie production codes of the 1930s and 1940s. By the 1950s, however, and especially with the growth of television and the decline of attendance at the box office, moviemakers abandoned the code and incorporated increasing violence, explicit sex, and vulgar language. As the public gradually became accustomed to this type of content, the industry pressed farther, using these themes to attract audiences, transgressing traditional norms even more. Stated as systematic theoretical propositions, the theory goes like this:

**1.** Our movie industry (like other media) operates in a system of economic capitalism in which making profits is a major and highly approved goal.

**2.** Making profits with a movie follows classical principles of competitive and market-driven capitalism. It means not only keeping costs down but also maximizing the audiences who pay in one form or another to see the film. Sex, violence, and vulgarity attract larger audiences.

**3.** Our First Amendment offers few or no political restraints on what any medium can present to the public. What they show is largely left to audience tastes and cultural norms that define what people will or will not tolerate.

**4.** A large proportion of the movie audience, particularly the young, care little for controls based on conservative tastes and restraining cultural norms as they actively seek pleasure and excitement via exposure to sexual depictions, vulgarities, and violence. The number of active and vocal critics is relatively small.

**5.** Therefore, moviemakers, seeking maximum profits, will constantly increase depictions of sex, violence, and vulgarity until the public reacts strongly—stopping temporarily if criticism is strong but resuming after the public becomes accustomed to the new standard.

they supply the public with what it appears to want, and back off only temporarily when critics raise a significant fuss.

## Censorship and Politics

Sex, violence, and vulgarity have not been the only categories of content at the center of outcries against movies over the years. Politics too has been the basis for censorship efforts. Many films with political themes were widely criticized during the 1930s. Battles to organize unions, fights between unions and producers, charges that some unions were tools of Communists, and accusations that some films were Communist propaganda split Hollywood in the years before World War II. During the war, political differences were submerged as the industry united behind the war effort. However, when fear of communism ignited again in the late 1940s and 1950s, political censorship came to Hollywood as never before. The House Un-American Activities Committee, an official group of the U.S. Congress that had been active since the 1930s, held hearings and charged scores of people, including many in the film industry, with Communist activity. The hearings were followed by some prison sentences and **black-listing** of people in the film, broadcast, and print industries.

Blacklisting was the work not of government but of private groups, and it was decidedly not a democratic activity. Various lobbying groups put together lists of people they suspected of being Communists, circulated the lists privately, and threatened to boycott advertisers who sponsored shows, newspapers, or magazines that hired anyone on the list, as well as producers who gave listed people work. Most of those blacklisted were not publicly accused, so they had no chance to defend themselves. Some actors, producers, writers, and others did not even know they were on such a list until no one wanted to hire them and their careers crashed. For a time performers had to be "cleared" by one of the anti-Communist groups before they would be hired. This period, when unsupported charges were frequent, is one of the darkest in media history. Postwar fear of communism was the culprit, and the film industry was hard hit by the informal censorship that resulted.

Many groups outside the movie industry have exerted influence on the content of films.

During the 1950s, some in the nation feared that "Communists" were trying to take over the country. Congressmen Scherer, Clardy, Velde, Moulder, and Doyle (left to right) were on the Un-American Activities Committee of the U.S. House of Representatives. Its mission was to investigate the activities of many writers and actors in order to try and root out Communist influences. Critics note that the reputations of many people suffered from accusations made during the period. (UPI/Corbis-Bettmann)

Congress has summoned actors and directors to public hearings, the Supreme Court has tried to define what is and is not obscene, and church groups and local officials have tried various strategies to shape, suppress, or ban American movies. The result is a constraint on the artistic freedom of film-makers, but little if any useful feedback for them. The groups pressuring the filmmakers are too small and their interests too narrow for their efforts to con-stitute effective feedback for a medium intended for a mass audience. Never-theless, their efforts can seriously distort communication between filmmaker and audience. Still, consumers of films have the same First Amendment rights that filmmakers do, and this includes the right to protest against content they do not like.

## ▼ Evaluating Films: Criticism and Awards

Film ratings or public protests are only part of the many assessments that film-makers receive. The writings of critics, the selections made for film festivals and awards, and surveys of public opinions of films provide other evaluations. These assessments might suggest that there are uniform standards of excel-lence in films, but that is not the case. Although occasionally there may be widespread agreement on which film was the best of a year or decade, there are about as many standards for criticism as there are critics and awards.

### The Critics

Some people distinguish between **reviewers,** who make assessments for a gen-eral audience, and **critics,** who judge a film by more artistic and theoretical criteria and try to ascertain its social importance. The terms are used inter-changeably by most people, but they can connote significant differences. Re-viewers see films, discuss their content, popularity, and merits in newspaper columns or other media, and make recommendations to the public. Critics do much the same. However, they are not interested in a film's popularity. Critics have their own standards against which they judge a film, although they vary from one individual to another. Because film has gained status as an art form, some critics judge a film on the basis of artistic potential and compare it with other films and theatrical productions. They consider factors such as the film's originality and its ability to project universal themes. A critic might be inter-ested in any number of things about a film: the technical aspects such as pho-tography, sound, use of close-ups, and color; the quality of the screenplay as a piece of writing; the performance of the actors; and the unity and cohesiveness of the production. Some critics discuss the film in terms of the way it fits into a particular actor's or director's career. For example, a critic might discuss whether the direction and acting in the latest Woody Allen film are as good as in his previous films.

Film criticism appears in many places. Specialized industry magazines speak mainly to the movie community and to film scholars. Many magazines and newspapers have movie reviews and criticisms. *Time* and the *New York Times,* as well as others, publish annual "ten best movie" lists. NBC's popular "Today" show offers regular movie reviews. PBS has a half-hour show devoted to movie reviews called "At the Movies," which is a sort of "consumers' guide" for what is worth seeing. Local television and radio stations review films on the air. Various Internet services also list, critique, and rate films. Sometimes it seems like more energy is devoted to reviewing and criticizing films than to making them. There are even annual awards for the best film criticism.

## The Awards

Most organized human endeavors offer various kinds of symbolic rewards to individuals or groups that perform well. It may be a medal for wartime bravery, a diploma for completing a degree program, a plaque for selling the most insurance, or a cup for catching the biggest fish. Individuals who organize and control such awards understand their importance. As long as people take them seriously, awards satisfy needs for status recognition and give both prestige and publicity to that particular arena of competition.

Moviemaking is no exception. It has its own system for recognizing high performance and for publicizing those accomplishments. The granddaddy of all the movie awards is the Oscar—the gold-plated statue about a foot high awarded each year in a nationally televised spectacle by the Academy of Motion Picture Arts and Sciences. The Oscars are prizes from the industry itself to its honored few, and even though the little statues themselves are rather tacky and cheaply produced, they are the most coveted of all the movie awards. Receiving the awards has real economic value, because films that win them are usually rereleased, with attendant publicity, and draw thousands more viewers and box-office receipts.

The Academy makes awards in many categories, and the list is almost endless: it includes best picture, best director, best actor, best actress, best supporting actor, best supporting actress, best screenplay adaptation, best original screenplay, best cinematography, and best foreign-language film. There are also awards for art direction, sound, short subjects, music, film editing, and costume design, as well as honorary awards, scientific and technical awards, and various awards for service to the industry.

The Academy Awards have not been without their critics. Some charge that those giving the awards concentrate on the most popular films rather than on the best or most socially significant. There is some truth to this argument. For example, one of the best films of all time—Orson Welles's brilliant *Citizen Kane* (1941)—got only one award, for best screenplay. Still, the list of Oscar winners is a kind of "Who's Who" of well-known films and filmmakers.

Other honors and prizes are less well known. Both the Writers Guild and the Directors Guild give awards, and there are a number of awards by groups independent of the industry. The National Board of Review Awards are given for films that are recommended for children. Both the National Society of Film Critics and the New York Film Critics give annual awards for exemplary films, and the foreign press corps covering Hollywood gives annual Golden Globe Awards. The awards at these festivals usually honor artistic quality.

Finally, there have been a number of efforts to identify the greatest films of all time by surveying directors and critics. One of the most ambitious efforts to identify such a film was carried out by the American Film Institute in 1977. The 35,000 members of the Institute across the nation—including film scholars, critics, and industry people—were asked to select five choices, in order of preference, for the best American film. Some 1,100 titles were mentioned in the balloting, and the institute compiled a list of the top fifty films. The list was heavily weighted with films produced since 1970, and the silent era, in particular, was underrepresented. Andrew Sarris, critic for the *Village Voice*, commented, "I suspect that many AFI voters were simply not familiar with many great films."

Nevertheless, the Institute unveiled the list of the top fifty films at a dazzling ceremony attended by the president of the United States. Keeping in mind that no film on the list was made after 1977 when the survey was conducted, the top ten films on the list are:

1. *Gone With the Wind* (1939)

2. *Citizen Kane* (1941)

3. *Casablanca* (1942)

4. *The African Queen* (1952)

5. *The Grapes of Wrath* (1940)

6. *One Flew Over the Cuckoo's Nest* (1975)

7. *Singing in the Rain* (1952)

8. *Star Wars* (1977)

9. *2001: A Space Odyssey* (1968)

10. *The Wizard of Oz* (1939)

To balance all the self-congratulation of the movie industry and its friends, the *Harvard Lampoon*, with tongue in cheek, presents annual worst movie awards. There has been no great study to identify a list of all-time turkeys. However, films have been produced and released that are so bad that it is difficult to imagine what possessed people to produce them. Perhaps the worst film of all time was an unbelievably tacky Western with the title of *Terror of Tiny Town*. It had an all midget cast, a small saloon, and very small ponies for the hero and villain!

# CHAPTER REVIEW

▼ Motion pictures have a technological history that includes inventions in optics, photography, and electronics and discoveries in the psychology of the perception of motion. By 1886, short, primitive pictures showing motion were being exhibited in America.

▼ The movie theater as we know it began after the turn of the century with the nickelodeons. Within a few years, movies were being made for the middle class, and the industry expanded to become a popular mode of family entertainment.

▼ As society changed rapidly after World War I, movies mirrored the new ways of life. Conservative people were alarmed at portrayals of alcohol use, easy money, fast cars, and loose morals. Extensive efforts to control movies arose, and research on their effects began.

▼ Between 1930 and 1960, the great golden age of movies dawned and then declined. The American film industry has gone through many changes in its short history. For the most part, it has been a medium for entertainment.

▼ Every film is a product of technology, artistry, managerial skill, and showmanship. Making a film involves a wide range of professionals and craft workers. At various times different members of the filmmaking team have tended to dominate in shaping films.

▼ The content of a film is influenced by conflicting forces: the desire for efficiency, a view of what the audience wants, and an individual's desire to shape the film. The result of this conflict has been a wide range of genres and styles in American films.

▼ Traditional film (shown in theaters) was once a more important medium of entertainment than it is today, but the industry has responded to the demands of new competition, changing technology, and changing audiences. Because it has adapted so well, the moving picture show, in one form or another, will remain a large, lively, and significant medium.

## CHAPTER 6

# Radio

## The First Broadcast Medium

*U*ntil a little over a century ago, lack of communication technology was a severe handicap in coordinating complex human activities, and had been since the dawn of history. In fact, inability to communicate quickly over distance had more than once altered the fate of the entire world. For example, in 1588, Philip II of Spain sent the Armada, a great fleet of 130 war ships under the command of the Duke of Medina Sidonia, to crush the English, who were helping Spain's enemies. The plan was for the Spanish ships to pick up the army of Alessandro Farnese, the Duke of Palma, on the shores of Flanders and take them across the channel to invade and conquer England in order to reestablish Catholicism.

Up to that time, this was the greatest naval and military venture in the history of the world. It should have succeeded because the English had no standing army. However, as it turned out the venture was a miserable failure. The problem was a lack of adequate communication. The Armada and Palma's army never found each other. English ships harried the Armada in the channel, doing little actual damage, but forcing them northward. Problems of coordination mounted. Unable to contact the nearby army he was supposed to meet and, indeed, uncertain that it was even there, Sidonia abandoned the invasion plan.

Bad storms arose as the ships tried to return to Spain by way of the Atlantic to the west of Ireland. Dozens of vessels foundered with great loss of life, and the whole effort ended in disaster. If the commanders of the Armada and the shore-bound army had possessed just one little CB radio each, they could have coordinated their efforts effectively. The entire history of the world would have changed, and we would probably all be speaking, reading, and writing Spanish today!

Communication devices that could conquer distance at high speed were a dream extending back to ancient times. Giovanni della Porta, a sixteenth-century scientist, described in his book the "sympathetic telegraph" for which learned men had long been searching.[1] It was a device that would be able to "write at a distance" (in Greek, *tele,* far off, and *graphos,* to write). In the imagination of those searching for a way to do this, the instrument would be prepared with a special *lodestone* (a magnet) that would sensitize two needles so they would act "in sympathy." The needles were to be mounted on separate dials, something like compasses, but with the letters of the alphabet around the edge. If one needle were to be moved to a given position on its dial, such as to point to the letter A, the other would move to a similar position immediately, even though the devices were far from each other. With such a sympathetic telegraph, messages would be sent and received rapidly over distances.

It was a great idea. Unfortunately the special lodestone was never found. However, there was a slow accumulation of science during the next three centuries, and more rapid acceleration in technology during the nineteenth and twentieth centuries. The result was that communication devices were developed that would have astounded Giovanni della Porta.

Starting in the 1840s, the new technologies came quickly, one after the other, within a span of about fifty years. The first was the electric dot-and-dash telegraph (1844). It was followed by the telephone (1876), the wireless telegraph (1896), and finally the radiotelephone (1906). Then, with adaptations of radiotelephone technology in the early 1920s, radio became a mass medium for household use. We saw in Chapter 5 that the movies also came into existence during the last decade of the nineteenth century. By the mid-1920s, even the principles needed for television had been developed.

To appreciate how rapidly all of this took place, we can imagine a person born in 1843—just before Morse transmitted his first telegraph message. In that year, a message could move only as fast as a galloping horse, or at most a flying pigeon. Few increases in speed had been made since prehistoric times. Then suddenly, remarkable changes came. When a person born in 1843 was only ten years old, the telegraph was regularly sending messages at a mind-boggling 186,000 miles per second between distant points in a large network. By the time that individual was about forty, he or she could have telephoned friends at distant locations. By eighty-five, he or she could have listened on a home receiver to regularly scheduled radio programs transmitted over a nationwide network. If that same individual had survived to an unusual 105 years, he or she could have watched news, sports, and entertainment programs on a home television set.

This chapter focuses on only part of that set of swift changes—the development of radio. As will be clear, radio and television share a common background of technological development. They also share a common economic base and a system of societal control. For that reason, the events of history common to both media will be reviewed in this chapter, but what is unique to TV will be presented in Chapter 7.

## ▼ The Growth of Broadcasting Technology

To understand the ways in which the development of communication by broadcasting was a part of more general trends taking place, we need to review very briefly what we have said in earlier chapters about society itself at different times during the nineteenth century. Few citizens at the beginning of the period could have imagined the changes in lifestyle that would soon take place in the industrializing countries. During the early 1800s, people still traveled between towns on foot or by animal power. Trips to distant places often took months. Goods to be purchased were handcrafted rather than factory made. Food was either grown at home or produced on nearby farms. Only a limited selection of items came to a community from distant places. Long-distance communication was by sailing ship, or postal and courier services that used horses. The pace of society was slow indeed, and most people lived a simple rural or small-town existence.

The century was not even half over before travel time had been drastically reduced. Awesome machines, belching smoke and steam and pulling long strings of wagons, rolled across the countryside on iron rails at what were then considered incredible speeds. Powerful ships, thrust forward by steam-driven paddle wheels, plied the nation's waterways. Power-driven factories spewed forth standardized goods. The scope and pace of commercial activities had increased greatly. Thus, even before the Civil War, the Industrial Revolution had transformed much of the nation.

After the war ended, railroads soon connected most major American cities with scheduled service, and steam-driven ships regularly crossed the great oceans. In addition, hundreds of factories were producing shoes, farm implements, clocks, guns, cooking pots, woven cloth, tools, and a great variety of other manufactured goods. Small towns had become cities, and large metropolitan centers thrived. Food came not just from local farms but by rail from more distant sources. The Industrial Revolution had generated a parallel revolution in the production, distribution, and consumption of goods and services of many kinds.

The development of radio was a part of these great changes. As we have already suggested, it was by applying principles discovered in the basic sciences that practical devices were developed to communicate rapidly over long distances. For example, unraveling the mysteries of electricity was a first step toward broadcasting. The Greeks marveled at static electricity but did not understand its nature. By the 1700s, Europeans were generating gigantic static charges, but they still did not understand the nature of electricity. Then, researchers succeeded in revealing how electricity works, how it could be stored in batteries, and how it could be used in practical applications. Discoveries of scientists such as Volta, Ampere, Faraday, and Maxwell laid the scientific foundations for applications such as the telegraph, and later, radio and television.

## Communicating over a Wire

The great dream of the sympathetic telegraph seemed increasingly achievable as the nature of electricity and ways to control it began to be understood. At the end of the 1700s, devices had been developed by which electrical impulses could be used to send a message over wires. They were very cumbersome and limited to short distances (such as between two rooms). The system relied on static electricity and separate wires connecting cards—one for each letter of the alphabet. A charge applied at one end of a wire caused the letter card at the other end to flop down. With great patience, and constant resetting of the letters, a message could be sent. Actually, it was a lot faster and easier just to walk from one room to the other. Nevertheless, this fascinating toy showed what problems needed to be solved to develop an electric telegraph. To start with, the device would have to be based on a single wire.

The American Samuel F. B. Morse is usually credited with inventing the long-distance telegraph. What he actually did was develop a more practical system than certain earlier innovators. The first important discovery came in 1819 when Hans Oerstead found that a wire carrying a pulse of electrical current over a considerable distance could deflect a magnetic needle. He also noted that reversing the direction of the current would reverse the deflection of the needle. With ways of patterning and interpreting the deflections of the needle, the device served as a crude telegraph. A number of scientists, including André Ampère and Karl Gauss, then studied and improved the process. By 1837, Wilhelm Cooke and Charles Wheatstone developed a working telegraph system based on this needle-deflection principle. It was actually used by railroads in England.

A much more efficient system, based on the electromagnet, was developed by Morse in 1844. The electromagnet itself was discovered by William Sturgeon in 1825 and then refined by Michael Faraday and Joseph Henry. It was a rather simple device. If a bar of soft iron, about the size of a wiener, is wrapped in copper wire and a steady flow of electricity from a battery is passed through the wire, the bar becomes a fairly strong magnet. Stop the electricity and the bar loses most of its magnetic property. By starting and stopping the flow of electricity, an operator can make the electromagnet attract and release another piece of iron. Using this principle, Morse constructed a telegraph machine and devised a code for each letter by using long and short pulses of electricity. He was also able to attach a pencil to the piece of metal that his electromagnet attracted so as to leave a record of the transmission on a moving strip of paper.

Samuel F. B. Morse did not invent the telegraph in its entirety. Others had built workable systems in England. However, his machine was very simple, practical, and reliable. An important contribution was his simple code used to transmit messages. It was so practical that it was adopted worldwide and is still in use today in a few applications. (North Wind Picture Archives)

By today's standards Morse's was a crude system. But by comparison with what was available at the time, it was a fantastic practical advance in communication technology. After the device proved reliable, Morse was able to obtain a grant from the U.S. government to field-test the system. He had a copper wire strung on poles between Baltimore, Maryland, and Washington, D.C., a distance of about forty miles. From Baltimore, on the morning of May 25, 1844, he sent the dramatic message, "What hath God wrought?" It was received in Washington with wild cheering and awe. No longer was the movement of a message limited to the speed of travel or of a carrier pigeon or locomotive. Information could be flashed to a distant location at the speed of lightning. It did indeed seem to many observers like something that God had personally wrought.

Within a few years, with wires on poles along the railroad lines, most of the major cities of the United States were connected by telegraph. Business, the military, and—as we saw in Chapter 3—newspapers began to depend on the system for rapid communication. Undersea cables were laid, even before the Civil War. Regular service between the United States and Europe was available by 1866. Yet the telegraph obviously was not a medium for the general public. It would be more than half a century before ordinary people would have a device in their homes for instantaneous mass communication without wires.

The telegraph not only initiated the era of instantaneous communication, it also set the model for the structure of ownership that would eventually characterize the electronic media in the United States. Even though the federal government had paid for Morse's experimental line between Baltimore and Washington, it declined to exercise control over the telegraph. The medium became the property of a private corporation to be operated for profit. This decision was critical because it set the pattern of development for the telephone, radio, and television.

## Communicating with Radio Waves

Meanwhile, a German scientist, Heinrich Hertz, had been experimenting with some curious electromagnetic phenomena that he had produced in the laboratory. By 1887, he had constructed a simple transmitter and receiver and had demonstrated the existence of what we know today as radio waves. The accomplishment electrified the scientific world, and experimentation with these new waves that traveled at the speed of light began in laboratories in many countries. This discovery in basic science was to become the foundation of radio broadcasting.

**Marconi's wireless telegraph.** A few years later, Guglielmo Marconi, a twenty-year-old Italian youth from a wealthy family, had read everything he could find about the Hertzian waves. He bought the necessary parts, and on his father's estate he built his own devices to produce and detect these waves.

▶

By 1895, Guglielmo Marconi had found a way to transmit a message via radio over an impressive distance on his father's Italian estate. He synthesized Heinrich Hertz's discoveries of electromagnetic waves that traveled instantaneously without wires and the concept of transmitting messages encoded into dots and dashes via the electric telegraph. The result was a telegraph that worked without wires. It was one of the great inventions of all time—the starting point for the modern era of electronic media. (Culver Pictures, Inc.)

He experimented with different wavelengths, types of antennae, and other features of the system. His idea was that by systematically interrupting the wave as it was being generated, he could send and receive messages in Morse code—without wires.

By 1895, Marconi had succeeded in sending coded messages over a considerable distance across his father's estate. Thinking that his invention probably could have important uses, he offered it to the Italian government and tried to persuade them to help finance his work. But his government, deciding the device was only a novelty without practical importance, was not interested. Undaunted, and at the urging of his English mother, Marconi took his ideas to London, where in 1897 he was able to obtain a patent as well as financial backing to develop further his "wireless telegraph." Soon after, by 1901, he had built a much more powerful transmitter and succeeded in sending a message across the Atlantic.

Radio, in this dot-and-dash form, had enormous practical advantages over the land-based telegraph that required wires. Ships at sea could communicate with each other and with stations on land. A number of remote stations could all hear the broadcast of a central station simultaneously. For England, as for other nations with numerous colonies, a large navy, a huge merchant marine, and far-flung commercial enterprises, the wireless telegraph was a godsend.

The principal drawback of the earliest sets was that they required large, heavy equipment to achieve long-range transmission. An early set could barely fit into a room. Not being a scientist, Marconi had chosen the wrong end of the frequency band. He reasoned that long radio waves would go farther than short ones. However, it took great electrical energy to transmit them over long distances. Thus, his system required powerful electric currents, heavy wiring and switches, and massive antennae. If he had used the very short waves, he could have developed a much smaller, more portable machine. Within a few years that became evident.

Marconi was not only an inventor but also a shrewd businessman. He successfully fought patent challenges to protect his ownership and established profit-oriented corporations to exploit wireless communication. He founded the American Marconi Company in 1899, and by 1913 it had a virtual monopoly on the use of the wireless telegraph in the United States. By that time radio had come into worldwide use, and Marconi became a rich man indeed. As earlier with telegraph by wire, the principle of private ownership and profit in broadcasting was established from the outset.

Marconi also invented a device for generating and detecting a particular wavelength for the more precise transmission of signals, and he patented it in 1904. This device was important because it allowed the transmitter to broadcast on a specific wavelength or "frequency." With the receiving instrument "tuned" to a similar wavelength, signals on other frequencies could not interfere. We still tune radios to specific frequencies in this manner for transmission and reception.

**The radiotelephone.**   During the first decade of the twentieth century, radio quickly became more than a wireless telegraph. On Christmas Eve in 1906, radio operators along the lonely Atlantic sea lanes could not believe their ears when suddenly they heard a human voice over their sets. A man read from the Bible, then played a phonograph record and a violin. Up to that time, only dots and dashes had ever come out of their earphones. It was Reginald A. Fessenden broadcasting from an experimental station near Boston. He used a telephone mouthpiece as a "microphone" and a special alternator to generate his radio waves. The dot-dash receivers were able to detect his complex signals.

It was Lee De Forest who in 1906 brought the radio into its own by inventing the **audion,** a three-element vacuum tube, which allowed much more sophisticated circuits and applications. De Forest's tube made amplification of radio signals possible. This in turn permitted the development of small reliable receivers. As a result, portable radio transmitters and receivers about the size of a bread box played important roles in World War I. By 1918, radio communication had advanced sufficiently for a pilot to receive and transmit from an airplane to people on the ground. Basically, however, radio at this time was either the older dot-dash wireless system introduced by Marconi or a laboratory device used for experimental purposes. It was by no means something that people used at home to listen to scheduled broadcasts. In other words, it was a private rather than a public medium.

Nevertheless, radio captured the imagination of the public in the early days. It seemed like a scientific marvel at the cutting edge of new technology. People had the same fascination with it that later generations would have with early space vehicles. For example, when ships got into trouble it was possible to summon aid by radio. One of the first examples occurred in 1898, when radio signals were used to bring aid to a vessel in difficulty. A really dramatic rescue at sea, though, took place in 1909. When the SS *Republic* began to sink off New York, the wireless operator sent out a distress signal. Other ships detected it and came as quickly as possible to the position indicated. All the passengers were rescued. It made great newspaper headlines, and the public was enthralled.

A historic rescue effort in 1912 was less successful. When the "unsinkable" *Titanic* struck an iceberg in the North Atlantic, the wireless operator tried to alert nearby ships, but their radio crews had gone to bed for the night. However, he was able to make contact with a shore station (in Wanamaker's department store in New York), whose stronger signal could reach more distant points. The young operator, David Sarnoff, stayed at his post for many hours, making contact with other vessels. Unfortunately, by the time those ships arrived the next morning, the great passenger liner had gone to the bottom. Some 1,500 people drowned, including the *Titanic's* heroic wireless operator, who tried all night to summon aid until he went down with the ship.

## ▼ *The Development of Radio as a Mass Medium*

In increasing numbers, amateur radio fans were attracted to the medium after World War I. Although assembled sets could be purchased, they were expensive; and so thousands bought parts and put together their own receivers. Plans for **crystal set** radio receivers appeared in popular magazines aimed at the home mechanic and tinkerer. Companies marketed kits through the mails for crystal sets that even a bright child could put together. With a length of copper wire wrapped around a Quaker Oats box, a device to slide along the resulting coil to tune the device, and the right kinds of crystal, battery, earphones, and aerial, the home listener could pick up audible signals. Radio was the scientific wonder of the age, and the public expressed a broad interest in the medium even before regular broadcasting began.

### The Period of Transition

Before radio broadcasting could be a mass medium, it had to make the transition from a long-range, rather cumbersome device for maritime, commercial, and governmental communication to an easy-to-use system that would bring program content to people in their homes.[2]

First, radio sets had to be small enough for use in the home. In part, the home-built set helped fulfill that need, but many people wanted to purchase their sets ready-made. Second, therefore, their price had to be brought within the means of large numbers of families. Third, there had to be regularly scheduled programs to which people would want to listen. This barrier was a real one, because there simply were no stations providing content that would interest most potential listeners. Fourth, reception had to be reasonably clear—that is, without annoying static and overlap between stations. This meant that there had to be a means of regulating the use of the airwaves, either by voluntary agreements or through some government licensing scheme. Not everyone who wanted to broadcast would be able to do so without interfering with others on the same wavelength. Fifth, and perhaps most important of all, there had to be a means of paying for the broadcasts.

Although by today's standards, the transmission equipment itself was not all that expensive, space had to be provided to house the station, with its attendant costs of heat, light, rent, and so forth. Salaries had to be paid to engineers, to people who said things over the air, and even to janitors who cleaned up.

Within a few years all of these barriers would be overcome, and the transition to a true mass medium would take place very quickly. In 1916, David Sarnoff (who played a part in trying to summon aid for the *Titanic*), had gone to work for the American Marconi Company. He wrote a now famous memorandum to his boss that outlined the way radio could become a medium for home use:

> I have in mind a plan of development which would make radio a "household utility" in the same sense as a piano or phonograph. The idea is to bring music into the house by wireless . . . The receiver can be designed in the form of a simple "Radio Music Box" and arranged for several different wave lengths, which should be changeable with the throwing of a single switch or pressing of a single button.
>
> The "Radio Music Box" can be supplied with amplifying tubes and a loudspeaking telephone, all of which can be neatly mounted in one box. The box can be placed on a table in the parlor or living room, the switch set accordingly and the transmitted music received.[3]

Sarnoff went on in his memo to suggest that people listening at home could receive news, sports scores, lectures, weather reports, and concerts. He also suggested that such machines could be manufactured and sold by the thousands. All his scheme needed was the addition of advertising as a source of financial support for regularly scheduled broadcasts, plus government control over frequency allocation, to make it a very accurate description of the future of radio as a mass medium. Sarnoff's proposal was rejected by his superiors as impractical and too visionary. However, by 1919, he became the manager of a new company called the Radio Corporation of America (RCA) and played a major role in bringing radio to the public.

**Scheduled programs begin.** The broadcasting of regularly scheduled programs over the airwaves did not begin in all parts of the country at once. A sort of amateur version of such broadcasts started in Pittsburgh in April of 1920. An engineer, Dr. Frank Conrad, was developing transmitting systems for the Westinghouse Corporation. He needed to test equipment after hours, so he built a transmitter over his garage at home. It was licensed as station 8XK, and with the help of his family, Conrad began making regular broadcasts two evenings a week. People sent him postcards and called on the telephone requesting particular **Victrola** records. This feedback from the audience enabled Conrad to understand the reach of the signal.

Westinghouse, seeing the growing public interest in home radio in 1920 and intrigued by Conrad's example, decided to establish a radio station to produce regularly scheduled broadcasts in the Pittsburgh area. The idea was to provide programming for people who bought the home receivers that Westinghouse  manufactured and sold. The firm built a transmitter in a tin shack on top of its building in Pittsburgh and licensed it as radio station KDKA. To dramatize the establishment of the station, they announced that for their first broadcast they would transmit the returns of the 1920 presidential election (Harding versus Cox). Actually, the station received its election information from a local newspaper by phone. Nevertheless, several hundred people with sets in the Pittsburgh area learned from signals sent over the evening sky that Harding had won. The event was a dramatic success, greatly stimulating the sale of receivers. The station continued to broadcast regularly, presenting music, religious services, sports information, political talks, and even market reports. Its signal carried over a long distance, and people in many parts of the country tuned in. Radio station KDKA is still on the air and is recognized as the oldest station in continuous operation in the nation.

▶

On November 2, 1920, KDKA became the nation's first commercial radio station to begin continuous scheduled operation. Its first broadcast consisted of news about the Harding-Cox presidential election. A running account of the returns was phoned in from a newspaper office and read over the air. Between announcements, banjo music was played. (Courtesy KDKA Radio 1020, Westinghouse Broadcasting, Inc.)

Within months, dozens of other stations went on the air in various cities. Soon there were hundreds, and the infant mass medium became a chaotic mess. Transmitters were paid for and operated by just about anyone who wanted to transmit messages. This included department stores, wealthy individuals, automobile dealers, corporations, churches, schools, and of course, manufacturers of radio equipment. By the end of 1922, some 254 federal licenses had been issued for transmitters that complied with the provisions of the Radio Act of 1912. By 1923, dozens were going on the air every month. About six hundred were broadcasting by the end of the year. There simply were not enough locations on the frequency spectrum to accommodate everyone. Each position had at least one and sometimes several stations. Furthermore, the amplitude modulation (AM) broadcasting system in use could carry over very long distances, especially at night. People trying to listen to a local station would at the same time hear a jumble of broadcasts from other parts of the country.

**Regulating the airwaves.** Because radio transmissions respect no national boundaries, it was clear from the beginning that international agreements of some sort were needed to maintain order on the airwaves. An international structure designed to regulate telecommunications already existed, long before radio was even developed. It was the International Telegraphic Convention, organized in 1865 by twenty-five European countries to work out agreements on telegraphic and cable operations. It was quite successful, and it provided a model that by extension could be used to forge agreements on radio broadcasting.

The first conference devoted specifically to radio was held in Berlin in 1903, and important rules were agreed upon. For one thing, it was decided that humanitarian and emergency uses of the medium would get the highest priority. Thus, when ships needed aid, or during other emergencies, commercial interests were to be set aside. In 1906, a second Berlin Convention set forth further restrictions and rules on international and maritime broadcasting.[4] However, all of this had nothing to do with home radio.

The U.S. Congress confirmed these international rules in the Radio Act of 1912, which replaced a number of earlier attempts to develop laws suitable for radio. One feature of the 1912 act was that it provided for *licensing of transmitters*. However, as it turned out, that feature failed to solve enormous and unanticipated problems in the development of a home radio industry. Although it required citizens to obtain a license to operate a transmitter, it provided no real way that the government could turn anyone down. Furthermore, it established no criteria for approving the operations of a new transmitter, such as a broadcasting frequency, its power, or time on the air. In fact, it really gave the Secretary of Commerce (head of the licensing agency) no way to turn anyone down who wanted to transmit!

Because the 1912 legislation did not prescribe a frequency for a new station, its owner could choose the one that he or she preferred. If several operators decided to use the same frequency, as often happened, interference and overlap increased. Some stations solved the problem by agreeing informally to broadcast only on certain days or hours. Others, less cooperative, simply increased their power sharply to blast competing stations off the air. There was some experimentation with networks, with several stations sending signals on the same frequency. However, none of these solutions were effective.

As more and more stations began transmitting, the overlapping of frequencies and broadcast hours finally made it virtually impossible to tune in any clear signal. The chaos first brought the establishment of new stations to a halt, then sharply reversed the growth trend. Hundreds of stations simply went off the air and never returned.[5] They had no way of recovering their costs and their signals were lost in a chaos of noise.

Obviously, some sort of tight government control was needed to make the system work. However, the federal government was very reluctant to try to control the new medium. It was still a time when Americans looked on government regulation of anything as unwanted interference. Decades earlier Congress had shied away from taking over the telegraph, and it was not about to step in and be charged with trying to limit free speech through control of the airwaves.

The Secretary of Commerce at the time was Herbert Hoover. He tried to assign frequencies to new stations on an informal basis as licenses were granted, and it did seem to help for a while. However, the courts decided in 1926 that his agency lacked the legal power to do even that. The chaos that had prevailed earlier started to return and again threatened to ruin the fledgling industry.

Finally, Congress stepped in, held lengthy conferences and hearings, and provided new legislation—the Radio Act of 1927. This legislation established a very important principle: the *airwaves belong to the people,* and this gave the government the right to regulate their use in the public interest. Thus, the Act of 1927 temporarily gave the government new authority to regulate virtually all technical aspects of broadcasting. The act provided for a Federal Radio Commission (FRC) with broad new powers. In particular, the rules for licensing became very demanding, and those who wanted to transmit had to agree to do so only on assigned frequencies, at specified power levels, and at scheduled times. Even

Herbert Hoover's name is familiar mainly because he became the president of the United States during the late 1920s and was in office at the time of the stock market crash in 1929. He was, however, a remarkably effective Secretary of Commerce earlier. He played a key role in developing federal policies to govern the new radio medium that grew rapidly during the 1920s. (UPI/Corbis-Bettmann)

though the 1927 act brought strong and effective controls to the medium, it was applauded by the industry, which had been totally unable to regulate itself.

The interim Radio Act of 1927 prevailed during the new mass medium's early years of growth and development. Within a few years, it would be replaced by the Federal Communications Act of 1934, with complex legislation administered by a permanent Federal Communications Commission (FCC) that could oversee licensing and issue rules as needed. The 1934 Act, with numerous revisions, remains the legislative foundation governing the broadcast industries, as well as all other forms of radio transmission in the United States.

## Establishing the Economic Base of the New Medium

Radio was so new that no one was sure how to pay for the costs of transmitting or, in particular, how to make a profit from the broadcasts. At first, there seemed to be a number of alternatives. After all, each of the other media available at the time—newspapers, magazines, the movies, and even the telegraph system—paid their way and made money.

**Paying for the broadcasts.**   At first, the costs of acquiring and operating a transmitter were not great. For about $3,000 one could set up a station and start broadcasting. Operating expenses ran about $2,000 a year. Almost immediately, however, expensive, technically trained personnel and greater transmitter power were needed. Costs began to escalate. How to recoup those costs was an important question.

Clearly, operation by the *government* was one possible answer. That was the solution settled on by many societies in different parts of the world. In such a system, radio and television are operated by government bureaucrats and the content of the media is rigidly controlled. In the United States, however, few citizens wanted that kind of arrangement. The basic values of democracy conflict with government intervention in the flow of information. Therefore such a government operated and controlled system was never seriously considered.

Some visionaries thought it would be best to use a *subscription* system, where each owner of a radio receiver would have to get an annual license to operate it and pay a fee that would support the programming. Although that system was adopted in Great Britain, it was never seriously tried in the United States.

One system that was actually tried (by AT&T) was the *common carrier* approach. The principle here was similar to providing a truck or train line to carry whatever goods people might want transported and delivered. Applied to broadcasting, the transmitter was to be leased to whoever wanted to go on the air to broadcast whatever content they prepared. However, there were not enough takers and the idea was abandoned.

Another possibility was the *endowment* idea. Rich philanthropists would be invited to endow the stations with large money gifts, and then the station could use the earnings on investments to pay the costs of broadcasting. That system had worked well in funding universities, museums, and libraries. However, no rich philanthropists stepped forward.

**Advertising as the source of profit.**    The challenge, then, was how to make a profit by broadcasting programs to a general public who could tune in and listen for free. About the only obvious possibility was to transmit advertising messages over the air and charge the advertiser for the time, just as newspapers made a profit by presenting such messages in print. However, there was great resistance to the use of the airwaves for advertising, at least at first. Radio seemed to most people to be a wonderful new medium at the forefront of human accomplishment and destined for nobler purposes. To use it crassly for advertising seemed a disgusting idea. Herbert Hoover strongly opposed the idea, saying, "It is inconceivable that we should allow so great a possibility for service, for news, for entertainment, and for vital commercial purposes to be drowned in advertising chatter."[6]

In spite of these early airwave "environmentalists," advertising won over good taste. There simply did not seem to be any alternative solution that could make the medium financially viable. Although scattered uses of advertising over the airwaves had been tried earlier, the system as we know it was initiated by station WEAF in New York, which made the decision to lease time to present advertising promotions. There was no particular limit on the amount of time (the idea of brief "commercials" sandwiched in between segments of a program would come later). In the summer of 1922, a real estate firm leased a ten-minute segment to extol the virtues of some apartments in New York. It cost the firm $50.

After the idea caught on, advertisers warmed to the idea of becoming regular sponsors of weekly programs. These might be dance music, readings of the news, ball scores, and so on. With the number of home-owned receivers growing astronomically (see Figure 6.1) it soon became clear that radio was a very important medium by which advertising messages could reach consumers.

Early radio advertising was very polite and restrained. The initial model was *institutional* advertising; that is, the corporation sponsoring a particular presentation or program would be identified by name, but no information was provided about a specific product that it produced. For example, advertising in the early days of radio would have consisted of a dignified voice saying, "This program is sponsored by the XYZ Pharmaceutical Corporation and we are pleased to present the following program." That was it!

Today, advertising messages openly identify a specific product, such as a brand of laxative, and go into grim details about such matters as "constipation," the "softening effects" of the product, the time it takes to "gain relief," and feelings of comfort and joy that result from such an act. The public in radio's early days would have been truly horrified by the mention of such matters over the air, and the resulting outcry would have caused the station's license to be withdrawn. Obviously, times and standards of taste have changed.

## Trends in Media Use

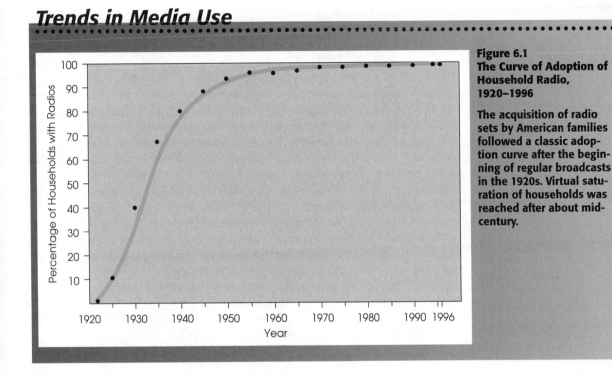

**Figure 6.1**
**The Curve of Adoption of Household Radio, 1920–1996**

The acquisition of radio sets by American families followed a classic adoption curve after the beginning of regular broadcasts in the 1920s. Virtual saturation of households was reached after about mid-century.

**Acquiring receivers for home use.** Throughout the early 1920s, manufacturers marketed various kinds of sets and the public eagerly bought as many as could be produced. For several years demand often outstripped supply. By 1922 an estimated half-million sets were in use. In 1925 that number escalated to about 5 million. By the end of the decade, some 14 million radio receivers were in American homes. (Radios no longer required batteries and were operated on house current.) In 1926 the National Broadcasting Corporation (NBC, led by David Sarnoff) initiated network broadcasting. The Columbia Broadcasting System (CBS) and others soon followed, and near the end of the decade, people all over the country could simultaneously hear a broadcast of the same radio program.

Thus, in the brief span of a single decade, radio was transformed from a long-distance signaling device serving limited interests into a medium that served an entire nation with broadcasts to home receivers. A great industry had come into existence. It was privately owned, dedicated to making a profit, and linked firmly to the world of commercial advertising. Unlike other media, it was regulated to a considerable degree by government, especially in terms of the mechanics of broadcasting. Listening to the radio was rapidly becoming one of everyone's most important leisure-time activities. Marconi's device had truly become a mass medium.

# EXPLAINING MEDIA EFFECTS
## *Uses and Gratifications Theory*

By the 1940s, during the Golden Age of radio, it was clear that mass communications had limited and selective influences on individuals exposed to a particular message. However, a different kind of question began to be asked by researchers of the time. Why did audiences deliberately seek out some kinds of media content and completely ignore others? Why did people intentionally listen to particular kinds of radio broadcasts? Why did they buy a particular kind of magazine or book? Why did they turn first to a particular section of the newspaper? Why did they peruse the latest advertisements of movies so as to find particular kinds of films?

The researchers began to realize that these are very goal-oriented forms of behavior, which indicated clearly that audiences did not simply wait placidly to receive whatever content happened to come their way. Audiences were seeking content from the media that they anticipated would provide them with certain kinds of practical information and satisfactions. In other words, receivers wanted to *use* the information in some way or to obtain *gratifications* that they anticipated.

After several massive studies of the audiences for the daytime radio serials of the late 1930s and early 1940s, media researchers formulated the **uses and gratifications theory** to try to explain why audiences do not passively wait for media messages to arrive. It sought to explain why audiences are active, deliberately seeking out forms of content that provide them with information that they need, like, and use.

This theory focuses on psychological factors—each member of the audience has a structure of interests, needs, attitudes, and values that play a part in shaping selections from the media. Thus, one person, with a particular set of needs and interests, might seek satisfactions through exposure to sports, popular music, wrestling and detective dramas. Another, with a different psychological makeup, might prefer wildlife programs, political analyses, symphonic music, and literary classics.

The central propositions of the uses and gratifications theory emerged from a long list of investigations completed over a number of decades. It has remained an important explanation of why people se-

lect the media content that they do. Although it has not previously been stated in formal propositions, in summary its basic ideas can be expressed in the following statements:

1. Consumers of mass communications do not *passively* wait for messages to be presented to them by the media.

2. Members of audiences are *active* in that they make their own decisions in selecting and attending to specific forms of content from the available media.

3. Those choices are made on the basis of individual differences in *interests, needs, values, and motives* that have been shaped by the individual's socialization within a web of social relationships and social category memberships.

4. Those psychological factors *predispose* the person to select specific forms of media content to obtain diversion, entertainment, and respite, or to solve problems of daily life in particular ways.

5. **Therefore,** members of the audience will actively select and *use* specific forms of media content to fulfill their needs and to provide *gratifications* of their interests and motives.

## ▼ *The Golden Age of Radio*

During the years between 1930 and America's entry into World War II in December 1941, radio continued to develop into a medium of increasing national and worldwide importance. Following the war, radio would enjoy only five additional years, from 1945 to about 1950, of unchallenged dominance as our nation's major broadcast medium. It would then have to meet the challenge of television. Thus, we can identify the fifteen-year period between the mid-1930s and about 1950 as the Golden Age of radio.

The programs and diversity that we see on television today are contemporary versions of much of what was on radio during its golden age. It offered an enormous variety of content. Its comedians became household names and made the entire nation laugh. Its broadcasts promoted popular dance bands and singers who gained national followings. Radio presented sports events to which millions of fans listened. The medium was used by politicians to get elected and to persuade the public to support new programs. News broadcasts were an immediate source of important information for huge audiences. Radio brought a constant flow of fads. Broadcasts promoted everchanging dance styles and new forms of popular music. Millions of housewives listened eagerly to "soap operas" during the day. Above all, it sold the nation's goods. Radio's advertising revenues soared to stupendous levels. It was, in short, a great medium that became a significant part of almost everyone's life.

◀

Franklin Delano Roosevelt used radio effectively, both to get his campaign messages across to voters and to assure the American people during times of national crisis. His calming voice during the Great Depression and after the Japanese attack on Pearl Harbor reassured the nation and marshalled public support for his programs. (The Bettmann Archive)

## Radio During the Great Depression

If ever there was a population in need of free entertainment, it was the people of the United States during the 1930s. At the depths of the Great Depression, fifteen million workers were unemployed in a population of about half of what we have today. That calculates to about 20 percent of the labor force. Today people feel that times are bad if the rate exceeds about 6 percent.

There was no national system of public relief, unemployment compensation, food stamps, social security for older people, or medicaid for the poor, and no government programs of public works to absorb the unemployed (all would come later in the 1930s). Farmers could not sell their crops; factories could not sell their goods; many businesses simply shut down and locked out their employees. Mortgages went unpaid and families were evicted from homes and farms. People went without meals, without medical treatment, and even without shoes. Hundreds of thousands of children wandered without adult supervision; hungry people foraged in the streets. Anyone who had a steady job was among society's fortunate, no matter how mean the work.

But people did have radio. It was free in the sense that all one needed to do was plug a receiver into a socket. It brought them comedy broadcasts by such former vaudeville stars as Fred Allen, Jack Benny, Eddie Cantor, and Ed Wynn. Listeners laughed at the antics of "Amos and Andy" (a show with two white actors working in blackface in the old minstrel tradition). They thrilled to the heroism of the Lone Ranger, who brought simple justice to the old West. They were kept in suspense by The Shadow, a mysterious figure who vanquished the forces of evil. Children were excited by the airborne adventures of Sky King and the incredible space exploits of Buck Rogers. For those with more rural tastes, there were regular programs of country music. Urbanites probably preferred the dance music of the "big bands," which transmitted live "swing" music from various hotels and ballrooms. News programs reported the latest policies of the Roosevelt administration and called attention to events overseas, such as the military buildup of Hitler in Germany and Mussolini in Italy. All that did not seem very important to most listeners; few Americans were interested in the political problems of places like Europe or Japan.

Although one might think that the Depression should have held back the development of the medium, that was not the case. An increasing number of stations came on the air and an ever-growing number of homes purchased radio sets. Advertising revenues grew sharply, from about $40 million per year in 1930, just as the Depression began, to over $112 million in 1935, as it reached bottom. Programming became more and more diversified and sophisticated, attracting a growing number of listeners. The networks continued to expand and dominate broadcasting.

In the mid-1930s two things happened that were very important to the future of broadcasting. One was the establishment of the federal legislation we noted earlier (the Federal Communications Act of 1934), with a new government agency (the FCC) to supervise broadcasting in the United States. The other was the development of an entirely different technology for broadcasting called frequency modulation (FM).

**Frequency modulation (FM) broadcasting.** In 1933, a relatively obscure inventor, Edwin Armstrong, developed and patented a new kind of radio signal based on frequency modulation (FM) rather than on amplitude modulation (AM). The world took little note because Mr. Armstrong did nothing to publicize his innovation. The advantages of the new system were that it was static free and that it could carry much higher and lower audio frequencies, making it an ideal carrier for music. At first, it seemed that its disadvantage was that at most parts of the frequency spectrum, FM reaches only to the horizon. In contrast, AM signals travel from the transmitter in all directions. They go up to the ionosphere where they are then reflected back to earth, and they can bounce back and forth between the two far beyond the horizon. Thus, AM can carry signals over very long distances (such as across the Atlantic). The FM signal is different. At very high and ultrahigh frequencies (VHF and UHF), it simply goes in a straight line in all directions and does not bounce up and down. Because the earth is not flat, such broadcasts cannot be effectively detected beyond the horizon. Furthermore, a big building or mountain that gets in the way of FM signals can garble or even stop them.

These might sound like serious limitations, and for some purposes they were. However, FM turned out to be exactly what was needed as a basic carrier of the audio signals for the new system of television with which RCA and other corporations were experimenting. The FM audio carrier was ideal for TV because it could confine a signal to a local area and not interfere with other transmitters some distance away, meaning that TV channels could be kept from interfering with each other. The same was true for radio stations that wanted to confine their broadcasts to a local area.

Unfortunately, Armstrong had to fight RCA in the courts when they started using his system for TV broadcasts. Although his case was ultimately won, his bitterness and frustration led him to commit suicide some years before the settlement.

**Radio and the news.** Another great battle fought during the period was over who had proprietary rights to the news. In 1930, Lowell Thomas, who was to become a well-known radio news personality, began a trend by reading the news over the air. Frightened by the competition radio was giving them, newspapers tried to stop local stations from using the early editions of papers as the source for their news, claiming that the radio stations were violating copyright laws. However, the courts ruled that although the particular expression of a writer can be copyrighted, the factual content of news is in the "public domain"—thus, no one "owns" the news. The radio stations could broadcast news shows even if they could not afford to hire their own reporters. As it

▲

Radio reached its zenith as a global news medium during World War II. One of the most effective foreign correspondents was Edward R. Murrow, whose nightly reports to American listeners on the German bombing of London set standards for radio reporting that have seldom been approached since his time. (UPI/Corbis-Bettmann)

turned out, radio coverage actually stimulated rather than deterred interest in newspaper reading. The brief news broadcasts and bulletins provided by radio caused people to follow up to get more detailed accounts in print. Before long, the major networks had developed their own separate news-gathering operations—a system that still brings us the broadcast news today.

## Radio During World War II

Radio became a global news medium as the world was plunging into war. Even before the U.S. entry into World War II, reporters around the world were able to transmit live "eyewitness" reports on major events by short wave to New York. From there they were picked up by the major networks and relayed over standard frequencies to listeners at home. Americans heard dramatic firsthand accounts from Edward R. Murrow, reporting from London in 1940 during the bombardment by the German Luftwaffe. Later, such news personalities as Robert Trout, H. V. Kaltenborn, and Elmer Davis used the medium to bring reports and interpretations of the war in Europe.

On Sunday, December 7, 1941, American families could scarcely believe their ears when they learned by home radio that the Japanese had attacked Pearl Harbor. More than two hundred Japanese carrier-based bombers devastated the U.S. Pacific Fleet and killed more than two thousand American servicemen and a number of civilians. Radio played a key part in mobilizing the nation. As the war progressed, firsthand news reports came from battlefields in strange places people had never heard of—Guadalcanal, Attu, Anzio, Iwo Jima. Throughout, President Roosevelt calmed the American public with frequent radio talks, reassuring the nation of ultimate victory and setting the goal of "unconditional surrender." Finally, the Allies defeated Germany, and then U.S. atomic bombs forced the Japanese to surrender and the dreadful conflict came to an end. By this time, radio was the unchallenged news medium of America.

The importance of the expansion of radio news to worldwide coverage is that it built the foundation of audience expectations for which contemporary broadcasters provide news on a global basis. For example, when CNN Headline News presents summaries of what is happening "Around the World in Thirty Minutes" on a 24-hour basis, it follows a tradition pioneered by radio broadcasters during the late 1930s and the dark days of World War II.

# ▼ *Radio and the Challenge of Television*

After World War II, radio lived on in its glory for roughly five years. However, starting in 1948, television stations began to go on the air with regular broadcasts. Early in that first year, only seventeen were in operation. Before the end of the year, however, the number more than doubled (to forty-eight). Sales of television sets increased 500 percent, and the audience for TV broadcasts grew at an astounding 4,000 percent in only two years! Coaxial cables began to connect communities, and the same networks that had fostered radio enthusiastically developed the new medium. No one in radio knew quite what to do. Many radio executives announced that TV was only a fad and that audiences would remain loyal to the original broadcast medium that had served them so well.

As television continued to take over audiences, radio was in deep trouble. In fact, it was in danger of disappearing altogether as a mass medium. Profits plummeted and radio audiences melted away as both talent and audience interest switched to television. Radio might have died completely had it not been for its resourceful response to the challenge of television. At first, the medium tightened its belt and took on advertising accounts that could not afford costly television commercials. Then it made changes across the board that permitted it to survive on a more permanent basis.

The major form of adaptation was that the *content* of radio broadcasts changed sharply. Out went the well-developed radio drama, the soap opera, the quiz program, and other amusement fare that had been the mainstay of radio entertainment. All of that type of programming could now be found on television. In came the disc jockey, continuous music, frequent spot news, weather reports, and call-in talk shows. For the most part radio ceased to be a national medium. Network-type programming decreased, and radio became a medium providing services to local rather than national audiences. In effect, then, radio drastically changed its functions. It gave more emphasis to music, news summaries, and talk, and less attention to its earlier forms of entertainment. In this way radio survived as an intimate and community-oriented medium.

One additional set of changes that influenced radio (as well as television) was the development of public broadcasting. As early as 1941, the FCC had reserved a number of FM channels for noncommercial use. In effect this meant educational broadcasting. However, Congress provided no funding for such programming. A number of small radio stations eked out an existence with support from churches, colleges, and universities. Some lived on public funds, some from donations or from foundation support. In 1967, however, Congress passed the Public Broadcasting Act, creating the Corporation for Public Broadcasting (CPB), serving both radio and television. The CPB was not actually a corporation in the sense of a profit-oriented business, and it was not exactly an arm of government. The CPB was set up as an independent, nonprofit organization that receives federal funds and allocates them to local stations within networks. The radio part of the CPB package was National Public Radio (NPR). This division not only links radio stations into a network, but also produces various kinds of noncommercial programming for broadcasts. Today, there are about two hundred FM radio stations in the NPR system. They all produce some programs and make at least some use of the nationally produced material. Such stations also solicit local donations and sponsors. For the many people who tire of regular AM or FM stations—with their continuous broadcasts of rock and roll, country-western, or classical music, and frequent commercial advertising—NPR is a pleasant relief. The nationally produced content is heavy on news, public affairs analyses, interactive talk shows, and information about music, theater, and the arts. There is even some attention to sports.

In its various formats radio is surviving the challenge of television. FM broadcasting has now become the dominant system with the majority of the radio audience in the United States.[7] FM stations tend to present news and analyses, more "oldies," low-key background-type music, and classical programs. NPR is thriving, with a small but dedicated following. In contrast, AM radio tends to be more oriented toward faster-paced popular music, nonintellectual talk shows, and some news summaries.

## ▼ Radio as a Contemporary Medium

In the late 1990s, radio continues to be America's most widely attended to medium of communication. A total of just over 11,000 radio stations stretch across the country, with numerous signals reaching every community and neighborhood.[8] Studies show that 96 percent of the population over age twelve listens to the radio during an average week. This compares favorably to television viewing (90 percent) and newspaper reading (76 percent). Among the reasons so many people listen is that radio is the most portable of the broadcast media, being accessible at home, in the office, in the car, on the street or beach, virtually anywhere at any time. Because radio listening is so widespread, it has prospered as an advertising medium. Radio stations reach local rather than national audiences, and are thus very useful for merchants who want to advertise their wares and services to people in their community. Furthermore, radio serves small, highly targeted audiences, which makes it an excellent advertising medium for many kinds of specialized products and services. As we explained in the case of magazines (Chapter 4), this feature appeals to advertisers, who realize it would be inefficient and prohibitively expensive to tout a special-interest product to heterogeneous audiences drawn to nationally popular entertainment programs.

## Radio's Role in the Media Mix

In 1997, there were an estimated 588 million radio sets in the U.S.—with 375 million in homes, and 213 million in cars, offices, and other settings. Thus, this medium can reach every set of ears in the United States.

Between 10 and 11 percent of all money spent on media advertising in the United States goes to radio. This percentage has remained quite stable for more than a decade, which has meant substantial growth in actual dollars brought in by radio. In 1977, for example, total radio advertising amounted to about $2.6 billion per year. By 1996, it was over $12 billion—almost a fivefold increase.[9] According to the Veronis, Suhler and Associates' *Industry Forecast,* this growth has exceeded that of the overall economy, reflecting the radio industry's robust progress.[10] Surveys show that radio gets more than 75 percent of its revenues from local advertising, about 22 percent from national advertising, and a tiny sliver (around 1 percent) from network compensation.

What is accounting for radio's renewed economic success? Experts say it is the high cost of commercial television time, which is still prohibitive for many local advertisers who can afford radio's more reasonable ad rates. Another key factor may be the emergence of remote control devices and VCRs, which allow viewers to avoid watching TV commercials and thus cut the effectiveness of television advertising. The radio audience, on the other hand, is more captive and not able to tune out commercials easily. In addition, the advertising sales forces for radio stations offer a good deal of assistance to local advertisers in preparing their spots for broadcasting. It is thought that radio's ability to attract local advertisers hurts mainly newspapers, because its low costs are attractive to small, local businesses.

Radio adapted to the development of television during the 1950s by changing the kind of programming it delivered. It is a medium that does not demand the level of concentrated attention required by print or television, thus allowing people to drive, jog, sunbathe, or do any of a number of other things while listening. Popular music plays a dominant role, appealing largely to younger listeners. However, AM and FM programming includes fare for other segments of the American audience, including news, talk shows, and classical music. Because of these features, radio will probably survive as a medium. (Spencer Grant/Photo Researchers, Inc.)

Like movies and television, radio can at times be quite controversial. In Chapter 5 we discussed the "creeping cycle of desensitization." A counterpart can be found in certain kinds of radio programming. For example, some talk

# Media and the Liberal Arts

## Talk Radio and the American Public    A Linchpin to the Sociology of Public Opinion

Leon Panetta smiled and nodded. At a February 1997 conference in Washington D.C., the former White House chief of staff acknowledged that President Clinton was not "relying on second hand information" when he lambasted talk radio hosts for misrepresenting his record and "misleading the American people." No, said Panetta, the President does know what's going on and what's being said about him. "You'd be surprised at how closely he listens and the details he remembers."[11]

In this respect the President of the United States was like most other Americans who listen to talk radio, although he and others who actually call in to a show are part of a decided minority. The President, who often talks about the Internet and appears continuously on television, does pay attention to radio as an opinion medium. Like Ronald Reagan and George Bush before him, he makes Saturday radio addresses to the nation and also knows what is being said about him on the radio.

Rush Limbaugh, the most popular and listened to of the talkmeisters, has a lot to say about Clinton and it is mostly negative. Other nationally and regionally syndicated talk show hosts, including Oliver North and G. Gordon Liddy, are also politically conservative and mostly opposed to the President and his policies. To some critics, this provides a counterpoint for conservatives in their opinion war with the mainstream media, which they regard as politically liberal. But do the radio talk show hosts and their lively call-in programs reflect public opinion in any accurate sense?

To this question, pollster Andrew Kohut, who heads the Pew Center for People and the Press, answers, "no." Says Kohut:

Rather than genuinely reflect widespread public disquiet, these voices often caricature and exaggerate discontent with American political institutions. Notably, the vocal minority sounds a conservative tone on many issues and is much more critical of President Bill Clinton and his policies . . . than is the average American. At a time . . . when active public expression in the form of talk radio, letters to the White House and Congress and newer forms of electronic populism are being venerated, the voices of a vocal few represent a significant advantage of the GOP over the Democratic Party.[12]

Kohut's study and others underscore the representative nature of listeners of talk radio—nearly 50 percent of Americans—but the unrepresentative nature of those who call in—more likely to be Republicans than Democrats, men than women, older people than younger ones.

To media critic Tom Lewis, a professor at Skidmore College, Rush Limbaugh and other talk hosts are show hosts, like Howard Stern, have adopted a style in which vulgar language is frequently used. Others, like G. Gordon Liddy, are accused of being "hate-mongers" in that they cater to callers who express very negative views about politicians, members of minorities, or other kinds of people and issues.

An example of radio programming that some claim pushes across the boundaries of good taste was found in 1996 on a Boston radio station.[13] It provided racy morning programming aimed at a teenage audience. It was highly successful in that it attracted an astonishing 37 percent of the twelve- to seventeen-year-old listeners in its market (a total of some 150,000 teenagers). Many listeners were even younger. A problem for many parents was with the

part of a long tradition stretching back to the early days of radio when a Kansas physician, Dr. John Brinkley, used his radio program to dispense medical advice and political views. Similarly, the controversial Louisiana politician Huey Long raged against "lying newspapers" and promised "every man a king" on the radio in the 1930s. About the same time a fiery priest, Father Charles Coughlin in Detroit, attacked the "Red Menace and international bankers" as well as then President Franklin D. Roosevelt. And for six decades from the 1930s through the 1990s, the staccato intonations of commentator Paul Harvey have also stirred public sentiments. Indeed, some of the most vivid images of radio are in talk shows, though listener call-ins actually date from the late 1940s when a Chicago radio host, Jack Eigen, created the first modern radio talk show. Perhaps better known was Walter Winchell's radio programs, which featured celebrity interviews, political news, and heavy-breathing analysis. In the modern age, Larry King drew heavily on Eigen's approach and to some extent followed the example of Winchell in building

his nationwide radio (and subsequently TV) audience.[14]

Talk show host Diane Rehm, who conducts an informative public radio talk show out of Washington D.C., calls these efforts "America's electronic backyard fence."

If the radio talk shows don't actually reflect and represent the public in the opinions expressed by hosts or by those who call in, then what is their role as an opinion medium? Like letters to the editor, which similarly are not representative, they provide a safety valve, an outlet for those who are discontented with government or politicians, regardless of party. They are a feedback mechanism in a media system that is all too often controlled by a tiny number of gatekeepers. They are interactive and stimulate public debate and criticism. In some instances, they have been enormously powerful—for example, in an instance a few years ago when talk radio campaigned against Congressional pay raises. Some say they have kept corruption in campaign financing on the public agenda and allow a forum for radical or highly critical ideas that cannot find a hearing elsewhere.

While much of talk radio is grassroots communication, often reflecting the views of the disaffected, it is also a showcase for politicians seeking votes (from the courthouse to the White House), authors selling books, and other people pushing ideas in the public marketplace. Radio industry experts say that talk radio has had a vigorous impact on the health of radio itself with Rush Limbaugh at one time single-handedly keeping many AM stations on the air with abundant advertising messages and revenue.

If to some radio was a forgotten medium, the maiden aunt of the media family, the reemergence of talk radio in the 1990s was proof positive that it is still a viable and vigorous medium with considerable appeal even in an age of television and cyberspace. And radio, which was once mostly an entertainment medium with dramatic programs and music, takes on the opinion function with gusto at a time when robust opinion is less important in television (largely an entertainment, news, and advertising vehicle) and opinion magazines have only tiny readerships.

lyrics of some of the songs. One such song advocated "Go do it. Then find someone else and do it again." Another, delivered by female vocalists, asked, "Do you mind if I stroke you up?" "Do you mind if I stroke you down? Get it up; Ooh that's what I want to do."[15] The singing was accompanied by moaning, which puzzled some of the younger listeners who really did not understand the meaning of the lyrics. On the other hand, radio stations have universally banned TV porno star Robin Byrd's song, "Bang Your Box." She says that it is about a piano, but many disc jockeys doubt that.

On a more positive note, radio provides much for ethnic communities. There are Spanish, Native American, and African-American radio stations (and even a national African-American network) as well as stations that feature programming in Greek, Irish, Scandinavian, Chinese, Japanese, and other languages. (Cable television, too, serves widely as a medium for ethnic programming, but radio is cheaper to produce than cable.)

Public radio, especially NPR, (mentioned earlier) and other forms of non-commercial broadcasting, provide important services and typically reach a large, upscale market, especially in university communities. Many noncommercial stations are owned by educational institutions, religious organizations, cities and towns, and other groups. However, most U.S. radio, like U.S. television, consists of commercial stations that rely on advertising sales to stay on the air.

## The Future of Radio

Today, radio prospers. As we have noted, it still commands the largest cumulative audiences in America, and it is gaining strength. As cable and satellite TV, the Internet, and VCR usage intrude on the ability of television to capture the attention of large audiences, local advertisers are returning to radio. As revenues from local advertising increase, the worth of radio stations increases, which helps their prospects for future profitability. This trend will probably extend into the foreseeable future.

Another significant trend has been the decline in number of listeners of AM stations and the steady increase in those tuning into FM stations. This pattern of change has been steady for over the last two decades. Before about 1977, more people listened to AM stations. After that year, the pattern switched and FM listenership grew increasingly dominant. Today, nearly 70 percent of radio listeners are tuned into an FM station. The future of the older, more static-prone, AM band is less and less clear.

Overall, radio has proved itself a versatile medium, one that supplies a good deal of information and entertainment, some opinion, and effective local advertising. It will continue to readjust and recalibrate itself as audience tastes and interests change. Like all media today, radio is sometimes owned by medium-specific companies (that have mostly radio properties). Increasingly, however, stations are being purchased by large media companies that are likely to own newspapers, magazines, television stations, databases, and other communication enterprises. Radio continues to have a market niche both in its command of audiences and its ability to sell advertising and generate other revenues.

# CHAPTER REVIEW

▼ Radio developed as a logical extension of the electric telegraph, which became a reality in the 1840s. Reliable electric telegraphy was not possible until after the invention of the electromagnet, which was at the heart of the system developed by Samuel F. B. Morse.

▼ When Morse sent his famous message, "What hath God wrought?" over forty miles of wire between Baltimore and Washington, D.C., the speed with which information could move changed from that of a train or a flying pigeon to that of lightning. It was a truly startling advance.

▼ Radio shares its early history with the telegraph. The wireless represented the achievement of an ancient dream of conquering both time and long distance to communicate quickly without wires. The first wireless patent went to Guglielmo Marconi, who spanned the English Channel with a wireless telegraph message in 1897 and then the Atlantic in 1901.

▼ The new form of telegraphy was an enormously useful device for communicating with ships at sea and with far-flung business, military, and diplomatic enterprises around the globe. Radio took on an aura of glamour very early when it played a critical role in rescue efforts at sea. Although it would be many years before it would even start to become a household communications medium, it quickly gained a large and enthusiastic following in the population.

▼ During the early 1920s, under existing legislation virtually anyone could obtain a license, build a relatively inexpensive transmitter, and go on the air. Hundreds did just that. Soon, the airways were cluttered with conflicting signals. With considerable reluctance, Congress first passed the Radio Act of 1927 and finally the Federal Communications Act of 1934, which brought radio broadcasting under the technical control of the national government.

▼ An important problem that had to be solved before radio could become a household medium was how to pay for the broadcasts. After several alternatives were considered, the answer came in the form of selling air time to advertisers—a close parallel to selling space to advertisers in the print media. Selling air time permitted the development of sponsored shows, regularly scheduled broadcasts, and a star system.

▼ The golden age of radio was between the 1930s, after the medium had matured, up until it was almost displaced by television during the early 1950s. Many important features developed during the period, including worldwide radio news, FM broadcasting, and the ultimate adjustment of radio to its current format and style.

▼ As a contemporary medium, radio is surviving well, largely as a local medium. Listening is widespread and radio captures about 10 percent of the nation's expenditures for media advertising. Its formats and content range from various kinds of music through talk shows, news, and sports. The majority of listeners today tune into FM stations.

▼ Radio's future seems secure. It has worked out its own niche in our system of mass communications. It is a flexible medium capable of responding to changes that may come in the future. At present, in financial terms, radio enjoys a period of relative prosperity.

## CHAPTER 7

# Television

## The Most Popular Medium

*T*elevision was born in controversy and remains controversial today. Some claim that it is the most important medium ever developed. Others believe that it is harmful as the cause of many undesirable conditions in our society. Debates about television began early in its history with claims as to who actually invented it. Following World War I, scientists in various parts of the world—England, Japan, Russia, and the United States—began experimenting with the idea of sending visual signals over the air using radio waves. Although the earliest television technology may not have been exclusively American, there is little doubt that in the United States it was developed swiftly as an enormously popular mass medium. Transmissions began as experiments in laboratories in the 1920s. By the late 1930s, it was a fledgling broadcast medium whose signals were being transmitted a few times a week in the New York City area to several hundred people using amateur-built receivers in their homes. Although its development was temporarily halted during World War II, by the end of the 1940s it was poised to sweep through society as a mass medium for home use. During the 1950s it did just that.[1]

During its brief history, television has been a remarkably volatile medium. Its technology has steadily changed; its content has constantly evolved; its audiences have grown hugely; and large numbers of critics have continued a flow of condemnation because of its presumed effects. In spite of all that, TV quickly became and remains America's favorite, and arguably most influential, medium.

At first, the typical factory-built receiver offered small black-and-white pictures about the size of a man's wallet. They were of poor quality by today's standards, but people were fascinated with the idea that moving pictures could be broadcast over the air and received in the home. Even the commercials seemed interesting because they *moved.* Before long, however, the novelty wore off and audiences became more selective and demanding. They wanted larger screens, clearer pictures, more channels, and color. Still later, they wanted greater control over what they viewed.

As new technologies arrived to satisfy these wishes, Americans gleefully adopted them. Screens grew much bigger than the early versions. Better transmitters and receivers made the picture more stable. Cable hookups brought more channels with greater choices of programs. Color made TV more pleasurable to watch. VCRs transformed the TV set into a little movie screen in the living room. Hand-held remote controls, routinely supplied with new sets, enabled audiences to exorcise ruthlessly the bothersome commercials sandwiched between segments of programs. As we will see, that upset advertisers, who started to turn to alternative media—which reduced the earnings of the networks, eroded the income of advertising agencies, and generally threw the whole television industry into turmoil. Finally, direct signals from satellites and a transformation to digital technology clouded the picture even more. Television remains in a condition of "vast uncertainty" today.[2]

## ▼ *The Birth of Television*

The history of television goes a lot further back than many people suppose. In fact, in 1884, a German experimenter, Paul Nipkow, developed a rotating disk with small holes arranged in a spiral pattern that had unusual properties. It would be the basis of the earliest TV experiments. If a strong light was aimed at a picture or scene it reflected patterns of light and dark back toward the disk. Those patterns of light passed through the holes in the rotating disk to be registered in light-sensitive electric devices. This produced a very rapid scanning effect that was somewhat like the movements a human eye makes while scanning across a page. It was realized quite early that the perforated whirling disk could produce patterns of electrical impulses that could be sent along a wire so as to transmit pictures. Later, the same patterns would be transmitted by radio. The **Nipkow disk** became the central technology for further experimentation on the transmission of images, both by wire and later by radio waves. This scanning concept is at the heart of television, even today, although it is accomplished by electronic means rather than by a mechanical disk.[3]

Although the scanning disk was unique to early TV experiments, the entire histories of radio and television are closely intertwined. All the inventions and technologies that made radio broadcasting possible are also part of the history of television. In addition, the social and economic organization of the industry was already set before TV became a reality. The medium is supported by advertising. That was never an issue. It is governed by the FCC. That, too, was never an issue. Its content is an extension of that developed in radio. The three major television networks that dominated early television were radio networks first. They were the same companies that pioneered commercial radio broadcasting.

Early in the 1920s, such corporations as General Electric and RCA allocated budgets for experiments with television, and other corporations soon followed. The idea seemed farfetched and futuristic to many in the industry, but television research was authorized in the hope that it would eventually pay off. General Electric employed an inventor, Ernst Alexanderson, to work exclusively on the problem, and within a short time he had developed a crude but workable system based on the Nipkow disk. However, it was not to be the system that the industry finally adopted.

▲

Early forms of new technology are often crude and cumbersome. Here, for example, is a picture of Felix the Cat transmitted over an experimental television system in the mid-1920s. The system was based on the Nipkow disk, which was soon replaced by a much superior electronic scanning system. It was many years before sufficient advances were made to permit television to become a home medium. (RCA Corporation; Courtesy of AT&T Archives)

## Developing an Electronic System

Perhaps the most remarkable of the inventors who played a key role in developing the needed electronic technology was a skinny high school boy in an isolated part of the United States. Philo T. Farnsworth was a poor youngster from a large family in Rigby, Idaho, a small farm community. As a child he had started reading about electricity, and in 1922 he astounded his high school science teacher by showing him diagrams for electronic circuits that would make it possible to transmit and receive moving pictures over the air.

Philo had studied reports of television experiments based on the Nipkow disk. He correctly reasoned that such a system was primitive and clumsy. He had reached the conclusion that electronic devices were needed to sweep across a scene or picture rapidly in a series of horizontal lines, detect points of light and dark along these lines, and transform those variations into signals that could be broadcast over the air. Parallel electronic devices for reception and viewing were also needed. He had come up with designs of circuits for each apparatus and calculations as to how they could function. Philo's teacher enthusiastically encouraged him to try to perfect and patent the system.

During this same period, just after World War I, a talented Russian, Vladimir K. Zworykin, had come to the United States to work on radio research at Westinghouse. He had been a communication specialist in the army of Tsar Nicholas, where he had worked on early television experiments before the Russian Revolution. He asked for permission to continue development of television at Westinghouse. Directors of the huge corporation thought it was a long shot, but decided to finance the work. Zworykin was also unimpressed with the mechanical disk approach and believed that electronic systems were needed for practical television transmission and reception. He set out to work on them with the full facilities of the great Westinghouse laboratories.

Meanwhile, as Zworykin was closing in on the problem, a friend of Philo Farnsworth took him to California and provided him with a place to work and funding for his experiments. There, on a shoestring budget, Farnsworth transformed his circuits and drawings into a working apparatus, which he built in an apartment where he kept the blinds drawn. (The neighbors thought he was

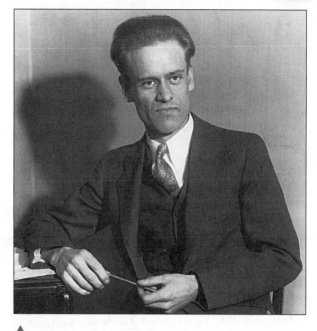

▲
In 1922, a young high school student from remote Rigby, Idaho showed his science teacher drawings for circuits that would make it possible to broadcast and receive television pictures based on electronic technology. Philo Farnsworth's system was a significant advance over the mechanical ones being used in experiments at the time. Later, with financial backing from friends, he constructed the apparatus and filed a patent application shortly before similar steps were taken by major corporations. The situation created an uproar, but Farnsworth prevailed in the courts. (UPI/Corbis-Bettmann)

a bootlegger running a still, and he was raided by the police.) Then, in 1927, the young man was able to make actual transmissions. He showed his friend how his apparatus could broadcast and receive both fixed images and small scenes from motion pictures. It was a remarkable achievement.

Having created a working system, Farnsworth took his drawings to federal authorities and applied for the first electronic television patent. His application created an uproar. The great radio corporations, taken completely by surprise, were shocked and outraged that an obscure nobody had invented, built, and asked to patent a system that Westinghouse, RCA, and others had spent fortunes trying to develop and were themselves about to patent. They immediately contested the application.

After a great deal of controversy and legal maneuvering, Farnsworth won. To regain control, RCA haggled with Farnsworth, who held out for a very profitable royalty settlement. Although Farnsworth reached his solution before Zworykin, the latter invented some of the most critical components of television technology: the iconoscope (electronic picture tube) and the image orthicon camera. Also in the 1920s, Scottish engineer John Logie Baird invented a television system that was adopted by the BBC.

## The Early Broadcasts

The earliest experimental television receivers used tiny screens based on cathode ray tubes about four inches in diameter. Cameras were crude and required intense lighting. People who appeared on the screen had to wear bizarre purple and green makeup to provide contrast for the picture. Nevertheless, in 1927, a picture of Herbert Hoover, then Secretary of Commerce, appeared on an experimental broadcast.

By 1932, RCA had built a TV station, complete with studio and transmitting facilities, in New York City's Empire State Building. RCA set aside a million dollars to develop and demonstrate the new broadcast medium. In 1936, it began testing the system, broadcasting two programs a week. By that time, a few hundred enthusiasts in the New York area had constructed or obtained TV receivers and were able to pick up the transmissions in their homes. Meanwhile, the federal government had developed procedures for awarding licenses to transmitters and had granted a limited number. Thus, by early 1941, the medium was set to take off.

Suddenly, the whole world changed. After the Japanese attack on Pearl Harbor in December 1941, the war effort completely monopolized the country's attention. Along with almost every other aspect of American life, the manufacture of the new television receivers was temporarily delayed. All the electronics manufacturers turned to producing equipment for the armed forces, and not until 1945 did these companies return to making products for the civilian market. In the immediate postwar years, however, television stations were quickly established in a number of major cities, and the public was ready to buy sets. TV was finally ready for home use.

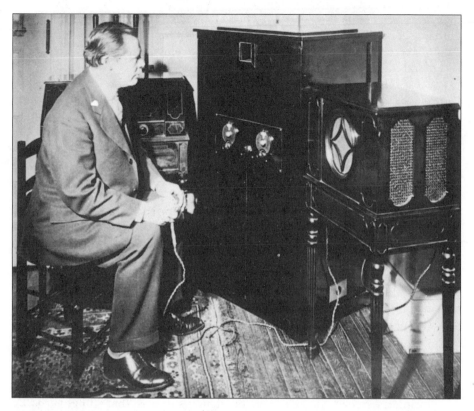

By the end of the 1920s, TV broadcasts were being made on an experimental basis, and receivers somewhat resembling their modern counterparts were being developed with an eye toward an eventual consumer market. In this 1928 version, the screen of the cathode ray tube is about the size of a business card. The speaker is at the right, and the man is using the controls to adjust the picture's quality. The set received only one channel. (The Bettmann Archive)

## ▼ *The Period of Rapid Adoption*

By 1946, the FCC had issued twenty-four new licenses for television transmitters. The networks and advertising agencies eagerly waited for the new medium to enter American homes. It seemed clear to all concerned that television might become a truly important broadcast medium. There was a great scramble to take part.

The manufacture and sale of home receivers began that same year. As sets became available, Americans rushed to buy them. However, they were quite expensive. In 1947, a set with a picture about six by seven inches cost around $400. That was more than a month's wages for many blue-collar working families, and did not include the special antenna that had to be installed on the roof. A truly deluxe set, with a fancy wood cabinet and a mirror system for making the picture seem larger, sold for about half as much as a modest car. Obviously, only more affluent families could afford such a luxury, and so a TV set became a new kind of status symbol. Families who had receivers often invited their envious neighbors in to watch the transmissions (and to see visible evidence of their affluence). Stories circulated of people who put up an antenna to make their neighbors think they had TV, when all they really had was the antenna—with no set hooked up below. In fact, TV was regarded as such a luxury that if a family receiving welfare was found to have a television set, it was regarded as a moral outrage.

One establishment that could afford a set was the local tavern. By 1948, a television set was a central feature in almost every tavern in the country. Sports programs were the favorite, and big crowds would gather to watch the games. It is probably no exaggeration to say that the local tavern was a significant element in demonstrating and popularizing the new medium.

## The Big Freeze

By the beginning of 1948, the FCC had issued approximately one hundred licenses. Some cities had two or even three stations, although most still had none. Soon, however, problems developed of the kind that had troubled radio in the early years. The signals of one station sometimes interfered with those of another. This led the FCC to conclude that drastic action was needed to avoid upcoming difficulties. Beginning in 1948 and extending through 1952, the commission ordered a freeze on the issuance of new licenses and construction permits (previously licensed stations were allowed to start up). As a result, TV transmitters could not be built in many American communities until after the freeze was lifted. The FCC wanted to study thoroughly the technical aspects of television and related broadcasting so that it could allocate frequencies to TV, FM radio, and other kinds of transmissions appropriately.

During the freeze, the FCC developed a master plan that still governs TV over-the-air broadcasting today. The system prevents the signals of one television station from interfering with those of another, thus avoiding the chaos that characterized early radio broadcasting. When the freeze was lifted in 1952, television spread quickly throughout the United States. Within a remarkably short time, it became so ubiquitous that most American families had a set. Social commentators began to speak of the "television generation" of Americans born after World War II who never knew a world without TV. The medium is presumed to have shaped their lives in significant ways.

## Becoming a Nation of Television Viewers

Figure 7.1 shows how rapidly the American public adopted television. In 1950, less than 10 percent of American homes had a set. In 1960, only ten years later, nearly 90 percent had a receiver. By 1980, ownership of sets had virtually reached saturation level in American households. Today, it is very unusual to find a family without a television set, and most have more than one.

Another index of the popularity of television can be seen in terms of viewing time. The television set has been in use during an ever-growing number of hours per day for almost four decades. In 1950, those who owned sets had them on four-and-a-half hours daily on average. That number rose sharply

# Trends in Media Use

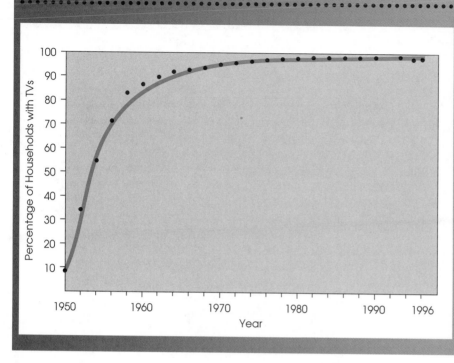

**Figure 7.1**
**The Curve of Adoption of Television 1950–1996**

The adoption of television by U.S. households followed a classic adoption curve, although it took place very rapidly by comparison with other media. Television was introduced about 1947, when a limited number of stations went on the air. The big freeze of 1948 to 1952 slowed early adoption slightly. However, as soon as it was lifted, adoption soared as new transmitters went on the air. By 1970, television had reached virtual saturation, with only a few late adopters still holding out.

year after year to more than seven hours per day in recent years (see Figure 7.2). Today, it is becoming increasingly difficult to determine patterns of television viewing because a TV set can be used in so many ways. One can watch regular broadcasting, signals from satellites, cable channels, and of course, VCR cassettes. And with multiple sets in about two-thirds of American homes, one person may be watching a broadcast of a ball game, another a soap opera on cable, and still another a movie on a VCR.[4] But whatever the specific time allocations among these various forms, it is clear that Americans are spending many hours a day with their television sets turned on.

## The Coming of Color

Color television got off to a slow start. Experiments had been performed with color test pictures as early as 1929, and there was much talk about commercial broadcasts in color, even as early as 1940. There were problems, however, in settling on the best technology. By 1946, two separate color systems had been perfected. CBS had developed a system based on a rotating disk that actually gave very good results. However, it had one major problem: the FCC insisted that the system for color transmission be such that existing black-and-white television sets could still receive a picture (though not in color), and with the CBS system that was not possible. A new set was required. In 1953, the FCC

## Trends in Media Use

**Figure 7.2
Daily Use of TV Sets in
U.S. Households,
1950–1996**

For decades, American families increased their daily use of their TV sets. In the early days of television, with a limited number of channels to view, the set was on only about four and a half hours per day on average. As the number of over-the-air and cable channels increased, that average time increased to over seven hours a day, where it has apparently leveled off. However, this does not mean that people always pay close attention to programs. We now know that people do many things—visiting, eating, cooking, tending to children, etc.—with the television on in the background.

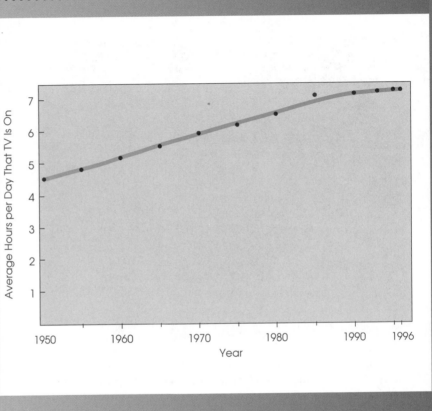

approved a different system, developed by RCA. Although it produced less refined colors, it did allow existing black-and-white sets to receive programs.

For a variety of reasons, the networks exercised a great deal of caution in delivering color broadcasts. At first they transmitted only a few programs in color. By 1967, though, most network programs were in color, and even local stations began to produce programs in this mode. As a result, all the black-and-white cameras had to be phased out and new technicians trained. However, the industry made the transition to the new technology smoothly. By the mid-1990s, almost all American homes had color television receivers.[5]

### Television's Golden Ages

Two rather different periods can be called the golden age of television. The first is the time when the medium was experiencing its most rapid period of growth—roughly from 1952 to around 1960.[6] The second is a longer period, from about 1960 to around 1980, when network television still had few competitors.

Those who identify the earlier period do so not only because of the rapid growth of the medium but also on the basis of some of the programming. Some point to it as a golden era by noting dramatic programs of high quality that were broadcast, such as "Playhouse 90." These appealed to more sophisticated viewers. Others note that it was a time when family situation comedies, sports, and variety-vaudeville shows were new features of home viewing that had very wide appeal. Among the latter, Milton Berle's "Texaco Star Theater" and Ed Sullivan's "Toast of the Town" are often cited as examples of how great television programs were in those "good old days." Among the performers often identified as among the "greats" of the period are Sid Caesar and the late Jackie Gleason. Today, the long-running series "I Love Lucy" (starring the late Lucille Ball) is routinely mentioned as a classic. Many younger people who view these programs today are at a loss to understand the glowing classifications. To them the early shows can seem naïve and even dull. Whether the programming of the period should be regarded as "art," simple slapstick, or mindless and trivial pop culture of a particular era could be debated endlessly.

On other grounds, the two decades between 1960 and about 1980 can be regarded as a rather different kind of golden age of television. It may not have been so in some ideal sense of audience satisfaction or in terms of classic programming. On the contrary, at that time the public showed many signs of frustration and dissatisfaction

Television technology has constantly undergone change. At first, large cumbersome antennae were needed on rooftops to pick up the broadcast signals. In some areas little "rabbit ears" were sufficient. Today, analog television signals are delivered via cables and digitized ones arrive from satellites. Early satellite dishes were as large as barn doors. Now, a dish the size of a large pizza works very well. There is little doubt that these systems will continue to evolve. (Copyright © Kathy Ferguson, PhotoEdit)

with the medium. The period was one of turmoil in American society, beset by such issues as civil rights, the Vietnam War, and increasing crime and violence. Many blamed TV for social ills, believing it to be a powerful medium that was eroding the moral standards and stability of the nation. As we will see later, such charges generated a great deal of interest in the effects of television.

The same two decades spanned a time when the medium was dominated by three major networks with virtually no competition. Their profit margins were very high from advertising revenue and they commanded the attention of virtually the entire viewing audience during prime time. Cable had yet to spread to more than a small proportion of American households, and there were no VCRs for home use. The networks competed with each other, but the three of them almost totally dominated the medium. If one wanted to watch TV during the period, there were very few alternatives to viewing network programming. A small proportion of Americans did view programs on educational stations and the Public Broadcasting Service (PBS—the television arm of the Corporation for Public Broadcasting set up in 1967), but they had to do so in inconvenient ways on obscure UHF channels. Thus, it was a golden age for the networks, in the sense that their profits were at a maximum.

Network television was widely criticized for broadcasting too much violence and for keeping the intellectual level of its programs low. Programs presented during the period were often designed with the tastes of the lower middle class in mind. Violence and fantasy were persistent themes. The lower middle class viewers in America were the ones who purchased the most beer, soap, detergent, toothpaste, soft drinks, and other nationally distributed products that could be advertised so effectively on television. The cumulative purchasing power of this vast majority was mind-boggling, and programming was directed toward that aggregate monetary bonanza. That translated into simple tastes and material at a relatively undemanding intellectual level. The majority of Americans loved that kind of TV content. At the same time, more sophisticated viewers understood that, in the words of Newton Minnow (then chairman of the FCC), network television was a "vast wasteland" of mindless comedy, unrealistic soap operas, staged wrestling, cartoons, spectator sports, quiz games, and shallow portrayals of family situations.

Somehow, though, for both of the periods mentioned above, time has transformed what many critics regarded at the time as "trash" into the "good old days" of TV. That assessment may arise in large part from the fact that the content of the period was carefully designed to fit the limited tastes and intellectual preferences of the majority. Those same people are now older, but their tastes have not become noticeably elevated. Moreover, their children have similar tastes. It is little wonder, then, that as they look back to the programs of the earlier periods they see classics, and the people who starred in those presentations as "significant performers."

# ▼ Alternatives to Broadcast Television

Three technological advances play a critical role in the reshaping of the American television industry. One is the growth of cable television. The second is the widespread adoption of the video cassette recorder. The third is the entry of direct satellite broadcasting into the mix. All three are relatively recent events.

## The Spread of Cable Systems

Cable TV began innocently enough. It was needed in certain locations because of the line-of-sight nature of the TV signal. For example, a community that is blocked by a large hill between it and the nearest television transmitter cannot receive the signal. The same is true for people who live in a valley or among a lot of tall buildings that block the transmission.

In the 1950s, a number of local and very small systems were set up to overcome such obstacles. The solution was to put a large community antenna in a favorable location, and to wire people's homes via coaxial cable to this central facility. Usually, the signal was amplified to make reception very clear. It worked just fine, and was especially attractive to people in rural areas and other hard-to-reach locations.

At first, the number of households that were "wired" in this way was very small (less than 2 percent of TV homes in 1960). It was actually a kind of "mom and pop" industry, with some 640 small systems each serving only several hundred or a few thousand clients. Then, the whole concept began to expand, largely because cable brought better pictures and more selection. This development angered the broadcasters, who saw the cable operator as a "parasite" who was pirating their programs off the air and selling them for a profit. Then, as the cable companies developed better technology, they began to offer their clients television signals that had originated in cities a long way off—effectively diminishing attention to local broadcasters. Even worse, some of the cable companies started originating their own programming!

Lawsuits were filed by almost everyone against almost everyone else. Finally, it was resolved that the FCC had the right to regulate the cable companies, just as though they were broadcasting over the air. The broadcasters persuaded the FCC to impose stiff, complex regulations that effectively stopped the growth of more cable systems. By 1979, however, many of those restrictions were relaxed and local governments were given the right to grant franchises to private cable companies to provide service in the local community. Out of that came a great surge of development. In 1980, less than 20 percent of American homes were wired. By 1995, the proportion had soared to 66.3 percent as the adoption curve continued to rise (see Figure 7.3).

The increasing adoption of cable by American households has significantly altered the whole television industry. First, it has reduced the **market share** (proportion of the total television viewing audience) that watches regular network television. Indeed, the networks have suffered a slow but steady decline in market share for a number of years. Second, it has begun to segment the viewing public along the lines of their tastes and interests. With dozens of channels to choose from in a typical cable system, one no longer needs to view whatever the networks happen to be broadcasting at the moment. It is possible to find on most cable systems at any given time some form of program content that will fit almost anyone's interests. Thus, a pattern is developing much like that for magazines when the large general circulation periodicals gave way to the more focused specialty magazines. Advertisers are following these developments with keen interest. If one has a special product to advertise, it is more than likely that a program interesting potential customers can be found in the cable TV lineup.

Currently, there is considerable discontent with cable channels like HBO, USA, and MTV. The programming is often repetitive. Monthly fees are said to be too expensive, and cable channels now incorporate about as much

## *Trends in Media Use*

**Figure 7.3**
**The Curve of Adoption for Cable Television in the United States, 1960–1995**

Cable television started on a small scale with community antenna systems wired to households in local areas where there was difficulty in receiving an over-the-air signal. The majority of Americans are now connected to a cable system. In spite of many conflicts and limitations, the adoption of cable television has followed a rather typical s-shaped curve.

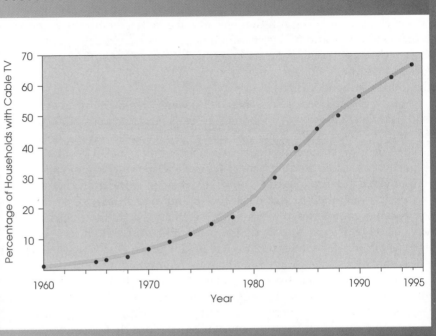

advertising as traditional over-the-air broadcasts did earlier. Furthermore, critics complain, there has been no noticeable elevation of aesthetic tastes or intellectual standards. One used to find such content as wrestling, bowling matches, and soap operas on broadcast television channels. Now one finds them on cable channels, along with new contenders, such as direct marketing, real estate ads, and rock music videos.

These criticisms appear to be valid. However, the 11,800 cable systems in the U.S. still serve the same public with the same tastes that broadcast TV always has served. There is little reason to assume that the majority among the audiences media communicators want to reach will demand more sophisticated programming just because it is being delivered by cable. We can safely conclude, therefore, that the intellectual level and aesthetic tastes of most programming on cable will remain similar to what has always been found on broadcast television.

### The Video Cassette Recorder

Like so many electronic devices, the VCR is an American invention and a Japanese success story. The Ampex Corporation in New York developed the original machine. In 1952, Charles Ginsberg, along with several other Ampex engineers, set out to develop a device that could be used to record television programs on magnetic tape.[7] Four years later they had succeeded. The first videotape recorder was about the size of a suitcase and used large reels of two-inch-wide tape. It was quickly adopted by the TV industry as a means to record material for later broadcasting. Used in this way it was very practical. No longer did everyone have to perform live. Programming errors could be edited or changes spliced in, allowing mistake-free programs at air time.

At the beginning of the 1970s a number of American companies saw the consumer potential of the device and set out to manufacture and market a small home version. However, they could not agree on the size and standards of the tape and other aspects of the system. By the middle of the decade some five different standards were used in the machines on the market. All were very expensive, and the prerecorded material available might or might not fit the machine purchased.

The Japanese stepped in. They standardized the systems and technology, brought prices down, and sold millions of the machines, so that today more than two-thirds of American television households have a VCR. Figure 7.4 shows the pattern of adoption of the VCR for home use in just over two decades. The device gave birth to a whole new industry. Today, one can rent a movie for a very modest fee at a rental agency specializing in cassette tapes, or in some cases in supermarkets, convenience stores, or even gas stations. To feed this market, the movie industry has begun to produce films in this form. A movie on cassette can generate enormous profits long after the film has exhausted its market at regular theaters. A host of other kinds of cassettes—ranging from exercise programs to bass fishing and home repair instruction tapes—have made the VCR even more popular.

When practical VCRs for home use arrived during the 1980s, hundreds of small "mom and pop" video stores sprang up to provide rental movie cassettes. Within a decade, however, these stores were largely replaced by chains. The smaller stores could not compete. Today, virtually any kind of content can be found on cassettes, and providing them for both sale and rent has become an important part of both the TV and the movie industry.
(AP Photo/Rick Bowmer)

# Trends in Media Use

**Figure 7.4**
**The Curve of Adoption for VCRs in the United States, 1978–1995**

The home use of the VCR as a device for recording television programs or viewing other content was delayed for many years after its invention in 1952. In its earliest form, it was used mainly by the TV industry to record programs for replay. After unsuccessful attempts by U.S. manufacturers to standardize the device for home use, the Japanese took over its development and manufacture. During the last half of the 1980s, its use soared. The majority of American homes now have a VCR, and there is a classic curve of adoption.

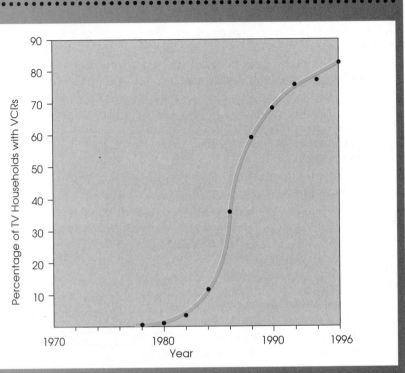

The proliferation of home VCRs was seen at first as a threat by moviemakers and broadcasters who feared that people would record movies and programs off broadcast or cable TV, thus reducing video rentals and the effectiveness of TV advertising. That fear turned out to be unfounded. For the most part VCRs are used to play rented or purchased cassettes. Studies show that the majority of VCR users do not even know how to program their machines to record material off the air.

The tape technology at the heart of the VCR may be heading for obsolescence. With more sophisticated systems under development, it will very likely be replaced with more efficient and reliable alternatives. Movies are now becoming available on CD/ROMs. Digital storage techniques have made it possible to squeeze an entire movie on a compact disk. With a small CD player, the movie can be seen on a TV screen. The pictures produced have a higher quality than those seen from the older tapes. Other, even more efficient, digital storage systems are under development. Thus, the VCR that everyone now has may become as much of a curiosity in the future as the wind-up Victrola of the early part of the twentieth century.

## Direct Broadcast Satellite

It has been possible to receive television signals from satellites for many years. Such reception required a large satellite "dish"—about the size of a barn door—stationed near the house. It had to be capable of being lined up and re-aligned on demand to point directly to the satellites from which the signals were being transmitted. The system was complex and awkward. Because of the complexity, appearance, size and cost, few American families made use of this technology, although it did serve people in rural areas who were far from both regular television stations and cable systems.

In more recent years, a number of corporations have been marketing hardware and services that bring television signals from satellites directly into the home with the use of a dish about the size of a large pizza. In some cases, the equipment is purchased; in others it is leased. In either case, the dish is permanently fixed on the roof where it is pointed at the satellite and does not have to be moved or repositioned.

Unlike the older network broadcasts, these signals are not free. The system for making a profit for the services provided is essentially like that used by cable operators. The user pays a monthly subscription fee. A variety of "packages" is available. A "basic" package provides a bare bones number of channels that are essentially similar to what a basic subscription to a cable system provides. The user can pay additional fees to add a number of movie, sports, or other special channels that contain programming of interest to the subscriber.

Direct broadcast satellite systems are beginning a strong pattern of increasing adoption. They generally offer more viewing options—that is, a greater number of channels—and their signals produce a sharper picture on the typical TV set than is often the case with cable. At present, it is difficult to say what the outcome will be for the cable systems, or even for local television stations. If programming can be originated in major cities on each of the coasts and then distributed via satellite to the entire country, there may be less and less need for local **affiliates** (local television stations that distribute network and other programming to people in a given market).

Clearly, the VCR, cable TV, and the hand-held remote control that can mute television sound or change channels, have made serious inroads into traditional broadcast television. The growing use of direct broadcast satellite systems and the shift to CD-delivered movies will bring further inroads. We have seen the impact of new technology on existing media in previous chapters. Earlier, alternate sources for news brought a significant decline in newspaper subscriptions. The large-circulation general magazine was a victim of the shift to TV advertising. Television viewing almost destroyed radio, and it seriously displaced moviegoing. Today, it is network television that is in trouble—or more precisely, broadcast television of all kinds—undercut by technologies that give viewers more of what they want. Numbers of viewers are down, and consequently advertising revenues are declining. Many who advertised their products almost exclusively on broadcast TV are now turning to direct mail,

▶ The hand-held remote control, now in almost universal use, poses a problem for network television. In the late 1980s and early 1990s, many considerations have reduced the percentage of total viewers who tune in to network broadcasts. Although their audiences are still large, the networks have been hurt by the growth of cable systems, the rapid adoption of the VCR, and the "zapper," which mutes the sound. (Dick Luria/FPG International)

cable itself, specialty magazines, the World Wide Web, and any other medium where they can still reach their potential customers.

## Video via the Internet

Currently, the Internet is a relatively crude system on which to view video, because in some cases our modems are too slow. Less easily remedied is the fact that the copper wires over which most of the signals are transmitted from a source to one's computer at home are too "narrow" (electronically speaking) to carry quickly enough the amount of information needed for realistic movie-like pictures in motion. Those who are technologically sophisticated refer to the problem as *bandwidth.* The analogy often used is that transmitting action video through the existing telephone wires is like trying to deliver a large amount of water through a small-diameter hose. It can be done eventually, but it can take a long time. If the hose were a lot bigger, the same amount of water could be delivered very quickly.

As the technology of telephone lines and cable systems develops, new kinds of wires will replace the copper ones now in wide use. Fiber optic lines are much more efficient. They will replace our current telephone lines and television cables within a relatively short time. Indeed, many systems have already made the switch. When that transformation is complete, digital video will zip through the new systems more easily. With a faster modem one will be able to view a movie on a computer screen, the same movie will be seen on a television screen as the two systems (TV and computers) merge. Beyond that, with

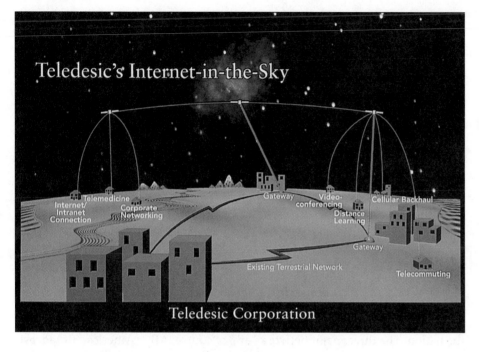

Teledesic's Internet-in-the-Sky

Teledesic Corporation

Communications technologies constantly undergo change and improvement. One system now being developed is *teledesic,* which will consist of 840 small satellites circling the earth, receiving and sending signals to carry swiftly delivered digital video via the Internet. This will result in greater convergence between computers and television. (Courtesy Teledesic Corporation)

more sophisticated mainframe computers (now becoming available) at the transmission source, *interactive* video and *movies on demand* will be possible. Not only will a viewer be able to request a movie (or other kinds of programming) of his or her choice at the time the person wants to view it, but also it may be possible to jump around to alternative plots or endings as the movie is being viewed to achieve outcomes that the customer desires.

There is a caution to keep in mind when discussing new technologies. Driven by the same profit orientations that have motivated development and adoption of the mass communication system in the United States in the past, such new systems will have to face the ultimate test of the marketplace. Just because a system is technologically possible does not mean that it will shoulder its way into the mass media markets of the nation. Three-D movies were technologically workable in the late 1940s, but they did not survive the test of the market. The same will be true of the futuristic technologies that dazzle us today. Some will find their place in our living rooms; others will fail and disappear. One thing seems certain, however: Americans will continue their love affair with the popular entertainment, sports, and news that express their own tastes and interests. That content will be delivered to them by a system they can afford and use within the technical skills they have. At present, the Internet is both complex to use and expensive to access. Therefore, its role as a medium of popular entertainment in this marketplace is not entirely clear.

# ▼ *Television as a Contemporary Medium*

Like radio, from which it was derived, television is both a technology and a complex medium of communication. As its history amply demonstrates, it is also an economic system made up of communicators, advertisers, programs or content, and a large and diverse audience. And it has become an omnipresent medium—the major form of mass communication preferred by the American public. As indicated earlier, on average, the television set is on more than seven hours a day in American households. At the same time, it is a medium that is little understood by its public. The majority of viewers know little about the behind-the-scenes dramas involving technology, ownership, or conflict among the individuals and groups that make up television systems.

## The Economics of Competing Systems

Television signals are received from local stations over the air (or on cable). These local stations are still the backbone of the system. In 1997, there were only 1,181 commercial and 363 educational television stations broadcasting in the nation. The three major networks are, of course, ABC (American Broadcasting Corporation), CBS (Columbia Broadcasting System), and NBC (National Broadcasting Corporation). All three have been in business for decades. Much newer are the Fox network and CNN (Cable News Network). The Fox system is owned by Rupert Murdoch, whose holdings (as noted in Chapter 3) also include a newspaper empire. CNN is not actually a network, but a specialized system that delivers programming to cable systems. In addition, there are regional systems formed of local stations that band together and share programming and promote advertising. Finally, the U.S. government operates a large television network overseas. Ostensibly for members of the armed forces, AFRTS (Armed Forces Radio and Television Service), as it is called, reaches into seventy countries and is seen not only by people in the armed forces but also by millions of U.S. and foreign civilians.

Over the years, the number of independent (not network-affiliated) stations has increased. This has given rise to **barter syndication**. (The idea of syndicates for newspapers was discussed in Chapter 3. The same structure exists for broadcasters.) Thus, a local station can get taped content from program syndicators who sell their wares to independent, nonnetwork stations, creating what amounts to a series of small networks. Syndicated programming competes directly with network offerings. Much of the content of such syndicated programming consists of older reruns. For example, "I Love Lucy" episodes are available for independent stations in this way. Other programs (such as *Jeopardy*) are syndicated and available on a first-run basis.

From the standpoint of a family viewing their TV set at home, the sources that deliver television programs can be a confusing jumble. What they see on their screen at any given time may originate from one of several networks, from an independent local station, from PBS, from their basic cable service (perhaps with add-on subscription fees), via satellite, or from their video cassette recorder.

This variety in sources really makes little difference to viewers. A given movie provides the same viewing experience regardless of who delivers it. The same is true of a ball game, cartoon, or nature documentary. What do viewers care how it comes to them? Because it looks the same on the screen, regardless of what delivery system is being used, most families do not attach a great deal of importance to the various vendors and systems from which they get their entertainment, sports programs, or even news. The main thing for them is that the programming they want to view is *there*.

However, for the players involved, what source viewers use is of *paramount* importance. It is the basis for consuming battles for profit and economic survival within the system. Thus, *competition* among the sources that deliver programming to audiences is the central factor in understanding the economics of contemporary television.

Competition has always existed among the various networks. Every year they vie for dominance in terms of commanding the largest audiences. And in recent years, competition started between network television and its alternatives (cable TV and the VCR) as these systems came on line. That competition resulted in significant changes.

From the early days of TV up until the mid-1980s, regular broadcast television was very popular because of the relationship among networks, advertisers, those who produced TV content, and the audience. Advertising revenues brought high earnings to the major networks, permitting them to produce expensive programs that were well received by audiences. Thus, a kind of reciprocal system was in place. Television advertising was very costly. However, because the commercial messages shown on the popular programs reached huge audiences, advertisers were willing to pay enormous fees for tiny segments of air time (like thirty seconds, or even fifteen). And because of this great income, the networks were able to produce still more expensive programs with even greater appeal to the public. Thus, advertising revenues spiraled up and up, along with the size of the audience.

At the heart of this mutually profitable system is *audience attention*. The worst nightmare of both the advertiser and the television network executive is that people will not view the programs on which their wares are advertised. Various kinds of survey and polling techniques have been used to determine what kinds of people were viewing what kinds of television programs during what periods of time. For many years, the techniques used were rather simple. Some were based on diaries that carefully selected panels of people kept at home, or on verbal reports of audiences contacted by phone or mail about what they had been watching.

Those ratings, whatever their limitations, became *institutionalized*—that is, deeply established—as the ultimate measure of whether a given program would be kept on the air. They remain so today. Thus, what can be called the **law of large numbers** was the prevailing principle determining the television agenda presented by the major networks. The more eyes and ears a program attracts, the more valuable it is to an advertiser whose message is displayed during the transmission and to the broadcaster who profits from the sale of the time. If a program's ratings fell, even by a few points, it was in jeopardy. Many programs were simply dropped from the air if their ratings did not seem to justify what it cost to produce and broadcast them, and especially if they did not draw enough advertisers to generate sufficient profits.

The use of such ratings as the ultimate criterion by which the networks assessed the worth of a particular program was just fine with the advertisers who supported the system. It ensured that the programs on the air, and so the advertising commercials, commanded the attention of the largest possible numbers of potential consumers. For several decades this was how the system worked. Thus, in spite of competition among networks, the system as a whole remained rather stable for many years and the networks continued to dominate television. The law of large numbers continues to prevail today.

In recent years a new factor has entered the competitive arena. That worst nightmare of the advertiser and the television network executive has become a reality. It came in the form of the "zapper"—the hand-held remote control, with its buttons for muting the sound or changing channels without leaving the chair or couch. It has brought a significant reduction in the amount of attention that viewers give to television commercials. Actually, the idea had been around for a long time before the more contemporary versions came into wide use. The earliest version (as far back as the early 1950s) was called the "blab-off." It had a long wire between the viewer and the speaker circuit in the set, and by pressing a single button the sound could be turned on and off. A limitation of the device was that it had to be purchased separately and installed by a technician. That was a lot of trouble, and thus not many people used it. In later years, however, manufacturers began building remote controls directly into the set, with infrared light beams providing the link between set and hand unit. Today, they are extremely common.

The remote deeply troubles advertisers, who worry that the expensive commercials they are paying for are not actually getting through to television audiences. That issue is an especially serious one for network television, which is still where the bulk of the most expensive advertising messages appear. The networks have had a hard time countering the charge that the remote is eroding attention to TV commercials.

In Chapter 8 we will discuss the "people meter." This device created new headaches for network television when it arrived about a decade ago. We will note that it is a relatively simple recording device—a gadget operated by the home viewer, who is part of a panel of hundreds of people carefully selected and managed by one of the audience-measuring services. The system provides a way of obtaining relatively accurate records of who watches what in ways that are more reliable and accurate than the older systems.

When the people meter was introduced, it created a great stir because it revealed patterns of viewing that were quite different from those indicated with the older ways of calculating ratings. This was very disturbing, particularly when the new device seemed to show that the actual audiences for particular programs were really much *smaller* than had been suggested. In particular, the people meter made it possible to determine rather accurately when people were viewing cable or using their VCR, rather than being tuned to network television. It was very clear that overall attention to network television was on the decline. This realization caused many advertisers to reconsider how much of their advertising budgets they wanted to devote to network TV, as opposed to other media.

The significance of the zapper and the people meter in the economics of television is easy to document: for the first time in history, advertising rates went *down*. (Later they did recover, though.) Pundits began to debate whether the television networks that had dominated the medium for so long were dinosaurs ready for extinction. Such conclusions appear to have been premature. Today, network television is in a slow decline in terms of its share of the total viewing audience. At the same time, however, as Figure 7.2 indicates, the total amount of time that American families spend with their sets has been rising ever since the medium was first introduced. Thus, network television still commands a huge audience, and will very likely be an important player in the system for some time to come. Still, the viewing mix continues to change, and the ultimate impact of cable TV, the VCR, or any other system cannnot be predicted at this time.

## The Television Industry in Transition

It is difficult to separate television as a signal transmitting business from media as an economic institution generally. Increasingly, television is a global industry with programming moving across national borders. As we have pointed out, many U.S. television stations are owned by large corporations, although the number that a single owner can have is limited by law to twelve stations not covering more than 30 percent of the population of the country. Media ownership, along with that of many other business enterprises, is global. Although FCC regulations place limits on foreign ownership of broadcast properties, complex patterns of conglomerate ownership are common.

Television profits are a function of the total annual revenues of the whole industry—advertising sales, annual volume of advertising, network and station television billing, market ratings, and other indicators. The major players are networks, local stations, and barter syndicators who provide independent sources of programming. As mentioned earlier, the competition of cable, VCR, satellite, and syndication services has brought a downturn in the economic fortunes of TV networks. But the networks nevertheless can still deliver impressive audiences, even though their share of total time spent with the medium is down.

In spite of the fact that a great deal is known about the social, cultural, and economic structure of the American population (as we will see in Chapter 8), one of the poorly charted aspects of television audiences is their actual composition. For example, TV industry market researchers give only superficial attention to the demographic characteristics of network television viewers. Cable services and public television sometimes claim to deliver "quality" or upscale audiences of viewers who are relatively well educated and affluent in comparison with the general population. However, those claims are not backed with data from well-designed studies, and television as a whole does not conduct the precise and careful research on audiences in the same detailed ways that marketers of many other products and services do.

An important concept for television stations is the *market* as an area. A **market** in this sense consists of a community and a contiguous area in which a substantial number of people live who can be reached by a station's signal. In practical terms this translates into a metropolitan area that includes a city. Some markets are relatively small, like that in which Little Rock, Arkansas, is located. Others are huge, such as that of Los Angeles or Philadelphia.

Finally, the economic fortunes of television in all its forms, as we have stressed, revolve around *advertising.* Today, the revenues from that source are by no means evenly distributed among the competitors. For example, cable—which receives its basic support from subscriptions and fees—receives only about 7 percent of all advertising spent on television. Television stations broadcasting to markets receive a whopping 54 percent; that is understandable because they account for virtually all of the local or community-level advertising. Still, the networks, whose advertising is mainly for nationally distributed products and services, retain 32 percent of the total. Barter syndicators are a minor player, with only 7 percent.

▶

An important concept for television broadcasters is the *market.* A market consists of the people who live in a particular geographical area, which usually includes a town or city. The population in a market provides the audience for local news and potential customers for goods and services advertised by the area's businesses. An example of a middle-sized market is the city and surrounding metropolitan area of Portland, Oregon. (Copyright © Bob Collins, Image Works)

As we suggested earlier, patterns of television advertising are changing. As noted, the ratio between advertising revenues of local stations versus the networks is 56 to 36. Ten years ago, the percentage was about the same, 55, for the stations, but it was 45 for the networks. This change brings into sharp focus the problem now faced by the networks resulting from such factors as the zapper, the people meter, and alternatives such as cable. A decade ago, none of these revenues went to cable or to syndicators. The drop from 45 percent of the total to only 36 percent works out to a 22 percent reduction—a truly substantial loss for any business—and it poses very difficult times for the networks.

## ▼ The Future of Television

The future of TV will be one of somewhat unpredictable change coupled with constant debate. New technologies include a device built into newly manufactured sets to enable parents to control the programs seen by their children. Entirely new systems for delivering signals to the home are under serious development. These systems include not only direct satellite broadcasts that are already coming into increasing use, but may also include fiber optic and even microwave systems operated by telephone companies for delivering signals to homes (although the telephone companies may back out). Other changes will occur in the shape and clarity of the picture seen on the screen.

One change that began on February 3, 1997 is the system of ratings that can be used in connection with the "v-chip," now required in all newly manufactured receivers. With such a set, parents can presumably program the set to control what comes into their home. A major problem in developing this system was how parents could tell whether a program that they were about to receive contained content they did not want their children to view. To provide an answer, the television industry devised a system of ratings to be shown at the beginning of each program. However, a great controversy began in 1996 over the nature of the rating system. The basic idea was that the ratings should identify how much violence, vulgar language and sexual content was contained in each TV show. Then, the parents could control their set so that their children did not see the show, or if they have the equipment they could use the v-chip to prevent it from appearing on their screen.

To provide for this screening, the industry opted for a system very similar to that used in the movie industry. It is a very simple system with only six categories:

- TV-Y: specifically for children of all ages
- TV-Y7: for children 7 and over
- TV-G: for all audiences
- TV-PG: parental guidance suggested
- TV-14: parents strongly cautioned
- TV-M: mature audiences only

Many spokespersons for parents and other groups objected to this age-based system on the grounds that it provided no real information about whether or how much violence, vulgar language, or sexual content was actually contained within a show. A number of critics wanted a content-based system, like the one used in Canada—a system often cited as an ideal model.

At first glance, the Canadian model seems simple and effective. It is based on the same basic categories of violence, bad language, and sexual depictions. However, the system also provides points for each category, ranging from 0 to 5. For example, a program rated V-0, L-4, and S-2 would have no violence, a lot of vulgar language, and a limited amount of sexual content. On closer examination, however, the Canadian system has not worked well. Its problems came about from difficulties in identifying exactly what constitutes depictions of violence and sex. For example, "The Lion King," a popular animated feature designed for children, had violent episodes between some of the cartoon-like characters and was rated high on that dimension. It would probably have been screened out if a v-chip system were in use. Similarly, "The Nanny" (which contains a great deal of sexual innuendo) was rated in the Canadian system the same as "Sesame Street." Moreover, with some 600,000 programs produced by the TV and movie industries every year, the sheer task of analyzing them within the Canadian system proved to be an awesome one. For these and other reasons, Canadians are now abandoning their complex approach and are testing various simpler alternatives. Thus, the ultimate outcome of the debate over the nature of TV ratings remains to be seen.

Older problems remain. The zapper will continue to trouble advertisers and they will actively explore alternative media, such as newspapers, magazines, radio, and even direct mail. However, offsetting these negatives for TV advertising is another trend (shown in Figure 7.2). That trend is the increase over the years of the total time people spend using their television sets. However, it now appears to have stabilized, presumably because there is only so much time that people can devote to viewing and possibly because some people now spend more time on their home computers. Whatever the reason for that trend, television today presents a complex situation and there is little doubt that further changes are in store. The fortunes of the industry will continue to shift as new players arrive on the scene.

An important aspect of television's future that makes it difficult to predict is changing technology. Looming on the horizon are a number of technological systems that will vastly extend the number of choices viewers will be able to make in their homes. These include a number of new ways of delivering the signal via satellites, optic cable, telephone lines, and wireless systems making use of microwave signals. Telephone companies at one time announced they would invest heavily in systems that delivered a variety of signals and services to the home. Many have now backed off as they realized the costs of rewiring their systems and equipping each home with new receiving devices.

One technology that is about to arrive is digital television—sometimes referred to as **HDTV** (High Definition Television). The Japanese began its development a number of years ago, but their approach was based on an older (analog) transmission and reception technology. (Essentially it is the same as in contemporary TV sets in wide use today.) The United States rejected that technology for HDTV and moved forward to develop digital television. It was a move that paid off as this system has some clear advantages. For one, it provides for a much clearer picture. The HDTV screen is somewhat wider than the ones we use today, and because it has more lines it gives a much sharper image—a picture equal to a fine photograph. Second, digital television information is compatible with computers, which are also based on digital technology. There is little doubt that digital television is coming and that convergence with computer systems represents the future. It is just a matter of how soon HDTV can be received in homes. A nagging problem holding back development has been the standards that will be used. Conflicts between the computer and the television industries slowed its adoption by broadcasters. Additional channels are needed over which to broadcast the signals. How these should be allocated to broadcasters by the FCC has been a subject of intense political debate. Finally, one of the troubling features of the new system is that in order to use it in its full capacity, Americans will have to buy new TV sets capable of receiving the digital signal and showing the pictures on the screen. Older TV sets will be able to continue receiving the analog signals. Although the television and computer industries have not totally agreed on the technical standards that should be used when the new system starts, sufficient consensus was reached late in 1996 so that broadcasts could begin in the near future.

One thing about the future of television is entirely clear. The tastes and preferences of the American audience will undoubtedly remain *precisely where they are* whether the signals come from satellites, phone wires, optic cable networks, computer systems, or HDTV. Therefore, we will not undergo a revolution in program content that will parallel the new technological developments. Thus, whatever spectacular home TV sets are in store for us, perhaps with wall-sized pictures as clear as the real world and with hundreds of choices of channels, we will see the usual array of soap operas, sitcoms, infotainment news, quiz games, sports, home-shopping opportunities, religious evangelists, negative political campaigns, and so on. Mixed in will be a scattering of offerings for the more serious viewer, but the great number who support the industry through their consumer purchases of breakfast foods, laxatives, and other commonly advertised products will want more of the same. Thus, the law of large numbers will prevail in the future to dictate the nature of much of the programming as it has in the past.

# CHAPTER REVIEW

▼ Pioneering experiments on sending pictures by radio began in several countries just after World War I. The earliest attempts made use of a revolving "Nipkow disk," a mechanical system that created a scanning effect when used with a beam of light. It was not until electronic scanning was developed that television became practical.

▼ The first patent for an electronic television system was awarded to Philo T. Farnsworth, an obscure inventor, who had worked out the basic design while still a high school student. With minimal funding he built a working model in a small apartment in Los Angeles. Vladimir Zworykin, of Westinghouse laboratories, also invented an electronic system. Court battles resulted but Farnsworth won.

▼ By 1932, a transmitter was installed in the Empire State Building in New York City. Regular transmissions began on a limited basis in 1936, with two broadcasts per week. A few hundred amateur enthusiasts who had built or purchased sets could receive the signals in the New York area. By 1940, television was capable of becoming a mass medium for home use. However, when World War II began in 1941, the need for war production temporarily halted development of the new medium.

▼ The period of rapid adoption of home receivers began just after the war. Between 1950 and 1960, nearly 90 percent of American households acquired a television set. This rapid adoption happened in spite of a freeze on the licensing and construction of new television stations imposed by the FCC between 1948 and 1952.

▼ Television quickly became a part of family behavior patterns across the nation. The number of hours with the set in use in homes climbed from about four and a half per day in 1950 to over seven in recent years. During the 1970s, color sets all but completely replaced black and white.

▼ Two periods can be identified that might for different reasons be called television's golden age. One, based on the popularity of certain programming and television personalities, was roughly from the early 1950s to about 1960. The second, defined more in terms of the predominance and profitability of the television networks, was from about 1960 to 1980.

▼ Alternative ways to use the TV set at home have now become a significant part of the total picture. Cable systems were not a major factor in the industry until the 1980s. During that decade, the proportion of American homes receiving cable transmissions increased sharply. The VCR was developed in the 1950s by an American company. Since the mid-1980s the Japanese have sold millions of the sets in the United States. Currently, digital television and especially direct satellite broadcasts may change the picture still further.

▼ As an industry, television broadcasting is undergoing a number of changes. New patterns of ownership are emerging. Large corporations and conglomerates are increasingly making TV stations and even networks part of their holdings. The result is changing patterns of competition within the industry. Also, the original networks have lost a large share of the market in terms of advertising dollars. Both cable and VCRs are more widely used than ever before. Further changes lie ahead as this dynamic industry continues to evolve.

▼ Technological changes, convergences, and trends are in store for the medium in the near future. Digitally based HDTV will be available within a short number of years. It will change the format and clarity of the picture seen on the screen. Cable TV will be challenged by systems of delivery via phone wires, microwaves, or satellites. These technological improvements will offer more channels but are unlikely to create a revolution in the nature of television content.

# The New Media

## Computers and Communication

From the earliest times, changes in technology have signaled the development of new communication media. The invention of movable type and high-speed printing presses made print the dominant form of communication for centuries until motion pictures, radio broadcasting, and television ushered in electronic communication, which soon took a foothold. Now both print and electronic media are merging with new digital technologies, namely the computer, to create an age of new media. Technology—that is the methods and materials used to achieve industrial or commercial objectives, such as public communication—is the product first of invention, then of application and marketing where consumers make choices leading to winners and losers. The new media include such television technologies as cable services and pay-per-view, and computer applications like electronic on-line services and various cyberspace home pages on the Internet and World Wide Web.

## ▼ *Factors Influencing the New Media*

The new media are the result of a major shift from a society that mostly depended on agriculture and manufacturing to one based on what sociologist Daniel Bell calls the "manipulation of information," which makes us an information society wherein more people are employed in various information and communications industries, including the media, than in all other sectors of the economy. The new media, which would have been possible only in science fiction two decades ago, were made possible by the merger of television and computer technologies or what is called **convergence**—the coming together of all forms of human communication in an electronic-based, computer-driven system.[1] Some commentators say this happened when television sets began to talk to computers or at the time of what Harvard University's Anthony Oettinger calls "compunications," the merger of communications—all kinds of communications—with computers. The communications revolution or information society evolved over a twenty-year period as electronic systems designed to retrieve, process, and store information and data were developed and integrated with each other. What once only collected statistical data could now bring together text, data, sound, and image. One of the authors of this book called this "the united state of media" made possible by more portable, cheaper, and more user-friendly technology. It is what some commentators have called "the digitalization of almost everything," which is explained by Nicholas Negroponte of the MIT Media Lab as a situation where "formerly mass media evolve into a personalized two way street of communication. Information is no longer pushed at consumers; instead people or their digital agents pull or help create the information they need."[2]

## Convergence

Communication, thanks to the new media, is *interactive* (or interacting with and talking back instantly to an information source) and can be stored and retrieved in electronic form. Not all new media technologies result in public communication, however. Some like **e** (for electronic) **mail** are person-to-person communication whereas on-line chat groups are simply electronic bull sessions for groups of people who want to talk to each other and share information about a common interest, ranging from Middle Eastern cooking to advanced mathematics. In this chapter we focus on the new media that are part of public communication rather than interpersonal media or those that are not interacting with more traditional media such as newspapers or television. What are currently called new media are made possible by the convergence or coming together of various media industries that previously maintained quite separate identities and relationships with citizens and consumers. For example, cooperative ventures between and among broadcasters, telephone companies, cable firms, and computer software companies, unimagined in the past, are creating new media. One dramatic example is MSNBC, a joint venture of Bill Gates' giant Microsoft and NBC News. This new medium takes two forms—a 24-hour cable television network and a cyberspace news and information service that are linked to each other and to those who want to "retrieve" them on the Internet or on the local cable system.

▲

An important component of the new media now emerging is the personal computer linked to the Internet. This system can be a mass medium (point to multipoint transmissions to audiences) that is either interpersonally interactive (as in e-mail) or selectively interactive (where the user can tour through content by clicking on preset "buttons"). (Copyright © Tony Freeman, PhotoEdit)

Without convergence, the new media would not be possible. That convergence or coming together, as we will explain later, has required revolutionary changes in the economics—structure and operation—of the media industries; that is, they must work together for new media to occur. A newspaper company might, for example, work with a telephone company, cable company, and broadcaster to produce an electronic newspaper. Similarly, the hardware and software must also be able to interconnect and work together and, finally, the laws and rules under which communications operates must also cooperate and, in fact, blend together. Separate laws and privileges for print media and the broadcast media do not work in the new media environment. An electronic database offering news and information as well as video games is a new medium, not an old-style magazine or a conventional broadcaster.

An example of media convergence is MSNBC, a joint venture between Microsoft and NBC News. A digital news service and a 24-hour cable network are linked together in such a way that content can be retrieved on either the Internet or on a TV cable system. Whether or not such convergent systems will survive will depend on their ability to yield a profit for their investors. (Copyright © Gifford, Liaison)

## The Internet and the World Wide Web

To Martin Irvine of Georgetown University the typical answer to the question, what is the Internet? (Answer: the global network of computer networks) is not enough. To Irvine, who heads a culture, communication, and technology program, the Internet has three components:

- a *worldwide computer system* using a common means of linking hardware and transmitting digital information
- a *community of people* using a common communication technology
- a globally distributed *system of information*

He quickly adds that the Internet (or Net) in practical and functional terms is

- a *24-hour nonstop global forum and communication system*
- an *on-line library and international information system*
- a *business and corporate communications medium*
- a *distance and remote education system*
- a *commercial transactions medium*
- a *multimedia delivery system for news and entertainment*
- a *government information service*
- *all of the above simultaneously*[3]

Originally organized in the 1960s by the U.S. Department of Defense, the Internet was at first mostly used by scientists and university professors as vari-

The Internet and all modern computer applications were made possible because of the development of the first digital electronic computer. The ENIAC (Electronic Numerical Integrator And Computer) was over 100 feet long and eight feet high, it used more than 18,000 vacuum tubes and hundreds of miles of wire. It was programmed by wiring boards and setting 6,000 switches by hand. Hailed as a scientific marvel at the time, it had only a small fraction of the power of today's laptop computers. (UPI/Corbis-Bettmann)

ous technical problems were worked out. Until the early 1990s, few ordinary people had ever heard of the Internet or the **World Wide Web,** which is a system for delivering hypertext and multimedia files on the Internet. Hypertext is a type of document that has links to other documents. Especially important to Internet development worldwide was the 1993 introduction of Mosaic, an early Web browser.[4] To technology expert Wilson Dizard, "The Internet is a major factor in redefining the meaning of mass media," but he admits that the distinctions between old and new media are rapidly blurring as people grapple for terms to describe what the new digital information services can and might do in the future.[5] In 1997, it was estimated that there were 50 million people worldwide using the Internet and the World Wide Web both for individual messaging and for communication to audiences large and small, institutions, and organizations. There are, of course, various closed-system and proprietary on-line services that are not technically a part of the Internet. In fact, the major services like America Online and CompuServe existed long before they provided an Internet gateway for their clients. By 1996, when demand for the Internet exploded, most commercial on-line services and private networks owned by AT&T and Microsoft moved to the Internet.

Al Sikes of Hearst New Media and a former chairman of the Federal Communications Commission calls the Internet "today's new media conundrum." He says, "The Internet is expensive to access, artistically primitive, painfully slow, and overpopulated with garbage. And it is wonderful. It gives voice to those who don't have a radio or TV frequency or a printing press. It transcends boundaries; while some contend that it is a source of disunity, if you are thinking globally it is a source of unity."[6]

Although there are many books and manuals about the Internet, its protocols and uses, it is important to remember that every e-mail address using the "network of networks" has three aspects: a user name, a host name, and a domain name. The user and the host are always separated by the @ sign and usually distinguish individual users from the organization of which they are a part, such as a university or a company. The domain name indicates the kind of institution to which the user belongs. The domains and the percentage of users they had in January 1996 are listed here:

*.edu*—Educational and research organizations (8%)

*.com*—Commercial (business) organizations (45%)

*.gov*—Government nonmilitary organizations (16%)

*.mil*—U.S. military branches (15%)

*.org*—Nonprofit organizations (23%)

*.net*—Network organizations and access providers (24%)[7]

## Convergence in Three Dimensions

Thus, there are three kinds of convergence: economic convergence, which blurs and merges the once-clear lines between print and electronic media and allows mergers and new economic arrangements; technological convergence, in which the new machines talk to each other through an intelligent network; and regulatory convergence, which removes legal roadblocks.

Without the advent of communication satellites that beam messages all over the globe, personal computers, and various computer networks and software, the new media would not exist. However, the new media are more than new technical inventions. They are instead a process in which several social forces combined to create a powerful new communications capacity with, as mentioned earlier, technological, economic, and regulatory applications.

**Technological invention and applications.**   The invention of compact, high-speed computers, appropriate software, and a worldwide network of networks—the Internet—were key to new media development. Complex information, storage, and retrieval technology, once found only in massive university and industry computer labs, were available to ordinary individuals at relatively low cost. Software programs called *search engines* allowed for instant retrieval of information and thus made it possible for people to navigate the complex, interactive digital world, which is called *cyberspace*. In the modern medium, various computer systems and networks were linked to others, not just in a local, geographic area, but worldwide.

**Economic demand and consumer needs.** All the computer inventions and new tools or games in the world would have little meaning if the economic system was not friendly and if consumers did not want the products produced. What was called "the media wars" in the 1980s—in which various media industries like newspapers fought telephone companies and others to hold onto their special relationship (or franchise) with readers (or news consumers)—gave way to mergers and various relationships that connected once quite separate industries with each other. For example, in the 1980s the ABC television network merged with Capital Cities Communication, a newspaper company and broadcaster. In the 1990s, the combined company became part of the entertainment giant, Disney, known mostly for movies and amusement parks. Time, Inc.—a magazine, book publishing, record producer, and cable firm—merged with Warner Communications—an entertainment company—and merged and connected many interests. Thus, consumers were able to get various communication "products" from the same firm, which welcomed new media ventures that would draw on their various resources to create information and entertainment content. This meant economies of scale for the communications companies that run the mass (and more specialized) media, and cost savings for the consumer.

Users of the Internet and the World Wide Web have a vast variety of choices of content to receive on their computer screens. These include one-to-one typed conversations with other individuals and similar exchanges with chat groups. Other content includes games, databases of technical information, advertising, and entertainment material for every interest and taste. User-friendly search software has made it far easier to use the system than it was earlier. (Courtesy Ko Photo)

**Regulatory connections.** Many of the new media would have been blocked if it had not been for the deregulation of communication industries. This took place in various government rulings and legislation. The most important was the Communications Act of 1996, which relaxed many rules that in the past made it illegal for various media industries (for example cable and telephone companies) to work together. Because much of broadcasting and other electronic communication are regulated by the government in the United States and in other countries, greater freedom—and less regulation—has been friendly to the coming of new media. In the past, many of the new agreements between computer software makers, broadcasters, newspapers, and others would have been prohibited by laws passed to prevent monopolies and too much control by any one media company. Previously, the government regulated the "scarcity" of communication, such as a limited number of TV channels, but in the new media age there is an abundance of communication with scores of new cable channels and an unlimited access to the Internet.

## ▼ *Understanding Differences: Three Domains*

In his book, *Mediamorphosis,* Roger Fidler says all communication and media can be seen in three domains: interpersonal, broadcast, and document. The first, as he puts it, is the *interpersonal domain*, which consists of one-to-one forms of oral/expressive communication whose content is not structured or influenced by external mediators. This also includes communication between human beings and computers and might involve specific on-line information searches. Examples are on-line chat, e-mail, and computer games.

The second is the *broadcast domain*. This is point-to-multipoint communication, where information is transmitted from few to many. Generally, messages here consist of forms of aural/visual communication whose content is highly structured. They are sent to audiences sequentially from beginning to end in relatively fixed locations and in scheduled, predetermined periods of time. Examples are cable TV, FM radio, and music videos.

The third is the *document domain*. Again, this is transmitted from a few senders to many receivers. The messages here are in large part textual, with some visual communication. This kind of content is packaged and presented to individuals primarily through the World Wide Web and other kinds of hypertext documents.[8]

A one-time newspaper editor and graphic artist, Fidler helped pioneer electronic on-line services for newspapers and eventually wrote a book that allowed him to think more deeply about media and technology—why some things work and others do not. He called the process "mediamorphosis," which he defines as "the transformation of communication media, usually brought about by the complex interplay of perceived needs, competitive and political pressures and social and technological innovations." Thus, the process by which new media come about is, as we have explained earlier, the interaction of three interrelated forces involving various forms of invention, money, and politics.

To Bill Gates, chairman of Microsoft, the new media wonders of the present will evolve into a virtual world where all TV sets and computers are linked to a global intelligent network that can carry out transactions for people drawing, for example, on the three domains just mentioned. Eventually, says Gates, in his book *The Road*

▲
Visionaries, such as Bill Gates of Microsoft, foresee a brave new world ahead where people everywhere are linked into one vast information system. In spite of earlier forecasts that the world would become a "global village," as a consequence of the spread of television, traditional problems of war, ethnic hostility, poverty, and disease are likely to continue. Increases in the capacity to communicate may or may not help alleviate such difficulties. (Copyright © 1994 Michael A. Schwarz, The Image Works)

*Ahead*, communication and human behavior will merge and will become invisible with the so-called media as simply tools of no more interest to most of us than are the component parts of automobile engines.[9] This idea suggests a high degree of reliance on new media technologies, something that the novelist E.M. Forster warned about in a short story written before 1914 called "The Machine Stops." In Forster's story, people lived under the earth in compartments and relied completely on a massive, global communication system called, "the machine."[10] As he put it in his imaginary tale: "The machine," they exclaimed, "feeds us and clothes us and houses us; through it we speak to one another; through it we see one another, in it we have our being. The machine is the friend of ideas and the enemy of superstition; the machine is omnipotent, eternal; blessed is the Machine." Forster adds, "the machine was still the creation and implement of man, but in practice all but a few retrogrades worshipped it as divine." Eventually, the machine gets out of hand and "year by year it was served with increased efficiency and decreased intelligence. The better a man knew his own duties upon it, the less he understood the duties of his neighbor and in all the world there was not one who understood the monster as a whole." Eventually, this proves disastrous as the Machine slows and stops, leaving the world and humanity to perish.[11]

On August 17, 1996, some people wondered if their "machine," or access to the Internet, had stopped. That was the day America Online crashed. News and information services, business travel, and other functions of everyday life were massively disrupted. The disruption led to serious concern about the extent to which people depended on new communication systems, which can break down.

## Big On-Line Crash Frustrates Businesses

A network blackout at America Online left many small businesses and home-office workers without electronic mail and other network services yesterday, illustrating the growing importance of on-line communications to modern commerce.

The outage also caused America Online's dozens of information publishers to lose many thousands of dollars in access fees and advertising revenues.

America Online, the nation's largest operator of an on-line computer network with six million subscribers, said its service went down during a regularly scheduled maintenance update and software installation, beginning at 4 A.M., Eastern daylight time, yesterday. Service was not restored until nearly 11 P.M.

Network crashes are not uncommon in the on-line world. But for America Online, which casts itself as the user-friendliest service, yesterday's crash was an embarrassment.

In recent years, the number of users of the Internet grew so rapidly that major service providers, such as America Online, have at times been unable to keep up with the demand. AOL's system was so heavily used in 1996 that on August 17 of that year it crashed and caused great annoyance and difficulties for millions of subscribers. More recently, AOL and CompuServe have merged into one huge online provider. (Copyright © 1996 The New York Times Company, reprinted by permission)

# ▼ *Winners and Losers in the New Media*

Futurists often forecast new media developments decades ahead of their actual development and some new technologies turn out to be disappointing. Some analysts of media say one should not take a new medium technology seriously until it has the capacity to reach 50 percent of the population, whereas others say that is too severe a test and does not account for smaller, segmented audiences that can give a new medium a start before it becomes popular. Technology scholar John Carey reminds us that it took one hundred years for the newspaper to reach the magic 50 percent figure; the telephone, seventy years; radio, only about ten years; and television less than that. By contrast, cable was invented in the 1950s and took nearly forty years to reach a majority of American households.

## On-line Interactive Services

Consumer on-line interactive services such as America Online, Prodigy, and CompuServe, which offer information on demand and e-mail, succeeded in a field where other new media efforts failed. On-line services trace their origins from early experiments in the United States and Britain. They were called either **teletext** or **videotext**, both of which used the lower lines of the television screen (the vertical blanking interval), rather than computers. The Knight-Ridder Company set up Viewtron, the first videotext service in the United States, and operated it in Miami between 1979 and 1986 as a bold new media experiment. They had to call it quits due to lack of consumer demand and advertising support. The Viewtron failure, according to media technologist and author Roger Fidler, was due to a failure to understand consumers and other considerations. He says that

- What consumers wanted wasn't more information;
- It wasn't a newspaper;
- The cost was too high;
- The medium was not compelling.[12]

Another bold experiment, and eventual failure, was Warner Amex's QUBE system in Columbus, Ohio. It was an interactive television system that allowed viewers to make programming choices and engage in "electronic democracy" through electronic town meetings and regular polls. This service, which existed between 1977 and 1985, was also eventually abandoned because it failed to make money for the owners; had limited, crude technology; and made consumers worry about their privacy. The two failed experiments, like that of facsimile, which was used for so-called "radio newspapers" in the 1930s and 1940s and

# Media and the Liberal Arts

## Electronic Democracy Through News Groups and Listserves
### A Linchpin to Political Science, Speech Communication, and Technology Studies

Although the United States has the longest continuous democratic governmental system in the world, what some say is a "two-hundred-year-long march toward political equality for all citizens" is changing and changing radically. Why? According to Lawrence K. Grossman it is "the explosive growth of new telecommunications media, the remarkable convergence of television, telephones, satellites, cable, and personal computers." This, says Grossman, a former president of PBS and NBC News, is creating an electronic democracy where citizens can "see, hear and judge their own political leaders simultaneously and instantaneously."[14]

Part of this is the interactive capability of the new media and the platforms for content they provide through news groups, listserves, and other "cybersalons" that let people connect with each other on various topics and interests, but also talk back to each other in multifaceted ways. That this can be done cheaply through the Internet also makes the prospect of electronic democracy, where people can vote electronically on political, cultural, social, commercial, and other matters that concern them, a reality. Instead of complex voting procedures or even cumbersome market research studies, the computer and

new media have made instant communication and feedback possible for the first time.

Some critics think this has ushered in an era of electronic town meetings, in concept much like the New England town meetings of early America when all citizens gathered in the meeting house or on the village green to discuss and debate common concerns and interests. The new town meetings can connect people in a local area through simple e-mail, cutting down on the need for telephone calls or face to face meetings. It can also facilitate electronic town meetings between and among like-minded people sharing common interests anywhere on the globe. All this is changing our sense of community, reinforcing the old geographic communities (because people do have much in common with those who are their physical neighbors) but also creating new communities of chocolate lovers, gamblers, the disabled, and an infinite number of others.

Although hailed by many as a boon for democracy and human communication with a new medium stimulating new kinds of content, others worry about the potential negative effects of electronic democracy. Such instant and specialized communication could fragment the nation and world, some say. Others

say that it creates an "information anxiety," which makes it difficult to make sense out of the world and focus on information that helps people function or solve problems. Richard Sal Wurman has proposed new graphic signposts that help people "organize their cities, their lives and their interests."[15]

Cyberpundit David Shenk worries about the unsettling impact of information overload or "data smog" on our individual emotional and physical well-being and on society at large. Shenk warns that the current age is moving toward an electronic Tower of Babel and that we must find a return to meaning. The trick, he says, is figuring out how to become empowered by information, rather than smothered by it.[16]

The promise outlined by Lawrence Grossman and the warnings issued by David Shenk will benefit by a clearer understanding of the history of technology and its meaning for society as well as by rhetorical studies that consider how to develop, deliver, and channel messages through new media in the most effective fashion. Just how the enormous range and promise of new media can be harnessed to sense making for individual and social benefit is one of the greatest dilemmas of the information age.

delivered to dumb terminals in the home, may have died because their owners lacked patience. Technologist Paul Saffo, like John Carey, says that a successful, new technology often takes as long as thirty years to move from the laboratory to widespread consumer use.[13]

## The Most Popular News Web Sites

Throughout the 1990s, American newspapers began offering their readers on-line electronic services delivered on the home PC via the Internet or in some instances other dedicated networks. Among successes was the *Raleigh* (N.C.) *News and Observer*'s "Nandonet," which attracted home users, connections to schools, and even advertising revenue from elsewhere on the globe. The *San Jose Mercury News*'s Mercury Center project was also widely hailed for its innovative graphics and fast-paced information, keyed also to stories in the newspaper, thus extending the reach of one medium into another. By 1997, there were more than one hundred such electronic news experiments tied to newspapers and several others that were developed by news magazines, business magazines, business information firms, and others. These Web sites were grappling with ways to measure their audiences and attract advertising as this was written. In early 1997, the most popular Net news sites were

1. *USA Today*
   www.usatoday.com

2. CNN Interactive
   www.cnn.com

3. *Washington Post*
   www.washington.com

4. *New York Times*
   www.nytimes.com

5. MSNBC
   www.msnbc.com

6. *Jerusalem Post*
   www.jpost.com

7. *Los Angeles Times*
   www.latimes.com

8. *Christian Science Monitor*
   www.csmonitor.com

9. *San Jose Mercury News*
   www.sjmercury.com

10. *Chicago Tribune*
    www.chicago.tribune.com [17]

This roster of news services on the Web shows how consumers draw on different kinds of news organizations for information. And the mix of long-standing, mainstream newspapers alongside cable services and those developed by software companies demonstrates the many sources of media services and the practical meaning of convergence.

## ▼ *The Information Superhighway*

Vice President Al Gore has for some years promoted the concept of an "information superhighway" in which all persons would be part of an interactive communications process with instant access to global information. The term **information highway** goes back at least to 1909 when an ad for AT&T described the Bell System as "a highway of communication."[18] In its current use, it is mainly a visionary notion that all people everywhere should be able to connect with all information everywhere. Such an idea assumes that computers have the capacity to gather, process, and retrieve all information, entertainment fare, and other human communication. The technology of computer systems would presumably make this possible and the result would be accessible to people through computers or advanced (sometimes called smart) television sets. Of course, this is a distant goal. However, the information superhighway is frequently discussed in terms of the Internet and the "television of

Vice President Al Gore has long been an active promoter of the "information superhighway," a term he frequently used for what is now the Internet and the World Wide Web. He saw that providing school children with access to personal computers and the information that access could bring to them as a key factor in reducing the troublesome knowledge gap between rich and poor. (Copyright © Mark Richards, PhotoEdit)

abundance," which imagines up to five hundred channels in the home. By the late 1990s, the term has come to mean connecting with all of the content on the Internet and World Wide Web as well as all that comes over the television set, mainly on cable channels. Thus, the information superhighway is the system or infrastructure that lets communication companies offer services on TV or on the computer screen. It is also the content produced—whether TV programs, on-line services, electronic newspapers, or whatever. It is also the interactive trafficking of people using the system. Computer scientist Michael Dertouzos of MIT says the information superhighway is not a "highway" or two-way road system at all, but instead a communications marketplace where all kinds of media companies and other interests bargain with and for information.[19] Of course, the global superhighway could reach people everywhere only if they have access to computers with the capacity (and memory) to handle all the information.

## The Superhighway and Media Industries

Anthony Smith and Wilson Dizard, both leading experts on communications and media technology, speak of old and new media; for example, *Time* is an old media product, whereas Time Warner's Pathfinder news service, which one finds on the Internet, is new media. One is a printed product of ink on paper distributed by mail; the other is a menu of news and information material retrieved electronically on the PC screen. Both have similar content, although the new medium—Pathfinder—has infinitely more material, the equivalent of thousands of pages, which allows consumers to "create" their own electronic magazine. This is a version of what the MIT Media Lab had in mind years ago when they created a newspaper called the *Daily Me*, in which every individual reader becomes an "editor" by virtue of making choices on an electronic menu. Although many new media ventures have been started by small firms—mostly young computer hackers with editorial and business interests—old media companies quickly realized that they also needed to be "players" in the marketplace. They adapted their content and activities to new media technologies, sometimes called "platforms." Newspaper and magazine companies, therefore, have developed on-line news services that transmit their content to homes and offices electronically and often add additional material. Radio and television stations have done the same thing with news, and moviemakers have even created web sites for individual films.

Much publicized was the development by Microsoft of an on-line magazine called *Slate*, edited by Michael Kinsley, formerly editor of the opinion magazine, *The New Republic*, and a commentator on CNN's contentious program, "Crossfire." To many the Kinsley appointment at *Slate* underscored the differences between the young, hip cyborgs who live and work in the virtual world of cyberspace and older, more traditional media types. Kinsley doubts that the differences are so great or that there is anything "fundamentally differ-

There have always been fears among media owners and managers that new technologies would eclipse the need for older forms. For example, some media experts predicted that computers and the Internet would bring about a collapse of both the book and magazine industries. People would get their information online and not from magazine racks and book stores. The fact is that the rise of the computer generated a huge industry of print publications related to their use. (Copyright © David Young-Wolff, PhotoEdit)

ent about the nature of communication, the nature of thought, of human relations because of the Internet."[20] Kinsley was portrayed as a refugee from old media in publications like *Wired* or its cyberspace version, *Hot Wired*.

## Reflecting on New Media

No one is quite sure what is the precise definition of "new media," but they most certainly include the emergence of new platforms or technologies used to deliver messages to audiences in an interactive fashion. People in new media can talk back directly to those who bring news and information, entertainment, opinion, and advertising—and can even initiate the communication process themselves. There are, of course, differences between the home pages and web sites of giant media entrepreneurs—backed by thousands of workers developing content, the capacity to promote and advertise their wares, and other advantages of size and resources—and those developed by students or other individuals as a means to communicate with friends and acquaintances.

From early writings about the benefits of new media technologies, commentators have argued that one of the eventual results would be more democratic communication, opportunities for people to communicate with and through media to get information, debate issues, solve problems, and forecast the future. Former NBC News President Lawrence A. Grossman sees the new media and new telecommunication systems as potentially "redistributing political power" and fostering an electronic republic.[21] Others argue that the new media will instead foster fragmentation and move us away from the more unified world of mass communication where a few large entities, mainly broadcasters, could command massive audiences and therefore "speak" to the nation, if not the world. The new media and their complex networks allow for greater access and greater reach than ever before, but not necessarily larger audiences—due to the competition of thousands upon thousands of news services, home pages, and other services.

Futurists see the new, interactive media eventually employing high-definition television with sharper pictures and better sound to link up with virtual reality, which allows the viewers/participants actually to take part in the programming they are watching. Scores of other innovations and new media forms are being talked about and experimented with.

As we indicated at the outset of this chapter, there have always been new media. In the last two centuries those new media have included the telegraph, which brought us wire services; modern telephone (the phone system) radio and television (over-the-air broadcast communication); and cable (broadband communication) and others. Some new media inventions begin subtly and then have a larger impact than is expected. For example, the invention of a software package called the Aldus *Pagemaker* in the 1970s allowed news organizations to design and lay out pages electronically with greater ease than had earlier been the case. The system was developed by a newspaper and computer company executive, Paul Brainerd, who was once the editor of the student *Minnesota Daily* at the University of Minnesota. Although he worked for old media—newspapers—Brainerd created software that made him "the father of desktop publishing." As a result of his invention and cheap offset printing processes, many individuals and organizations developed their own highly professional newspapers, newsletters, and magazines, which previously would have required costly investments in printing equipment and typesetting. Access to communication opened for many people who were not previously able to communicate with such ease and cost effectiveness. In the same way that the personal computer and Internet expanded access to information and the communication process, so did the Aldus *Pagemaker*, which Brainerd eventually sold for tens of millions of dollars. He now runs a charitable foundation in Seattle, Washington.

## ▼ *The Future of New Media*

As we have indicated, the nature and definition of new media keeps changing, but the digital revolution is quite different than anything human beings have experienced previously with communication messages crossing borders and returning from all points on the planet. The new media of the present engage in instantaneous and interactive communication. They merge text and data with sound and pictures. They mostly use personal computers, but can also be linked to the television set.

Some critics say there is a burning appliance war between the television set and the personal computer with some doubt about who will win. Many think that both will win and attract certain followings and interfaces. Others think that a new device or appliance will emerge and render both obsolete. It is well to remember that new media refer to the technology of delivery (the machine used), the software or systems that allow the communication process to occur, and the actual content that is communicated.

Whether a new medium is largely concerned with *information* (like on-line services), *entertainment* (video games and pay-per-view movies), *opinion* (bulletin boards, chat groups, and cybersalons), or *advertising* (home shopping services on TV and on the PC screen), in the end it will compete with other existing media. Some will supersede old media, taking over their functions. For example, the newspaper industry for years blocked telephone company entry into the on-line news world because they feared that electronic classified ads would eventually kill newspapers, which depend on these important revenues. Most new media live alongside old media and the most successful of them integrate with the older media enterprises and eventually the public does not know the difference. At one time cable television was seen as the mortal enemy of over-the-air television broadcasting. After all, cable was a scavenger taking its content from over-the-air TV and redistributing it to viewers. Now, cable is a delivery system on which traditional television relies as well as a programming service with its own distinctive networks like CNN, Arts and Entertainment, ESPN, The History Channel, and many others.

## CHAPTER REVIEW

▼ From movable type to modern computers, new technology that challenges time and distance has signaled the development of new communication media.

▼ Older print and electronic media have recently merged (or converged) with digital technology to create what are called "new media."

▼ New media are part of a communications revolution or information age, which historically follows the agrarian or agricultural age and the Industrial Revolution.

▼ Convergence is the coming together of all forms of electronically based, computer-driven media into a single system.

▼ The Internet is a global network of computer networks that is (1) a worldwide computer system, (2) a community of people, and (3) a globally distributed system of information.

▼ The Internet and World Wide Web were initiated by the Defense Department and subsequently used by scientists and academics before spreading to the general public.

▼ Two of the most famous and widely used "closed" Internet services available for a cost and useful as a link to the Internet are America Online (AOL) and CompuServe.

▼ Convergence has three interrelated dimensions—the technology or invention; economic demand and consumer need; and regulatory or legal systems—all of which work together to allow new media to exist, win financial support, and have permission to operate.

▼ New media embrace three domains of communication, including (1) interpersonal, one-to-one communication, (2) broadcasting to a mass audience, and (3) documents that allow people to retrieve material of personal interest.

▼ Consumer adoption of new media takes time and scholars remind us that it took one hundred years for the newspaper to reach 50 percent of the public; seventy years for the telephone; ten years for radio, and forty years for cable.

▼ Newspapers in the United States (and many in other countries) are scrambling to be part of the electronic age and new media by establishing web sites with news and information.

▼ Some of the most popular news web sites are *USA Today*, CNN Interactive, *The Washington Post*, *The New York Times*, and MSNBC.

▼ The information superhighway is an infrastructure that potentially allows people everywhere to communicate with each other. The two delivery systems for the information superhighway are (1) cyberspace and various digital services and (2) cable television, which allows multiple channels of information for viewers.

▼ New media differ from old media in that they are instantaneous and interactive, allowing users or consumers more control in shaping their messages. Its future depends largely on success with consumers.

# PART THREE

# Media Industries
# and Audiences

▼ **C H A P T E R  9**

# *News*

## The Information Function of the Press

Since newspapers came into existence, the press has served as the "eyes and ears" of society. The term *press* today includes all the print, broadcast, cable, and computer media that bring news reports to the public. Through its monitoring of the social environment, the press gathers, processes, and disseminates the news. By attending to what is selected and presented, the public comes to comprehend, in greater or lesser degree, a selected agenda of topics summarizing at least some of what has happened in their community, region, nation, and the world.

Defining what is news can be a complex problem. Hundreds of definitions have been advanced since scholars began writing about the topic. For our purposes, however, we can define news in a very simple way: *News is current or fresh knowledge about an event or subject that is gathered, processed, and disseminated via a medium to a significant number of interested people.*

Of critical importance for understanding the nature of news are the four terms: *gathered, processed, disseminated,* and *public.* These four are at the heart of the **news process**—a series of steps by which accounts of events in reality flow through news organizations and eventually reach the public. Those steps consist of (1) gathering relevant facts or details selectively, (2) preparing them into stories judged to be newsworthy and suitably encoded for particular media, (3) transmitting those accounts via a mass medium to an audience, which then, (4) in varying degrees, attends to and comprehends what has been presented.

A broader idea that places the news process in perspective is the "surveillance function of the press." The main idea here is that the press (news media generally) keeps an eye on what is going on for citizens, and through the news process described previously, gives them reliable reports about what appears to be important. Thus, citizens supposedly have trustworthy information enabling them to make informed decisions about events and issues that are of significance to them and the society. This idealized interpretation of the function of the press in our democracy is the justification for according the news media special protections and privileges not extended to other kinds of profit-making businesses.

If the news process works well—that is, if the information presented is reasonably complete and accurate as a representation of reality—the public gets a valid picture of what is actually going on. This picture, at least presumably, creates a close correspondence between what Walter Lippman called the "world outside" and the "pictures in our heads." However, as this chapter will make clear, there are many reasons to believe that the news presented by the press has only a *limited* correspondence with what is actually happening in the real world.

Recognizing the limitations of the news process, as we do in this chapter, is not the same as condemning it. To show that the "pictures in our heads" that we create from the news media's presentations of "the world outside" are *distorted* is not to say that journalists or the media deliberately set out to dupe us. An alternative conclusion is that such distortions are an inevitable product of the forces, factors, and conditions within which the press, as we have developed it, must operate to survive. At the same time, as this chapter will show, in some instances the press can and should be criticized—strongly in some cases—for policies and decisions that have been made by owners and managers. A major purpose of this chapter, therefore, is to examine the news process objectively so as to provide a better understanding of how well, or how poorly, the press actually performs its surveillance function, and why.

On the whole, the contemporary news industries are impressive. It is quite true that the press reports thousands of events of a trivial nature to the public. However, the press also brings us information about truly significant events, situations, and changes that can have a profound impact on our lives. Furthermore, it does so today with a swiftness and to a degree of detailed coverage that people in earlier times could not have imagined. Today the proliferation of media and technologies that permit the gathering, processing, and dissemination of information allows the press to provide far greater coverage of events, gathered from more places, delivered in richer detail, and presented much more quickly than ever before.

## ▼ *The News Process in Earlier Societies*

In ancient times, a major means of transmitting the news was by *news specialist*—that is, by messengers of various kinds who developed ways of remembering long accounts with many details. The availability of speech greatly expanded human beings' ability to store information in memory. Studies have shown that people who have only oral language, and who have to remember complex information, develop elaborate techniques that help them recall details. One such technique is the poetic structure. We still keep some details in our heads by memorizing little poems. For example, for recalling the number of days in each month, who can forget, "Thirty days hath September, April, June, and November . . ."

Ancient communication specialists, however, had to commit truly important and complex information to memory in such a way that elaborate details could be recalled and retold accurately. To do so, they used several kinds of memory devices. For example, in classic times, news was packaged into epic poems (from the Greek word *epos,* meaning "tale"). The standardized verbal rhythms and structures of the poems provided aids to memory, and epics were widely used in preliterate societies. Perhaps the best-known example is the *Iliad*, in which (in about 1200 B.C.) the poet Homer described the Greeks' ten-year siege of Troy. At the time, the Greeks had no written language, and the complex story of Troy had to be remembered with the help of the *Iliad's* 16,000 lines of dactylic hexameter.[1]

In the Middle Ages, minstrels and traveling bands of troubadours went from one village and estate to another. They sang, staged little plays, and danced to entertain the local gentry. More important, however, they organized songs and recitals around important tidings that they brought from centers of power. It was in this manner that many locals learned of such events as the birth of an heir to their throne, an important marriage among the nobility, or the death of a royal person.

Even today, *interpersonal transmission*—word-of-mouth telling and retelling—is still very much a part of our contemporary news process. Such transmission takes place when individuals who experience events firsthand (or are directly exposed to news stories transmitted by media) tell others what they have learned. Their listeners, in turn, tell still others, and the information moves along through chains of people.

Although word-of-mouth diffusion remains important, the majority of people receive their news directly from media, and it is to them that we must turn to understand the news process. It begins with the stage of gathering information from which to construct news stories.

Throughout history, people have eagerly sought news about happenings at home and elsewhere. As societies became more complex, political life and commercial activities became increasingly significant concerns. During the sixteenth and seventeenth centuries, demand for both domestic and foreign news grew, but few printed media published timely and detailed information. Thus, social gathering-places, such as taverns and coffee houses, became centers for the diffusion of information by word of mouth. At times, as this engraving shows, discussions of the news could grow heated. (Dept. of Special Collections, Memorial Library, University of Wisconsin–Madison)

# EXPLAINING MEDIA EFFECTS
## *The Theory of the Two-Step Flow of Communication*

Although most people get their news and other kinds of information directly from the mass media, information continues to diffuse through societies by word-of-mouth. Thus, even in our sophisticated information society with its satellites, computers, and news media with worldwide reach, word-of-mouth communication is still a part of the mass communication process.

In a now-classic study of the role of the mass media in the 1940 presidential campaign of Franklin D. Roosevelt versus Wendell Wilkie, communication researchers Lazarsfeld, Berelson, and Gaudet rediscovered the importance of the diffusion of information through interpersonal communication.[2] To their surprise, they found that many of the people they were interviewing did not get their information about the issues and candidates from the media at all, but from *other people* who had read about the campaign in the newspapers, or who had listened to the broadcast speeches of the candidates.

The researchers found that such "opinion leaders" passed on information to many others who had much less contact with the media. As they did so, they had an influence on the way the information was interpreted. Thus, the term "opinion leaders" described not only their activity of transmission but also their role in exerting personal influence. Out of that famous research project came a theory that has come to be called the **two-step flow of communication.** It is important in understanding the word-of-mouth transmission of news to a larger audience than just those who

## ▼ *Categories for Surveillance*

Reality, of course, is the ultimate source of all news. The problem is reality's mind-boggling complexity. In the words of philosopher William James, the world is a great "blooming and buzzing confusion." Thus, the news is drawn from a reality made up of an enormous variety of issues, events, conflicts, trends, and a host of other happenings. But whatever the perplexing nature of reality, the first step in the news process is that it must be observed, understood, interpreted, and recorded by reporters whose task is to prepare initial comprehensible descriptions for public consumption.

To understand this initial stage of the news process, we need first to look at how practicing journalists reduce the complex world to a limited number of *categories* so as to divide up the task of surveillance. A brief look at each of these categories will help in understanding the initial stage of news gathering.

### Territories, Topics, and Organizations

One of the principal advantages of dividing up reality into categories is that it allows for an orderly division of labor in assigning reporters to cover different kinds of events. These divisions have grown out of the practical experience of journalists over the years and have become deeply established by tradition.

are initially exposed. The two-step flow of communication has been widely studied since it was first formulated in the 1940s.

Most of us can recall learning of some major news event this way, but modern research on word-of-mouth transmission of news has shown that it is not a very reliable or accurate system for moving complex information that includes many details. However, it does work well for short messages of a dramatic nature, such as "the space shuttle blew up," "the president has been shot," or "we won the big game." The theory has been well verified, and can be summarized in the following terms:

**1.** The mass media present a constant flow of information about a great variety of topics of interest and importance to people in contemporary society, but most people attend only *selectively*.

**2.** Some people, at all levels of society, *attend more fully* to the media than others and become more knowledgeable than their families, friends, or neighbors in certain areas of media content.

**3.** Among those who attend more fully are people who become identified by others as *opinion leaders*—persons like themselves, but who are especially knowledgeable and trustworthy as sources of informa-

tion and interpretation about certain areas of media content.

**4.** Such opinion leaders often *pass on* information they obtain from the media about specialized topics to others who have turned to them for information and interpretations about those topics.

**5. Therefore:** Mass communications often move in *two stages* —from the media to opinion leaders, who attend directly to media presentations about selected topics, and then by word-of-mouth to other people whom they influence by their information and interpretations.

They are shaped in part by journalists' conceptions of what will interest the public, and in part by their beliefs that there are some things that the public should know about in a democratic society.

One important set of categories is the somewhat natural division of geographic *territories*.[3] Thus, facts for news stories come from events that are *local, regional, national, or international.* Each of these rather imprecise territorial definitions refers to rather different types of facts that hold different levels of interest for particular segments of the public. Some in the audience are "cosmopolitans," who follow the international and national news avidly, but who care little or nothing about what is happening locally. Others are "locals," who keep well informed about what is happening in their immediate community or region but have limited interest in national and international events.[4] These audience preferences have become well understood by professional journalists, who balance their news reports to meet the needs of these different kinds of people.

Within each territory there are additional well-understood classifications based on *specialized topics*. Typical of such topics are politics, the economy, science, health, education, sports, fashions, weather, entertainment, space, crime, and so on through a long list. These play a key role in structuring the nature of the surveillance engaged in by the various media.

Still another broad category has to do with the *organizations* from which facts for developing news stories are often obtained. Thus, at a national level, reporters are specifically assigned to cover the White House, the Pentagon, or the Congress. Assignments at the local level may be the police department, city hall, or the local university. These categories and subcategories represent different focuses of attention in the ongoing activities of the society, and they represent different subject matters and degrees of interest to various segments of the population. Using them as the basis for a division of labor in a news organization allows reporters to become specialized and thereby "expert" in one or more categories. Thus, some reporters confine themselves to international affairs, or even to a particular area of the world. Others focus exclusively on a particular topic or kind of activity, such as fashion, science, or education. This kind of specialization helps reporters develop unique skills and perspectives in locating, understanding, and writing about the important facts that are central to the territory, activity, or organization over which they exercise surveillance.

## Time as a Category

A rather different kind of distinction among news stories can be made, within any of the previously mentioned categories, on the basis of the *extension of the story through time*. Some news happenings are of short duration and are essentially one-time events. For example, at the local level, a house may burn down or an explosion occur. Such events provide **spot news**—a staple of the industry. Spot stories have no history. The event occurs; it provides facts for a news story; the account is prepared; it is disseminated to the public; and that is it.

In contrast, other stories can be classified as *developing*. They occur in stages, like the acts of a play. New stories are generated as the action or situation unfolds. Eventually, however, each story comes to an end and is no longer newsworthy to the same degree. An example at the national level was the highly publicized explosion and crash of TWA Flight 800 that took place over Long Island Sound on July 18, 1996. One aspect or another of the crash made news for months as new information became available. The first act began with eyewitness accounts and versions offered by spokespersons for federal agencies investigating the causes of the crash. Additional acts came when bodies were counted and memorial services were held; still others were in the news as people of note speculated about the cause and as additional pieces of wreckage were recovered. By early 1997, the story had moved into its final act as only an occasional report was generated about the incident.

A rather different time-related category is *continuing* news. Here, there is no clear beginning or end, but only an ongoing series of related happenings. Each time some related event occurs, stories can be generated about the ongoing process. A good example is the issue of abortion. Protests, counterprotests, court cases, and political debates about women's rights to have abortions have provided a continuing theme around which stories have been developed for more than a decade. It is a story focus that is unlikely to come to an end. Other examples of continuing news are issues related to the use of drugs, nuclear waste dumps, development versus the environment, the death penalty, assisted suicide, and the American trade deficit.

## Hard versus Soft News

Two additional categories that are somewhat time-related can be seen in the distinction between **hard news** and **soft news.** The former is what most ordinary people think of as news. Something actually happens on a particular day—a bank is robbed, a murder is committed, a bridge collapses. Time is an important consideration in such stories. They are news precisely because they are today's fresh happenings, and must be reported to the public as rapidly as possible.

Soft news, on the other hand, is not as time-critical. It focuses on situations, people, or events that have "human interest." Such stories are seldom based on events that are restricted to a particular day, and can be used in the news whenever they are needed. A classic example is the story of a pair of male and female eagles in the Syracuse, New York, zoo. Captured originally as part of a breeding program to reestablish eagles in the wild, the pair finally bred and the mother incubated an egg until a chick hatched. Then the mother died. Observers predicted disaster. Surprisingly, however, the male eagle took over the job of raising the newly hatched infant. The father fed the baby regularly, cleaned it, and so on, until it grew large enough to be released in the wild. The local media and the public loved it and these events provided an ongoing series of touching stories—a classic example of soft news.

▲
News comes in many forms. A common variety, which is the bread and butter of the industry, is spot news. This refers to stories about real events such as a fire, robbery, or airplane crash, as opposed to "pseudoevents" such as people saying things, planning things, or meeting about things. Spot news stories have no history and are neither developing nor ongoing. The reporter on the spot transmits his or her version of what happened to the newsroom, where it is processed for dissemination via some medium. (© John Burr/The Gamma Liaison Network)

## ▼ *How News Facts Get Distorted*

To what sources do news gatherers turn to obtain facts, and what problems with each source can cause a story to depart from reality? In this section we identify a number of traditional sources and others that have come with the technological developments of our time, plus some of the ways facts from such sources can be unwittingly distorted.

# Media and the Liberal Arts

## The Press as a Representative of the Public
### A Linchpin to Philosophy and Ethnic Studies

It is not uncommon for members of minority groups to criticize bitterly the mainstream American media. Their unhappiness with the press might be reduced to a single word: representativeness. African-Americans, Asian-Americans, Latinos, and Native Americans (as well as other groups that have historically lacked much social or economic power, such as women, the handicapped, the elderly, and gay people) have argued that the mainstream press does not fairly represent them or their interests. Further, they claim, one of the reasons for this state of affairs is that the important decision makers on the staffs of American newspapers, magazines, and broadcast stations tend not to be representative of any of these groups.

That news content and coverage should fairly and accurately represent what a given group or interest is doing in society does not sound like an unreasonable expectation. Its basis, though, is the cause of some debate both in the media community and in the courts. The question is whether the concept of representation, which enjoys an honorable history in public law and philosophy, squares with freedom of the press. The "command of the press" clause of the First Amendment states only that "Congress shall make no law . . . abridging the freedom of speech, or of the press." It says nothing about requiring the press to be fair, objective, or representative. Indeed, the framers of the

Constitution believed that the rationale for a press unconstrained by censorship was twofold: to give the public a free flow of information and to provide a forum for opinions of all kinds.

Still, the idea of the press as a representative of the people is an assumption on which most journalists operate and that permeates many details of their day-to-day work. This concept was discussed in the 1947 Commission on Freedom of the Press, which declared that the public deserves "a truthful, comprehensive and intelligent account of the day's events." The Commission went further, arguing that the news media should provide "a representative picture of the constituent groups of society."[5] Some scholars have linked this formulation with the concept of representation as it is defined in political science, wherein the press has a role much like that of the more formal aspects of representative government such as the legislature and the executive.[6] In fact, the idea of the press as the fourth branch of government—the fourth estate—is directly linked to the idea of representation.

The great British legal commentator William Blackstone wrote that every person has "an undoubted right to lay whatever sentiments he pleases before the public: to forbid this is to destroy freedom of the press."[7] Blackstone's work provided a legal framework for the integration of ideas from such seventeenth-

and eighteenth-century philosophers as John Milton, John Locke, Jeremy Bentham, Thomas Hobbes, and Jean Jacques Rousseau; their views provided a basis for freedom of the press, drawing on such notions as self-expression, tolerance, the free flow of ideas—indeed, freedom itself. Direct links between these thinkers and others as seen in the letters of Cato and in *The Federalist Papers* were said to influence both the framers of the Constitution and subsequent legal commentators. Later such philosophers as James Mill and John Stuart Mill argued that freedom of the press was necessary to representative government.

For a long time the idea of the press as a representative of the people was buried in little-used treatises by philosophers, but in the 1970s the idea emerged again in U.S. Supreme Court decisions. In one case Justice Lewis Powell opined that "the press is the necessary representative of the public's interest . . . and the instrumentality which effects the public's right."[8] Recently, the concept of representation is most often invoked as a moral and ethical imperative by critics who argue that the press ought to give the public an accurate picture of what is actually happening in society. This objective, they assert, would be enhanced by a media workforce that is culturally more diverse—an idea most major media organizations are committed to at least in theory, if not always in practice.

Perhaps the source of news facts that most readily comes to mind is *direct observation*. Such "on-the-spot" covering of events or situations presumably gives the news gatherer the fullest access to the facts. A related source, which is very traditional in news gathering, is the *reports of witnesses*, who themselves have observed an event and who in interviews can provide eyewitness accounts. Another related source is the *expert*, who may not have observed the particular event in question, but who is knowledgeable about that general class of occurrences.

Many less personal sources are also used. One is the **news release**—a prepared handout provided to reporters by an organization (for instance, the Pentagon or a major corporation) to summarize the "official" version of some event or situation. Another impersonal source of facts is the many published *documents* news gatherers use, such as reports of business, educational, or governmental groups; technical journals; census reports; or summaries of economic trends. These can be found in libraries or in many cases via on-line computerized databases. Finally, *public records*, such as court, tax agency, or property ownership records, are widely used as sources of facts. Some are paper records; others are filed on magnetic tapes or other computer storage media.

Although professional standards prevailing among news gatherers demand a high degree of accuracy in observing and assembling facts, much evidence suggests that unwitting errors, biases, and misrepresentations of reality are inevitable when *any* of the previous sources are used. That is not to say that reporters or others in the news industries deliberately falsify the accounts they prepare. On the contrary, the majority try very hard to be factually meticulous. Nevertheless, for reasons that we will show, distortions always occur; it is largely a matter of degree. Furthermore, some sources pose far more problems of this nature than others.

## Problems of Selective Perception

Contrary to what many people suppose, direct observation of an event by a reporter does not guarantee accuracy in a news story. To understand how this can be, we need to understand how a reporter proceeds when trying to observe a situation in order to put together a coherent account of what happened.

Good reporters trying to understand an event do exactly what all human observers do. They focus on what appears to them to be the central details or core of the matter and proceed from there. They cannot possibly notice and comprehend every detail about an occurrence, even if they see it firsthand. Like all human beings, they perceive, interpret, and recall events *selectively*. Exactly what they observe and recall will be a product of their own unique sets of needs, beliefs, attitudes, values, and other cognitive factors, such as memory schemata, that inevitably bias their interpretations.

For example, to perceive and make sense out of an occurrence, a reporter must use categories of thought defined by the *language* with which he or she is familiar. To illustrate the point, imagine a reporter who has just arrived on a scene where hundreds of people are watching a smaller number of people

▶

Reporters covering an event such as a riot must describe what happened using the words that they know in their daily language and that will be understood by readers or viewers. Often, the meanings commonly aroused by those words have a poor fit with the actual facts of the event. Thus, a disturbance on a street corner can be called a "riot," which enhances the drama for the audience but distorts the actual facts. (© Gregory Foster/The Gamma Liaison Network)

milling around, shouting, and looking angry. The term that he or she uses to think about such an event is *mob*. Therefore, the reporter "sees" a "mob." Suppose, then, that a handful of the individuals get mad, begin to throw stones or bottles, and even smash a few windows. A word commonly used to describe such behavior is *riot*, and the reporter "sees" that behavior through perceptual glasses provided by this term. Suppose further that a few of the people in the crowd decide to run away quickly after seeing stones and bottles being thrown. When this happens, the reporter "sees" people *panic*.

Putting it all together, the reporter's habitual modes of perceiving and thinking about such events are shaped by the meanings we all share for words in our language. These meanings lead to the preparation of a story about "an unruly mob that participated in a riot and caused people to panic." From the reporter's point of view, those are the *facts*—he or she was there and "saw it all firsthand." The additional facts that the majority of the people were merely onlookers, did not throw anything, and did not run away, will probably not be central features in the resulting news story. The member of the media audience on receiving this account will imagine hordes of terrified people fleeing in confusion. They will not imagine that such activity was confined to a few and that the majority were just standing around.

The point is that every firsthand observer perceives and recalls a unique pattern of interpretations and recollections. Firsthand reports are always based on selective experience and cannot represent the full range of reality as it actually exists. This is not to criticize reporters, who may indeed do better than most

The news process begins when a reporter observes an event or interviews eyewitnesses who give accounts of what happened. Whether the reporter's story is recorded on tape or in writing, it contains distortions because all observers see and interpret sequences of events selectively. Reporters are undoubtedly quite objective, but even they perceive events selectively, couch their reports in a particular language, and depend for interpretation on their own attitudes and values. Because these factors introduce bias, the story can never be a full and totally accurate account of what really happened (Spencer Grant/The Picture Cube)

of us in describing what happened in a given situation. Nevertheless, news reports prepared by on-the-spot observers always contain biases arising from the selective nature of perception that characterizes all human beings.

## Compounded Selectivity

But what about secondhand accounts? For most events in the news, reporters are not eyewitnesses but must rely on the recalled accounts and claims of others. Here, we have a situation of *compounded selectivity*. Reporters often try to minimize biased viewpoints by interviewing more than one witness, seeking "corroboration" from such sources. Yet this is really no guarantee of either accuracy or objectivity. Every witness who actually observes an event firsthand puts together an account based on his or her own unique interpretations and perceptual biases. However, insofar as we all share a similar language and culture, parallels are inevitable. These parallels do not mean that the witness reports reflect reality accurately. Even though they appear to corroborate each other, both parties could simply be creating the same distortions. Moreover, the reporter will selectively perceive and recall the accounts of witnesses—adding his or her own distortions to theirs.

To understand an event being reported in the news, reporters may seek the interpretations or advice of an "expert." Because such individuals may understand the type of event well, the expert may seem a far better source than an untrained witness. However, if the expert did not personally see the event under discussion, his or her "facts" are but interpretations, conjectures, and assumptions based on past observations of similar cases that have led to generalizations about what usually happens. No specific event is an exact du-plicate of others in a class of events. The ancient saying *exceptio probat regula* (the exception probes the rule) remains true. Whether the opinions of any ex-pert about what *usually* takes place are a close representation of what *actually* took place in a particular instance is anyone's guess.

Thus, the reporter interviewing witnesses and experts exercises a second level of selectivity when assembling the results of interviews into a story. He or she may have posed the questions in a biased or leading way, or misunder-stood or ignored comments by the witnesses. Any witness may be reluctant to disclose some of what he or she saw or heard. The point here is that—even with the best of training and intentions—the more removed the reporter is from direct observation of the actual events, the less correspondence there will be between the report prepared and the true nature of what happened.

## "Idealized" News Releases

Even more troublesome are accounts of an event or situation prepared for reporters by the public affairs (read public relations) personnel of an organi-zation. Often, reporters have no opportunity to see the situation or event first-hand or even to interview people who were actual participants. They go to the relevant group's spokesperson (read public relations officer), who conveniently provides them with a written or verbal account of what the group *claims* took place. Indeed, as we pointed out in a previous chapter on the nature of pub-lic relations, such accounts are used very heavily by the press. Because all groups and agencies have their own agendas, and a need to protect them-selves, there is every reason to suspect that such handouts or press conferences provide idealized accounts of what transpired. That does not mean that they present false accounts. It can mean that what is presented is quite selective. Again, the distance between the resulting news story and the actual events it presumably represents has increased, and correspondence with reality is an unknown.

## Limitations of Public Documents

Today, few knowledgeable reporters go directly to a library and start rummag-ing through published reports from government, industry, educators, or wher-ever. They first undertake searches of on-line databases for the information they need. The thousands of databases available contain summarized or com-plete documents pertaining to almost any subject about which someone has published an article or written a book. Many newspapers now maintain sub-scriptions to such database services as Lexis/Nexis (providing full text of thou-sands of news-oriented publications) or more technical databases that contain summaries of hundreds of publications.

Can distortions be present in such documents? Of course they can. Indeed, the distortions can be significant. Just because a document resides in a library or a computer file does not guarantee that it is any more accurate than one obtained from any other source. In particular, summaries and abstracts are by definition abridged versions of originals. As such, they are inherently likely to be selective.

Another problem with public documents is *access*, especially to the electronic records produced by public agencies. At all levels of government, records of every kind are increasingly being kept not on paper, which is cumbersome and expensive, but on computer data tapes. Although the federal governments, and each of the states, has freedom of information laws, they often do not provide the access to records journalists want. For example, in Massachusetts it is not possible to obtain the computer files containing the records of felony convictions. The reason, says the legislature that promulgated this particular statute, is that this protects the privacy of those who have "paid their debt to society." Justifying this position, supporters of the law point out that the trials in which such people were convicted were open to the public. The fact that no one could possibly attend hundreds of such trials, or that information on offenders is often needed long after the trial is over, seems not to be relevant. Thus, in situations of this kind, reporters are barred from the facts even before they undertake to prepare a news story that includes information about a crime that took place at an earlier time.

## ▼ *Encoding Strategies for Packaging the News*

The second major stage in the news process occurs as stories are **encoded**—that is, transformed within news organizations into versions deemed suitable to be transmitted to the public by their particular medium. Encoding is different for newspapers, magazines, radio, television, or the Internet. Modifications and repackaging of news stories occur at this stage for a variety or reasons. One encoding strategy is based on the need to emphasize certain *news values* in selecting stories, so as to make the report interesting enough to capture and hold the attention of the audience. Another encoding strategy is based on the need to *format* news stories, so as to organize the ways or sequences within which its facts are presented. Finally, encoding strategies must fit with the *journalistic style* preferred by a particular newspaper, magazine, broadcasting group, or on-line service. Each of these encoding strategies will be discussed in more detail.

A second consideration in encoding arises from the ways in which the newspapers, magazines, and broadcasters *organize their daily agenda* or list of stories actually printed or broadcast. Stories received from reporters are positioned in the paper or news broadcast along with advertising and other content. That position may be more or less prominent or obscure—on the front page or back near the obituaries, at the beginning of the broadcast, or following the weather report. All of these decisions influence the way people interpret a story and can erode the relationship between news reports and truth. Journalism scholar Walter Lippmann said it very well in 1922, when he wrote:

> "Every newspaper when it reaches the reader is the result of a whole series of selections as to what items shall be printed, in what position they shall be printed, how much space each shall occupy, what emphasis each shall have. [Thus] . . . news and truth are not the same thing, and must be clearly distinguished."[9]

For many understandable reasons, then, Lippmann's dictum aptly describes the news—*news and truth are not the same thing*. In addition to the problems of selective perception, many kinds of judgments must be made by editors, news directors, and others in the chain of command, about story size, content, location, balance with other reports, ethical status, ideological slant, and general suitability for the particular medium. The end result of this processing by the organization is that the medium's news stories present versions of reality to the public that are far removed from the actual events that actually happened. This does not imply a deliberate attempt to mislead the public. Such distortions result from the ways in which news media function within our particular society.

## Traditional News Values

In organizing facts into an actual news story, a crucial requirement is that the account of what happened must be as interesting and understandable as possible. If the audience finds it either dull or too complex, communication will fail. This requirement introduces a number of ways in which news accounts are encoded. Thus, decisions have to be made about which stories will be selected, how they will be written, and where they will be positioned in the daily paper or broadcast. As these choices are made, they result in quite different versions of reality.

Journalists have developed convenient criteria for judging the "newsworthiness" (that is, potential interest level) of stories. These criteria are called **news values,** and the account prepared must incorporate as many of them as possible. Both print and broadcast journalists use a number of considerations to judge the general newsworthiness of a story. These criteria have been derived over a long period and represent a kind of historically distilled wisdom as to what the public wants to read, hear about, or view in news presentations. Thus, these news values are of considerable importance to reporters when they initially decide what is worth covering and when they prepare their initial accounts of what happened. News values also guide editors and news directors in making final decisions about what to print, put on the air, or put on the Net.

At least seven major criteria can be applied in assessing a particular story as an attractive candidate for presentation to the public. Few stories fit all. And, of course, some stories may be of great importance even if they fulfill none.

# EXPLAINING MEDIA EFFECTS
## Lippmann's News Distortion Theory of the Press

In 1919, Walter Lippmann, a journalism scholar, published an important article in which he advanced the earliest version of this theory. He expanded it in his now-classic work, *Public Opinion,* published in 1922. He developed the thesis that there are often significant differences between the descriptions of events and situations described by the newspapers and the meanings for those events that were reconstructed by the people who read about them.

Lippmann provided numerous examples of the great gap between the beliefs people entertain about the world and the factual features of that world. He pointed to the outbreak of World War I in Europe (which was a current situation in his time) and noted that for weeks after that terrible conflict erupted, many people had no idea that it was going on. (The press operated at a much slower pace in his time than it does today with worldwide satellite coverage.) People continued their lives and businesses as though they were still in peacetime.

Later, after the press falsely reported that an armistice had been signed five days before it actually was, people rejoiced that the war had ended. Meanwhile, the soldiers on both sides continued to fight. Significant numbers of men died on the battlefield while other people were celebrating, under the false belief, obtained from the press, that the terrible conflict had stopped. Thus, the actions taken by those rejoicing were terribly inappropriate in relation to the factual nature of reality.

The proper role of the press, said Lippmann, was to create "pictures in our heads of the world outside." But too frequently, he maintained, the process functioned poorly and the pictures presented by the press were false. Inevitably, then, the meanings and understandings people derived from press reports about the events of the world were also false. As a consequence, those false beliefs often led to behavior by the public that was sometimes tragic in its consequences.[10]

Strictly speaking, Lippmann's **news distortion theory of the press** pertains to the newspapers of his time. However, it is an early version of more contemporary theories that explain the role of all of the mass media in presenting "social constructions of reality" to the public— that is, meanings for the world, which they then use as guides to action. In that sense, it is as modern as today's network newscast. Although Lippman never put forth his theory as a set of systematic propositions, it can be summarized in the following terms:

**1.** The press continuously *monitors* events and situations occurring in the physical and social environment to identify potential news stories (the "surveillance" function).

**2.** To prepare news reports, the press *selects* from those events and situations those that news personnel believe will be of importance or interest to the populations that they serve.

**3.** Many factors beyond their control (time, technology, money, or opportunity) *limit the ability* of the press to investigate, describe, and transmit full details of all events and situations that come to their attention.

**4.** Because of these factors, news reports are often characterized by *selectivity, omissions,* and *distortions* in spite of efforts by the press to be objective, fair, and factual.

**5. Therefore:** When audiences construct their own meanings of news reports ("pictures in their heads") they often have *limited correspondence* with the facts of reality ("the world outside"), leading people to behave in ways unrelated to the original events and situations.

Nevertheless, in a practical sense, the news values listed next provide important guidelines for judging the newsworthiness of any particular story:

1. *Impact.* This criterion refers to the number of people whose lives will be influenced in some way by the subject of the story. For example, if workers in a local bakery decide to strike, it may have only a minor impact on the

majority of the community. There may be some inconvenience, but most people will be little affected. However, if postal workers go on strike, everyone is affected because no one will get mail. Thus, a news report about a bakery strike will have less impact than one about a postal strike and will be less newsworthy.

2. *Timeliness.* One of the most important features of news is that it should be presented to the public while it is fresh. News that is stale has less appeal. Thus, stories of recent events have higher news value than those about earlier happenings. Of particular value are stories brought to the public ahead of the competition. An older term for such a story is "scoop." Journalists like to claim, "You read it (or heard it, or viewed it) here first."

3. *Prominence.* Stories about people who are in the public eye have much higher news value than those about obscure people, even if the occurrences are the same. Thus, a story about a well-known football or basketball star who has a major problem would be more newsworthy than one about some unknown individual who had a similar difficulty. An example in recent years was the intense attention paid to the O.J. Simpson trials, or the death of Princess Diana in 1997. If they had been ordinary citizens, their tragedies would not have commanded the attention of the news media.

4. *Proximity.* Stories about events and situations in one's home community are more newsworthy than events that take place far away. A rather grim hypothetical example often used by journalists to illustrate the point is to equate the news value of various numbers of deaths at various distances. If a thousand people drown in a flood in a faraway country, the story has about the same news value as one describing how a hundred drowned in a distant part of the United States. That event, in turn, has about the same news value as a story concerning ten flood victims in one's own state. And finally, a story about those ten has about the same value as one describing a flood that drowns a single person in the local community.

5. *The bizarre.* An example that illustrates this criterion well is the oft-quoted definition of news attributed to John B. Bogart, who was the city editor of the *Sun* in New York during the 1880s: "When a dog bites a man," Bogart is purported to have said, "that's not news, because it happens so often. But if a man bites a dog, that is news." In any case, odd or peculiar events have always seemed more newsworthy than those of a routine nature. For that reason, the news media can usually be counted on to give space or time to sightings of Bigfoot, the appearance of a likeness of Mother Teresa on a cinnamon bun, reports of UFOs, or disappearances of ships or planes in the Bermuda Triangle.

6. *Conflict.* The rule here is that harmony is dull, but strife is newsworthy. Stories that describe such events as messy divorces or child custody battles, rebellions, personal vendettas, and other kinds of clashes are high in news value. Thus, what transpired at a meeting of an organization devoted to promoting lasting peace might make dull news, unless a fist fight broke out—that would make a good story.

7. *Currency.* More value is attributed to stories pertaining to issues or topics that are in the spotlight of public concern than to those about which people care less. Thus, as we entered the late 1990s, President Clinton's problems with Paula Jones and the alleged unethical behavior of Newt Gingrich were high on the public's agenda. Stories related to those topics had high value. They were replaced with alleged campaign finance violations during much of 1997. Those too were replaced with more current concerns in the ever-changing news agenda.

Essentially, then, the news industry greatly prefers stories that their accumulated wisdom identifies as those in which public will be most interested. The cost of using such criteria to define newsworthiness is that many stories will be ignored that are in fact truly significant from other points of view. For example, discoveries by scientific researchers may be of historical importance, contribute to betterment of the human condition, or advance the frontiers of knowledge. However, they may be judged as dull. If so, they are likely to be found in the back pages or in the last part of the newscast (if they appear at all).

## Story Formats

A second major encoding consideration is that the story itself must be packaged in one of the *formats* that prevail in the relevant news medium, so as to make it understandable while maintaining or increasing its interest. Over many decades, journalists have worked out effective ways of organizing news stories that will accomplish those objectives. By tradition, one general format for a well-written newspaper story is that it tells *who* did *what, where, when* and *why.* These "five w's" set forth the essential features of any good news story and are the basic format that every beginning journalism student learns. In large part, they remain the way in which working print journalists package most of their stories. This plan for story organization is also used in broadcast journalism. However, the requirements of radio, and especially television, are quite different from those of print and allow enhancements to the standard print format.

A second traditional way in which news stories are organized is the so-called *inverted pyramid.* It too has long been used by all of the news media, but is especially relevant to newspaper stories. The basic idea is that the most important ideas should appear first. Journalists learned early that many people read only the headlines. Others read the "lead" sentence, or perhaps the first paragraph or two, and then go on to the next story. Thus, the important ideas need to be set forth at the beginning, and overall the account should both be interesting and make few intellectual demands. Journalists have little confidence in the willingness of the average citizen to linger over complex details or sophisticated analyses. Many maintain that in writing stories they always use the KISS system (keep it simple, stupid).

Broadcast journalists, of course, must also use formats. Radio and television news stories often use the criteria of news values, the five w's, and the

▶

Broadcast journalists use a variety of more or less standard formats to encode their stories. Some are more complex and expensive than others, but can be used to enhance viewer interest. A common but expensive format is the "standup with package," in which a reporter on the scene interviews a witness and provides interpretation or comment. (Copyright © B. Daemmrich, The Image Works)

pyramid. However, a radio or television newscast has much greater flexibility and can use many variations to maintain audience interest. Radio news can incorporate "actualities"—sound effects, such as the noise of a log being sawed in a news report on a lumber mill. Television is even more flexible. For example, the simplest format for a TV newscast is the **word story,** where the anchor person is shown behind a desk telling what happened. A variant is to provide a graphic that appears in the upper corner of the screen, with an identifying phrase keyed to the story. Another TV format is the **VOT** (voice-over tape), in which the viewer first sees the anchor person, but is then switched to a video tape with the anchor's voice over the ongoing picture. Still another is the **stand-up,** in which the anchor switches to a reporter in the field who makes comments at the scene. The **stand-up with package** is similar, with the reporter interviewing someone at the scene. Several versions of such formats are regularly used in producing TV news in an effort to create audience interest and to provide richer information. All of these have the possibility of introducing meanings into a story that modify it in selective ways.

## Alternative Journalistic Styles

Finally, while the ideals of fairness, objectivity, and accuracy continue to be approved by the news industry, a number of alternative **journalistic styles** can be used. These, too, can reshape meanings. Styles are based on the idea that a particular set of facts can be combined into a news story in a variety of ways. A considerable number of such styles have emerged within journalism over the years. Some are far more widely used than others, but each has had its period of popularity, and each has left its mark on the contemporary news industries. Morover, each presents the story within a different framework of meaning.

**Sensational journalism.**   This style characterized the press from the late 1800s to about 1920. It stressed shocking details, bizarre events, and sometimes appalling transgressions of the social norms. The newspapers of the time thrived on implications of scandal and sin in high places. For example, if a murder had been committed, the crime was described with special attention to the appearance of the corpse, the look of the blood, suggestions of illicit sex, and the insidious nature of the killer. Facts, in such an account, are of secondary importance. The sensational style is alive and well in such tabloids as the *National Enquirer* and similar publications sold chiefly in supermarkets.

**Objective journalism.**   Sensationalism gave way to objectivity, which generally prevailed until about mid-century. In 1950, Alan Barth of the *Washington Post* wrote with pride, "The tradition of objectivity is one of the principal glories of American journalism."[11] In reality, that opinion was not universally held. As an examination of the trade journals of the 1940s and 1950s quickly shows, objectivity had been under fire for generations. For a few years, however, there was almost complete consensus among most journalists and consumers that objectivity was a vast improvement over the sensational journalism that characterized the earlier American press.

Generally speaking, objectivity is a style that has traditionally been characterized by three aims: (1) separating *fact from opinion*, (2) presenting an *emotionally detached view* of the news and (3) striving for *fairness and balance*—giving both sides an opportunity to reply in a way that provides full information to the audience. By world standards, American reporters had long been (and still are) relatively objective. For decades they have tried hard to separate fact and opinion, keeping factual accounts in the news columns and opinion on the editorial page. However, beginning in the 1960s an increasing number of critics have denied that this can be done. They claim that no human being is capable of complete objectivity. Anchorman Dan Rather maintains that objectivity is an impossible goal and urges reporters to adopt fairness as their standard instead.

The challenge to objectivity occurred in part because critics had come to feel that American journalism was lifeless—unemotional and incapable of dealing with great social problems. There is much to be said for this view. For example, during the first half of the century, the press had virtually ignored the predicament of blacks, other minorities, and the poor, and the rising tide of civil rights frustration. Many American journalists acted as if objectivity were an established characteristic rather than a yet-to-be-achieved ideal. The typical response to those who said coverage was unfair or inadequate was, "We just report the news." This claim that the press was objective seemed to many to be a rather arrogant refusal to face complaints, and it often enraged critics.

During the 1960s, the press was criticized with a vigor it had not encountered before. In this fate it had much company; during the same period most American institutions were challenged by widespread distrust and a search for new approaches. The outcome was that several alternative styles for presenting news stories emerged, and although they did not revolutionize the press, they have influenced contemporary journalism. To understand how, we can examine a few of these alternatives more closely. They included the *"new"*journalism, along with *advocacy* and *precision* journalism. Today, objectivity is still dominant, but these newer styles are currently used to some extent in both the print and broadcast media, although because of government regulation, most of them are more difficult to implement in broadcasting.

**The "new" journalism.**    This style was never an issue of great concern to the public, but it did alter the reigning definitions of news and writing forms within the profession. The first stirrings of the new journalism came from three sources. One was journalists on newspapers and magazines who felt restricted by the traditional formats such as the inverted pyramid. Another was literary figures, especially novelists, who wanted to say something in a direct way about the nation's discontents. The third was broadcast journalists eager to explore less conventional sources and language.

Journalists looking for change felt that traditional procedures were not effectively capturing the essence of the great social movements of the day or the changes in lifestyle. They felt that both the customary reliance on official sources (mainly public officials) and the conventional avoidance of rich description prevented them from capturing the tone of the great changes taking place during the 1960s and later. As a result, they maintained, it was impossible to give the public the full story of what was happening. For example, the so-called "counterculture," which influenced millions of young people during the period, was not presented fully in newspapers and newscasts because it was not tied to "authoritative" sources.

The result was that several young writers began experimenting with new techniques. The new journalists engaged in *scene setting,* using many descriptive adjectives to give the reader a sense of being there. Another technique was *extended dialogue.* Instead of using a few well-honed quotations, the new journalists used long passages of dialogue to capture the essence of a person's language. Rather than trying to be detached and objective, they provided a *point of view*—sometimes allowing the attitudes or values of their sources to dominate their stories. To portray the thoughts of the people who were the news sources, as the sources reported them to the journalist, an *interior monologue* might be included. Finally, instead of quoting all sources by name, the new journalists sometimes created a *composite character* who brought together the characteristics of several people and stood for, say, the average prostitute or police officer.

All these devices are old tools of fiction writers. The new journalists claimed that these methods allowed them to offer a richer and truer portrait than the traditional news style permitted. These new journalists were not necessarily political activists; they wanted to observe and report on America's manners and morals in an exciting way instead of merely quoting official sources. The methods of fiction writers helped them do so.

Despite controversy and criticism, the new journalism style continues to influence the conventions of the media generally. By the 1980s and continuing into the 1990s, the new journalism's techniques were commonplace in radio and television documentaries, magazines, nonfiction novels, and newspapers. For the most part, however, the influence of the new journalism has been not overwhelming or revolutionary but rather subtle and indirect.

**The advocacy style.**    Another alternative to objectivity is the **advocacy style.** Here, the reporter and the story identify with and "advocate"—that is, try to promote—a cause or position. Unlike editorial writing, advocacy journalism appears in news columns and is not a simple statement of opinion. In a sense, it is a kind of hybrid news story that promotes a particular point of view. Thus, it departs from traditional journalism, and from investigative reporting, which we discuss in a later section.

Advocacy journalism appears mostly in magazines, although a few well-known broadcast journalists, such as Geraldo Rivera, are unabashed advocates, doing stories with no pretense of balance or fairness. Rivera, a controversial figure, broke into broadcasting with his exposés of such situations as mental hospital conditions, inner-city corruption, and negligence toward the poor and minorities. Advocacy journalists see themselves as torchbearers for justice and pursue their mission knowing that plenty of people are promoting an opposite point of view. Critics see them as undisciplined mouthpieces for a single side of an issue. Advocacy reporting is not widely practiced, and most studies of journalists show that it is not particularly admired in the field.

**Precision journalism.**    A very different style that is becoming increasingly important is **precision journalism.** Essentially, it is a style of reporting and writing that makes use of some of the methods of the social sciences to gather and analyze quantitative information for the purposes of preparing news stories. It takes two forms: in *active* precision journalism, reporters actually conduct surveys or other research projects; in *reactive* precision journalism, they use reports already assembled by government agencies, universities, and private firms and develop stories around the data the reports provide.

The basic goal of precision journalists is to present to the public understandable analyses based on quantitative information relevant to significant issues in the news. For example, traditional journalists often interview people selected casually or conveniently so as to portray the opinions of "people in the street" concerning a forthcoming bond issue to build a new convention center. In contrast, the precision journalist would interview a sample of citizens, selected according to the rules of scientific sampling, so as to obtain a more representative summary of the views shared in the community.

Although precision journalism is not the same as scientific research, its goal is to obtain quantitative information that permits more accurate analyses of issues in the news. It makes extensive use of tables and graphs, often supplemented by interviews that serve as examples. Thus, it cannot be applied to many kinds of stories. It does not replace traditional journalism; it simply makes the news more accurate where quantitative information is important. Reporters using this style must have training in basic methods of the social sciences, including the use of statistical tests and computer data processing.

**Civic or public journalism.**    This recently developed style of journalism often involves projects aimed at diagnosing and solving community problems. It is a journalistic effort to promote and achieve "civil society"—voluntary efforts that improve the quality of life for the public. It moves beyond just telling the news into attempts to revive civic life and to improve public dialogue. Widely practiced by today's newspapers and some television stations, its goal is to keep the press grounded in the concerns of ordinary people, rather than in those of the elite. Essentially, this form of journalism identifies problems to be solved, such as a high crime rate in the community, political corruption, or taxes that are imposed unevenly in different neighborhoods, and attempts to assist in their solution. The newspaper or TV station reports on citizens' meetings, assemblies and other cooperative efforts where problems are aired, often taking sides in controversies.[12]

Advocates argue that traditional journalism is no longer trusted by the public and that this strategy can restore confidence. Journalism needs a rebirth, they maintain, as a more democratic profession concerned with the problems of ordinary people. Critics warn that it moves journalism away from its traditional impartial and disinterested stance to that of political activists pushing a

One of the problems of the news industry is that far more stories are available every day than can be fit into the newspaper's space or into the time available in a typical half-hour TV broadcast. Decisions must be made as to which stories to accept, whether they need to be shortened, and where to place them in the paper or broadcast. These are gatekeeping and agenda-setting decisions made by editors and news directors using a variety of criteria. (Copyright © John Neubauer, PhotoEdit)

particular agenda. They reject the notion that social problems can be fixed through journalism by having news columns take sides in local disputes. Such efforts are inappropriate, they maintain, or even arrogant. Although at present the movement toward civic journalism appears to be growing, its ultimate fate is unclear. The term means different things to different people. It is today's journalistic chic, but in the long run it may turn out to represent either a long-term trend or merely a fad.

## Social and Cultural Influences on Decisions in News Organizations

Two sets of social and cultural factors play a significant part in shaping decisions as to what is finally transmitted to the public after specific news stories are passed from reporters to editors and news directors. First, influences arise from the *social organization of newsrooms*. These include a number of particular editorial and production roles within the teams that decide news policy, selecting the final assortment of stories that will make up the paper or the newscast. The second set of influences is broader, consisting of the *cultural constraints* on news organizations posed by the basic nature of private enterprise itself, as defined within our society. Both are important in shaping and reshaping the meaning of a news story.

**The social organization of the newsroom.**   Each news medium—newspapers, magazines, radio, and television—has a pattern of social organization. These patterns influence encoding decisions and therefore the nature of the news story as it is finally produced. At the top are those that own the organization as a business enterprise. We have already reviewed patterns of ownership among the major media (Chapters 3, 4, 6, and 7). The owners, or their corporate representatives at the top, seldom exert direct control over specific news stories. However, they do set broad guidelines as to which styles of journalism are to be emphasized and where the organization will locate itself along a liberal to conservative continuum.

Managers make up a second stratum. Upper-level managers are generally sensitive to the orientations of the owners. Theirs is the task of running the organization on a day-to-day basis, setting its more specific operating policies, and making certain that it achieves its goals. Below them are the middle managers—editors, directors, and producers whose daily task it is to assemble the content of the newspaper, get the magazine ready for the printer, or produce the news program in final form for broadcasting. Often, the personal preferences and values of these managers influence the ways in which news stories are finally shaped.

News stories flow to the newsroom from reporters, stringers, freelancers, and the "wires." Here they are reviewed and reshaped by this hierarchy of editors and managers. At the core of this reshaping is the fact that so much is happening in the world, the nation, the state, and the local area that there is simply not enough time or space to bring it all to the attention of the public. In producing the daily newspaper, for example, the various ads and announcements that provide financial support must be accommodated first. If they were not, the paper would soon go broke. Certain other material that is not news must also appear in the daily paper: weather reports, stock market quotations, editorials, the crossword puzzle, the comics, and so on. As noted in Chapter 3, the space that is left— generally only about a quarter or less of the paper—is called the *news hole*, and it is into that 20 to 25 percent of the paper that the news of the day must be fit. Because there is always more news than space, only two kinds of decisions can be made to fit the news into the hole. They are to drop or to shrink stories prepared by the reporters. The editor, often with a heavy hand, removes details that seem expendable—and again the gap widens between reality and its description in the news story.

To deal with the excessive number of stories that flow into the newsroom via the "wire" (by satellite today), wire editors read all the stories that accumulate up to a particular time and select ones they view as important and suitable. Once again, through a process of selection, the gap widens between what happened in the "world outside" and what is reported in the newspaper.

In the television or radio news organization a similar process takes place. The thirty minutes allowed for the newscast includes time that must be set aside for introductory and closing material, the various commercials that support the program, and mandatory features such as weather, sports, and reports on the stock market. The time left can be used for presentation of the news. After the amount of time left over is identified, the editing process begins. News directors review the stories prepared by reporters and those received from network sources. They select the ones to be included and complete the process of fitting the material into the available time. Editors review taped reports, shorten scenes, drop details, and sometimes cut entire stories. The end result is the station's version of what happened today. It may or may not be close to what actually took place. Chances are that it is not.

These processes of selection and elimination of details or even entire stories are called **gatekeeping.** This complex process is a central part of all news editing and production systems. Individuals at different positions—editors, news directors, and others—have to make decisions about including or excluding material from news presentations.[13] Obviously, gatekeeping significantly influences the selective construction of reality to be reported by the press.

**Consequences of the profit motive.**    Real people invest real dollars in newspapers, magazines, broadcasting stations, cable, and on-line systems. Logically enough, they expect to make real profits. What critics protest is not so much the idea that media owners make a return on investment, but *what the owners do* to maximize their profits. However, Americans value a profit-driven market economy—so much so that we now avidly support its development in all parts of the world. There is no denying that the profit motive will continue to exert powerful influences on what the public receives as news.

# EXPLAINING MEDIA EFFECTS

## *Gatekeeping Theory*

The need for a newspaper or broadcaster to select a particular line-up of stories from those available begins with the fact that the press continuously exercises a *surveillance* function. News gatherers constantly feed into editorial offices or newsrooms a huge number of stories about what is happening out there in the community, region, society, and world. There is so much going on, however, that far more stories are generated than can be included in the daily news presentation of a particular paper or news broadcast. Therefore, some system for *screening* and *selecting* must be in place to sort out what will be reported to the public and what will be ignored. That process of screening and selecting has come to be known as *gatekeeping*.

The term "gatekeeping" was first used in this way (to label screening, decision making, and selecting) as a result of an important study conducted for the government during World War II.[14] The federal government sponsored research designed to determine how housewives could be persuaded to buy, prepare, and serve to their families cuts of meat (kidneys, heart, liver, and so on) that were not needed to feed the armed forces. It was conducted by Professor Kurt Lewin, a distinguished social psychologist of the time. Logically enough he first

made a thorough study of how decisions were made by housewives (who at the time normally purchased foods and prepared family meals) to select specific kinds of foods, including meats. He used the analogy of a *gate,* letting certain products through to the family table and keeping others out. Lewin reasoned that knowing who the *gatekeepers* were, and the *criteria* they used in making their selections, would provide essential information for designing persuasive campaigns directed toward those gatekeepers to increase the selection and consumption of organ meats during the war.

This research came to be widely read almost at once. As a consequence, the term "gatekeeping" came to be applied to a variety of decision-making functions, including the flow of news. Thus, only four years after World War II ended, David Manning White realized that the editor in charge of the wire service, who selected many of the stories that would appear in the daily newspaper, was acting as a "gatekeeper." He decided to make a study of his own gatekeeping role, and how his decisions were made. An article that he published in 1950 spelled out what he discovered. Since that time, gatekeeping has come to be seen as an important part of the process by which news is

collected, edited, and published as part of the daily news agenda.

**1.** In exercising its "surveillance" function, every news medium, whether newspaper, radio, television, or other, has a *very large number* of news stories brought to its attention daily by "wire" services, reporters, and other sources.

**2.** Due to a variety of practical considerations, only a *limited amount of time or space* is available in any medium for its daily presentations of the news to its audience.

**3.** Within any news organization, there exists a *complex set of criteria* for judging a particular news story—criteria based on organizational policy, personal preferences, definitions of newsworthiness, conceptions of the nature of the relevant audience, and beliefs about fourth estate obligations.

**4.** Those complex criteria are used by editors, news directors, and other personnel who *select a limited number* of news stories for presentation to the public and encode them in ways that the needs of the medium are met.

**5. Therefore:** Personnel in the news organization become *gatekeepers*, letting some stories pass through the system but keeping others out, thus limiting and controlling the public's knowledge of the actual events occurring in reality.

Nowhere is the problem better illustrated than in the case of network television news. A little over a decade ago, news gathering and broadcasting were supported by all of the other programming offered by the networks. The news programs themselves were not expected to show a profit. Their ratings were not as high as those of entertainment programming, and advertisers did not flock to news programs as a context for their commercials. Subsidizing the news was seen as similar to the system in newspapers. The news part of the paper is not expected to operate profitably on its own. The revenues from the newspaper as a whole provide funding for news gathering, editorial functions, printing, and the like.

However, when cable and the VCR began to eat into audience shares for network television, both corporate leadership and news policies changed significantly. The new policies declared that the news had to earn its own keep. It had to develop ways of offering the news that would increase ratings so as to make news broadcasts more attractive to advertisers. Under these new policies, the networks pared news teams down sharply to cut costs. Even cameras were automated to save labor costs (Tom Brokaw's three cameras at NBC—privately called "Curly," "Larry" and "Moe" after the "Three Stooges"—are computer-operated; the former human operators were laid off).

Far more important, however, were corporate decisions to define news program content in different ways. It had to be more fun to watch, so as to bring in more viewers. Less funding was to be available for such frills as investigative reporting, on-the-spot coverage, camera teams in foreign lands, or opinion and analysis. Instead, new kinds of programming were designed, sometimes even "staging" or "recreating" news events. For example, when NBC News initiated a series called "Bad Girls," critics called it lurid sensationalism. The same group came up with "Women Behind Bars," and a kind of syndicated tabloid called "Hard Copy," openly oriented toward sexual content. CBS News introduced "Saturday Night with Connie Chung," in which actors were hired to play parts. ABC did not go to such lengths, but it did produce "Prime Time Live," in which Diane Sawyer and Sam Donaldson provided entertaining interviews with interesting people. The relationship of such programs to news in a traditional sense is remote. Indeed, critics used the term "trivialization" of the news to describe such programming.

Out of these transformations of news substance came the concept, *infotainment*—a merging of information and entertainment—and now an important criterion for gatekeeping. From all that is available to news directors and editors, many selections appear to be made for their entertainment value, rather than because of their newsworthiness or their essential importance to society.

In greater or lesser degree, pressures toward trivialization exist in all of the news media, but it is a special problem for the networks. As the emphasis on infotainment has gradually become the television standard, most thoughtful analysts feel that the nation is being poorly served. Indeed, the question can be raised as to whether the reasons for protecting the TV news media with the First Amendment and with a body of shield laws and other legislation unique to this category of business make sense any more.

# ▼ Contrasting Conceptions of the Nature and Functions of News

Individual newspapers and broadcasters vary in how they resolve the conflict between the obligation to inform the public fully and the need to be profitable. The choice involved can be very well illustrated by comparing two almost completely opposite prevailing conceptions of the nature and functions of news. These are the *marketing approach*, which avidly pursues the goal of maximizing profits by selling news as a product and sharply limiting public service; and the *adversarial approach*, which sees news as information needed by the public and which emphasizes the watchdog functions of the press, often at the expense of profits. That these strategies coexist in sharp contrast shows the two very different paths our nation's press may follow in carrying out its surveillance function in the future.

## The Market Approach: News as a Product to Sell

A news organization that uses the market approach devotes considerable resources to the task of understanding what the audience wants to find in a news medium. Then, it makes certain that it serves those interests. The idea is to market the product—that is, the news—in much the same way as any other commercial commodity, like beer, soap, or breakfast cereal, is marketed.

This approach begins with extensive market research that assembles statistical data on the interests, media habits, and concerns of the audience. These data are then used as guidelines in determining what material will be offered, and especially, in what manner. Thus, both the content of news stories and the style in which they are offered to the public are selected on the basis of research findings that define what the audience wants most.

Of course, newspaper editors and publishers for decades have been concerned with what will and will not sell papers. The marketing approach, however, takes this concern a giant step further. News organizations using this strategy invest a great deal of time and money to find out what the public wants to read about, and what formats and styles they like best. The organizations then apply the answers methodically to shape their products. Thus, the marketing approach institutionalizes concern with the audience so as to enhance revenues, and it gives this concern priority stature in the process of selecting and encoding the news. Whether or not the resulting news accurately portrays the "world outside" is a secondary concern.

Marketing the news is not really a new idea. For many years, the marketing approach was used heavily by broadcasters. Newspapers were actually slow to adopt methods that broadcast stations had used routinely to calibrate their product to their audience. For example, the marketing approach has been applied to television news almost from its beginning, with changes in format and style often made to attract a larger audience. For years, print journalists often treated this practice with contempt. But in the early 1970s, managers and owners of metropolitan daily newspapers were appalled by their declining circulations per household. Soon print journalists had their own "news doctors." There seemed to be many causes for the declining circulation; competition from television, the growth of the suburbs, new life styles, and a lack of relevance in the papers were all blamed. The newspapers responded with market research designed to diagnose the "ills" causing the decline.

To end declines in newspaper circulation, the market researchers prescribed *change*, advising the newspapers to add new sections on topics such as lifestyles, entertainment, gardening, and housing—sections that help readers "use" their communities and their environment. These new sections are hardly "news." They are edited and written for audience interest and approval—infotainment. In some ways they represent extended and repackaged coverage of topics that have always been in the paper. For example, many newspapers covered real estate for years, but as a result of the marketing approach, some renamed the section "Shelter" or "Home" and began to treat the topic from the consumer's point of view—adding, for example, very personal stories about how to find an apartment or remodel a house. Similarly, in their lifestyle sections the newspapers print advice from "experts" on how people can solve their everyday problems—from how to get rid of stubborn stains to how to deal with a sulky child or a spouse's infidelity.

The best-known example of a newspaper that relies heavily on the marketing approach is the nationally circulated *USA Today*, which was designed on the basis of market research and which continues to make heavy use of research findings that indicate audience interests. *USA Today* not only selects its topics of coverage on the basis of guidelines from research, but has also pioneered the use of color, new styles of graphic presentation, and brevity (some say superficiality) in writing.

Does the marketing approach serve readers better, or does it pander to the lowest tastes? Philip Meyer, a leader in the precision journalism movement, suggested that it helps newspapers obtain and respond to feedback from their audiences and

*USA Today* has successfully become a national newspaper with a unique design. It makes effective use of market research to keep tabs on what kinds of news stories people like to read about and what encoding formats they like best. The newspaper's use of color, graphics, and a brief but clear writing style have contributed to its success. (Copyright © R. Lord, The Image Works)

thus to communicate with them more effectively.[15] Others maintain that it leads to trivialization of the news, especially in broadcasting. The consultants sometimes seem more concerned with the hairstyles of anchor people than with the substance of the stories. Perhaps it is too early to predict the marketing approach's lasting effects. As the approach has become increasingly commonplace, however, the definition of news has shifted further away from an emphasis on reports on public affairs and specific events, moving instead toward infotainment material that will gratify the audience.

## The Adversarial Approach: Watchdogs of the Public Interest

The role of the press as an adversary of government is the one most honored in the traditions of journalism. In this capacity the press has sometimes been called the *fourth estate*. Thomas Carlyle (1795–1881) attributed the phrase to Edmund Burke (1729–1797) who called the reporters' gallery in the English Parliament "a Fourth Estate more important by far" than the other three estates of Parliament—the lords, bishops, and commons.

It was because the right to speak out freely acted as a check on government, holding it accountable, that the American founders nurtured the principles of freedom of speech

▲ In recent years, some news media have relied heavily on the "marketing approach." News is regarded as a product to sell, like any other commodity. Extensive research is conducted to determine what subscribers or audiences want to read or hear about. Here editors choose attention grabbing photos to accompany stories. Although this strategy may not achieve the goal of a well-informed public, it does ensure that the medium will have audience appeal and improves its chances of making a profit. (© Jeff Albertson/The Picture Cube)

and protection of the right to public dissent. Today, the adversarial approach makes a critical contribution to society by increasing accountability and by exposing unsatisfactory conditions in both government and the private sector.

**Traditional investigative reporting.** Central to the adversarial approach is *investigative reporting*. This is a kind of news gathering in which the reporter probes deeply into a situation and assembles evidence that discloses whether or not there is something unusual, unethical, illegal, or even outrageous going on. Although the fact gathering may be done by a single reporter or a team of individuals working together, the decision to undertake such an investigation is made by editors who must provide the financial support and be ready to disclose and defend reports on what is uncovered.[16]

The professional organization, Investigative Reporters and Editors (IRE), defines such reporting in the following terms: *It is reporting, through one's own work product and initiative, matters of importance that some persons or organizations*

During the last century, investigative journalism was established as an important function of the American press. One of the pioneers of this tradition was Elizabeth Cochrane, who wrote under the byline of "Nellie Bly." In the 1870s and 1880s, she reported on many deplorable conditions that prevailed among poor working women and other disadvantaged groups. Her greatest investigative work was the exposure of the dreadful conditions that existed in an insane asylum on Blackwell's Island in New York. (The Bettmann Archive)

*wish to keep secret.* The three basic elements in this definition are that the investigation be the *work of the reporter*, not the report of an investigation made by someone else; that the subject of the story involves something of *reasonable importance* to the reader or viewer; and that others are attempting to *hide these matters* from the public.[17]

Investigative reporting started in the nineteenth century. Some view the first such investigation to have been conducted in the 1840s by James Gordon Bennett, the energetic publisher of the *New York Herald.* Dissatisfied with the usual stories of reporters covering the courts, he sought a way to provide more interesting accounts of serious crimes. He chose the occasion of the spectacular murder of a young prostitute. He personally went to the "fancy house" where she worked, interviewed the "madam," poked through the victim's personal papers, and even examined the unfortunate girl's remains. The resulting story, rich in details about the place and the people involved, made very interesting reading.

Investigative reporting reached dramatic heights late in the nineteenth century. An adventurous young woman, "Nellie Bly" (a *nom de plume;* her name was actually Elizabeth Cochrane), became famous as a result of her investigative report of Blackwell's Island, an insane asylum in New York. In an elaborate scheme, she posed as a mentally ill person and was committed to the asylum. There, continuing the deception, she saw firsthand how patients were treated. The doctors and staff had no idea she was a reporter, and she received very bad treatment for about ten days. Fortunately, she had prearranged with her newspaper, Joseph Pulitzer's *New York World,* to extricate her. They did so, and her exposé of conditions in the hospital gained worldwide attention.[18]

Early in this century, the journalists of the muckraker tradition investigated many private and governmental institutions (see Chapter 4). They uncovered and exposed corruption, abuse, and crime that characterized both private industry and government at the time. The contribution of the muckrakers to American society was far more than just interesting reading matter. Their exposés led to reform and legislation that still affect us today.[19]

American journalists have kept that great tradition alive. During the 1920s, they played an important part in exposing the Teapot Dome scandal, in which Secretary of the Interior Albert B. Fall leased drilling rights to federal oil reserves to private developers and received a large loan and gift in return. Fall was tried and convicted of receiving a bribe and was sentenced to a year in prison. Also implicated but never convicted was Harry M. Daugherty, U.S. Attorney General. The *New York Times* and other newspapers disclosed many details about the mess and kept the affair before the public. Although President Warren G. Harding was apparently not directly involved, the affair broke his presidency. (He died soon after the extent of the scandal became known.) Upton Sinclair, a controversial Pulitzer Prize-winning novelist and one of the original muckrakers, wrote *Oil,* a book about the scandal.

An extraordinary example of investigative reporting from the 1970s was the Watergate disclosures concerning the Nixon administration. Beginning in mid-1972 and continuing through 1973, the series of stories was developed by investigative reporters Carl Bernstein and Robert Woodward of the *Washington Post.* Their revelations dominated American news media for months, exposing a conspiracy by the White House staff, the CIA, and others to cover up a number of covert illegal activities carried out during the 1972 presidential election by White House aides. The ensuing congressional investigation eventually implicated the president and led to his resignation.

Today, investigative reporting seems to be on the increase in the American press. Although such reporting is expensive, new sources of information and new tools of analysis have become available. Advances in computer use for both data storage and information recovery permit reporters to develop stories based on a broader body of information than ever before.

**Using on-line information retrieval services.** On-line data services, operated by commercial vendors, are especially valuable for obtaining background material for the development of a story or an investigation. Starting in the 1970s, a few on-line information services became available. At first they were used mainly for bibliographic retrieval; that is, a user could find out from a database who had published what in, say, the scientific journals. Today, the thousands of different databases to which access can be obtained for fees contain information ranging from stock market prices and airline schedules to complete files of scientific articles on every conceivable topic. With a desktop computer and a modem permitting telephone access to large mainframe computers at remote sites, a user can retrieve vast amounts of information on virtually any subject.

**CAIR: Computer-assisted investigative reporting.** Government agencies at the national, state, and even local levels, have been moving away from the preparation and maintenance of vast files of paper records. In their place, they store the information much more efficiently in electronic data files on magnetic computer tape.[20] This trend actually began during the 1950s, but was largely ignored by journalists. They had no idea *how* such records could be examined, or indeed if they legally could be examined at all. Even if one knew how, it was not clear *why* one might want to undertake such an analysis.

During the next decade, Congress passed the Freedom of Information Act (FOIA), which supposedly made almost all government records available for inspection by the public. It was not clear at first whether FOIA also applied to electronic records. As it turned out, it took many court battles before interested citizens could have access to government computer tapes. Agencies preferred to keep their operations from public scrutiny, frustrating many would-be users. However, in the early 1970s a few pioneering newspapers, such as the *New York Times*, began to examine tapes produced by the NYPD—the city's police department. The goal was to check up how the police were handling their job and to make disclosures where irregularities were found. Such early analyses represent the beginnings of **CAIR,** or **computer-assisted investigative reporting.**

The analysis of computerized records is increasingly paying off for those who can access the data. Sometimes it is not all that difficult. An oft-quoted example that illustrates the advantages of the procedure is the "School Bus Driver" story developed in 1985 by reporters Elliot Jaspin and Maria Johnson of the *Providence Journal-Bulletin* (Rhode Island). Here is what happened: A series of tragic deaths of children in school bus accidents in Rhode Island prompted the newspaper to investigate to find the causes. Jaspin and Johnson began by getting a list of the several hundred school bus drivers in the state. Each driver had been screened by local police chiefs who had certified that he or she was a good and moral person with a safe driving record. Wondering if that were true, the reporters obtained the state's tapes on traffic offenses for the previous three years. They matched the bus drivers' names against those on tape and found that many school bus drivers actually had dreadful records. Some had driven under the influence of alcohol or drugs; others had invalid licenses, or none at all; some had been in serious accidents more than once. These findings led the now very suspicious reporters to get the court records of felony trials from the state and again compare names. They found that a number of drivers had been convicted, some for very serious crimes. Needless to say, there were a great many red faces among those who had certified the drivers. The final result was a major shakeup in procedures for certifying school bus drivers in the state.

Much more massive electronic records are generated at the federal level. Because of their extraordinary size, large and powerful mainframe computers must be used for their analyses, along with sophisticated software and advanced statistical techniques. This has virtually locked out journalists who want to look into the operation of some of our most important federal agencies. An example of such an analysis is that conducted by CAIR analyst Margaret DeFleur. Working with investigative reporter David Burnham, her objective was to examine the electronic records of the U.S. federal courts. These consisted of the complete records of all charges brought against individuals and all criminal and civil trials, plus all appeals transactions, for the ninety-two judicial districts in our fifty states for a seventeen-year period. The total was more than five-and-a half million charges, trials, and appeals. The analysis of such a body of information challenges the capacity of even the largest and fastest supercomputers.

The CAIR analysis revealed disquieting trends and comparisons that had never been exposed before. For example, there was evidence that over the most recent eight years there had been a considerable increase in the use of plea bargaining to dispose of federal cases. Moreover, in spite of our presumption of equal application of the law, great variations were found among the districts in terms of what types of cases (for example: violent crime, drug offenses, or organized crime) had been pursued by each prosecutor. Using the findings, supplemented by more traditional investigative techniques, reporters developed stories about their communities for a number of major newspapers around the country.[21]

There is a major lesson to be learned both from the school bus story and from the large-scale CAIR analysis of federal court records. It is that computer-assisted investigative reporting can reveal situations *that could never have come to light* using only traditional techniques—that is, leaks from informants, examination of selected paper documents, and personal interviews. These techniques remain valuable, but close examination of an agency's entire computer files opens a Pandora's box in which many well-hidden secrets come to light. These new technologies give some indication of what investigative reporting will be like in the twenty-first century, when the use of computers will continue to add to the traditional tools of journalism.

Generally, then, adversarial journalism has a long tradition and a clear future in the print media. However, today it is also found in the world of broadcasting, where one of the brightest spots of television is the weekly CBS News program "60 Minutes." The program takes on targets from faith healers to public officials, coming down hard on consumer fraud and corruption, and vividly presenting the conflicting statements of its sources. For years it has often been number one in the Sunday evening ratings, which argues against the idea that the public wants merely to be entertained. The continuing popularity of "60 Minutes" shows that people are very interested in having the media serve their traditional role as watchdogs of the public interest. That fact seems to have escaped the notice of media managers who are leading the movement toward infotainment.

# ▼ The Final Step: The Agenda-Setting Function of the Press

The final stage in constructing the daily news is deciding on *which stories* to present to the public and the degree of *prominence* they deserve. Communication scholars refer to this final part of the news process as **agenda setting.** It means deciding on which positions within the newspaper or broadcast the stories of the day should appear. Some, it will be decided, should be very prominent. These will be on the front page and have a large headline. They may have a photo or many column inches. Others, which seem less important, will have a smaller headline, be short, have no photo, and will be relegated to back sections of the paper. In the case of broadcast news, some stories can appear early in the presentation, perhaps be given more time, be accompanied by some

▶ Each medium packages the news in a different way and is given different kinds of attention by audiences. Newspapers present a portable cafeteria of news that can be consumed in a variety of settings and at a pace selected by the reader. However, reading requires undivided attention. Radio's news bulletins and brief summaries require only a short attention span and can be heard while people are doing other things. Viewing TV news requires being in place before a set and attending closely to the presentation. There is no chance for review at one's own pace. (© John Blaustein/Woodfin Camp & Associates, Inc.)

background information, and have some video footage taken on the scene. Others can be presented in less dramatic and simpler form toward the end of the broadcast.

In the final setting of their medium's agenda, those who make the decisions about content and prominence have already considered which news values to emphasize, what story or broadcasting formats will be used, whether to use a market approach, an adversarial position, and whether concerns over ethical, legal, or profit matters have been met. Thus, the final set of stories that appears in the newspaper or broadcast of the day has undergone a very complex news process beginning with the surveillance of the environment for story possibilities and ending with decisions of what will be the actual content and positioning of the news of the day to be transmitted to the audience served by that particular medium.

Communication scholars and researchers have discovered that the agenda defined by news professionals, as just outlined, has a counterpart among the audiences that attend to their media. It is that, when people are asked about their personal ranking of importance of the news stories of the day, their selections usually reflect the degree of prominence given those same stories in newspapers and broadcasts. Simply put, people believe that story is important if it is given a position of prominence by the press. This statement may seem

Each medium transmits the news to its audience in different ways. Each of these ways has advantages and disadvantages. TV is visual and dramatic but must be received at the site of the set. Radio news can be heard in many settings but cannot be revisited. Newspapers are very portable and can be read and reread at the user's own pace without the use of equipment. For that reason they are likely to survive. (Copyright © Tom McCarthy, PhotoEdit)

hardly surprising, but it is an important issue. What it means is that those who set the agenda of the press have a significant influence on the public in terms of what people believe to be important among events taking place in their society. If people believe something is important, it catches the eye of politicians who want to be elected or stay in office, and this often becomes an influence on the kinds of laws and policies that they formulate. Thus, the agenda-setting function of the press is more than an interesting relationship uncovered by researchers. It can have profound influences on the direction the nation takes in developing new policies and laws.

## ▼ Transmitting the News: Unique Features of the Different Media

Once news has been gathered and packaged, a vital next stage in the news process is delivering the information to the audiences of the several media. In the United States this is accomplished by newspapers, magazines, radio, television, and the Internet. The news industry operates within a complex media environment. It makes use of all these channels to deliver to the public a daily tidal wave of information on what is happening in the world.

# EXPLAINING MEDIA EFFECTS

## *The Agenda-Setting Theory of the Press*

A theory concerning the influence of the press on peoples' beliefs and evaluations of the topics reported in the news was first developed by Maxwell McCombs and Donald Shaw.[22] The theory explains how individuals come to regard some events and situations that they encounter through news reports in the press as more important than others. Thus, agenda setting implies a relationship between the treatment of an issue or event in newspapers, television and radio news, and the beliefs about its importance or significance on the part of individuals who make up the news audience.

The agenda-setting theory grew out of studies of the presidential political campaign of 1968. Its authors studied how people in a community decided which issues, among those that received extended news attention, were important. As it turned out, the public did develop a kind of ranking in their own minds about the importance of the different issues discussed in the news. The authors of the theory found a high level of correspondence between the amount and kind of attention paid to a particular political issue by the press and the level of importance assigned to that issue by people in

the community who had received information about it from newspapers and other news sources.

It was the press, therefore, that determined during a political campaign what issues people would discuss among themselves and how much importance they would attach to different ones. In other words, the press developed its own agenda concerning what issues were news and how much space and prominence to give them. The agenda of the press then became the agenda of those who followed the news of the campaign. This does not imply that the press tells people *what* they should think and decide about the issues. However, it does imply that the press tells people what they should think *about* and what issues were important enough to require their decisions.

Hundreds of research projects have been carried out by communications scholars since McCombs and Shaw first published their theory, and its basic ideas have been well verified. The theory is applicable mainly to the relationship between political issues as these are discussed in the press and the beliefs about their importance by those who follow campaigns in the

news. It may not apply to news about other topics. In any case, its basic propositions are these:

**1.** The press (news media in general) *select* a number of issues, topics, and events from its continuous surveillance of the environment to process and report daily as the "news."

**2.** Because of limited space and time, and because of journalists' convictions as to what is "newsworthy," many issues and topics are *ignored* and do not become part of the news.

**3.** The press gives each of the news stories selected greater or lesser *prominence* in its reports by assigning it a particular position, or giving it more or less space or time, in their print and broadcast news presentations.

**4.** The selection of stories presented, with their different levels of prominence, space, and time, forms the *news agenda* of the press.

**5. Therefore:** When the public attends to these news reports they will perceive the order of prominence assigned by the press in its agenda of stories and will use it to decide on their *personal rankings of importance* of the issues and topics that make up the news.

Perhaps the major point to understand in looking at the various channels by which news is transmitted from organizations to the people who make up the news audience is that each does so in a unique way. The daily newspaper, for example, brings a once-a-day cafeteria of news stories and other information to people's homes (or to newsstands or dispensers). It presents its stories in greater detail than do any of the other news media, with the possible exception of magazines. However, it often does so after people have initially heard about the events elsewhere. On the other hand, newspapers offer coverage of the most events. They contain items of news that would never appear on network or even local television.

The newspaper has certain advantages as a medium. (The newsmagazine has some of the same ones, but newspapers play a much larger role in disseminating daily news.) The newspaper is a channel that can be used at the person's own pace, and the individual can go back and read a story again and again to understand it better. Furthermore, newspaper reading is an activity in which readers shut other people out. It may be done in a social environment, but full attention is usually given to the printed account. It is a very convenient medium, because it can be carried around and read in almost any context. People read newspapers or magazines on the subway, at lunch, at work, in bed, or while eating breakfast.

Because of these features, which help the newspaper offer completeness of coverage, it is thought to be the most effective medium from which people learn about the news. It clearly is the slowest, however, and for that reason people often hear about an event through other media and then get more details from reading a newspaper account later.

Radio, on the other hand, is a very different medium and presents news in a dissimilar pattern. People seldom sit down for extended periods of time to listen attentively to a lengthy radio news broadcast. They used to before television was available, but today they listen to the radio while driving their cars, perhaps before going to sleep at night, while fixing meals, or while doing something else.

Although radio listening is often a secondary activity, it is more convenient than newspaper reading because it can be done while doing other important things. Radio newscasters understand this very well, and therefore present their reports frequently and in brief "bursts." A radio news report offers few details, and opinion and analysis are rare (except on public radio). Thus, radio news presentations touch on the main points and come in the form of news headlines or brief news summaries that seldom last more than five minutes.

These features all suggest that radio is relatively ineffective compared with newspapers when it comes to audience comprehension of the news. On the other hand, it does have the factor of immediacy. That is, it can get news bulletins out to the public far faster than any other medium, and when truly significant events take place, such as the outbreak of war, the assassination of a leader, or a serious explosion, the majority of people hear it first on radio, or from someone who heard it from that medium.

Television, too, has its own characteristics as a channel for dissemination. Because most sets are not really portable, viewers have to watch at a fixed location, increasingly one linked to a cable. Thus, TV is not as convenient as either the newspaper or radio. Like radio, television requires the viewer to receive the information at the medium's pace rather than his or her own. However, because it is a visual as well as an aural medium, it requires a different kind of focus than does radio. It is definitely not something one does while driving, for instance, and one can attend only partially while fixing a meal or doing some other task that requires attention.

Television news viewing, then, has its own pattern. Generally, people sit down to watch the news at the end of the work day, or before retiring. However, this often becomes a social ritual as well as a learning experience. People fix drinks, admonish children, munch on snacks, talk to each other during the broadcast, or engage in other kinds of activities that tend to reduce the level of concentration with which people attend. Thus, although a TV newscast is usually much longer and more complete than a radio version, it is still a source from which audiences comprehend the news only to a limited extent.

Multimedia presentations on the World Wide Web of the Internet represent still another unique channel. Here, the audience concentrates on their computer screen, scrolling through and reading text. Even so, reading news from such a screen is a different experience than doing so in a newspaper. Those who write for multimedia use a special style—often one that permits "jumps" within the text from a topic to a more detailed or related set of information. The point here is that news presentations prepared for this medium are different from those developed for broadcasting or other forms of print, which has an influence on what details are presented, in what way, and in what order. These factors influence the ways in which people will reconstruct meanings and interepret the information presented.[23]

# ▼ The News Audience: Selection, Comprehension, and Recall

The final stages of the news process take place as members of the public selectively attend to news reports, understand and recall their content to varying degrees, and differentially act upon what they see or hear. It is very clear that this is an extraordinarily complex stage. Some people never attend to the news and know very little about what is going on in their community and society. Others pay occasional attention in selective ways, learning about some events but ignoring others. A few are "news junkies," who avidly keep up with the flow of news reports, using a variety of media from which they get multiple exposures.

## How Closely Do People Follow the News?

We saw earlier that people select content from each of the mass media in ways consistent with their demographic backgrounds and personal characteristics. The *uses and gratifications theory* (Chapter 8) explained that the American population is an "active" audience. People seek out and attend to content consistent with their interests, which provides gratifications and fulfills their needs.

Similarly, the news audience is not "passive," merely waiting until messages arrive. However, research on what factors lead people to select and learn about particular news topics does not show consistent results. Also, findings are often at such a general level that they offer little real insight into the actual news-learning experiences of the audience. Nevertheless, a number of conclusions can be reached regarding who attend to the news and what they generally prefer.

Some research shows that people do expose themselves to the mass media—both print and broadcast news—to a remarkable degree. However, the situation is perplexing because, whether or not people are exposed to the news, research also shows that the majority of our population actually retain relatively little *knowledge* about individual news stories. Few can explain major social and economic trends (such as changes in foreign policy, interest rates, or the stock market). They do not appear to have insight into the nature of most events of major political significance (for example, trade treaties, bills passed by Congress, or policies advocated by the president). The majority do not know the names of major public officials (like the Secretaries of State and Defense, the Chief Justice of the Supreme Court, or even the vice president).

Leo Bogart, who for many years directed research for the Newspaper Advertising Bureau (NAB), is one of those who believes that most Americans attend widely to various media: "In contemporary America, there is almost universal daily contact with the three major media. In the course of an average weekday, 83% of the adult public watch some television . . . and 68% listen to the radio, while seven of ten read a newspaper."[24] Bogart goes on to note that this high level of attention does not necessarily mean a large audience for the news. Still, he concludes that, on any given weekday, only 8 percent fail to receive news from any medium. Bogart offers evidence to support this claim. He concludes that from 60 to 80 percent of the population (depending on educational level) are "exposed to news." He reaches this conclusion because respondents claim in interviews that they "read a newspaper yesterday." The comparable figures for radio range from 41 to 61 percent (depending on education); for television news the figure is 64 percent for all educational levels.

These figures seem to indicate that people do indeed follow the news closely. However, it is not clear what "reading the newspaper (or listening to radio or watching TV) yesterday" really means. Some people read only the comics, watch sports on TV, and listen to rock music on the radio, encountering news only incidentally. They may have been exposed "yesterday," but they will likely have trouble remembering any news they saw, heard, or read.

From all this research it is clear that it is difficult to make sweeping statements about the effectiveness of the various news media in keeping us informed. The overall evidence is inconsistent, to say the least. A better approach to understanding the depth of news exposure in the audience is to look more closely at the personal and social characteristics of different kinds of people and see how such factors can make a difference.

## The Influence of Personal and Social Characteristics

A considerable body of evidence indicates that different types of people differ greatly in how much they can remember a news story once exposed. Generally, however, their level of recall is remarkably *low*. Some of this evidence comes from experimental studies of news recall; some from testing people on issues that recently have been well publicized in the news; and some is from surveys in which people are interviewed right after seeing a news broadcast on TV (these reveal levels of comprehension without regard to day-to-day exposure). Although there are variations among these findings, there are a number of consistent patterns. What are the personal and social factors that lead to high and low attention to the news? There are no final answers to that question, but we can put together a kind of general picture.

Essentially, a person's position in the *social structure*, in terms of education and income, and one's classifications by age, gender, and ethnicity provide one set of answers as to how likely it is that he or she will attend closely to the news. Still another set of answers comes from the individual's *personal characteristics*—that is, beliefs, preferences, interests, attitudes, and values.

No variable shows a closer relationship with attention to the news than *education*. Simply put, the farther down the educational attainment ladder one goes, the less people know about the news. At the same time, the differences appear to be greater for print news (in both newspapers and newsmagazines) than for televised news.[25] This conclusion has been well supported by research in a number of countries.[26]

Much the same conclusions have been found for *income*. Poor people pay far less attention to the news than do the middle class and the affluent. However, this may actually reflect education, which is closely linked to type of occupation and therefore to income. Those at higher socioeconomic levels generally have greater knowledge of news from all media than do those who are less affluent.

The factor of *age* is directly related to high or low exposure to news.[27] Few children below about age fifteen follow the news, except for sporadic attention when adults have the TV set on or when the radio is on in the car. Similarly, although they may read the comics, they seldom read news stories in other parts of the paper. That pattern prevails well into the teens—a segment of the population notorious for its disinterest in public affairs. Contact with the news increases with age among adults. The older a person is (to a point), the greater his or her attention to the news. The real news addicts are people over sixty, but not over seventy-five.

Although research on the matter is scarce, to a certain degree, *gender* has also been linked to interest in the news, and consequently to patterns of exposure.[28] The limited research available suggests that women have somewhat lower levels of interest in news, especially if it deals with violent themes, and this brings about lower levels of attention.

Still another characteristic that predicts whether a given individual will attend to and retain the news is the person's *race* and *ethnicity*. Generally, members of minority groups are less likely to follow the news avidly than are the more dominant segments of society. However, this too can be misleading because income and educational levels tend to be lower among minority groups, and the reduced interest in the news is probably due to these factors.

Other factors related to news exposure are *occupation* and *area of residence*. Some people work in situations where they can pay little attention to the news: for instance, on ships, at remote sites, or during odd hours of the day. Generally, urban dwellers contact news more than others. However, people may live in inner-city environments where keeping up with the news is not a cultural tradition. Some people are outside the flow of news simply because the media are not available. Such people may lack a stable home situation. Some are traveling; others are stationed in foreign lands for either business or military purposes; still others are sick or institutionalized.

Another set of considerations arises because of the psychological make up of different kinds of people. The factors just discussed—age, sex, education, and so on—lead to distinctive patterns of *interest* in different news topics. These patterns of interest, in turn, lead to different patterns of exposure. For example, young males may have a heavy interest in sports that is simply not shared by females. Affluent people may actively seek out business news, which is totally uninteresting to many working-class families. Older people are generally more interested in politics and economic trends than are younger. And so it goes. In a complex and heterogeneous society, a host of factors and variables determine the topical interests of various categories of people. The general principle is that interest in different kinds of news is determined by a person's psychological profile and by the demographic factors that define his or her position in society.

Finally, *daily habits* are important in news exposure. For example, the medium one habitually turns to for exposure to the news is a critical factor. Robinson and Levy have examined the role of television versus other media as vehicles for learning the news. It is clear that TV is the main source for the majority of people. However, in reviewing fifteen studies conducted over a twenty-year period, it was clear that viewers of TV newscasts were less informed compared to those who depended mainly on print media. This was a result of viewing habits. Many people watch TV news while preparing meals, eating, socializing with the family, and so on, and their attention is less focused than, say, while reading a newspaper. Television, then, is the main source for news for most people, but it is also the medium from which they learn and retain the least information.[29]

The bottom line is that the de facto audience for the news—people who attend regularly and who learn quite a bit about what is happening on a daily basis—is much smaller than many journalists would like to believe. Only a handful are avid news consumers who use all the media and know virtually everything that happens. A large number follow the news very selectively gaining a grasp of only a few topics. Most people are somewhere in between.

## CHAPTER REVIEW

▼ News can be defined in a common-sense way as current information made public about an event or subject that is of interest to a significant number of people.

▼ That information is gathered, refined, and disseminated to an audience through a news process consisting of several steps, including gathering relevant facts, preparing them into stories judged to be newsworthy, and transmitting them to the audience, which, in varying degrees, attends to and comprehends what has been presented.

▼ The public entertains "pictures in their heads" of "the world outside," but the correspondence between the two depends on many factors and may not be accurate, because there are numerous points in the news process where stories are shaped in ways that result in unintentional distortions.

▼ Reporters who observe events use personal perspectives to write about what they see. They also use reports of witnesses. Accuracy can suffer substantially because of the selective nature of perception, recall, and interpretation.

▼ News organizations try to make stories both interesting and understandable. They are judged within a set of news values and prepared according to a number of alternative formats. Various styles of journalism exist within which basic facts can be developed into news accounts. These styles include sensational, objective, and "new" journalism, plus advocacy, precision, and civic journalism.

▼ Social and cultural influences in news organizations play a central role in decision-making about what stories will be disseminated, in what order of prominence, and in what form.

▼ Two very different kinds of goals often sought in the development of news are represented by the marketing and adversarial approaches. The former stresses news as a product packaged to please the audience and maximize profits. The latter is aimed at protecting the public interest by performing the watchdog function of the press.

▼ Each of the media is used in a different way as a means of disseminating the news. The differences among these media in terms of learning and comprehension of news by those who use them are increased by the different behavior systems associated with each.

▼ Some studies suggest that the majority of Americans are exposed to some degree to news on a daily basis. Other studies reveal very low levels of comprehension and recall of the news. In terms of personal and social characteristics, those who best understand and recall news stories are the older, more affluent, and well educated. Television is the main source of news for the majority in the United States, but it is also a source from which comprehension is relatively low.

# Popular Culture

## Entertainment, Sports, and Music

A once-famous photograph of two boys carrying a garbage can had this caption: "What are you throwing away that will be valuable tomorrow?" A visit to any antiques or collectables shop will quickly tell you what throw-away items of the past are now regarded as valuable. Items such as old signs and postcards, medicine bottles, calendars, medals, buttons, and comic books are part of that inventory. These and other artifacts or objects are clues to the meaning of popular culture—what ordinary people enjoy, use, and consume. The totality of popular social and artistic expression is usually referred to as **popular culture,** distinguishing it from elite or high culture, which is discussed later in this chapter.

Some examples of popular culture are not part and parcel of the mass media—such as printed legends on T-shirts, messages on milk cartons or beer cans, folk songs and new dance steps, not to mention fashion and hairstyles, which are always-changing indicators of the popular culture. However, much of media, from videocassettes and comic books to advertising symbols and icons and many others, are clearly integral to media industries.

At the end of the twentieth century, as the millennium or year 2001 approaches, a sort of millennia mania begins to occur as television and movie producers, futurists and scholars, as well as business people speculate about the meaning of the new century. As a result, souvenirs of all kinds begin to appear, as well as new books, articles, TV programs, and other media fare designed to celebrate the millennium. Although some historians regard the rundown to the new century as fundamentally silly, they also remind us that from the 1400s on, the end of every century has stimulated such activity. In the late nineteenth century people flocked to futurist writings such as *Looking Backward,* a Utopian work by Edward Bellamy that predicted the future of communication, architecture, travel, and other aspects of life. In the late 1990s, the press frequently features articles about the most popular travel spots as people begin planning where they will spend New Year's Eve 1999, even though the millennium really begins on New Year's Day 2001.[1]

When the Industrial Revolution of the nineteenth century introduced factories with regular work days, it also defined and expanded people's leisure time. With larger blocks of free time available, the demand for amusement and entertainment expanded, and with it came popular culture, which we now associate closely with our contemporary mass media. Before they arrived, the rich and otherwise well-off had their cultural amusements and sports, but people who worked in factories and their families also had their own distinctive brand of entertainment. As historian Richard Maltby writes,

> The city amusements of the late nineteenth century were prototypes for ephemeral consumption: saloons, dance halls, pool rooms, and roller-skating rinks; dime novels and

illustrated papers, circuses, amusement parks, burlesque shows, and professional sports; melodrama and cheap seats in the theaters and concert halls.[2]

Meanwhile, the burgeoning industrial production in the United States and Europe needed more consumers to buy products—a development that led to organized promotion and advertising. The means of promoting consumption went hand in hand with the rise of popular entertainment and mass media, which aided in the process of consumption. Eventually, Maltby writes, popular culture became "something you buy" as opposed to traditional folk culture (games, songs, crafts, etc.), which was "something you make."[3]

# ▼ The Nature and Importance of Popular Culture

The mass media, as they existed and evolved over time, became players in the creation and promotion of popular culture from the beginning. Some "media products" like dime novels provided entertainment, whereas others like billboards, newspapers, and magazines were vehicles for advertisements that helped sell goods and services being produced. Eventually, much of the entertainment once offered only to small audiences used the media to expand its reach. Thus, cheap novels were also serialized in newspapers and magazines, and live drama eventually made its way into radio and television. Likewise, sports that began on the playing field quickly became fodder for newspaper stories and electronic media broadcasts.

## The Media and Popular Culture

The content of popular culture was, by definition, aimed at large audiences of mainly middle and lower classes of varied education and income. Thus, there was an attempt to reach the *largest audience possible* with pleasurable, easily understood fare. Critics constantly complained the popular culture offerings of the media were debasing, drove out so-called high culture or art, and had an overall negative effect on people.

Early in the debate between the defenders and critics of popular culture, the terms "lowbrow" and "highbrow" were coined. They were first used by the journalist and critic Will Irwin in a series of articles in the *New York Sun* in 1902 and 1903. The inevitable "middlebrow" came later. A lowbrow was a person of vulgar or uncultivated tastes, whereas a highbrow was said to aspire (or pretend to) to "a high level of cultivation and learning." A "middlebrow" simply accepted and sometimes celebrated mediocre fare somewhere between the other two.[4]

Scholars, critics, journalists, and others have continued to debate and discuss these terms as they assess and examine both the content and effects of popular culture. All these concepts and others are explained later in the chapter, which discusses the entertainment function of the media. It focuses on media content as soap operas, comic strips, television sitcoms, advertising art, play-by-play spectator sports, and other examples of popular culture. While considering both the content and supposed impact of this material, this chapter also considers the "money connection," because popular culture is *big business* when presented through the mass media.

Much of the content of the mass media is popular culture that is sold for a profit and integral to the economics of the media. Audiences are courted to consume popular culture, ranging from popular entertainment to sports and even pornography. People will probably argue forever about whether a given image or presentation is popular culture or not. So, too, will they debate the probable impact of such material: whether or not it is harmful; and whether it drives out better-quality programs, high-caliber design, and more elegant writing.

## A Definition

But just what is popular culture? Like many other topics of debate, it has been defined in many ways. Critic Ray Browne, who has written several books on the subject, broadly defines popular culture as "all those elements of life which are not narrowly intellectual or creatively elitist, and which are generally though not necessarily disseminated through the mass media."[5] Additional features are provided by scholar David Madden, who writes "It is anything produced or disseminated by the mass media or mass production or transportation, either directly or indirectly and that reaches a majority of people."[6]

Even more inclusive definitions can be found. British historian Lord Asa Briggs wrote a book titled *Victorian Things,* treating such objects as tools, medals, hats and other artifacts of popular culture.[7] In fact, buttons (as in campaign buttons) or T-shirts are themselves expressions of popular culture. Sociologist Herbert Gans has written musingly about T-shirts and the slogans and legends on them, indicating that the messages and advertisements displayed on the ones worn by women tend to be different from those on the ones worn by men.[8]

Some students of popular culture study virtually anything that people use in everyday life—the lettering on cigar boxes, beer cans, and wine labels; advertising in print and electronic media, billboards, and other messages that actually communicate very effectively. The American Museum of Advertising in Portland, Oregon, has exhibits going back to ancient Greece showing how advertising signs and other symbols communicated with everyday people over the years. There is even a set of long-forgotten "Burma Shave" signs from the 1930s, recalling a time in America when successive phrases on humorous roadside advertisements provided amusement for motorists. For example, a "Burma Shave" series advertising a now-defunct shaving cream proclaims "Free, free, a trip to Mars for 500 empty jars!"

Communication scholars define popular culture very broadly. It can include music, sports, movies, television programs, and virtually any product or service that is designed for amusement and diversion and sold for a profit. Even t-shirts with funny messages and slogans would fit such a definition. (Copyright © Lee Snider, The Image Works)

All of these phenomena of everyday life hold their own fascination. In this chapter, however, we will not discuss in detail elements of popular culture that are not specifically part of the mass media, although some of them, such as fast food and clothing styles, rely on the media for popularization. Somewhat arbitrarily, then, we can formulate a definition of popular culture as it will be discussed in this text. Simply put: It is *mass-communicated messages that make limited intellectual and aesthetic demands—content that is designed to amuse and entertain media audiences.* Popular culture, in this sense, is presented by all of the print, film, and broadcast mass media. Indeed, the term covers most of what they disseminate. although serious popular culture theorists would probably complain that our definition is too narrowly focused on media popular culture, it covers what we will address—namely, such media presentations as game shows, soap operas, spectator sports, crime drama, movies, popular music, and indeed, most of what could be classified as entertaining media content.

## Why Studying Popular Culture Is Important

Debates over the value of the popular arts and the supposed superiority of high culture have gone on for decades, with the idea that much that is popular is unworthy junk. Thus, each generation seems to decry the reading habits, musical tastes, and other popular addictions of the young. One reason for all educated people to observe and understand popular culture is simply a matter of *keeping up with what is happening in society.* As musician Bob Dylan wrote in

▶

One of the most obvious forms of popular culture is music. The first popular music was ragtime, which caught on in the early 1900s. Just after World War I it was replaced by Dixieland jazz. In the 1930s came swing, with boogie following in the 1940s. Today country and rock remain popular in many forms. One of the original creators of Dixieland was Dominick LaRocca and his band, who coined the word "jazz." (Brown Brothers)

his "Ballad of a Thin Man," a response to attacks on popular culture: "You've been through all of F. Scott Fitzgerald's books/You're very well read, it's well known/But something is happening, and you don't know what it is, do you, Mr. Jones?"

In the 1980s and 1990s, public funding of popular arts led to considerable controversy. Photographer Robert Mapplethorpe received support through federal funding for exhibits of his work. Many people who came to see the exhibit were surprised, and not a few were shocked, to find that some of his photographs showed nude males and homoerotic themes. The fact that federal funds were used for the exhibits ignited a national controversy. Conservative senators demanded that funding be withdrawn from the National Endowment for the Arts, or at least that strong rules be imposed on the agency. This proposal, of course, raised questions about popular culture and freedom of expression. The debate over the issue has never been fully resolved and it has implications for the entire issue of what is acceptable in popular art. The Mapplethorpe photographs were widely published in various media, most of them fringe, and were the topic of heavy media coverage.

Some social scientists, such as Japanese sociologist Hidetoshi Kato, maintain that, "the mass media can be seen as one of the most decisive factors shaping the populace of a society." Kato continues: " . . . the belief systems and behavior patterns of the younger generation in many societies today are strongly affected by the messages they prefer to receive (or are forced to receive) either directly or indirectly through mass media."[11]

# Media and the Liberal Arts

## The Strange, Sad Case of Amy Fisher as Popular Culture
### A Linchpin to Sociology and Cultural Studies

In 1997, five years after she went to jail after a celebrated trial and a media feeding frenzy, tabloid television shows were still chronicling the prison antics and complaints of Amy Fisher. As a teenager on Long Island, she was arrested and subsequently convicted for shooting a woman named Mary Jo Buttafuoco, the wife of her lover. Thus began a sad and violent story that quickly attracted the attention of racy tabloid newspapers and equally exploitative TV programs. The trial was short, because Fisher admitted guilt and plea-bargained a five-to-fifteen-year prison sentence.

The story had many elements of sensationalism, including sex, crime, and a supposed love triangle. In addition, Fisher was an attractive eighteen-year-old. It also left open many questions: Who was telling the truth and who was lying? What was the role of Joseph Buttafuoco, the alleged lover who denied intimate involvement with Fisher? Was the affair the fantasy of a teenager or a real-life drama?

In December 1992 and January 1993, three made-for-television movies aired on CBS, NBC, and ABC networks dramatizing Amy Fisher's story. As a *New York Times* article put it, "Surpassing the expectations of network officials, each of the three made-for-television movies based on the Amy Fisher case . . . was a stunning success, and two of the three are likely to emerge as the most popular television movies of the season.[9] Each movie took sides—one portrayed Amy Fisher sympathetically and blamed Joseph Buttafuoco for her plight, while another took the Buttafuocos' point of view and depicted Fisher as a lying, duplicitous girl with emotional problems.

At the same time, the TV tabloid show "Hard Copy" managed to acquire X-rated videos of Amy and another boyfriend and broadcast them on the air. Before long, popular national talk shows such as "Donahue" and "Geraldo" got involved in the case, inviting the Buttafuocos on the show, where they were heckled and hooted by a studio audience in one case and subjected to a mock trial in another. What began as a serious case of domestic violence involving virtually unknown people in a local community was trumpeted in the print and electronic tabloids and became the subject of hundreds of magazine articles, scores of TV shows, and three network TV movies. In addition, deals for paperback books were quickly in the works. The case and its protagonists were suddenly the "stuff" of popular culture. What had been a matter for the police blotter and the courts became everybody's business as people speculated about the parties in the case, their honesty, and their ethics. Ruth Slawson, senior vice president for movies at NBC, said that the massive public interest "stunned" her. As she put it. "I don't believe there was anything so unique or gripping to this story to make it that special."[10] On reflection, Slawson thought that Fisher's age might have been a factor in luring young viewers.

From the original facts of the case, about which there is disagreement, came fast and loose TV movies that took considerable license in telling the story. What had been a racy but still fairly factual news story became a quasi-fictional treatment as a TV movie and more fodder for what University of Michigan scholar John D. Stevens calls the "wretched excess" that is so common among the tabloid media.

Although none of the people involved in the case were thought to be particularly attractive by newspeople and commentators, their story had taken off as a popular tale and became an artifact of popular culture. Popular culture portrayals like this can have staying power, but many do not and simply recede from public consciousness as new and more gripping stories emerge.

▶ One of the best-known events focusing on popular culture was Woodstock. It was a 1969 rock music festival held near Bethel in upstate New York. The event attracted thousands of young people who participated in what was then called the "counterculture," which emphasized sexual freedom and included the use of marijuana and other drugs. (Copyright © J. Dominis, The Image Works)

This kind of influence on audiences is what communications scholar Michael Real calls "mass-mediated culture," and he argues that although it may be distasteful to some, there are good reasons for studying popular (or mass-mediated) culture.[12] Some include the following:

1. It offers delight for everyone;
2. It reflects and influences human life;
3. It spreads specific ideas and ideology internationally;
4. It raises far-reaching policy questions, challenging education and research;
5. It is us.

Although these reasons may seem self-evident to today's students, many universities have been reluctant to allow the serious study of popular culture. Author Arthur Asa Berger, for example, had a very difficult time getting his Ph.D. committee at the University of Minnesota to let him write his dissertation on Al Capp's comic strip character "L'il Abner." Few English departments in American universities are interested in having their students study pulp fiction or Gothic romances, although these books command a far greater audience than the most respected literary classics. Art history courses are not much interested in advertising art, although it is produced by an impressively large labor force and consumed by millions. American history classes do not take note of the meteoric rise of the fast-food industries, although groups like McDonald's have delivered enough sandwiches to their customers to form a line from earth to the outer reaches of the solar system. In other words, the study of popular culture seems "tainted" to most intellectuals even though it influences us in many powerful ways.

In this chapter we reject the position that popular culture can just be dismissed with a wave of the hand. Some reasons for taking popular culture seriously in the study of communication are: (1) it reaches almost all of the public in one form or another; (2) whether we like it or not, it influences the way we think, act, dress or relate to others; and (3) it has a tremendous economic impact on the media and strongly influences almost all mass communication content.

Further, what is today's popular culture might become tomorrow's high culture. For example, editor Tad Friend, writing in *The New Republic* maintains that, "Popular entertainment that outlasts its era gets re-examined by new critics, re-presented to a new audience, elevated and enshrined."[13] Some examples include Matthew Brady's Civil War photographs, the movies of Charlie Chaplin and Buster Keaton, and the music of Patsy Cline and Jim Morrison. And, even though many deplore it, historians often study an era through its popular culture because it tells a great deal about what people liked and enjoyed.

Closely associated with popular culture studies are two kinds of media research. One studies *heroes* and the other focuses on *images*. The popular heroes of any period—athletes, rock stars, film sex goddesses, and even some of our military leaders and major politicians—are

▲

Popular culture makes few intellectual demands on its consumers. Often, it emphasizes youth, beauty, and sexuality. Most students of popular culture agree that its products are intended for immediate gratification as opposed to long-term rewards. Its themes are seldom intended to reflect deep concerns of society or lasting values. (AP Photo)

"products" of mass media portrayals. Similarly, one learns a great deal about a given culture by its media portrayals of the images of women in advertising or the images of minority groups like African Americans, Latinos, and Native Americans in news photographs. The frequency with which people appear and the way they are depicted say a great deal about the values of a society and the decisions that media people make. In the early 1940s, for example, the *New York Times* and other newspapers mentioned African Americans mostly under the grisly topic of "lynching," rather than covering them for their achievements. Even earlier, many media stereotyped various ethnic groups in denigrating ways, again indicating social values by the content of what popular culture portrayed.

▶

One of the most popular entertainers of all times was Charlie Chaplin, shown here in a 1936 movie entitled "Modern Times." Produced for mass audiences in the 1930s as popular culture, it was designed mainly to make money. The film is now proclaimed by some to be a great classic and an example of high culture. Such transformations of popular culture celebrities and their products to icons are not uncommon. (Copyright © C. Topham, The Image Works)

# ▼ *Popular Culture as Entertainment*

Virtually all popular culture has an entertainment function. It is typically designed to amuse and serve as a pastime. However, it can also be argued that some popular culture content, such as advertising, is deadly serious about promoting a product or a point of view. Not all entertainment is associated with the media. An example is the circus, which is promoted and advertised in the media but stems from a circus tradition dating to the Romans. However, the media are the important delivery systems for most kinds of popular culture today, and indeed, they would not exist at all in the absence of mass communications.

Of the media we discuss in this book, it is the content of television and film that is mostly concerned with entertainment. Newspapers, once a major source of entertainment, continue to provide utilitarian information. However, they do carry a considerable amount of entertainment. When they do, they rely heavily on *feature syndicates* to bring in entertainment fare. (The role of feature syndicates in newspaper publishing was discussed briefly in Chapter 3). Radio, once an important news medium, is now mainly devoted to entertainment, with its emphasis on music, talk shows, and sports broadcasts. Cable is both an entertainment and an information medium, but clearly entertainment is the dominant concern. Books, our oldest medium, also deliver both serious information and entertainment.

## Media Influences on Consumer Art

One of the most controversial (and most fascinating) social and cultural effects of the media is the invention and spread of a constant deluge of popular songs, cheap paperback novels, formula TV drama, low-grade film thrillers, comic strip characters, and other unsophisticated content. Such material reaches enormous proportions of the population and becomes a part of people's daily lives. People hum the latest popular tunes, suffer the latest problem of a soap-opera heroine, exchange analyses of the latest big game based on news reports, and organize their activities around the weekly television schedule. This media output is at the heart of popular culture. The development of well-articulated theories concerning the sources and influences of popular culture represents a frontier of theory development that has been widely but not systematically explored. In this section, we look at this area of mass communications and offer a tentative theory that tries to explain why our media are so preoccupied with this type of content.

People have debated the artistic merits of media-produced culture and its impact on society for generations.[14] Media critics and defenders have disagreed hotly about whether deliberately manufactured mass "art" is blasphemy or blessing. These analyses of mass communication and its products as art forms take place *outside the framework of science.* Media criticism is an arena of debate where conclusions are reached on the basis of personal opinions and values rather than carefully assembled data. Nevertheless, those who praise or condemn the content of mass communication perform an important service. They offer us contrasting sets of standards for judging the merits of media content. We may choose to accept or reject those standards, but by exercising some set of criteria we can reach our own conclusions about the merits of popular music, soap operas, spectator sports, and so on.

In the sections that follow we review a tentative theory of mass communicated popular culture induced from discussions of two issues: (1) the merits of various forms of popular culture manufactured and disseminated by the media, and (2) the levels of cultural taste that characterize segments of the American population served by our media. These discussions are based on the *strong opinions, clear biases,* and *personal sets of values* of a number of critics. You may find these admittedly biased opinions consistent with your own views, or you may disagree violently. In either case, they illustrate the types of analyses found in debates over popular culture. Hopefully, they will clarify your own thinking about popular culture.

To understand popular culture and why it is so ubiquitous as a form of content in the American media, we first need to place it into a more general context of artistic products. Critics tell us that prior to the development of the mass media there were essentially two broad categories of art. These were **folk art** and **elite art.**[15] Both, it is said, are genuine and valuable. However, there is an important relationship between the two, according to the popular culture theory we are developing.

**Folk art.**    This category of artistic products consists of those that are developed spontaneously among anonymous people. Such art is unsophisticated, localized, and natural. It is produced by many unknown artists who are talented and creative but who receive no recognition for their contributions. It is a grassroots type of art created by its consumers and tied directly to their values and daily experiences. Thus, villages, regions, and nations develop characteristic furniture styles, music, dances, architectural forms, and decorative motifs for articles of everyday use. Folk art never takes guidelines from the elite of society but emerges as part of the traditions of ordinary people. It does not consist of widely known classics.

**Elite art.**    Products of elite art represent "high culture" deliberately produced by talented and creative individuals who often gain great personal recognition for their achievements. Elite art is technically and thematically complex. It is also highly individualistic, as its creators aim at discovering new ways of interpreting or representing their experience. Elite art includes the music, sculpture, dance, opera, and paintings that originated mainly in Europe and received the acclaim of sophisticates from all parts of the world. Although it has its great classics, it is marked by continuous innovation and is now produced in many countries. Novelists, composers, painters, and other creative artists constantly experiment with new forms and concepts.

**Kitsch.**    In modern times, many critics maintain, both folk and elite art are threatened by a tragically inferior category. The rise of privately owned, profit-oriented media brought radical change and created a completely new kind of popular art. With the advent of cheap newspapers, magazines, paperback books, radio, movies, and television, this new form of art made its debut, catering to massive, relatively uneducated audiences with undeveloped aesthetic tastes.

The content of this new art form, say its critics, is unsophisticated, simplistic, and trivial. Its typical literary forms are the "whodunit" detective story and the sex magazine; its typical musical composition is the latest rock hit; its typical dramatic forms are the soap opera, game show, the comic strip, and the sexually explicit or violent movie. A term that has been widely used to label such mass-mediated art is the German word *kitsch.* Like the English word "junk," **kitsch** refers to trashy and garish products that are in bad taste and have no artistic merit. According to the popular culture theory we are developing, it is the unrelenting demands of the media for entertainment content that produces a constant flow of kitsch.

**Criticisms of kitsch.**    Critics charge that in manufacturing kitsch, those who produce it for the media often "mine" both folk and elite art for crass commercial purposes. They do so "the way improvident frontiersmen mine the soil, extracting its riches and putting back nothing."[16] As Clement Greenburg wrote:

> The precondition of kitsch . . . is the availability close at hand of a fully matured cultural tradition, whose discoveries, acquisitions and perfected self-conscious kitsch can take advantage of for its own ends.[17]

Why do critics see kitsch as such a problem? They maintain that the older separation between elite and folk art once corresponded to the distinction between aristocracy and common people. Although they do not necessarily approve of the aristocracy, they believe that it was critical to the existence of the most developed forms of art. Prior to the emergence of mass communication, critics claim, folk art and elite art could coexist because they had clearly defined constituencies.

Then came the dramatic spread of the media to all classes of society. They were geared to the largest numbers of consumers with purchasing power. The tastes of these consumers were not linked to either folk art or elite art—they were best satisfied with content characterized by low intellectual demand. The result was a deluge of inconsequential kitsch.

Some would maintain that a painting of Elvis on black velvet represents the ultimate form of *kitsch*. However, there is little doubt that he was one of the most popular singers of the twentieth century. Media-produced culture and celebrities can have an influence on people for generations. Large numbers of fans interested in Elvis still buy such memorabilia and find gratification in his memory. (Copyright © Jim Corwin, Stock Boston)

Kitsch affects all levels of society and art because it competes for the attention of everyone. Its constant presence and attention-grabbing qualities are the source of its popular appeal. Thus, critics conclude, people who earlier would have read Tolstoy now turn to one of a few dozen formula writers of mysteries and romances. Those who might have found entertainment at the symphony, ballet, or theater now tune in on Madonna or wrestling; those who would have gained political wisdom from modern versions of Lord Bryce and Alexis de Tocqueville now watch the latest "analyses" of Geraldo Rivera.

In other words, popular culture theory states that products in low artistic taste drive out elite art and higher culture, just as bad money drives out good money. In assessing the principal characteristics of popular culture, Dwight MacDonald maintains that:

> It is a debased, trivial culture that voids both the deep realities (sex, death, failure, tragedy) and the simple, spontaneous pleasures. The masses, debauched by several generations of this sort of thing, in turn come to demand trivial and comfortable cultural products.[18]

Furthermore, the theory maintains, kitsch represents a double-barreled form of exploitation. Those who control the media not only rob citizens of a chance to acquire higher tastes by engulfing them with less demanding media products, they also reap high profits from those whom they are depriving.

If true, this theory of popular culture leads to three major predictions: First, kitsch presumably diminishes both folk and elite art because it simplifies their content, and in using them exhausts the sources of these arts. Second, it deprives its audiences of interest in developing tastes for more genuine art forms. Third, it is mainly a tool for economic exploitation of the masses.

These predictions represent serious charges. To try to see if this theory has merit, we can attempt to determine if at least one of these three conclusions is true. To do this, we can look at one aspect of popular culture—the heroes created by the media. Does the presence of media-created idols of kitsch tend to diminish the stature of genuine heroes as the theory predicts? Moreover, does a fascination with such media-created heroes lessen interest in meritorious accomplishments in real life? Furthermore, is economic exploitation a real factor?

**Heroes of the media as kitsch.**  As just suggested, one way of inferring whether our theory of popular culture has merit is to look at the kinds of heroes that our mass media have created. In early America, critics say, heroes and heroines were extraordinary individuals with rare personal qualities who performed admirable deeds. The list of heroes admired by eighteenth and nineteenth century Americans included such notables as George Washington, Robert E. Lee, Sacajawea, Daniel Boone, Harriet Tubman, Geronimo, Davy Crockett, and Harriet Beecher Stowe. These men and women were real people who performed deeds that truly had a significant impact on history. They did not win acclaim because they were pretty or entertaining but because they had powerful determination to succeed in situations requiring courage, dedication, and self-sacrifice.

Even as the media rose in the twentieth century, the tradition of heroes lingered. Alvin York and Eddie Rickenbacker emerged as the great heroes of World War I. After that, however, (following the rise of the new media) the number of real heroes of the deed thinned out noticeably. Perhaps the last great hero and one of the most adulated of all time was Charles A. Lindbergh. His solitary flight across the vast Atlantic in a single-engine aircraft required steel nerves and an iron will. In his single deed were focused all those qualities that Americans admired, and he was the most acclaimed hero of the twentieth century—at least until the full development of film and broadcasting.

When the media became established in our society, our heroes changed. In a famous classic study, the sociologist Leo Lowenthal examined biographies in popular magazines, believing that ordinary people best understand history and contemporary affairs in terms of famous people. He looked at political, business-professional, and entertainment heroes. Heroes, Lowenthal concluded, are a product of the values and tastes of the time. For example, in the early years of the twentieth century, *idols of production* in fields like business,

# EXPLAINING MEDIA EFFECTS

## *The Theory of Origins and Functions of Popular Culture*

Although human beings have always enjoyed light entertainment, simple diversions, and sports, they played only a minor role in the economic affairs of societies until relatively recent times. Before the Industrial Revolution, most ordinary people toiled from daylight to dark on their farms or at other forms of work. They had little leisure time to enjoy entertainment, so there was no great need for popular culture.

With the coming of the Industrial Revolution, factory work became scheduled rigidly by the clock and people began to have at least some leisure time. However, diversions were fewer than they are now. People could turn to print media if they were literate. Or, if they had an afternoon or day off they could attend circuses, amusement parks, dance halls, roller skating rinks, and so on.

As leisure time increased, there was a great need for simple forms of diversion that could be enjoyed at home, or by traveling a short distance and paying a modest fee. The movies provided just such entertainment and they began to produce popular culture after the turn of the century. Then came home radio, with its soap operas, quiz shows, evening drama, comics, sports broadcasts, and other forms of entertainment. With each additional medium came an increasing flood of popular entertainment fare. After television arrived, the airways were flooded with sports, sitcoms, daytime serials, old movies and cartoons, and the Age of Popular Culture became an ever-present reality. After cable and the VCR joined the available media, the pace increased even further.

Thus, popular culture is a product of our dependency on mass communication and our increasing inability to gratify our needs for diversion by social contacts with our family and neighbors. Today, our society requires a relentless flow of new entertainment content that plays a critical role in the competitive struggle among the media for audience attention.

Those who produce popular culture turn to any source that can be turned into simple entertainment for the masses. Elite art and high culture are often simplified and used for commercial purposes in the production of popular culture. Critics maintain that the consequent production of *kitsch* debases high culture, exploits the public who must pay, and diminishes interest in real-life heroes who make significant contributions to our civilization. These ideas can be summarized as the *theory of popular culture*, which explains both its sources and its influences on art and the public. Its major propositions are as follows:[19]

**1.** Our privately owned mass media are dedicated to maximizing their *profits* by presenting advertising messages, increasing their circulations, viewers, and so on.

**2.** This profit motive locks them into an economic dependency on attracting and holding the attention of the *largest number of people* who make up the potential media audience, regardless of their level of artistic tastes.

**3.** The simple tastes of most people in this audience are not linked to either folk art or sophisticated elite art, but to unsophisticated entertainment (emphasizing popular music, sports heros, talk shows, games, sensational stories, etc.) that makes *limited intellectual demands* on its consumers.

**4.** To maximize profits from advertising, subscriptions, movie admissions or direct sales, the media produce and disseminate an endless flow of such content—that is, *popular culture* (cheaply produced products with no redeeming artistic value, which are often labeled as "kitsch").

**5. Therefore,** the economic and consumer taste systems driving the media result in a constant production and consumption of kitsch, which exploits and drives out artistic products by mining their themes. The result is a *destruction* of both folk art and elite art, economic *exploitation* of the public, and a *diminishing* of the significance of real-life heroes.

politics, and industry dominated magazine biography, but later *idols of consumption*, persons from entertainment, the arts, and sports, moved ahead in popular appeal.[20]

Hero study traces its origins to an essay by the historian Thomas Carlyle published in 1885, who demonstrated how forceful personalities have shaped history. Although the great man or woman theory of history is now on the wane, scholars and media critics still find the study of heroes useful in examining people's attitudes and values. In effect, heroes become symbols for public hope and aspirations and, according to cultural critics, serve a social function.

Are the days of true or real-life heroes gone? Some people feel that they are. As the media assumed a greater presence, many critics maintain, a new *hero of kitsch* began to replace the hero and heroine of the *deed*. These new objects of public adulation are not individuals with extraordinary personal qualities. Instead, they are media-created idols known for their sex appeal, their alluring voices, and their athletic or acting ability.

It is greatly to the advantage of the media and those who create and supply popular culture to convince the audience that their products are *truly important*. One way that this is done is through highly publicized "competitions" in which a multitude of awards (Oscars, Tonys, Emmys, Heisman trophies) are presented to the creators of kitsch, usually in highly publicized, televised ceremonies. These events powerfully reinforce the illusion that these are the people in our society that really "count." Yet, critics ask, are they simply modern versions of "The Lone Ranger," who was, as sociologist Richard Quinney noted "nothing more than a creation of commercial enterprise"—a creature who had no real existence aside from images on film?

Thus, the view posed by popular culture theory is that most contemporary heroes are media creations of kitsch whose fame derives not from extraordinary deeds that inspire and benefit society, but from words on paper, images on the screen, and sounds from CDs and tapes. Some are actual people who sing, dance, act, and play sports. Others are pure inventions—imaginary characters who have no real existence aside from movies, the soap opera, or prime-time sitcom. There is ample reason to believe, say the critics, that in treating these illusions as though they are important, our society has merged fantasy with reality in a final commitment to kitsch.

We can identify several categories of such media-created heroes. First, there is the *hero of ball and stick*. A long list of athletes have been made into celebrities through media attention, from Babe Ruth and Red Grange to today's Michael Jordan and Tiger Woods. Clearly these individuals are superb athletes and have received extraordinary financial rewards. Yet critics say it would be difficult to account for their immense popularity on any other grounds than the status conferred on them by the media.[21] Striking a ball skillfully with a bat, racket, or club contributes little to the national destiny. Athletic skill is scarcely the stuff of which advances in civilization are made.

Another significant category is the *hero of the titillating tune*. Famous singers are instantly recognized by millions of fans. Not many members of the older generation in the United States would fail to identify the voices of Bing Crosby or Frank Sinatra. Today, the sounds of Toni Braxton and Mariah Carey command instant recognition. The songs that these and other musicians have made famous through the media constitute an important part of today's kitsch. Here, the dependence of popular culture on folk and elite art is especially clear. Many songs that have made the top of the popularity lists are based on either classical music or American folk traditions, such as early American ballads and grassroots jazz.

Of even greater interest are the *heroes of superhuman power*. Characters of the imagination have long intrigued people. For example, one could easily speculate that the various "supermen" of today's media are the counterparts of ancient mythological deities with fantastic powers who appeared in human form. There is a timeless attraction to fantasies of power and success. Millions have been entertained by the unusual deeds of a long list of fictional characters with superhuman capacities. Generations of readers have admired and coveted the powers of such fantasy creations as Superman, Spiderman, Wonder Woman, and Batman.

Other contemporary media characters have human limitations, but are remarkably capable of combating the forces of evil. Here the critics include the police *heroes of screeching tires,* the cloak-and-dagger *heroes of international spydom,* and the steely-eyed "private eye." The list would not be complete without the *heroes of the legal ploy* and the venerable *heroes of suture and scalpel.* What hard-working private eye measures up to Magnum? Who can defeat James Bond or Dirty Harry? The capacities of real people in the real world are pale and flabby by comparison.

How, then, can we evaluate this theory of popular culture? The charge that popular culture draws from elite culture can clearly be substantiated in many cases. However, whether popular culture should be *condemned* for doing so is an open question. The conclusion that the public is forced to pay for popular culture also seems correct, for the public ultimately pays the high salaries of media heroes and heroines because they are added to the costs of advertising and marketing the products of sponsors. On the surface this does rather look like "economic exploitation of the masses," but the final assessment must be decided on the basis of one's personal values.

Finally, the charge that media heroes diminish interest in accomplishments in real life may also have some validity. Most of the significant achievements of "ordinary" people that make the news do so in the back pages of the paper. The accomplishments of scientists, artists, and others who make significant contributions to our culture seldom receive much recognition, whereas gossip about celebrities often makes front page headlines. Overall, then, the theory of popular culture makes important arguments. However, the degree to which these aspects of popular culture actually represent a *threat* to the public as a whole remains a matter of personal judgment.

## Taste Publics as Markets for Media Presentations

The theory of popular culture makes important assumptions about taste levels among the public. Just what are the different levels of taste among those that the media serve, and how are these tastes linked to the production of kitsch? We can take a brief look at these issues in this section. However, the analysis of taste publics, like debates about the merits of popular culture, is also outside the framework of science and proceeds from individual opinions and standards. Judgments must be made about whether enjoying a particular artistic product represents "high" or "low" taste, or something in between, and judgments about "good" and "bad" taste depend on subjective values, not scientific criteria. Nevertheless, such analyses focus our attention on significant factors in the basic support system of American media.

Because the task is difficult, and the risk that others will disagree strongly is great, not many scholars have analyzed taste publics in the United States. Sociologist Herbert Gans, however, has used the method of qualitative observation to identify five major levels of taste in American society.[22] In the sections that follow, we describe these taste publics and the content they tend to prefer. Our description is based largely, but not exclusively, on Gans' analysis. Education seems most important in defining taste levels, but many other factors are also involved.

The **high culture taste public** likes the products of "serious" writers, artists, and composers. High culture is found in the little magazines, in off-Broadway productions, in a few art-film theaters, and on rare occasions on educational television. It values innovation and experimentation with form, substance, method, overt content, and covert symbolism. Styles tend to change often. Art, for example, has been dominated at one time or another by expressionism, impressionism, abstraction, conceptual art, and so forth. In fiction, high culture emphasizes complex character development over plot. Modern high culture explores psychological and philosophical themes, among them alienation and conflict.

Clearly, this form of culture would have little appeal to the majority of the media's usual audience. For this reason, it is seldom found in mass communication. Members of the small segment of the public that prefers high culture consider themselves elite and their culture exclusive.

The **upper-middle taste public** is concentrated in the upper-middle socioeconomic class—which is composed mainly of professionals, executives, managers, and their families. These people are well educated and relatively affluent, but are neither creators nor critics. For the most part they are consumers of literature, music, theater, and other art that is accepted as "good."

To characterize the upper-middle-class public, one might generalize that they prefer fiction that stresses plot over characters or issues, and that this group favors stories about people like themselves who have successful careers and play important parts in significant affairs. They tend to like films and programs about likable upper-middle-class people in upper-middle-class settings. They read *Time* or *Newsweek* and enjoy the kind of new media fare that appears in *Wired*. They might well be familiar with classical music and opera but dislike contemporary or experimental compositions. They purchase hardcover trade books, support their local symphony orchestra, and occasionally attend the ballet. They subscribe to magazines like *The New Yorker*, *National Geographic*, and *Vogue*.

Although this group is fairly large, its influence on media content is actually quite limited. Some television dramas, public affairs programs, and FM radio represent the upper-middle level, but most media content is at the level below it. The reason is that although they are relatively affluent as families go, there is simply not enough of them. Taken as a whole, their aggregate purchasing power does not add up to an impressive part of the total of the nation.

The **lower-middle taste public** is the dominant influence in mass communication for two reasons. First, the lower-middle taste public includes the largest number of Americans; second, it has sufficient income to purchase most media-advertised products. The people of this level tend to be white-collar workers (for example, public school teachers, lower-level managers, computer programmers, government bureaucrats, druggists, and higher-paid clerical workers). A substantial number are college-educated, many with degrees in technical subjects. This public often consciously rejects the culture preferred by the taste levels above it, but occasionally uses some of their forms, especially after they have been transformed into popular culture.

The lower-middle public continues to support religion and its moral values. It tends to like books, films, and television drama in which old-fashioned virtue is rewarded. Thus, it disapproves of positive portrayals of gays, promiscuity, or other "deviant" lifestyles. The lower-middle public likes unambiguous plots and heroes. They loved the late John Wayne, who espoused traditional virtues. Neither complexity of personality nor philosophical conflicts are dominant themes. People of lower-middle tastes commonly read *Reader's Digest* or subscribe to *People*. They also purchase millions of paperbacks with fast-action plots. They enjoy television programs such as "Melrose Place," family and situation comedy, cop-and-crook dramas, musical extravaganzas, soap operas, and quiz shows. Earlier, they tuned into "All In the Family" (many even supported main character Archie Bunker's racial and ethnic biases). In music, Lawrence Welk (recently revived on television) remains most appealing for older members of this group, and groups like the Beach Boys for the younger generation. Such music makes few intellectual demands from its listeners.

The **low culture taste public** consists mainly of skilled and semiskilled blue-collar workers in manufacturing and hands-on service occupations (factory line workers, auto repair, furnace servicing, routine plumbing). Their education level is likely at the vocational school level or less. Younger members of this category attend vocationally-oriented community colleges. Although still numerically large, this taste public is shrinking. More blue-collar families are now sending their children to four-year colleges, and many manufacturing industries are rapidly being replaced.

This taste public dominated media content in the 1950s and 1960s and still plays a part. But because its purchasing power is currently somewhat less than that of the lower-middle level, it is being replaced by that category as the dominant influence on the media. However, the media continue to produce a substantial amount of unsophisticated content for this audience.

The taste public for low culture likes action—often violent action—in film and television drama. Thus, to please this public the media resist efforts to censor the portrayal of violence. This group enjoys simple police dramas, comedy shows, and western adventures. Popular are programs with a lot of slapstick (older examples are the Lucille Ball and Jackie Gleason shows), as well as "Wheel of Fortune," wrestling, and country-western music. For reading, they like the *National Enquirer,* confession magazines (for women), and *Wrestling* (for men).

The **quasi-folk taste public** is at the bottom of the socioeconomic ladder. It is composed mainly of people who are poor and have little education and few occupational skills. Many are on welfare or hold uncertain or unskilled jobs. A large portion are nonwhite and of rural or foreign origin. Although this group is numerous, it plays only a minor role in shaping media content, primarily because its aggregate purchasing power is low.

The art appreciated at this bottom level of taste resembles that of the low culture level. This taste public tends to like simpler television shows, and in many urban areas foreign-language media cater to their needs. This group also preserves elements of their folk culture. For example, they may hold religious and ethnic festivals and social gatherings and display religious or ethnic artifacts and prints on the walls of their homes. Colorful murals adorn the streets of some urban ethnic neighborhoods.

## Implications of Popular Culture Theory

As the previous sections have made clear, popular culture as media content must be understood in terms of both the aggregate purchasing power and taste preferences of various segments of the public. Regardless of the protests, claims, and counterclaims of the critics, the media *must* continue to produce content that appeals to the largest taste publics because it attracts attention that they sell to sponsors in order to stay in business. There is little likelihood, given these dependent relationships, that on their own the media will bring about a cultural revolution by emphasizing high or even low upper-middle culture. The obvious prediction for the future is that lower-middle and lower tastes will continue to dominate American mass communication. Thus, no matter what the future holds in bigger screens, clearer pictures, more channels, or alternative modes of delivery, the taste of the lower-middle category will continue to dominate and define the nature of the majority of mass media content.

## ▼ *The Feature Syndicates as Sources for Popular Culture*

One of the most durable of the delivery systems that bring entertainment content to the print media are the feature syndicates. We discussed these earlier in terms of newspapers. However, they have become the model for television syndication as well.

As we noted in Chapter 3, the earliest syndicate was organized just after the Civil War. Others quickly followed suit, and by the late nineteenth century Irving Batchelor and S. S. McClure (who later became famous as magazine publishers) and others organized feature syndicates—a formal system for distributing a particular feature, such as a regular political analysis, comic strip, or gardening column to newspapers that subscribe to the service. William Randolph Hearst organized his King Features Syndicate in 1914. By the early 1900s, syndicates were offering opinion pieces, political cartoons, and comic strips as well as columns on fashion, personal problems, politics, and other topics, with considerable competition among them. Almost from the beginning the syndicates played an important role in making the work of particular writers and artists popular among millions of readers.

Unlike the wire services, which distribute their wares to both print and broadcast media, the syndicates aim almost exclusively at the print media. However, the major broadcast networks (ABC, CBS, NBC, and PBS) as well as some independent companies distribute material that is to local television and radio stations what syndicated material is to newspapers and magazines. Local radio and television news and evening magazine programs often include material that comes from the networks, a kind of syndicate of the air.

## What the Syndicates Provide

To understand the source of much popular culture that winds up in the media, it is necessary to understand the role of syndicates. In particular, the syndicates provide a great deal of the entertainment and opinion material for newspapers, including serializations of popular books, columns by noted political commentators, comic strips, and editorial cartoons. Other syndicates serve the television industry. In addition, some syndicates sell design services, graphics, and even newsstand racks. To the print media, they promise that their material will bring circulation gains, something every newspaper covets, and readership studies indicate that the syndicates are sometimes right.

King Features Syndicate claims to have the greatest array of comic strips for the Sunday papers. This syndicate has feature columnists who cover everything from astronomy to zoos. It offers many old favorites that go back a couple of generations, and also carries material from the rock magazine *Rolling Stone*. In addition, subscribers have access to puzzles and game columns.

Tribune Media Services (formerly the New York Daily News-Chicago Tribune Syndicate) offers "Dear Abby," the nation's most widely read advice column, and a variety of other columnists and comics. Along with crossword puzzles and other amusements, the syndicate carries editorial cartoonists Jeff MacNelly and Wayne Stayskal, as well as "Youthpoll," which keeps track of young people's opinions. Tribune Media Services gets about 60 percent of its revenues from its comics; the rest comes from the text features, puzzles, and a graphics service. Washington Post Writers Group claims to offer "bylines that build readership." Among its services are political commentary by George F.

Will and David S. Broder, economic analysis by Hobart Rowen and Jane Bryant Quinn, and media criticism from Sander Vanocur and Charles Seib. It also provides columns by Ellen Goodman, illustrations by Geoffrey Moss, editorial cartoons by Tony Auth, and the Book World Service.

## How the Syndicates Work

A former syndicate editor, W.H. Thomas, wrote, "Of all the outlets available as a market for creative talent, none is so little understood or so ill defined as the newspaper syndicate, that insular and elusive shadow-organization which exercises so much power within the various communications media."[23] Little is written about syndicate organizations, probably because even the largest of them are modest in size and complexity. However, in spite of this lack of publicity and the variations among the syndicates, we can make some generalizations about how they work.

Syndicates coordinate many people and tasks, including contracts between the creators of syndicated material and the syndicate itself and contracts between the syndicate and subscribing newspapers. They also handle the flow of money from the newspaper to the syndicate and the payment of royalties to the writers and artists. A production staff prepares material for distribution to various media outlets. Additionally, syndicates promote and market their products through personal contact, advertising, and other means.

**Acquiring material.**   First the syndicates must acquire the content that they want to distribute. To do so, they maintain regular contacts with writers, artists, designers, and others. Acquisition can be complicated and secretive, as in the negotiations for a president's memoirs, or it may result from opening the morning mail. Freelance writers and artists frequently send material to syndicates. The syndicates often serve as representatives for their writers and artists, much as literary agents represent authors. Contracts must be negotiated; the new "property" (strip or column, for example) must be prepared for marketing; then the material is sold to clients.

The syndicate usually offers a newspaper a contract for a variety of materials for a specified time at a specified cost. Like the wire services, the syndicates have a sliding scale of fees; papers with small circulations pay less. Some syndicates make it financially attractive for a newspaper to take several of their offerings, but most often, newspapers buy material from several syndicates. Sometimes there is vigorous competition for a feature.

**Managing and marketing.**   Syndicates must manage and market their wares like any business that produces a product. New items are added constantly; unsuccessful columns and cartoons are dropped. Bob Reed, former president of the Tribune syndicate, once said that syndicates are always on the lookout for new talent but are extremely cautious in signing new artists and writers. A property succeeds or fails on the basis of the numbers of papers signed. Sometimes unique circumstances intervene. For example, in the late 1970s, Reed "discovered" editorial cartoonist Jack Ohman, then a sophomore at the University of Minnesota, where he drew cartoons for the *Minnesota Daily*. Ohman, at the age of twenty, moved on to the *Columbus Dispatch,* where his work was syndicated to other papers. Later, the syndicate's star cartoonist, Jeff MacNelly, took a year's vacation, and young Ohman was picked to take his place. Instantly Ohman's work began appearing in nearly three hundred newspapers. MacNelly later returned to cartooning, but Ohman continued to draw successfully for the syndicate from his new base, the *Oregonian*.

Sometimes syndicate personnel must coordinate many talents. For example, in 1917, John F. Dille was a creative businessman with experience in advertising when he founded the National Newspaper Syndicate. Although Dille was neither an artist nor a writer, he is credited with originating adventure comic strips. The most notable accomplishment of his syndicate was the science fiction strip "Buck Rogers." Dille got the idea for "Buck Rogers" from a science fiction article in a magazine. He talked the author into writing for a strip based loosely on the story. Then he hired an artist to work with the writer, and "Buck Rogers" was born. Dille's involvement with the strip did not end there. He knew scientists at the University of Chicago and often talked with them and reported their ideas about the future to his artist and writer. Perhaps more important, Dille convinced newspapers to buy the new strip. It prospered, appearing in some 287 newspapers at the height of its popularity.

Thus, syndicates are multifaceted organizations that broker a wide variety of creative energies to potential outlets. Syndication can be carried out by large organizations or by the self-syndication efforts of a writer or artist. Syndicates are brokers, but they can also be quite creative, as was John Dille. Some syndicates are responding to the communication revolution and making substantial changes. Tribune Media Services, for example, became an information service with a broader mandate than it previously had, and ceased calling itself a syndicate in the 1980s.

## The Influence of Syndicates

Whether and to what extent feature syndicates have influence is not a purely academic consideration. In the late 1980s, a syndicate controversy erupted in Dallas, Texas, when several popular columns and comic strips distributed by Universal Press Syndicate moved from the Dallas *Times-Herald* to the Dallas *Morning News.* The *Times-Herald* lost "Doonesbury" by Gary Trudeau, "The Far Side" by Gary Larson, "For Better or For Worse" by Lynn Johnston, and "Herman" by Jim Unger, as well as "Dear Abby" by Abigail Van Buren, "Erma Bombeck," and "A Conservative View" by James J. Kilpatrick. A lawsuit was filed and an angry dispute ensued.[24]

This was not the first time that a tug of war between various features would be settled in the courts. The reason? "Syndicates have an enormous influence, especially in competitive markets, and the potential for abuse exists," says Roy E. Bode, editor of the Dallas *Times-Herald*.[25] But this may depend on how many features a given paper gets from a single source. According to Steven S. Duke of the Chicago *Sun-Times*, "I don't think syndicates can dominate newspapers. At least not here. We don't buy that many pieces from a single syndicate. If we lost them all, it wouldn't cause any significant damage."[26] However, the late editor and publisher of the Oakland *Tribune*, Robert Maynard, came down somewhere in the middle, when he wrote:

> When I became editor [of the *Tribune*] I found the *San Francisco Chronicle* had exclusive contracts with all their major syndicates. Every feature we wanted, we couldn't have. We sued and finally settled. The settlement enabled us to get all the features we wanted on a phased-in basis. I came to understand that syndicates are middlemen, distributors. Some find and develop powerful features and then control who can buy them. The question is, is it smart business or undue influence? There is no easy answer.[27]

Nevertheless, the debate over the impact and influence of syndicates and their services continues.

## ▼ *Sports as Popular Culture*

Sports is a form of popular culture that is deeply rooted in modern society. From neighborhood games to school, college and professional sports, it is so pervasive in society that even presidential debates have to step aside rather than compete for public attention and approval. In the 1996 presidential campaign, for example, the timing of the Olympics was key to scheduling of the debates, and no political party would have dared suggest preempting a game for a debate to pick the next president of the United States. In the midst of an important tennis playoff a few years ago, the "CBS Evening News" was delayed for several minutes, and Dan Rather stomped off the set in a famous incident, which again pointed up the apparent economic and psychological value sports has for television.

Sports as conveyed in media also has considerable international clout. Several years ago when the United States had no diplomatic relations with China, it was media coverage of ping-pong matches between Chinese and American teams that brought a breakthrough. Sadly, the Olympics has also been used as a tragic staging ground for international politics, as in the 1972 Munich Olympics when Israeli athletes were attacked and killed by terrorists. In 1980, then President Jimmy Carter blocked U.S. participation in the Moscow Olympics to protest Soviet downing of a Korean aircraft in violation of international law.

There is also a whole sports-culture industry, ranging from toys and games to cards, calendars, magazines, books, T-shirts and clothing, and other items. The demand for such items is promoted by media coverage of sports and by advertising that features sports and sports figures. Sports has also been a major source for America's heroes. Baseball figures like Babe Ruth, Lou Gehrig, Joe DiMaggio, and Mickey Mantle cast a long shadow across the sport and American life. In virtually every sport there have been great "heroes" such as Joe Louis and Muhammad Ali from boxing. Whether it is hockey, tennis, golf, basketball, football, or baseball, each sport has its great figures, which Americans know for their athletic feats and for their personalities far better than they know their national leaders or powerful figures from other fields.

If the amount of attention given to an aspect of popular culture is any indication of its importance, then sports heads the list of popular culture fare. Sports coverage in the media, whether in newspapers or on network, cable, and pay-per view television, is dominant in terms of the time and space it occupies and the revenues it brings to media. In the late 1990s, such coverage occupied 20 percent of all newspaper space and 25 percent of television's weekend and special-event coverage. Roughly 19 percent of all newspaper reporters cover sports, as do 21 percent of all consumer magazines. No other subject gets as much media attention.

Sports is a vital form of popular culture and has wide appeal. Images of winners and losers, success and failure, pain and pleasure are drawn from sports. Without muscular sports metaphors in the language, American businesses would probably not communicate at all. The most valuable and expensive advertising time on television is during the Super Bowl, World Series, and Olympics.

The earliest sports journalism in the United States and elsewhere emphasized the pastimes of the wealthy, such as hunting and horse racing. Pastimes of the poor or common people received less attention. Although this has changed greatly over time, sports journalism today has a middle-class bias and covers mainly baseball, football, hockey, and a few other major sports. Upscale sports like skiing, golf, and tennis also get considerable coverage; the down-home pastimes of less affluent people such as bass fishing, professional wrestling, and stock car racing are rarely covered in the sports pages.

In a very real sense, media industries and sports both date from the Industrial Revolution, when people began to have more leisure time. Newspapers at first paid little attention to sports, and some leading editors such as the legendary Horace Greeley of the *New York Tribune* seemed ambivalent about sports and its coverage. As historian John D. Stevens points out, Greeley once devoted six columns of coverage to a prizefight and a one-column editorial denouncing the brutality of the sport in the same issue. Still, sports and newspapers grew up together, and as the Penny Press of the 1830s developed, sports coverage helped draw ordinary people to these inexpensive, highly popular papers.

Henry Chadwick, an Englishman who came to America in 1824 at the age of thirteen, became America's first important sports writer and was especially influential in popularizing baseball. He wrote for the *New York Times,* Greeley's *New York Tribune,* the *Brooklyn Eagle,* and the *New York Clipper*—where he covered, promoted, criticized, and helped standardize the rules of baseball.

The development of spectator sports was in many ways an outcome of the Industrial Revolution. Individualistic sports, such as hunting and fishing, were carried on in frontier or rural environments. Games such as croquet and tennis began as activities for the family at home. However, as more and more people crowded into urban-industrial areas, sports were needed as diversions for large numbers of spectators who could pay only limited fees. Such games as football and baseball met this need. Henry Chadwick, the first important sportswriter in the United States, popularized baseball and helped standardize its rules. He is widely regarded as one of the "fathers" of the game. (The Bettmann Archive)

Although Chadwick did not invent baseball, he was known in his lifetime as the "Father of the Game." According to John Stevens, until the advent of baseball there were no specific games that were played uniformly across America. Baseball at first was an entirely amateur affair, but by the late 1860s players were being paid, sometimes under the table. The Cincinnati Red Stockings was the first team to admit having professional players, which came after a season of 57 wins, no losses, and one tie.

Chadwick played an important role in covering and commenting on baseball during this period, and published the first annual baseball guides. He noted that there was little agreement about the number of players on a team and the specific rules of the game. In his compilations, he summarized rules and helped institutionalize baseball. People in distant places who had never seen the game played learned it from Chadwick's writings. This remarkable man urged the use of gloves and chest protectors for catchers, criticized team owners, and helped organize the first professional sportswriters organization. Chadwick is credited with helping to make baseball the national pastime, and was one of the first nonplayers elected to the Baseball Hall of Fame in Cooperstown, New York.

Sports columns like those written by Chadwick became sports pages and eventually sports sections of newspapers. They were also the forerunners of sports magazines. Sports coverage spread over time, and along the way other artifacts of popular culture such as sports books, baseball cards, and other materials appeared. With the advent of radio, actual coverage including play-by-play action was possible, and the dominant role of sports in the press, while still important, was never the same again. Television ushered in a new era of sports media fare and also a new era of media economics, wherein the rights to broadcast games of popular teams, the Olympics, and the Super Bowl generated huge revenues.

Sports broadcasting was largely invented and defined by two important events: David Sarnoff's coverage of the Dempsey-Carpentier championship boxing match in 1921, and the 1958 National Football League championship game between the Baltimore Colts and the New York Giants. Author Huntington Williams says the first event launched prizefighter Jack Dempsey, one of the most popular and mythic sports figures of all times, as a hero of popular culture and established Sarnoff and his fledging National Broadcasting Company (NBC) as the leader of post–World War I radio—and eventually television. The NFL game coverage established professional football as the first money-sport of the television era.

The narrators of sports programs on radio and television became legends in their own time as well. In the 1920s, Graham McNamee, who first covered the 1923 World Series, understood the game and communicated it well to the public with a rich, baritone voice and colorful play-by-play announcing. He was such a popular figure that he once received 50,000 letters during a World Series. And, of course, he and others who joined him in the broadcasting booths in stadiums all over America brought their listeners the heroic exploits of great teams and players, which themselves became legends in sport.

In the television era, ABC Sports, an independent company owned by the ABC network, did not treat sports as mere entertainment or as a subset of news, but as a subject of its own. With live productions of sporting events, the network staged extravaganzas and harnessed new technology to dazzle the public with instant replays and other marvels of the electronic age. Under the leadership of Roone Arledge, one of the greatest programmers in modern broadcast history, and with the collaboration of engineer-technologist Julius Barnathan, ABC Sports harnessed satellites, employed minicams and developed computer graphics long before they were used by other networks for sports, news, or entertainment. Most visible to the public through three decades of television's championing of sports was announcer Howard Cosell, sportscaster for "Monday Night Football." With a distinctive style and personality, Cosell became the most famous figure in television sports. He dominated the screen with his opinionated interviews, analyses, and play-by-play action. He even appeared in movies playing himself.

Television revenues took professional sports from a mostly local, modest enterprise to billion-dollar enterprises. By the 1990s, as the television networks fell behind cable as a competitor for the best sports fare, the sports industry was itself again in charge, and television was more of a vehicle for its distribution. The ESPN network, a 24-hour, all-sports service on cable, became a regular feature of most fans' TV diet.

There is no doubt that sports programming will remain as one of the most popular forms of popular culture. Although there are significant segments of the population who have little interest in, or even detest, spectator sports, the ability of such content to attract attention makes it an advertiser's dream, at least for many kinds of products.

# CHAPTER REVIEW

▼ A great need for popular culture was created by the industrial revolution of the nineteenth century. Factories established regular workdays, which defined and expanded people's leisure time. With larger blocks of free time available, the demand for amusement and entertainment expanded, which came in the form of mass communicated diversions, amusements, and entertainment.

▼ Much of the content of the mass media today is popular culture that is sold for a profit and integral to the economics of the media. Audiences are courted to consume popular culture, ranging from various forms of entertainment to sports and even pornography. People will probably argue forever about whether a given image or presentation is popular culture or not.

▼ Somewhat arbitrarily, for purposes of this text, we can formulate a definition of popular culture. Simply put: It is mass-communicated messages that make limited intellectual and aesthetic demands—content that is designed to amuse and entertain media audiences.

▼ Some reasons for taking popular culture seriously in the study of communication are: (1) it reaches almost all of the public in one form or another; (2) whether we like it or not, it influences the way we think, act, dress or relate to others; and (3) it has a tremendous economic impact on the media and strongly influences almost all mass communication content.

▼ People have debated the artistic merits of media-produced culture and its impact on society for generations. Media critics and defenders have disagreed hotly about whether deliberately manufactured mass "art" is blasphemy or blessing. These analyses take place *outside the framework of science.* Media criticism is an arena of debate where conclusions are reached on the basis of personal opinions and values, rather than carefully assembled data.

▼ Folk art consists of products that are developed spontaneously among anonymous people. It is unsophisticated, localized, and natural. It is produced by many unknown artists who are talented and creative but who receive no recognition for their contributions. It is a grassroots type of art created by its consumers and tied directly to their values and daily experiences.

▼ Elite art is deliberately produced by talented and creative individuals who often gain great personal recognition for their achievements. It is technically and thematically complex as well as highly individualistic, as its creators aim at discovering new ways of interpreting or representing their experience.

▼ In modern times, many critics maintain, both folk and elite art are threatened by kitsch—a tragically inferior category. With the advent of cheap news-

papers, magazines, paperback books, radio, movies, and television, this new form of art made its debut, catering to massive, relatively uneducated audiences with undeveloped aesthetic tastes.

▼ To assess the theory of popular culture, one form of mass communication provides evidence—the heroes created by the media. The presence of media-created idols of kitsch tends to diminish the stature of genuine heroes as the theory predicts. Moreover, a fascination with such media-created heroes lessens interest in meritorious accomplishments in real life.

▼ The theory of popular culture makes important assumptions about taste levels among the public. Several different levels of taste exist among those that the media serve. The largest is the lower-middle level, which has the greatest aggregate purchasing power and therefore its preferences dominate the production of media content.

▼ One of the most durable of the delivery systems that bring entertainment content to the print media are the feature syndicates. Syndicates coordinate many people and tasks, including contracts between the creators of material and the syndicate itself, and contracts between the syndicate and subscribing newspapers. They also handle the flow of money from the newspaper to the syndicate and the payment of royalties to the writers and artists.

▼ Sports is a form of popular culture that is deeply rooted in modern society. From neighborhood games to school, college, and professional sports, it is so pervasive in society that even presidential debates have to step aside rather than compete for public attention and approval.

▼ If the amount of attention given to an aspect of popular culture is any indication of its importance, then sports heads the list of popular culture fare. Sports coverage occupies 20 percent of all newspaper space and 25 percent of television's weekend and special-event coverage. Roughly 19 percent of all newspaper reporters cover sports, as do 21 percent of all consumer magazines. No other subject gets as much media attention.

## CHAPTER 11

# *Advertising*

## Using the Media in the Marketplace

*A*dvertising is ubiquitous in American society and in most of the rest of the world, too. It is seen on television and on the pages of magazines and newspapers, on billboards and in specialty items such as matchbooks and pencils as well as in cyberspace. Advertising, as we will explain later in this chapter, is a process, a commercial activity, an industry, a career, a source of media content, and a social institution. It is also an influence on people, organizations, culture, and society. Advertising is so omnipresent that sometimes people pay it little attention, thinking of it as part of the media landscape. At one time there were some predictably advertising-free zones such as public schools (where it was formally forbidden), movie theaters, cable television, and text-only magazines such as *Reader's Digest.* In recent years, however, all of those venues have opened themselves up to advertising so that there are fewer and fewer places where advertising is not highly visible. Advertising uses the names of college football bowl games, electronic screens in taxis, even some business voice mail systems. Similarly, the Internet and World Wide Web, once the private preserve of noncommercial scientists and academics, began to transmit interactive advertising in the late 1990s.

As the English historian and essayist Thomas B. Macaulay wrote, "Advertising is to business what steam is to industry—the sole propelling power. Nothing except the Mint can make money without advertising." Almost without exception, Macaulay's principle holds true for businesses today, and it is especially true for the mass media. Their solvency as businesses depends to a great extent on advertising, and advertising, in turn, depends heavily on the mass media as its vehicle. It is impossible to imagine the American mass media without advertising, for they have grown up together and each depends on the other. Although many people deplore ads on TV or elsewhere, advertising is regarded as the key to persuading consumers to buy particular goods and services. Its persuasive effects result in jobs throughout the entire complex chain of systems that either turn raw materials into finished products or perform service activities for profit.

Advertising revenues support newspapers, magazines, radio, and television in the United States. Funding and control by government is unacceptable to Americans. As the Internet and the World Wide Web continue to develop, ways will have to be found to pay all of their costs and to make a profit for investors. It seems clear that, in the long run, advertising will have to play a major part. (Silicon Graphics, Inc.)

Advertising is the main source of funds for the American system of mass communication. It is one of two streams of revenue that support American communications industries. Advertisers use communications media to market products and services to consumers, or "end users" as economists call them. Not surprisingly, the other revenue stream for communications are end users themselves—individuals and families who buy magazines, subscribe to newspapers or cable services, and consume records, videotapes, and other media products.

If there were once advertising-free zones in American society as we have suggested earlier, that condition also described much of the rest of the world, especially the communist states of the former Soviet Union, Eastern Europe, and elsewhere. One could visit Russia, China, North Korea, and other countries where there were no neon signs or billboards advertising commercial products. There were, however, signs promoting the government or the leader in power. With the decline of communism and transformation to more democratic media, advertising as part of a capitalist market economy became commonplace. Even in authoritarian China, which once forbade advertising as "bourgeois capitalist decadence," commercial messages now flourish. Only in a few places today, such as North Korea, is commercial advertising virtually unknown. Thus, it appears that advertising is essential to the modern market economy. There are no known instances where there are free market *and* an advertising-free society, although some international broadcast systems, such as the BBC, pride themselves on not carrying commercial announcements.

As tightly controlled societies turned in recent decades from centrally managed economies to those based increasingly on private enterprise, advertising became more common and essential. In Russia, for example, advertising was forbidden and unnecessary twenty years ago. Today, as the trend toward a market economy accelerates in Russia, the advertising of products and services is becoming much more common. (Reuters/Corbis-Bettmann)

This chapter examines both the content and function of advertising as communication. We look briefly at how it developed and how advertising messages are manufactured. We will give attention to the industry, its messages, its structure, the connection of advertising to public taste, and criticisms of the outcomes it supposedly produces.

# ▼ *Advertising as Communication*

Advertising is a social institution in its own right—a deeply established part of American culture. It is not a mere appendage to the mass media; that is, it has a structure and existence of its own, and it is an important factor in the U.S. economy. Moreover, as economic historian David M. Potter wrote:

> Advertising now compares with such long-standing institutions as the school and the church in the magnitude of its social influence. It dominates the media, it has vast power in shaping popular standards, and it is really one of the very limited group of institutions which exercise social control.[1]

Viewed in this broader context, then, advertising is a central feature of our urban-industrial society—one that needs to be understood in relation to society's other institutions and processes. However, advertising takes so many forms that it is not easy to sort out the central principles that need study. For example, consider the following: a television commercial, a catchy slogan, a full-page spread in a magazine, a pencil with the name of a firm embossed on its side, a poster above your seat on a bus or subway. All these are forms of advertising, but what do they have in common? Thus, this examination of advertising begins with a look at its definition, functions, content, and history.

## What Is Advertising?

Perhaps the answer many people would give to the question "What is advertising?" would be similar to the common reply to "What is art?" That answer is, "I can't define it, but I know it when I see it!" Nevertheless, it will be helpful to examine attempts to provide a definition and then develop one that incorporates the most essential features.

A dictionary definition suggests that advertising is simply "the action of attracting public attention to a product or business [as well as] the business of preparing and distributing advertisements."[2] Another, provided by the American Marketing Association, states that advertising is "any paid form of nonpersonal presentation and promotion of ideas, goods and services by an identified sponsor."[3] Neither of these definitions, however, notes the role of the mass media in advertising. To correct this deficiency, a leading advertising textbook defines advertising as "controlled, identifiable information and persuasion by means of mass communications media."[4]

Each of these definitions provides at least a part of the answer. Advertising is *controlled* in that it is prepared in accordance with the desires of the firm or other group it represents. Unlike a person who grants an interview to the press not knowing how his or her words will appear, the advertiser knows exactly what the message will say. Furthermore, advertising is identifiable as *communication*. The message may be subtle or direct, but you know it is advertising and not, for example, news. Advertising can be entertaining, but few would claim that entertainment is its primary goal. If advertising entertains, that is only a means to an end. That end is to increase sales. Thus, advertising tries to inform consumers about a *particular product* and to persuade them to make a *particular decision*—usually, the decision to buy that product. Its avowed goal is to guide and control buying behavior, to move the consumer toward one product instead of another. Thus, it is a form of *social control,* urging the consumer to conform within a range of product choices, "providing norms of behavior appropriate to current economic conditions."[5]

Taking a more theoretical approach, one could define advertising in terms of the meaning construction theory of mass communication's effects presented in Chapter 17. In these terms, it is an attempt to establish, extend, substitute, or stabilize people's meanings for symbols that label the advertiser's products or services. Advertisers seek to influence language conventions, individual interpretations, and the shared meanings associated with such symbols so that people will make choices favorable to the advertisers' purposes. In other words, they hope that through communication they can get people to know about, like, and purchase their clients' wares.

Each of these attempts to define advertising has merit. However, each also emphasizes only one or two important features of the process. Thus, in order to set forth clearly what this chapter is about, we can develop the following more comprehensive definition: **Advertising** *is a form of controlled communication that attempts to persuade an appropriate audience, through the use of a variety of appeals and strategies, to make a decision to buy or use a particular product or service.* Because advertisers make use of many other channels of communication, this definition does not specify that the message must be transmitted via the mass media. However, a huge amount of advertising is presented via mass media, so we focus on that in this chapter.

## The Content of Advertising

To accomplish their ends, advertisers must make a *persuasive appeal.* Sometimes that appeal is simple and descriptive; sometimes it is subtle and sophisticated. Communication scholar James W. Carey says that advertising is persuasive— and thus acts as a form of social control—mainly by providing information.[6] Indeed, some advertising content is direct and makes rational appeals, mentioning characteristics of the product, its relative advantages, and price. A General Tire commercial that features babies, for example, talks about the durability of the tire and its role in keeping the family safe.

Much advertising, however, has little to do with direct information or rational appeals. Instead it attempts to manipulate the consumer by indirect appeals. Research in the 1990s on Americans' favorite commercials indicated that those with fantasy scenes, such as the ads for the California Raisins or Kibbles 'n Bits dog food, are more popular than those featuring celebrities. Economic historian David Potter maintains, "Advertising appeals primarily to the desires, the

▶

McDonald's "golden arches" have become one of the most durable symbols in American advertising, whose messages typically change rapidly. Anyone who sees these arches easily recognizes the products with which they are associated. Another example of an enduring symbol was the "Marlboro man," who was instantly recognizable to millions. (© Elaine Braithwaite/ Peter Arnold, Inc.)

wants—cultivated or natural—of the individual, and it sometimes offers as its goal a power to command the envy of others by outstripping them in the consumption of goods and services."[7] If this is true, advertising may try to get you to buy a product not because of its advantages and not because of your existing needs, but because of a need or desire that the advertisement itself tried to create.

Potter's analysis has much merit. Almost every appeal imaginable has been used in advertising. Some ads have traded on prestige; others have used fear. Some have promised glamour and the good life. Some have embraced fantasy, and others have been firmly fixed in reality. To make these appeals, advertisers associate products, verbally and visually, with other images, symbols, and values that are likely to attract consumers. For example, advertising for the auto rental firm Avis appealed to the love for the underdog when it promised, "We try harder." Historically, another kind of dog—the trustworthy family dog—was used by RCA Victor, an early manufacturer of the record player that advertised the Victrola with the slogan "His Master's Voice" and a picture of a dog listening to recorded music. The starched but debonair look of "the man in the Arrow shirt" provided a model for the well-dressed man. Elegant, tastefully designed advertisements for Cadillacs convey an image of quality and excellence. Coca-Cola's successful "It's the Real Thing" advertisements show happy, fun-loving, youthful people drinking Coke with upbeat music playing in the background—without saying anything about taste, nutritional value, or price.

The advertising industry places a high premium on creativity in finding new images that will appeal to the public. Table 11.1 lists some winners of the

**Table 11.1**

| Category | Client & Ad (or Series) | Advertising Agency |
|---|---|---|
| Local Campaign | The Amy Burack Company; "Bill Gates," "Gandhi," "Keith Richards" | McConnaughy Stein Schmit, Chicago, IL |
| Apparel/Fashion | Nike; "Leslie" and Levi Strauss & Co.; "Dockers" | Elias Associates, New York, NY<br>Foote, Cone & Belding, San Francisco, CA |
| Automotive Products | Pioneer; "Epicenter" | BBDO West, Los Angeles, CA |
| Banking/Financial | John Hancock Financial; "Subway," "Shepherds," "Triple Squeeze" | Hill, Holliday, Connors, Cosmopolus, Inc., Boston, MA |
| Beverage/Alcoholic | Anheuser-Busch; "Football," "Fisherman," "Earthcore" | Atherton & Associates, New York, NY |
| Cinematography | Anheuser-Busch; "Football," "Fisherman," "Earthcore" | Goodby, Silverstein & Partners, San Francisco, CA |
| Home Entertainment | Segasoft; "Egg" | Ground Zero Advertising, Santa Monica, CA |
| Home Products | Fire Ant Killer; "Sole Contribution" | BBDO West, Los Angeles, CA |
| Media Promotion | HBO; "Chimps" | BBDO, New York, NY with Quiet Man, New York, NY |
| Music Adaptation | Levi Strauss & Co.; "Dockers" | Ren Klyee Sound/Music, Mill Valley, CA |
| Print Advertising | Pioneer; "Turbulence," "Earthcore" | BBDO West, Los Angeles, CA |
| Performance | McDonald's; "Sophisticated Chicken" | World Wide Wadio, Hollywood, CA |
| Animation—Computer | Nissan; "Toys" | Vill Vinton Studios, Portland, OR |
| Special Effects | Segasoft; "Egg" | Sight Pix, Venice, CA |
| Visual Style Direction | Segasoft; "Egg" | Morton Jankel Zander, Hollywood, CA |

1996 Clio awards, which are given annually to the best, most effective ads. Even the sometimes prosaic area of outdoor or billboard advertising has been on the lookout for striking, appealing ads. In 1992, for example, that industry's Creative Challenge contest sponsored by the Gannett Outdoor Group honored an ad showing a mighty dam holding back a waterfall. Above the dam appeared a single word: "Huggies." Said the *New York Times*, "This unexpectedly imaginative way of advertising one of the most mundane products [disposable diapers] has won a hefty prize in a contest intended to persuade agencies that creativity in outdoor ads is no oxymoronic concept." The winners of the $10,000 prize were three employees of the advertising agency Ogilvy &

Mather; the big winner, naturally, was the advertiser itself—Kimberly-Clark, producer of Huggies.[8]

Not all advertising focuses on a specific *product,* such as diapers. A form called **institutional advertising** is much less direct. For example, a firm that makes paper and other forest products presents a television ad or a colorful full-page magazine ad describing the virtues of a beautiful, well-managed forest. The advertisement shows cute animals but says nothing about its specific product, providing only the corporation's name. The goal is, of course, to get the public to associate the corporation with the "selfless" ad and lovely images.

The visual and verbal content of advertising has changed considerably over time. In the last hundred years, styles have included the ornate and highly decorative soap and cosmetic ads of the 1890s, the clean lines of the art deco designs of the 1920s and 1930s, and the psychedelic posterlike ads of the 1960s and early 1970s. More recently, the clean, orderly, Swiss Gothic look of the 1980s yielded in the 1990s to more traditional and formal design, possibly in response to an economic recession and later recovery. It is, says design expert Roy Paul Nelson, all a matter of coordinating art and typography with content.

These changes reflect the efforts of creative professionals and entrepreneurs to fashion effective messages. In order to be effective, an advertisement must appeal to its audience and reflect shared values. Advertising that works is therefore an index of popular culture. That was recognized as far back as 1917, when writer Norman Douglas claimed, "You can tell the ideals of a nation by its advertisements."[9] Thus, changes in advertising over the years have been closely tied to changes in American society as a whole.

## ▼ Advertising in America: A Brief History

Until recently, social histories all but ignored advertising. Even histories of journalism failed to deal with advertising's role in creating the modern mass media. However, the American Museum of Advertising in Portland, Oregon, has examples of advertising going back to the Greeks and Romans and much material from colonial America. Since our country's beginnings, advertising has had an important place in the life of the nation. As historian Daniel J. Boorstin has written:

> Advertising has remained in the mainstream of American civilization—in the settling of the continent, in the expansion of the economy, and in the building of an American standard of living. Advertising has expressed the optimism, the hyperbole and the sense of community, the sense of reaching which has been so important a feature in our civilization.[10]

American society provided one important precondition for advertising: abundance. It seems clear that advertising can thrive only in a society where abundance exists. When resources are scarce, there is little or no need for manufacturers or producers to promote their wares. As economic historian David Potter wrote:

> It is when potential supply outstrips demand—that is, when abundance prevails—that advertising begins to fulfill a really essential function. In this situation the producer knows that the limitation upon his operations and upon his growth no longer lies, as it lay historically, in his productive capacity, for he can always produce as much as the market will absorb; the limitation has shifted to the market, and it is selling capacity which controls his growth.[11]

The United States has usually provided the relative abundance necessary for advertising to be useful. And American businesses, with the help of advertising, have been very successful at increasing sales. The result is what economists have dubbed the "consumer society."

Although historians often date modern advertising to the 1880s, advertising is actually much older than that. The earliest advertising messages were those of criers or simple signs above shops. Modern advertising has its origins in the trademarks used by crafts workers and early merchants to distinguish their wares from those of others. With the advent of printing and expanding world trade, there was even more advertising. The watermarks of printers were distinctive forms of advertising. Coffee, chocolate, and tea, to name a few items, were hawked in messages on broadsides and in newspapers and other periodicals. Proving that advertising could be compelling and useful, the *London Gazette* in 1666 published an advertising supplement to help lost and homeless fire victims get in touch with one another.

In the American colonies, advertisers used many media—newspapers, pamphlets, broadsides, and almanacs. Early communications media thus became factors in the marketplace for goods and services. However, advertising was not a very important source of revenue for early newspapers. They depended more on government printing contracts and the price paid by the reader. Advertising in colonial times was somewhat subdued by modern standards and rarely overshadowed the editorial content of the papers. Still, it often received front-page billing, probably because the news often consisted of less-than-fresh reports from distant Europe, whereas the advertising was current and local.

It was the Industrial Revolution, with its huge increase in the production of goods, that made advertising so essential. From the early 1800s on, advertising grew naturally as markets expanded and factories tried to sell their goods. As the nineteenth century progressed, advertising accounted for an increasing proportion of the content of newspapers and magazines—and for more and more of their revenue. Like the press during this time, advertising was fiercely local and was paid for by local merchants.

Around the middle of the nineteenth century, **national advertising** developed. In the United States, the first advertising aimed at a national audience appeared in magazines, which were really the first medium of nationwide communication. Many of the new national magazines appealed to women. Therefore, soaps, cosmetics, and patent medicines were among the products frequently advertised in their pages.

These ads created markets for new products; that is, advertising proved that it could accelerate acceptance of new products and get people to change their buying habits. For example, in 1851, people still bought soap by the pound. Then a soap manufacturer named B.T. Babbitt introduced the bar of soap. When the public was unresponsive to the product, Babbitt introduced a history-making innovation. He offered a **premium:** For every twenty-five empty soap wrappers a buyer presented, Babbitt promised a handsome colored picture in return. The lure attracted buyers, and the idea of premiums took hold. We have been living with premiums ever since. They are common today on cigarette wrappers, cereal boxes, and other products.

The nineteenth century saw the use of another advertising strategy: the **testimonial.** Some firms used photos of beautiful or prominent women, such as the First Lady (without her permission), to promote their products. Later, movie stars, athletes, and television stars would lend their names and images to particular products. The testimonial has also become part of our culture.

In the late nineteenth century, a combination of new postal rates favorable to regularly issued publications, improved transportation, and the desire of business for nationwide markets stimulated the growth of national magazines and consequently national advertising. Magazine publishers, following the lead of Benjamin Day and the nation's newspapers, adopted the idea that the reader should be able to buy a magazine for a fraction of its actual cost (that is, less than the cost of production) whereas advertising revenue should pay for the rest and produce profits. By the 1890s, nickel and dime magazines flourished, even though the cost of production was much higher than five or ten cents.

In the twentieth century, as new mass media were developed, the importance of advertising in promoting products accelerated greatly. Radio and television were ideal as advertising media, and as we have seen in earlier chapters, they soon became dependent on its revenues. Whereas a newspaper or magazine required the receiver to purchase a subscription, broadcast messages were free and difficult to avoid; consequently broadcasting was added to print as a major advertising medium. Thus, as the industrial society developed, a symbiotic relationship provided the financial foundation of the American system of mass communication. It has been said that "Marconi may have invented the wireless and Henry Luce may have invented the news magazine, but it is advertising that has made both wireless and news magazines what they are in America today."[12]

The captains of American business fought vigorous battles for larger sales in an expanding economy. One of their weapons in this war was advertising. At first, essential goods and services were advertised, then luxury items, and then an almost infinite list of products and services. Advertising became the expression of the nation's commercial self. As the advertising industry grew, newspapers and magazines developed advertising departments catering to commercial interests that wanted to buy advertising space. Publications began to compete aggressively for advertisers' business, especially in towns where there were competing media. Large retail organizations placed large amounts of advertising, and eventually they too established advertising departments to plan and place their ads. By the 1930s, intermediaries facilitated the relationship between the commercial enterprise and the media organization. At first, these intermediaries were merely space brokers who arranged for the placement of ads. Later, they expanded their operations and became the world's first **advertising agencies**—organizations that eventually provided creative and research assistance and advertising strategies to large numbers of clients.

Thus, the main features of the modern advertising industry were established early in this century. Its development both depended on and stimulated the growth of the mass media; it could not have flowered without businesses eager to expand. And, of course, neither of these would have been possible without consumers with money to spend. Thus, advertising has become a great social institution linking the nation's productivity, its mass media, and its consuming public.

## ▼ *The Contemporary Advertising Industry*

The advertising industry exists for the purpose of putting businesses who want to market and distribute goods and services in touch with consumers who want to buy and use them. Viewed in this way, the advertising industry today is a kind of facilitator of communication between advertisers and the public. Components of the industry include

1. Advertising agencies
2. Media services organizations
3. Suppliers of supporting services ranging from public opinion research to commercial art
4. Advertising departments of retail businesses
5. Advertising media, including print and electronic media, outdoor advertising, specialty advertising, direct-mail advertising, and business advertising (also the various departments of these organizations that deal with advertising)

These are only the bare bones of the industry, and everything on the list comes in several sizes. For example, there are massive national advertising agencies with offices in scores of cities in the United States and abroad, and there are small, local agencies with only a few accounts.

Although the advertising industry is made up of independent business interests and is by no means a tightly controlled national entity, it is held together by various voluntary organizations and associations. There are, for example, associations of advertisers and advertising agencies, including the important American Association of Advertising Agencies (or 4As) and the Association of National Advertisers (the clients of agencies), as well as regional and state groups. There are also media associations concerned with advertising, including the Newspaper Advertising Bureau, the Outdoor Advertising Institute, the Television Bureau of Advertising, and the Cable Advertising Bureau, to name only a few.

These organizations and others produce regular publications that carry news of the advertising industry. Some are general-interest periodicals for advertising (for example, *Advertising Age*); others are very specific (for example, *Art Direction*, which deals with graphics). Each category of advertising (direct mail, outdoor signs, packaging, and so on) has its own publications. Information and research services as well as publishing houses also produce much on the subject of advertising.

All this adds up to a huge industry with a substantial economic impact. Forecasters estimate that by 2001, U.S. businesses will spend $411 billion per year on advertising, including media advertising and such other approaches as direct-mail marketing. (A list of the leading advertisers appears in Table 11.2.)

Of the total amount of advertising spending, media get about 60 percent, with the rest going to sales promotion, direct marketing, package design, and other activities. It is estimated that the top one hundred advertising agencies—the principal "middlemen" between advertisers, the media, and the public—were getting about 36 percent of this amount, which represented a slight but noticeable decline. It is also estimated that more than 226,900 people are employed in advertising, approximately 157,900 of them in advertising agencies in the United States. The U.S. Bureau of the Census estimates that there are nearly 14,000 establishments engaged in the advertising business, including 9,800 advertising agencies.

The trend toward concentration into large firms that we see elsewhere in the communications industries also characterize advertising. A list of the top grossing agencies, as shown in Table 11.3, sections A and B, reveals that a small number of giant New York agencies predominate in the industry. To grasp the magnitude of the business that these companies do around the world, remember that the value of billings for each firm is several times that of the income figures displayed in the table.

The various elements of the advertising industry are interrelated parts of a dynamic system in which competition is intense. The image of the harried advertising account executive often presented in movies and on television may be an overstatement, but advertising is a field marked by stress and competitiveness as agencies and other firms do battle for accounts.

**Table 11.2  Top Ten National Advertisers**

| Rank | Advertiser | Ad Spending in 1996 (in millions) | Percentage Change |
|------|------------|-----------------------------------|-------------------|
| 1 | Procter & Gamble Co. | 2,622.7 | −3.9 |
| 2 | General Motors Corp. | 2,373.4 | 14.0 |
| 3 | Phillip Morris Corp. | 2,278.9 | −10.8 |
| 4 | Chrysler Corp. | 1,419.7 | 13.8 |
| 5 | Time Warner | 1,409.9 | 8.0 |
| 6 | Sears, Roebuck & Co. | 1,317.1 | 3.3 |
| 7 | Walt Disney Co. | 1,288.8 | −0.6 |
| 8 | PepsiCo | 1,268.8 | 5.1 |
| 9 | Grand Metropolitan | 1,257.4 | 40.8 |
| 10 | Ford Motor Corp. | 1,179.2 | 1.1 |

Source: *Advertising Age*, September 29, 1997.

## Advertising Agencies

Advertising agencies have come a long way since the nineteenth century, when they were essentially space brokers. Today, there are two main types. One is the full-service agency, which performs virtually every aspect of the advertising process for its clients. The other is the boutique agency, which is a much smaller operation.

**Full service agencies.**   The **full-service agency** employs writers, artists, media experts, researchers, television producers, account executives, and others as part of the organization. Advertising professor John S. Wright and his colleagues identified three main functions for the full-service advertising agency.

1. *Planning.* The agency must know the firm, its product, the competition, and the market well enough to recommend plans for advertising.
2. *Creation and execution.* The agency creates the advertisements and contacts the media that will present them to the intended audience.
3. *Coordination.* The agency works with salespeople, distributors, and retailers to see that the advertising works.[13]

Within the full-service agency are several major functions and groups:

1. *Account management.* The account executive and his or her staff provide services to a firm or product. An account management director is responsible for relations between the agency and the client.
2. *The creative department.* The creative director supervises writers, directors, artists, and producers, who write and design the ads.

**Table 11.3    Rankings of Advertising Agencies by Income (in millions)**

| A. Top Ten U.S. Agencies by Worldwide Gross Income (in millions) | | Percentage Change |
|---|---|---|
| 1 | McCann-Erickson Worldwide, New York | $1,386.1 | 14.1 |
| 2 | BBDO Worldwide, New York | 1,280.2 | 8.6 |
| 3 | Young & Rubicam, New York | 1,271.2 | 13.3 |
| 4 | DDB Needham Worldwide, New York | 1,266.1 | 16.6 |
| 5 | J. Walter Thompson Co., New York | 1,119.1 | 6.8 |
| 6 | Ogilvy & Mather Worldwide, New York | 986.5 | 10.5 |
| 7 | Grey Advertising, New York | 935.5 | 9.2 |
| 8 | Leo Burnett Co., Chicago | 866.3 | 7.5 |
| 9 | Foote, Cone & Belding, Chicago | 798.9 | 7.9 |
| 10 | Ammirali Puris Lintas, New York | 775.4 | 6.6 |

| B. Top Ten U.S. Agencies by U.S. Gross Income (in millions) | | Percentage Change |
|---|---|---|
| 1 | Leo Burnett Co., Chicago | $393.7 | 6.2 |
| 2 | J. Walter Thompson Co., New York | 375.2 | 8.1 |
| 3 | Grey Advertising, New York | 352.2 | 7.8 |
| 4 | McCann-Erikson Worldwide, New York | 329.6 | 21.2 |
| 5 | Foote, Cone & Belding, Chicago | 299.9 | 12.0 |
| 6 | BBDO Worldwide, New York | 289.3 | 11.5 |
| 7 | Saatchi & Saatchi Advertising, New York | 274.1 | −0.9 |
| 8 | DDB Needham Worldwide, New York | 271.9 | 11.7 |
| 9 | Y & R Advertising, New York | 241.9 | 17.5 |
| 10 | Ogilvy & Mather Worldwide, New York | 233.3 | 11.4 |

| C. Top Ten U.S. Cities for Advertising by Billing (in millions) | | Percentage Change |
|---|---|---|
| 1 | New York | $34,208.9 | 15.5 |
| 2 | Chicago | 10,002.5 | 11.7 |
| 3 | Los Angeles | 7,256.2 | 12.3 |
| 4 | Detroit | 5,943.5 | 7.9 |
| 5 | San Francisco | 4,734.7 | 18.2 |
| 6 | Minneapolis | 4,259.4 | 16.1 |
| 7 | Boston | 2,753.2 | 19.6 |
| 8 | Dallas | 2,679.4 | 16.4 |
| 9 | Connecticut | 1,674.5 | 16.2 |
| 10 | New Jersey | 1,411.6 | 20.0 |

Source: *Advertising Age,* April 21, 1997.

3. *Media selection.* A media director heads a department that chooses the specific media to be used for particular ads.

4. *The research department.* This group protests advertising messages and gathers data to help the creative staff fashion a specific design and message. The research director supervises in-house research and hires public opinion firms for more extensive national and regional studies.

5. *Internal control.* The administrative operations of the agency, including public relations, are concentrated in one department.

An administrative director runs the agency. Of course, large agencies have a board of directors and the usual trappings of a big business.

**Boutiques.** A **boutique agency,** unlike its full-service counterpart, has more limited goals and offers fewer services. It is essentially a creative department and may hire other agencies for particular clients and products. Often a boutique works closely with an in-house agency—that is, a small ad group or department formed by a business to handle its own products. Most boutiques are small agencies established by people who once worked for full-service agencies.

Once, most advertising agencies and the preponderance of the advertising business were based in New York City, mainly on and around Madison Avenue. Although there were strong regional centers, such as Chicago, Los Angeles, and a few other cities, serious national advertisers usually looked to New York for big-time agencies. In the 1980s and 1990s, with the advance of new technology, many local and regional agencies in smaller cities such as Atlanta, Minneapolis, Seattle, Portland, and Kansas City began to pick up major national accounts outside of their own regions. The industry is still firmly planted in New York, the capital of the communications business, but observers are closely watching the regional developments (see part C of Table 11.3).

**Inside the agency.** What an advertising agency offers is service, and it is confidence in that service that brings clients to pay 15 percent of their total billings to an ad agency. Just what happens from the initial contact between an agency and a client to the finished advertising campaign varies considerably, depending on the size of the agency and the nature of the account. Essentially, this is how it works.

The **account management director** either calls on a business—say, a local company that manufactures solar heating devices—or someone from the business contacts the advertising agency. Indeed, the company may contact several agencies and ask all of them for proposals, with the understanding that only one will receive the account. The account management director then selects an **account executive** from within the agency, who arranges a meeting between company executives from the solar heating firm, the account management director, and other appropriate people from the agency. They discuss potential advertising objectives: Who are likely customers for the device? How can they best be reached? Through what medium? With what appeals?

Then the account executive goes to work inside the agency. The **research department** conducts studies or assembles information to answer some of the questions about potential consumers. The agency's **creative department** holds brainstorming sessions, discussing ideas for a potential campaign. Artists and writers draw up *sample ads*. These may be rough sketches of newspaper and magazine advertisements as well as broadcast **story boards,** which are a series of drawings on a panel indicating each step of a commercial. Depending on how complex and detailed the campaign will be, a variety of other specialists may be involved, such as sound engineers, graphic artists, lightning experts, and actors.

The result of all this is the sample ad, which is then *pretested* on potential consumers. The agency's research department goes over this pretesting and suggests which of several approaches would be best for the client. In recent years, copy-testing has grown in importance: All elements of a print ad or broadcast commercial are tested for consumer reactions. This process removes some of the risks of advertising and generally pleases the client. The research also guides the agency and client in deciding what media to use. Various options are print, broadcast, outdoor advertising, matchbook covers, buses, and so on.

The account executive then gathers this information and, along with other agency personnel, conducts a *presentation* for the client. First, however, potential costs are clearly laid out so that the company can evaluate the proposal. The presentation is often elaborate, with slide and tape presentations and sample ads. Research and creative personnel are called in to discuss the ads, and people from the **media department** discuss the advantages and disadvantages of using particular media for the campaign. Now the ball is in the company's court. The executives either accept or reject the agency's proposal. Their acceptance may, of course, be conditional on various modifications.

Once the go-ahead is given, the account executive coordinates activity within the agency to produce the actual ads and works with the media department to contact the appropriate media and arrange for the advertising campaign to reach the public. The research department prepares to *evaluate* the campaign so that the agency can present evidence about whom the campaign has reached and with what effect—and thus ensure that the account will be renewed in the future. Finally, the advertisement reaches the consumer. The success or failure of the campaign depends on whether an ample number of consumers head toward a local store to buy the product.

## Media Service Organizations

Advertisements must be placed in appropriate media, and space or time has to be arranged. Specialized organizations exist that spend their time buying space in the media at reasonable rates and negotiating with advertising agencies for it. Many people in these **media service organizations** once worked for advertising agencies.

One type of media service organization is the national advertising representative, who has special expertise in network television rates and knows the ideal times to display particular kinds of products. Often national advertising representatives buy blocks of television time in advance and then sell the time to various advertising agencies for particular accounts. They get involved with an account late in the game, usually after a lot of planning has been done. Other kinds of media service organizations include independent design firms and television production companies. Usually they work with the advertising agency and not directly with the advertiser.

## Advertising Departments

Whole industries, as well as large department stores, sometimes have **advertising departments.** Unlike advertising agencies, which are independent "middlemen" serving several accounts or businesses, the advertising department of a business works with that firm's products and is part of its staff. This department has an intimate knowledge of the business or industry and makes proposals for advertising plans and strategies. Its main concern is the outcome: increasing sales or heightening the awareness of a particular product or service. Advertising departments work closely with advertising agencies, which compete for their business and present alternative proposals for the campaigns. Some retail advertising departments resemble small advertising agencies and place advertising directly with local media. For more complicated transactions that involve research and other specialties, they look to agencies for assistance.

## Advertising Media

All of the standard mass media are, of course, advertising vehicles. Newspapers, magazines, TV stations, radio stations, cable companies, and other media outlets have advertising departments. At both the national and the local level, the media compete vigorously for advertising dollars. Each of the major media has some kind of national advertising association that gathers data and tries to show that it is the "best buy" for reaching a particular audience. At the local level, advertising salespeople who work for media organizations sell space to businesses either directly or through an advertising agency or media service organization.

In selecting a medium, the business or advertising agency considers the target audience to be reached, the cost of advertising, and the effectiveness of a medium for reaching the desired audience. Various sources report slightly different data, but it is clear that among the traditional mass media, newspapers get the largest share of the advertising dollar (24.1 percent), followed by television (21.7 percent), direct mail (19.3 percent), Yellow Pages (7.2 percent), radio (6.7 percent), magazines (5.2 percent), and all other types (15.8 percent). Table 11.4 indicates how advertising volume in the United States is divided.

The other types of advertising include **retail advertising** (signs and displays in stores), **specialty advertising** (pencils, calendars, and similar items),

**Table 11.4   National Ad Spending by Medium**

| | 1996 | | 1995 | | |
| Medium | Millions of Dollars | Percentage of Total | Millions of Dollars | Percentage of Total | Change (%) |
|---|---|---|---|---|---|
| Magazine | $11,213.8 | 6.4 | $10,057.8 | 6.2 | 11.5 |
| Sunday Magazine | 942.4 | 0.5 | 955.4 | 0.6 | (1.4) |
| Newspaper | 13,928.9 | 7.9 | 13,338.6 | 8.2 | 4.4 |
| National Newspaper | 1,437.0 | 0.8 | 1,136.5 | 0.7 | 26.4 |
| Outdoor | 1,107.5 | 0.6 | 1,115.0 | 0.7 | (0.7) |
| Network TV | 14,739.6 | 8.4 | 12,402.2 | 7.6 | 18.8 |
| Spot TV | 14,017.7 | 8.0 | 13,017.2 | 8.0 | 7.7 |
| Syndicated TV | 2,326.1 | 1.3 | 2,316.8 | 1.4 | 0.4 |
| Cable TV networks | 4,728.4 | 2.7 | 3,418.8 | 2.1 | 38.3 |
| Network Radio | 805.9 | 0.5 | 776.5 | 0.5 | 3.8 |
| National Spot Radio | 1,463.9 | 0.8 | 1,352.3 | 0.8 | 8.3 |
| Yellow Pages | 10,849.0 | 6.2 | 10,236.0 | 6.3 | 6.0 |
| Measured | 77,560.0 | 44.3 | 70,123.0 | 43.0 | 10.6 |
| Unmeasured | 97,670.0 | 55.7 | 92,807.0 | 57.0 | 5.2 |
| **Total** | **175,230.0** | **100.0** | **162,930.0** | **100.0** | **7.5** |

Source: *Advertising Age*, September 29, 1997.

**outdoor advertising** (billboards and other signs), **transit advertising** (posters on buses and other vehicles), and **business advertising** (special advertising directed to an industry or business, as in trade magazines and trade shows). There is also **electronic advertising** on videotext systems and on-line data services delivered through personal computers. There are even rather exotic forms, such as an electronic headline advertising service in taxicabs, and commercial messages posted over toilets in public restrooms. This list, however, gives only a hint of the diverse media for advertising. There are firms that specialize in exhibits for trade shows and fairs, firms that do skywriting, and many other outlets.

Not to be overlooked as a major advertising medium is **direct mail,** which is growing very rapidly. It began with post office deliveries of letters, brochures, broadsides, and other materials, but recently added electronic mail, automatic telephone messages, fax, video appeals, and on-line advertising on the Internet. Here new technology is amplifying a longstanding advertising medium.

Since the late nineteenth century, media that carry advertising have dominated the mass communications industries and have produced the lion's share of media revenues. By 1997, however, that certainty seemed to be changing. Such segments of the media industry as video rental outlets, pay-per-view TV networks, video shopping networks, business information services, on-line advertising, and other individual person-to-person media have become important factors in the media mix. These new media including those just described are already getting notice on Wall Street as vibrant and growing segments of the media industries.

Increasingly, audiences are being asked to pay more of the "freight" for their media fare. For example, newspapers and magazines have recently raised their prices considerably, and pay-per-view productions such as prizefights and wrestling matches may charge as much as $50 for a single evening's event. Fax newspapers and various specialized newsletters, including those delivered on the Internet, may charge hundreds if not thousands of dollars per year. In such a climate, it is probable that advertising will play a slightly less significant role than in the past, and certainly the idea that people pay little or nothing for their media because of advertising will no longer be true.[14]

# ▼ Advertising Research

The advertising industry is a great generator of research. Each of the advertising media hires research firms, rating services, and other groups to gather data showing its pulling power. Agencies conduct applied communication research on the effectiveness of their ads, awareness of their clients' products, and the public's response to them. And, of course, academics—including sociologists, psychologists, and anthropologists—conduct theoretical research on the industry and its effects, studying topics such as product appeals, the psychology of advertising, and consumer behavior. Market researchers probe the effects of different appeals on various audiences, and mass communication researchers examine audience trends among particular media.

Reports on such research can be found in trade publications and academic periodicals, such as the *Journal of Advertising* and the *Journal of Advertising Research*. Some associations and groups will provide a copy of a research report (for example, on the ability of magazines to sell a particular product) to anyone who asks for it.

Much of the applied research on the effectiveness of advertising, however, is *proprietary*—owned by those who produce it and hidden from the public. Some of it is gathered by research firms and then sold to the highest bidder; some of it is conducted by a specific company for its own use; some of it is conducted by agencies for particular clients. Moreover, much of this research is self-serving, designed to demonstrate that an advertising agency or business should take a certain action. As a result, there are always questions as to its objectivity. Businesses sometimes hire consultants to help them sort out the various claims of these kinds of researchers.

## Studying the Effects of Advertising

Advertising researchers may conduct surveys, panel studies, or experiments. In surveys, researchers systematically interview people about their consumer preferences. In panel studies, researchers select a carefully selected sample of subjects and analyze their attitudes or behavior over time. In experiments, they set up "treatment" and "control" groups to determine the effect of advertising messages. Whatever the method, Russel Colley claims, good research on advertising effectiveness must make a systematic evaluation of the degree to which the advertising succeeded in accomplishing predetermined goals.[15]

What are these goals? If advertising is successful, says Colley, it results in sales, and to do that it must carry consumers through four levels of understanding: (1) *awareness* of a brand or company, (2) *comprehension* of the product and what it will do for them, (3), a *conviction* that they should buy the product, and (4) *action*—that is, buying the product.[16] Colley urges advertisers to use precise research, including the following types, to evaluate whether an advertisement has succeeded:

1. *Audience research* involves gathering basic data on the audience to be reached, including the numbers of people in various groups (based on age, sex, religion, and so on) who see and respond to advertising.

2. *Media research* involves studying the particular characteristics of each medium and what it can do, including comparisons of the pulling power and persuasiveness of various media.

3. *Copy research* consists of making comparisons of audience reactions to particular advertisements. For example, researchers might compare the effectiveness of ads using an underdog appeal with those that arouse fear, instill pride, or reinforce old values.

## Consumer and Lifestyle Research

More accessible than studies of advertising effectiveness is **consumer behavior research,** although some of it is also privately funded and proprietary. From their studies of consumers, researchers help businesses and ad agencies learn who their most likely consumers are and what kinds of advertising are most likely to reach them. They might study how needs, drives, and motives affect consumers' buying, how perception of an advertisement might vary among consumers, and what opinions, attitudes, beliefs, and prejudices should be taken into account in fashioning a message.[17] Some researchers focus on one group, such as children. These specialists might examine children at different stages of their development and then predict what kinds of things children like at certain ages and how they may influence their parents' purchases of toys, food, and so on. Advertising agencies may then use this information to prepare commercials for Saturday morning cartoon shows.

Another area of study is **lifestyle research,** which grew out of surveys studying trends in Americans' living patterns and buying behavior. These studies inform advertisers about the changing attitudes and lifestyles that characterize potential consumers at different ages—information that can be immensely helpful in fashioning an advertising campaign. For example, if older people today are moving out of large old houses into small new apartments

Lifestyle research shows that the markets for various kinds of products are sometimes rigidly segmented. Teens tend to be the only significant part of the population that purchases popular music CDs. Older citizens are virtually the only consumers of liquid meal supplements in cans. Affluent upper middle class families constitute the major market for expensive French wines. Advertisers understand this very well and tailor their messages to such markets. (Copyright © Bob Daemmrich, Stock Boston)

where they live alone, and if they are interested in simplifying their domestic tasks and having more free time, then they are new potential consumers for several types of goods, such as single-serving frozen food dishes, microwave ovens, and airline tickets.[18] It might be worthwhile, then, for companies producing these items to use ads that have special appeal to older people.

Generally, advertising research is *applied* research. Its purpose is to help stimulate sales. Not surprisingly, this use of research in attempts to find ways to manipulate people has aroused considerable criticism. Although the research tries to demonstrate the effectiveness of particular advertisements and campaigns, no scientific cause-and-effect relationship can be established between a given ad and the product or service it seeks to sell. As social scientists have said, there are just too many uncontrollable variables in any situation to prove that advertising actually works. The important thing, though, is that many people believe it does, and they are the ones making decisions to spend millions of dollars on it. Advertising is part of the corporate strategy of most firms that sell products. Advertising researchers try to gather the best evidence available to show what advertising can do, but their efforts fall far short of absolute proof.

## An Age of Market Segmentation

Although advertisers would like to sell their wares to everyone, they know that is not possible, and so they go after a particular *segment* of the market. As we discussed in Chapter 9, that segment may be defined by age, income, gender, education, race, and so on. Once, most advertising was *product-oriented*; that is, the content was mainly concerned with a persuasive message about the attributes of the product. Now most advertising is *user-oriented*, with messages aimed at the specific needs, interests, and desires of particular groups of consumers. As historian Daniel Pope put it:

> Segmentation campaigns are user-focused and concentrate on consumer benefits rather than product attributes. They show people with whom the target audience can identify; people who represent a credible source of authority for them or who express their latent desires and dreams. Marketers hone in on consumers whose lifestyles and personalities have been carefully profiled.[19]

This new emphasis also suggests problems for the ethical presentation of advertising. It is much easier to apply a truth-in-advertising standard to statements about the qualities of a product than to indirect appeals to the desires of a segment of the audience. The trend toward market segmentation has also led to some specialization in advertising agencies and promoted the growth of media that appeal to a specific rather than a general audience.

Recently, a considerable amount of research evidence is emerging from what John Phelan of Fordham University calls "noble hype," or information campaigns focused on good causes, such as the prevention of AIDS, heart disease, and other social problems. A lot of money has been poured into studies of information campaigns that use direct advertising strategies and messages. The dramatic success of the AIDS information campaign—which is credited, in part, for the decrease in sexual activity likely to spread the disease—seems in a preliminary way to bode well for advertising effectiveness. At the same time, other researchers and critics say that AIDS is a special case that does not apply generally, because the threat of death is a great motivation in changing behavior.

## ▼ Criticism and Control of Advertising

Few people doubt that advertising has a significant impact or that it plays an important role in the United States. Most would agree that it reflects the culture and ideals of this country—although many also find that idea disturbing. Noting its importance, however, is very different from granting approval, and advertising has been criticized on many grounds. Some disparage advertising in general for its economic and social effects; others criticize the content of some ads or their effects on some groups. These criticisms, as we will see, have led to attempts to regulate advertising.

### Economic and Social Criticisms

A favorable view of advertising claims that it *stimulates competition*, which is good for the economy, and encourages the development of new products,

which is good for consumers. Proof of the pudding, defenders say, is that people choose to buy the new products. And consumers are happier because they can choose from a great variety of goods—a diversity stimulated by advertising. Advertising helps keep the economy and the number of jobs growing by encouraging people to buy more. And, by giving consumers information, advertising also helps them buy wisely. Advertising, then, is a key cog in the economic machine that can give Americans the good life and the fruits of capitalism—the so-called American dream.

Critics have many answers to these comments. First, a great deal of advertising has nothing at all to do with objective information and does not help consumers make wise choices. Yet, even though they do not benefit, people must pay for advertising because its cost raises the price of the goods they buy. Therefore, they say, advertising is wasteful.

What is more, critics say, rather than stimulating competition, advertising contributes to *monopoly*. Larger firms can easily afford to invest in expensive national advertising, whereas smaller firms cannot. Larger firms can then perpetuate and even expand their hold on the market. For example, there are few local brands of soft drink that can compete with Coca-Cola or Pepsi-Cola, although there were once many successful local and regional beverages. Even in the absence of an actual monopoly, some economists see advertising as hindering the development of perfect competition and leading to the condition

Many people champion the role of advertising in bringing together people and goods and thus stimulating the economy, but there can be a darker side. During World War I, tobacco companies convinced soldiers that smoking was manly, relaxed them, and brought luck. After the war, advertisers worked hard to convince women to smoke and were able to double the cigarette market. Meanwhile, lung cancer, which was very rare in 1919, had become the leading cause of cancer deaths by 1990. Today, it causes more than 140,000 deaths per year in the United States. (The Bettmann Archive; The Bettmann Archive)

# Media and the Liberal Arts

## How Advertisers Persuaded Americans to Smoke
### A Linchpin to Public Health and Demography

In 1919, Dr. George Dock, chairman of the department of medicine at Barnes Hospital in St. Louis, called his students together to witness an autopsy. The patient had died of a rare disease. Dr. Dock said that it was unlikely that most of them would ever see such a case again. The disease was lung cancer.

In 1989, an estimated 155,000 new cases of lung cancer were diagnosed in the United States and 142,000 people died from the disease. Cigarette smoking was the cause of an estimated 85 percent of those deaths. Lung cancer has a very low rate of survival. Only one in ten who contract the disease can be cured. The other nine die rather quickly.

If anyone doubts the great power of advertising when it sets out to persuade people to buy a particular product, the case of cigarettes offers dramatic evidence to the contrary. Thus, a considerable lesson can be learned by reviewing the history of cigarette advertising in the United States. We do not do so in order to condemn tobacco companies or to assess the wisdom of those who take up the habit. A purpose more relevant to our analysis is to show that, under certain conditions, advertising campaigns can be extremely effective, with a cumulative influence on individual behavior, demographic trends, and the public health of society as a whole, persuading people to behave in dangerous ways.

Before World War I, few people in the United States smoked cigarettes. Men who did so were regarded as effeminate. Real men smoked either cigars or pipes, or they chewed tobacco. In retrospect, both were very unhealthy habits, but they did not lead specifically to lung cancer. Women rarely smoked; those few who did so in public were generally regarded as "loose."

At the turn of the century, automatic cigarette-rolling machines were acquired by major tobacco companies and production rose sharply. Between 1910 and 1919, the number of "tailor-made" cigarettes produced increased by well over 600 percent. More than any other factor, it was the events of World War I that hooked American men on cigarettes. A major tobacco company and a group called the National Cigarette Service Company (a creature of the industry) distributed millions of free cigarettes to the boys in France. They were regarded by the military, from General Persh-

known as *imperfect competition*. Several consequences may follow, including, according to critic Neil Borden, "improper allocation of capital investment," "underutilization of productive capacity and underemployment," "relatively rigid prices," and increasingly severe cyclical fluctuations in business, from inflation to recession and back again.[20]

According to Borden, even the diversity of goods stimulated by advertising is not beneficial. Consumers, writes Borden, "are confused by the large number of meaningless product differentiations and consequently do not make wise choices."[22] Other critics point to more general effects on individuals and society attributed to advertising. Advertising is often believed to be manipulative and deceptive, indirectly teaching us that other people are objects to be manipulated and deceived. By creating new wants and desires, advertising is also said to distance people from their "true" selves, contributing to their alienation and dissatisfaction, and making life an unending and hopeless quest for trivial goods or the perfect image.

ing on down, as an important factor in keeping up morale. Lighting up was said to provide relaxation under conditions of great tension and anxiety. The use of cigarettes lost their earlier wimpish image. It was replaced by the much stronger one of a soldier under fire coolly lighting up a smoke just before going "over the top." The free cigarette program was repeated during World War II. All field rations provided for the troops in combat contained small packages of cigarettes to be enjoyed with each meal.

During the early 1920s, with the habit firmly established among men, the tobacco companies faced the fact that half of the population did not smoke! The next step was to destroy the concept that women who did so were somehow immoral. Advertisers began their campaigns. Ads began to appear suggesting that it was all right for women to smoke cigarettes. For example, one now famous ad showed a young man and woman, both ele-

gantly dressed, on a grassy river bank enjoying a picnic. The man held a cigarette with a smoke plume rising. The woman was leaning longingly toward the man and the smoke. The ad copy indicated that she was saying "Blow a little my way."

Meanwhile, movies, novels, magazine stories, and virtually every other portrayal of everyday life showed people smoking and offering each other cigarettes. During the 1950s and 1960s, intensive advertising campaigns portrayed smoking as "masculine" for men, but "sophisticated" for women. They touted cigarettes as completely safe, relaxing, and even beneficial to health. Thousands of ads convinced people that smoking would promote digestion, protect the throat, and even help avoid wrinkles. Meanwhile, the death rate from lung cancer rose sharply. In 1930, it was less than 5 per 10,000 of population per year. By 1950, it had quintupled to more than 20. Today, it exceeds 70.

As medical understanding of the smoking-cancer linkage grew, starting about 1960, the federal government and consumer groups began conducting vigorous antismoking campaigns. Tobacco companies were prohibited by law from making claims that cigarettes are harmless. They have been barred from advertising on television and forced to label their product as dangerous. As a result, smoking has significantly declined in the United States. By 1985, 41 million Americans had quit smoking.

The implications are that when advertising is unrestrained, and supplemented by public relations efforts, it can be very persuasive indeed. However, when a consistent advertising message is challenged by contrary claims and evidence from authoritative sources, even deeply established habit patterns can be turned around. Advertising, therefore, can have great power, but only over an extended period in which other conditions are supportive and few challenges exist.[21]

We certainly cannot evaluate point by point either the economic or social analysis advanced by advertising's critics, and we have stated their complaints rather briefly. However, note that advertising depends on mass communication, and the principles we will review in later chapters regarding the media's influence on individuals and society apply in general to advertising. You should not assume that advertising messages are "magic bullets" that cause uniform effects among all who receive them. Moreover, you would be ill-advised to consider the people seeing or hearing the messages as passive dolts receiving them helplessly. Nor should you think of advertising as a single, isolated cause of behavior, such as a decision to purchase a product. Reactions to advertising messages are determined by complex causes and influences that we discuss in Chapter 13 related to the nature of the audience. Only a great deal of careful research will reveal the answers.

If you have taken a course in economics, you may recall how little attention textbooks in that field devote to advertising. The distinguished Harvard economist John Kenneth Galbraith said that there is a good reason why such texts downplay its importance. Economists like to believe that consumer wants are held deeply within the human psyche. They subscribe to the idea of consumer sovereignty. But Galbraith writes:

> So long as wants are original with the consumer, their satisfaction serves the highest of human purposes. Specifically, an original, inherent need is being satisfied. And economics as a subject matter or science thus becomes basic to the highest human service. But [this] holds only if wants cannot be created, cultivated, shaped, deepened, or otherwise induced. Heaven forbid that wants should have their source in the producer of the product or service as aided and guided by his advertising agency.[23]

Thus, it would downgrade some of the most basic principles of economics if it were true that consumer wants were actually generated by advertising and not by human nature itself.

## Children and Advertising

Few aspects of advertising have generated more concern or research than advertising directed at children, particularly TV commercials. Critics fear that such advertising creates wants that cannot be fulfilled and that it prompts children to ask their parents for innumerable things that they cannot afford. Thus, children's advertising may generate tension and conflict in the family and teach many wrong lessons because children mistake advertisements for realistic portrayals of the world. In defense of such advertising, supporters maintain that it helps children learn to be consumers, a role that is vital to the economy.

Any evaluation of advertising's effect on children requires answers to several questions: To what extent do children pay attention to commercials? What, if any, effects do commercials have on children's thinking processes? Can they, for example, distinguish between fact and fantasy in a commercial? What, if any, influence do children exert on their parents' buying as a result of commercials? Government, foundations, ad agencies, and other businesses have spent a lot of money to answer these and similar questions. Research by advertisers and ad agencies, however, is devoted understandably to one purpose: determining how to make better and more persuasive commercials. Although their results are usually kept secret, we are beginning to get some answers to these questions from outside researchers.

To date, the findings suggest that the younger the child, the fuller the attention he or she pays to commercials. However, trust in commercials declines with age.[24] Very young children do not know the difference between commercials and programs. They pay a good deal of attention to commercials that would seem to be irrelevant to them, such as ads for beer or household cleaning products. Perhaps they are simply using the commercials to learn about what is unfamiliar to them. As they get older, children pay less and less attention to commercials, and by the time they are adolescents, they usually scorn them. The evidence so far indicates that children do pressure their parents to buy the products they have seen advertised. Overall, however, we do not yet know enough about advertising's effects on children, and many questions have yet to be explored in depth.

Meanwhile, critics, such as Action for Children's Television, are taking their concerns to the government and seeking controls on advertising. In the controversy over advertising appeals to children, particular media (such as television) have debated with consumer groups and government. In 1988, the *Wall Street Journal* noted that although network television had high standards for children's advertising, independent stations usually did not. The networks barred the overglamourizing of a product or the use of exhortative language such as "Ask Mom to buy . . . ," but independent stations were quite lax on these and other points. As criticism mounted, the Better Business Bureau urged local TV stations to be more vigilant, and eventually the board of the Association of Independent Television Stations endorsed guidelines for children's advertising. Later the same year, the U.S. Senate passed legislation to limit the number of commercials aired during children's programs.[25]

▲ Children often accompany a parent to the supermarket. Products such as breakfast cereals are advertised heavily on TV programs aimed at children. The extent to which preferences created by this advertising influence what parents select from the shelves has been debated for decades. Overall, the relationship of children and advertising is a complex one that varies greatly depending on age. There are no simple answers. (© Jane Scherr/Jeroboam, Inc.)

An unusual and highly controversial effort at TV advertising began when "Channel One," Whittle Communications' news program for public schools, went on the air in 1990. The Whittle organization supplied free video equipment to thousands of public schools, and they broadcast, into classrooms, news programs complete with paid advertising. Regarded as a boon by some school administrators who readily accepted the equipment and programming, "Channel One" was attacked by others, including the consumer-oriented Action for Children's Television, which found the service odious. What bothered critics was that "Channel One" invaded the public schools with advertising messages. Schools, critics said, should be off-limits from commercial exploitation. On the other hand, defenders of Whittle's efforts said that children could learn to be better consumers if they got advertising messages in the classroom where teachers might critique them. School authorities in New York and California barred schools from accepting the equipment or programming. At about the same time, a noncommercial service was started by Cable News Network. Meanwhile, the debate over whether (and if so, how much) advertising should be directed to children is an ethical dilemma for policymakers who have to weigh potential harm against the reality that "advertising revenue is considered

▶ Controversy over advertising aimed at children—a long-standing issue—took on a new slant when Chris Whittle's Channel One, a TV service for in-class use, included paid advertising with its programming. Citizens, educators, policymakers, and media researchers debated the implications of commercials in the classroom. (Copyright © David Young-Wolff, Photo Edit)

essential for the existence of children's programming,"[26] according to media scholar Katharine E. Heinz of the University of Washington. Another scholar, Ellen Seiter, in her book *Sold Separately* says that advertising for children's products is an important part of their culture. "Children's interest in consumer culture involves much more than greed, hedonism or passivity." Advertising for children helps them build a sense of community and freedom from adult authority. Additionally says, Seiter, "As a mass culture, toys and television give children a medium of communication."[27]

## Sources of Control

Whatever the general effects of advertising, the content of many ads has been attacked for poor taste, exaggerated claims, or annoying hucksterism. As a result of these specific sins, some controls on U.S. advertising have developed. Shabby practices led to a gradual erosion of the ancient principle of *caveat emptor* ("let the buyer beware") in favor of *caveat venditor* ("let the seller beware")—that is, toward regulation. Advertisers today live with certain constraints, some imposed by the government and some by the industry itself.

**Control by government.**    As early as 1911, *Printer's Ink*, an industry magazine, called for greater attention to ethics in advertising and proposed a model statute that made fraudulent and misleading advertising a misdemeanor. Before long, with a strong push from the Better Business Bureau, most states enacted it as law. Although there is doubt about its effectiveness, the statute was a statement on advertising ethics as well as a standard setter. A few years later, in 1914, the Federal Trade Commission (FTC) also set up some ground rules for advertising. In administrative rulings over the years, the FTC has written rules related to puffery, taste, and guarantees and generally has taken considerable interest in the substantiation of advertising claims. At times, the FTC has demanded "effective relief" for those wronged by misleading advertising and levied fines against companies engaging in unfair, misleading, and otherwise deceptive advertising.

As we saw in Chapter 10, the Federal Communications Commission (FCC) also scrutinizes advertising. In addition, several other federal agencies, including the Food and Drug Administration, the U.S. Postal Service, the Securities and Exchange Commission, and the Alcohol and Tobacco Tax Division of the Internal Revenue Service, influence advertising. State and local governments have passed laws on lotteries, obscenity, occupational advertising, and other matters. Government controls over advertising, however, relaxed considerably during the era of industry deregulation in the 1980s and 1990s under Presidents Reagan, Bush, and Clinton.

**Industry codes of ethics.**   In the private sector, various advertising organizations and individual industries have developed codes of ethics to govern advertising. The broadcasting industry, for example, has codes that set standards for the total amount of nonprogram material and commercial interruptions per time period. (However, the amount of time commercials could air for each hour of programming for adults was expanded during the deregulation of broadcasting in the 1980s. In fact, say some critics, today some programs are nothing but hour-long paid advertisements. These so-called *infomericals,* airing late at night or on weekends, promote business-success seminars, real estate deals, "classic" CDs, juicers, personal care items, and phone consultation with psychics.) In many states, local industry organizations such as advertising review committees and fair advertising groups promote truth in advertising. The National Advertising Review Council promotes ethical advertising and fights deception, and Better Business Bureaus prepare reports on particular firms and their advertising.

**Court rulings.**   In recent years, both the public and private sectors have followed closely various court decisions regarding whether or to what degree the First Amendment's guarantee of freedom of speech and the press extends to advertising. To date, the courts have distinguished between advertising that promotes an individual's or group's views, which *is* protected by the First Amendment, and advertising that is designed only for commercial gain, which is *not*—although at times it is difficult to separate the two. Typically, courts have stoutly defended what they call "political speech," or expression that promotes public discussion of public affairs. The courts have until recently been less kind to "commercial speech," which is aimed at selling products. Now all that is changing, as commentators recognize that separating public and private speech is difficult at best.

**Consumer groups.**    In addition, many consumer groups monitor advertising and protest when they object to particular content. These groups range from the National Consumer Union to religious organizations and environmental groups.

Advertisers have in the past responded to public criticism, and advertising itself has undergone constant change. For example, for many years radio and TV commercials included very few African Americans, Latinos, or other minorities. When they were featured, portrayals were often trivial or demeaning. By the late 1960s, however, advertisements began to include minorities more often and more realistically. Some would argue that such changes are not always for the best. In a recently exposed practice, producers of malt liquors (with a higher-than-normal alcohol content) have allegedly targeted blacks (some say teenage blacks specifically) with their ads.

Changes have also begun to take place in advertising's images of women, who have traditionally been shown behaving either idiotically in domestic situations or as passive sex objects. Similarly, elderly people, who often appeared as doddering simpletons, are sometimes portrayed more respectfully in today's ads.

Although there have been improvements, advertising still often deals with stereotypes. In the 1960s, feminist writer Betty Friedan drew attention in *The Feminine Mystique* to sex-role stereotypes in advertising. Twenty years later, researchers Thomas Whipple and Alice E. Courtney write that there have been only relatively cosmetic changes. In fact, they found that the use of women as sex objects in advertising is on the rise:

▶

For many years, African Americans did not appear in advertisements for products other than those typically used mainly by blacks. In more recent times, advertisers have come to realize that middle-class African Americans make up a large market for many consumer products and services. Advertising specifically aimed at such families has become more common. (Copyright © David Austen, Stock Boston)

Nudity, seminudity, innuendo, double-entendre and exploitive sex are being used with increasing frequency and intensity in advertising. . . . [It] continues to exploit [women], show violence and aggression against them, and cause widespread offense.[28]

Many advertising professionals would take issue with these critiques, saying that advertising reflects public tastes and that feminism has had a definite impact on advertising content. Other advertisers, as Whipple once stated in an interview, are likely to say, "Gee, I'd really like to avoid these stereotypes, but I've got to use them to survive."[29] Whipple argued that research shows that avoiding stereotypes can be effective and urged a re-education of advertisers.[30]

If a large part of the public becomes unwilling to accept demeaning stereotypes, advertising will probably soon follow that lead. After all, advertisers are not trying to mold society or public opinion—although they may in fact influence both. They are trying to sell goods, and they will change their message if need be to appeal to the public. If critics can arouse people to complain enough or can convince advertisers that the public is annoyed, they have a good chance of changing specific aspects of advertising messages. Critics argue that they want to raise the standards of ad content, not censor communication.

It is likely that the debate over sexual stereotyping in advertising will continue for a long time. Many advertisers appeal blatantly to sex appeal, and much of what they put before the public is clearly sexist. Occasionally, various groups representing women, religious interests, and other social forces protest and even urge the boycott of particular products. Because advertisers almost always want to avoid controversy—after all, they want to sell products, not enrage consumers—some of these protests have worked.

Formerly, sex appeal in advertising was largely aimed at men and exploited women in the process. However, this has changed in recent years as suggestive poses of men are now commonly featured, displaying males as sex objects in an explicit manner heretofore unknown in advertising. Thus far, few men have objected. Sometimes such advertising has curious origins. For example, in the 1990s, rap star Marky Mark of the group Funky Bunch was pictured in *Interview* magazine wearing only his underwear, disrobing being one of the trademarks of his performances. Designer Calvin Klein saw the photo and decided to use the irreverent rapper in his ads. Photos done for the ads concurrently appeared in book form in time to compete with a similar photo essay book featuring a teasing nude Madonna. In 1996, Calvin Klein was again in the news with controversial ads, this time featuring sexually suggestive poses of teenage boys and girls, which were eventually withdrawn after considerable public protest, even from the White House.

At no time does the serious role of advertising in America as a consumer communication channel get more attention than during the Super Bowl.[31] Top commercial interests vie for precious minutes and seconds. In 1997, some 140 million viewers saw messages from thirty advertisers who paid $1.2 million each for a thirty-second ad. This price tag puts the Super Bowl as an advertising venue far ahead of its closest competitors including the Academy Awards, the NBA finals, the World Series, and programs like Seinfeld and ER.

It is possible, of course, that advertising does not influence people as much as its critics claim. Sociologist Michael Schudson argues that advertising is not nearly as important, effective, or scientifically targeted as either advocates or critics imagine. Advertisers are often quite cautious in deciding on their advertising outlays and take few chances. In the end, says Schudson, advertising rarely has a chance to create consumer wants, and instead reinforces what already exists. In assessing the role of advertising in American society, Schudson makes the following observations:

1. Advertising serves a useful informational function that will not and should not be abandoned.

2. Advertising probably has a socially democratizing influence, but one with an ultimate inegalitarian outcome.

3. The most offensive advertising tends to have the least informational content.

4. Some advertising promotes dangerous products or promotes potentially dangerous products to groups unlikely to be able to use them wisely.

5. Nonprice advertising often promotes bad values, whether it effectively sells products or not.

6. Advertising could survive and sell goods without promoting values as bad as those it favors now.

7. Advertising is but one factor among many in shaping consumer choice and human values.[32]

Critics who object not to specific aspects of some advertisements but to advertising's broader effects on individuals, society, and the economy will not see the changes they desire any time soon. Government is unlikely to impose stringent controls. As long as they think the messages work, advertisers are likely to continue to appeal to people's desires to be more attractive, liked, and somehow better than the neighbors—in short, to have more or better of just about anything—whatever may be the psychological, cultural, or economic effects of these appeals. Furthermore, advertisers are likely to continue to engulf us with their messages unless there are monumental changes in the economy and society.

All of these considerations lead to a reaffirmation of our central thesis: The media, the economy, advertising, and the population as consumers are inextricably linked in a deeply institutionalized way. Thus, advertising is a central social institution in American society.

# CHAPTER REVIEW

▼ Advertising is a form of controlled communication that attempts to persuade an appropriate audience, through the use of a variety of appeals and strategies, to make a decision to buy or use a particular product or service.

▼ Advertising is essential to the mass media insofar as it is the principal source of revenue for most of them. Without advertising, Americans would not have the great variety of mass communications from which to choose what they now enjoy.

▼ The history of advertising is related not only to public taste but also to the growth of the American economy and the mass media. Unless there is relative abundance in a society, businesses are not likely to find advertising worthwhile.

▼ The nineteenth century saw the growth of national media, national markets, and national advertising in the United States. Advertisers showed that they could create markets for new products, and newspapers, magazines, and broadcast stations eventually became dependent on advertising for most of their revenues.

▼ As advertising grew, organizations specializing in the production of advertisements developed. Today, advertising agencies are staffed by managers, writers, artists, researchers, and other specialists. Boutique agencies and various media service organizations offer more limited, specialized services, and many businesses and media organizations have departments that deal exclusively with advertising.

▼ Advertising by 2001 will be a $411 billion industry that employs nearly a quarter of a million people in the United States. However, concentration into large firms seems to be the trend here as in other industries.

▼ The advertising industry has many critics. Some economists claim that it is economically wasteful in that it decreases competition, increases consumers' costs, and channels investment away from more productive uses. Other economists claim that advertising promotes competition, diversity, and wise buying decisions.

▼ Some critics are concerned that advertising somehow debases individuals and cultures. Still other criticism is directed more specifically at advertising that makes exaggerated claims, is in poor taste, is directed at children, or presents negative stereotypes of particular groups.

▼ Those who recognize the importance of advertising but want it to be carried on with higher standards have set up guidelines to prevent misleading, offensive, and excessive advertising.

▼ Although advertising can be criticized on many grounds, it will be with us for the foreseeable future. It plays a critical role in promoting the economy's goods and services, and is a deeply established social institution.

## CHAPTER 12

# Public Relations

## Influencing Images and Actions

For centuries those in power have sought ways to influence the beliefs, attitudes, and actions of their followers by using effective communication strategies. Almost universally, their goal was to inspire awe and respect on the part of their supporters and fear on the part of their enemies. To accomplish those purposes they had their scribes record glowing accounts of their accomplishments. They built palaces and monuments, staged elaborate parades and ceremonies, and monitored carefully what both their friends and enemies said about them. For example, almost four thousand years ago the Babylonian King Hammurabi (Chapter 2) had his scholars develop a set of laws to govern his empire. He had the laws inscribed on huge blocks of stone that were placed in the center of each city in his domain. On each he had carved a representation of himself receiving those laws from the Sun God. This communication was designed for the purpose of convincing people of his special status and the lofty origin of his laws. In this ancient public relations effort, the medium was stone. Nevertheless, given the limitations of the time, this strategy was as modern as any professional communicator could devise today to enhance the king's public image.

Some scholars argue, and the preceding example suggests, that even though they did not call it by that name, people have been engaging in public relations communication for a very long time. For many centuries much of the purpose behind public discourse and public rhetoric has been for reasons of **publicity**—expanding the number of people who are aware of some policy, program, or person. In addition, public relations is often associated with **propaganda,** persuasive communications designed to gain people's approval—or as we might say today, to capture their hearts and minds—concerning some policy or program. (The term "propaganda" originally referred to the Roman Catholic Church's efforts to "propagate the faith" through the communication efforts of missionaries.)

Certainly both publicity and propaganda played major roles in the American colonies before the Revolution, when committees of correspondence sought to win the support of the public. Also, many American presidents have had a need to sway public opinion in a direction favorable for their policies. Abraham Lincoln, for example, had a definite "public relations problem" with his Emancipation Proclamation of 1862. It freed all slaves in states and territories at war with the Union, but not in those fighting on the Northern side. Several states not in the Confederacy were reluctant to give up the idea of slavery, and Lincoln had a "hard sell." If he had been able to use public opinion polls at the time (they did not exist) he might never have issued his Proclamation until he prepared the population for it with public relations efforts. Similarly, in 1939, President Franklin D. Roosevelt began (unsuccessfully at first) to persuade the

▶

Since ancient times, great national leaders have understood the value and strategies of effective public relations. By providing the media of his time with dramatic opportunities to photograph massive passive resistance, Gandhi was able to engineer the independence of India. More recently, by effective use of the media, Nelson Mandela was able to promote international support for democracy in South Africa. (AP Photo/Anna Zieminski/POOL)

American people that it was in the country's best interests to come to the aid of the British in their fight against Hitler. By 1941, he had begun to turn the situation around with his speeches and policies. However, the need was eliminated after the Japanese bombed the Pacific fleet at Pearl Harbor. During the twentieth century, other national leaders such as Ghandi and Martin Luther King became masters of communications designed to promote approval of their social and political goals. Thus, throughout both ancient and recent times efforts to change public beliefs and commitments through the use of effective communication strategies have been a part of human society.

## ▼ The Development of Public Relations

As a professional field, public relations has a much briefer history. It grew out of reactions to the "public be damned" attitude that characterized American big business at the turn of the twentieth century. As the 1900s began, the "captains of industry" who ran the nation's corporations did as they pleased regardless of what people thought. Eventually, however, the public became aroused over their excesses—especially after many of their practices were exposed by the "muckraker" journalists of the time (Chapter 4). To counter this negative trend, many of the large corporations began to use public relations in one form or another to head off confrontations.

## Birth of the Public Relations Agency

A forerunner of the modern public relations *agency* was the Publicity Bureau of Boston, founded in 1900 by three former newspapermen. They set an important pattern in the way that public relations services were provided for clients. For a fee they would promote a company's causes and business interests by getting favorable stories in the newspapers and by other forms of managed communication. The bureau's early clients included AT&T, Harvard University, the Fore River Shipyard, and Boston Elevated (trolley lines).

By 1911, the Bureau had died, but other public relations and press agencies quickly formed in its place. For example, publicist and former journalist Ivy Lee, after working for political candidates and the Pennsylvania Railroad, recognized the value for businesses of a positive public image and the possibilities of creating such an image systematically through favorable publicity. He set up a firm providing services that we would now call public relations activities to help businesses communicate with the public. His clients eventually included perhaps the most famous "captain of industry," John D. Rockefeller, Jr., and his infamous Standard Oil Company. Another early publicist was Pendleton Dudley, who at Lee's urging opened an office on Wall Street. According to Scott Cutlip, Dudley denied that early public relations efforts were in direct response to the muckraking journalists.

During these early days, public relations specialists were called "publicity men," or sometimes "press agents." In 1919, the newspapers of New York took a census of the number who worked regularly in that capacity in the city and found that there were about 1,200 actively employed.[1] Furthermore, their functions were well understood by that time. Journalism scholar Walter Lippmann noted that it was their task to use the media (mainly newspapers at the time) to provide the public with interpretations of events related to their clients:

> The development of the publicity man is a clear sign that the facts of modern life do not spontaneously take a shape in which they can be known. They must be given a shape by somebody, and since in the daily routine reporters cannot give a shape to facts, and since there is little disinterested organization of intelligence, the need for some formulation is being met by [press agents and publicity men].[2]

Thus, there was a thriving public relations industry by the time of World War I. Its professional communicators performed the same services as their modern counterparts, although they had only the print media to work with as they attempted to create meanings and images about those whom they represented.

Today, the field of public relations has grown into a sophisticated and complex occupational field, with most of the work carried on either by relatively large agencies or by public relations departments of many kinds of corporations,

government agencies or nonprofit groups. Even today, some old-fashioned publicity agents (still using that name) continue to work, especially in New York
City, serving the needs of people and groups in such high-visibility fields as the
entertainment and fashion industries.

## Defining Public Relations Today

Although it is a complex field, it is not difficult to define the basic nature of
public relations in terms of what its practitioners actually do. **Public relations**
is an organized communication process, conducted by people who make a living as professional communicators. It can be defined in terms of conducting the
following activities:

> Paid professional practitioners design and transmit messages, on behalf of a
> client, via a variety of media to relevant and targeted audiences in an attempt to
> influence their beliefs, attitudes or even actions regarding some person, organi-
> zation, policy, situation, or event.

This is a complex definition and, although it sets forth the basics of what practitioners actually do, it does not provide enough details so that nonspecialists
can actually understand the field. Taking each of the ideas in the definition and
explaining them more fully will help.

**Practitioners.**   Professional public relations practitioners are usually people
whose education and perhaps prior employment was in a field in which writing and producing other forms of messages was a major focus. Such practitioners serve many types of clients. They may work in an agency that contracts for
services, as discussed earlier, or they may be salaried employees of a corporation, government agency, or a nonprofit group, such as a charity, museum, or
university. They may have titles such as "information specialist," "public
affairs officer," or "press secretary," but their activities are similar regardless of
the setting in which they work.

**Messages.**   Public relations specialists prepare many kinds of messages, news
releases, information campaigns, and communication policies. Most are of
a routine nature. Examples are *brochures* that provide information about a
corporation, government agency, or nonprofit group. Other examples are
*newsletters* that are distributed to various "stakeholders," such as alumni, employees, stockholders, and so forth. *Annual reports* on the status, activities, and
accomplishments of an organization is still another example. They also assist
in preparing *news stories* and other information to be released to the press.

**Clients.**   There are almost as many kinds of clients served by public relations
practitioners as there are individuals and groups in the United States that produce materials and services for the public. These include corporations and industries that manufacture goods, local, state and federal government agencies,
the military, institutions that provide for health care services, investment firms,

banks, schools, college and universities, organized charities, religious groups, and so on. To this comprehensive list could be added public personalities, such as prominent actors, singers, politicians, preachers, and musicians who need a constant flow of publicity in order to retain the image of their importance in the public eye.

**Media.** Virtually every kind of medium used for communication today plays some part in the activities of public relations specialists. Information is prepared and transmitted using newspapers, magazines, radio, and television. Increasingly, information about their client or employer is prepared for distribution via the Internet or in the form of a CD/ROM. In addition, they design special events, such as trade show displays and formal presentations of new products. They write speeches and magazine articles for their employers. They provide briefings, talking points, and practice interviews. They help prepare clients and employers for formal speeches, public appearances, and interviews by the press. In addition, their clients or employers may sponsor sports events—ranging from golf competitions to bass fishing contests—that are designed for public relations purposes.

In some cases, they prepare messages intended to achieve **damage control.** If the airplane crashes, the train derails, or the tanker spills oil, public relations specialists help to design measures and messages that will limit the negative impact on their client. That does not mean that they either avoid responsibility or misrepresent the situation (which can happen in some cases). More often, they help design measures or help management focus on steps that the public sees as meeting their responsibilities. Serious mistakes are made by those who try to cover up, deny, or lie about a bad situation.

The historic oil spill that occurred when the tanker *Exxon Valdez* went aground in Alaska's Prince Edward Sound created a public relations nightmare for Exxon, the vessel's operator. Americans were deeply disturbed that hundreds of miles of beaches were contaminated and thousands of animals were killed. The corporation spent millions of dollars in clean-up efforts as part of its public relations "damage control" campaign. The goal was to clean up its public image as well as the environment. (© Bill Nation/Sygma)

**Audiences.** The messages developed and transmitted by public relations specialists are prepared for many different categories of people. Obviously, some are broadly defined and are intended to be read or viewed by the public at large—as in a news release prepared for the readers of a local newspaper or an interview designed as a TV news story. Beyond that are more narrowly defined groups, such as the constituents of an officeholder, the employees of a large company, or the personnel of a major military organization. Another group might be the investors who hold stock in a large corporation. Sometimes the intended audience is very narrowly defined. For example, information may be prepared specifically for the surviving family members of an air crash or a military accident. In any of these cases, the public relations practitioner must understand the nature of that audience and the impression that will be made among them after receiving the specific information being prepared.

**Influences.**    The bottom line in public relations is to have the messages transmitted accomplish the purposes for which they were designed. There are many such purposes and each depends on the complexities of the situation. For example, a long-range public relations campaign may be designed to alter the behavior of the public regarding some form of action that has national significance. An example is the Smokey Bear public service campaign conducted by the U.S. Forest Service. Starting in 1949, the cartoon-like bear wearing the wide-brimmed hat has for fifty years been saying "Only YOU can stop forest fires!" Smokey and his message are known by almost every person in the United States. The campaign was so effective that the public reacted very negatively when in 1992 the Forest Service wanted to set some fires deliberately to burn accumulated dry branches and other materials on forest floors to reduce the danger of fires caused by lightning.

Public relations messages often have less dramatic goals. Many are designed to turn the public around regarding some person, issue, or event that has taken a negative turn. For example, in the 1990s, film star Rob Lowe was the object of a well-publicized scandal in which he was videotaped in a sexual encounter with two teen age girls. Lowe sought to express remorse for his earlier behavior, redeem his reputation, and build an audience for his upcoming new movie titled "Bad Influence." He enlisted the help of public relations specialists and followed an orchestrated strategy to restore his public image as a credible, if sometimes wild, young actor. In a carefully planned media tour, Lowe made the rounds of television talk shows to promote his film. The guest spots were the actor's first public appearances after the scandal. Much of the credit for Lowe's successful comeback was due to the help of public relations professionals, who understand the tools needed to engineer a favorable image for celebrities and other public figures.

The majority of messages are much more mundane than either of these examples. Indeed, many are prepared to inform rather than persuade. They may consist of a news story concerning a new CEO taking over the reins of a corporation, the release of a new model of a product, an explanation of a new policy by a government official, or a briefing about a campaign by a military spokesperson.

## Public Relations versus Advertising

The preceding discussion may make public relations and advertising seem somewhat alike. Like advertising, public relations is a communication process; it is planned and organized and depends in large part on the mass media to convey its messages. Unlike advertising, however, which makes use of purchased slots of media space and time, public relations does not have such easy access to mass communications. Some critics call advertising space "captive media," because an advertiser buys and uses it according to his or her own discretion. Public relations messages are not bought and paid for in the media, but instead are offered persuasively to editors, news directors, and others who then determine whether that information is worth using or not.

Although some public relations campaigns involve advertisements, such as those that promote tourism, or the general integrity of a corporation like Dow Chemical, public relations specialists often use more indirect, persuasive means to build a favorable climate of opinion or achieve other goals. Moreover, public relations efforts are not always identifiable. We know an advertisement when we see it on television or in a magazine, but we do not always know that the source of a news article or the staging of a golf tournament, bowling contest, or other public event is the result of a public relations campaign. Rarely do public relations people announce exactly what they are doing or for what purposes. Public relations personnel may use advertising as part of their overall activities, but they are much more involved than advertisers in the total process of communication, from initiating the message to getting feedback from the public.

In summary, public relations is a complex professional field in which paid communicators design and distribute messages for a great variety of purposes. Overall, it is a field representing a very broad spectrum of communication activities. Some are clearly essential for the adequate functioning of the society. Others are less significant, except to the people involved. In either case, public relations is deeply dependent on the mass media. Through the activities of its practitioners, much of what is learned by the public about people, activities, and organizations in their society is generated to accomplish one or more of its goals. In the final analysis, then, public relations is a way of *manipulating meanings*, in ways that are not always apparent to the target audience, to influence their interpretations of messages about the person or group represented by the communicator. However, this does not necessarily mean that such manipulation is necessarily deceptive or unethical.

## ▼ Public Relations Settings and Activities

Public relations practitioners today go by many names, among them public relations counselors, account executives, information officers, publicity directors, and house organ editors. They are found virtually everywhere—in the private sector in business, industry, charities, churches, labor unions and so on; in the public sector they are in all levels of government from the White House to the local school or fire station. The number of people employed in public relations is impressive. The U.S. Department of Labor estimated in 1950 that there were 19,000 people engaged in public relations and publicity work. By 1970, this had grown to 76,000. Today there are more than 170,000 working in jobs with those words in their title. This estimate is very low because the figures include only the rather narrow category of "public relations and publicity writers." In contrast, the U.S. Bureau of the Census reports that nearly half a million persons are currently engaged in various forms of public relations work. Of this number, about 45,000 work for public relations or management firms.

Public relations activities are carried on in a variety of organized ways. Most are team efforts by various kinds of groups: Perhaps most common is the independent **public relations counselor** or **agency.** This person or organization operates much like an advertising agency or law firm, taking on clients and representing them by conducting public relations activities on their behalf. The client may be an individual who wants better understanding from the public, or a large company that wants an experienced firm that can provide special services. These services may include conducting research and designing publications to help the company's own in-house public relations staff. Agencies represent only a relatively small part of this labor force.

Somewhat related is the **public relations department** within a particular business, industry, or other setting. These departments act as part of the overall management team and attempt to interpret the firm to the public and internal constituents. They also provide channels for feedback from the public to management. In industry, these departments are expected to contribute to the firm's profits by helping it achieve its overall business goals. The public relations department of General Motors, for example, sets communication goals to support and enhance the corporation's economic achievements. Public relations departments of a similar nature also exist within nonprofit or educational institutions. Publicity for organizations such as colleges and labor unions usually involves a range of internal and external activities, from publications to fund drives.

Public relations departments also provide services within governmental agencies at the federal, state, or even local level. In government, the terms "public information" and "public affairs" refer to any activity that communicates the purposes and work of an agency to the general public or to users of the agency's services. For example, welfare recipients need to know about the policies of the state social services department, and taxpayers need to know how their money is being spent. Similarly, a metropolitan police department typically has a "public affairs" department to provide information about its services and accomplishments to citizens.

Another way in which organized public relations activities are carried on is by **specialized consultants.** These range from political advisors who work exclusively on public relations problems during election campaigns to information specialists who are experts in communications in a specific field such as health, transportation, or insurance.

A related form of organized public relations activity is provided by **policy consultants.** These specialists suggest courses of action to public and private institutions that want to develop a policy for the use of information resources. They may want to influence the policies of Congress or the Federal Communications Commission, or develop an early-warning system to assess and trace the impact of a particular issue or program on corporate clients. This new area of public relations expanded considerably during the 1990s.

Finally, the field includes communication specialists in **technical areas.** For example, in Chapter 8 we discussed television consultants who try to improve the ratings of a station's news programs. Others include specialized firms that work with corporate clients to help them better understand and work with television, training programs for company presidents who serve as spokespersons, and placement services that get corporate clients on the air in various cities. Technical specialists also include graphics practitioners who provide full-service publication assistance, producing publicity messages that fit into an organization's overall public relations plan.

As in any dynamic industry, new ways of accomplishing goals constantly emerge. For example, a number of advertising agencies have recently acquired many established public relations firms or have set up new ones within their own organizations. Many public relations practitioners and media critics fear that public relations, if it becomes a branch of advertising, will become a servant of product promotion and not maintain ethical practices. They assert that the credibility of an independent public relations agency is greater than that of a public relations program under an advertising agency.

Recent changes in the communication industry have complicated the world of public relations. Independent public relations agencies are becoming less common as advertising agencies acquire and subject them to the corporate requirements of the parent company. It is too early to predict whether this trend within the industry will continue and what it will mean for public relations practice.

## Typical Tasks and Work Assignments

As the preceding discussion suggests, the actual tasks and work assignments of public relations practitioners vary widely from one professional setting to another. Much depends, of course, on the position of the individual within the power hierarchy of the agency. In some businesses, the vice president for public relations is a high-ranking person who is involved in all major corporate decisions and a part of the policy-making team. In other firms, the public relations officer has less power and is brought in only to provide "damage control" through publicity. Still others are the drones of public relations—entry level or low-ranking employees who do the many day-to-day tasks that are necessary in a public relations campaign. Thus, at the top end of the organization are those who engage in tactical and strategic planning while those at lower levels perform more routine tasks involved in such plans.

Top-level policymakers set long-term objectives and usually agree on some realistic expectations for results. This somewhat abstract agreement is then channeled into specific approaches, using publicity tools ranging from sponsored events to television presentations, press conferences, and information pamphlets. Thus, the complete public relations process involves planning and implementation—both in overall thinking and precise technical work—that make achievement of the campaign goals possible.

Lone practitioners or people in small firms usually do everything, ranging from designing both strategy and tactics to writing copy for press releases. In any case, there are a number of specific tasks that must be accomplished in implementing a campaign. In larger firms with a significant division of labor, the work assignments may be highly specialized. For example, a particular specialist may spend most of his or her time writing news releases for a political candidate. Another may specialize in communicating new, high-tech information to nurses or engineers. In smaller firms, personnel handle a wider range of duties. However, regardless of the size of a public relations agency or department, certain categories of work assignments are common. Cutlip and Center list common tasks and specific forms of work:

1. *Writing*—producing news releases aimed at the general media and drafting copy for specialized publications, brochures, posters, catalogues, and other pieces intended for distribution to the public.

2. *Editing*—revising and checking texts of speeches, company magazines, newsletters, and electronic bulletin boards.

3. *Media relations and placement*—getting clients in the newspaper and on the air and coordinating media coverage of events.

4. *Special events*—organizing media events such as anniversaries of organizations, openings of new programs, sponsored performances, donations of money, dedications of new facilities, and similar ceremonies.

5. *Speaking*—writing and delivering speeches to various groups on behalf of the client organization.

6. *Production*—working with designers, typesetters, editors, and producers to present material in printed or visual form.

7. *Research*—evaluating programs, developing questionnaires for surveys, and analyzing media coverage of an event or issue.

8. *Programming and counseling*—developing a plan for the client or department and giving advice about how to handle a particular event or limit negative publicity.

9. *Training and management*—providing training services to employees, advising them on how to set a proper climate in a firm and coordinating employees of varied skills and backgrounds to ensure the success of a program.[3]

In addition to being able to perform these kinds of work, effective public relations practitioners usually must have certain personal qualities. Publicists usually have excellent written and oral communication skills, are at ease socially, have a thorough knowledge of the media, management, and business; and have the ability to function both as problem solvers and decision makers. Other common qualities include stability, common sense, intellectual curiosity, and a tolerance for frustration.

## Public Relations Campaigns

Public relations practitioners or agencies work in systematic ways. Typical of their activities on behalf of clients is the **public relations campaign,** which is an organized way of communicating carefully designed messages with specific meanings to targeted audiences that are important to the client. In contrast to a single news release, speech, or television interview, a campaign orchestrates many kind of messages that are presented in many different ways making use of a number of media to achieve its goals.

Public relations campaigns become necessary for businesses and other organizations under many kinds of circumstances. Some have positive goals in mind; others may not. For example: (1) A business has been causing industrial pollution and is gaining a bad reputation. The firm now wants to convince the public that it is dedicated to protection of the environment. (2) A health maintenance organization (HMO) wants to erase the stigma of being too profit-oriented to the detriment of the quality of health care provided. (3) An educational institution has experienced a bad sports scandal with consequent negative publicity. Enrollments have dropped, and it now wants to attract students and resume alumni donations. (4) A government agency promoting prenatal child care for the poor wants women to make better use of its services. All these groups achieve their goals with public relations campaigns.

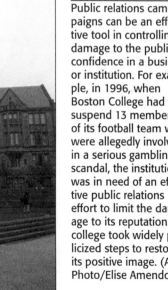

Public relations campaigns can be an effective tool in controlling damage to the public's confidence in a business or institution. For example, in 1996, when Boston College had to suspend 13 members of its football team who were allegedly involved in a serious gambling scandal, the institution was in need of an effective public relations effort to limit the damage to its reputation. The college took widely publicized steps to restore its positive image. (AP/Photo/Elise Amendola)

## Media and the Liberal Arts

### Shaping a Sympathetic Image of Kuwait During the Gulf War
A Linchpin to History and Political Science

On August 1, 1990, the forces of Iraq's Saddam Hussein invaded and seized control of the independent nation of Kuwait. Months later, in January 1991, the United States led a coalition of allies and went to war with Iraq to free the tiny, oil-rich nation.

Just how the United States and its allies decided to go to war was influenced by a carefully organized effort by the White House and other interested parties. The image that was successfully propagated was of the government of tiny, overpowered Kuwait helplessly waiting for outside help to wrest its country from Iraq. Not so. The government of Kuwait was closely in touch with

U.S. government and military authorities from the beginning and left nothing to chance.

Ten days after the invasion, Dr. Hassan al-Ebraheem, a professor of international politics at Kuwait University, visited the Washington, D.C. offices of the public relations firm Hill and Knowlton, Inc. Kuwait thus became a client of Hill and Knowlton and in the next ninety days spent $5.6 million dollars trying to win the hearts and minds of the American people.

It is not unusual for nations, multinational firms, or political movements to use professional public relations firms. In fact, there are few that

do not. Because public relations companies, lobbyists, and others doing work for foreign governments in the United States have to file reports with the U.S. Justice Department, detailed information about Kuwait's use of Hill and Knowlton is available. How was the money spent? Apparently $2.9 million was for professional fees and $2.7 was for other expenses, some of which are detailed here:

| | |
|---|---|
| Research | 1,100,000 |
| Video production (probably for news releases) | 644,571 |
| Printing (PR kits) | 436,825 |
| Advertising | 43,217 |

According to Cutlip and Center, any effective public relations campaign must be designed around four basic stages or steps:

1. *Fact-finding and feedback.* This stage involves background research on the desired audience, including impressionistic observations by knowledgeable observers and careful studies of public opinion. The public relations practitioner uses this information to define the problem and to identify the audience to be reached.

2. *Planning and programming.* The publicist uses the information from the fact-finding stage to plan a broad strategy for the entire public relations program. This strategy includes a timetable, media, budgets, and possible targets for the message.

3. *Action and communication.* In this stage the publicist initiates the actual communication process using the media and the appropriate publicity tools. Pamphlets are distributed, speeches are given, news releases are sent to media organizations, and so on.

4. *Evaluation.* After the program is initiated and carried out, it is assessed in several ways: by measuring changes in attitudes and opinions among

That so little was spent on direct advertising demonstrates the ability of public relations firms to get free publicity. In the Kuwaiti case, this involved direct lobbying of Congress, governors, and other leaders, rallies on college campuses, and support for an instantly manufactured group called Citizens for a Free Kuwait.

One of the more outrageous aspects of the campaign came in the midst of a Congressional debate when fifteen-year-old Nayirah (only her first name was given) testified before Congress on October 10, 1990. She claimed to have witnessed Saddam's soldiers taking babies out of hospital incubators and leaving them to die on the hospital floor. It was "a PR masterstroke" orchestrated by Hill and Knowlton, according to the *Washington Monthly*.

So what was wrong with bringing in the girl to testify about the mass murder of Kuwaiti babies? First of all, the story was manufactured: secondly, the girl was not an ordinary Kuwaiti, as had been reported, but the daughter of the Kuwaiti ambassador to the United States. Only months later was this incident revealed in John R. MacArthur's influential book, *Second Front: Censorship and Propaganda in the Gulf War*. Incidentally, Hill and Knowlton was famous for having considerable influence at the White House, with several of their top people having close ties with President Bush. At the same time, the firm was known for its bipartisan clout: It also employed top Democrats.

Propaganda is, of course, part of virtually every war. Almost as much energy is devoted to this quieter side of warfare as to the actual engagement on the battlefield. In World War I, for example, the British and the Germans both engaged in a vigorous propaganda war that influenced their entry into that conflict. Prior to World War II, the German propaganda machine under Hitler created massive support among the German people. Later, during the Vietnam War, there was a feverish battle to sway public opinion as that war became increasingly unpopular. It was the memory of the loss of the public opinion war at home during the Vietnam conflict that is credited with giving the military in the Persian Gulf a special impetus to supply government-controlled information and cooperate with the Kuwaitis in certain efforts (like those by Hill and Knowlton).[4]

particular publics, counting the number of news clippings or reports on radio and television to evaluate the success of contacts with the news media, or by interviewing key opinion leaders. If carried to its logical conclusion, evaluation should affect future public relations activity, depending on what worked and what did not.[5]

In actual practice, a public relations campaign begins with the recognition of a problem or the perceived need for an image change of some sort. Let us say, for example, that the tourism board of the state of New York is unhappy with the state's revenues from visitors and thinks it might be due to a poor public image. The group decides to investigate further and hires a public relations firm. The firm conducts research among selected publics such as regular vacationers, travel agents, and travel writers for newspapers and magazines. Surveys assess what these people know about vacation possibilities in New York State. The results indicate a lack of public awareness or misconceptions, and reveal concerns that keep tourists from vacationing in the state.

Next, the public relations firm prepares a campaign proposal suggesting a variety of measures likely to increase tourism in New York. Suppose that because all Americans obviously cannot be reached through a limited campaign, the firm decides to direct its efforts at travel writers, hoping they will say something positive in their articles about the state as a vacation spot. To influence the writers, the firm will distribute news releases, hold press briefings, and even organize tours. In addition, it will send special mailings to travel agents to encourage them to direct their clients to select New York State as a vacation site. If they decide to try to reach the general public, the firm proposes to place a series of advertisements on national television and in newsmagazines. Based on advice from advertising agencies and research on the demonstrated effectiveness of particular media, the firm selects the best media for the purpose.

As a next step, the firm presents the campaign proposal to the leaders of the tourism board. Assuming that the board accepts the proposal with a few modifications, it then commissions the public relations firm to carry out the campaign. At the end of the campaign, the firm conducts an evaluation that includes another survey of the same groups who provided the initial evaluation of attitudes and opinions to see if they have changed. In addition, the firm looks at subsequent tourism figures and attempts to ascertain whether the campaign actually had any effect on them.

This hypothetical example reveals one of the real problems with public relations: The people who carry out information campaigns are not disinterested social scientists but *profit-making entrepreneurs* (or perhaps government employees eager to advance in their jobs). Thus, they look for "proof" that their information campaign has worked. If it clearly has not, publicists may try to convince their clients that uncontrollable factors, such as a poor economy, too many crime reports in the media, or preexisting negative stereotypes about New York, caused the public relations program to fail. Naturally, clients who hire the firm are free to make their own judgments about what works and what does not. Scholarly evidence about such public relations campaigns—and there is far too little of it—suggests that many such efforts are unsuccessful. However, practitioners dispute this evidence with practical and often compelling examples.

Leaders in public relations are quick to point out that their work involves much more than mass communication. Sometimes they distinguish internal from external communication. *Internal communication* is communication within an organization directed to its members. For example, a labor union communicates to its members through newsletters, meetings, bulletin boards, and other internal media. This kind of communication is aimed at a discrete group of people, not at the general public through mass media. In contrast, *external communication* transmits messages via the mass media to a large, diverse audience or to particular segments of the population outside the organization.

## Managing Election Campaigns

A relatively new, or at least considerably expanded, kind of organized public relations work is that of consultants serving as managers of political candidates' campaigns during elections. They key their efforts to opinion polls.

Although they usually stay out of the public eye, such consultants occasionally appear on CNN and various network talk shows to speak on behalf of their clients. Typically, however, they avoid the limelight and engage in a kind of guerrilla warfare, plotting strategy and modes of attack, and designing defensive responses for their clients when they are under fire.

This kind of organized activity brings together public opinion research, strategic planning and more traditional public relations. According to Jerry Hagstrom of the *National Journal*, who is an expert on this new form of public relations, there is an elite corps of about forty Washington-based polling and media firms that play a profound role in national presidential campaigns and other races. Similar firms exist across the country and typically serve the Republican and Democratic parties. And, although national campaigns are the most prestigious races, Hagstrom observes that the most elite consultants usually center their efforts on statewide campaigns because they are more financially lucrative.

Hagstrom states that this new cadre of consultants has virtually replaced state and local political bosses and party chairpersons as behind-the-scenes power brokers. What was once done intuitively by political operatives is now in the purview of consultants. In dealing with the media, public relations campaign managers often engage in what has come to be called **spin control** (a term from billiards, where a left or right spin can be put on a ball, making it curve to one side or the other as it moves across the table). They do so with carefully controlled use of language. If a political figure has unintentionally made an error in reporting the use of campaign funds, a political *spinmeister* may advise his or her opponent to characterize the situation as a "disgraceful scandal" and claim that "people who violate decent standards of behavior should never be allowed to hold public office." Spin control from the other side will claim that "unintentional mistakes are being escalated by my opponent using wild claims in a political vendetta."

Carefully orchestrated spin-control measures during election campaigns can make a difference. For example, during the 1996 presidential and congressional elections, advisers to the Democrats persuaded them to characterize Republican proposals to slow slightly the rising rate of expenditures on entitlement programs (e.g., Social Security and Medicare) as "slashing aid to senior citizens." This phrase was repeated endlessly during the campaign and was intended to convince older people that they would suffer actual reductions in their Social Security benefits and access to health care. Republican spin-control advisers, on the other hand, were successful in attaching the meaning of irresponsible "give-away" tax increases and spending programs to the word "liberal." This term was used repeatedly in describing the intentions of Democrats were they to be elected. The intention was to scare taxpayers that new social programs planned by Democrats to aid the poor would eat into their family incomes. Thus, language providing interpretations of situations that arise in connection with candidates is couched in ways intended to reflect more favorable (or more damaging) meanings and images. What often spins out of control in such situations are the facts.

# ▼ *Public Relations and the Media*

We noted that there is an important difference between advertising messages and most of the messages that are prepared by public relations practitioners. Advertisers simply purchase the time or space in print or broadcast media and place their messages where they want. Public relations practitioners can do this, of course, but they are far more likely to try to get the media to accept (without cost) news releases, interviews, and other messages that are favorable to their clients, but that are not easily seen as public relations efforts.

Individuals or interests that want to achieve a positive public image by using the mass media in this way face at least two barriers. First, the media are independent entities with their own goals, which may conflict with those of the publicity seekers. For example, a politician's desire for positive coverage on the evening news obviously would conflict with the local television station's intention to disclose the same politician's alleged wrongdoing. Second, there is great competition for limited space and time in the media and other public forums, and many worthy individuals and causes simply cannot receive the media attention and public exposure they desire.

## The Agenda-Setting Process

An important theory explaining how the media select only a limited number of news stories to print, or air in a particular edition or broadcast, is the *agenda-setting theory of the press* (discussed more fully in Chapter 9). This theory is important in understanding the complex relationship between public relations and the media. It states that those who select the content for the daily newspaper, news broadcast, or on-line news site do so by using a number of criteria to decide what is "newsworthy." They realize full well that there is only a limited amount of time or space available. Only those stories judged to be most important, or those in which their audience will be most interested, will be given priority. Those that meet these criteria will be selected from the abundance of stories available to them from reporters, wire services, and the like. The latest news release from a public relations agency, press secretary, or political consultant may not survive this test. Indeed, unless it has some special quality that the editors and news directors feel is important, they are likely to ignore it.

On the other hand, public relations practitioners know this full well. They have no illusions that editors will eagerly accept and make public any kind of news release or other information handout that they prepare. To help in opening the channels, a public relations practitioner will try to become acquainted with those who make news decisions. An effective public relations specialist will establish good relationships—intended to generate and maintain confidence and credibility—with reporters, editors, and news directors. However, journalists often remain wary and are not likely to trust just any public relations person who approaches them with information.

## A Relationship of Mutual Dependency

Adding to this complex relationship between public relations and journalism is the fact that these two groups *need* each other. A careful examination of a daily newspaper or a television news broadcast will reveal that a very large proportion—as much as 70 percent—of what appears in the news has its origin in someone's news conference, news release, or some other form of material prepared by a public relations or public affairs specialist. The press, however, does not blindly make public whatever practitioners provide. Reporters follow up, interview people with other points of view, and so on. Nevertheless, much of the agenda in the daily press has its start in information released by public relations specialists of one sort or another.

To illustrate, if a plane crashes, a grisly crime is committed, or a corporation is caught harassing women or mistreating minorities, some spokesperson for the relevant organization (airline, police department, corporation) will hold a news conference or otherwise appear before reporters. Their purpose is not only to provide information, but also to put the best possible interpretation on what happened, what they are doing about it, and so on. Those are not casual appearances. Most such presentations are carefully rehearsed with the aid of public relations specialists who warn of damaging questions that are likely to be asked and who develop ways of deflecting those questions likely to create harm to the agency or authorities. The reporters, on the other hand, *need news*. They have very little time to generate alternatives to what the practitioners are providing for them. About all they can do is to flesh out the story with a few quotes from experts, someone who represents contrary points of view or some background information.

Thus, in spite of their basic distrust of each other, public relations practitioners and journalists live in a state of *mutual dependency*. Not all of the stories in the daily press come from dramatic events. Indeed, many are products of much more routine happenings in business, education, politics, and so on. Even here, however, reporters depend on those who speak for the major institutions, corporations, and other agencies of society. It is out of their complex interactions and exchanges that much of the daily news is generated and shaped. It is not difficult to understand, therefore, why people and institutions who want public understanding usually cannot achieve it on their own. They need help in seeking it, and it is exactly that set of societal conditions that has given rise to the public relations industry.

## ▼ Lobbying as Public Relations

A special form of public relations is **lobbying,** although some experts would not see it as part of the field. Notwithstanding, lobbying has many similarities

▶
The words "lobbyist" and "lobbying" were in use before the Civil War. Many legislators ate lunch at the historic Willard Hotel, which is very close to the Capitol Building in Washington, D.C. Individuals wanting special consideration waited in a long lobby near the dining room and plucked at the sleeves of politicians as they passed through. Even President Lincoln, who stayed at the hotel for weeks before moving into the White House, received their attentions. (The Bettmann Archive)

to the kinds of activities we have described as constituting public relations. Lobbyists are defined as persons employed "to influence legislators to introduce or vote for measures favorable to the interests they represent."[6]

To achieve their influence, lobbyists rely mainly on interpersonal communication and informal contacts with those whom they try to influence on behalf of their clients. Nevertheless, they are persons or groups paid to engage in efforts to influence the beliefs, attitudes, and actions of specifically defined target individuals through the use of deliberately designed messages. In that sense, they fit quite well within the broad definition of public relations. The main differences are that they seldom use the mass media and they focus their influence attempts narrowly on legislators.

When they were first identified in the nineteenth century as a distinct group of influence peddlers, they stood in the lobby of Washington, D.C.'s venerable Willard Hotel, which still stands only a short walk from the White House and a few blocks from the Capitol building. Many politicians walked to the hotel to have lunch or an evening meal. When officeholders came through the lobby, these importuners clutched at their sleeves and tried to get their attention (much as had influence-seekers at centers of power since organized government began). In time, they came to be called "lobbyists." Even today, the Willard Hotel proudly tells its guests that the name was born right there.

Lobbyists represent a great variety of groups and interests. These include trade associations, veteran's groups, labor unions, political action committees, consumer advocates, professional associations, churches, foreign governments, and many more. There are literally tens of thousands of organizations and individuals who want to influence the legislative process. A lobbyist might be a lawyer, public relations practitioner, or policy expert who has been hired to influence the work of Congress. Not all work at the federal level; some represent clients at state and even local centers of government.

Federal law requires that lobbyists register with the Records and Registration Division of the Capital Hill Lobbying Office. There are over 6,000 registered individual and group lobbyists in Washington, D.C. alone. They represent more than 11,000 active and about 28,000 inactive clients (those who have not been represented on Capitol Hill for the last three months). Some of the groups identify themselves as lobbying specialists. Others are public relations agencies, law firms, and "think tanks" (various mission-oriented institutes and centers).

Lobbying and lobbyists have always been a subject of controversy. Some critics regard them with deep suspicion. Early in 1993, lobbying got on the news agenda very quickly when the late Ron Brown, former chairman of the Democratic National Committee, was appointed Secretary of Commerce by President Clinton. Brown had been a member of a well-known and very influential lobbying firm, Patten, Boggs and Blow. The group had represented many special interests in Washington, D.C. over the years. Questions were raised as to whether Brown would favor those whom his firm had represented in the past. His untimely death took this concern off the agenda, but the issue remains regarding others who make similar moves from a lobbying firm to government office.[7]

A move by any person between lobbying and government, or the reverse, illustrates a continuing focus of criticism. There is a constant rotation of individuals between government service and private influence-seeking roles. The problem that many people see is that former government officials or employees who return to or take jobs in lobbying will use their inside knowledge and contacts to give an unfair advantage to the special interests they represent. There are now laws that prevent them from doing so for several years after they leave office

For a number of years, the two largest lobbying and public relations firms in Washington, D.C. have been Hill and Knowlton, Inc., and Burston-Marstellar, Inc., each with ties to advertising and public relations groups on a worldwide basis. Clients pay huge fees to be represented by such groups, and their annual billings are in the millions of dollars. Such firms use every conceivable tool and process to promote, change, or impede legislation pending before Congress that can have an influence on their clients. Sometimes even getting a single word changed in a bill (e.g., from "shall" to "may" or from "never" to "seldom") passing through a committee can mean millions to a client. Similar to the work of more traditional public relations firms, they organize events, do research, develop communication strategies, or sometimes shape news, on behalf of their clients. Lobbyists at both federal and state levels write articles, make speeches, design campaigns, buy advertising, influence journalists, and guide public officials.

Although many critics deplore all lobbying and lobbyists, others point out that they have a legitimate role in the process of government. Lobbyists do bring to the attention of officeholders a great deal of information that should

▶
Although lobbying cur-
rently has a negative
connotation for many
critics, some lobbyists
provide legitimate and
necessary services that
go beyond gaining bene-
fits for special-interest
groups. Representatives
of various causes that
are well regarded by the
public often bring to of-
ficeholders' attention information that can be
critical to promoting the
well-being of their con-
stituents. Thus, lobbyists
can help busy legislators
see an issue from a
number of perspectives.
(Bob Daemmrich, Stock,
Boston)

be taken into account as laws are formed or modified. They bring together those who have legitimate interests with those who can have powerful influ-ences on those interests. Often, legislators need to know who will be affected by the outcome of bills under consideration. The downside comes when spe-cial interests gain an advantage over the public good and scandals arise. Fortu-nately, consumer groups, the press, and our government constantly monitor lobbyists for ethical and other kinds of violations.

## ▼ Public Relations as an Emerging Profession

As the field was being established, no particular credentials were required to become a public relations specialist. Indeed, many of the earliest practitioners were ex-journalists who had an understanding of the workings of the press and how to get stories about their clients into the pages of the newspapers. More-over, it was all done by the "seat of the pants"; that is, there was no body of concepts and principles that had been developed by systematic research. It was a field where intuition, creativity, insights, and lore held sway. Often the guesses and inspirations of practitioners led to success; sometimes they did not.

Today, there is a strong movement among its practitioners and educators to try to transform public relations into a *profession*. Whether this will be successful or not depends on what one means by that label. The word "profession" is an ancient one, going back to the Middle Ages, when there were only three basic "learned professions": divinity, law, and medicine. What set them apart from other vocational pursuits were these major criteria: (1) Each had an extensive *body of sophisticated knowledge* requiring long periods of formal study to learn and master. (2) Their practitioners used that body of knowledge on behalf of the public *within a set of ethical norms*. And (3) their practitioners *monitored each other* to ensure compliance with the norms, rejecting from their ranks those who engaged in unethical practices.

The label "professional" is now widely applied by the public to designate virtually any specialized occupational group. Thus, we hear of "professional" hairdressers, prizefighters, bartenders, and even dog groomers. However, it is the traditional meaning of the term, and its prestige, to which public relations practitioners and educators aspire, and there is evidence that at least some progress is being made. Today, two major factors play a central role in the evolution of public relations as a professional field. One is the increasing establishment and acceptance of courses and degree programs in higher education. The other is systematic research and scholarly inquiry aimed directly at developing concepts, principles and practical solutions related to public relations.

Both education and research would appear to satisfy the traditional criterion of developing a body of sophisticated knowledge that requires lengthy training to master. However, whether the field's practitioners use that knowledge for the benefit of the public within an ethical framework is another matter. Furthermore, whether they monitor each other and reject those who transgress the ethical norms is something else altogether. In the section that follows, we focus on public relations within the framework of the three criteria of a true profession.

## Public Relations Education

Public relations has been taught in universities since 1923, when Edward Bernays organized the first course at New York University. Early on, it was taught mostly in journalism schools, which were largely newspaper-oriented and not always hospitable to the inclusion of public relations in the curriculum. This prejudice toward public relations has faded over the years, although a few journalism schools still bar it from the curriculum. The first formal undergraduate degree program in public relations was established at Boston University in 1947. In more recent times, departments of speech communication also have added public relations programs, as have many comprehensive communication schools and colleges. In addition, there are individual courses in public relations at community colleges and industry trade schools.

Today, public relations is not only a rapidly growing field of study in higher education, but also it has taken other important steps to establish itself as a profession. For example, the organization that periodically examines and approves of journalism curricula in the United States also reviews public relations course work in specific institutions to determine if it qualifies as an "accredited" sequence. (Other regularly reviewed areas of study are news-editorial, magazine, and radio-television news.)

There are several hundred teachers of public relations in journalism and communications schools and in speech communication programs in the United States, and every year thousands of students major in the field. Student internships are available with public relations firms, businesses, government agencies, and professional associations. Dozens of textbooks and a number of technical journals reporting research results are devoted to the field. Public relations practitioners also have their own national organization called the Public Relations Society of America (PRSA) with student chapters on many campuses as well.

A formal curriculum in public relations at the undergraduate level usually includes substantial work in the liberal arts and sciences. Typically, a public relations major takes an overview course on public relations as a communication field, an advanced course in public relations methods, and other specific courses of instruction in various aspects of the field, depending on the size of the program. Public relations curricula at the graduate level usually involve formal communication theory courses and research training as well as instruction in the field's areas of specialization. Over the last three decades, public relations has become one of the most popular communication majors as students in the information age realized the importance of the field and other media consulting activities. The fact that the field pays more than most other media-related industries is an added attraction.

The purpose of public relations education is to promote the field as a professional communications activity, to produce a well-educated workforce, and to foster research. However, this does not mean that people who aspire to work in public relations must major in public relations at a university or college. Although there is a great and growing demand for people formally educated in public relations, many still get into the field by working for newspapers or other media. Some people come into public relations as specialists—for example, they may have a background in public health and take up a public relations assignment in that area. Thus, there are many pathways to a public relations career. At the same time, most university-based public relations programs have the advantage of having close links with the industry and are better positioned to help their students get jobs in the field.

## Public Relations Research

A second significant area of development in public relations is research. This, too, represents an effort to gain full professional status by fulfilling the first criterion of having an extensive body of specialized knowledge. However, as will be clear, in many ways that body remains to be developed.

Much of the research done in the field stems from practical rather than theoretical considerations. Clients want to see what kind of "bang" they have received for their "buck." This means that "research" consists mainly of assessing the results of a particular campaign or determining the needs of a client in order to develop an appropriate strategy. Although public relations was once carried out with little formal evaluation, businesses and governmental departments increasingly require that public relations practitioners document expenditures and provide reliable evidence that some kinds of benefits flow from those costs.

Increasingly, however, much of the impact and influence of public relations can be understood in the general context of more sophisticated media and communication research. Thus, research on such general topics as the process of persuasion; the nature of opinion, attitude, and attitude change; and how media agenda-setting takes place, is pertinent. Moreover, a growing field of applied research more specifically focused on problems and practices in public relations has also emerged. Some public relations agencies and departments conduct in-house assessment studies simply to take stock of their activities. Other research is done in universities by public relations scholars. This type of academic research is broader in scope and less parochial than the applied research of public relations practitioners. Academic research typically aims at establishing general concepts, patterned relationships, and theories that help explain processes and effects in the field.

Public relations scholar John V. Pavlik has identified at least three motivations for public relations research: One is understanding public relations as *communication*, which involves building communication theory and studying the effects of public relations activity on the individual, group, and society. A second is *solving practical problems* in the field, including monitoring the public relations environment, measuring social performance, and auditing communication and public relations. A third motivation stems from the need to *monitor the profession*, by taking stock of how public relations practitioners, individually and collectively, are performing technically and ethically.[8]

Much of the in-house public relations research done by agencies gives clients feedback and helps them improve communication with their constituencies. Some critics say that such research is manipulative, but defenders say it is simply intelligent, systematic information that can make the client more sensitive to the desired audience. How public relations people use such information is up to them—hopefully most will use it ethically.

The state of proprietary public relations research and its actual use by people in the field is difficult to ascertain. The largest and most powerful public relations firms and government departments spend a considerable amount of time and money testing their messages and monitoring campaigns for evidence that they are having some effect. At the same time, many small public relations firms and individual practitioners make limited use of research in their work. Some publicists do not use research at all, preferring an intuitive "seat of the pants" approach. General usage on a day-to-day basis of the kinds of public relations research typically reported in academic journals is limited. Yet such research contributes to that much-needed body of knowledge that can help imaginative and thoughtful practitioners and planners move toward professional status.

## Ethical Issues and Criticisms

As public relations continues its struggle to be recognized as a profession, one of its major problems lies in the public image of the field and in developing and enforcing a meaningful code of ethics. As we noted earlier, almost from its beginnings public relations has had its detractors. Critics charge that public relations activity is manipulative, self-serving, and unethical; that it distorts and blurs issues in its attempts to persuade the public, and that publicists will use just about any means to assure a favorable image for their clients.

Such charges are not without foundation. There are unscrupulous people in public relations. The same is true of physicians, lawyers, and any other profession. However, in public relations, questionable or unethical practices become especially visible because of the nature of what practitioners do. Unlike the botched surgery or the ineptly handled legal case, the products of public relations practitioners are open to scrutiny. Public-spirited groups and the news media make special efforts to try to ferret out deceptive activities. As a result, public relations practitioners who transgress norms almost immediately receive unfavorable press coverage. In addition, even if not detected immediately, unethical practices sometimes backfire and at a later time harm the image that public relations is meant to polish.

To its credit, the field makes extensive efforts to reduce poor practices. To be *accredited* by the Public Relations Society of America, a practitioner working professionally in the field must pass tests of communication skills and agree to abide by a code of good practice. In addition, many college and university programs include courses on public relations ethics. Hopefully, these conditions taken together will eventually limit flagrant deceptions of the public.

In spite of these efforts, those who criticize the basic task of public relations focus on a more fundamental problem: They raise the question as to whether there is something less than honorable in a business devoted to enhancing the image of a corporation or individual by suppressing truths that would bring criticism and emphasizing only favorable meanings. To the critics this is a serious charge, and it is this aspect of the basic mission of many public relations campaigns that is most troublesome. Defenders say that a corporation or individual has every right to put on the best face possible before the public. Moreover, public relations practitioners do provide useful information to people in an increasingly complex and bureaucratic world—although most would agree that in an ideal world such information should be balanced with information from more objective sources.

As efforts toward professionalization of the field continue, such negative views of the field may change. One reason is that during the past twenty years, "public accountability" is an important concept that has found increasing favor among public relations specialists. This idea has received much attention and has been integrated into public relations education, thinking, and practice. The accountability concept is tied to the idea of "corporate social responsibility," which stipulates that a business ought to contribute as much to the common good as to its own economic success.

According to this idea, a responsible corporation should make a positive contribution to local communities or the nation as a whole in which it is allowed to function. As a business, however, public relations still has a long way to go in this respect and often appears to lack accountability. For example, after Hurricane Hugo hit the Caribbean islands in 1989, promoters of tourism quickly organized information about what islands and resorts were still open for business—even though they had been hit by widespread destruction and were in the midst of relief efforts. Although some criticized this seemingly insensitive campaign, others argued that the future employment and prosperity of the islanders depended on sustaining the tourist trade. In such a case, critics of public relations may charge that no one represents the consumer. On the other hand, publicists may counter that their own ethical standards prevent them from deliberately misleading the public, and that the promoters did a service by providing accurate information in the midst of rumor and misinformation. There are no easy answers, and there will be none until the canons of ethics for such complex public relations situations are further developed.

Today, one of the major ethical sore points among critics of the industry lies in the area of public relations during elections. Political campaign consultants often approach and sometimes cross the ethical borderline. Negative or "attack" ads provide a case in point. These can be both deceptive and unfair. A classic example, often cited, was developed by Roger Ailes, who worked for George Bush in his successful 1988 presidential campaign against Michael Dukakis. The campaign Ailes designed ran negative television ads that many critics said appealed to racial fear in voters. The most cited was the so-called "Willy Horton" ad, which showed convicts going through a revolving door (to represent a prison furlough policy approved by Dukakis). The meaning conveyed was that Dukakis was insensitive to the fact that a convicted African-American murderer was let out on furlough and committed another terrible crime. In addition, Ailes admitted that he planted doubts in reporters' minds about Dukakis, knowing full well that the imputations were false. Ailes and other political consultants who "play hardball" in their public relations efforts are often criticized by the press and their colleagues. However, as long as they successfully accomplish

During elections, both sides use materials that make their opponents look bad. So-called "attack" ads often contain scowling or mean-looking photos of the opposition in not-so-subtle efforts to discredit the competing candidate. If a "sound-bite" (often taken out of context) can be used along with such a picture, the result can be persuasive and cause shifts in voter preferences. (AP Photo/Mark Wilson)

their goals in getting people elected, it is doubtful that they will change their tactics.

Attack ads played a significant role in the 1996 presidential campaign. Democrats targeted Newt Gingrich (Republican from Georgia and Speaker of the House), in particular, with negative ads that many citizens felt crossed the line. On the other hand, candidate Bob Dole's consultants focused forcefully on President Clinton's personal troubles toward the end of the campaign with very negative ads.

Research shows that even though many voters say that they deplore attempts to influence their votes with negative advertising, such attack ads work. Elasmar and his colleagues reviewed the accumulated research on the issue and studied their influence in the 1996 New Hampshire primary.[9] It was clear that such ads brought about changes in vote intentions among the electorate. Given such findings, it is likely that public relations consultants advising candidates and helping design their communications will continue this practice.

## ▼ The Future of the Field

Although many efforts are being made by public relations to be identified as a "profession" in the traditional sense, it is clear that the field has a long way to go. The current status of the field can be assessed against the three criteria previously discussed. Progress is clearly being made on the first criterion; that is, the field is assembling through research and scholarship a *body of complex knowledge*. Moreover, that accumulated knowledge is now being taught in formal courses and degree sequences in colleges and universities. There is less certainty as to how well the second criterion is being met; that is, it could be hotly debated whether public relations practitioners *serve the public* with their knowledge. In some ways they do, but there are grounds for concluding that for the most part they serve only those well-heeled clients who can afford their fees. Indeed, many critics believe that public relations campaigns often deliberately fool the public by suppressing damaging information and emphasizing only positive messages about their clients. Finally, there is, as yet, no codified set of ethical norms to which public relations practitioners universally subscribe, and there certainly is no way in which those who cross the line on ethical standards can be drummed out of the profession. Therefore, it will be interesting to see, in the years ahead, if the field can resolve these problems and gain the public trust that has largely failed to develop over the years.

One way in which public relations will continue to change in the future is through the development of new strategies to *reach* relevant publics. That is not to say *serve* the public—the benefits go to clients who pay the bills. In any case, practitioners seek ways to make use of technological advances in communication systems within the United States and all over the world. With new media available, public relations specialists have been able to design new formats, such as home pages on the World Wide Web, CD/ROMS that present information to clients and the public, video news releases, and other ways of presenting messages about their clients to relevant receivers.

## Computer Technologies

Today public relations messages compete with other kinds of information for public attention in an environment that includes many kinds of media and a great variety of sources. Through personal computers connected to the Internet and its World Wide Web, people access a vast array of specialized information. E-mail enables people, both within and between groups, to transmit and receive information of many kinds. Computer-based teleconferencing brings small groups together for discussions, even though they may be at sites remote from each other. Public relations agencies, consultants, and individual practitioners make use of all these media for a variety of purposes. For example, World Wide Web home pages have become very common. Many are sophisticated and "interactive" in that a person contacting them can access various kinds of information by clicking on "buttons" designed in the system. Often, an agency will post important information for potential clients or journalists on such a system; this makes it easier for them to receive it, as opposed to telephone calls with their inevitable recorded voices and requests to press different numbers to reach specific people.

This continuously evolving world of privatized communication does not rely on mass media at all. It is targeted to specific individuals, within both established groups and new constituencies. The electronic services offer a more precise way of reaching a desired audience than, say, the special-interest magazine. In fact, the most specialized publication probably has a more diverse readership than the audiences currently being targeted by new data services. There is also a considerable on-line news industry now growing rapidly. Special-interest newsletters, often transmitted electronically, reach chocolate lovers, travelers to certain countries, and many other "publics" that desire highly specific information.

The idea of using various kinds of new technologies to achieve public relations goals was understood well by the Chinese student groups who in 1989 led the protest in Tiananmen Square against corruption in their government. They quickly learned to provide information to American and European print and broadcast journalists by fax and e-mail. They used these media to transmit their news releases and interpretations across national boundaries into the court of world opinion. The Chinese government, which strongly disapproved of their actions, was slow to make use of such channels or even to shut them off. At first they stonewalled requests for information and later tried to persuade reporters and others that the protests were simply disruptive and illegal. When that strategy failed, the government crushed the protest in a bloody massacre. Many student leaders were subsequently executed, jailed, or forced into exile; yet images of the students bravely demanding democracy in the face of violent governmental opposition will likely be remembered for a long time. Since that time, the Chinese government has begun to exercise very strict controls over the Internet, denying citizens unrestricted access to e-mail.

▲
The lessons of American public relations were not lost on the Chinese students in Tiananmen Square in 1989, when they used the "Goddess of Liberty" to capture the attention of television viewers (especially Americans). (© Chip Hires/ Gamma-Liaison)

## The Video News Release

A good example of the way in which public relations practitioners constantly search for new ways to present their messages to targeted publics is the **video news release** (VNR)—a self-serving promotion of a person or organization presented on videotape. Originally used by companies to promote their general image or to respond to a crisis, VNRs are now increasingly used by political candidates. By 1996, more than 10 percent of television stations were using VNR material from the major presidential candidates in the primaries and general election.

Producers of VNRs control the style, content, and tone of the message, which may be picked up and aired by broadcasters. VNRs represent another example of the dependency that exists between public relations and the media. From the standpoint of television stations, VNRs conveniently provide much-needed visual material for the news. Moreover, they reduce filming costs. In some instances, the only way a local station can get direct access to major candidates is through VNRs or satellite news conferences, both of which are paid for by the candidates. Thus, the stations get the material cheaply and do not have to spend time and resources digging it up independently. The practitioners get their message on the air for their clients in the format they want.

An ethical problem associated with this kind of communication concerns identification of the source. When television stations do not identify the VNR as such, they do their viewers a disservice. Yet stations do not always give the public due warning that self-serving VNR material is produced by the candidate or company represented and was not subject to usual journalistic checks for accuracy.

VNRs are distributed either on videocassette or via satellite transmission. Like a printed news release that may emphasize favorable elements to convey a positive image, the video news release seeks to communicate a certain point of view or argue a case. For example, VNRs have been used by various industries to dispute environmental claims and by environmental groups with equal fervor. When a firm is in the midst of a major crisis, the VNR allows the company spokesperson or CEO to put the firm's position forward to employees without press intervention. Supporters of corporate VNRs say that this is an appropriate use of corporate communications in an era when it is difficult for a firm to get its message across without constraints or disruption from the press. Sometimes VNRs are used to save time and money when a firm or interest wants to get its message across in several markets without extensive travel or personal appearances from its executives. In effect, the VNR is an advisory from an organization making a plea for publicity and understanding. Media organizations are then free to use the material verbatim, edit it heavily, or identify it as a statement from those appearing therein.

In a basic sense, the future of public relations is not difficult to predict. The field has developed rapidly over the last century and regardless of its critics, there is no doubt whatever that it will continue to be an essential part of our complex society in the future. Organizations producing goods and services that are important to the public need public relations to maintain good will and favorable attitudes on the part of those that consume their products. The public, on the other hand, benefits when such organizations continue to function—employing people, providing things, and conducting activities that the society requires. There is also a relationship of dependency between public relations and journalism. Reporters, editors, and news directors need the information supplied by public relations because it makes up a large part of what journalists report to the public. In turn, public relations practitioners are dependent on the news media to transmit many of their announcements, campaigns, and releases to their audiences. Thus, public relations is a field intricately interwoven into the major activities and affairs of society. It is completely unrealistic to assume that its importance will diminish in the years ahead.

## CHAPTER REVIEW

▼ Public relations can be defined as the work and outcomes of paid professional practitioners who design and transmit messages, on behalf of a client, via a variety of media to relevant and targeted audiences in an attempt to influence their beliefs, attitudes, or even actions regarding some person, organization, policy, situation, or event.

▼ Some scholars believe that communication strategies used today in public relations have ancient origins. The case of Hammurabi's laws dates back about four thousand years. However, the field's more modern origins lie in the "publicity men," "press agents," and agencies that developed in New York City early in the twentieth century. Their task was, much as it is today, to improve the image of clients.

▼ Most public relations efforts make extensive use of mass communications. Practitioners constantly try to draw attention to their clients by information transmitted by the media in news reports, talk shows, or in any form of print or broadcast content that can show their client in a favorable light.

▼ A somewhat uneasy relationship exists between the field of public relations and the media—more specifically, journalism. Each needs the other. Much of what appears in the news has origins in events or information released by public relations practitioners. However, such practitioners are deeply dependent on the media as a means of transmitting their messages to their desired audiences.

▼ Lobbying can be considered a special and controversial form of public relations. Lobbyists use a variety of communication techniques to try to influence legislators as they initiate, modify, and pass laws that can have an impact on their clients.

▼ Today, there is a strong movement among its practitioners and educators to try to transform public relations into a *profession*. Whether this will be successful or not depends on how well the field meets three major criteria: (1) developing a body of sophisticated knowledge, (2) using that knowledge for the public good within a system of ethical norms, and (3) ensuring compliance to those norms by monitoring practitioners.

▼ The accomplishment of the field in both education and research would appear to satisfy the first criterion. There is considerable doubt that the field's practitioners always try to use that knowledge for the benefit of the public within an ethical framework. Furthermore, efforts to monitor each other and reject those who transgress the ethical norms have not been impressive, to say the least.

▼ Therefore, the field has a number of problems to solve before it can gain professional status in the classic meaning of that term. It will be interesting to see, in the years ahead, if the field can resolve these problems and gain the public trust that has largely failed to develop over the years.

## CHAPTER 13

# The Audience

## Demographics of the American Audience

*I*n 1854, in his literary classic *Walden,* Henry David Thoreau wrote that "If a man does not keep pace with his companions, perhaps it is because he hears a different drummer. Let him step to the music which he hears, however measured or far away." Like Thoreau's marcher, we all step to a different drummer when it comes to attending to mass communications. We do so because each of us is a unique individual, with distinct preferences in what we want to read, hear, and view. What this means is that the American audience for the mass media is one of great *diversity*, with each person different from all others. That uniqueness is derived from two basic sources. One is from each individual's inherited attributes, which in part shape past learning experiences in their family, among friends, at school, and in the community at large. The second is each person's positioning in particular kinds of *social categories* in their community and society—his or her age cohort, gender, educational attainment, income level, and race or ethnicity.

Taken together, these psychological and social characteristics produce *individual differences* in each person's psychological organization of beliefs, attitudes, values, tastes, and interests. These differences, in turn, determine what he or she will select and attend to from the vast flow of mass communications available to all of us every day. Moreover, those individual differences will determine what *meanings* various members of the audience will assign to the media messages they receive, how much they will *like* or *use* them, and what *actions* they will take as a result.

This chapter focuses on the second of those sources of individuality—the distinctions that can be found among us in terms of such characteristics as age, gender, income, education, race, and ethnicity. It also discusses ongoing changes in significant social processes like urbanization, migration, and family composition, which play a part in determining how people respond to the media. All of these *demographic characteristics and trends* need to be understood because they lead different kinds of people to select, interpret, and act upon different kinds of content in different ways for different media. In the sections that follow, then, the general demographic features of the American population are discussed insofar as they define the nature of the audience for our complex system of mass media.

A second major issue addressed in the chapter is how these various differences among the audience are assessed so that professional communicators can obtain an understanding of their interests and preferences. Various kinds of rating systems and other ways of measuring audience attention to media presentations reveal their size, composition, and patterns of attention.

By looking closely at the American population as media audience, this chapter looks at the *receiving end* of the linear model of mass communication presented in

Chapter 1. In the six stages of that model, we noted that the process begins with professional communicators who decide on the nature and goals of the message; additional steps are encoding the intended meanings and transmitting the message via the specialized technologies of print, film, and broadcasting. In Chapters 2 through 7 we discussed those technologies and indicated how they transmit their messages. It is that final stage of the model in which members of the large and diverse audience selectively attend to, perceive, and assign meanings to what they read, view, or hear to be influenced in their feelings, thoughts, or action.

As we have made clear, ours is a system of mass communication that rests solidly on individual ownership, free enterprise, and competition in the marketplace. Although there are exceptions, the bottom line in that system is that it is designed to earn money from its audiences, either directly or indirectly, in order to produce profit. Content is prepared for the media that audiences will buy directly, or that will attract their attention to advertising designed to motivate them to purchase goods and services. Thus, an understanding of the tastes and interests of the audience that bring them to make selections from the media are the *sine qua non*—the absolute necessity—for anyone who attempts to be successful in the mass communication business. And, because audience tastes and interests are linked to the distinct personal and social characteristics of individuals that make up the population, the sources of their diversity need to be fully understood. Thus, it is important to examine the population's demographic structure, including its trends and changes.

The sections that follow do not try to sort out details about which specific media reach exactly how many people with particular kinds of content. We have tried to do that in previous chapters. Instead, the discussions focus on the nature of audiences and on the techniques used by the major media to assess them. These sections also do not try to identify the kinds of influences mass communications have on audiences. That will come later (in Chapters 16 and 17). Instead, this chapter focuses on the *range and sources of diversity* that exist in the American population. It discusses the sources of that diversity and how it is undergoing changes that will have implications for mass communications. We will help make clear why we indicated in our discussion of the linear model that the "multitude of receivers will have a multitude of ways in which to assign meaning to incoming mass communicated messages."

Essentially, the first section of our discussion of the American population as audience reviews three major issues. One is the *size* of the population and how that continues to change. A second is its complex *composition.* By composition we refer to such factors as age, gender, education, income, race, and ethnicity. All these factors

# EXPLAINING MEDIA EFFECTS
## *The Selective and Limited Influences Theory*

Research on the effects of mass communication began during the late 1920s with the Payne Fund Studies of the influence of movies on children. At first, the results seemed to support the "magic bullet" theory indicating that motion pictures had widespread and powerful effects on their audiences. However, newer research seemed to offer a different interpretation. In 1940, a major study of a presidential election conducted in Erie County, Ohio, seemed to show that the influence of the media was quite limited. The political campaign presented by the media did have limited effects. It *activated* some people to vote who might have stayed home and it *reinforced* the views of others. However, very few people were persuaded to *change* their vote from one party's candidate to the other. In addition, it led to the conclusion that two kinds of factors were important as influences on what people selected from the media to read and hear. These were their *social category memberships* and their *social relationships* with friends and family.

Other research, done by the U.S. Army during World War II, also led to a conclusion of selective and limited effects. Soldiers who were shown the *Why We Fight* films learned a number of facts from their exposure, but they underwent only minor changes in their opinions. They did not change their more general attitudes about the war or patterns of motivation to fight as a result of seeing the films. What changes did occur were linked to their individual differences in such matters as intelligence and level of formal schooling.

lead to multicultural and personal diversity in our media audiences, and provide the basis for modern counterparts of what Thoreau had in mind when he posed his metaphor. Because each of us is different in our personal combinations of social identities, we do indeed hear different drummers as we select our content from the media. Each of us steps to music that may not be perceived in the same way, or even heard at all by other kinds of people, as we think about or act upon these selections.

## ▼ *The Changing American Population*

The sheer number of people in a population can be critical to the success or failure of particular kinds of media at particular times. We saw earlier that one reason magazines failed in colonial America was that when they were introduced the population was too small and too scattered to provide a viable market. In addition, we saw that it was the growth of population in such urban centers as New York City, and generally along the more populated eastern seaboard, that provided the initial audiences for the penny press—the forerunners of modern newspapers.

Following the war, a number of experiments by psychologist Carl Hovland and his associates confirmed that exposure to, interpretation of, and response to a persuasive message were influenced by a host of factors. The degree to which a person was influenced was related to both the characteristics of the message and the personality of the receiver.

This accumulation of research made it necessary to abandon the earlier "magic bullet" theory that forecast powerful, uniform, and immediate effects of mass communication.[1] It was necessary to develop explanations that took into account the fact that different kinds of people selected different kinds of content from the media and interpreted it in different ways. Thus, the new theory emphasized both selective and limited influences. Although formulated in retrospect, the theory that emerged can be summarized in the following terms:

1. People in contemporary society are characterized by great psychological diversity, due to learned *individual differences* in their psychological makeup.

2. People are also members of a variety of *social categories*, based on such factors as income level, religion, age, gender, and many more. Such categories are characterized by subcultures of shared beliefs, attitudes, and values.

3. People in contemporary society are not isolated, but are bound together in webs of *social relationships* based on family, neighborhood ties, and work relationships.

4. People's individual differences, social category subcultures, and patterns of social relationships lead them to be interested in, select, attend to, and interpret the content of mass communication in *very selective ways.*

5. **Therefore,** because exposure to media messages is highly selective and interpretation of content varies greatly from person to person as a function of individual differences, social categories, and social relationships, any specific mass-communicated message will have only *limited effects* on the public as a whole.

Today, with our population exceeding 266 million, there is little danger that there will be too few people in the nation as a whole to support any major medium. On the other hand, that population is not evenly distributed among the states and local areas. This uneven distribution can influence decisions as to where to locate a TV cable system, where to establish home delivery of a newspaper, or whether it is economically feasible to develop a movie theater in a local mall. Furthermore, the size of any population—local or national—*changes* over time, which can have significant influences on the viability of particular media. That is particularly true at the local level. If a town or city is gaining or losing population, its newspapers, radio stations, and even its movie theaters may fall upon hard times as the numbers they serve decline. The opposite is obviously true if the community is growing. We need to understand, therefore, what factors determine population size and change, both at a national level and in particular areas or communities.

## A History of Rapid Growth

The size of any population in any particular area at any particular time is a product of three specific factors: the number of *births* that add population during a particular period; the number of *deaths* that occur during that period and remove people from the population; and the pattern of *migration* into or out of the area that results in a gain or loss of residents. If one knows the past trends in these three factors and can anticipate their nature in the years ahead, predictions of population size are not difficult, at least on a short-term basis. These are important data, then, in management decisions on whether or not to provide various kinds of media services.

A problem is that all three of the preceding factors can change rapidly and rather sharply. The birth rate in a particular area can rise or fall as people make decisions about starting, expanding, delaying, or stabilizing the size of their families. That can happen when the economy waxes or wanes. The death rate generally rises or falls with the availability of medical treatment and as public health measures (clean water, effective waste disposal, and food inspections) deteriorate or improve. Migration can be a wild card as people move into or out of an area due to the availability of work, welfare benefits, housing, protection from crime, religious or racial intolerance, and so forth. In fact, the American population and where people choose to live has changed greatly during the twentieth century as a product of just such factors.

To gain an appreciation of how population size, and numbers of people available for media audiences, can change as a result of these three factors, we can review our pattern of population change at the *national* level during the twentieth century. It was during this period that our mass media saw their major patterns of growth. Whereas the print media were already well established as the century began, radio, the movies, and television in all its forms developed after 1900.

As Figure 13.1 shows, there has been a long-term expansion of the American population since the beginning of the twentieth century. Actually, that expansion started earlier, as soon as the 1800s began. By 1840, large numbers of immigrants were already pouring into the United States. Near the end of the century, the population had reached over 76 million from its mere 5.3 million in 1800. That is an astonishing 1,335.7 percent increase in essentially three generations (of about thirty years each). This was one of the largest human migrations in the history of the world.

All during the nineteenth century, attracting immigrants was a deliberate national policy. The United States acquired vast territories, and undeveloped land is an open invitation to external aggressors. Settlers were needed to farm and secure millions of square miles when the nation's geographic boundaries expanded as a result of two huge land acquisitions. The first was the Louisiana Purchase of 1803—which for a mere $15 million added what are now the states of Arkansas, Iowa, Kansas, Missouri, Nebraska, North and South Dakota, and most of Minnesota, Montana, Oklahoma, Louisiana, and Wyoming. The second, following a successful war with Mexico, was the result of the 1848 treaty of Guadaloupe-Hidalgo. This treaty permitted the United States to acquire, for another $15 million, what became California, New Mexico, and Utah, plus major parts of what are now Arizona, Texas, Colorado, and smaller sections of other states.

These monumental real estate bargains opened enormous territories to settlement. In 1862, during the Civil War, the federal government established the

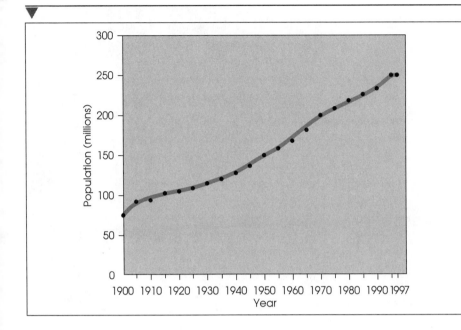

**Figure 13.1**
**Growth of the U.S.**
**Population, 1900–1997**
The American population has been characterized by one of the fastest rates of growth in history. Even during the twentieth century, population continued to rise sharply as wave after wave of immigrants arrived from Europe and other parts of the world.

Homestead Act, which allowed any citizen, or even an alien who had filed a declaration to become a citizen, to acquire ownership of up to 180 acres of public land free of cost by residing on the site and farming for five years. Entire regions were populated by immigrants taking advantage of this extraordinary offer.[2] To develop the nation's agriculture more rapidly, Congress, through the Morrill Act of 1862, granted tracts of land to the states to establish colleges where offspring of the settlers could study the "agricultural and mechanical arts." (These have become our great land-grant colleges and universities.) Thus, during the nineteenth century, the majority of the population lived on farms. We reached the 50 percent farm residence point in the 1920s. Today, less than 2 percent of Americans continue to live on farms.

## Immigration and Cultural Diversity

In 1997, the American population was just over 266 million—up 190 million from 76 million at the beginning of the 1900s. That is a growth of 250 percent—which is enormous, but far less than the rate of expansion in the previous century. One of the important features of our current rate of population growth is that it is largely a result of immigration, through which we continue to add population. In fact, according to the Bureau of the Census estimates, we have added another 25.4 million during the 1990s alone.[3] Although the birth rate is declining in the United States, large numbers of immigrants (legal and illegal) have and will come from Mexico. Others will arrive from Asian countries, South America, and the Caribbean.

▶

Just before and after the turn of the century, unprecedented numbers of immigrants poured into the United States from all parts of the globe, but mainly Europe. Shown here, eating lunch in the main dining room, is a group of immigrants passing through Ellis Island. Some called it the "Golden Door" to their life in the New World. The result of this massive immigration was a society of great ethnic, racial, cultural, and religious diversity. Such diversity remains an important feature of the audiences for mass communications in the United States. (AP/Wide World Photos)

Because of the legality of slavery prior to the Civil War, millions of Africans arrived in the United States over a span of more than two hundred years. Their offspring remain our largest distinct racial minority and an important category contributing to diversity in the American population. In addition, millions of Europeans came as part of the earliest large-scale immigrations in the 1800s to settle in the northeastern and midwestern states. These vast parts of the country were virtually empty of farms and settlements at the time, and those in charge wanted immigrants from Europe very badly. The fact that Native Americans were already there did not trouble the young nation. They were either killed or forced onto reservations. The immigrants who replaced them during the early and mid-1800s were mainly from England, Ireland, Scotland, France, Scandinavia, and Germany.

Toward the end of the nineteenth century, the origins of the immigrants shifted to southern and eastern Europe as millions of Italians, Poles, Russians, Czechs, and Hungarians arrived through Ellis Island. Many remained in cities on the eastern seaboard, but others went on to the upper midwest and found work in mines, mills, and factories. The importance of these immigration patterns is that they produced a nation of great ethnic, racial, and cultural diversity. In this sense, the emerging United States was a different kind of nation than those in Europe and Asia, where the racial and ethnic composition of populations remains more or less stable.

As Table 13.1 shows, by the 1990s the population of the United States was one made up largely of the offspring of immigrants. The grandparents, or even parents, of many contemporary American families arrived in this country late in the nineteenth or early in the twentieth century. The cultural values and

**Table 13.1   U.S. Population by Ethnic Group**

| Ethnic Group | Population (thousands) | Ethnic Group | Population (thousands) |
|---|---|---|---|
| **European** | | **Hispanic** | |
| English | 49,596 | Mexican | 7,693 |
| German | 49,224 | Puerto Rican | 1,444 |
| Irish | 40,166 | Cuban | 598 |
| French | 12,892 | Dominican | 171 |
| Italian | 12,184 | Spanish/Hispanic | 2,687 |
| Scottish | 10,049 | Colombian | 156 |
| Polish | 8,228 | Spanish | 95 |
| Dutch | 6,304 | Ecuadoran | 88 |
| Swedish | 4,345 | Salvadoran | 85 |
| Norwegian | 3,454 | Total | 13,017 |
| Russian | 2,781 | | |
| Czech | 1,892 | **Asian** | |
| Hungarian | 1,777 | Chinese | 894 |
| Welsh | 1,665 | Fillipino | 795 |
| Danish | 1,518 | Japanese | 791 |
| Portuguese | 1,024 | Korean | 377 |
| Total | 207,099 | Asian Indian | 312 |
| | | Vietnamese | 125 |
| **Middle-Eastern** | | Total | 3,384 |
| Lebanese | 295 | | |
| Armenian | 213 | **Other** | |
| Iranian | 123 | Jamaican | 253 |
| Syrian | 107 | Haitian | 90 |
| Total | 738 | Hawaiian | 202 |
| | | Native American | 6,716 |
| **African** | | French-Canadian | 780 |
| Afro-American | 20,965 | Canadian | 456 |
| African | 204 | Total | 8,497 |
| Total | 21,169 | Grand Total | 253,904 |

Source: U.S. Bureau of the Census, *Statistical Abstract of the United States,* 111th ed. (Washington, D.C.: 1991).

lifestyles that were brought with them are still to some degree alive and well in the United States. We can see that in our ethnic neighborhoods, our foods, folk festivals, and diverse religious groups.

During the period of the great immigrations, the national policy was that of a "melting pot," in which all immigrants would drop their foreign ways and

▶

At the turn of the century, the nation's school systems emphasized a "melting pot" approach. This meant forbidding children of immigrants to speak anything but English, discouraging evidence of "foreign" appearance or behavior, and "Americanizing" them as soon as possible. Today, diversity is lauded and bilingual instruction is offered in many languages. (Credit T/K)

merge into a single American culture. It was an important policy at the time, and one that had been deliberately adopted. The melting pot concept was intended to unify the nation politically and reduce the risk that age-old blood hatreds and ethnic animosities would create destructive political conflict in the United States. (Currently, one can see the result of such problems in Canada, where French descendants seem bent on dividing the nation. The same is true in the former Soviet Union and in the Balkan countries that made up the former Yugoslavia.)

In retrospect, the melting pot policy worked very well at the time. We did not form a checkerboard of separate cultural, religious, or political identities. We now share a common language, even though others are also spoken. Moreover, although there are people in this country with almost every conceivable ethnic and religious background, there is a widely shared general American culture. On the whole, we are able to function very well within our secular democratic institutions that separate church and state. At the same time, the melting pot is now seen by many Americans as a dreadful idea that brought disrespect to other people's cultures, prejudice, discrimination based on ethnicity, and conflicts between parents and children. With our general culture well institutionalized and the secular government unchallenged, many advocate a contemporary policy of cultural pluralism in order to avoid these consequences.

## Internal Population Movements

A factor that works in the other direction—to reduce certain kinds of differences between people in audiences—is *internal* migration. A number of distinct major shifts in population within our borders have taken place during the twentieth century, which resulted in redistributions of the population into various regions. The most visible of these internal migrations have been: (1) The great *westward* movement, which has been extended into modern times. This movement has caused high rates of growth in most of the western and southwestern states during recent decades. (2) The *farm-to-city* movement attracted millions of rural people to cities and factory towns as opportunities arose through the growth of industry, and greatly accelerated the growth of the urban centers of the northeast. (3) A large *south-to-north* movement of population took place as African Americans left the harsh conditions of the south to seek work in the industrial north. The majority of the urban black communities that exist in northern cities today grew sharply as a result of this trend. It was accelerated greatly during the two world wars, when factory hands were badly needed in war industries. (4) There has been a continuous *exodus to the suburbs* as the white middle class escaped from crime, racial tensions, and other stressful conditions of the city. This exodus led to vast expansions of suburban communities in all parts of the nation.

During the past two decades, some of these trends have been partially reversed. Increasing numbers of people have moved to the *sun belt states*. They sought economic opportunities as these states changed from agriculture to other types of industries. Many older Americans wanted more favorable weather conditions and lower living costs for their retirement. There has also been an *expansion of small towns* that are within commuting distance of large cities. Finally, with the *gentrification* of formerly run-down areas in some cities, many younger middle-class families have moved back to more urban areas.

## Implications for Mass Communication

Both the massive immigration and internal migrations of population that have characterized the American population have had significant implications for mass communication. Adding millions of people from a long list of foreign countries to the population of the United States left a legacy of *cultural diversity* resulting from the racial and ethnic subcultures that continue to exist. This factor can create barriers to communication, conflict, and animosity. For example, African Americans, Native Americans, Hispanics, and indeed all other racial and ethnic groups, are sensitive to their treatment in the media. This sensitivity has become abundantly clear over the years. To be "politically correct," encoding of media messages must be done with a clear understanding of the beliefs, attitudes, and values of people from diverse backgrounds. Professional communicators ignore this principle at their risk.

The cultural diversity existing in the population has produced media aimed at specific populations. In Chapter 2 we noted the existence of a substantial

▶ Four great streams of internal migration have characterized the American population over the last century. One was the westward movement, which brought people to newly acquired territories, displacing Native Americans. A second was the South to North movement of African-Americans, from subsistence farming or sharecropping to urban ways of life. A third was the farm to city movement, bringing rural people into urban environments. Finally, an exodus from the cities to surrounding areas concentrated middle-class whites in the suburbs. All of these movements played a part in structuring the American audience for mass communications. (Joe Munroe, Photo Researchers, Inc.)

ethnic press. In a similar way, a number of magazines, radio programs, movies, and television shows are produced mainly for persons who identify with one racial, religious, or ethnic group or another. These media serve not only as a means to preserve cultural differences, but also as vehicles for advertising, political debate, and entertainment for the groups involved.

Although we have shown that immigration from abroad and other sources of cultural differences have been significant factors in creating diversity, other factors have had a reverse effect—leading toward cultural similarities. For example, the American population is also one that has constantly been on the move, migrating and relocating within the nation's expanding borders. Over the generations, diverse people have mixed in ways that have reduced their differences, producing a strong and unifying *general American culture*. Thus, our internal population shifts have to some extent resulted in a kind of "homogenization effect" in national tastes for certain kinds of media content. Because of the relatively predictable nature of the general American culture, the media have been able to present entertainment—soap operas, evening crime drama, game shows, films, and other kinds of content—that is not bound to particular subcultures. Each major socioeconomic level has media products that appeal to their tastes and interests in all parts of the country, creating a true *national* audience for our print and broadcast media.

# ▼ Contemporary Sources of Diversity

We have reviewed a number of changing characteristics of the American population that resulted from various kinds of migrations. However, additional contemporary sources of social differentiation in media audiences can be seen in its demographic composition. Important among them are *age, gender, education,* and *income.* There are other factors as well, but these four have a particularly strong influence on what people select from the mass media.

## Age

No factor is more important in the process of mass communication than age. Significant trends have taken place in the American population with respect to this demographic factor. The most pronounced among them is that we are now living much longer on average than we were at the beginning of the twentieth century, and there is every likelihood that the aging trend will continue. As Figure 13.2 shows, in 1900, the average life expectancy at birth was 47.3 years.[4] By 1995, it had risen steadily to 76.3. Estimates indicate that this will continue to rise, reaching 76.7 in the year 2000 and will be even higher in the decade to follow. Figure 13.2 illustrates how this has meant an increasingly aging population, which of course, has significant implications for media audience interests, tastes, and preferences.

Although there are many specialized subcultures in any complex society, such as the United States, a general culture provides stable and predictable ways for conducting most daily affairs and interpersonal exchanges. The general culture enables a diverse population to live together in coordinated ways. The mass media are an important agent in displaying and reinforcing the general culture. (Copyright © Remi Benali/Liaison International)

▼
**Figure 13.2
Changing Life Expectancy of Individuals in the U.S., 1900–2000**
Americans are now living much longer than they were at the beginning of the twentieth century. Life expectancy (the average age at death of people born during a given year) has risen by nearly thirty years. For the most part, this rise has been due to relatively simple measures, such as improving water quality, more effective disposal of human wastes, inoculation and vaccination to prevent the spread of diseases, and related public health measures. Life expectancy will continue to rise, however, as scientists continue to discover ways to keep older people in better health. This has significant implications for mass communication as audiences will be made up of older individuals.

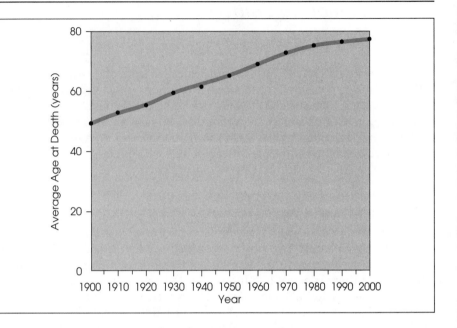

The causes behind this extension of the average human life expectancy are not as obvious as they may seem. It is clear that advances in sophisticated medical treatment have made a contribution. However, the trend is less associated with heroic surgical interventions that replace organs, or miracle drugs that cure dreaded diseases, than with much more mundane measures. For the most part, the extension in life expectancy is a result of rather simple public health practices and basic preventive measures that have reduced the influence of infectious diseases as our leading causes of death. To illustrate, at the turn of the century, such diseases regularly struck large numbers of people. In 1900, 200 people for every 100,000 in the population died of influenza and pneumonia. In fact, during the influenza epidemic of 1918–19 alone, more than 500,000 Americans died of the dread disease.[5] By 1960, the rate of deaths due to this cause was down to a mere 0.2 fatalities per 100,000—a 1,000 percent drop in the rate! The number of deaths from smallpox, tuberculosis, diphtheria, typhoid fever, dysentery, whooping cough, scarlet fever, and malaria showed similar declines.

Older people were particularly vulnerable, and mortality from these diseases kept the average age of the population low, as it had been for centuries. The benefits of preventive measures that now seem simple and obvious to us were not understood. However, medical experts increasingly discovered the microorganisms that caused these diseases and took steps to control them. Steps included sanitary sewage disposal, purification of water, quarantining those already infected, and the use of effective vaccinations and vaccines.

These public health measures, coupled with more attention to industrial accidents—a major cause of deaths among males in particular—began to extend the average life expectancy of our population. Today, this trend continues. The effects of smoking have been uncovered, and we are moving rapidly toward a smokeless society. The relationship between diet, exercise, and health is now clearer to many Americans and they are taking steps that will extend their lifetimes.

Even more subtle factors adding to life expectancy are related to retirement and years spent in the labor force. To illustrate, the age at which a worker entered the labor force in 1870 was thirteen on average. That age increased steadily in this century, and by 1950 it was 17.6 years. The trend continued to an average age at present of 19.1 years. Age at retirement was another factor. In 1870, there was no expectation of "retirement." Workers continued on the job as long as they were physically able, usually until they died. (So much for the "good old days!") The idea of a "normal retirement age" at 65 was not recognized as part of our culture until the years of Franklin D. Roosevelt, during the 1930s. Today, the average age at retirement is 63.6. Thus, workers are spending fewer years on the job, and are therefore subject to less stress and possible occupational accidents. Even working at home on such chores as washing, ironing, mowing the lawn, shoveling snow, and the like have declined (from 1,825 hours annually in 1870 to 1,278 in 1990). Thus, older people today have much more leisure time, fewer risks from work, and (as we will see later) they have more income and live longer than they did in earlier years. Finally, because of a sudden rise in the birth rate during the two decades following World War II (the so-called "baby boom") the sheer number of older people in the population will start to increase sharply, starting in about 2010. All of these factors, trends, and events are important in understanding age as an important demographic category related to the composition of media audiences.

## Gender

Males and females do not select identical kinds of content from the mass media. Thus, gender is an important demographic factor in trying to determine what kinds of material will work well to achieve the goals of professional communicators who design advertising, news programs, sports presentations, popular culture for entertainment, and so on. A review of past trends and the current composition of our population in terms of gender can help in understanding the American media audience.

For reasons that are not entirely clear, there are more males than females born in all human populations. The number of males per 100 females in a population is called the **sex ratio.** Worldwide, about 106 boy babies arrive every year for each 100 girls. This sex ratio of 106 is perhaps nature's way, based on long evolution. In prehistoric times, many males were killed in the hunt, and as human societies became more complex and competitive, more men died in battle. Consequently, the male death rate was always higher than that of

**Figure 13.3**
**Numbers of Males and Females in the U.S. Population, 1900–1997**
The gender composition of a population is of great importance to mass communicators. More males are born in any given year than females. However, by the time they reach retirement years, females outnumber males. This influences the gender composition of older audiences. Moreover, during this century, the proportion of the population that is male in any given year has declined steadily. The earlier surplus of males was a product of immigration. More males than females left their native lands to immigrate to the United States.

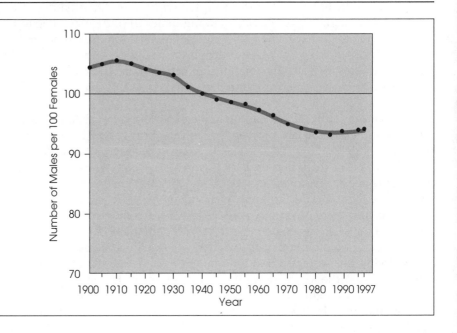

women. In fact, it still is! Today, females outnumber males in our population. As Figure 13.3 shows, for every 100 females there were only 95.9 males in 1997. The ratio of males per females dropped steadily during the present century until the early 1980s. Since that time there has been a slight reversal of the trend.

One reason for the changing sex ratio in American society is that the number of males at the beginning of the century was greater because of the typical pattern of immigration; that is, males came to the United States in larger numbers than females. Some—but not all—later sent for their families. Then, as the factor of immigration declined in importance, the higher risks for males in the labor force and in wars altered the ratio.

Today, many women survive their husbands and live on as older widows. Thus, the sex ratio is more evenly in balance among younger adults than is the case for seniors. Among the elderly, women continue to outnumber men to a considerable degree. This feature is important in understanding the older audience and in developing programming specifically for them.

## Education

Educational attainment in the American population has been rising for many decades. This fact has truly significant implications for the content people want in mass communication. The overall trend is clear. Educational attainment has increased greatly since World War II. For example, in 1940, the average years of education among the American population was 8.4. The majority had less than a high school education. Since that time, the number of high school graduates has increased steadily and the percent of the population with a college degree has risen sharply. Today, the average number of years spent in formal education is thirteen. Among adults twenty-five years and older, nearly 15 percent have a bachelor's degree. That is a six-fold increase from 1950. Therefore, we have, as a nation, become far more educated than was the case before World War II. That trend is expected to continue as more and more young people continue their education through college.

This great advance in education is a product of the several factors. One is the history-making concept of free (tax-supported) and mandatory education for all children that was introduced by Horace Mann in Massachusetts in 1834. Before that, it was mainly the children of the relatively affluent who became educated. At the time it seemed to conservative elements a wild and radical idea, and they opposed it bitterly. However, it spread to all the states, and as a result, we have a population deeply devoted to education today. Our system of state-supported education extends beyond secondary school to community colleges, four-year institutions, and great public research universities that are all funded in part by tax revenues. We also enjoy the largest number of private schools, colleges, and universities in the world. These, along with government-supported programs, such as the GI Bill, Pell grants, and student loans, have opened educational doors to almost all individuals who have the motivation and intellectual capacity to earn degrees. In that sense, the United States is unique. Currently, support for higher education is high. Not only do the majority of parents want their children to go to college but also new programs are being developed in Congress that will make it financially possible for them to do so. As will be seen in the next section, education is a critical factor in the lives of citizens as well as in the functioning of the media.

## Income

Income is a critical demographic factor in understanding media audiences. It is a central factor in decisions about producing media content at various taste levels. Obviously, the higher one's family income, the more big-ticket items one can afford and this plays a part in advertising certain kinds of luxury goods. However, those who design and produce media content are not deeply concerned with the affluent, because there are simply not enough of them! What drives media decision makers in designing content is the *number* of families who will be able to purchase a long list of mundane products. For example, there is a huge number of families with enough income to purchase items as toothpaste, breakfast cereal, soft drinks, and paper towels. Because there are millions of them, their collective purchases represent a huge source of income for those who manufacture and market such products. Influencing purchasing decisions by attracting attention to advertisements that appear on television, radio, or in printed media, then, is a factor that drives the majority of decisions about the nature and taste level of media content.

Income is not distributed equally among the various kinds of people we have discussed thus far. For example, in earlier decades, large numbers of older citizens were near the bottom of the income distribution. Since World War II that has changed. With increased numbers of companies and other organizations providing their workers with pensions, with the Social Security system supplementing the incomes of many, and from increases in investments, seniors are not now the poorest age group. That distinction goes to those between eighteen and twenty-four years of age. Nevertheless, about 50 percent of those sixty-five or older live on Social Security income as their sole source of income.

Income is closely related to education. Simply put, for all categories in the population, the more education one has attained, the higher one's income (on average). An example is the way income differs by *gender*. Again simply put, men make more money than women (on average). Table 13.2 shows these relationships as of 1995.

Another important condition related to income is race or ethnicity, as we can see in Table 13.3. On average in 1995, African Americans had a lower monthly income than their white counterparts. Similarly, those of Hispanic origin also had lower monthly incomes. In each case, however, a critical factor was their level of education.

## Implications for Mass Communication

Age, gender, education, income, and ethnicity, then, are basic demographic factors that have a truly significant influence on the media habits and content

**Table 13.2    Monthly Income by Education and Gender**

|  | Not a High School Graduate | High School Graduate | Some College | Bachelor's Degree | Master's Degree |
|---|---|---|---|---|---|
| Males | $1,211 | $1,812 | $2,045 | $3,430 | $4,298 |
| Females | 621 | 1,008 | 1,139 | 1,809 | 2,505 |
| Total | 906 | 1,380 | 1,579 | 2,625 | 3,411 |

Source: U.S. Bureau of the Census, *Statistical Abstract of the United States,* 1996.

**Table 13.3    Monthly Income by Education and Ethnicity**

|  | Not a High School Graduate | High School Graduate | Some College | Bachelor's Degree | Master's Degree |
|---|---|---|---|---|---|
| Whites | $951 | $1,422 | $1,649 | $2,682 | $3,478 |
| Blacks | 713 | 1,071 | 1,222 | 2,333 | 2,834 |
| Hispanics | 786 | 1,106 | 1,239 | 2,186 | 2,605 |
| Total | 906 | 1,380 | 1,579 | 2,625 | 3,411 |

Source: U.S. Bureau of the Census, *Statistical Abstract of the United States,* 1996.

selections of the American audience. Different tastes and preferences exist among these categories, and those who make decisions about what type of content will characterize our media understand this very well. For example, it is well established that older people have very different preferences and media habits than younger. They follow the news avidly (both in print and broadcasting); they attend fewer movies and select ones that are different from those that appeal to youths and young adults. Seniors also watch more television, perhaps because they have more time. They have very different preferences in music, and therefore their radio listening tends to be very different from that of younger people.

Gender is not as powerful a factor in determining selections from media as age and education. However, women do have different preferences in content than men in many ways. As a category, they have less interest in sports and they tend to dislike violent films. They are more likely to read romance novels than adventure or war stories. For understandable reasons they attend more closely to presentations about child-rearing, fashions, and beauty products. Because significant numbers are not in the labor force, women attend far more often to the daily soap operas than men. At the same time, women are similar to men within specific age and educational categories. They have about the same interest in public affairs and political news.

No conditions of the audience play a greater role than the combination of education and income in determining what selections people make from available media content. Those that are well-off and well educated, as compared to less affluent people with limited schooling, select different books, read different parts of newspapers, attend different films, prefer different types of TV programming, and listen to different radio programs.

In summary, as the previous sections have shown, age, gender, education, and income, as well as race and ethnic background, are factors that have importance in two related ways. They are the guidelines used by those who design and produce content for the purposes of attracting particular kinds of consumers to particular kinds of media content or programming. The reverse side is that these factors are significant influences that determine what people select from the daily flow of media content and how they interpret and respond to those messages.

## ▼ *The Changing American Family*

Media messages are received and interpreted mainly within the context of our families. They influence not only what we attend to but also how we understand and act upon what we receive. It is within the decision-making context of this important human group that most people decide on what products or services they will purchase, for what candidates they will vote, what pundits they will believe, whether they will contribute to a particular charity, or what

**Table 13.4    Numbers of Males and Females in the U.S. Population, 1900–1997**

| Year | Number of Males | Number of Females | Males per 100 Females |
|------|-----------------|-------------------|-----------------------|
| 1900 | 38,867 | 37,227 | 104.4 |
| 1905 | 42,965 | 40,857 | 105.2 |
| 1910 | 47,554 | 44,853 | 106.0 |
| 1915 | 51,573 | 48,973 | 105.3 |
| 1920 | 54,291 | 52,170 | 104.1 |
| 1925 | 58,813 | 57,016 | 103.2 |
| 1930 | 62,297 | 60,780 | 102.5 |
| 1935 | 64,110 | 63,140 | 101.5 |
| 1940 | 66,352 | 65,770 | 100.9 |
| 1945 | 70,035 | 69,893 | 100.2 |
| 1950 | 75,539 | 76,146 | 99.2 |
| 1955 | 82,030 | 83,246 | 98.5 |
| 1960 | 89,320 | 91,352 | 97.8 |
| 1965 | 95,609 | 98,694 | 96.8 |
| 1970 | 100,266 | 104,613 | 95.8 |
| 1975 | 105,366 | 110,607 | 95.3 |
| 1980 | 110,888 | 116,869 | 94.9 |
| 1985 | 116,648 | 122,631 | 95.1 |
| 1990 | 121,600 | 127,789 | 95.2 |
| 1995 | 128,569 | 134,321 | 95.7 |
| 1997 | 130,440 | 136,050 | 95.9 |

*Population figures are in thousands.

Source: U.S. Department of Commerce, Bureau of the Census, *Current Population Reports,* Series P-25, Nos. 519, 917, 1045, 1057, 1095, and PPL-57.

they will consume in the way of popular entertainment. Because the family is such a significant influence on media behavior, its characteristics need to be discussed briefly.

Our families have changed significantly during the twentieth century—and especially since World War II—in terms of size, decision making, women working outside the home, and in aggregate purchasing power. Each of these trends has had important consequences for mass communications.

## Trends in Family Size

At the beginning of the century, when Americans were mainly farmers, the extended family was common and households included a larger number of people. The grandparents, parents, and their children—three generations—often lived in the same farmhouse. Other relatives, such as a widowed aunt or aging father-in-law, might also have lived in the same home. In addition, families included on average a larger number of children than they do today. For example, in 1940, the average size of family in the United States was 3.76. By 1995, this had fallen to 2.61, which is a decline of over 30 percent. Today, there are far more single-parent families, persons living alone, and couples with no children. Obviously, such smaller families will attend to and use almost all forms of mass communications in ways that differ from those families with many children.

## Relationships Between Husbands and Wives

During the twentieth century, the American family changed from one that was male-dominated to our current more egalitarian pattern. As the century began, few husbands preferred their wives to work. Men were supposed to be the "breadwinners," supporting the family by their earnings alone, and they fully accepted that obligation. In their capacities as providers, they felt entitled to make the major decisions in the family, and for the most part, their views and preferences prevailed over those of their wives and children. Women were supposed to be submissive and to serve as child-bearers and homemakers. They had little power, no right to vote, and until relatively recently, were not even allowed to own property. Women could not initiate a divorce, take out a mortgage in their own name, or obtain credit at a store. In general, then, the traditional

One of the most significant changes in the American family since the turn of the century has been a reduction in the number of people in an average household. In earlier times, the norm was the extended family, consisting of several generations and often including aunts, uncles, or other relatives who had to be provided for in a society without a national welfare system. Today such large family units are the exception, and many families consist of a single parent and one or more children. (Stock Montage, Inc.)

**Table 13.5     Women in the Labor Force, 1900–1995**

| Year | Number of Females of Working Age* | Number of Females in Labor Force† | Percentage of Women Who Work |
|------|------|------|------|
| 1900 | 28,246,000 | 5,319,000 | 18.8 |
| 1910 | 34,553,000 | 8,076,000 | 23.4 |
| 1920 | 40,449,000 | 8,550,000 | 21.0 |
| 1930 | 48,773,000 | 10,752,000 | 22.0 |
| 1940 | 50,688,000 | 12,887,000 | 25.4 |
| 1950 | 54,293,000 | 18,412,000 | 30.9 |
| 1960†† | 61,582,000 | 23,240,000 | 37.7 |
| 1970 | 72,782,000 | 31,543,000 | 43.3 |
| 1980 | 88,348,000 | 45,487,000 | 51.5 |
| 1985 | 93,736,000 | 51,050,000 | 54.5 |
| 1986 | 94,789,000 | 52,413,000 | 55.3 |
| 1987 | 95,853,000 | 53,658,000 | 56.0 |
| 1988 | 96,756,000 | 54,742,000 | 56.6 |
| 1990 | 98,399,000 | 56,554,000 | 57.5 |
| 1992 | 100,035,000 | 57,798,000 | 57.8 |
| 1994 | 102,447,000 | 60,239,000 | 58.8 |
| 1995 | 103,555,000 | 60,994,000 | 58.9 |

*From 1900 to 1930, the U.S. Department of Labor defined those of working age as "noninstitutionalized civilians aged 16 years and older." From 1940 to 1960, 14-year-olds and older were included in the working age population. After 1960, the definition became "noninstitutionalized civilians aged 16 years and older" again. From 1940 to 1970, those of working age included people in the armed forces, as well as civilians.

†Includes both unemployed and employed.
††First year for which figures include Alaska and Hawaii.

Sources: U.S. Bureau of the Census, *Historical Statistics of the United States,* Colonial Times to 1970, Series D, Nos. 11–25; Statistical Abstract of the United States, 1996.

family was almost completely *male-centered*. It had a clear-cut division of labor—one in which neither wives nor children had much of a voice in their own destiny.

Because of these characteristics, the American family at the beginning of the twentieth century was a very different economic and consuming unit than it is today. Because few women had control of the family purse strings, they played only a minor role in purchasing decisions. Typically, their husbands doled out an allowance for them to purchase their clothing and the family food. As Figure 13.4 shows, few women (18.8 percent) were in the labor force.

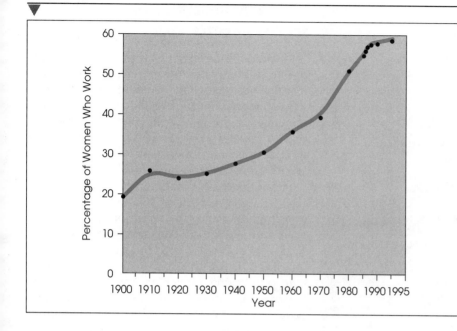

**Figure 13.4**
**Women in the Labor Force, 1900–1995**
The role that women play in American society is of great concern to professional mass communicators. One of the most significant trends in the twentieth century has been the movement of women into the labor force. This has altered their disposable income, their media habits, and their patterns of consumption. Today, more women work outside the home than at any period in U.S. history. This leads them to select different media content, attend to different advertisements, and purchase different kinds of products than during earlier periods.

Most of these worked as teachers, domestic servants, or factory hands. There were almost no professionals, such as doctors, lawyers, or professors.

Today, drastic changes have taken place. The movement for equal rights for women began to coalesce when in 1848 the first Women's Rights Convention was held at Seneca Falls, a small community in upstate New York. In the twentieth century the movement's greatest achievement was woman's suffrage. Women gained the vote when the Nineteenth Amendment to the Constitution was ratified in 1920. Although the movement waned for several decades, women began to change their situation following World War II, during which many entered the labor force temporarily. They earned high wages and learned to enjoy financial independence. During the years that followed, a new *feminism* evolved that has drastically altered the status and freedoms of women in our contemporary society.

Although patterns of sexual harassment and limitations on women's economic opportunities remain, the American family is now very different than it was just a few decades ago. Power tends to be shared and husbands increasingly take responsibility for household chores, including shopping for domestic products. Women have a much greater voice in decisions about major purchases. For example, automakers have found out that women constitute a large market and have changed their designs and products accordingly. Even children have money to spend and freedom to make choices—a fact not lost on those who advertise such items as food, clothing, athletic shoes, popular music, and films.

# Female Participation in the Labor Force

No feature of family life has undergone more drastic change than the movement of women into the world of work. We noted earlier that few women worked at the beginning of the century. However, as the century moved on, the proportion of females of working age who held jobs outside the home increased steadily over the entire century. Many attribute the change to women entering the labor force to work in factories during World War II, but it started long before and has continued into the present.

This trend toward two-income families had a heavy impact on the mass media industries. For one thing, it considerably increased the aggregate purchasing power of American families. Perhaps it is more accurate to say that it kept disposable income from eroding as inflation in society increased. And, in spite of the financial difficulties of the early 1990s, families with both the husband and wife employed will continue to have more discretionary income than if we returned to the male breadwinner pattern.

Many women who work today are single, largely as a result of divorce. The proportion of our society who are divorced has risen sharply in recent years. For example, in 1970, only 3.2 percent of the population were divorced. By 1995 that had risen to 8.3, an increase of over 153 percent in just twenty years! There are more divorced

As more and more women have entered the labor force, relationships between husbands and wives have changed. Power tends to be shared, and husbands have taken greater responsibility for domestic chores. Women who earn a share of the household income are much more involved in purchasing decisions. These changes have altered advertising directed at women as consumers of various products and generally changed the nature of the audience for mass communications. (© James H. Karales/Peter Arnold, Inc.)

women in society than men—largely because divorced men tend to remarry rather quickly. If children are involved, the courts tend to follow legal tradition and award custody to the ex-wife. This practice has created a significant number of families in our society in which a working mother provides the sole or major support for her children. These are largely low-income families, because women lose the purchasing power of the husband as the marriage is dissolved, even if child support is paid. There are other single-parent families, with some made up of never-married women and others of divorced men. In all these families, patterns of media usage tend to differ from those of intact families.

## Implications for Mass Communication

The changing American family is the foundation for understanding many of the purchasing decisions and media habits of contemporary Americans. For that reason, understanding the size, structure, and processes of decision making within families is critical for media professionals who want to influence purchasing with advertising and other persuasive appeals. Today, the family is smaller, less likely to include members other than the parents and children, and it is far more democratic in its decision making. The majority of women of appropriate age are employed outside the home, and they are now much more important as consumers of a variety of products than they were just a few decades ago. Even children have considerable aggregate money to spend.

Generally, the trend toward two-income families has increased family purchasing power, or at least kept it from serious erosion during a lengthy inflationary period. At the same time, other family-related trends have had a negative impact on women's aggregate purchasing power. In particular, the increase in the number of single or divorced mothers raising their children alone has created a growing number of consumer households with very limited income.

Overall, these changes in the American family, along with all of the demographic factors of population growth, race, ethnicity, age, gender, and education, have created a complex and constantly changing audience for mass communicators to sort out as they try to discover and chart who attends to their messages with what effects. Because all the trends we have described will continue in various ways, the audience of the future will be *unlike* that of yesterday or today. However, whatever its size and composition at a given point in time, the many social categories involved will continue to play a significant part in shaping the beliefs, attitudes, and behavior of every individual who turns to the mass media for news or entertainment, and who receives information about products to buy. The bottom line is that at any particular time there are many audiences of varying size and diversity in that heterogeneous and multicultural population, each composed of its unique pattern of demographic factors and individual differences.

## ▼ Assessing Audience Composition and Attention

Each of the media faces the task of discovering and continuously *assessing* the size and composition of its audience. If professional communicators did not know the nature of their receivers and how they were responding, they would soon be out of business. But as this section will show, the assessment of audience size and composition is carried on in a variety of ways.

In principle, there could be three kinds of information flowing back to professional communicators from their receivers. Having effective feedback would make it easier for professional communicators to reach the largest number of people, tailor the nature of their messages to the capacities and interests of their audience, and prompt them to take some form of desired action (buy, vote, donate, etc.). One very limited kind of information is **simultaneous feedback,**

## *Media and the Liberal Arts*

### How the Audience Rules in "Adopting" New Technologies

#### A Linchpin to the Spread of Material Culture

John Carey, a genial communications technology expert, has a favorite question. He seriously asks his audiences, "Would you buy a dog that could fly?"

He then explains, "It's an odd question, but no more odd than questions people are asked everyday in telephone surveys that try to determine the likelihood of consumers buying futuristic communications services." Says Carey, "In responding to a question about a hypothetical, genetically engineered flying dog, you might respond positively on the grounds that you would be the envy of all your neighbors, or negatively if you considered the problems associated with

walking such a dog." In either instance, Carey wonders aloud with his audiences, "How much confidence should the person asking the question put in your answer?"[6]

Carey and other advisers to high-technology companies producing new media try to get the best possible intelligence for their clients. After all, no one wants to manufacture a new device, appliance, or service that people say they want but will not pay for. In a sense, new technological devices ranging from VCRs to picture phones and electronic notebooks are like orphans when first introduced by manufacturers. They are produced because they are technologically

possible and because the manufacturer wants to make money. The big question is, Will the public buy the new product? In some instances, new technologies start out as institutional services. For example, when the telephone was first introduced, it was not practical for individual households but used in offices. Eventually, it was "adopted" by people in their homes and then even in their cars. By contrast, early facsimile machines in the 1930s and 1940s were test-marketed in people's homes. Consumers reacted by saying "This is interesting, but why should I pay for it?" and for decades the fax was dead. It came back in the 1980s, first in offices and institu-

such as takes place in face-to-face or interpersonal communication. A second more common one is **delayed feedback,** such as occurs in letters to the editor or phone calls to the studio after a broadcast. Finally, the most widely used is the **audience-assessment information** obtained from various agencies and services that make a business of measuring audiences for the various media. This kind of feedback is systematically gathered in the form of circulation audits, ratings, and polls.

Only in a very limited sense is simultaneous feedback a part of the mass communication process. As we pointed out in our discussion of the linear model of mass communication, there are very few occasions when receivers are actually visible to a professional communicator while he or she is delivering a message. It can happen, as in the case of a news report where a reporter is among a crowd of people, or in a call-in type of program on radio or television, where at least some members of the audience can be in direct touch with the communicator. For the most part, however, simultaneous feedback messages from the audience are not available as the message is being formulated or transmitted.

Delayed feedback is another matter. Indicators of approval or disapproval come from many sources. For example, a considerable amount of commentary and criticism often flows from individual members of the audience back to the

tions and later in private homes. Today, people can get faxes through their laptop computers and electronic notebooks on airplanes.

Carey, a guru of consumer adoption of new technologies, says there are four factors worth watching when considering the possible success or failure of a new technology.

First, the price has to come down dramatically from where it started. Phone calls were exorbitantly expensive when first introduced (as much as a full day's pay for a three-minute call between New York and Chicago), as were radios, color TV sets, and pocket calculators. Affordability is key.

Second, technology needs to reach a point of explosive growth so that it can penetrate a significant number of households to be a serious contender for audience affections. For some devices, such as radio and television, the explosion

came immediately, but for others, such as the VCR, growth came more slowly. VCRs were once seen as a luxury for the rich who could afford to *buy* a whole library of videotapes. The *rental* store was the trigger that made the technology affordable and useful for ordinary people. Today, 75 percent of Americans own a VCR.

Third, some technologies get off to a fast start only to fail later because they are fads and the public is fickle about them. Citizen-band (CB) radios in the 1970s and 3-D movies of the 1950s are examples of fast-moving, exciting new technologies that had short life spans. This does not mean that a new technology, like the fax, won't come back when there is public demand.

Fourth, sometimes small competitive disadvantages perceived early at the start may escalate and eventually spell doom for a new

technology—for example, the battle between VHS and Beta formats in the video cassette market ended with the dominance of VHS. The public, says W. Brian Arthur, senses even a tiny competitive edge in a product and favors winners over losers. People watch publications such as *Consumer Reports* or TV consumer shows that indicate what will be the best product in the long run. Here, the role of information is crucial and critical.

Brilliant inventors, enthusiastic manufacturers, and skilled marketers all work in concert to curry public support, but it is the consumer in the end who votes at the cash register and determines which of the thousands of "orphans" in the marketplace will be "adopted." As David Poltrack, head of research for CBS, says, "for the commercial television industry, (the product) is its audience."[7]

communicator. Newspapers regularly print at least some of their "letters to the editor," in which individuals denounce or applaud news stories or other material that has been printed. Large metropolitan papers get several thousand of these a year (but print only about 10 percent). Most other newspapers receive from one hundred to about five hundred a year, depending on their size. Similarly, people write or call in to radio or television stations to air their views about particular broadcasts. Even filmmakers receive mail with comments on their products. The limitation of such material is that it is scarcely representative of the views of the majority of the audience. Such delayed feedback tends to come mainly from disgruntled people with an axe to grind who are sufficiently motivated to write or call to take issue with the communicator.

Sometimes such delayed feedback takes a more organized form. From time to time, various groups take strongly critical positions on the content of mass communication. A religious group may object to the way in which sacred ideas or events are depicted in a film and organize demonstrations at theaters where they are being exhibited. An organization representing a minority group may put pressure, through threats of boycotts, on local or national media concerning the way their people are portrayed. An organization of educators, mothers, or even physicians may deplore the content of television and seek the assistance of

For the film industry, the ultimate form of delayed feedback is the number of people who pay at the box office to see the movie, plus other forms of profit. Those who produce films have little opportunity to assess audience feedback while their messages are being encoded. For that reason, moviemaking is an industry with great risks as well as the chance for large profits. (Copyright © D. Young-Wolff/ PhotoEdit)

Congress to bring about change. Many professional groups, such as police organizations, seek change in the content of television, the movies, and even the recording industry. Some mount nationwide petition drives to put pressure on professional communicators for change.

Are the media sensitive to such pressures from their audience to a point where they actually alter the nature of their messages? The answer is "sometimes." We saw in Chapter 5 that, in its early years, the film industry became very concerned about public criticism and adopted a strong production code that completely cleaned up the movies—for a while. However, during the 1950s, the code became ineffective when television reduced movie attendance sharply. Films then turned to violence, sex, special-effects, gore, or whatever would result in paid admissions without creating too much of an uproar. At one time or another, codes and conventions pertaining to virtually all of the media have been formulated by various groups. The problem with almost all such agreements is that they are voluntary and lack effective enforcement provisions. The result is that when financial pressures arise, they become ineffective or are forgotten.

Awards and prizes are still another form of delayed feedback. Each industry has its contests at which its products are judged for various (largely symbolic) recognitions. The movies have their Academy Awards; the newspapers have Pulitzer Prizes; the advertising industry awards Cleos for ads judged by various professional criteria; and so it goes.

The ultimate form of delayed feedback to the media is *profit*. If a particular kind of film fails to bring in the dollars at the box office (or video rental store) it is unlikely that others will be produced within the genre. If a television series fails to attract the advertisers that the network needs, it will not be on the air very long. If a newspaper's or magazine's circulation falls below a certain level, it will be out of business. Thus, audience approval in the form of paid admissions, rentals, subscriptions, purchase of products, and so forth, in the final analysis, is the only truly effective form of delayed feedback.

The media themselves understand very well the need to assess their audiences in terms of size, composition, interests, tastes, and purchasing power. A number of organizations providing such services have been developed over the years to measure the numbers of people who attend and to determine their demographic characteristics. This information is critical to each of the media, and they use this form of delayed feedback continuously to design and redesign their presentations in order to gain the attention of their audiences, to satisfy their interests and needs, and to elicit from them behavior they deem desirable. In the sections that follow, we outline briefly the major forms that such audience assessment takes for print and broadcast media.

## Measuring Circulations of Print Media

The basic assessment of audience size for a newspaper or a magazine is its *circulation,* which means sales through paid subscriptions plus other sales by mail or single copies. Obviously, large numbers of readers attract advertisers who want their message seen by as large a number of people as possible. Early newspapers and magazines were often guilty of exaggerating the numbers of their readers and subscribers. To end this practice and promote reliable, impartial reports, a group of advertisers, advertising agencies, and publishers formed the Audit Bureau of Circulations (ABC) in 1914. It is essentially a combination research organization and auditing firm that makes periodic checks on circulations reported by newspapers and magazines making use of its services. Today most newspapers and magazines in the United States are ABC members. The data assembled by ABC provide an important form of delayed feedback to the medium, and critical data to advertisers and advertising agencies who want precise numbers before deciding whether to place their ads. Market penetration, as represented by circulation, is an important indicator of audience composition and the apparent value of the medium to the advertiser.

ABC sets standards for circulation (such as solicitation methods and subscriptions) and requires a publisher's statement of circulation and other data every six months. The statements are checked, processed, printed, and distributed by ABC. Once a year an ABC auditor goes to the offices of the newspaper or magazine and examines all records and materials necessary to verify the claims of the publisher's statement of circulation. Information provided by ABC in its semiannual reports includes audited, paid-circulation figures for the six-month period, with breakdowns for such things as subscriptions versus newsstand sales and data on regional, metropolitan, and special-edition circulation. The report also includes an analysis of a single issue of the publication in terms of the market area it reaches and much more.

The criteria used by ABC generated a conflict in 1982, when *USA Today* began publishing. A dispute arose between the organization and the paper's owner, the Gannett Company, when ABC refused to count *USA Today*'s bulk paper sales to airlines and hotels as part of its audited, paid circulation. ABC maintained that only individual subscriptions and newsstand sales would be counted while Gannett argued for a broader definition of circulation. In the end, the newspaper also used reader estimates from the Simmons market-opinion studies to assess how many actual readers the paper had.

Several other organizations and groups provide basic circulation data for the print media as well as audience figures for broadcast stations. Among them are Standard Rate and Data Service, which reports audited audience/circulation figures and lists advertising rates, policies, and practices. Still more audience data are available from the Association of National Advertisers, the American Newspaper Publishers Association, the Magazine Publishers Association, and others.

## Assessing Movie Audiences

As suggested earlier, the most significant means of gauging the response of any audience to any message transmitted by any medium is by determining the amount of *profit* that it eventually derives for its owners. For films, measuring profit—and thereby the response of the audience—is relatively straightforward. The total number of dollars derived from paid admissions to movie theaters—box office receipts—is the major form of delayed feedback.

A daily trade newspaper, *Variety*, keeps track of the earnings of each film released and shown in the United States. Every week, a report is prepared showing the earnings of and several other kinds of information about the fifty films that lead the list. Each is followed week by week until its earnings are low enough that it falls out of the top fifty. The necessary data for *Variety*'s Weekly Box Office Report are derived from a systematic survey, by an independent research firm, of some 1,600 theaters that are located in approximately twenty cities. It is a simple and reliable system and the results are closely followed by the entire industry. They provide a clear-cut means of assessing whether Americans like what has been produced well enough to pay for a ticket. However, it is not the only form of delayed feedback indicating a measure of a film's success. Once a movie has been shown in most theaters around the country, it is released in video form for purchase and rental. In addition, many American films are shown in large foreign markets. A movie may not be a top box office success at home but do well in the home video market or in other countries.

A number of other approaches to analyzing audience response to films are used—both before release and after. Some studios make use of *focus groups*. These are composed from a dozen to about twenty carefully selected people who see the movie before it is finally edited. If they dislike certain parts of it, it may be edited. Some consultants analyze film scripts even before they are produced in an attempt to forecast whether it will have audience appeal and why. Still other analysts interview people or persuade "sneak preview" audiences to fill out a questionnaire immediately after they have seen a film. All of these techniques can provide useful information.

## Ratings and the Broadcast Audience

The paid circulation of a magazine or newspaper, and the amount of money people pay to see a movie, can be audited rather easily. But getting reliable information about the audience for a broadcasting station or a network is more difficult. Here, no physical object, like a ticket, newspaper, or magazine passes from one hand to another. Moreover, broadcast messages can occupy long periods of time and reach their audiences in different ways and at varying levels of intensity. Consequently, wrote broadcast historian Sydney Head, "no single universally accepted way of measuring broadcast consumption has evolved. Instead, several research companies using rival methods compete in the audience measurement field."[8] They use different procedures to chart audience size, characteristics, and behavior. Over the last twenty or thirty years they have frequently changed these methods to keep pace with new techniques for using surveys and statistics.

Broadcast audience assessment, in one form or another, has been around a long time because radio, from its early days, and later television, have had to justify their worth to advertisers who agreed to sponsor certain programs.[9] In addition, *ratings*, which involve audience as well as program and advertising analyses, have played a central role in determining the shape of broadcast content in America since the 1930s. The first ratings were done by advertising agencies, but before long the networks organized their own research departments. Later, independent research rating services joined in. Today each of the major networks has a large research department that investigates such topics as the influence of television on children and also tries to determine which programs will succeed with the audience.

In the world of television, the influence of ratings has gotten more intense in recent years, as cable and other new technologies have attempted to capture the traditional broadcast audience. For decades, the various techniques of assessment were quite crude. They were based on telephone interviews and a number of other procedures, such as diaries. Essentially, such efforts measured simple factors, as when TV sets were turned on, not who actually watched and with what degree of attention. (As we will note, that limitation has now been reduced somewhat through the use of new devices and techniques.)

At one level, broadcast ratings have generated increasingly complex quantitative assessments of who is watching, when, for how long, and with what intensity. At another, these "number crunching" ratings have inspired the ire of critics, who have called for new assessments. Their objections may be justified as dense numerical ratings are quite limited in what they tell us about the *quality* of television and its overall effect. The issue of critical examination of the social and cultural consequences of television raised in industry circles is echoed in universities, where scholars argue that quantification can lead to self-fulfilling results and does not necessarily yield much new knowledge about either the medium or its audience.

**Types of ratings.** One way to measure the audience in an area is to relate the number of receivers in working order to the total number of households; the result is the relative saturation, or **penetration,** of the broadcast medium in a particular area.[10] Obviously this figure is not a precise measure of the audience, because it says nothing about the viewing habits of people, who may or may not be using their TV sets regularly. Penetration (or saturation) measures reveal the *potential* audience.

The search for more precision in calculating the broadcast audience led to systems in which the *relative audience size* for a particular time slot or program is calculated. Various measures are used in this approach. One kind are *instantaneous rating reports* that indicate the audience size at a particular moment; another are *cumulative reports* that give figures for a period of time—thirty minutes, for example.

More specifically, three measures frequently provided by audience measuring services are the "rating" of a particular program, the "share" of the total audience that is tuned to a station at a given time, and an index of "households using television" (again at a given time). These provide a set of comparative indices that tell within a specified market area how well a particular station is attracting viewers, along with how well the programs they offer are competing for the audience that is viewing at a particular time. The differences among these forms are important. They can be expressed as follows:

A program's **rating** is defined as the number of households receiving the program, divided by total TV households in the market area (times one hundred). Or, in terms of a calculating formula:

$$Rating = \frac{\text{Households watching a particular program}}{\text{Total households in area with TV sets}} \times 100$$

Thus, in general terms, the rating is the *percentage* of the potential audience, made up of TV-set-owning households in an area that could be watching or listening to a particular program aired in a particular time slot. It is a critical measure of program popularity.

Another important index is *HUT*, which stands for "households using television." This does not tell much in itself, but this percentage is needed in order to calculate the share of the active or viewing audience at any time that a particular station or program is attracting. **HUT** is defined as the number of households in the area with their TV sets turned on, divided by the total number of households that own sets (again, times one hundred). In terms of calculation:

$$HUT = \frac{\text{Households in the area with the TV set on}}{\text{Total households with TV sets}} \times 100$$

A third index is a program's or a station's **share.** Share can be defined as the percentage of the audience presumed to be viewing programming offered by a particular station at a particular time. This index is often used as a measure of the success of the station (rather than the program) in competing for its slice of the available audience pie. This index can be calculated by the following:

$$Share = \frac{\text{Households tuned to a particular station}}{\text{Households in area with TV sets on}} \times 100$$

These measures may seem complex, or at least a bit confusing, but each provides somewhat different information that is helpful to both broadcasters and advertisers in sorting out how many people are attending to a station or a program at any given time. Rating services also provide estimates of the composition of the audience, with some demographic data about age, sex, education, and so on.

Research on the broadcast audience has undergone many changes over the years; today the audience is examined in terms of its overall size potential, its actual size, its stability over time, how much actual time it spends with particular programs, and the degree of viewer loyalty, which is called **tuning inertia.** In addition to national television and radio ratings, there are also local station and market ratings for broadcasting, as well as relatively new services that measure the cable audience.

Cable ratings have proved difficult. They involve measures of cable penetration (the percentage of overall viewers actually on the cable) and audience viewing patterns across many more channels than is the case with conventional broadcasting. Radio research typically measures a much smaller audience than television, because there are so many radio stations, and they aim at limited segments of the audience with their specific formats (rock, country-western, news).

Obtaining ratings.    Radio and television ratings are obtained in rather similar ways. In all audience research, after the area or "market" has been designated, some more or less representative set of people—a sample—must be selected. The people are contacted; data obtained from them are recorded in some way so that it can be analyzed; and reports are prepared for users. More than fifty companies conduct research on a national level, and scores of others do local and regional research that leads to ratings of some kind. Their first step is to define the local population or area of interest. Two major broadcast rating services, Arbitron and Nielson, provide national and local ratings. Arbitron developed one method for defining the areas of interest in the television industry. They divide the United States into over 260 market areas called "areas of dominant influence" or ADIs. Nielsen uses another term, "designated market areas." Each of the nation's 3,141 counties is assigned to one of the areas and the markets are ranked according to the number of television households. The ADIs range from New York, with more than 7 million television households, to Pembina, North Dakota, with just over 6,500. The information is used by media advertising buyers to try to capture specified audiences.[11]

Researchers use various techniques: telephone interviews, in-person interviews, listener/viewer diaries, or receiver meters. Arbitron, which conducts research for both radio and television, asks a sample of about four thousand listeners or viewers to keep a weekly diary of their viewing/listening behavior. Radio listeners, for example, are asked to indicate the amount of time they listen and the stations they are listening to, including the specific program and the place they are listening (for example, at home or away from home, including in a car). Samples are drawn from each market area and are weighted to provide a picture of the viewing or listening habits of the people who are asked to keep diaries. Needless to say, the system has many limitations. People forget to fill out the diaries. Some put in data to make it seem like they listened, even if they really did not. Less than half of the diaries distributed to the sample come back to Arbitron with usable data.

For years, the Nielsen ratings, from which the television network programs were ranked, were based on data accumulated from a device called an **audiometer.** It was attached to television sets in a sample of about 1,700 American homes. All it recorded was how long the set was on and to what channel it was tuned. It provided no information as to whether someone was actually viewing. However, the device delivered the information to a central computer through a telephone wire network. This allowed rapid daily processing of data, which were analyzed for the national prime-time ratings. For ratings of local programs, Nielsen also used diaries. In addition to diaries and audiometers, a considerable amount of telephone sampling added to what the electronic media knew about their audiences.

The people-meter controversy.    In the late 1980s, as computer-driven audience research became more precise, a new technique for audience assessment was introduced by Nielsen, Arbitron, and other firms. The **people meter** consists of a small box that sets on top of the TV set and a hand-held gadget (like a remote channel changer) by which people can record what they say they are viewing. Nielson uses about four thousand such systems in a supposedly random sample of households. Each provides information on various demographic factors for the rating company. While viewing, members of the family press buttons that record times and stations. As viewers turn on their people meters and record their viewing, the information goes instantly over phone lines to a central computer, which yields almost instantaneous rating analyses. Originally tested on an experimental basis, people meters proved so popular that they replaced the diary system. They seem to work well, with about 90 percent of the households providing usable data.

Although people meters attracted little sustained attention outside of the trade press, experts regarded this new tool as the most dramatic development in audience measurement in decades. However, it was not immediately accepted by all parties because it gave different results than earlier techniques. CBS especially objected to some of the earliest findings derived from the people meter, feeling that the new system undervalued part of the television audience that had typically been loyal to CBS, namely people in the Midwest, especially in small towns. Corrections were made and eventually all the networks, advertising agencies, advertisers, and other parties accepted the new system. People meters, with their presumably more precise records, also helped the cable industry, because for the first time cable and VCR use received serious ratings attention.

Problems remain with the use of people meters and all other approaches to obtaining ratings. Some critics are concerned because any system of sampling has its flaws. For example, they maintain that young, urban viewers with a "high-tech" orientation would be more likely to let Nielsen come into their homes and wire them for people meters. It was also thought that people who would cooperate with the people meter measurers would be more likely to be cable viewers. Finding a reasonably accurate assessment of the viewing audience from which generalizations can be drawn will remain difficult, making assessment of audience size for any station, cable channel, or program educated guesswork at best.

Audiences for the news.   News programs have not been immune to the probes of researchers and rating services, and their audiences are regularly measured in the same way as other programming. In addition to the rating information, news broadcasters frequently make use of *consultants*. These are individuals and firms who, for substantial fees, analyze a station's news operation and advise it as to how its ratings and share can be improved. Thus, such companies as Frank N. Magid Associates and McHugh and Hoffman are really marketing experts concerned mainly with "packaging" the news to achieve the greatest possible audience. Their recommendations often have much less to do with journalism as such than they do with theater and nonverbal communication. As two educators have written:

> Few [of the consultants' suggestions] deal with the complexities of news writing, best uses of resources, lines of communication, controversial reporting, or other journalistic topics. They have traditionally convinced station managers that the anchorwoman needs to convey more warmth on the air, the sportscaster needs to have silver teeth fillings replaced with more telegenic porcelain fillings, the weathercaster needs to practice getting rid of his lisp.[12]

Outrageous and superficial as these examples seem, they do reflect the kinds of recommendations that the consultants make. They may urge the station to build new and better sets, suggest more elaborate weather-forecasting equipment, and tell the anchorman to get a new hairpiece or wear a sweater vest. In recent years, the most visible sign of the news consultants' work for local stations has been "happy talk" news in which anchor people deliver the news

Packaging, that is encoding, local television news includes attention to visual factors present in the studio as well as accurate information on stories that are reported. For example, broadcasters assume that ratings to some degree depend on the visual characteristics of people who appear on camera. Therefore, television news is often presented by happy smiling people whose hairstyles are immaculate, and who chatter together in a friendly manner. (Copyright © B. Daemmrich/The Image Works)

in chatty fashion with frequent friendly comments to sidekicks who are on camera. Other evidence of the consultants' advice is the "action news" format, which includes more stories of shorter length. This format is the result of the consultants' conviction that viewers are not too bright and have short attention spans.

Station managers take these recommendations seriously, although many news directors have resisted them. In some places the consultant's recommendations have virtually dictated major changes; in others the information is used advisedly in reshaping the format of a program. Many consultants do have an undeniable talent for boosting ratings. In any event, the use of these consultants shows clearly that news programming on radio and television, like entertainment programming, competes vigorously for an audience. Better ratings mean a bigger share of the market and thus greater profits.

Generally, whether measuring audiences for radio or TV, for entertainment or news, all rating services have problems gaining acceptance in homes. Some people simply refuse to cooperate; others do so halfheartedly or provide flawed data. These forms of resistance distort the results, although the rating services say they try to correct for these problems. No one outside these very secretive and competitive organizations really knows for sure how severe these distortions are, because the services do not readily share information about their methods and procedures. (An exception is Arbitron, which publishes a book explaining its methodology.) Regardless of the actual quality of the ratings, however, they are taken very seriously by the broadcasting industry. Indeed, these ratings sometimes cause major losses in advertising revenues, people's jobs, and careers.

## Ratings and Audience Diversity

Finally, all of the ratings services try to break down the broadcast audience in terms of the categories we discussed earlier: age, gender, education, income, ethnic background, and so forth. As we indicated, it is these indicators' diversity that are the matrix within which tastes and preferences are formed and consumer decisions are made. Precise knowledge of such characteristics has become increasingly important as broadcasters try to attract specific kinds of audiences.

In addition to rating information organized around such categories, various kinds of commercial researchers probe the size and stability of the audience, seasonal variations, the hours spent viewing, and other factors. A number of market research firms look at audiences as potential consumers. The Axiom Market Research Bureau, for example, uses a large national sample (25,000) and collects information to learn how people use products and the media and how different categories of people make their buying decisions. It offers its subscribers information about some 450 products and services, 120 magazines, 6 newspaper supplements, the nation's major newspapers, network television, and television usage as well as radio usage by type of program. The resulting data can help an advertiser decide which medium to use to sell laxatives, perfume, beer, or some other product to specific types of people.

Readership or viewership and product data are also correlated by W. R. Simmons & Associates Research, which studies the composition of audiences of magazines, newspaper supplements, national newspapers, and network television programs in terms of selective markets. Other firms, like Opinion Research Corporation, provide selective market information about the reading patterns of categories such as executives and teenagers. Another firm, Lee Slurzberg Research, focuses on the black consumer and black media.

Other market research firms collect and disseminate information about advertising rates and mechanical specifications, advertising volume, and advertising effectiveness. One such firm, Daniel Starch & Staff, Inc., studies different categories of readers of consumer magazines, general business and trade periodicals, daily newspapers, and other publications. The firm also notes reading intensities or the reactions of readers to particular typographical devices and approaches.

Individual newspapers or broadcasters sometimes hire firms to probe the composition of their audiences in more detail. The circulation losses of American newspapers over the last two decades led to a good many of these studies. One study, commissioned by a large metropolitan newspaper, examined what was in the paper and what various categories of people read. The confidential report described the study's recommendations in the following terms:

> The prescription outlined here is: It points out what kinds of things might be cut out of the paper to improve readership, and also what kinds of things readers seem to want more of. It points out how differences in readership are related to such things as the subject of a story, its orientation, where it takes place, where it appears in the paper, the writing approach used in the story, the length of the story, the size and quality of its headline, the size of the newshole and the number of items on the page where the story appears, and the size of any photographs used to illustrate the story.[13]

Clearly, specially commissioned studies of this kind offer recommendations that, if followed, would alter the newspaper in the hope of gaining a larger and more dedicated audience. Thus, the various rating services and market researchers do not provide static indicators of audience preferences, but do provide information that can be used to change the content or format of a program or publication.

Most of the information we have been discussing is gathered for internal use by advertisers and media organizations. Sometimes, as in the case of the Nielsen ratings, the information is published widely in the press, but still its main use is internal. The public sometimes sees the consequences of the ratings but rarely knows much about how the ratings were determined or why decisions were made. On rare occasions, a disgruntled Nielsen employee has revealed anecdotes about the internal operations of the firm. Beyond this kind of insider's view, however, little is known about these audience-assessment organizations, which have so much influence on the media.

# CHAPTER REVIEW

▼ Each of us attends to and acts upon mass communications because of our individual differences in tastes, interests, beliefs, attitudes, and values. These are shaped by our experiences in the different social groups and categories in which we are members.

▼ American society is rich in diversity. That diversity is based in large part on the history of the nation, during which a huge and constantly growing population was brought together in the largest migration in human history from virtually all parts of the globe.

▼ Our population has always been characterized by various internal migrations within our borders. These have included flows of population westward, from south to north, farm to city, city to suburbs and to sunbelt states from those farther north. These migrations tended to mix people and eventually produce a general American culture.

▼ Most of our citizens are of European origin. Immigrants from northern Europe came first, followed by others from southern and eastern Europe. In addition, many came from Africa. In more recent times, the greatest numbers of immigrants have come from Latin American and Asian countries.

▼ Our contemporary sources of diversity are based both on the ethnic and racial mix of our population and on demographic characteristics, such as age, gender, income, and education. Each plays a part in determining what people select from the mass media and how they interpret and respond to it.

▼ The family is the most significant consuming unit and its trends and current status are important for professional communicators. American families are now smaller and organized differently than in earlier times. Relationships have changed between husbands and wives, with the latter gaining power and economic influence.

▼ The women's movement of the nineteenth century and its more contemporary phase completely altered the role of women in the American society. They now exercise considerable economic power as consumers. Their power increased in particular after the majority of women entered the labor force.

▼ The media depend mainly on delayed feedback in one form or another to judge how well their messages are being received by the complex audience and if their goals are being achieved. A variety of groups have developed ways to assess the size and composition of the audiences for each of the media.

▼ Newspapers and magazines depend on the Audit Bureau of Circulation to monitor their claims about readers and subscribers. These figures are used by advertisers who must judge where their print advertising will attract the attention they seek.

▼ The movie industry depends on box office receipts to judge how well audiences like their products. These data are systematically gathered and reported by *Variety*, an industry periodical.

▼ Various approaches have been taken to measuring audiences for the broadcast media. These approaches have changed in various ways through the years. They have included passive devices that merely recorded when the sets were on, diaries completed by samples of people, phone surveys, and the people meter.

▼ Billions of dollars are at stake from advertising and other sources. Therefore, the assessments of audience size, interest, and behavior are of critical importance to mass communicators. Any technology is likely to be criticized by one group or another. Indeed, all of them have flaws and none provides completely reliable and valid data.

## CHAPTER 14

# International Media

## Communication across Borders

*I*n the 1960s, the Canadian media guru Marshall McLuhan envisioned a global village of instantaneous communication linking all peoples of the world. With the help of satellites and computers, it would be possible for individuals and institutions, including the mass media, to move messages across borders to any point on the globe.[1] At a time when most media organizations had quite limited reach—many, like national newspapers and broadcast systems, staying mostly within their own countries—this seemed a fanciful idea, more like science fiction than cold reality.

International communication has been part of the American scene since the first colonists brought newspapers, books, and broadsides with them and waited patiently for news to come by ship. It was the invention of the telegraph that separated transportation and communication and allowed information to travel across time and space without benefit of horse, rail, or water travel. For years, international communication meant wire services like Reuters of Britain or the U.S.'s Associated Press. Most major countries—France, Germany and Italy, for example—also had their news services that crossed borders and oceans by wire and cable, although most of their business was in their own country.

## ▼ *Dimensions of International Communication*

To understand how the world communicated and what impact that activity had, diplomats, journalists, and scholars have developed a body of ideas and knowledge about three broad topics. One is *international news coverage*—that is, how the United States and the rest of the world cover news about foreign countries and the planet generally. A second broad topic focuses on *comparative journalism and world press systems*. The concern here is how the media of the world are organized and how they operate. The third is referred to as *mass media and national development*. The main topic here is how media play a role in what used to be called "underdeveloped" countries of the so-called third world. The term "third world" has been carried forward from the cold war era, when it referred to countries that were not aligned with either the United States and its allies or with the Soviet Union. Today it usually means parts of Africa, Asia, and Latin America that are not as modernized as the countries in Western Europe or North America. The labels for such countries in these areas have changed over time to be "politically correct." In the last century they were commonly referred to as "backward." That changed to "underdeveloped," which in turn gave way to the more polite (and current) "developing." Other terms have undergone similar transformations. Polite discourse no longer uses the term "foreign" in certain contexts. It has been replaced with "international," which refers to anything involving two or more nations or nationalities, such as an "international student," or an "international incident." More recently, people concerned with communication across borders talk about "globalism" and the "global media," which means just what McLuhan talked about—communication that can reach anybody, anywhere, anytime—or almost.

One of the most visible examples of global communication is Ted Turner's Cable News Network, which although based in Atlanta, Georgia, brings news and information from every continent—even such closed societies as Myanmar (formerly called Burma) and North Korea. Delivered in the United States over cable television systems, CNN employs communication satellites to move news, information, and pictures from nearly two hundred countries and maintains a global army of correspondents. CNN can be seen in most countries of the world, in business offices and hotels as well as in rural villages. In Asia, Star TV, owned by the media mogul Rupert Murdoch, has a huge footprint and several channels of programming across the most populous countries in the world—China, India, and Indonesia. Of course, the various news services, old and new, like the Associated Press or Bloomberg (mentioned in Chapter 11) also have worldwide connections and cover the globe, but principally for U.S. media outlets. At the moment, CNN is one of the most visible examples of global communication with the instantaneous ability to bring news from the scene of the latest coup or natural disaster virtually anywhere in the world.[2]

International communication today is so efficient that reporters can beam television stories live from scenes of action thousands of miles away. During Desert Storm, CNN's Peter Arnett was able to present news from Iraq, via satellite directly from Baghdad, even as that country was being attacked by American and allied air and ground forces. (Copyright © William Johnson/Stock Boston)

# ▼ How World Media Are Organized

Before considering the various global and international media, it is important to understand how different press and media systems are organized in various regions and countries of the world. Until the early 1990s, the world's media could be divided mostly between those that were part of the West or Capitalist world and those that belonged to the Socialist or Communist world. During the cold war between East and West from 1945 to 1991 or so, Western-style media were largely independent of government and professed press freedom. Media in the countries of the former Soviet Union, China, and elsewhere were part of the machinery of government in totalitarian states (still true in China, North Korea, and Cuba at this writing).[3]

Western media watch groups such as Freedom House then and now referred to the news media of the world as "free, partly free, or not free," based on whether the press was independent and free of direct governmental control. Most of what was called the "free press" got its funding from advertising or reader-viewer subscriptions in the private sector. Exceptions were state broadcasters in Europe, like the BBC, which was sanctioned by the government but got its revenues from a license fee paid by all taxpayers. In the United States, public broadcasting—radio and television—began with government funding, but eventually got support from the private sector, especially from charitable foundations and businesses.

What Westerners called the "free and independent media" usually had free press guarantees from government and could appeal to an independent judiciary in times of conflict. In the Socialist states, however, newspapers, magazines, and broadcasting were part of the government with different bureaucracies supervising different aspects of their operations. For example, the Russian newspapers *Pravda* and *Izvestia* had a government- or party-supervised editorial staff, and did not own their own presses or distribution system. Printing was done by another government bureau and distribution by yet another. This was very different from the Western model, where a newspaper would produce its own editorial content, operate its own presses, and hire its own carriers to put papers on doorsteps or at newsstands.

## Changes at the End of the Cold War

With the collapse of communism across Eastern Europe, the former U.S.S.R., in the Balkans, and elsewhere, the role of the media in former Socialist societies changed greatly. About the same time, many military dictatorships in Latin America and Asia also collapsed and once-controlled media in those countries also made changes, often looking to the West for examples. In Eastern Europe, for example, the role of media in society changed radically. Instead of being party or government monopolies, new independent media sprang up and some old party papers proclaimed their independence and their new links with the market economy and capitalism. The changes for the media of the former "second world"—as the Communist states had been called—meant such important changes as redefining

- *the role of media and government*
- *the basis of financial support* (from government subsidies to free market advertising, subscriptions, etc.)
- *the role of the journalist* (from government employee to private sector professional)

- *the definition of journalistic content* (from official news sanctioned by government, to more diverse news, often critical of government)

- *the role of the audience* (moving from guaranteed "captured" audiences to competition for news consumers.)[4]

## Contemporary U.S. Versus European News Models

As the press of the newly independent states of the former Soviet Union and Eastern Europe grew from one-time underground sheets, called the *samizdat press*, to mainstream news organizations, many Western observers and consultants arrived on the scene. The fledgling new presses in Eastern Europe were besieged by Western media companies, mostly from Germany, France, Britain, and Scandinavia, who wanted to "invest" in the new enterprises. German media giants like Bertelsmann and Axel Springer quickly bought up many newspapers. In Hungary, for example, within two years there were no locally-owned daily papers.

When it came to editorial content, many of the papers followed the European model of interpretative news, which blends fact and opinion with analysis. Others were enthusiastic about American-style journalism, sometimes called "the journalism of fact," which tries to distinguish news stories from opinion and advocacy material on editorial pages. A battle over which style of journalism should prevail ensued as some papers in Poland and the Czech Republic, for example, preferred the U.S. style of journalism and others sought more politically oriented material with a definite point of view or editorial slant. That battle continues as this is written.

## The Developed Media of Western Europe

Much like the complex media of the United States, the media of Europe are highly developed products of an industrialized and information society. Of course, European media predate the media of the United States by hundreds of years and American newspapers were modeled on those of England, France, and other countries.

Newspapers and magazines have remained strong in Europe with a mix of national and provincial sheets, many of them closely associated with or connected to political parties much as the U.S. press in an earlier period. Europe's electronic media, like the BBC, have also been powerhouses, but usually formed as public service enterprises with either partial or full government support. Although the U.S. broadcasting system—radio and television—lived in the commercial market and depended on advertising, most European media did not. In fact, advertising on the air came quite late in several countries.

The structure of European broadcasting also limited its growth and in several countries a single network or two dominated the airways for most of the twentieth century. Now, with privatization and the lifting of some government

A modern counterpart of the nineteenth-century newspaper baron is Rupert Murdoch. He is a controversial figure who has developed an international communications empire that includes newspapers—such as the *New York Post* and the London *Times*—and television stations, as well as holdings in film, book publishing, and magazines. Originally from Australia, he lived in England and later became an American citizen in order to meet U.S. requirements for media ownership. He has many critics in the world of mass communications. (Peter Marlow/Magnum Photos Inc.)

controls, Europe's television operations are blossoming, though they still lag behind the United States in growth and development of multichannels as well as of cable. In fact, one British observer, Jeremy Tunstall, says "the media are American,"[5] meaning that the U.S. style of media, especially television, dominates much of the world these days and sets a standard for the European and other regional media.

One fact of European media that should not be overlooked is its growing ownership concentration by moguls, who often have holdings in the United States and elsewhere in the world. British firms are strong in book publishing, for example, wheras the Germans have vast newspaper, electronic media, and magazine interests as do French and Italian companies. Names like Berlesoni (Italy), Bertelsmann (Germany), Hachette (France), and Murdoch (Britain/Australia) are dominant powers in world media.

## Asia's Dynamic and Distinctive Media

Even before the collapse of communism, profound economic and social changes came to Asia, and a part of the world once regarded as underdeveloped and poor, especially at the end of World War II, soon had some of the richest nations in the world. Except for China and North Korea, which are still Communist states with monopoly media, other Asian countries mostly follow a democratic model in their governments. As a consequence, they have independent media. Examples are Japan, Korea, Taiwan, Singapore, Malaysia, Thailand, and Hong Kong (which was governed by the British until midyear 1997).

It is ironic that Asian media are only now developing so rapidly. After all, Asia is where much of communication began—paper was invented there and the first newspaper appeared hundreds of years ago. That legacy, however, was lost to history and has little to do with the modern Asian media. Although the emerging media of East Asia, like their counterparts in the West, deliver information and news, convey opinion, and offer entertainment and a marketplace for goods and services through advertising, their editorial voices and other content differs greatly. That difference is philosophical. Whereas our media in the United States and elsewhere in the West are the product of Western Enlightenment with an emphasis on freedom and individual rights, the media of much of Asia are influenced by Confucian philosophy, which stresses consensus and cooperation. As one study puts it, "thus what may look the same is actually quite different in function."[6]

Some communist states, such as North Korea, control their media rigidly. Contacts with international media or even with visiting foreigners are very limited. Thus, people are aware of only the information and interpretations that those in charge want them to receive. Such a controlled flow of information results in social constructions of reality designed to maintain the power of political leaders. (Copyright © Bonnie Kamin/PhotoEdit)

The consensus model of Asian media has meant more cooperation with government than in the West, where conflict and adversarial disputes are more often the case. Thus, in many countries the kind of investigative reporting that embarrasses government or business so common in the West is not welcomed. In some instances—in Singapore, for example—the restrictive media system has little formal censorship, although journalists often engage in self-censorship. Singapore's longtime leader and now a senior minister in the government, Lee Kwan Yew, opposes Western-style freedoms and any absolute notion of freedom of the press, arguing that Western values have led to a breakup of families and a disruption of government. Singapore and some other countries keep a tight leash on their press in an otherwise free market economy and sometimes penalize foreign media who "abuse their welcome." For example, both *Time* and the *Wall Street Journal* have been fined and banned in Singapore for reporting on the government and military in unflattering articles.

Outsiders in several Asian countries cover international news at their own peril and sometimes are expelled for angering local authorities. Asia's media scene, like that of Western Europe and North America, is highly diverse and complex ranging from national dailies in Japan with millions of readers to a vast array of magazines, television programming, a movie industry, advertising and public relations enterprises, and various new media cyberspace ventures. At the same time, rural Asia relies on community radio and small, often poor vernacular newspapers and broadsheets. As with other parts of the world, there are vast differences between urban and rural communication in Asia.

## ▼ Developmental Journalism and Information Imbalances

In some parts of Asia, Latin America, and sub-Saharan Africa, *developmental journalism* is advocated by government and other leaders of society who argue that their countries are fragile, fledgling democracies with many internal and external threats. Developmental journalism in the media, print and broadcast, is part of a larger notion of using mass media as tools of national development. Countries using this strategy believe that a pesky, Western-style press can undermine and destabilize the government and that their local press should transmit values in support of their leaders' visions for development. In such a system, teaching the language and helping foster new agricultural methods are more important than covering the news or criticizing the government.

Striving for national cohesion, rather than diversity or disruption, is strongly urged by the leaders in countries like Malaysia and some West African states as well. The important role of the media in promoting health, nutrition, agricultural production, and safety cannot be denied, and many countries that gained their independence from Western colonial powers like Britain, France, and the Netherlands wanted to bolster their economies and improve their standards of living.

Arguments over the role of the press and media in the development process have ensued for decades. For more than twenty years, a debate has continued over a press policy usually referred to as the *New World Information and Communication Order.* At the center of this debate is concern over an "information imbalance." Supporters argue with considerable evidence that most news and information is "manufactured" in the West and imposed on developing societies, with the United States and Western Europe getting most of that coverage in most countries. Less developed (but still highly populous) countries like India, Indonesia, and Nigeria get relatively little attention, which hurts their economic development and political influence in the world.

The NWICO concept has often been vigorously supported by its advocates in the United Nations, where the leaders of developing countries line up against those from the more developed West. In 1997, the issue resurfaced when a number of dictatorial heads of state in highly controlled societies again demanded that the basic ideas of NWICO be implemented with international controls over the press. In the West the whole idea is generally viewed as a threat to the establishment of democracy, and especially to press freedom, because a central feature of the advocated plan calls for the licensing of journalists—not uncommon in some countries. This practice has repeatedly been loudly denounced in the West.

This debate will not end soon. NWICO supporters argue that the United States and other Western nations have a disproportionate amount of the world's information resources and technology. Because people in the West write and control the news, they determine the images of much of the rest of the world, the critics argue. This concept has been called "global communication dominance."[11] In this discussion the United States is seen as a ruthless information superpower with enormous influence because of its great wealth and the presence of global media like the AP and CNN.

It is quite true that the economically and politically powerful nations manage and control news coverage of the whole world, with the United States and

▼

Many third world countries, such as India, have huge populations. However, they are often virtually ignored by the news media of the Western world. Far more news and entertainment content flows into such countries from the West than flows in the other direction. Many critics see this as a pattern of domination and cultural imperialism aimed at "Westernizing" such countries. (Copyright © 1989 Sujoy Das/Stock Boston)

## Media and the Liberal Arts

### American Media Imperialism and Dominance
A Linchpin to Cultural Studies and International Relations

Ethicist William May has called the modern media one of the three great "teaching authorities" in history, the others being the church and the school. As "teaching authorities" media are said to construct social realities showing people how to act, dress, eat, cut their hair, and behave with others. This rather bland description sometimes makes people overseas "see red" when it comes to the dominance of American media, especially the movies and television, on the rest of the world.

All media, whether transmitting entertainment or news, convey images and values. Critics assert that the U.S. dominance in media of all kinds has a deleterious effect on other countries and their cultures.

Close to home, Canadians strongly condemn the impact of U.S. media images, especially television, on their own popular culture and cultural identity. Thus, Canadians insist that their own television stations and networks carry locally-produced programs, rather than simply buying from and rebroadcasting American products. Canadians argue convincingly that their literature, art, and overall cultural heritage is being drowned out by American products coming over the border via satellite and computer, not to mention various forms of transportation.

More dramatically, some Asian leaders in Singapore and China, for example, have tried to control satellite earth stations (or dishes) and have proposed software that would censor the Internet for both cultural and political reasons. "We simply don't want our culture and values overrun with Western images," one Chinese official told one of the authors of this book, a view he heard again and again throughout Asia.

If fear of imperialist American media images is an issue in countries that are, in fact, trying to Westernize, imagine the resentments stirred up in such Islamic countries as Iraq, Iran, Saudi Arabia, and Syria. Even though some of these countries have been allied with the West, they worry that distinctive Moslem views on dress, hairstyles, and personal behavior and speech will be eroded. American programming prevalent in several Islamic countries is offensive to the religious values and moral convictions of these people.[7]

the West getting most of the attention in most countries. Less developed, but still highly populous countries like India, Indonesia, and Nigeria get relatively little attention. It is undoubtedly the case that this limits their economic development and political influence in the world. Here again, we see the great importance of independent newspapers in major and provincial cities, well-developed radio for both news and entertainment, a growing television industry, various new media, and on-line services. When these are in place, there is clear evidence of development.

With the growth of democracy and the rise of a robust middle class, Latin America has seen a massive growth of magazines and cable. Much of the Latin American press, itself part of an old media system dating back to the late 1700s, looks to North America for role models. For example, the *Wall Street Journal* has a Latin American service that is heavily used by the major papers in most countries. Latin America is known for its *telenovella* or soap operas, which are not only seen in Latin America (including Central America and Mexico), but also in the United States, which has an increasing number of Spanish cable chan-

Leaders in developing countries, most of which are poor, worry that U.S. television programming, films, and rock videos promote unnecessary demands for consumer products that people do not need and cannot afford. Suddenly people want fancy cars, expensive food, clothing, and jewelry as well as electronics of all kinds.

At the same time, defenders of American popular culture argue that its producers are entitled to disseminate their wares and seek markets wherever they can. And it can further be asserted that in most instances, broadcasters and movie theaters buy U.S. cultural products because they are popular with their audiences. The process of cultural imperialism may still be present no matter who is in charge of selecting material for various overseas audiences. At the same time, increasingly satellites and the World Wide Web cross borders with ease and without invitations. They can communicate wherever they are in the world.

What is said of American cultural imperialism can also be said of some other countries although their products at present constitute a small part of the global market. For example, Venezuela, Mexico, and Brazil produce *telenovellas* or soap operas, which make their way to the United States and also to Europe and Asia, where they have a large following.[8]

Because the United States is the world's largest and most influential media system, it is inevitable that U.S. culture will have a large footprint on the rest of the world. Still there have been efforts to be sensitive to local conditions by some media people. For example, the colossally popular Sesame Street on PBS has been adapted in scores of countries where local images, stories and, of course, the language can be integrated into the project. The result is country-sensitive Sesame Street programming in several countries. Although the media are conduits for cultural transmissions

of all kinds, the overall study of that process and impact are found in courses in cultural and international studies as well as related fields.

Why is this important? Some critics like Anthony Smith of Britain or Walter Wriston in the United States believe that eventually nation states will decline in power and have less influence and control over their own people and their cultures. Although much of the world in the post-cold war era is generally defined as democratic and seeking market economies, most countries still have and want to keep their own original local cultures and traditions. This is especially true in the quite different world of the Middle East and other Islamic countries. This debate is likely to be even more heated as the easily accessed Internet continues to spread in influence.[9]

nels, and even in Europe and Southeast Asia. One Caracas-based company, Phelps-Granier, exports its *telenovellas* to several countries where they are either played in Spanish or dubbed into other languages. Only Communist Cuba stands apart from the rest of Latin America in the rise of democracy, market economies, and independent media.[12]

## ▼ The Elite Press: Influencing the Influential

Virtually every major country of the world—and some smaller ones too—have important and highly visible newspapers, variously called "quality, class, prestige and elite journals," according to John Merrill, an authority on international media. Says Merrill, "In the vast global wasteland of crass and mass journalistic

# EXPLAINING MEDIA EFFECTS
## Cultural Imperialism Theory

A theory associated with international communication is often termed *cultural imperialism*. The basic idea is that the mass media, along with other industries in Western societies, follow a deliberate policy designed by powerful economic and political interests to transform and dominate the cultures of other people. This process is focused in particular, say those who oppose it, on countries that during the cold war came to be called the "third world." This transformation is said to be displacing traditional values, beliefs, and other important features of the way of life in those societies. It takes place, say those who subscribe to this theory, in spite of efforts on the part of the non-Western societies to resist such change.

At the heart of this process of domination are the mass media, which convey news and entertainment to people in many parts of the world. The content of these media, say the critics, emphasizes contemporary events in Western societies, secular beliefs and values, and the material culture of Europe and the United States.

The foundation for this theory came from three areas of scholarly concerns about the role of the media in international communication. The first was a body of research and analysis from the 1950s and 1960s that led to the conclusion that mass

media were a very important factor in *national development*. The media were found to be useful in bringing about rapid social change in those societies that valued this goal. The second was an often-heated debate within UNESCO during the 1970s and 1980s protesting the domination by Western organizations of the *flow of news* throughout the world that emphasizes the developed societies. Many third-world leaders resented this and fought for significant changes. A third area of concern is the contemporary predominance in foreign markets of the products of American entertainment industries, particularly *films* and *television programs.* For many decades, American movies have been widely distributed throughout the world. Currently, American TV programs are also widely distributed and viewed in every part of the globe.

These processes of international communication have come to be interpreted by critics as *imperialistic.* The critics claim that American and European powers deliberately use the media to impose Western material culture and the many kinds of freedoms embodied in democracies on people who prefer to retain their traditional values, beliefs, political structures, and ways of life.[10]

**1.** The content of print and broadcast news, plus movies and

television programming, produced by organizations in the United States and Europe is widely distributed throughout the globe to non-Western and "developing" countries.

**2.** Citizens who live in such societies have only limited choices for media-provided information and entertainment outside those brought to them by Western global distribution systems. (Local systems lack resources to compete.)

**3.** Those in less developed societies who receive the content produced and distributed by those global systems are exposed to what many in the audience perceive as attractive alternatives to their own material culture, values, and traditional ways of life.

**4.** Such audiences are led to adopt, or want to adopt, the goods, services, values and lifestyles that they see portrayed in the Western media, which creates both political unrest and markets for goods that can be exploited by Western powers.

**5. Therefore,** the developed societies deliberately engage in cultural imperialism by distributing media content that systematically undermines and replaces traditional beliefs, values, and lifestyles, leading people to prefer the political systems, material goods, and perspectives of Western populations.

mediocrity is a small coterie of serious and thoughtful internationally oriented newspapers that offers a select group of readers an in-depth rational alternative."[13] Merrill says these papers are mostly found in the "information societies," countries with highly educated populations, technological sophistication, and well-developed media systems.

## Influential International Newspapers

Elite international papers are typically defined as cosmopolitan in scope; serious in general tone; and wide-ranging in coverage of politics, economics, the arts, and other matters of significant concern. They also have an "institutional identity," which involves good writing, high quality journalism, and a strong and distinctive editorial voice, all produced by a high caliber staff. The elite press is not sensational, tabloid fare. One recent roster of elite papers—a top twenty world list (including some high quality American entries) was

*Asahi Shimbun* (Japan)

*Berlingske Tidende* (Denmark)

*Christian Science Monitor* (United States)

*Corriere della Sera* (Italy)

*Daily Telegraph* (Britain)

*El Pais* (Spain)

*Frankfurter Allgemeine Zeitung* (Germany)

*Globe and Mail* (Canada)

*Le Monde* (France)

*Los Angeles Times* (United States)

*New York Times* (United States)

*O Estado de S. Paulo* (Brazil)

*Suddeutsche Zeitung* (Germany)

*Svenska Dagbladet* (Sweden)

*Sydney Morning Herald* (Australia)

*Wall Street Journal* (United States)

*Washington Post* (United States)

## Other Newspapers and Magazines with International Reach

Although most newspapers in the United States serve a single city, state, or region, several U.S. media organizations have exceptional international outreach, even if their circulations are modest. Such papers include the venerable *International Herald Tribune*, published in Paris and jointly owned by the *New York*

*Times* and *Washington Post. USA Today,* owned by Gannett, has international editions in Europe and Asia. Dow Jones publishes the *Asian Wall Street Journal* and the *European Wall Street Journal* as well as an insert service for Latin American newspapers. The *Christian Science Monitor,* funded by the Christian Science Church, bills itself as "an international newspaper" and is distributed worldwide. Two American newsmagazines—*Time* and *Newsweek*—both have international editions, as do such business magazines as *Business Week.* International publications with considerable presence in the United States include two from Britain: *The Economist,* a weekly newsmagazine that has a larger circulation in the United States than in the United Kingdom; and the *Financial Times,* a worldly competitor to the *Wall Street Journal* with strong European economic coverage. *The European,* originally founded by the controversial late press baron Robert Maxwell, also reaches an audience in the United States. For people near the U.S.–Canada border, Toronto's prestigious national newspaper, *The Globe and Mail,* also has a following.

## ▼ *Covering the Global Village*

How does the gatekeeping process work in international communication as practiced by the press? For many Americans, international communication means world news coverage in U.S. media. Making sense of the rest of the world is a major challenge for newspapers with a "shrinking news hole." For television, news programs have only a limited twenty-two minutes of content in a half-hour period. Therefore, rigid controls must be exercised in the gatekeeping process. Typically a set of about four rather general criteria have guided editors in selecting international news stories for U.S. audiences. These are

1. political importance
2. economic importance
3. security relationships
4. breaking news, such as natural disasters

As noted earlier in the discussion of NWICO, countries that play a vital role in the world, such as major powers like Russia, Britian, and Germany, usually get high news priority. Similarly, countries and regions with strong economic ties to the United States such as Japan, Canada, and Mexico get covered. Because of cultural ties to American citizens, Israel receives a great deal of coverage, considering its size and importance on the world scene. Those who pose potential threats to our security also get high priority for news coverage, which accounts for continuing extensive coverage of China and Iraq.

For many editors, the cold war—the clear division between East and West politically and economically, capitalism versus communism—was a strong organizing principle for news. With the end of the cold war, no new organizing principle has been found, and the media face what *Foreign Affairs* editor James F. Hoge, Jr. calls "the end of predictability."[14] Hoge says the end of the cold war added confusion to our understanding of "what is important" and also encouraged a kind of journalistic isolationism with more emphasis on the domestic scene. The Associated Press's Louis D. Boccardi says that his journalistic "army" has been redeployed and that news coverage now includes major world events and happenings, as well as such global themes as the economy, the environment, international security, world health, and others. This refocusing takes news coverage beyond what author and correspondent Mort Rosenblum described in his book *Coups and Earthquakes: Reporting the World for America.*[15] One of the authors of this book, in a speech at Tufts University, called for a systematic approach to "covering the whole world" by making sure that major topics and countries do not get left out.

Visitors to the United States and virtually all international students who have ever spent time at an American university complain about the lack of coverage of their country in U.S. media. There has been a steady decline of international news in major newspapers and on network television in recent years, but considerable coverage in many specialized magazines and on-line services. Still, some critics rightly complain that whole sections of the globe, notably the Islamic world and Middle East generally (other than Israel), are virtually invisible. One study showed that nonadvertising content of newspapers devoted to international news over a ten-year period ranged from a low of 2.8 percent to a high of 9 percent.[16] At the same time, one editor of a large Midwestern daily listened patiently while a French professor lambasted him for lack of coverage of France. He responded coolly, "We don't edit this newspaper for visiting Frenchmen."

A different perspective on international coverage by American newspapers comes from Alabama editor H. Brandt Ayers. He has urged more coverage of international affairs in the "heartland press because virtually every local community has businesses which are either owned by foreign interests or whose major competition is overseas." John Maxwell Hamilton in a book called *Main Street America and the Third World*[17] also argued for more coverage of developing countries because of their growing connection to the United States.

## New Media Worldwide

The development of new media made possible by the convergence of traditional systems with advanced computer technology such as the Internet and World Wide Web has great potential for increasing international communication. However, these systems are not deeply established in many countries and in some parts of the world are still largely unknown. Although global information and retrieval systems give individuals increasing access to international sources, the success of on-line services, cybersalons, electronic newspapers, and other new media products are still undetermined.

As the new technologies continue to develop, key issues will be the reform of telecommunication industries and the policies of state-owned telecommunication authorities to allow more public access to electronic communication. Many companies, including the global media giants, have invested hugely in new media operations and they continue to experiment while they hope for growing consumer interest—and adoption.

## International Media Organizations

Several groups and organizations monitor international communication. For example, the International Press Institute, an industry-oriented group based in Vienna, Austria, tracks issues like freedom of the press. A similar mission is undertaken by the New York-based Freedom House. The Committee to Protect Journalists monitors threats and violence against journalists internationally, calls attention to their plight, and even petitions governments. The International Institute of Communications in London takes a special interest in international broadcasting and telecommunications developments.

Among educators' professional groups, the International Communications Association encourages research, as does the International Association for Mass Communication Research. Virtually all media industries have international associations, conventions, and publications. The same is true with such media and media-related interests as publishers, public relations practitioners, advertising industry personnel, television executives, and others. Clearly, globalism—communicating with others with shared or common interests elsewhere in the world—is now commonplace in the media industries.

## CHAPTER REVIEW

▼ International communication involves media with an international reach as well as the media industries of other countries and regions. It also includes news coverage of the world in U.S. media and the uses of media in national development. Increasingly, media enterprises are global, being connected to a global economy.

▼ Trends worldwide include more independent, free market media in the wake of the end of the cold war. International news coverage in the United States has declined in mainstream media, but can still be found in specialized publications and services.

▼ Different parts of the world have different approaches to news gathering and dissemination. For example, the European model seen in Western Europe and increasingly in the former Socialist states of Eastern Europe is interpretative and analytical and is usually linked to a political party or philosophy. Unbiased or objective reporting is not claimed or advocated.

▼ European media are contentious, however, and like those of the United States are derived from ideas first introduced during the Enlightenment—individual rights and critical press freedom. By contrast, the Asian model is one that promotes cooperation and harmony rather than conflict. This comes from Confucian philosophy and is dramatically different from ideas of press freedom and independence common in North America.

▼ In sum, the field of international communication develops understanding of other press systems. Its scholars watch how the U.S. media cover international or foreign affairs. They realize that in some countries "developmental journalism" is the norm, where the media are either urged or required to assist with national development and nation-building, rather than being an independent and critical—often adversarial—force of their own.

# ▼ PART FOUR

## Media Influences
## and Issues

## CHAPTER 15

# Limited Effects

## Short-Term Media Influences on Individuals

*A*s soon as the penny papers began to circulate in the nineteenth century there arose an enormous outpouring of complaints about their negative influences on their readers. These condemnations focused on the problems that the new papers were supposedly causing, and were based on the widely held assumption that the media of the time had *great power* to influence individuals, particularly in unwholesome ways. Similarly, as film and broadcasting arrived during the twentieth century, people became deeply concerned about the problems for society that these new media were presumably creating. These criticisms have left in our society a "legacy of fear" that our mass media have *immediate, uniform, powerful,* and often *harmful* effects on their audiences.

A critical issue for understanding mass communications today is whether or not these anxieties are *justified*—whether the "legacy of fear" is *still* a valid perspective for assessing the impact of our media on individuals within our society. More specifically, do mass communications present false pictures of the world to the public? Do our media promote unacceptable behavior among our children or among adults? Can mass media messages be used as instruments of persuasion so as to shape our beliefs, attitudes, and behavior? Are mass communications dominating our political process and limiting intelligent decision making?

Questions of this kind point to a serious challenge to basic democratic values. If the answer is "yes" to any of them, it follows logically that the broad concept of "freedom of the press" may not be such a good idea. Allowing anyone who controls a medium to print, broadcast, or display any content that they wish, for any purpose that they wish, may not be in the best interests of our society as a whole. If some kinds of mass communications unfairly *control* or even *harm* large numbers of people, perhaps the content of the media should be more closely controlled—or even censored so as to eliminate content that creates unacceptable effects.

It is an important issue, but the dilemma is that a cure may be worse than the problem. Most Americans would find such controls unacceptable. Obviously, this issue goes to the heart of the issue of freedom of expression and our cherished constitutional guarantees. Therefore, it is little wonder that debates about effects of mass communications are conducted with such vigor.

Another problem is how do we decide whether or not a particular medium or form of mass communication has effects that are personally or socially destructive? Most scholars take the position that among the alternatives, *research* conducted within the scientific perspective provides the most trustworthy answers. No one would claim that research findings are always right. Studies can be done poorly, or they can pursue the wrong questions. However, *in the long run,* scientific investigation is the most effective way to gain reliable information to make decisions about complex and perplexing questions, such as those that concern the influences of mass communications.

In this chapter we will review a number of large-scale investigations that have become "milestones" in the search for trustworthy knowledge about the influences of mass communications on individuals within our society. During the six decades since systematic research began, an interesting mixture of insights emerged from the milestone studies, plus hundreds of others that focused on the process and effects of mass communication. Although some yielded conclusions that are still quite *correct,* others were *inconsistent.* Still others (seen in hindsight) were just plain *wrong.* However, we will see that as the ability to conduct research on the influences of the media improved, additional understandings were provided by each new investigation. Thus, as the "cutting edge" of research moved forward, incorrect conclusions were gradually eliminated, to be replaced with alternatives that more adequately described the realities of mass communications and their influences. It is this *self-corrective* feature of science that makes it an attractive means of gaining trustworthy knowledge.

This chapter presents a *developmental* view of our increasing understanding of the process and effects of mass communication—a kind of historical tracing of the paths that research took. In particular, it shows how increasingly adequate theories explaining the effects of the media gradually emerged and how inadequate ones were abandoned. Thus, we must interpret with caution any one of the investigations to be presented. We cannot simply take the conclusions of a study done long ago, when both the media and the society were much younger, and say that they are perfectly valid for interpreting influences of our media today. It is the larger picture that counts; the improvement of understanding over time. In the early studies, the research methods used were crude and often inadequate. The theoretical perspectives developed from them were quite simple, and in some cases, they are now obviously invalid. However—and this is a major point of this entire chapter—during the sixty-year period represented by these studies, *there has been a slow but steady accumulation of knowledge* about how our media function, what the media do, and what they do *not* do, to individuals in our society. That kind of development is exactly what research is all about.

# ▼ *Early Evidence Supporting a Belief in Maximum Effects*

Empirical research on the effects of mass communication lagged far behind the development of the media themselves. Large-scale studies did not begin until the late 1920s. The reason for the delay was that the necessary research procedures, strategies, and techniques required to conduct such investigations were not available until the century was well underway. By then, research designs, measurement, and statistical procedures were sufficiently developed within the social sciences—mainly psychology and sociology—for investigation of the effects of mass communication to become possible.

In the decade following World War I (the 1920s), when the first communication researchers began their work, sweeping changes were taking place in society as well as among the media. The frontier was gone. Millions of immigrants had arrived; the forty-seventh and forty-eighth states (New Mexico and Arizona) had just been admitted to the union (in 1916). Not only was the U.S. population growing rapidly but also major internal migrations were taking place—east to west, south to north, and farm to city.

Thus, the nation had become more complex as the "master trends" of *migration, urbanization, industrialization,* and *modernization* continued with special vigor. Something like a "mass" society had emerged—increasingly made up of unlike people with weak ties to one another—or even animosities toward people unlike themselves. It did not resemble a "traditional" society, in which similar people have close personal ties based on longstanding loyalties and family obligations developed over generations. America was a jumble of newcomers thrown together, with significant psychological, economic, ethnic, and religious differences that kept them apart psychologically and socially. With communication based on strong interpersonal ties on the decline, it is not surprising that the new mass media of communication played an increasingly important role. People came to *depend* more and more on the mass media, and less and less on each other, for information they needed (see dependency theory in Chapter 1). The developing mass media were themselves an integral part of the master trends. As the twentieth century began, the movies arrived. Within twenty years they had become a major form of family entertainment. Radio became a household medium during the 1920s, and in the 1930s and 1940s new kinds of magazines and television came on line. Computer-mediated communication followed late in the century.

Against this background, large-scale empirical research on the influence of mass communications began and continued. At first it was relatively unsophisticated, and the methods used had many shortcomings. Furthermore, the beliefs that prevailed among social scientists during the 1920s about the basic nature of people and society guided the investigators. Those beliefs stressed the idea that human beings were guided by their *inherited* instincts and that

# EXPLAINING MEDIA EFFECTS
## *The "Magic Bullet" Theory*

The earliest general theoretical perspective on the influence of mass communication is implicit in the writings of late nineteenth century social scientists. Although its basic assumptions were widely shared when empirical research began, it was never developed formally as a specific set of propositions. This has been done here for the first time, but for several decades scholars have referred to its essential ideas as the *magic bullet theory*. In spite of its colorful name, and even though we realize today that it never matched reality, it was a beginning point for considering the process and effects of mass communication.

This theory grew out of the evolutionary perspectives of Charles Darwin. Before he published his *Origins of Species* (in 1854), thinking about the nature of humankind emphasized *religious* interpretations. Human beings were said to be unique "rational" creatures formed in the image of God. After Darwin, scientific thinking began to stress the importance of inheritance and biology as causes of human behavior.

Influenced by this genetic perspective, social and behavioral scientists rejected interpretations of "rational" human beings and stressed the *animal* side of human nature. They assumed that there was *continuity* between the behavior of higher animals and that of human beings. For example, animals within a particular species presumably all behaved in more or less the same way because of their *uniform inherited instincts* (derived from their evolutionary history). It was assumed, therefore, that human beings were

the social ties between individuals were *weak* because of the heterogeneous nature of "mass" society.

As we follow the story of media research across seven decades, we need to understand (1) the *basic theories* that researchers developed over the years, (2) how they used increasingly sophisticated *research methods* for studying the effects of mass communication, and (3) how new findings sometimes forced them to *change* or even abandon some of their theories. All of these developments contributed to our contemporary understanding of the process of mass communication and its influences on individuals and society.

## Research Begins with the "Magic Bullet" Theory

Around the start of the twentieth century, both social scientists and the public believed that the mass newspapers of the time were powerful instruments that could control and sway the thoughts and behavior of the members of mass society. As we explained in Chapter 1 in our discussion of dependency theory, intellectuals of the period were convinced that people in the modern urban-industrial societies that were developing lived in social isolation from each other in a kind of "lonely crowd." People, they said, lacked the strong ties to neighbors, family, and friends that had characterized the older, preindustrial and traditional societies. It was, as Gustave Le Bon, the French sociologist, put

also uniformly controlled by their biologically based "instincts," and that they would react more or less uniformly to whatever "stimuli" (situations confronting them) came along. Under this conception of human nature, responses made by human beings to stimuli were thought to be shaped either by "instincts" over which people lacked rational control, or by other "unconscious" processes that were not guided by intellect.[2]

This was a frightening view, and it had a strong influence on thinking about the power of mass communications. It portrayed human populations as composed of irrational creatures that could be swayed and controlled by cleverly designed mass communications "stimuli." This theory led people early in the century to believe that those who controlled the media could control the public. Thus, the magic bullet theory implied that the media have direct, immediate, and powerful effects of a uniform nature on those who pay attention to their content. The theory, representing both popular and scientific thinking, assumed that a media message reached every eye and ear in the same way, like a symbolic "bullet," bringing about the same changes of thought and behavior in the entire audience.

1. People in "mass" society lead *socially isolated lives* with very limited social controls exerted over each other because they are from diverse origins and do not share a unifying set of norms, values, and beliefs.

2. Like all animals, human beings are endowed at birth with a *uniform set of instincts* that guide their ways of responding to the world around them.

3. Because people's actions are not influenced by social ties and are guided by uniform instincts, individuals attend to events (such as media messages) *in similar ways.*

4. People's inherited human nature and their isolated social condition leads them to *receive and interpret* media messages in a uniform way.

5. **Therefore,** media messages are like symbolic "bullets," striking every eye and ear, and resulting in effects on thought and behavior that are *direct, immediate, uniform,* and therefore, *powerful.*

it in 1895, an age of *crowds,* without ties between people, as opposed to an age of *community,* where people were linked by strong social bonds.[1]

A general set of beliefs about media influences prevailing at the time has come to be called the **magic bullet theory.** Although formulated in a systematic manner only in retrospect, it represents the prevailing convictions about the features of the new industrial society, and why people believed that the mass media had very powerful effects on people. It predicted immediate, direct, and uniform effects upon everyone who received a media message. Thus, it was a general theory within which both social scientists and the public interpreted the mass media when empirical research started. As it turned out, these interpretations of the power of the media would not be easy to alter because they seemed so logical and were so widely believed.

## The Payne Fund Studies of Movies and Children

Social scientists interested in large-scale research on the effects of mass communication first focused on the movies. There were clear reasons for this choice. During the first decade of the new century, movies were a novelty. During the second decade, they became one of the principal media for family entertainment. By the end of the 1920s, feature-length films with soundtracks were standard, and the practice of going to the movies for entertainment was deeply established.

▶

During the 1920s, the public became deeply concerned about the influence of the new motion pictures on children. In 1929, more than 17 million children under the age of fourteen attended the movies every week. The films presented stories about crime, love, war, and horror. Especially worrisome were themes that seemed to emphasize immoral behavior. Early research on the influence of films appeared to confirm the public's worst fears. (Brown Brothers)

Meanwhile, the public had become uneasy about the influence of the movies on children. In 1929, an estimated 40 million minors, including more than 17 million children under the age of fourteen, went to the movies weekly.[3] Critics raised alarming questions about their effects. Were the picture shows destroying parents' control over their children? Were they teaching immorality? Films with unwholesome themes—horror, crime, immoral relationships, and the illegal use of alcohol (during Prohibition)—were especially troubling.

No government agency existed to give money to investigators who wanted to assess the impact of films on children, but a private agency (the Motion Picture Research Council) decided to seek research data in order to develop a national policy concerning motion pictures. This agency called together a group of social scientists to plan large-scale studies to probe the effects of motion pictures on youth. A private foundation called the Payne Fund was persuaded to supply the necessary money.

When its thirteen reports were finally published in the early 1930s, the Payne Fund Studies were the best available evaluation of the impact of motion pictures on children. These researchers used approaches that ranged from collecting and interpreting anecdotes to experiments measuring and analyzing responses to questionnaires. However, by today's standards of research many of these studies seem quaint and naïve. Later, some became quite controversial. Technical details about the way data were collected and the conclusions reached by the Payne researchers were widely criticized by research specialists for a decade. On the other hand, the public did not care about these controversies. They were frightened by the results. The technical criticisms of research procedures seemed to the lay person like debates over fine points of navigation conducted while the ship was sinking. Above all, the overall results of the

Payne Fund Studies seemed to confirm the charges of the critics of the movies and the worst fears of parents. To illustrate the approaches, data, limitations, and conclusions of the studies, we can look briefly at one example. The study dealt with the question of how the movies influenced the everyday behavior of children.

**Influences on everyday behavior.**   One of the most interesting, if least rigorous, of the Payne Fund Studies was done by sociologist Herbert Blumer.[4] Blumer wanted to provide a general picture of how viewing films influenced children's play, their everyday behavior—such as dress, mannerisms, and speech—their emotions, their ideas about romance, their ambitions and temptations, and their career plans. His method was simple. He had adolescents and young adults recall (in autobiographical form) influences from films they had seen years before in their childhood. Eventually, Blumer collected accounts from more than 1,200 people. Most were college and university students, but some were office and factory workers. The result was an immense number of recollections about how people *thought* that seeing films had influenced their daily behavior.

Blumer attempted to draw conclusions from these accounts, but he did not subject them to quantitative or statistical analysis. He preferred to "let the facts speak for themselves" by quoting liberally from the autobiographies to illustrate his conclusions. The movies were, he said, a source of *imitation, unintentional learning,* and *emotional influence.*

According to Blumer, the movies had an especially powerful impact on children's play. Youngsters impersonated cowboys and Indians, cops and robbers, pirates, soldiers, race-car drivers, and every conceivable hero and villain they had seen in films. Reenacting movie plots, children battled each other with wooden swords, spears made from broom handles, and shields from washboiler tops. They rode horses made of scraps of lumber, shot rifles and pistols made of sticks, and flew airplanes built with apple crates. They dug trenches in their backyards and assaulted forts in vacant lots. They became Dracula, Cleopatra, the dreaded Dr. Fu Manchu, Tarzan, the Red Baron, and Mary, Queen of Scots. Most of it was remembered as fun. For the most part, these activities seemed to have little lasting influence on later life.

More significantly, Blumer concluded that children and teenagers copied many mannerisms, speech patterns, and other behaviors from the people portrayed on the screen. There were hundreds of accounts in the autobiographies of how youngsters tried to imitate the way a favorite movie star smiled, leered, smirked, laughed, sat, walked, or talked. Their attempts were usually unsuccessful and short-lived, and they often mystified parents.

Although it would seem harmless for children to adopt hair and dress styles from film characters, remember that the 1920s were the age of "flaming youth" and "flappers." The movies showed speakeasies, easy money, powerful cars, and fast women. Parents were accustomed to books and magazines that followed the strict standards of the Victorian era. By the time of World War I, however, Victorian morality began to fade, and the automobile was being used for

▶

Many of the movies pro-
duced during the late
1920s alarmed the older
generation, whose moral
values grew out of the
Victorian era. Films that
depicted gambling and
easy money, fast cars,
illegal drinking, and
"loose" morals were
feared as unwholesome
influences on children
and young people.
(Culver Pictures, Inc.)

more than just transportation. When they saw movies mirroring the new styles
and the new "looser" morality, many people believed the movies were the *cause*
of the changes (a common *non sequitur* in interpreting mass communication).
By showing that children copied the behavior they saw in films, Bloomer's findings seemed to support this view; this worried parents a great deal.

Blumer's study revealed another facet of the movie experience. Movie
viewing was often an intensely emotional experience. His subjects reported
that often while watching films they experienced what he called *emotional
possession*. As the plot unfolded, they had intense feelings of terror and fear,
sorrow and pathos, thrills and excitement, or romantic passion and love. They
often left the film emotionally drained, anxious, or sexually stimulated—
depending on the film. This effect also worried parents and fueled the fires of
critics of the movies.

What can we learn from Blumer's research and its conclusions? Can
Blumer's study tell us whether the films *caused* certain behaviors? Can it give
any objective measure of the influence of films on children today, or even on
Blumer's subjects at the time? Can it tell us whether any influence they might
have had lasted over the lifetimes of the subjects?

The answer to each of these questions is *no*. First, whatever Blumer found
out about the first generation of moviegoers has completely unknown applications to today's youth, who have a great deal of experience with other kinds of
media and a very different culture. Second, the methods of Blumer's study are
not adequate to provide indisputable answers even to his own questions. Notice first that Blumer's *sample*—the subjects who wrote the autobiographies—

might have been unrepresentative or biased in many ways. Moreover, his ways of measuring influences were merely anecdotal and retrospective.

Stated in more technical terms, Blumer's study falls short in meeting two fundamental criteria for scientific research: *validity* and *reliability*. A procedure is valid if it measures what it claims to measure. It is reliable if it yields consistent results. We are not certain that Blumer's autobiographies validly and reliably show the influences movies had on the children under study. Similarly, a study is reliable if a repetition of the study using the same techniques would yield similar results. Would his findings have been the same if Blumer had repeated his research? Or, if another researcher had duplicated the study, would the conclusions have been parallel? We simply do not know. Yet, in spite of all of its "warts," we do not want to write off Blumer's study as inconsequential. It was very imaginative and opened important lines of research that we still follow today. His study remains a historic landmark.

**Implications of results: confirmation of fears.**   Other studies conducted as part of the Payne Fund series were more systematic. Large-scale "before and after" experiments were conducted in which children's attitudes toward a topic were measured prior to seeing a film and then afterward to detect changes. Some movies did seem to alter children's attitudes toward minorities or topics of the time such as prohibition, war, and gambling. These findings also convinced many in the public that the movies were powerful and were producing unwholesome effects on children.

From the overall findings of the Payne Fund Studies, which were published in the early 1930s, the magic bullet theory seemed to have considerable support, and the conclusions reinforced the legacy of fear. The views of the strongest critics of the media, who argued that the media were both powerful and harmful, seemed justified. However, not everyone came to such conclusions. Even when the studies were first published, experts criticized their technical shortcomings, but to the public, that seemed like quibbling over technicalities of navigation while the ship was sinking. The Payne studies *reinforced public fears* that the movies were responsible for bad ideas, bad morals, and bad behavior among the nation's youth.

## Radio Reports the Invasion from Mars

On October 30, 1938, horrible creatures from Mars invaded the United States and killed millions of people with death rays. At least, that was the firm belief of many of the 6 million people who were listening to the CBS show "Mercury Theater of the Air" that evening. The broadcast was only a radio play—a clever adaptation of H. G. Wells's science fiction novel *War of the Worlds*. However, it was so realistically presented in a "newscast" format that the many listeners who tuned in late missed the information that it was only a play. They thought that Martian monsters were taking over.

**Reactions to the "news" of the invasion.**   If there had been any doubt that a mass medium could have a powerful impact on its audience, that doubt was dispelled by the next day. Among those who believed that the show was a real news report, large numbers panicked. They saw the invasion as a direct threat to their values, property, and lives—as the end of their world. Terrified people prayed, hid, cried, or fled. A high-school girl later reported:

> I was writing a history theme. The girl upstairs came and made me go up to her place. Everybody was so excited I felt as [if] I was going crazy and kept on saying, "what can we do, what difference does it make whether we die sooner or later?" We were holding each other. Everything seemed unimportant in the face of death. I was afraid to die, just kept on listening.[5]

Among those who believed that the Martians were destroying everything and that nothing could be done to stop them, many simply abandoned all hope:

> I became terribly frightened and got in the car and started for the priest so I could make peace with God before dying. Then I began to think that perhaps it might have been a story, but discounted that because of the introduction as a special news broadcast. While en route to my destination, a curve loomed up and traveling at between seventy-five and eighty miles per hour, I knew I couldn't make it though as I recall it didn't greatly concern me either. To die one way or another, it made no difference as death was inevitable. After turning over twice the car landed upright and I got out, looked at the car, thought that it didn't matter that it wasn't my car or that it was wrecked as the owner would have no more use for it.[6]

Such accounts showed that the broadcast was accepted as real by many people, who thought they were going to die.

In fact, the Mercury Theater and the actors had no intention of deceiving people. The script was written and the program was presented in the tradition of telling "spook stories" for Halloween. It was clearly identified as a play before and after the broadcast and in newspaper schedules.[7] However, the newscast style, the powerful directing, and the talented performances of the actors conspired to make the presentation seem very real. The result was one of the most remarkable media events of all time.

Immediately after the broadcast, social psychologist Hadley Cantril hastily began a research study to uncover the causes of panic in a general sense, as well as reactions to the radio broadcast. More specifically, he sought to discover the psychological conditions and the circumstances that led people to believe that the invasion was real. Although the scope of the investigation was limited and its flaws numerous, the Cantril study became one of the milestones of mass media research.[8]

Actually, only 135 people were interviewed in depth. Most were people who had been frightened by the broadcast, and all came from the New Jersey area, where the Martians were said to have landed. Most of the subjects were located as a result of the interviewers' personal initiative. No pretense was made that those interviewed were a representative sample. In addition, just prior to the start of the interviews, two extensive tabulations of listeners'

On October 30, 1938, Orson Welles and the CBS "Mercury Theater of the Air" broadcast an evening radio play designed to resemble a news broadcast. Modeled after H. G. Wells nineteenth-century novel, the play portrayed a fictional "Invasion from Mars" by dreadful creatures armed with deadly ray guns. Not realizing that it was only a play, six million people in the nation panicked, often responding in bizarre ways. Others, who checked the authenticity of the broadcast, remained calm. (UPI/Corbis-Bettmann)

comments, commissioned by CBS, were made available to the researchers. All the mail received by the Mercury Theater, CBS station managers, and the FCC was analyzed, and 12,500 newspaper clippings related to the broadcast were systematically reviewed. The results provided a sensitive study of the feelings and reactions of people who were badly frightened by what they thought was the arrival of Martians.

The researchers concluded that "critical ability" was the most significant variable related to the response people made to the broadcast. Critical ability was defined generally as *the capacity to make intelligent decisions.* Those who were low in critical ability tended to accept the invasion as real and failed to make reliable checks on the broadcast; for example, they did not call authorities or listen to other stations.

Especially low in critical ability were those with strong religious beliefs, who thought the invasion was an act of God, and that it was the end of the world. Some thought a mad scientist was responsible. Others were disposed to believe in the broadcast because war scares in Europe (World War II did not begin until 1939) made catastrophe seem more plausible. Those high in critical ability tended *not* to believe the broadcast was real. They were more likely to be able to sort out the situation even if they tuned in late. These people tended to be more educated than those low in critical ability. In fact, statistical data obtained from CBS revealed that amount of *education* was the single best factor in predicting whether people would check the broadcast against other sources of information.

**Implications: powerful effects, but only on some.**   The conclusions derived from the Cantril study posed something of a dilemma. In some ways the magic bullet theory was supported, but in other ways it was not. For example, it was clear that the radio broadcast brought about some very powerful effects. Yet, *they were not the same for everyone.* This result was not consistent with the theory. To be consistent, the broadcast should have had about the same effect on everyone who heard it. The Cantril study, however, isolated individual characteristics of listeners that strongly influenced their response: critical ability and amount of education. Thus, although for the public the "War of the Worlds" broadcast seemed to reinforce the legacy of fear of the media, many researchers began to suspect that the magic bullet theory had flaws.

## ▼ *Beyond the Magic Bullet:*
## *Selective and Limited Effects*

We next review two classic studies that were milestones in replacing the magic bullet theory: one examining soldiers in training during World War II and the second analyzing the presidential election of 1940. Both studies helped build new ways of understanding how and to what extent the media influence ideas, opinions, and behavior.

### The "Why We Fight" Film Experiments during World War II

By the time of World War II, social scientists had developed fairly sophisticated techniques of experimentation, measurement, and statistical analysis. The military therefore felt that they could contribute to the war effort. In particular, the Army formed a special team of social psychologists to study the effectiveness of a special set of films that had been designed to teach recruits about the background of the war and to influence their opinions and motivation.[9]

When America entered the war in 1941, many young men were ill-informed about all the reasons for America's participation. It was a society that was without television—our main source for news today—and people were generally less educated and less informed. Everyone knew about Japan's attack on Pearl Harbor, but not everyone knew about the rise of fascism, Hitler's and Mussolini's strategies, or the consequences of militarism in Japan. Moreover, the United States was (and still is) a nation with diverse regions, subcultures, and ethnic groups. The newly drafted soldiers included such diverse categories as farmers from Nebraska, ethnic men from big-city slums, small-town youths, and young men from the ranches of the West. All were plunged into basic training, and many understood only dimly what it was all about.

**Goals and conduct of the experiments.**    The chief of staff, General G. C. Marshall, had decided that the troops needed to be told *why* they had to fight, *what* their enemies had done, *who* their allies were, and why achieving victory would be a *tough job* that had to be seen through to unconditional surrender by the Axis powers. Because no one knew about the atom bomb, which ended the war in Japan, everyone thought that the terrible conflict would drag on for several additional years after Hitler was defeated.

General Marshall believed that special orientation films could give the diverse and poorly informed recruits the necessary explanations of the causes of the war and provide understanding of why it would not end soon. He hoped that showing these films would also result in more positive attitudes and higher morale.

A top Hollywood director, Frank Capra, was hired to produce seven films—a series called *Why We Fight*. The Army gave the job of studying their effectiveness to social psychologists in the Research Branch of the Information and Education Division. The basic plan was to see if exposure to such a film would result in measurable influences on the understandings and orientations of the soldiers. These included a firm belief in the right of the American cause, a realization that the job would be tough, plus confidence in our side's ability to win. The Army hoped that by presenting the facts the films would create resentment of Germany and Japan for making the fight necessary. Finally, they anticipated that seeing the films would foster a belief that through military victory the political achievement of a better world order would be possible.

We can summarize the procedures used rather simply: Four of Capra's *Why We Fight* films were used in a series of well-conducted experiments. Great control over the experimental conditions was possible, because the subjects were under orders to participate in the experiments, and were under the watchful eyes of tough sergeants to see that they took it seriously and none "goofed off." (Few experimenters today could match this!) Under such conditions, several hundred men who were undergoing training were given a "before" questionnaire that measured understandings of *fact*, various kinds of *opinions*, and overall *attitudes.* These questionnaires were carefully pretested on at least two hundred soldiers in order to minimize ambiguities in their language. Then the men were divided (by company units of about one hundred men each) into experimental groups and a control group. Each company designated as an experimental group saw one of the four films from the *Why We Fight* series. The control group saw a different film that did not deal with the war. After they had seen a film, all subjects answered an "after" questionnaire. It measured the same variables as the first questionnaire, but the questions were rephrased so that repeated exposure to the test could not account for changes in responses. Thus, by comparing the amount of change in each experimental group with that of the control group, the effect of the films could be assessed.

Actually, no dramatic results were obtained! The films did produce minor changes in their audiences, but the changes were *very limited*. For example, seeing The "Battle of Britain" (one of the films in the series dealing with the Royal Air Force's defense of England) increased the recruits' factual knowledge about the air war over Britain in 1940. As a result of knowing those facts, it also changed specific opinions about some of the issues treated in the film. However, it produced no broad changes, such as increased resentment of the enemy or greater willingness to serve until the Axis powers surrendered unconditionally. The results were much the same for the other films studied.

**Implications: media have limited effects.**    Generally, the researchers concluded that the *Why We Fight* films—with powerful propaganda messages—were modestly successful in teaching soldiers facts about events leading up to the war. They were also modestly effective in altering rather specific opinions related to the facts covered. However, they clearly had no great power to fire soldiers with enthusiasm for the war, create lasting hatred of the enemy, or establish confidence in the Allies. Moreover, the effects were different for soldiers with low, medium, and high levels of education. Generally, soldiers with more education learned more from the films.

These results certainly did not confirm earlier beliefs in all-powerful media. And the finding that variations in education modified the effects flatly contradicted the old notion that communications were *magic bullets* penetrating every eye and ear in the same way, creating similar effects in every receiver. For all intents and purposes, the older theory of uniform influences and powerful effects *died* at this point. The Army film studies were models of careful research, and they left no room for doubt about either the precision of their methods or the validity of their conclusions.

After World War II, research on mass communication blossomed. Social scientists were armed not only with new theories of the nature of human beings but also with increasingly precise research techniques. Some researchers tried to sort out the factors in communication through simulation experiments. Professor Carl Hovland, for example, launched a large-scale research project involving anthropologists, sociologists, and political scientists.[10] He and some thirty associates explored several broad issues, including the nature of the communicator, the content of the communication, and the response of subjects exposed to messages. However, real-life media campaigns and mass communication were not part of this research. It used mostly student subjects. The research produced advances in theory, but the applicability of the program's findings to the real world was not clear.

## Effects of the Media in a Presidential Campaign

One major study, conducted in 1940 but published several years later, did focus directly on real-life media. Sociologists Paul Lazarsfeld, Bernard Berelson, and Hazel Gaudet probed the web of influences within which voters made up their minds during a presidential election campaign. In this election the Republican nominee, Wendell Wilkie, challenged Franklin D. Roosevelt, the incumbent Democrat. In particular, in a now-classic work called *The People's Choice,* the researchers studied the role of mass communications as influences on voters.[11]

This study is a landmark for two reasons. First, its scale was large and its methodology sophisticated. In fact, even today, few studies have rivaled it in these respects. Second, the findings revealed completely new perspectives on both the process and the effects of mass communication.

**Great improvements in research methods.** Lazarsfeld and his colleagues interviewed some 3,000 people from both urban and rural areas of Erie County, Ohio. Interviewing began in May and ended in November of 1940, when Franklin D. Roosevelt defeated Wendell Wilkie. All 3,000 subjects were interviewed in May, and they agreed to give further interviews as the election campaign progressed.

The research strategy used was new at the time and very clever: A random sample of 600 was selected from the 3,000 interviewed and designated as the *main* panel. The remaining 2,400 were randomly divided into four additional panels of 600 each. Those in the main panel were interviewed each month from May to November for a total of seven interviews. The other four groups served as *control* panels and each was to be interviewed only one more time. One control panel was given a second interview in July, another in August, and another in October. At each point, the results of these interviews were compared with those of the main panel. This procedure allowed researchers to see how *repeated* interviews affected the main panel compared to a fresh panel. After three such comparisons they found that the repeated interviews had no measurable cumulative effect, and they decided that a fourth was not necessary. Thus, the researchers could feel confident that their findings were meaningful and not an artificial result of their multiple interviews of the main panel.

Some respondents decided early for whom to vote; some decided late. Some shifted from one candidate to another; some who had firmly decided fell back into indecision. Always the interviewers tried to find out why the voters made these changes. They also focused on the social characteristics of the subjects. Rural and urban dwellers were compared; people at various income levels were contrasted. People of different religious backgrounds, political party affiliations, and habits of using the media were studied. Using complex methods, the researchers found that these category memberships could be used with fair success to *predict* voting intentions and actual voting behavior.

**How the media influenced voters.** Then, and even more now, much of a political campaign is waged in the media through both news reports and paid advertising. However, Lazarsfeld and his colleagues did not find all-powerful media controlling voters' minds. Instead, the media were just one part of a web of influences on voters. People's personal characteristics, social category memberships, families, friends, and associates, as well as the media, helped them make up their minds. Furthermore, the media did not influence all voters in the same way. When the media did have an effect, three kinds of influences were found. The researchers called them *activation, reinforcement,* and *conversion.*

**Activation** is the process of getting people to do what they are predisposed to do by their social category memberships—pushing people along in ways they are headed anyway. For example, for almost fifty years in Erie County most well-to-do Protestant farmers usually voted Republican; most Catholic, blue-collar, urban workers usually voted Democratic. Indeed, all across the country, many voters tend to have certain socially based predispositions for and against the political parties. Yet even though as the campaign progressed, many voters in Erie County said they were undecided, the media helped activate voters to follow their predispositions.

Although activation by media influences changed no one's mind, it did influence the election's outcome through the following four steps:

1. The political propaganda in newspapers, magazines, and radio broadcasts increased *interest* in the campaign among potential voters.

2. This increased interest led to greater *exposure* to campaign material.

3. However, the exposure was *selective.* Personal characteristics (e.g., age, gender, education) plus social category memberships (e.g., rich Protestant farmers versus Catholic urban workers) led people to read or listen to the output of just one party.

4. As a result of increasing interest and selective exposure, the voters' intentions eventually *crystallized* in directions that were generally predictable from the voters' personal and social characteristics.

**Reinforcement** is a different process. Fully half of the people studied already knew in May for whom they would vote in November. They made up their minds early and never wavered. Does this mean that the media had no effect on such voters? Not at all. The media were also important in strengthening the voters' intentions. Political parties can ill afford to concentrate only on attracting new followers; the intentions of the party faithful must be constantly reinforced through communications that show they have made the right choice. The media are used to provide this reassurance. Clearly, reinforcement is not a dramatic effect. It merely keeps people doing what they are already doing.

Finally, **conversion** was rare. The presidential campaign in the mass media did move a few voters from one party to the other in Erie County, but the number was small indeed. Most people either made up their minds in May, went with the party they were predisposed toward, or paid attention only to the campaign of their own party. Conversion took place among a very small number who had only weak party affiliation to begin with.

Perhaps the major conclusion emerging from this study is that the media had not only selective but *limited* influence on voters. When people talk of the media's power, the ability to convert is what they usually have in mind. However, the researchers found that of their subjects, approximately 16 percent showed *no* effect from the media; 9 percent showed *mixed* effects; 14 percent were *activated*; 53 percent were *reinforced* (the largest influence), and a mere 8 percent were *converted*.

**Serendipity: The two-step flow of communication.**   One totally unexpected but extremely important finding emerged from *The People's Choice*. It was the two-step flow of communication, which we discussed at some length in connection with the word-of-mouth diffusion of the news in Chapter 11. Its discovery occurred almost by accident, in a way that scientists call "serendipitous." About halfway through the Erie County study, the researchers began to realize that a major source of information and influence for voters was *other people*. Individuals turned to family, friends, and acquaintances to obtain information about the candidates and the issues. Inevitably, those who provided the information also provided interpretation. Thus the two-step flow of information between people also included a flow of influence. The researchers called this **personal influence** (in contrast with **media influence**).

Those who served most often as sources of information and influence had two important characteristics: They had given great attention to the media campaign, and their socioeconomic status was similar to that of those whom they influenced. In other words, voters were turning for information and influence to people who were *like themselves* but whom they regarded as *knowledgeable*. Thus, in the two-step flow, content moves from the mass media to opinion leaders, who then pass it on to others whom they inevitably influence. Since *The People's Choice* was published, hundreds of other studies have tried to understand the nature and implications of the two-step flow theory and the personal influence of opinion leaders as part of mass communication.

**Implications: selective and limited influences.**   Without question, *The People's Choice* opened a new era in thinking about the mass media. Its large scope, sophisticated methods, and impressive findings set it apart as a major milestone in media research. It dismissed flatly the old theory that the media have great power. Instead it supported a new interpretation: that the media have selective and minimal consequences and are only one set of influences on people's behavior among many. Although several earlier studies had pointed in this direction, this particular study confirmed the need for a completely new theory of the effects of the media.

Meanwhile, as the century progressed, the social and behavioral sciences made great advances in understanding the nature of human beings, both individually and collectively. These discoveries would prove to be important in understanding the process and effects of mass communication.

Psychologists had discovered the importance of *learning* in human beings. They developed numerous theories and explanations of how this process played a part in shaping the organization and functioning of the human psyche.

It was clear that people varied greatly in their learned beliefs, attitudes, interests, values, and other psychological attributes. The key idea was *individual differences* leading to great interpersonal diversity. No two human beings were organized psychologically in exactly the same way. Each person, as a result of learning in his or her environment, had a different psychological organization through which the individual perceived and interpreted the world.

Sociologists and anthropologists, who had studied the emerging urban-industrial society intensively, also found a picture of great diversity. In this case it was based on the numerous *social categories* into which people could be classified. Societies had complex social class structures, based on such factors as income, education, and occupational prestige. People were grouped into other categories by their race, ethnicity, political preference, and religion. Within such categories, subcultures developed, bringing people within a given category to share many beliefs, attitudes, and forms of behavior.

Even more important, social scientists found that people did not live socially isolated lives in a "lonely crowd" existence. They still maintained strong social relationships, based on ties to family, friends, and acquaintances. These had truly significant influences on their interpretations and actions toward the world in which they lived.

These sources of diversity—individual psychological differences, social category subcultures, and patterns of *social relationships*—had powerful influences on the mass communications behavior of individuals. *The People's Choice* research on the presidential election revealed the foundations for a new general theory of the effects of mass communication based on such considerations. Although the authors of that study did not actually develop such a general theory, it was formulated within a few years, and it became the basic interpretation of the effects of the mass media as these were revealed by literally hundreds of experiments and surveys completed by social scientists and communications researchers.

As larger and larger numbers of research studies were published, it appeared that the **selective and limited influences theory** was well supported by the evidence. By 1960, Joseph Klapper stated the case in the following terms when he noted that there was

> a shift *away* from the tendency to regard mass communication as a necessary and sufficient cause of audience effects, toward a view of the media as influences, working amid other influences in a total situation. The old quest for specific effects stemming from the communication has given way to the observation of existing conditions or changes, followed by an inquiry into the factors *including* mass communication which produced those conditions and changes, and the roles which these factors played relative to each other.[12]

In other words, the new theory stated, the media do not have powerful effects, but only minimal influences that are modified by other "factors" (such as individual differences, social categories, and social relationships) that significantly limit those influences.

In fewer than twenty years, then, the view of the mass media's influence understood by social scientists changed drastically. No longer were media messages compared with magic bullets. Instead their influence was said to be both selective and clearly limited by a complex set of mediating factors.

# ▼ *Audience Uses and Gratifications in the Selection of Media Content*

Between 1940 and 1950, before television was widely available, a number of scholars were trying to understand what *uses* audiences made of the available media, and what *gratifications* they derived from exposure to what they selected. Soon, studies began to provide answers and an explanation was developed. It was called, appropriately enough, the "uses and gratifications theory." It was not an explanation of the "effects" of mass communications. Instead, it focused on a part of the "process" by which specific messages from specific media selectively reached specific segments of the audience. In that sense, it extended the factor of selectivity in the selective and limited influences theory.

The new theory saw the audience as *active* in freely choosing and selectively using message content, rather than as *passive* and "acted upon" by the media—as had been the case with the magic bullet theory. It stated that people themselves decided to what content they would attend from what medium, and that their decisions were influenced by their personal interests, desires, values, and habits of seeking gratification of various needs.

## The Foundation Studies

In one of the first studies of uses and gratifications, Herta Herzog interviewed those who listened to radio's daytime serials (soap operas). In 1942, she found that they did so for a variety of reasons.[14] Some identified with the heroes and heroines as a means of understanding their own woes better. Others did so to obtain emotional release. Still others engaged in wishful thinking about the adventures of the soap opera characters. Many felt that the serials were a source of valuable advice about how to handle their own family problems.

Another classic study of uses and gratifications was completed in 1945. Sociologist Bernard Berelson conducted an exploratory survey of people's reactions to a two-week strike by those who delivered New York City's newspapers.[15] He found that when people had been deprived of their newspapers for many days, they missed them "intensely." However, when the researcher probed more deeply into exactly what they missed, only a third said it was "serious" news presented by the paper—most kept up with that via radio. Actually, in response to detailed probing, ". . . different people read different parts

# EXPLAINING MEDIA EFFECTS
## *Uses and Gratifications Theory*

By the 1940s, during the Golden Age of radio, it was clear that mass communications have limited and selective influences on individuals who are exposed to a particular message. However, researchers of the time began to ask a different kind of question. Why did audiences deliberately seek out some kinds of media content and completely ignore others? In other words, why did people intentionally listen to particular kinds of radio broadcasts? Why did they buy a particular kind of magazine or book? Why did they turn first to a particular section of the newspaper? Why did they peruse the latest advertisements of movies so as to find particular kinds of films?

The researchers began to realize that these are very goal-oriented forms of behavior. They indicated clearly that audiences did not simply wait placidly to receive whatever content happened to come their way. Audiences sought content from the media that they anticipated would provide them with certain kinds of practical information and satisfactions. In other words, receivers wanted to *use* the information in some way or to obtain *gratifications* that they anticipated.

After several massive studies of the audiences for the daytime radio serials of the late 1930s and early 1940s, media researchers formulated the *uses and gratifications theory* to try to explain why audiences do not passively wait for media messages to arrive. Instead, it sought to explain why audiences are active, deliberately seeking out forms of

of the newspaper for different reasons at different times."[16] Some did miss information about public affairs. Others felt deprived because they regularly used the newspaper as a tool for everyday life (seeing what was on the radio log, selecting movies to attend, getting weather and stock market reports, collecting information from advertising, and even following the obituary notices). All of these catagories of newspaper content filled needs and provided gratifications that went unfulfilled during the strike. Other uses were "respite" (following the news so as to gain social prestige by seeming knowledgeable, gaining gratifications from personal advice columns or human interest stories, and vicarious participation in the lives of the rich and famous).

Other studies during the same period supported the general picture of uses and gratifications provided by the newspaper study. In an extensive study of comics reading, Katherine Wolfe and Margery Fiske concluded that children used the comic books for different purposes, depending on their age.[17] In a study of book reading, Douglas Waples and his associates concluded that readers selected their material on the basis of many predispositions that were derived from their individual personalities.[18]

As television swept through the population during the decade of the 1950s, this new theory would also play a role in guiding research. In fact, as we will see next, one of the largest studies ever of children and television was conducted within the theoretical perspective of uses and gratifications.

content that provide them with information that they need, like, and use.

This theory focuses on psychological factors—each member of the audience has a structure of interests, needs, attitudes, and values that play a part in shaping selections from the media. Thus, one person, with a particular set of needs and interests, might seek satisfactions through exposure to sports, popular music, wrestling, and detective dramas. Another with a different psychological makeup might prefer wildlife programs, political analyses, symphonic music, and literary classics.

The central propositions of the uses and gratifications theory emerged from a long list of investigations that were completed over a number of decades.[13] It remains an important explanation of why people select the media content that they do. Although it has not previously been stated in formal propositions, in summary its basic ideas can be expressed in the following statements:

**1.** Consumers of mass communications do not *passively* wait for messages to be presented to them by the media.

**2.** Members of audiences are *active* in that they make their own decisions in selecting and attending to specific forms of content from the available media.

**3.** Those choices are made on the basis of individual differences in *interests, needs, values,* and *motives* that have been shaped by the individual's socialization within a web of social relationships and social category memberships.

**4.** Those psychological factors *predispose* the person to select specific forms of media content to obtain diversion, entertainment, and respite, or to solve problems of daily life in particular ways.

**5.** Therefore, members of the audience will actively select and *use* specific forms of media content to fulfill their needs and to provide *gratifications* of their interests and motives.

## Assessing a New Medium

By the end of the 1950s, television was reaching almost every corner of the country, and just as the public grew alarmed over the movies during the 1920s, they now grew concerned about television. What was this new medium doing to them, and, most of all, what was it doing to their children? A trickle of research in the early 1950s did little to quiet the public's fears. It showed that when a family acquired a TV set it changed the lives of its children in a number of ways. For example, it reduced the time they spent playing, postponed their bedtime, and modified what they did in their free time. Children with TV spent less time watching movies, reading, and listening to the radio.[19] However, no one knew whether television viewing limited or broadened children's knowledge, raised or lowered their aesthetic tastes, changed their values, created passivity, or stimulated aggression. Research was urgently needed to clarify such issues.

Today, a huge literature has developed on the subject of children and television, but three investigations stand out as landmarks. The first was an early comparison of television viewers and nonviewers. The second was a series of studies on the relationship between portrayals of violence and aggressive conduct by children. The third was not a single investigation, but a synthesis of the findings of hundreds of studies done over a ten-year period between 1971 and 1981.

## Children's Uses of Television

In 1960, Wilbur Schramm, Jack Lyle, and Edwin Parker published the first large-scale American investigation of children's uses of television.[20] The study was concerned not with what television does *to* children but with what children do *with* television. In that sense, it was in the tradition of the uses and gratifications theory. The researchers looked at the content of television shows, the personalities of young viewers, and the social setting of television viewing. In eleven studies, conducted in both the United States and Canada, they interviewed nearly 6,000 children, along with 1,500 parents and a number of teachers and school officials. They used in-depth interviews and standardized questionnaires, with statistical analyses of the results. In the end they had an impressive mass of quantitative data plus detailed insights about children's viewing patterns and their uses of television.

**Patterns of viewing.**     Very early in the life of the children studied, television emerged as the most-used mass medium (it remains so today). By age three, children were watching about forty-five minutes per weekday, and their viewing increased rapidly with each additional year. By the time children were five years old, they watched television an average of two hours per weekday, and by age eight the average viewing time had risen to three hours. In fact, it startled Americans to learn that from ages three to sixteen, their children spent more time watching television than they spent in school! Only sleep and perhaps play took up as much or more of their time.

Of course, some children watched television much more than the average numbers of hours, and some much less. Compared with light viewers, the heaviest viewers had a characteristic profile: (1) They were in grades six through eight, and were about eleven to thirteen years old; (2) they were less intelligent; and (3) they were poor.

Children's tastes in television programs varied with their age, sex, and intelligence, but their families were the chief influence on taste. Middle-class children tended to watch realistic, self-betterment programs. Working-class children viewed more programs that provided sheer entertainment or fantasy.

**Uses of programs.**     For several reasons, *fantasy* was one of the most important uses: It gives the passive pleasures of being entertained, of identifying with exciting and attractive people, and of getting away from real-life pressures. It provides pleasurable experience free from the constraining limitations of daily living. Fantasy, in other words, provides both escape and wish fulfillment.

Children often turned to television for diversion, but in fact they often received *instruction*. This teaching was neither formal nor planned, nor did the youthful viewers intend to learn anything. Such unplanned, unintentional learning is called *incidental learning,* and is a very important concept that continues to help us understand the influence of television on children even today. What is learned is related, of course, to the child's abilities, needs, preferences, and patterns of viewing. The incidental lessons taught by television are not

One of the most important effects of the media, from the standpoint of those who support them through advertising, is the influence they have on consumer decisions. For example, the act of selecting products to purchase is the focus of costly efforts to influence consumers. The same is true for a variety of services. Hundreds of millions of dollars are spent every year to influence the beliefs and actions of consumers. Research that may reveal how their decisions are made or show how they can be influenced is of great potential value to producers and distributors of products. (Bowdan Hrynewych, Stock Boston)

necessarily objective or correct. TV sometimes portrays reality realistically, sometimes falsely. Whatever their validity, however, such lessons are a significant source of instruction for young viewers.

When the researchers compared children in an American community that received television signals with a similar Canadian community that had no television at that time, they found that children in the community with television had higher vocabulary scores and knew more about current events. This finding held true even among those with low mental ability. The researchers concluded that television accelerates a child's intellectual development during his or her early years.

**Implications: viewing television poses few dangers.** Overall, the findings from this massive study revealed *no truly dramatic problems* arising from television. Although the researchers found that children were preoccupied with viewing, they did not find that they were passive receivers of evil influences from it. Instead the effects of television depended on factors such as the child's family, mental ability, group ties, age, sex, needs, and general personality.

Although the study had some flaws in its methods, its findings remain important. It offered further evidence that the medium has both limited and selective effects. It showed that TV's influences vary among children with different individual characteristics and among those of one social category of children or another. In particular, the research evidence supported the central thesis of the uses and gratifications theory. Children actively selected what they viewed and that content fulfilled many needs and provided a variety of gratifications.

# ▼ *The Issue of Television and Violence*

The legacy of fear in modern dress was the source of the largest research effort ever aimed at understanding the effects of mass communications in America. It has been the case in American society that as each new medium appeared, vocal critics pronounced it to be the cause of society's mounting ills. The fact that these ills are rooted in the long-term trends of urbanization and industrialization is not readily accepted by most of the public. The media are visible targets to blame. Thus, it is not surprising that many people during the late 1960s saw television as the cause of the nation's rising rates of crime, mounting levels of violence, and changes in values among the young.

## The Report to the Surgeon General

As fears of the medium grew, public concern brought pressure on Congress to "do something." In March 1969, Senator John Pastore said he was "exceedingly troubled by the lack of definitive information which would help resolve the question of whether there is a causal connection between televised . . . violence and antisocial behavior by individuals, especially children." With Pastore's urging, Congress appropriated $1 million to conduct research into the effects of television.

The National Institute of Mental Health (NIMH) became the agency responsible for managing the program. NIMH appointed a committee of distinguished communication researchers to design the project and a staff to do the routine administration and to prepare a final report. However, all the distinguished researchers on the committee first had to be "approved" by the television networks. That is somewhat like asking the fox to designate who will watch the chickens! Some researchers who had published negative opinions about networks were actually blacklisted from participation. Needless to say, many highly qualified investigators thought that such exclusions were unethical and simply refused to play any part in the project.

In any case, the Surgeon General of the United States charged the committee with two goals: (1) to review what was already known about television's effects, and (2) to launch new studies on the subject. Eventually, in 1971, some sixty studies plus reviews of hundreds of prior investigations were published in five volumes, plus a summary volume.[21] Many issues were studied, including the impact of advertising, activities displaced by television, and the information learned from television. The focus, however, was on *televised violence* and its *influence on children*. We can review briefly some of the main findings on this topic.

**Network television's violent content.** Just how violent were network television shows at the time of the study? Volume 1 of the research report presented some striking answers. For example, one researcher studied a full week of prime-time television in the fall of 1969. He found that eight of every ten programs contained violence. Even more striking, the hours during which children viewed most were the most violent of all. Violence was carried out on the screen mostly by men who were free of family responsibilities. About three-fourths of all leading characters were male, American, middle or upper class, unmarried, and in the prime of life. Killings occurred between strangers or slight acquaintances, and few women were violent. (In real life most killings involve family members or people who know each other.) Overall, then, television's portrayals of violence were very *frequent* and very *unrealistic*.

**Social learning from models for behavior.**   Television content clearly presents large amounts of violence. Do such portrayals provide models that children imitate and that cause them to become more aggressive? In an attempt to answer this question, one volume of the report to the Surgeon General reviewed all the research that had been published on what psychologists call **observational learning.** This kind of learning is just what the term implies. As a result of seeing the actions of someone else, the observer adopts the modeled behavior, knowledge, attitudes, or values. We will review the idea in detail in Chapter 17, but some findings from research on modeling behavior are important to the issue of whether portrayals of violence on television provide models that stimulate aggression among children.

The most widely known studies of modeling were those done by psychologist Albert Bandura and his associates in the early 1960s.[22] Bandura had children watch a live (or sometimes a filmed) model strike a large inflated "Bobo" doll. In one experimental condition children saw the model *rewarded* for this aggressive behavior. In a second condition, children saw the model receive *no consequences* for such aggression. In a third experimental condition, the subjects observed the model being *punished.*

The children who had received these "treatments" were then left in a room full of toys, including a doll like the one the model had beaten. The children who had seen the model rewarded or receive no consequences showed a great deal of direct imitation: they too beat up the doll. Those who had observed the model being punished for aggression were much less likely to be violent.

Later, to check to see if the subjects had understood the actions of the models, the children in all three groups were asked to show the experimenter what the model had done. They were able to do so without difficulty. In other words, observational learning had taken place regardless of whether the model had been rewarded or punished. The children knew full well that the model had beaten the doll. However, whether the children imitated that behavior depended on what experimental condition they had been in; that is, on what they had observed to be the consequences of being aggressive.

What do such experiments mean? There is no doubt that children often imitate what they see others doing, and most psychologists believe that modeling is an important factor in personality development. Does this mean that children imitate violence portrayed on television? There are no clear answers.

Modeling influences in experiments may be very different than the effects of mass communication in "real life."

**Television and adolescent aggression.**   Other studies in the report to the Surgeon General did look at attitudes and behavior in real-life settings. In the volume entitled *Television and Adolescent Aggression,* eight projects are reported that attempt (1) to measure adolescent use of television, (2) to measure adolescent aggressiveness, and (3) to relate use of television to violent behavior.[23]

Perhaps the most interesting of these studies is one by Monroe Lefkowitz and his associates. This ten-year *longitudinal* project covered one set of subjects over a period of a full decade, which is unusual in communication research. Some 436 children in Columbia County, New York, were tested while in the third grade and again ten years later. The children were asked to rate themselves and each other on such characteristics as popularity and aggression. The researchers also interviewed the parents. The ratings and interviews revealed that a child who was unpopular in the third grade tended to be unpopular ten years later. It also showed that such children tended both to watch television more and to become more aggressive as they got older. Thus, frequency of viewing violence portrayed on television was related to level of aggression in the group studied, and the effects of viewing television violence were greatest for those who viewed most often.

Overall, the studies of adolescent aggression found that specific kinds of youths were more likely both to watch televised violence and to be aggressive. These were males, younger adolescents, those of lesser intelligence, and those in lower socioeconomic levels. Thus, among youths in these social categories, viewing violence on television and aggressiveness went together. At the same time, the relationship between these behaviors was not strong enough to imply that television *caused* the aggressiveness. This is an important point in interpreting such research: To show that two things tend to occur together is not the same as showing that one of those things causes the other.

**Implications: televised violence may cause aggression.**   The final report of the advisory committee, entitled *Television and Growing Up,* contains a summary of the findings of the previous and additional studies, recommendations concerning further research and public policy, and a statement about the relationship between televised violence and aggressive behavior. After reviewing the entire body of evidence, the Scientific Advisory Committee concluded that televised portrayals of violence *could be harmful to some children.* As they put it, the issue posed a potential public health problem:

> Thus the two sets of findings (laboratory and survey) converge in three respects: a preliminary and tentative indication of a causal relation between viewing violence on television and aggressive behavior; an indication that any such causal relation operates only on some children (who are predisposed to be aggressive); and an indication that it operates only in some environmental contexts. Such tentative and limited conclusions are not very satisfying [yet] they represent substantially more knowledge than we had two years ago.[24]

The Committee's conclusions from the research findings created a storm of controversy. Senate hearings were held in 1972 to explore what it all meant. The public, disregarding all the hedges, limitations, and qualifications of the scientists, focused on the idea that *television causes kids to be aggressive.* The television industry, seizing mainly on the shortcomings of the research and the tentative nature of the conclusions, declared the findings to be of little importance. Many media critics were outraged; a number of the researchers charged that their work had been misrepresented. Perhaps the final word went to J. L. Steinfield, the Surgeon General:

> These studies—and scores of similar ones—make it clear to me that the relationship between televised violence and anti-social behavior is sufficiently proved to warrant immediate remedial action. Indeed the time has come to be blunt: we can no longer tolerate the present high level of violence that is put before children in American homes.[25]

In effect, then, the Surgeon General of the United States concluded that *televised violence may be dangerous to your health*! However, that conclusion was still hedged with caveats that only certain kinds of children were influenced under certain kinds of conditions.

Perhaps most interesting of all is the clear contradiction between the implications of the findings from the studies of Schramm and his associates, a decade earlier, and those of the report to the Surgeon General. The first suggested that television posed no dangers to children, whereas the second suggested that, for some, the medium could be dangerous. Here, then, is the classic situation that often confronts a scientific community. Which is the

◄

Modeling theory explains that beliefs and behavior depicted by the media may be seen and adopted by individuals. This is particularly likely if the audience believes that what is presented represents someone or something that is attractive and if it appears to provide a solution to some problem for them. Contemporary youths who adopt Nazi paraphernalia, attitudes, and behavior may have been influenced by models seen in movies or on television. (Copyright © Mark Richards/PhotoEdit)

correct interpretation? As we indicated earlier, the answer must lie in further research leading to theories that more closely portray reality.

## The Second Report to the Surgeon General

By 1980, the pace of research on the effects of television had increased sharply. In fact, 90 per cent of *all* research ever done on the effects on behavior of watching television (up to that time) was done during the decade following the publication of the first report to the Surgeon General in 1971. So many research findings were available that it was difficult to grasp their overall meaning. Additionally, the report to the Surgeon General on children and violence had created many controversies and left many questions unanswered. Because of these two factors, Julius Richard, then the Surgeon General, asked the National Institute of Mental Health to undertake a *synthesis* and *evaluation* of the mass of research evidence that was then available. Thus, in 1982, a decade after the first report, a second was published.

**The increased pace of research.**    The new report to the Surgeon General, entitled *Television and Behavior: Ten Years of Scientific Progress and Implications for the Eighties,* was not based on new research sponsored by the government.[26] Instead, it was a compilation of the main findings of more than 2,500 studies of the influence of television on behavior, most of which had been published between 1971 and 1981.

Overall, this was an enormously valuable synthesis and evaluation of thousands of research studies on television, showing how the medium influenced a number of forms of behavior. Seven broad areas of influence were reviewed. These included (1) television and health, (2) violence and aggression, (3) prosocial behavior, (4) cognitive and affective aspects of viewing, (5) the family and interpersonal relations, (6) social beliefs and social behavior, and (7) television's effects on American society.

It is not possible to summarize in a few paragraphs the nature of the thousands of studies and details of findings of so massive an amount of material. We can, however, focus on that part of the report devoted to studies of violence and aggression. The report noted that television has been and remains devoted to showing violence. By the time of the publication, the portrayal of violence on television had continued unabated since the 1950s, with only a few minor fluctuations. In fact, over the decade covered in the report there was an *increase* in violence in children's weekend programs, which by the end of the period had become more violent than prime-time television.

**Implications: Televised violence does cause aggression.**    A major difference in conclusion between the first and second reports to the Surgeon General was that there is no longer any question that a relationship exists between exposure to violent television programs and increased tendencies toward aggressive behavior among individuals viewing such content. However, as is the case in the association between smoking and cancer, one cannot predict on an individual basis. It is not clear whether violent programs will cause a particular person to become more aggressive. However, the totality of evidence for inferring that viewing violent programs raises *rates* of aggression among children who are heavy viewers was even clearer than it was in the earlier report to the Surgeon General.

The question for research now, said the report, is not whether exposure to violence raises the probability that a person will engage in aggressive behavior. That conclusion has been well established. The problem ahead is to discover exactly what portrayals of violence, and what psychological factors, lead people with particular social characteristics to become more aggressive after being exposed.

# ▼ *The Bottom Line: The Research Evidence Reveals Only Weak Effects*

In this chapter we have reviewed a massive body of research that has accumulated over sixty years of investigation of the influence of mass communications. Some of these large-scale studies and projects involved hundreds of individual investigations. There have been literally tens of thousands of additional studies on a smaller scale that have not been included in this review, but their overall conclusions are consistent with what we have discussed.

This overall body of research has yielded several rather general conclusions. These can help in understanding the nature of research, why it is conducted, and in a very broad sense, what its "payoffs" have been.

First, it is clear that societal concern with the influence of the media on unapproved behavior, especially that of children, has been the *driving force* that stimulated several of the largest research efforts. Other very practical concerns of society provided resources needed to conduct other studies—determining how to motivate soldiers, understanding the role of mass communication in our political process, probing the relationship between violence shown on television and aggressive behavior. What this focus on public concerns implies is that research is as much a political process as it is a scientific endeavor.

Second, there was a progressive improvement and increasing level of sophistication in the *research methods* used in the study of the influences of the mass media. The early studies made many mistakes that now seem naïve and glaring. Yet, they were an important part of the development of our knowledge about the process and effects of mass communication.

Third, in spite of the back-seat status of the effort, there was between the late 1920s and the beginning of the 1980s a progressive development, modification, and improvement of *basic theories* explaining how people attend to the media, interpret their content, modify their beliefs or attitudes, and shape behavior because of such exposure. Although this development and modification did not follow a simple or even logical path, it did take place and it can be reconstructed somewhat as follows:

1. *The magic bullet theory was seen as incorrect.* Before empirical studies began, it was believed that the mass media produced direct, immediate, and powerful influences on all individual members of audiences. The earliest research findings did little to challenge that prevailing belief, and in fact, they seemed to confirm it.

2. *Selective and limited influence theories replaced the magic bullet perspective.* As research became more sophisticated, the factors causing people to expose themselves selectively to media were found to be *individual differences* (in psychological makeup), memberships in various kinds of *social categories* (age, education, gender, occupation, etc.), and finally, patterns of *social relationships* (with family, friends, work associates, etc.) that prevailed among the audience.

3. *The audience was found to be active and not passive in selecting media content for personal uses and gratifications.* Influenced by their individual differences, category memberships, and social relationships, people made their own decisions as to what they wanted to read, hear, and view from the media; they were not simply passive members of audiences who were "acted upon."

Thus, the preponderance of evidence about the effects of mass communication that emerged from decades of research led to the general conclusion that *the mass media are quite limited in their influences on people who select and attend to any particular message.* In short, six decades of research revealed an overall picture of weak effects.

## CHAPTER REVIEW

▼ Large-scale research on the effects of mass communication began with the Payne Fund Studies. These efforts of the late 1920s and early 1930s concluded that motion pictures had many influences on children. The early research was discredited by experts, but it confirmed the public's belief that the movies were a powerful and potentially dangerous influence on children.

▼ The Halloween broadcast by the Mercury Theater created a panic in the United States, as large numbers of listeners were unable to distinguish the play from news. It convinced many thoughtful citizens that radio was a medium with great power to influence people.

▼ Studies of films during World War II, which were used to teach soldiers about the war and to try to shape their opinions and attitudes, showed that they had far fewer influences than was anticipated. The films taught facts and modified some opinions, but they did little to create more powerful sentiments and motivations concerning the war.

▼ A large research project conducted in Erie County, Ohio, on the role of the media in a presidential election showed clearly that mass communications were not the powerful influences that people once believed them to be.

▼ A large, government-sponsored project (the report to the Surgeon General) focused on televised violence and its influence on children and adolescents. In content analyses, experiments, and surveys, all indicators pointed to the conclusion that under specific kinds of circumstances, repeated exposure to violence on television did raise the probability that some kinds of children would be more aggressive. Yet, the findings were not compelling, and debates over the research report triggered more heat than light.

▼ In a review of some 2,500 research studies of the effects of television (the second report to the Surgeon General) the link between exposure to violence portrayed on TV and aggressive behavior (among some types of children) was seen as somewhat stronger.

▼ Overall, the research reviewed in this chapter brought about the demise of the early theory that the media have powerful and uniform effects. Replacing that view were theories of selective influence on an active audience (based on individuals' differences, social categories, and social relationships) and a general conclusion that mass communications have quite limited effects.

## CHAPTER 16

# Powerful Effects

## Media Influences on Society and Culture

*T*hose who study and evaluate the process and effects of mass communications in modern society have long been troubled by a perplexing and recurrent dilemma. When they try to understand the influence of mass communications in our society, two totally contradictory conclusions can be reached. Both are clearly based on trustworthy sources of information. And—compounding the problem—both of those conclusions seem to be correct!

The dilemma is this: Looking at the research findings that have been produced over a number of decades leads to a clear conclusion that the media have only very *limited influences* on most people's beliefs, attitudes, and behavior. However, anyone who has even an elementary acquaintance with recent American history must reach the quite different conclusion that, frequently, the media have had very *powerful influences* on a number of social and cultural situations, trends, and processes within our society.

This perplexing dilemma has to be resolved. Did the research reveal a false picture of minimal effects? If so, that would contradict our earlier claim that science reveals trustworthy knowledge. Or, is our reading of recent history faulty when it seems to show that mass communications often have powerful effects on our society and culture?

To resolve that dilemma, we will show in this chapter that *both conclusions are correct!* The media do have weak effects, but they also have powerful effects. That may sound like impossible double-talk. However, the key to understanding this seemingly irreconcilable puzzle lies in recognizing the difference between *short-term effects* on individuals and *long-term influences* on beliefs, attitudes, and behavior that can change shared cultural norms and social institutions in society at large.

In this chapter a number of theories of long-term influences of the media are set forth briefly, along with historical examples of social and cultural changes that they explain. Included are *accumulation theory, adoption of innovation theory, modeling theory, social expectations theory, word-meaning construction theory,* and *stereotype theory*. These kinds of explanations of long-term media influences have been developed to provide guidelines for continuing research on the process and effects of mass communications.

One problem with such long-range theories is that they go *beyond* what can currently be confirmed by empirical research evidence. They deal with influences and effects of mass communications that cannot be readily uncovered by short-term scientific experiments or one-time surveys. Yet, these are more than just opinions and guesses. Powerful media effects can be revealed by careful observation of historical events and trends. To bring these influences under the scrutiny of researchers, not only new theories are needed for the decades ahead but also new methods and strategies of investigation.

# ▼ *Theories of Long-Term Influences*

It is not difficult to show that mass communications can play a vital role in stimulating social and cultural change. In this section we will look at two ways in which the media can be instrumental in bringing about change within a society. The first is by a process of continuous presentation over an extended period of media-provided interpretations of some particular event or situation in a society. Examples are reducing pollution, getting drunk drivers off the road, or ameliorating a widespread problem of public health. To explain the part played by the media in bringing about such changes, we will look closely at a **theory of the accumulation of minimal effects.**[1] This theory proposes that the impact of any one message on any specific person may be minimal (as the research very clearly reveals). However, it also states that even minor changes among publics do gradually *add up* over time. They do so as increasing numbers of individuals slowly modify their beliefs, interpretations, and orientations toward an issue repeatedly presented by several media that consistently emphasize a particular point of view. When this happens, significant changes in shared beliefs and actions take place on a long-term basis.

The second form of change is that which occurs within a society as people gradually adopt (individual by individual) some new form of technology, a new way of solving an old problem, or a particular new way of believing or behaving. That kind of change can be explained in terms of a theory focusing on the *adoption of innovation* over time. According to adoption theory, the media influence social change by bringing innovations to the attention of potential adopters, who, in turn, take up and begin to use new cultural items on the basis of information that is supplied.

## Accumulation Theory: The "Adding Up" of Minimal Effects

One way to understand long-term media influences is to identify the factors that must be present before minimal effects can "add up." We do this to show how the media can have a great deal of influence in shaping people's ideas and interpretations of a situation, even though any particular message they present to any one individual probably will have quite limited effects in a short-term sense.

Three factors must be present in a situation before accumulation theory can explain how significant changes occur over a long period. First, the media must focus *repeatedly* on a particular issue; second, they must be relatively *consistent* in presenting a more or less uniform interpretation; and third, the major media (newspapers, radio, television, and magazines) must *corroborate* each other with parallel content.

What evidence is there that powerful media effects are brought about under such conditions? Clearly, no such evidence can be derived from either experiments or from surveys completed at a particular point in time. However, historical analyses can supply examples that show the theory in action. We can identify very obvious and impressive examples of accumulative effects by looking at changing patterns of public response to certain events that have occurred in recent decades where media played a decisive role.

We begin with the sending of U.S. soldiers and Marines to Somalia, Haiti, and Bosnia. These episodes in our recent history show very clearly the dramatic consequences to society that can result from *consistent, persistent,* and *corroborative* media attention to human tragedies. However, to show that these actions were not something totally unique, we will also briefly examine several additional examples.

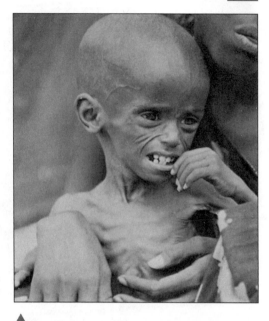

▲
If the conditions necessary for accumulation theory are present, the mass media can have powerful effects on a population. For example, for many weeks before U.S. Marines were sent to Somalia, television and other media repeatedly presented deeply disturbing pictures of starving children and adults. Each of the media conveyed much the same message, and none presented an alternative point of view. When a message is presented repeatedly in this way, with corroboration among the media, it can have a powerful cumulative influence on the beliefs, attitudes, and actions of audiences. (AP/Wide World Photos)

**Sending armed forces to Somalia, Haiti, and Bosnia.** Sending military forces of the United States to invade a foreign country is a drastic step in international affairs. This has happened three times in recent years. In the past, when the Marines have been dispatched to another country (such as Nicaragua and China earlier in the twentieth century) other nations strongly condemned the action. However, not only did the U.S. armed forces "invade" Somalia, Haiti, and Bosnia, but also they received the approval and gratitude of the majority of those country's citizens, and indeed the rest of the world.

How could this happen? Accumulation theory provides one answer. In 1991 and 1992, night-after-night on American television, viewers saw pictures of pathetic starving people in Somalia. These pictures showed little children in such a wretched state of starvation that they looked like skeletons. It was painful just to watch. The cause of their plight was shown to be the local "war lords" who were preventing humanitarian efforts to bring them food. No one claimed in any of the media that these people deserved their plight, that the war lords were justified, or that the United States should ignore the situation. In other words, the portrayals in all of the media were consistent, persistent, and corroborative. As a result, public sentiment built up to a point that President Bush was able, with a high level of approval, to take the extraordinary

Since the days of Theodore Roosevelt, who began the tradition of meeting with the press regularly, every U.S. President has developed his own style for these encounters. John F. Kennedy masterfully staged announcements at the State Department. Richard Nixon had a highly adversarial relationship with the press. Ronald Reagan met with its representatives infrequently and mainly in formal settings. George Bush had an informal style and often invited reporters aboard Air Force One, or even to his home in Maine. Bill Clinton faced a highly critical press early in his administration. (AP/Wide World Photos)

step of invading another country. Much of the world had seen the same pictures. They raised few objections; indeed most people in other countries applauded; a number even participated. However, without the accumulation of minimal effects to provide a strong base of public opinion it is doubtful that the invasion would have occurred. Later, during the first Clinton administration, television played much the same role by providing a constant flow of images of suffering in Haiti and later in Bosnia. In both of these cases, public support for sending U.S. troops into the areas was strong.

**Bringing down a president.**    A clear example of the accumulative influence of the media is Watergate. The press—that is, the news media in general—were in many ways responsible for slow changes in public opinion and resulting political pressures that eventually forced a president of the United States out of office. It was the only time that had ever happened in U.S. history. Of course the press did not do it alone; that is, the media did not create the actual events that finally led to the resignation of Richard Nixon from the presidency. The part played by the press was *relentless investigation and repeated disclosure* of the unfolding details of the Watergate issue. That disclosure consistently revealed the actions of the people involved, their efforts to cover up what they had done, and the negative interpretations of those who were not sympathetic to Mr. Nixon. Eventually, that negative orientation spread to the majority of citizens.

Facts and interpretations about Watergate were reported in the newspapers, on television, in magazines, and even in books, day after day and month after month, as the story unfolded. It preoccupied the entire nation for two years. At first, the public was not aroused, but Mr. Nixon slowly lost popularity and support as the reports in the press raised more and more questions about his credibility and honesty. As his public support faded, Mr. Nixon's political adversaries were able to move toward an impeachment process in the Congress, and the president resigned rather than face that outcome. That is a powerful effect!

It all started in June 1972, when a rather clumsy team of five burglars broke into the Democratic National Committee headquarters in the Watergate building in Washington, D. C. They apparently were looking for material that would be useful in the forthcoming presidential campaign. They were discovered, and two were arrested and convicted. It then became clear that the perpetrators and certain co-conspirators had ties to the CIA and to some of President Nixon's immediate aides in the White House. A persevering investigation by the *Washington Post* eventually revealed a complex plot that included attempts to discredit Mr. Nixon's political opponents. There were attempts to cover up the plot and any involvement of the president in the scandal. At its peak, virtually all media in the United States gave it extensive coverage. Outrage was expressed by everyone who disliked the president. That included many prominent journalists because Mr. Nixon and the press had developed a longstanding antagonistic relationship.

As the story developed, it provided wonderful opportunities for politicians to gain public attention and to posture before the TV cameras. Lengthy congressional investigations were held. The unfolding story made headlines and TV lead stories month after month. Ultimately, Mr. Nixon himself was charged with the responsibility for the situation and impeachment proceedings were initiated. President Nixon resigned and Gerald Ford took over the office. (His first official act was to pardon Mr. Nixon.)

The slow accumulation of negative interpretations, citizen by citizen, provided the base for the political actions that were taken. Without that transition, it would not have been possible to force an American president to resign from office. Without the press, however, it never would have happened. Thus, the news media were "necessary" but not "sufficient" conditions in the causal chain.

In one of the most successful examples of health communication in history, an anti-AIDS campaign raised public consciousness about the disease to the point where most Americans not only knew a considerable amount about it but also rated it the nation's top health threat. (In fact, the death rate from AIDS is relatively low when compared with that from cancer or heart disease.) There has been a longstanding controversy about the effectiveness of health advertising, but the AIDS campaign was definitely evidence of profound media effects. (Courtesy Centers for Disease Control and Prevention)

**Smoking and health.**   A third example of the accumulation of minimal effects is the twenty-five year campaign against smoking—waged largely in the media. The continuous, consistent, and corroborated portrayal of smoking as harmful to health in news and public service campaigns slowly but surely brought about a significant change in the thinking and actions of large segments of the public. Eventually, the public supported a variety of new laws concerning that habit.

## Media and the Liberal Arts

### The Media's Role in Defining Environmental Issues
A Linchpin to Environmental Science

Americans have been assaulting their environment since the first settlers arrived in the New World. Viewing nature as an obstacle to overcome, they cut down forests, drained marshes, diverted rivers, and used agricultural methods that destroyed topsoil while polluting water supplies. By the late nineteenth century, the air of many of the nation's industrial cities was heavily polluted by coal smoke, much of the nation's farmland and forests had been laid to waste, and many species of animals had been wiped out.

These developments received some important attention from philosophers and scientists. Their work, collected in some seminal books of the period, led to strong federal action to protect wild lands and wildlife, particularly during the administrations of presidents Theodore Roosevelt and his cousin, Franklin Delano Roosevelt.[2] But in general there was little sense of public alarm about the environment until the mid-twentieth century. With the publication of a single book in 1962, the environmental movement took root in the public consciousness virtually overnight.

That book was Rachel Carson's *Silent Spring*. In a lyrical prose style, it detailed with scientific rigor the effect of pesticides on animal habitats and life. A marine biologist by training, Carson at first felt ill-equipped to take on such a writing project, but her friend E. B. White encouraged her to go ahead with it. While dying of cancer, she finished the book. First serialized in *The New Yorker* magazine, the book stirred controversy even before its publication. *Silent Spring* became an instant best-seller and aroused the fury of politicians, chemical companies, and scientists alike, all of whom mounted smear campaigns against the book and its author. In time, however, Carson's thesis and her arguments withstood almost every challenge, leading the federal government to ban or restrict use of twelve of the most toxic chemicals the book discussed. But most importantly, perhaps, *Silent Spring* introduced the idea of ecology to the public imagination, taking a seemingly impenetrable topic out of academic circles and giving it a thorough and sophisticated public airing.[3]

Although old and new movies still show people smoking, media messages about its dangers became increasingly persistent, consistent, and corroborated across the media. Ultimately, cigarette ads were barred on TV, and no messages were deliberately presented to persuade people that credible authorities thought smoking was healthy and risk-free.

Many additional examples could be cited, showing ways in which effects slowly accumulate when consistent messages about a topic are persistently presented and corroborated across media. They would include our current emphasis on avoiding fats and cholesterol in our diets, our increasing preoccupation with exercise, and our shared concerns about the dangers of using drugs and alcohol. At one time the messages from the media concerning drugs were mixed. Now, the media have placed the negative aspects of these problems high on their agenda and have brought them sharply into focus for the public. Finally, in the same general category, we can note the role of the media in helping to define the dangers of AIDS and the benefits of "safe sex."

Eight years later, in April 1970, thousands of Americans across the country took part in the first Earth Day. TV, radio, magazine cover stories, and newspaper headlines proclaimed the environment a leading public issue. For a time, editors gave the topic great attention and reporters developed expertise in the field. Media coverage of several environmental disasters—such as the 1969 Santa Barbara oil spill, the burning of the Cuyahoga River in Cleveland, the biological "death" of Lake Erie, and the chemical quagmire at Love Canal—all galvanized public opinion. But the environmental movement of the 1970s had risen to prominence at least partly on the coattails of other issues—civil rights, nuclear weapons disarmament, the Vietnam war—and as they faded, so did environmental coverage.[4]

The environment began to regain salience as a public issue in the 1980s, even as official Washington, under the Reagan administration, virtually ignored it. Nuclear accidents at Three Mile Island, Pennsylvania, in 1978 and then at Chernobyl in the Soviet Ukraine in 1986 illustrated the global effect that a local environmental disaster could have. In 1989, the near ruination of Alaska's Prince William Sound by oil spilled from the Exxon *Valdez* outraged the U.S. public. For weeks TV pictures of the once pristine sound showed oily beaches, wildlife killed on a grand scale, a local fishing economy shattered, and a clean-up effort marred by incompetence and cynicism. In 1997, in what seemed a replay of history, an oil spill from a Soviet tanker off Japan caused another massive environmental disaster and television coverage reminded viewers of the Alaskan experience eight years earlier. The environment played a significant role in the 1996 presidential campaign and was frequently cited by President Clinton and Vice President Gore in their winning effort as an issue with top priority. Environmentalism has also gained ground in international media with the issue surfacing in post–cold war eastern Europe and Russia, Latin America, Asia, and even Antarctica.

Some communications scholars explain this renewed focus on environmental issues as a result of the accumulation of minimal effects theory of media impact. Others argue that, in the United States at least, the many environmental public interest groups are responsible for setting the public agenda and the media are merely second-tier players. Environmental scholars themselves often refer to the attention cycle theory of public interest, noting that worldwide concern for the environment has waxed and waned for nearly 200 years, often with significant effect. In any case, whatever the source of this latest concern, as the United States moves into a new century, more media are devoting more resources to environmental coverage than ever before.[5]

Generally, then, accumulation theory explains social and cultural changes in society that are influenced by the mass media as a slow "adding up" of minimal effects. The end result can be truly significant changes, with the media playing a relatively inconspicuous but nevertheless powerful role. Such effects are brought about when media repeatedly focus on a particular issue, present it in relatively consistent ways and corroborate each other from one medium to the other. It can be noted that there was no such consistency of reporting in the case of the O.J. Simpson trials. Varying interpretations, facts, and conclusions were presented by television, talk radio, the Internet, and print media. The result was that there was no consistent accumulation of effects—indeed public opinion remained polarized as a result.

## Adoption of Innovation Theory: The Role of the Media

A second perspective that includes a somewhat different type of accumulation process is *adoption of innovation theory*. Its basic propositions were set forth in

# EXPLAINING MEDIA EFFECTS

## *The Theory of Accumulation of Minimal Effects*

After several decades of intensive research, it became widely accepted that mass communications had only selective and limited effects. Hundreds of experiments and other kinds of research studying different kinds of persuasive messages aimed at changing people's beliefs, attitudes, and behavior failed to reveal any really strong influences on those who were exposed to them.

At the same time, year after year, changes could be observed taking place in society that many scholars believed were significantly influenced by the media. Thus, there was a dilemma concerning the ability of the media to influence people's ideas and behavior. Scientific research revealed a picture of weak media having only limited influence on people at best. However, systematic observation of ongoing events in society suggested a much more powerful role. For example it appeared to many observers that mass communication played a significant part in bringing about such changes as Richard Nixon's resignation due to the events of Watergate, the civil rights movement of the 1960s, the redefinition of the Vietnam War by people in the United States, and

many changes related to health behavior.

Clearly, some way of resolving this apparent dilemma was needed. Both the scientific research and the careful observation of historical events seemed to lead to sound conclusions—even if they were completely opposite. Finally, it came to be understood that almost all of the scientific research was based on short-term studies, making use of brief experiments and one-time surveys. The historical observations of changes in society extended over time. The resolution of the dilemma came when it was realized that both conclusions could be correct. In a short-term sense, the media may have very selective and limited influences. Over a long period, however, small changes in a few people at a time can eventually add up to a significant end result.

As it turned out, it was those issues on which the media focused repeatedly and in relatively consistent ways that changed people over time. If those conditions prevailed, and if the various media—print and broadcast—corroborated each other by presenting the same interpretations, truly significant changes

could take place in people's beliefs, attitudes, and behavior.[6] From these considerations the theory of the accumulation of minimal effects was developed. Its basic propositions are as follows:

**1.** The mass media begin to focus their attention on and transmit messages about a specific topic (some problem, situation or issue).

**2.** Over an extended period they continue to do so in a relatively *consistent* and *persistent* way and their presentations *corroborate* each other's.

**3.** Individual members of the public increasingly become aware of these messages and, on a person-by-person basis, a growing comprehension develops of the interpretations of the topic presented by the media.

**4.** Increasing comprehension of the messages supplied by the media begins to form (or modify) the meanings, beliefs, and attitudes that serve as guides to behavior of the audience regarding the topic.

**5. Therefore,** minor individual-by-individual changes *accumulate*, and new beliefs and attitudes emerge to provide significant changes in norms of appropriate behavior toward the topic.

Chapter 3 in connection with the increasing use of the daily newspaper by Americans over a number of decades. In chapters 4 through 7 we saw the adoption curves of the other media. However, the adoption process has far-reaching implications that go beyond the specific question as to how Americans took up and began to use radios, TV, and the Internet. In contemporary society, we are constantly confronted with *innovations*—that is, new technologies, new ideas, new fads and fashions, and new standards of behavior. Mass communications play a significant part in determining whether they catch on or just disappear. Some may be adopted widely (like VCRs and air bags in automobiles). Others, like 8-track audio tapes, may be introduced but never be adopted widely.

The source of many innovations is *invention* (although they can be borrowed from other societies). **Invention** is the process by which an individual or group brings together elements that already exist in the culture, putting them together into some new pattern—an innovation. We discussed the process at length in earlier chapters in terms of individuals combining existing technological elements to develop new devices related to mass communications (e.g., the telegraph, the movie projector, the radio telephone). Even popular music is a form of invention. Ragtime, Dixieland, swing, rock, and rap were innovations. Each had its own adoption curve at the time.

Obviously, people do not immediately adopt every innovation as soon as it is available, even if adopting it is logical and beneficial. It is an accumulation process; that is, it comes into use in a slow additive pattern as, individual by individual, people make up their minds to acquire and use it. Decades ago, for example, seat belts for cars were introduced. Many thousands of lives could have been saved by their immediate and universal acceptance. They were not particularly expensive, and they were not much of an inconvenience. Thus, they were good candidates for immediate adoption by all drivers. Yet, the vast majority of Americans simply ignored them. The federal government tried many media campaigns to increase the use of seat belts. Finally, enough people changed so that federal legislation requiring that all new cars have them was acceptable. Today, all recently manufactured cars have the devices, and many states have laws making their use mandatory. The majority of Americans apparently now use seat belts, but some of our drivers *still* do not use them regularly. Thus the seat belt is an innovation that has by no means been adopted completely.

For each such limited success, however, dozens of other innovations have been rapidly adopted with enthusiasm. Examples are the small hand-held electronic calculator, the digital display wristwatch, TV dinners, microwave ovens, hot tubs, cable TV, home computers, and so on. Other innovations are social rather than material. All around the globe, societies have been replacing age-old customs with modern ways. This process of social and cultural change has fascinated scholars and scientists for decades. Media researchers have been particularly interested in the adoption of innovations, and they have shown that mass communications can play a significant role in the spread of new ideas, forms of behavior, and products.

How does this adoption process actually take place, and just what is the part played by mass communications? Fortunately, a great deal of information has been developed about this *adoption process*. Studies of the spread of social change go back at least to the nineteenth century, when Gabriel Tarde said that "imitation" explained the spread of new social forms.[7] Later, sociologists made quantitative studies of the spread of such new cultural items as ham radios, hybrid seed corn, new teaching methods, and public health measures.[8] By the 1950s, research on this process was an established tradition in all the social sciences, and it can be viewed in terms of the s-shaped pattern that we described in connection with growth in use of the major mass media. People first become *aware* of the innovation. Then, a small number of adventurous early adopters *try it out*. If it seems to work for them, then increasingly larger numbers *take up the innovation*. Finally, the curve *levels out* and only a few late adopters continue to begin using it.

Where do the media fit into this? They create awareness. The spread of information via the media and the adoption and diffusion of innovations are closely related. In older societies innovations were adopted in the absence of mass communication; they came to people's attention by word-of-mouth. Today, information about an innovation can spread without resulting in adoption, but the first stage in adoption is *learning about* an innovation. Obviously, then, wide adoption of an innovation requires first that news of its nature and availability be made known. In modern society it is the mass media that facilitate the fast and widespread presentation of that information and thus stimulate social change.

In America today, the mass media present information on a great many possible innovations to large numbers of people. These range from such items as household products and cosmetics to new models of automobiles. Advertising is an obvious source of information about new consumer products. In addition, various kinds of media, such as magazines and newspapers, regularly report on advances made in medicine, physical science, biology, education, and various kinds of hobbies. Person-to-person communication supplements this media-initiated diffusion of information. As a result, Americans adopt many innovations over varying periods of time. Thus, adoption theory, explaining the communication and behavioral dynamics of the diffusion of innovations, provides an understanding of the contributions of the mass media to this kind of accumulative and long-term social change.

## Implications of Long-Term Theories

Both accumulation theory and adoption theory aid greatly in resolving the dilemma that we posed at the beginning of this chapter. It remains entirely true that from a short-term perspective mass communications have very limited and very selective influences on individuals. There is every reason to be confident in that conclusion. However, repeated exposure to a consistent message can change people. It may still be less than dramatic for any particular person, but it does happen, and such changes add up. Eventually, among large populations repeatedly exposed to relatively consistent interpretations presented and corroborated across media, an accumulation of individual influences eventually results in significant change.

# ▼ Socialization Theories: Incidental Lessons on Social Behavior

In chapter 15 we noted the preoccupation of researchers with the issue of televised portrayals of violence and their influence on children. This focus came about because parents and others have been concerned about the "socializing" influence of television—the *lessons* the media present to youthful audiences and the degree to which youngsters *learn* such instructions concerning the rules of behavior that prevail in the society. The fear is that television legitimizes the use of violence as a means of settling disputes between people. There are some grounds for that fear. As we saw, with repeated exposure over a long period of time, some children do appear to become somewhat more aggressive as a result of their attending to violence portrayed on television.

Although this set of relationships—between portrayed violence, youthful audiences, and their actual behavior—illustrates the idea of socialization, it is only one form of media content and one kind of behavior that comes within the broad concept. Socialization is a long-term process that every human being undergoes as he or she becomes a functioning member of society. It certainly includes much more than just learning from TV. Socialization refers to internalizing *all* of the lessons from many sources concerning ways of behaving that are approved and expected by society as individuals mature through every stage in the life cycle. Thus, as people pass from infancy to old age they must constantly acquire new habits, new ways of thinking about themselves, and new understandings of the groups in which they must participate. Briefly defined, then, **socialization** is that extended learning process by which the rules of behavior of a society, and all of the demands of its culture, are incorporated into the personal psychological organization of the individual participating in its social order.

To illustrate the long-term socialization influences of mass communications, we will review two rather different aspects of the process as it is influenced by portrayals in media content. The first—*modeling theory*—focuses narrowly on individual members who are exposed to depictions of certain forms of behavior that are seen as attractive and worth copying. A second look at socialization is much broader. It focuses on the rules and expectations for patterned social behavior that are shown as the media portray or describe people acting within groups. Thus, **social expectations theory** focuses on media-provided lessons about what constitutes acceptable behavior in various group settings. Both of these perspectives illustrate very well the idea of a long-term accumulation of influences.

## Modeling Theory: Adopting Behavior Portrayed by the Media

Because the dramas and other kinds of portrayals commonly found in the movies or on television show many aspects of human life, they provide depictions of behavior that can be imitated by members of their audience. To a lesser degree this may also be the case when behavior is described verbally in radio or in print. In either case, media portrayals "model" many kinds of actions and situations by displaying them on the screen or in other ways. Adopting such modeled behavior is one form of socialization.

The word "model" can apply either to the person who portrays an action or to the depicted action itself. Thus, under certain circumstances, members of an audience may imitate or reproduce behavior they find modeled in media sources. One of the most impressive findings of the Payne Fund Studies of the movies, undertaken in the late 1920s (chapter 15), was the extent to which children of the time readily imitated forms of behavior that they saw modeled on the screen. The same is true in more modern times of what people are shown doing in the movies or on TV. There is a great deal of imitation.

A theory has been developed by psychologist Albert Bandura to account for the acquisition of virtually any kind of behavior that people see being performed by others. In its more general form, it is called "social learning theory." It is not specifically focused on mass communication, but it attempts to explain how people take on new forms of behavior when they see them performed by others, whether by direct observation or in terms of media portrayals.

The term **modeling theory** has come into use to indicate the application of the more general social learning theory to the case where people acquire behavior forms that they find modeled in the media.[9] An important feature of modeling theory is that it can help explain long-term influences of mass communications; that is, it can help in explaining why minor changes take place among individuals, eventually to accumulate in major changes in society.

To illustrate modeling theory, we can cite an anecdote that actually happened: A middle-aged woman, new to the neighborhood, was invited by a group of local women to accompany them on a shopping trip to a nearby mall. After making a number of purchases, one of the group suggested that they stop at a cocktail lounge for a drink. The others seemed enthusiastic and the woman agreed, even though she was not a user of alcohol. Once the group was seated in the lounge, the waitress arrived to ask what each person wanted to drink. As the others were ordering various drinks by name, the woman realized that she did not know the name of a single drink, and she was embarrassed to display her ignorance. However, she suddenly remembered the "soap opera" that she had watched the previous day, in which a young couple met in a bar to discuss their marital difficulties. She recalled that the woman in the play was quite attractive and she wished she were like her. In any case, the young woman in the drama ordered a "Brandy Alexander." It was a colorful name and it stuck in the woman's mind. Therefore, when it was her turn to order, she asked for a Brandy Alexander, even though she had no idea what it would taste like. As

# EXPLAINING MEDIA EFFECTS
## *Modeling Theory*

The mass media, and especially television and movies, present many depictions of people acting out patterns of behavior in various ways. These can be ways of speaking, relating to members of the opposite sex, dressing, walking, or virtually any form of meaningful action. These depictions can serve as "models" of behavior that can be imitated, and people who see the action depicted may adopt it as part of their own behavioral repertoire.

One explanation of how and why this can take place is *modeling theory.* It was derived from a more general perspective called "social learning theory" originally formulated by psychologist Albert Bandura.[10] Social learning theory provides explanations of the acquisition of behavior by seeing it performed by someone else, whether the media are involved on not. When applied to learning or adopting forms of action portrayed by actors observed in the media, it has come to be called modeling theory.

The reason that modeling theory is particularly relevant to television and motion pictures is that they actually *show* actions performed by persons (models) who in the course of various kinds of dramas or other content, can be seen behaving in various kinds of social settings. Thus, the modeled behavior is depicted more realistically than if it were only described in verbal terms, as would be the case with radio and print.

Modeling theory does not imply any *intentions* on the part of the model, or even on the part of the viewer. The adoption of a form of action after seeing it portrayed in the media may be wholly unplanned and unwitting. Certainly there is no implication that those who designed or performed the media depiction intended them as models for others to adopt. Thus, viewers may imitate a behavior pattern whether or not the people who created the portrayal intended it to serve as a guide, and the effects of viewing a model can be completely unrecognized on the part of the receiving party.

The modeling process proceeds in stages. The receiver first encounters the model depicting the behavior. If the person identifies with the model, he or she may reproduce the form of action portrayed by the model. Before being permanently adopted, however, it must have some positive benefit for the observer. If that is the case, the behavior may be tried out, and if adopting it solves some problem for the person, it may be used again and again in similar circumstances.

Stated more formally, the theory can be summarized briefly in terms of the following propositions:

**1.** An individual *encounters a form of action* portrayed by a person (model) in a media presentation.

**2.** The individual *identifies with the model;* that is, the viewer believes that he or she is like (or wants to be like) the model.

**3.** The individual *remembers and reproduces* (imitates) the actions of the model in some later situation.

**4.** Performing the reproduced activity *results in some reward* (positive reinforcement) for the individual.

**5. Therefore,** positive reinforcement increases the probability that the person will *use the reproduced activity* again as a means of responding to a similar situation.

she discovered, it was a rather pleasant drink and she enjoyed it. Thereafter, on similar shopping trips when the group stopped for drinks, she always ordered a Brandy Alexander.

**The essential conditions.** This anecdote illustrates several essential features of modeling theory. It shows that the behavior was *modeled* in the media, where the woman first encountered it. She saw the actress as attractive and *identified* with her. She recalled the name of the drink, *imitating* what she heard in the soap opera, and used it to *solve an immediate problem* (what to order). That action was a *rewarding* experience—both in the sense that it provided a solution and that the drink was pleasant. She *adopted* the behavior as a more or less permanent solution to the problem when it arose again. Those are the essential stages and conditions of modeling theory, but the concepts of identification and adoption are particularly critical.

**Identification with the model.**    The second stage, identification, is central to modeling theory, but the term is not easily defined. In general, it refers to circumstances in which the observer approves of the portrayal and either wants to be like the person portraying the behavior or believes that he or she is already like the model. In some cases we can add another possibility: that the viewer finds the model different but attractive and therefore sees the modeled behavior as a suitable guide to his or her own actions.

**Imitating and adopting the portrayed behavior.**    A controversy has centered around the last stage of the modeling process. Under what circumstances will a viewer imitate a form of activity observed on television or in a movie? And, even if the person imitates the action once, what will lead him or her to adopt it on a more permanent basis?

One answer is that on at least some occasions a person is confronted with a situation to which some sort of response *must* be made, but for which he or she lacks an appropriate and previously learned way of acting to handle the problem. In the illustration, a mode of response remembered from a mass media presentation may seem worth trying. When that happens, and if it works as a way of responding to the situation, that alone provides positive reinforcement of the imitation. If the response generates even more valued rewards, such as approval from others or a strong feeling of self-satisfaction or achievement, then the reinforcement is even stronger.

## Social Expectations Theory: Learning Group Requirements

Another way of looking at long-term influences on media audiences is to note how, over time, people learn the rules and requirements for acting out parts within various kinds of groups by seeing them portrayed in media content. This process, too, is an important part of the socialization of the individual. However, here the focus is not on isolated specific acts that are acquired from mediated models, but on developing an understanding over time of the pattern of customs and routines of behavior expected within specific groups by seeing their portrayals in the media.

More specifically, what is it that must be learned by a particular individual for effective participation in a group, or for being accepted in any kind of social setting? In every human group there is a complex set of understandings of what behavior is expected. Those expectations must be acquired before the individual can act effectively in such circumstances. To understand this process we can begin by noting the essential features of any human group, large or small. First, groups are made up of people who come together to accomplish a *goal* that they deem important—and that cannot effectively be accomplished by the same number of individuals acting alone. Thus, it is the *coordination* of their actions into an organized "team-like" pattern that gives the advantage to the group over solitary action.

The rules of that team-like coordinated behavior—often called the group's *social organization*—are what set it apart from actions taken by individuals alone. Without such a pattern of social organization, learned and followed by each member of the group, their collective actions would be chaos. Thus, groups—from the smallest family to the largest government agency or corporation—have rules and expectations that define and govern the activities of each of their members if their collective goal is to be accomplished.

What are the major components of such a shared pattern of social organization, and how do human beings acquire their personal knowledge of such requirements? Briefly stated, **social organization** can be defined as that pattern of general group norms, specialized roles, ranking positions and the set of social controls used by the group to ensure reasonable conformity to its requirements. Each of these components of organized social activities is important in stabilizing a group and getting its members to work effectively for whatever goals brought its members together in the first place.[11]

**Group norms.** Every group has a set of general rules that all members of a particular group are expected to follow. These may have to do with the way people dress, use certain specialized language, greet each other, and so on through literally hundreds of activities that make up the behavior performed in the group. They differ greatly according to the type of group. The norms of Army life are very different from those of a religious order, and both are very different from the norms followed by members of a local labor union. Nevertheless, all such groups have some set of general norms that all members must learn, understand, and follow to a reasonable degree.

**Specialized roles.** These are more specialized rules that apply to persons playing particular parts or defined positions in the group. Such definitions of expected behavior must be understood not only by the person performing a particular role but also by those who must relate their own roles to it. For example, imagine a baseball team in which the batter, pitcher, and each other player understands only what he or she is to do in their position, but not what each of the other players are supposed to do under various circumstances. It would be chaos and the goal of winning could never be accomplished. Thus, the key ideas regarding roles are *specialization* and *interdependence*; in most groups, the role requirements for each position in the group are not only different (specialized) but are also interlinked with the specialized activities of other members. This feature of a coordinated "division of labor" makes groups far more efficient than the same number of uncoordinated individuals.

**Ranking.**    There are few groups, if any, in which every member has precisely the same level of authority, power, status, and rewards. Even in informal groups of friends some members are leaders and are looked up to, while others are followers and command less prestige. In large and complex groups many ranking layers exist. People at different levels have varying amounts of power and authority and they receive different amounts of respect and rewards. Such differences in ranking arise from many sources. Generally speaking, those at the top take the greatest responsibility; they possess scarce but critical skills; they have had extensive experience and they are not easily replaced. Those with opposite characteristics tend to remain at the bottom.

**Social controls.**    Maintaining the stability of a group takes place through the use of **sanctions.** These are the rewards and punishments used by a group to prevent excessive deviation from, and to reward conformity to, its social expectations. They can range from mild sanctions, such as words or gestures of approval and disapproval, to really significant actions of control, ranging from awarding medals to those who perform in a significantly positive way to executing those whose deviations are too great to tolerate. Many groups allow limited deviation from norms, some personal variability in the manner in which people fulfill role requirements, or even some disregard for rank. However, there are always limits beyond which sanctions will be invoked.

People in societies without media learn these social requirements by a slow process. Older members in the society teach the young, or they acquire the needed knowledge by a process of trial and error, which can sometimes be painful. In a media society, however, an enormous variety of groups and social activities are *portrayed in mass communications*. These can serve as a rich source of learning for their viewers. Social expectations theory explains that extensive knowledge of norms, roles, ranks, and controls can be acquired through a process of *incidental learning* by exposure to media portrayals of many aspects of social life and kinds of human groups.

An important caution is that the way various groups are portrayed in media—in movies, television programs or even in print—may be misleading, inconsistent, or just plain wrong. Nevertheless, such portrayals often provide audiences with a source from which they can acquire beliefs (right or wrong) about the requirements of many kinds of groups that they may have to deal with at some point in their lives.

## Implications of Socialization Theories

Socializing the young is an important kind of long-range influence of mass communications in our society. Media portrayals show people performing particular actions (e.g., smoking, drinking, being violent, engaging in sex) that can become guides for those who see them modeled. Those actions can become a part of the behavioral repertoire of those who imitate the modeled behavior. The media also portray hundreds of different kinds of groups. The patterns of social organization portrayed can be observed and learned by members of the

# EXPLAINING MEDIA EFFECTS
## *Social Expectations Theory*

One of the most important features of the socialization of the individual is the process by which he or she learns how to take part in, or at least to understand, various kinds of groups. These range from the family and peer groups early in life, to increasingly complex groups as the person goes on to school, begins work, and generally must understand and deal with a wide number of groups in the community.

Every human group has its own set of rules that must be followed—its customs and expectations for many kinds of social behavior. If the individual does not conform to these social expectations, he or she risks social criticism and even rejection.

What are the sources from which we acquire our knowledge about such social skills and learn the social expectations of others? The answer is that there are many. Obviously, we learn from our family, from peers, from schools, and from the general community. In our modern world, however, there is another source from which we acquire a great deal of information about the social expectations of people who are members of various kinds of groups. That source is our mass media.

By watching television or going to a movie, or even by reading, one can learn the norms, roles, and other components of social organization that make up the requirements of many kinds of groups. One can learn what is expected of a prisoner in a penitentiary, a father or mother, a nurse in a hospital, or a corporation president conducting a board meeting. Or, one can find out how to behave when at the horse races, in combat, gambling in a casino, or having dinner at an elegant restaurant (even if one has never been in such places).

There is, in short, an almost endless parade of groups and social activities, with their behavioral rules, specialized roles, levels of power and prestige, and ways of controlling their members portrayed in the media. There is simply no way that the ordinary individual can actually participate in most of these groups, so as to learn by trial and error the appropriate forms of conduct. The media, then, provide broad if unwitting training in such social expectations.

This influence of the mass-communicated lessons transmitted on such activities can be termed the *social expectations theory of media effects*.[12] Its essential propositions can be summarized in the following terms:

**1.** Various kinds of content provided by the mass media often portray *social activities* and *group life*.

**2.** These portrayals are *representations of reality* that reflect, accurately or poorly, the nature of many kinds of groups in American society.

**3.** Individuals who are exposed to these representations receive *lessons* in the nature of norms, roles, social ranking, and social controls that prevail within many kinds of common groups.

**4.** The experience of exposure to portrayals of a particular kind of group results in learning of behavior patterns that are expected by others when acting within such a group.

**5. Therefore,** these learned expectations concerning appropriate behavior for self and others serve as *guides to action* when individuals actually encounter or try to understand such groups in real life.

audience who may later actually enter such groups. That knowledge, right or wrong, can provide them with personal definitions of the social expectations prevailing in such groups. Personal definitions include what norms to use as guides to their behavior, how they should play their roles, how to show deference to authority, whether to accept the decisions of those in positions of power, and what they can expect in the way of rewards or punishments for either exemplary or deviant behavior. In this way, the depictions of social expectations shown in mass communications can have long-range, subtle, accumulative, but significant influences on the socialization of individuals.

# ▼ *Theories of Word-Meaning Relationships*

In this section we will look at two major ways in which mass communications help shape our personal and shared interpretations of the physical and social world around us through their influences on the meanings for words; this, in turn, can shape the way in which we understand reality.

The first way in which mass communications influence our conceptions of reality is in shaping the relationships *between labels and meanings* for many words we use to describe and think about things, events, and situations around us. The second way is by stabilizing **stereotypes**—"clusters of meanings" paired with words in our language used to label categories of people.

## Constructing Personal and Shared Understandings

An important explanation of certain long-range influences of mass communications on habits of perception, belief, and behavior among their audiences is called the **word-meaning theory of media portrayals.**[13] This interpretation of the influences of mass media sees the meanings people hold for various words as strongly influenced by their exposure to the content of mass communications. Those meanings, in turn, shape their understandings of, and actions in, situations with which they must cope in the real world.

Personal meanings for features of our physical and social environment are shaped in a variety of communication processes where our understandings for labels—that is, words in our language—are shaped, reshaped, and stabilized so that we can interact with others in predictable ways. These communication processes take place in our families, among peers, in the community, and in society at large. However, each is different from one society to another. In traditional societies, word-of-mouth is the main source for stabilizing word-meaning associations. In modern society, the mass media are a very important part of these communication processes. In a media-saturated society, not only do people attend to content directly from mass communications, but as we noted in discussing the two-step flow (Chapter 12) they also discuss such information in conversations and pass on news and interpretations in a process of diffusion.[14] In these exposures and exchanges our meanings for words are constantly shaped, reshaped, and reinforced. Thus, exposure to mass communications plays a singularly important part in forming our habitual ways of perceiving, interpreting, and acting toward the world around us by shaping our meanings for words. Therefore, we need to look briefly at the nature of words and how the media play a part in shaping their meanings, which in turn influences our actions.[15]

**Words as constructions of meaning for reality.**   Words are the basic units of communication with which we perceive, understand, and communicate about what we believe to be true. Each person's meaning for every word and grammatical pattern he or she uses is a record of personal experiences previously recorded (imprinted) in neural cell structures in the brain. Thus, meanings are "subjective experiences" that each of us has— "pictures in our heads," so to speak—for aspects of reality that those words label.

For every word in our personal vocabulary each of us has constructed a pattern of subjective meanings. Those meanings are undoubtedly different in some ways from the detailed and objective characteristics of the thing or situation for which the word stands. This difference exists because no word can capture *all* aspects of the objective reality to which it refers. Therefore, we do not communicate about actual realities; we communicate by referring to our own subjective meanings aroused by words. Others who receive our messages construct their interpretations of our words from their own subjective experiences. That may sound abstract, but that is the way human communication works.

Aside from communicating with others, we also *think* by using such word-linked meanings. After we learn a word, we soon become accustomed to following the shared rules of our culture concerning the subjective experiences that it is supposed to arouse in each of us. Then, we use the word not only to communicate with each other but also to *perceive* and *think about* the reality for which it is a substitute. Thus, words separate us from actual reality, focusing our attention on our own personal constructed meanings. This may be a complex idea, but it is critically important to understanding truly important influences of mass communications.

From this idea we can conclude that *the word itself becomes far more important to us in many ways than the objective reality for which it originally was a substitute.* In fact, most of us have never had any firsthand contact with the re-

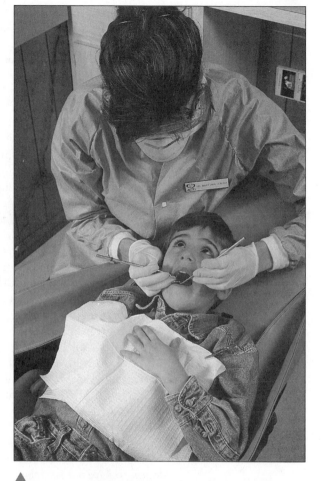

▲
Almost every child "knows" that going to the dentist is a dreaded and painful experience. Dental treatment today may be uncomfortable, but even root-canal therapy is seldom painful. Media-presented stereotypes of dentistry over many years have established the idea in our culture that even cleanings and fillings are modern forms of torture. (Copyright © Nancy Richmond/The Image Works)

alities to which the majority of the words we freely use refer! For example, only a few of us have ever put on "scuba" gear and dived to a tropical "coral reef" or flown a "jet fighter." Yet, because of the learned meanings we have acquired, we feel that we have a reasonably good understanding of what the scuba diving experience is like, what we would encounter upon reaching the reef, or what it would be like to pilot a jet fighter. Another example is "going to the dentist." Many children have never been there, but they "know" what it is like.

They can confidently confirm that it is a painful experience to be dreaded. In reality, modern dentistry is not actually painful. It may be uncomfortable and certainly expensive, but cleanings or even fillings do not cause pain. Nevertheless, most children share the meaning that dental treatment is a terrible experience.

What is happening here? We have never actually experienced many kinds of activities for which we have meanings. However, these meanings permit us to talk and think about scuba diving, fighter planes, the agonies of dentistry and a thousand other situations, actions, and things. What is happening is that in thinking and talking about such matters, we respond to our *subjective representations* of reality—meanings that we have acquired in processes of communication, rather than to the objective realities of actual experience.

Participating in our society's communication processes enables us to acquire and share *conventions* of meaning about almost anything that can be described in language or shown in media portrayals: life in the Arctic, ancient Greece, marriage, physicians, cowboys, and even beings on other planets. We "know" what these are because we participate in communication, even though we may never have been in the far North, visited Greece, been married, gone to medical school, or been a cowboy—and we certainly have not encountered people from another planet!

The important principle underlying the meaning construction theory of media portrayals is that *the personal and subjective interpretations we experience for words constitute the world to which we adjust.* We cannot relate accurately to the objective world of reality itself because our access to that world is both selective and limited. In the absence of direct experience with many aspects of that world, we create both our cultural and private worlds of meaning through communication. It is through these shared representations—the "pictures in our heads"—that we perceive, think, and shape our responses to the "world outside."[16] In short, the heart of the whole idea is that *our subjective and personal meanings shape our behavior.*

**Media portrayals as influences on meanings.**    How are the principles just discussed specifically related to the mass media? The obvious answer is that *by presenting endless portrayals of reality in its content, mass communications provide experiences from which we collectively shape our meanings for words.* Word-meaning construction theory explains that people learn or modify at least some of the meanings they associate with words through exposure to portrayals encountered in mass communications. Then, in their interpersonal communications, the meanings they derive from the media are further shaped, and reshaped, and into conventions about what words are supposed to mean that they share with others to become part of the general language and culture. The media also play a key role in stabilizing these meanings. Thus, the mass media are a source both of *changes* in language, as they modify meanings for individuals, and of *stabilization*, as they reinforce conventional usages. These influences of media content may be subtle, but they are real and of profound importance.

As an example of how meanings can be linked to a label by a medium in a forceful way, consider a television commercial for a well-known brand of deodorant that was shown on network TV. The commercial opened with a desert scene showing a gang of Mexican bandits on horseback galloping up to the foreground. When they stopped, the camera focused on their leader, who was a big, burly, hairy, and very dirty bandit. While glaring meanly out from the screen, he reached into his saddle bag and pulled out a can of a well-known brand of deodorant. Just as he was about to spray it under his arm, a voice in the background proclaimed, "If it can help him, think of what it can do for you!" The portrayal implied, of course, that Mexicans (the label) are the meanest, dirtiest, and presumably smelliest, people imaginable (the meaning). Needless to say, the commercial offended many people, and it was hastily withdrawn.

Through such portrayals, the media can modify the relationship between a word and the cluster of subjective experiences (the pictures in our heads) aroused by that word within an individual. In other words, the media can shape meanings for people exposed to their content and establish similar meanings among large audiences. The media may not *intend* to do this, any more than we intend to be influenced by them when we enjoy their content.

**Types of meaning modifications.** The influence that the media have on our meanings may be simple or complex. For example, by exposure to print, film, broadcasting, and the Internet audiences can learn new words that are added to our shared vocabulary. Or, after widespread use by the media, we can acquire new meanings for old words. Thus, our mass media have had a significant influence in transforming our shared vocabulary and standard meanings that are now widely shared.

According to word-meaning relationship theory, there are at least four ways in which media portrayals can play a part in shaping the process whereby we achieve new or modified social constructions of meanings for reality. These can be called *establishment*, *extension*, *substitution*, and *stabilization*. Each term refers to a relationship between a word and the learned subjective experiences of meaning to which it refers. These can be explained briefly.

**Establishment** is a process by which new words and new meanings become part of our language system through exposure to media portrayals. A word of clear media origin is "Rambo." Originally a name of a movie character, it has been established as a term to describe any person who takes bold and audacious, but reckless, action. More recently, "ebonics" has become a household word following widespread media usage. (It brings together "ebony" and "phonics" to describe street language structures used among some African Americans.) Similarly, the media spread to the larger population an understanding of teenage terms, such as "dweeb," and "dork" as labels for persons who do not fit into the lifestyles of those who regard themselves as more sophisticated. We also acquired foreign words from news reports, such as "perestroika" and "ayatollah."

**Extension**—that is, an expansion of meanings—can also take place as an outcome of media portrayals. In this way, people learn additional meanings that can be attached to symbols with which they are already familiar. For example, we now understand that "neat" may not mean orderly, as it once did, but likable or desirable. "Heavy" may mean more than weighty in the sense of pounds. A few years ago, the word "crack" was a physical defect that one found in a surface. After about 1985, widespread media usages extended its meanings to include a dangerous drug. Similarly, before the military action in Iraq and Kuwait "desert storm" referred to a weather disturbance in a dry region. It now also means that complex military intervention.

**Substitution** refers to a displacement of older meanings for a word and establishing newer ones as a result of media portrayals. For example, as a result of its widespread usage in movies, TV dramas and news reports, referring to a person as "gay" does not necessarily mean that he or she is jovial and light-hearted—a standard earlier usage. People today do not generally describe themselves as "gay" unless they wish to refer to their sexual preference. In addition, pressures from groups advocating "politically correct" language have altered media usages of terms like "deaf" and "blind." People in those conditions are now "hearing impaired" or "visually impaired." Many other substitutions have taken place: "Firing employees" is now "downsizing." "False teeth" have become "dentures." "Poor people" are now the "underclass."

**Stabilization** or standardization of meanings is still another outcome of certain kinds of media portrayals. In this case, members of the audience already share a more or less similar set of meanings for symbols in the portrayal. By repeatedly showing the accepted meanings for these symbols, the media reinforce (that is, more firmly establish) the conventions regarding their interpretation. For example, the public now holds certain beliefs about young black males living in the inner city. Many white Americans think they are dangerous and aggressive. Certainly some are, but the majority clearly are not. This may be a result of endless TV shows and movies in which members of this category of persons in our society have been portrayed as repeatedly engaged in drug-dealing, shootings, theft, and other deviant acts. Even the local TV news plays its part when it shows the evening round-up of crime stories. Many who are shown in the hands of police are young male African-Americans.[17]

Generally, then, although they do not invent new terms or combinations and force them on us, the mass media link words and our personal and shared meanings through their depictions and portrayals of reality in ways that play an important part in changing and stabilizing our language. Because our actions are shaped by the labels and meanings we use in responding to the world around us, the media have subtle, complex, and significant influences on our behavior.

## Stereotype Theory: Negative Meanings for Minorities

A special case of the more general word-meaning construction theory of media portrayals can be used to analyze specific ways in which our media reinforce

# EXPLAINING MEDIA EFFECTS

## The Word-Meaning Theory of Media Portrayals

One of the oldest explanations of human behavior is that people act on the basis of what they believe to be real; that is, *knowledge shapes action.* Furthermore, they obtain that knowledge—their beliefs, understandings, and meanings for the realities to which they must respond—from social sources in a process of communication. Both of these principles go back at least as far as the fourth century B.C., when Plato set them forth dramatically in his *Republic,* as he described his famous "Allegory of the Cave."

Today, we still deal with the world on the basis of knowledge derived from social sources. However, unlike people in Plato's time, we have the mass media as a central part of the process. The meanings that each of us associates with various words are significantly influenced by the ways in which the mass media present images, depictions, and interpretations of those aspects of reality to which our words refer. These media influences on the meanings of words can be stated in a theory.[18]

As we are exposed to the content of mass communications, the experience of reading, hearing, or viewing can *establish* meanings for new words that we learn (e.g., "modem," "carjacking," and "Irangate"). That experience can *extend* the meaning of existing words we already know, by providing additional meanings (e.g., "desert storm," "AIDS," and "star wars"). It can *substitute* different meanings for more traditional ones. For example, media reports on computers make use of terms like "bits" and "chips," which have very different traditional meanings. The same is true in news about sports, in which terms like "bowl" and "blowout" have little to do with their original meanings. Finally, the experience of exposure to the media can *stabilize* the relationship between familiar words and their customary meanings through repetition of standardized word-meaning linkages. Thus, the media present to us a complex flow of language and meanings that enrich, alter, and sometimes even confuse our interpretations of words.

In more specific terms, how does this process take place? In other words, how do the meanings of an individual become modified or stabilized by media exposure? The process of learning meanings from the media that then serve to guide actions is not difficult to understand. We can summarize the basic stages of the word-meaning theory of media portrayals in the following terms:

1. By presenting depictions of reality in print, audio, or screen form, the media describe objects, events, or situations in ways that link *labels* (language symbols, such as words) to *meanings.*

2. A member of the audience perceives such a portrayal and either *undergoes some change* in his or her personal interpretation of the meaning of a particular label or has its meaning *stabilized* around existing conventions.

3. The individual communicates with others using the label and its media-influenced meaning. In this interpersonal communication, such media-derived meanings are *further shaped* and/or *stabilized.*

4. This participation in mass and interpersonal communication is an important part of the development and maintenance of *cultural conventions* of meaning in our language community.

5. **Therefore,** individual behavior toward objects, situations, or events is *guided by the meanings* people hold for them. In this way, the media have played an indirect but significant role in shaping our thoughts and actions.

existing patterns of attitudes and behavior toward minorities in American society. The special case is what we will call **stereotype theory,** which brings together the word-meaning theory and the older idea of rigid beliefs that are a part of our shared culture.[19]

# EXPLAINING MEDIA EFFECTS
## *Stereotype Theory*

The term "stereotype" comes from the world of the roller printing press, where full pages of metal type were cast into a cylindrical form and attached to the roller. As the paper passed through the press, the stereotype produced thousands of pages that were exactly alike. Walter Lippman adopted the term in the 1920s to describe people who had rigidly formed ideas, usually of a negative nature, about a minority group and who treated all their members exactly alike.

Beginning in the 1930s, the concept was intensively studied by generations of social scientists. Commonly, they defined a stereotype as a structure of negative meanings thought to be characteristic of every member of a particular category of people. On the basis of such a structure of beliefs, each member could be treated in the same manner (usually rejected or discriminated against). Thus, a stereotype is a *schema* stored in memory—a set of beliefs held by individuals, but shared with others as part of a culture. It was an important concept in explaining both prejudice and discrimination and it came into common use in our language within that context.

Stereotypes function to keep minority people in positions of low power and prestige. For example, following slavery and well into the twentieth century, many whites were able to keep alive shared beliefs that African-American citizens were intellectually backward, lazy, oversexed, criminally inclined, and generally characterized by a long list of negative attributes. Therefore, they claimed, it was justifiable to deny them opportunity and to treat them as inferiors. The same was

Stereotypes are "clusters" of negative meanings that are shared widely for categories of people (such as minority groups). Generally, such negative meanings make it easier for those who are dominant to keep those categories in subordinate positions. For example, prior to the civil rights movement of the 1960s, it was to the advantage of whites to keep alive the idea that African-American citizens had low morals and were stupid, lazy, happy-go-lucky, and without ambition. Such beliefs seemed to make it reasonable to keep African Americans from voting, going to school with whites, living in white areas, and taking many kinds of jobs. Thus, to maintain their power advantage, dominant people perpetuated stereotypes about African Americans and many other religious, ethnic, and racial groups.

What kind of evidence can be assembled to see if this theory has any validity? One answer is extended and systematic observation of the content of mass communications as various categories of people are being portrayed. For example, before World War II, virtually all of our media were heavily involved in the portrayal of gross stereotypes about various kinds of minorities. For example, in the movies African Americans were almost always shown either as servants or as buffoons. They were never main characters playing significant roles. On radio such characterizations as "Amos and Andy" (two white actors in "blackface") brought the stereotypes of the ancient minstrel show traditions into the twentieth century. Newspapers seldom printed the

true of a number of other minorities. To maintain their advantaged position in the social order, dominant people perpetuated such stereotypes about many religious, ethnic, and racial groups.

During earlier decades, the movies were often criticized for their stereotyping of minority groups. Up until about mid-century, African Americans were routinely shown in subservient roles or in comic roles. Italian Americans were shown as gangsters and Asians were depicted as sly and sinister. Native Americans were most often shown as savages attacking wagon trains, but who were defeated regularly by the cavalry.

A theory of the influence of media depictions on stereotypes can be derived as a special case of the more general word-meaning relationship theory of media portrayals.[20] It can be used to analyze specific ways in which our media reinforce existing patterns of attitudes and behavior toward minorities in American society by perpetuation of stereotypes in media content. The essential ideas of stereotype theory can be expressed in the following propositions:

**1.** In entertainment content, and in other messages, the media repeatedly present *portrayals* of various categories of people, such as the aged, women, and major racial and ethnic groups.

**2.** Those portrayals tend to be *consistently negative;* that is, they often show such people as having more undesirable attributes and fewer positive characteristics than in portrayals of the dominant population.

**3.** Such portrayals are similar among the various media—movies, television, radio and print—providing *corroboration* of their nature.

**4.** These portrayals provide *constructions of meaning* for members of the audience, particularly for those who have only limited contact with actual members of the relevant categories.

**5. Therefore,** members of the audience incorporate those meanings into their memories as relatively inflexible *schemata*—stereotypic interpretations—that they use when thinking about or responding to any member of a portrayed category, regardless of his or her actual personal characteristics.

photos of African Americans, unless they were criminals (who were identified as "negroes"). Even in sports, the players and teams covered were white. The "Negro League" scores were seldom reported, and their photos were almost never found in the sports page. The list could go on and on: Italians were portrayed as gangsters, Orientals were sly and cruel, Native Americans were treacherous and always lost to the cowboys, Mexicans were lazy, and so forth.

After World War II, various reform groups and activists spoke out strongly against such portrayals and omissions. As a result, the American media sharply reduced their frequency. However, many kinds of stereotypes have survived. For example, older people are often portrayed unsympathetically as cranky and forgetful. Women are still portrayed as weak and emotional. All during the cold war, Soviet characters were portrayed as grim dullards whom we all loved to hate.

As the twentieth century draws to a close, the "incidental lessons" offered by media-portrayed stereotypes are undoubtedly less blatant than the mass-communicated curriculum of earlier decades. The process is still there, however, serving as the foundation on which meanings leading to prejudices and biases toward various categories of people can be learned from exposure to mass-communication content. An instructive example that seems to have a life of its own is the stereotyped portrayal of the mentally ill on television.

## The Mentally Ill: A Case Study in Stereotype Theory

To understand stereotype theory better, we turn to the issue of how the mentally ill have been portrayed on television in recent decades. The discussion is intended to illustrate some of the ways that portrayals in mass communication link meaning to particular words and to show how word-meaning construction theory in general helps us understand how mass communication may influence a particular set of interpretations and shared cultural beliefs. Our example will focus on the mentally ill because they make up one category of people whom the media continue to portray in grossly stereotyped ways. As we will see, the media have by no means invented the idea that mentally ill people are to be regarded negatively. What the media do is to perpetuate, stabilize, and reinforce our ancient and deeply established aversion to the mentally ill, and keep alive traditional meanings of insanity associated with them.

**Traditional meanings of insanity.**   The mentally ill have long been treated as social outcasts. To understand this pattern of social rejection, we need to look very briefly at the history of meanings for mental illness. In this way we can show the power of culture over individual interpretations and behavior and then illustrate the role of the media in perpetuating this particular set of stereotypes.

In medieval times, attitudes toward those we would now call mentally ill were far more benign than they are today. Later, during the Renaissance, the situation changed, and "madness" came to be feared and despised. The "mad" were often confined on ships that moved from place to place, exhibiting the "crazies" to people for a small fee.

"Ships of fools" crisscrossed the seas and canals of Europe with their comic and pathetic cargo of souls. Some passengers found pleasure and even a cure in the changing surroundings. Others withdrew further, became worse, or died alone and away from their families. The cities and villages that had thus rid themselves of their crazed and crazy could now take pleasure in watching the exciting sideshow when a ship full of foreign lunatics would dock at their harbors.[21]

Practices like confining people to ships of fools reinforced and stabilized the meaning of madness among Europeans. It became a repulsive state—an inherited curse to be concealed, a condition to be punished and dreaded. Children or other relatives who suffered such conditions were hidden in attics, confined to dungeons, or even killed, to keep people from knowing about "bad blood" in the family. Those afflicted were sometimes tortured to drive out the demons that "possessed" them.

**Establishing the "medical model."**   As the eighteenth century ended, changes had taken place. A few humanitarians successfully agitated for better treatment of the insane. The concept of providing them with sanctuaries or "asylums" was slow to come. However, during the last part of the nineteenth century, the belief spread that they should be placed in "hospitals" rather than chained in dungeons. In the early 1900s, psychoanalysts and other medical authorities provided a new view of insanity, arguing that it was not a curse indicating possession by demons or inherited bad blood but a sickness. This **medical model** of mental derangement was widely accepted by professionals by the early twentieth century. It redefined the insane as sick, as people with "syndromes" capable of being cured by treatment. This redefinition meant, of course, that after successful therapy they would be able to return to normal social roles.

Unfortunately, public attitudes lagged far behind these developments in the medical profession. Even today, they have been slow to change. Mental illness is still a dreadful stigma, and those who have been successfully treated have enormous difficulty in getting accepted as quite "normal," even though they behave in ways no different from other people. In fact, former convicts have better economic and social prospects for acceptance in our society than former mental patients. An important question is *why*?

Although the meanings associated with mental illness today differ greatly from those of earlier times, many elements of the older beliefs persist. In recent years the problems of the mentally ill have been compounded by the closing of many of the state-supported mental hospitals and asylums. This trend began when hospital costs began to rise dramatically and new drug therapies were discovered and used to control some of the symptoms of mental illness. Under such therapy, many patients who were in such institutions were able to function adequately in home settings—as long as they received medication.

Unfortunately, not all continued such therapies when they were turned out, and some now roam our cities with little or no support network. Many of today's homeless are people who either received institutional care at an earlier time or would be in such settings if the older system of hospitals and asylums still prevailed. Although the old system had many negative aspects, our nation has not developed a satisfactory alternative as yet for providing even basic care for such people. There is widespread apathy toward these unfortunate people, and they appear to have little hope of leading a normal lifestyle.

In any case, both those who were once mentally ill (and have recovered), as well as those still afflicted, suffer a considerable stigma. The term "mentally ill" remains a powerful label that is applied by the untrained public more or less uniformly across all categories of former and current patients. That label triggers strongly negative meanings that are widely shared. Above all, the stereotype implies that such a person is likely to be *dangerous*. A person so labeled is instantly stigmatized as one who is likely to exhibit bizarre and unpredictable behavior and should be avoided if at all possible. Reinforcing this idea is the fact that many criminals who perpetrate dreadful acts plead that they were "insane" at the time. This further links the ideas of mental illness and dangerous behavior.

Objective reality does not support the conclusion that people who are mentally ill are dangerous. The facts assembled by responsible medical and psychiatric research show clearly that mentally ill people as a whole are far less dangerous than the normal population as a whole! For every one of the handful whose crimes make headlines, thousands live obscure lives and pose no danger to others whatever. The truly dangerous segment of the population consists of clinically normal, young, urban males who are between ages sixteen and twenty-five. These "normal" people account for the lion's share of murders, rapes, and other crimes of violence committed in the United States. The mentally ill account for about the same proportion as adults over sixty-five, which is a tiny share indeed. In spite of the factual situation, however, the stereotype of the "mental patient" (including the "ex-patient") is one that continues to arouse fear.

**How the meanings of the stereotype are reinforced today.**    Why does the idea persist that mentally ill people are dangerous? What are the modern counterparts of the "ship of fools" that continue to show us that the mentally ill are mindless lunatics, only a hair's breadth away from deviant and dangerous behavior? One important factor is very clearly the way the *news media* report on mentally ill killers. Even though they are very rare—a few a year out of the 265 million citizens in our country—the press gives them enormous coverage.

The tradition of sensational reporting on "mad killers" was established as early as the 1880s, when the relatively new mass newspapers gave great attention to Jack the Ripper. The public was both fascinated and horrified, but the bottom line was that the stories sold newspapers. In fact, the public is still fascinated with the Ripper case more than a century later! Since World War II, there have been several notorious cases. The Boston Strangler, Charles Manson, the Son of Sam, John Gacy, Wayne Williams, Ted Bundy, Jeffrey Dahmer, and similar individuals have received *intense* attention from the modern media. Movies such as *Silence of the Lambs* add fictional portrayals of vicious mentally ill killers. These factual and fictional portrayals represent, for many people, about all one needs to know about the mentally ill. The fact that millions of other people who suffer mental illness are totally different and entirely harmless is ignored.

All of our mass media play a significant part in maintaining the stereotypes attached to mental illness. Books, movies, the comics, and television frequently portray the mentally ill in very negative ways. Their depictions are meant to amuse us, but unwittingly they influence the "pictures in our head"— our conventionalized constructions of meaning for "mentally ill."

**An example: television's portrayal of the mentally ill.**    To illustrate how stereotype theory aids in understanding the kinds of media portrayals that stabilize these meanings, we can review very briefly the results of a line of research using content analyses of evening television crime shows.[22] Both Goldstein, in 1980, and Diefenbach in 1995, reached similar conclusions. Goldstein's goal was to examine the portrayal of the mentally ill in all crime-adventure dramas broadcast by the major networks. First, a small "pilot study" was conducted. It showed that few other types of television programs had content related to mental illness. The mentally ill were mentioned (negatively) in a few news stories, and there had been a recent documentary and a movie dealing sympathetically with mental illness, but the overwhelming concentration of depictions of mental illness were found in the evening police and detective shows. For this reason, the study focused on thirteen action series in which various kinds of citizens, private detectives, or police officials sought weekly to outwit the bad guys.

Overall, seventy-five episodes of one-hour, prime-time, evening dramas were carefully analyzed in which official or unofficial representatives of law and order acted against wrongdoers or forces for evil. Thirty-one of the programs analyzed (41 percent) had content in which people portrayed as mentally disturbed openly committed serious deviant acts. A total of thirty-four such portrayals of mentally ill wrongdoers were identified and analyzed. (Several programs had more than one person portrayed as mentally disturbed.) Thus, portrayal of the mentally ill as *villains* was very frequent.

Each program was analyzed in terms of: (a) the details of the plot and the attributes of the characters; (b) descriptions of how the mentally ill were shown; and (c) a complete list of labels, words, and phrases used to describe or communicate about the mentally ill. For the "control" programs (explained next) a similar procedure was followed. Also, the programs were studied as "whole plots" so that the meanings of actions, labels, and incidents could be interpreted within their context.

In addition to those showing deranged criminals, twenty-one of the programs depicted serious deviance but *no* mental illness. These programs served as a control. The negative labels used to describe these "normal" villains—both number and quality—were carefully analyzed in order to see what *level of dangerousness* was implied for deviants who were not mentally ill. The purpose of this was to determine if mentally ill villains were portrayed in a more negative way than just plain crooks.

Assessing the level of dangerousness implied by each portrayal of wrongdoing allowed numerical comparisons of the actions of the mentally ill with the behavior of the non–mentally ill villains. In addition, the programs were classified into three categories: (a) those in which people were *verbally* identified as "crazy," "nuts," and so on, as they were shown carrying out deviant acts; (b) programs in which only *nonverbal* cues—such as closeups of strange-looking eyes, fixed grins, and odd twitches—indicated that a character engaged in deviant acts was "nuts"; and (c) programs that made extensive use of the *vocabulary* of madness but did not show mentally ill people acting in deviant ways.

Overwhelmingly, these nightly portrayals of mentally ill people were *unsympathetic* (to say the least). The scriptwriters were clearly using the mentally ill as the bad guys. They were murderers, rapists, slashers, snipers, and bombers. In other words, the cues, either verbal or nonverbal, that identified the actors as mentally ill were linked to activities that were extremely harmful to others. Moreover, by comparison with the (presumably sane) regular crooks, the mentally ill were shown as *far more dangerous.*

These portrayals were vivid. They provided powerful lessons that the meaning of mental illness includes elements of severe danger to others. The mentally ill offenders were not only shown to be dangerous but were also portrayed in ways calculated to arouse *fear* in the audience. As the mentally ill on the screen performed dangerous and harmful actions, they grimaced strangely, had glassy eyes, or giggled incongruously. Some laughed weirdly and then sobbed or cried. Others mumbled incoherently or screamed irrationally. One bared his teeth and snarled as he jumped on his victims to suck blood from their jugular veins. Still another squeezed raw meat through his fingers and rubbed it on his gun as he prepared to kill his next victim. Unusual music often accompanied these scenes to enhance the effect. In some shows dark scenes and carefully timed actions were used to startle and frighten the audience.

In addition to showing the overt behavior of the mentally ill in very negative terms, the stories made abundant use of the popular *vocabulary of madness*. Any kind of behavior that was unusual, eccentric, or merely difficult to explain with the facts at hand was likely to be categorized by the non–mentally ill actors as that of "kooks," "chuckleheads," "fruitcakes," "cuckoo-birds," and so forth. More technical terms for neurotic or psychotic conditions, such as schizophrenic and paranoid, were used far less frequently.

The essential conclusion from the analysis of these TV programs was that scriptwriters for these crime-adventure shows openly used the mentally ill to represent *evil*, against which the forces for right and justice could fight and win to protect society. Because the heroes and heroines of such shows were virtually invincible, the mentally ill never got away with their foul deeds. They were hauled off night after night to "hospitals for the criminally insane," where they presumably would remain forever.

Partly because of the reinforcement of the stigma attached to the mentally ill by the mass media, our daily language also continues to play a part in perpetuating the stereotype. Colloquial expressions that we all continue to use to describe irrational behavior are "nuts," "kooky," "kinky," "freaky," "wacky," "loony," and so on. Furthermore, many of us quickly judge as "sick"' or "weird" any behavior of which we do not approve. The list could go on and on. The point is that anything that departs from what someone thinks is normal— anything that seems alien, irregular, or merely inexplicable—is described in the terms that we use for the mentally ill. Thus, by repeatedly emphasizing the connection between the words we use to label mental illness and what we define as bizarre, we stabilize our meanings for madness. Our mass media continue to play a central role in the stereotyping process.

## Implications of Word-Meaning Relationship Theories

The basis of all complex communication is the link between words and the subjective meanings that they arouse within each of us. Insofar as those meanings ("pictures in our heads") are governed by shared conventions, we are able to communicate with each other more or less adequately. Given those conditions, it is clear that the part played by mass communications in establishing, extending, substituting, and stabilizing the links between words and meanings is of critical importance to society.

One of the continuing problems in any society is that of developing meanings for words that adequately reflect and incorporate the true characteristics of reality. There is considerable concern that our media are often doing just the opposite. Their portrayals emphasize ties between meanings and words that *misrepresent* the real physical and social world. The media clearly perpetuate incorrect and even harmful stereotypes that have come down from the past, as evidenced by research on portrayals of the mentally ill. The perpetuation of such stereotypes may be one of the ways in which mass communications can have powerful effects that are quite harmful to people. Although the portrayal of deranged and dangerous criminals on television is all very amusing, millions of people who are, or once were, mentally ill may continue to suffer if the medium continues to reinforce ancient stereotypes.

## CHAPTER REVIEW

▼ Two seemingly contradictory conclusions about the influences of mass communications on their audience can be derived. From massive research evidence, it seems clear that they have only selective and minimal influences on people. From observing events in society, such as Watergate, Somalia, and Bosnia, it appears that their effects are actually very powerful.

▼ This contradiction can be resolved by looking at media influences within two different perspectives. In a short-term and immediate sense, exposure to mass communications has limited effects on any particular individual. Over a long term, however, accumulation theory predicts that where information and interpretations supplied by the media are relatively persistent, consistent and corroborative, minimal changes in individuals can add up over time to significant changes in populations.

▼ Adoption theory explains a long-term influence in which significant social and cultural change takes place as large numbers of individuals gradually take up new technology and new ways of thinking and behaving.

▼ The media are a major source for bringing a flow of innovations of many kinds to the attention of the public and therefore they are a necessary (but not sufficient) condition in their adoption.

▼ In contemporary society, mass media play a central part in the overall socialization process by which individuals obtain their personal understandings of their culture and their knowledge of their social order. That socialization shapes everyone's patterns of perception, thought, and action.

▼ Modeling theory explains that one way in which people acquire new modes of acting is by observing behavior portrayed in mass communications. Such behavior is adopted if the individual identifies with the model and receives reinforcement for trying out the behavior.

▼ Another significant form of socialization is the acquisition of understanding about the requirements for behavior in groups. Social expectations theory explains that through exposures to media portrayals of social life and human groups, individuals learn about norms, roles, ranking, and controls.

▼ In their portrayals of the social and physical world, the mass media present meanings to their audiences for specific words, aspects of reality, social situations, and categories of people. Word-meaning relationship theory concludes that, once learned, those meanings and general interpretations provide a basis for people's behavioral decisions. This theory points out that every word in our vocabulary provides us with an associated set of understandings concerning some aspect of reality. Through their portrayals, the mass media help create and modify those understandings. Thus, mass communications influence our structures of meaning by establishing, extending, substituting, and stabilizing the meanings for words.

▼ An important application of the word-meaning relationship theory is the analysis of stereotypes, which aids in understanding how the media help perpetuate certain clusters of belief about particular categories of people. An illustration is the way in which television portrays the mentally ill, reinforcing the factually incorrect idea that all who are or have been mentally ill are extremely dangerous.

# *Controls*

## Policies, Politics, and the Media

J ust as the mass media must exist within a particular economic system with all
its realities, harsh and happy, so must they cope with government within a particular political system. Once it was easy to distinguish the relationship between
media and government in the United States simply by pointing to the former Soviet
Union. There, the media were a part of government rather than being independent
of it. Under such communist systems the missions of the media are defined as promoting the goals of government through the strict control of information—whether
it be news or entertainment. The media operate under the direction of propaganda
bureaus, supervised wire services, highly controlled newspapers, and broadcast and
film organizations.

In a society that regards its media system as independent, with guarantees of
press freedom enshrined in the constitution, a discussion of "controls" on the media
may seem curious. Control, after all, is at the other end of the continuum from freedom, and where there is complete and authoritarian control there can be little, if any,
freedom. In the American context, however, controls are in fact constraints that allow
the balancing of various individual and social interests with those of the media. Such
controls include communication policies that set standards and allow for resolution of
disputes as well as the political activity that shaped those policies in the first place.

In colonial America, people worried about royal charters that licensed the media
of the day and gave them permission to publish and disseminate information, which
we discuss later in this chapter. In the late 1990s, Americans and citizens of other
countries are concerned about potential controls or constraints on cyberspace and the
free flow of information. Although censorship may be technically impossible on the Internet, there have been efforts to block pornography in the United States and Germany, for example, and to stop political dissidents in China.

Not all controls involve government. Although censorship is an official act of a
government to block communication, merchants can refuse to stock certain objectionable CDs, videos, books, or magazines. Media owners can decide to carry a cable
channel or pay-per-view offering or not. Influence on advertisers from economic,
religious, educational, and other interests can also play a role in the communications
process. Thus, there are very real influences of policy and politics that shape our media
system, operations, and content.

With the fall of communism in the former Soviet Union and Eastern Europe, as
well as in the Baltics and the Balkan States, journalism and news media are being
reinvented in those parts of the world. New press laws have been drafted that generally give the media a role in society independent of government. There, as in the

United States, media are becoming part of a capitalist market economy. The roles of journalists and other communicators are being redefined. Furthermore, although the government still controls broadcasting to a considerable extent in many parts of the world, new and independent media industries are emerging, such as advertising and public relations.

This chapter describes the political conditions that confront the mass media in America. We make a distinction between the media as "the press"—which includes both print and broadcasting components—and mass communications, whose efforts are mainly directed toward entertainment or advertising. We will discuss both because, as will be made clear, it is often difficult to separate them clearly within a discussion of political controls. All are part of an integrated system and all are affected by the entire complex of political factors that relate media and government in American society.

Against a worldwide standard, American media, whether delivering news or entertainment, are separate from government; they operate independently and are not reliant on government funds or supervision. At the same time, it should be said that media systems in Latin America, Asia, and Russia, once tightly controlled by government, are moving toward full democratization. They are liberalizing, and the once stark contrasts with the United States no longer exist. However, exceptions remain in totalitarian states such as Cuba, North Korea, and China.

By deeply established tradition, the news media in the United States have an obligation to deliver information, debate, and opinion to the public and are often described as a "trustee" or "representative" of the people. They have been variously labeled the "watchdogs of the public interest," and even as the "fourth estate," implying that they are almost a branch of government. Quite often, this role puts the press in conflict with the government, as it did, for example, during the Watergate scandal in the mid-1970s, the Iran-Contra scandal in the late 1980s, or Whitewater in the late 1990s. Additionally, as we will discuss later, the press and government are often at odds during wartime. This situation has existed in the United States from the Revolution and through the short Persian Gulf War. In that conflict, the government not only controlled the conduct of the war, but it also attempted to control information about the war, especially that related to national security and military operations. The news media, in their desire to deliver information and form opinion on this important public concern, naturally resisted and even resented that control.

Sometimes conflict between press and government centers on particular individuals, for example by focusing on the alleged sexual or fiscal misconduct of members of Congress or the executive branch. Another area of conflict between government and the press is the coverage of elections, especially presidential elections. As might have been expected in the 1996 presidential election, the major candidates and their campaigns at some time were sharply critical of the press, charging bias and unfair portrayals.[1] Senator Bob Dole, the Republican candidate, decried what he called "the dangerously liberal press," but President Bill Clinton also smarted at media criticism of himself. In other countries, disputes with the press during elections have often led to censorship of a harsh nature. That has not been the case in the this country. Although politicians who are elected to office sometimes retaliate by withholding information or making the life of the press difficult, they have only rarely attempted censorship and punitive action. Still, the media are almost always wary of potential problems of this kind, knowing that the general public holds a generally negative view of the media. In fact, one recent survey suggested that if the public could reconsider the Bill of Rights in the U.S. Constitution, it would not grant so much latitude and freedom to the press.

Freedom of the press, as guaranteed by the First Amendment of the Constitution, is a basic tenet of American government. The Amendment guarantees the rights of assembly and speech, not only to private individuals but to all who operate our media as well. This principle has frequently been tested and interpreted by the courts so as to prevent censorship of the movies, to extend free expression rights to the electronic media, and even to allow advertisers and public relations practitioners to speak their minds—but within certain limits that we will discuss. Thus, direct government control over our media is very limited indeed. However, as we indicated earlier, communication in the United States (and elsewhere in the world) is largely influenced by economic competition, which exerts its own marketplace controls.

The political regime under which the mass media exist in the United States is complex and subtle, and government and the press frequently clash for a variety of reasons. One is the conflict over rights, described later in this chapter. Another is the desire of private and public interests in the country to communicate directly to the people through the press without any editorial interference. Although much of the content of the media is routine and noncontroversial, some material creates friction and, as we discuss in Chapter 11, supports the idea of an adversarial press attempting to check and balance the power of government. Of course, the government is not without means to fight back. This competition best characterizes the true nature of the way the media navigate in our political environment.

To survive in our system, the mass media perform two major functions: First, they provide a forum of communication for the nation, a *commonality of interest.* The daily agenda for public discussion is set by the press and this provides a sort of list of topics and issues to talk about. That agenda allows public opinion to form and emerge as people discuss its topics within the information provided by the press. Second, the media serve both as an *advocate* and an *intermediary* for the citizenry as they debate the topics on the news agenda from the standpoint of various social, economic, and political institutions.

The first function leads to consensus and cooperation, whereas the latter may lead to conflict. One allows the media to be a central nervous system for the nation, and the other is a correcting device that represents the people when other institutions need an independent evaluation. For example, a government agency that is performing poorly will not announce its shortcomings to the public, which deserves to know them. It is the responsibility of the press as watchdog of the public interest to report these shortcomings.

Thus, our news media exist in an atmosphere of both consensus and conflict. The balance between the two is closely related to the ability of the press to adjust to the political and governmental climate at the time. The news media both report on the activities of government and occasionally participate in it as petitioners in court or as supporters (or opposers) of candidates for public office.

To understand our press fully, it is vital to realize that for the most part, they see themselves as nonideological entities, or as instruments of fairness and impartiality in a world of self-serving politicians and government officials. Some citizens, especially those who are criticized by the news media, obviously have a different view. However, in comparison with news systems that openly declare partisan political allegiances, such as exist in Britain and France, our press is, to a large extent, politically independent and generally nonpartisan. Occasionally the press may endorse political candidates, but the media are not part of any political party or funded directly by the government—the hallmarks of media in other countries.

# ▼ Political Protections: The Constitutional Framework

Political as well as economic considerations place limitations on media in all democratic systems. In Great Britain, for example, although newspapers are privately owned it is a crime to publish anything from public documents unless prior authorization is obtained. Reporters are allowed to report only what is said at a trial, nothing more. Pretrial publicity is not permitted.

Although we have our First Amendment, the government frequently does prohibit the press from printing whatever it wishes. For example, in 1992, the Supreme Court of Minnesota ruled in a lawsuit against a newspaper that printed certain information. The case centered on whether an agreement between a reporter and a source (who had been assured of confidentiality) was a legally binding contract. In *Cohen v. The Minneapolis Star Tribune,* a reporter promised a Minnesota publicist that his role in leaking information would be kept confidential. The reporter's editors overruled the reporter and revealed the source's name—making him very angry. He sued, and after several appeals he finally won. The newspaper had claimed a First Amendment privilege to do what it wished with the information he had supplied. On appeal, the Court finally ruled that a verbal promise of confidentiality is a contract that must be honored, and, ignoring the First Amendment claim, awarded $200,000 in punitive damages to Cohen.[2]

As can be seen in the Cohen legal case, the political environment of the American media has two fundamental elements: First, a guarantee of freedom of the press is *clearly embodied* in the U.S. Constitution. Second, that freedom is *not absolute.* As it has come into conflict with other rights and freedoms, legal limitations on freedom of the press have been established. We begin an examination of these limitations by looking at the constitutional guarantee of a free press that arose from America's colonial experience.

## The Historical Legacy

As we discussed in Chapter 3, prior to the Revolution, the American colonies were ruled by England. Governors representing the Crown were appointed for each colony to ensure that English laws and English policies prevailed. With English law came a specific set of legal relationships between the press and the government. One principle embedded in those laws was that of **prior restraint;** that is, the government could not only punish those responsible for illegal publications, but could also prevent the publication of material it did not like. The government, in short, could censor publication.

In England, the Crown had not enforced its prior restraint laws for many decades before the Revolution although, as noted in Chapters 3 and 4, it had jailed or fined some individuals whose publications it did not like. English pamphleteers and newspaper writers in the eighteenth century often criticized the government without reprisal. However, in the colonies, where rebellions were an ever-present possibility, the Crown's governors sometimes required that any comment on the government's activities be reviewed and approved before publication. As detailed in our history of the newspaper, the governors would occasionally decide to crack down, as in the case of Ben Franklin's brother James, who was jailed and later forced to give up his paper for criticizing the government, and the celebrated case of John Peter Zenger, publisher of the *New York Weekly Journal.*

Zenger was charged with seditious libel for defaming the Crown and its governor. At his lawyer's urging, the jury found him not guilty because what he had published, although critical of government, was true. The jury's verdict thus asserted the right of citizens to speak out against the government. The Zenger case did not change the laws regarding libel, but it did put public opinion firmly behind the idea that newspapers should be allowed to print the

▶

Disputes between government and the press have taken many forms and had many levels of significance and complexity. The burning of John Peter Zenger's *Weekly Journal* on Wall Street in 1734 lacked subtlety, but was the beginning of a legal dispute that is of historical importance and symbolic value today. (Brown Brothers)

truth even if it is contrary to the wishes of the government. All during the remaining time of English rule, the principle of prior restraint remained a part of the legal system, although it was seldom enforced.

## The First Amendment

Curiously enough, despite the key role played by newspapers, pamphlets, and broadsides in mobilizing support for the Revolution, the framers of the U.S. Constitution did not mention freedom of the press in the original document. For one thing, they could neither agree on what the concept meant in practical terms, nor see how such a provision could be enforced. In addition, some of the members of the constitutional convention argued that there was no need to guarantee such freedoms.

Before the Constitution was finally ratified, however, several states insisted on a set of amendments that guaranteed a list of freedoms. These were accepted, and we have come to know them as the Bill of Rights. Prominent among these is the First Amendment, which states, "Congress shall make no law . . . abridging the freedom of speech, or of the press." These words are known as the free speech and free press *clause* of the First Amendment. (The amendment also includes guarantees of freedom of religion and freedom of assembly.) At first glance, the clause seems clear and unambiguous. Yet through the years, as additional media have come into being, the press and the government have become enmeshed in a tangle of issues that have confused the public, perplexed the ablest jurists, and placed a variety of constraints on those who operate the mass media.

How could such confusion occur? At the outset, we should recognize that even in the first days of the Republic, many of the founders had mixed feelings about the merits of a "free press" and the extent to which it should be unfettered. Some had qualms because it seemed obvious that newspapers were instruments of political power. For example, newspaper enthusiasts today are fond of quoting Thomas Jefferson, who wrote, "Were it left to me to decide whether we should have a government without newspapers, or newspapers without government, I should not hesitate a moment to prefer the latter." Less frequently quoted is the qualifying sentence that followed: "But I should mean that *every man should receive those papers and be capable of reading them*" (italics added). And almost never quoted are the disillusioned remarks of Jefferson after being opposed frequently by the press. He bitterly noted, "The man who never looks into a newspaper is better informed than he who reads them, inasmuch as he who knows nothing is nearer to the truth than he whose mind is filled with falsehoods and errors."

Almost all Americans will nod vigorously in agreement if asked whether they believe in freedom of the press. It ranks with motherhood, the Marines, and the American flag as a source of national esteem. However, when pressed on some specific case—such as pornography, criticism of their favorite public figure, or unfavorable stories about themselves—their assent to a free press is likely to vanish. Generally, then, support of freedom of the press is often based not on the idea that the government simply has no right to control the press, but on the belief that a free press is the best method for ensuring a well-informed public and a stable democracy. When the press appears to be doing a poor job of informing the public, support for its freedom is likely to diminish.

The issue of freedom of the press (media in general) is complicated by issues related to libel and offensive material (e.g., sacrilegious films, pornography, technical needs to control the airwaves, secrets during wartime, and many other issues). It is further complicated by jurisdictional boundaries between various courts. For example, over the years, most libel cases were fought in the state courts under state statutes. Federal courts rarely intervened to broaden press freedom until well into the present century. By then, the debate over freedom of the press had become more complicated with the appearance of film and the broadcast media.

Are movies, soap operas, and radio programs forms of "speech" and "the press," and therefore protected by the First Amendment? In 1915, the Supreme Court ruled that cinema was a "business, pure and simple, originated and conducted for profit" (*Mutual Film Company v. Ohio*). Therefore, the Court continued, it was not protected by constitutional guarantees of free speech and a free press. In 1952, however, the Supreme Court reversed this decision, after the state of New York forbade the screening of an Italian film ("The Miracle") in the state because it was "sacrilegious." When the case was appealed in the Supreme Court, it ruled that the state had no power to censor films on religious grounds.[3] The effect was that films gained the protection of the First Amendment.

Radio and television present a more complicated situation. Whereas in principle there are no limits to the number of newspapers that can be published or films produced, the number of frequencies that can be used for broadcasting is severely restricted. This difference between broadcasting and print has provided the basis for a host of government regulations regarding broadcasting. In other words, broadcast regulation has been justified by the scarcity of channels. Therefore, government regulates the owners of broadcast stations by granting and renewing broadcast licenses, as well as by regulating content to some extent. As we will see later in this chapter, regulations regarding broadcasting are generally compromised between the principle that "the public owns the airwaves" and the Constitution's guarantee of freedom of speech.

As the media developed, the idea of a scarcity of channels became obsolete. New technologies greatly expanded the means by which messages can be transmitted to audiences. For example, with the advent of cable television and direct broadcast satellite transmission, as well as such emerging technologies as fiber optics, we are entering a period not of broadcast scarcity but of *abundance*. Although this has led to a certain amount of deregulation, some of the old regulatory regime still reigns. Perhaps the greatest source of conflict over the right to a free press comes from the fact that it is only one among many other important rights. The right to a free press sometimes conflicts with society's right to maintain order and security. For example, the press's exercise of its freedom may conflict with the ability of the police and courts to do their jobs, or with the government's ability to maintain secrets it deems necessary for national security. Freedom of the press may also conflict with the rights of individuals, such as the right to privacy and the right to a fair trial. As a result of these conflicts, the courts have frequently ruled against the press's right to publish anything it pleases. The most important limitations on the press imposed by the courts concern *libel, coverage of trials, obscene material* and *government secrets*.

## Technology's Role—From Printing Presses to Cyberspace

Government controls have often focused on technology as a way of encouraging access to information or blocking it. From early printing presses (which were licensed) to cyberspace (which was the subject of official law in the United States and other countries), governments acting as agents for citizens (or for leaders or both) have always played a role. Without a royal license in many European and Asian societies, printers were not allowed to make copies of their works for distribution. Because absolute monarchs believed that they should control all communication—and thus have a clear sense of what was being said and by whom—they guarded this authority jealously. The right to freely print and distribute news, information, and opinions was central to revolutions in the United States, France, and other nations, and often still is, as undemocratic regimes are replaced. In the 1980s and 1990s, as communism fell in the former U.S.S.R and its satellites, military regimes were toppling in Latin America, and Asia was charged by new economic prowess. All three conditions led to much more freedom of communication, either guaranteed by law or encouraged by more democratic regimes. Still, even in the freest of societies, government agencies act as traffic cops to assign broadcast frequencies, register copyrights, prevent harmful advertising practices, or perform other social or citizen functions.

Much of the activity of government and other institutions trying to monitor, administer, or influence communication has been driven by technology. To prevent a kind of broadcast anarchy, it was necessary to assign frequencies and channels for radio and television. Later, cable systems were "franchised" in local communities; that is, they were given to a cable operator to develop because it was believed that only a monopoly system would be economically feasible. Telecommunication or telephone systems also benefited from the same kind of monopoly, much of which was subsequently broken. Federal agencies evolved to administer communications, trade, and other arenas where monitoring and adjudicating disputes was believed to be essential.

In the 1990s, as various media industries (telephone, cable, broadcast, motion pictures, newspapers) vied for control of new media enterprises, old regulatory schemes were scrapped for a new one. The Telecommunications Reform Act of 1996 was passed by Congress and signed by President Clinton. It permitted various business connections between media industries that previously would have been in restraint of trade and subject to antitrust laws, which exist to break up monopolies. The legislation also relaxed the rules for media ownership and content. For most observers the new act was profoundly important. To many in industry it deregulated a once highly regulated industry and allowed for more competition. To other critics the new law was the handiwork of big media companies and was a "license to make money" unconnected to the public interest. The Clinton administration, most often represented by Vice President Gore, said the new law was a tradeoff that freed broadcasters and other media industries from regulation in return for business growth and new jobs. There was also the hope that the law would spur the growth of the Internet and make it more widely available to school children in the classroom and all citizens at home within a few years. The law was still being evaluated and debated on its first birthday in early 1997.

One part of the Telecommunications Reform Act that drew considerable controversy was the Communications Decency Act, which banned indecent or patently offensive speech. The act imposed criminal sanctions for content deemed obscene or indecent that was transmitted over the Internet. The act made it a crime to use an "interactive computer service" to send minors "any comment, request, suggestion, proposal, image or other communication that, in context, depicts or describes, in terms patently offensive as measured by contemporary community standards, sexual or excretory activities or organs."[4] Although signed into law by President Clinton, many civil liberties and cyberspace groups objected, saying that any control over the Internet would "criminalize" speech and curtail the free and open system for which the Internet is known. In mid-1996, the case was reviewed in the courts and struck down by a federal court in Philadelphia, although it was sent almost immediately to the U.S. Supreme Court, which was expected to rule in 1997. The Internet and other forms of digital communication may have increased access to communication, but they have not ended government interest in monitoring and controlling. It is inevitable that every new technology will bring legal and other government control interests. Sometimes these reflect citizen interests—for example, parents in the case of the Internet, or specific industries trying to block new competition. In all disputes over technology, both sides cite the public interest as the rationale for their actions.

## ▼ *Protection from Libel*

Injunctions against making false, defamatory statements about others have ancient origins. Among the Ten Commandments is the injunction, "Thou shalt not bear false witness against thy neighbor." In ancient Norman law it was written that "a man who falsely called another a thief or manslayer must pay damages, and holding his nose with his fingers, must publicly confess himself a liar."[5] The idea that a person whose reputation was damaged by another's untrue public statements is entitled to compensation was passed on to the American colonies and on into our contemporary legal system through English law. Today, libel laws protect not only the reputations of individuals, but also those of corporations and businesses. With the development of media with huge audiences, it became possible to "bear false witness" and damage reputations on a very large scale, with very serious economic consequences.

### Libel Laws and the Media

Every year, libel suits are brought against newspapers, magazines, book publishers, and broadcast stations. They constantly test the principle of freedom of the press. The courts must weigh the right of the press to publish freely against the right of people to preserve their privacy, reputation, and peace of mind. The situation is complicated in the absence of any federal statutes concerning libel. It is a matter of state law, and each state has its own statutes.

· State laws usually give news reporters and the news media some protection against libel suits. They usually allow publication of public records and "fair comment and criticism" of both public figures and public officials. Unfortunately, it is not entirely clear who qualifies as either under the laws of the various states. However, various court cases have defined public *figures* essentially as persons who are well known. Examples include prominent sports stars, entertainment personalities, widely read novelists, or even well-known scientists.

In recent years, reporters and the media have also received constitutional protection from libel suits. In a 1964 case, the *New York Times v. Sullivan*, the Supreme Court considered for the first time whether state laws regarding libel might be overturned on the grounds that they violate the First Amendment to the Constitution. During the height of the civil rights conflict in the South, the *Times* had published an advertisement that indirectly attacked the Birmingham, Alabama, commissioner of public safety. An Alabama jury ruled that the *Times* had to pay $500,000 in damages because the advertisement included some misstatements of fact. However, the Supreme Court overruled the Alabama jury, holding that its decision violated freedom of the press. Essentially, the Supreme Court held that a full and robust discussion of public issues, including criticism of public officials, was too important to allow the states to restrain the press through their libel laws.

After 1964, it became very difficult for public officials to claim libel damages. According to the Supreme Court, only when public officials could prove that the press had shown "malice," "reckless disregard of the truth," or "knowing falsehood" could they sue for libel.

By no means was the libel issue decided once and for all in *Times v. Sullivan*. Since that time, courts have repeatedly redefined who is and who is not a public official or a public figure. And in a 1979 case, *Herbert v. Lando*, the Supreme Court ruled that courts could inquire into the state of mind of a reporter to determine whether there was malice present as a story was written. Furthermore, there have been many large libel judgments against the media.

## Multimillion-Dollar Libel Suits

Although the Supreme Court did not radically rewrite the law of libel in the 1980s, other conditions—mainly economic ones—called attention to the importance of libel as a constraint on freedom of the press. A number of dramatic libel suits captured headlines during the decade. General William Westmoreland, who led American forces during the war in Vietnam, sued CBS for his depiction in a documentary about the conflict but dropped his suit in the last days of the trial; a gubernatorial candidate unsuccessfully sued the *Boston Globe*; and Mobil Oil President William Tavoulareas successfully sued the *Washington Post*. Entertainer Wayne Newton sued NBC and won in a case involving charges that the singer had consorted with members of organized crime. In 1990, the *Philadelphia Inquirer* lost a multimillion-dollar libel suit to a local official. All of these cases had one thing in common: large amounts of money were involved, in what have been called "megabucks libel verdicts" involving substantial legal fees. Whatever their outcome, libel suits of this kind are extremely expensive and sometimes take years to litigate.

The rising cost of libel trials involves not only those judgments of the courts that penalize the media, but also legal fees and increasing libel insurance premiums. According to Henry Kaufman of New York's Libel Defense Resource Center, damage awards have increased more than 400 percent since *Times v. Sullivan* in 1964.

Today's average damage award in just a single media libel case where a plaintiff's verdict is entered comes very close to equaling the total of all awards requested in the cases surrounding Times against Sullivan, he claimed. The cost of libel, Kaufman declared, is "onerous and getting worse."[6] New laws are not being written by the courts, but statutes and court decisions long on the books are being enforced.

Some critics cite an increasingly conservative judiciary as one of the reasons for increasing libel costs, although David Anderson, a law professor at the University of Texas, argues that the media win nearly as many cases as they lose in the courts.[7] Still, win or lose, the legal costs are substantial. Some observers say that increasing costs have been responsible for diminishing investigative reporting (the so-called "chilling effect"), whereas others say that the costs check the growing power of the media in necessary ways. It should be noted that many large libel judgments are greatly reduced on appeal or by judges. Almost all knowledgeable observers agree, however, that the cost of libel has a significant effect.[8]

Libel law and libel cases always bear watching because the law in that area is complex, and it is relatively easy to bring a suit. Communication law scholar Donald M. Gillmor of the University of Minnesota points out in a widely cited book that although the media often win libel cases or have them thrown out of court, there is still a great cost due to legal fees that can be especially harmful to small publications and broadcasters. Gillmor sees public officials and celebrities as the culprits in many libel suits, and proposes to deny protection to those with "high visibility and the resources to communicate with broad sections of the public," saving the tougher provisions of libel law for ordinary citizens who are genuinely damaged by the media with little ability to fight back.[9]

A libel reform movement gained some publicity in 1989 when the Annenberg Washington Program mounted a proposal for libel reform and urged its adoption at the state level. However, it got few takers. Interest in libel reform typically comes from the media after major cases are lost, but to date it has had little public support. More importantly, the legal profession has little enthusiasm for reform, perhaps because lawyers would stand to lose huge fees under any such plan.

Other proposals have been made to circumvent libel and other media-public confrontations. One such proposal has been advanced by Robert Chandler, an Oregon publisher, who called for community complaint councils that would have less authority than press councils but would still offer a safety valve for public feedback.[10] The durable Minnesota News Council, mentioned elsewhere in this book, has also taken up cases on a trial basis in other states and has proposed a modest "nationalization" of their efforts. In the Pacific Northwest a journalism complaints council has also been developed. In 1997, as the fiftieth anniversary of the Hutchins Commission, which first introduced press councils to America, was being celebrated, a new push for news councils began. This time the leader was TV journalist Mike Wallace of CBS's "Sixty Minutes," who saw hope in the Minnesota News Council and wanted to see it implemented on a national basis once again.[11] At this writing, several foundations have expressed interest and convened projects on media fairness and journalistic improvement.

Lawyers rightly argue that libel and other press law issues have become increasingly complex in recent years as defendants from other countries have sued American media in foreign courts. For example, in the 1980s the prime minister of the Bahamas, Lyndon Pindling, sued *Time* magazine in Canada, where the libel laws are more restrictive than those in the United States. There are similar suits against U.S. media in Britain. Because the media are increasingly global and have a legal presence internationally, they are often susceptible to the laws of the countries where they operate, many of which run counter to press rights under the U.S. Constitution. This situation is likely to create a growing area of libel litigation.

## Libel and Congress

Members of Congress are virtually immune from libel suits. Statements they make on the floor of Congress or in committees are regarded as related to their responsibilities as public officials. Therefore, they can and often do make irresponsible public statements about issues and people protected by the knowledge that they will not wind up in court. The late Senator Joseph McCarthy provides a classic example of the abuse of this protection.

In the 1950s, McCarthy gained national and even worldwide attention by claiming that the United States was in the grip of powerful but hidden Communist infiltration. Using the media to whip up public fear of a vast Communist conspiracy, he accused prominent individuals in government, business, education, military, the film industry, and even the clergy of being "subversive," "fellow travelers," or "card-carrying members of the Communist Party." The media gave his outrageous claims worldwide coverage.

McCarthy's accusations helped create a climate of fear that wrecked reputations and ruined careers all over the nation. Finally, however, the media that had helped McCarthy's rise assisted in his downfall. As a result of his accusations, Congress held formal hearings on Communist influence in the Army, which were televised daily to a national audience. McCarthy's tactics were so outrageous that, after seeing him in action, the public concluded that he was an irresponsible demagogue. He lost credibility and his bid for power came to an end. Since then, McCarthy's name has become synonymous with unfair attacks without evidence. In presidential campaigns the term "McCarthyism" often reemerges, as it did in 1992, when Governor Bill Clinton accused President George Bush of using "guilt by innuendo" or McCarthy-like tactics.

## ▼ *Trial by Media*

The Constitution guarantees freedom of the press, but in the Sixth Amendment it also guarantees a fair and speedy trial to defendants. Sometimes publicity about a crime and the suspected criminal seems to make a fair trial impossible. The classic example of how the press can turn a case into a Roman circus and

▶

One of the most uncomfortable relationships in American society exists between the courts and the press. Unlike Britain, where pretrial publicity is forbidden, America allows its press virtually free rein. Recent cases receiving massive publicity were the O.J. Simpson murder trial and the trial of Timothy McVeigh, who was convicted of the Oklahoma City bombing. Many authorities feel that pretrial publicity can prejudice juries and their final decisions. (Agence France Presse/Corbis-Bettmann)

thereby deny the defendant's right to a fair trial occurred in the prosecution of Dr. Sam Sheppard in the 1950s.

Dr. Sheppard was a well-to-do osteopathic surgeon in Ohio. One night his wife was brutally beaten and stabbed to death under mysterious circumstances in their suburban home. The police were baffled because there were no witnesses and few clues. Long before the police investigation had been completed, the local newspapers decided that Sheppard was guilty. One headline read "Quit Stalling—Bring Him In;" another asked "Why Isn't Sam Sheppard in Jail?" Numerous editorials and cartoons proclaimed him guilty. Later, Sheppard was arrested and charged. The trial itself was overrun with reporters and photographers, and the jury was not adequately shielded from negative publicity about Sheppard. One newspaper even printed a photograph of Mrs. Sheppard's bloodstained pillow, retouched so as to "show more clearly" the alleged imprint of a "surgical instrument."

The prosecutor found no witnesses to the murder, and the only evidence he presented was circumstantial (for example, Sheppard was having an affair with another woman). Yet Sheppard was convicted and spent many years in prison before the Supreme Court finally reviewed his case. It declared his trial invalid, largely because of the publicity and improper legal procedures. Ohio tried Sheppard again and he was acquitted. By this time, of course, his life was shattered. He died in 1970, still a relatively young man. In 1997, new DNA analyses confirmed his innocence.

The American Bar Association took action to protect defendants against unnecessary publicity before trial. Because of the Sheppard case, along with the publicity surrounding accusations against Lee Harvey Oswald (the alleged assassin of President Kennedy), they convened a national commission to establish better rules for the protection of defendants. Led by Justice Paul Reardon of the Massachusetts Supreme Court, the ABA Commission in the late 1960s suggested rules to restrict the release of prejudicial information. For judges, court officers, attorneys, juries, prosecutors, and the police these rules carried the weight of law once they were adopted by federal and state courts.

For the press, the Reardon guidelines were voluntary. Nevertheless, in more than thirty states, beginning in the late 1960s, "fair trial–free press" committees charged with promoting recommended "codes of conduct" were set up. The guidelines were even issued on little cards for reporters, and for the most part they worked well. Then, in a Washington state case in the late 1970s, a judge used the voluntary guidelines as the basis for restricting press coverage of a murder trial. The fear that this could happen elsewhere quickly unraveled many, though not all, of the codes of the state committees.

Today, few reporters use the Reardon guidelines as such, and there is renewed discussion of the need for some voluntary curbs in a period when television, more often than newspapers, has become more sensational, a phenomenon journalism historian John D. Stevens has called "wretched excess."[12] However, screaming newspaper headlines that might be considered prejudicial are not a thing of the past. In covering many celebrated trials in recent years, supermarket tabloids like the *National Enquirer* or the *Star,* as well as big-city tabloids such as the *New York Post* or *Boston Herald,* have featured accusatory headlines about such highly visible defendants as William Kennedy Smith, televangelists Jim and Tammie Bakker, and others. Few examples of wretched excess outdistanced the massive and continuous coverage given the case of former football hero O.J. Simpson who was accused of a double murder in mid-1994 and tried for the crime in 1994 and 1995, and in a civil case in 1996. Sensationalism ruled, with almost continuous coverage on such television shows as those hosted by Geraldo Rivera, Charles Grodin, Larry King, and many others. Issues of violence and sex merged with race and social justice. The case consumed a major portion of news coverage during the first trial— one newspaper, the *Atlanta Constitution and Journal,* devoted nearly one-fifth of its entire national and international news space to the subject, and the major networks were not far behind.

Another sensational case that got massive coverage was the bombing of Centennial Park at the 1996 Olympics and the accusations against a security guard, Richard Jewell, who was subsequently cleared.

The Supreme Court in the case of *Gannett v. DePasqualle* (1979) suggested that the press could be barred from certain portions of trials. An uproar followed, in which many said the decision was a threat to the coverage of supposedly public trials. This interpretation was clarified somewhat in a 1980 Supreme Court decision, *Richmond Newspapers Inc. v. Virginia,* which gave specific constitutional protection for the media to cover public trials.

The intense publicity surrounding celebrated cases makes it common for defense attorneys to seek a variety of remedies to help their clients get a fair trial. One such remedy used by the courts, in addition to challenging potential jurors and sequestering the jury, is **change of venue,** such as occurred when the trial of the Los Angeles police officers in the Rodney King beating case was moved to nearby Simi Valley. The assumption is that in another location jurors would not be influenced by prejudicial publicity.

Celebrated trials in recent years—including those of General Manuel Noriega, the deposed leader of Panama; Marion Barry, the mayor of Washington, D.C.; and Colonel Oliver North of Iran-Contra fame—doubtless have received considerable prejudicial publicity. Just what can be done about this kind of media attention, which informs the public but also trammels individual rights, is uncertain. Some commentators have called for new rules for news gathering and a return to the Reardon Commission guidelines of the 1960s.

# ▼ *Moral Values: Obscenity and Pornography*

Do parents have the right to protect their children from seeing advertisements on the street for pornographic movies, or from seeing pornographic magazines displayed at the local drugstore? Many Americans would answer yes, but the Supreme Court's answers have been ambiguous. The most emotional issue in recent times has been child pornography: magazines and films depicting young children engaged in explicit sexual acts with adults and with each other. Public pressure prompted Congress to hold hearings on the issue in the 1970s, and various laws passed since that time have strictly curtailed the distribution of such material. As a result, the media are virtually forbidden to produce, distribute, or sell child pornography.

Two very different conceptions of the role of government underlie debates about regulation of obscene material. Liberals generally deplore censorship of such material, arguing that government should not attempt in any way to regulate the moral behavior of its citizens as long as the people involved are consenting adults. On the other hand, many conservatives are inclined to see censorship of obscenity as the proper duty of local or even national government. They tend to feel that a safe society can be maintained only through government regulation of personal behavior, such as sexual activity or the use of alcohol and drugs.

Over the years, the media have received strange and convoluted signals concerning pornography and obscenity: The Supreme Court seemed to side with the conservatives in 1957 when it announced "Obscenity is not within the area of constitutionally protected speech or press" *(Roth v. United States).* That statement may seem clear enough, but it has not been easy to determine what is or is not obscene. In the 1960s, material could not be declared obscene if it had "any redeeming social value" whatsoever. Then in 1973, the Court made it easier to ban materials by relaxing this standard. Moreover, it stated that material should be judged by local authorities according to standards that "prevail in a given community" *(Miller v. California)*. Thus, what is considered obscene in one community may not be obscene in another. Since this decision, however, the Court has overturned some efforts by local governments to ban materials. What can and cannot be censored on obscenity grounds remains far from clear.

In the face of public pressure, the media have censored themselves to some extent. Various industry associations have drawn up codes limiting the treatment of material related to sex. A classic example is the self-regulation of the movie industry in the 1930s, when the self-imposed Motion Picture Producers and Distributors Code became so puritanical that at one point not even butterflies could be shown mating. Later in the 1950s, the comic book industry voluntarily (if grumpily) curtailed production of horror comics in response to a public outcry. (Congressional hearings were held to determine whether such comic books were harmful to children.) Even as late as 1965, the American Newspaper Advertising Code prohibited such words as "girlie," "homosexual," "lesbian," "lust," "naked," and "seduce." It also ruled out horizontal embraces and comments on bust measurements.[13]

One of the most controversial issues that has confronted Americans in the past decades has been the legal status of pornography. Those who approve of it, own or manage porn shops, or show pornographic movies often claim that they are exercising their First Amendment rights. Many critics disagree, claiming that parents have a right to protect their children from exposure to such material and to bar its sale or distribution in their neighborhoods. At present, there are almost as many positions on this issue as there are porn shops and movie houses. (Copyright Ken Heyman)

Today, the National Association of Broadcasters forbids (rather unsuccessfully) the use of "dirty" words and explicit sexual content. The relative purity of broadcasting, however, is also a result of the Federal Communications Commission's enforcement of the Federal Communication Act's strict rules against obscenity. For example, in 1992 the FCC fined a Los Angeles radio station for airing allegedly obscene and off-color commentary by the controversial radio-TV host Howard Stern.[14] More recently, conflict has flared between feminists and producers of lurid, sexually explicit material. Here the old liberal-conservative split over censorship of pornography has come unglued, because many politically liberal feminists believe that pornography is so offensive and damaging to women that censorship is warranted.

Although we have dealt here with moral values as they are embodied in the law, the role of the media as a moral teacher and "enforcer" of values has also come up repeatedly in recent years. Arguing that the media are not taking

▶

Although the FCC tries to enforce its strict rules against obscenity, it has not been altogether successful. As the creeping cycle of desensitization theory explains, at least some performers constantly challenge existing norms in the use of obscene language and in the portrayal of explicit sex or excessive violence. Controversial radio talk-show host Howard Stern has been among those on whom the FCC has focused. (AP/Wide World Photos)

on the role once filled by the family, church, or school, critics urge more care and accountability among media professionals. However, this is strictly a voluntary matter, not something that can be enforced by the courts or other authorities.[15] As we have indicated earlier in this chapter, enforcement of morals is squarely at issue in the Communications Decency Act of 1996, which attempts to regulate obscenity.

## ▼ *The Government's Secrets During National Crises*

In times of national crises, such as wars, reporting some kinds of information can give the enemy a clear advantage. The classic example of the "scholarly spy" illustrates this danger. In 1940, before the United States and Germany were actually at war, a German undercover agent was smuggled into the United States on a mission to assess America's future capacity to produce air armaments. Such knowledge would play a vital part in Germany's preparations for air defense. Ironically, the spy did not need to sneak around airplane factories or army and navy airfields—he simply spent his time reading in public libraries. He carefully scrutinized the *New York Times Index* and the *Reader's Guide to Periodical Literature* for published accounts that mentioned aircraft facilities, plans for factories, and existing air armaments. After making copious notes, he returned to Germany and prepared a report for the high command. The report, later acquired by American espionage agents in Germany, turned out to be an extremely accurate prediction of U.S. production of military aircraft for the years 1941 through 1943. In fact, his assessment was more accurate than that made by the U.S. War Production Board for the same years. Yet, all the spy's data had come from newspapers, magazines, and books readily available to the public.[16]

Recognizing the security risks, Americans have generally accepted some form of censorship during wars. Even many fervent civil libertarians agree that the government deserves and requires protection during wartime. However, such censorship obviously contradicts the guarantee of a free press and limits the public's right to know.

In peace and war, government secrecy has led to many controversies. For example, in October 1983, when the United States invaded the small Caribbean nation of Grenada, military commanders barred the press from the island, and thus the war zone. Journalists and broadcasters vigorously protested the government policy as unprecedented and unwarranted censorship; the White House replied that it was trying to protect the lives of the media people. After Grenada, a commission involving military officers, government officials, and representatives of the press was set up. It recommended guidelines for the coverage of military actions and suggested the formation of a press-broadcast pool for future operations.

Only a few years later in 1989, the press got a chance to test these recommendations while covering the U.S. invasion of Panama, an action resulting in the ouster and arrest of Panamanian leader General Manuel Noriega. This time the press had greater access, and the pooling system for electronic media seemed to work. The arrangement in Panama offers a good example of press-government cooperation that balances the interests of both and is generally regarded as serving the public well. In August 1990, when Iraq invaded Kuwait causing the United States to send troops to Saudi Arabia, press access again became an issue in various foreign capitals and on the front lines with the troops.

The 1991 Persian Gulf War against Iraq's forces under Saddam Hussein revisited the conflict between press and government. From the beginning of what was a very popular war, in contrast to Vietnam, the press complained that the rules of access to information from the front were too restrictive and prevented effective coverage. A pool system representing the entire press corps was in effect, and military "handlers" who followed reporters to their interviews were heavily used. The Pentagon argued that it was simply trying to prevent the release of information that would undermine military operations or endanger the lives of troops. The result was tightly controlled information, released at formal press briefings, and little opportunity for reporters to pursue stories independently, especially if they required access to the battlefield. At the war's end, there was an almost universal agreement that the media had been kept at bay and, in effect, lost the information war.

Various conferences and meetings followed the war, as well as major reports and studies. A study with which one of the authors of this book was associated concluded that the Persian Gulf War witnessed severe restrictions imposed by the military on the press, including banning access to the war zone. A few media organizations and journalists fought the restrictions in court, but with no success. Although military officials have contended that they will look at each situation differently, they have also said that they plan to use similar controls in any future military conflicts.[17] Another report, published in Britain said, "The media and the military have fundamentally opposed information objectives during wartime; the military must protect operational security and the lives of armed forces, while the media seeks to satisfy the public's right to know and in so doing to gain new viewers and readers."[18]

So strong was media dissatisfaction with the restrictions that, after the war, a unified committee representative of U.S. print and broadcast media petitioned the Pentagon and the White House to consider a set of rules and procedures for future wars. Those rules are as follows:

1. Open and independent reporting will be the principal means of coverage of U.S. military operations.

2. Pools are not to serve as the standard means of covering U.S. military operations. Pools may sometimes provide the only feasible means of early access to a military operation. Pools should be as large as possible and disbanded at the earliest opportunity—within 24 to 36 hours when possible. The arrival of early-access pools will not cancel the principle of independent coverage for journalists already in the area.

3. Even under conditions of open coverage, pools may be appropriate for specific events, such as those at extremely remote locations or where space is limited.

4. Journalists in a combat zone will be given credentials by the U.S. military and will be required to abide by a clear set of military security ground rules that protect U.S. forces. Violation of the ground rules can result in suspension of credentials and expulsion from the combat zone of the journalist involved. News organizations will make their best efforts to assign experienced journalists to combat operations and to make them familiar with U.S. military operations.

5. Journalists will be provided access to all major military units. Special operations restrictions may limit access in some cases.

6. Military public affairs officers should act as liaisons but should not interfere with the reporting process.

7. Under conditions of open coverage, field commanders should be instructed to permit journalists to ride on military vehicles and aircraft whenever feasible. The military will be responsible for the transportation of pools.

8. Consistent with its capabilities, the military will supply public affairs officers with facilities to enable timely, secure, compatible transmission of

pool material and will make these facilities available whenever possible for filing independent coverage. In cases when government facilities are unavailable, journalists will, as always, file by any other means available. The military will not ban communications systems operated by news organizations, but electromagnetic operational security in battlefield situations may require limited restrictions on the use of such systems.

9. These principles will apply as well to the operations of the standing Department of Defense National Media Pool system.[19]

## Direct Censorship in Wartime

In past wars, the government has been able to use various indirect methods to protect its secrets. One of the earliest indirect ways used to control information was to deny access to telegraph, cable, and similar facilities. Reporters then either had to let military censors screen their copy or try to transmit it in some other way. For example, when the battleship *Maine* blew up in the harbor of Havana, Cuba, in 1898, the U.S. government immediately closed the Havana cable to reporters. Similarly, at the outbreak of World War I, the British immediately severed the cables between Germany and the United States. American reporters had to use the English-controlled cables between Europe and the United States and submit their copy to rigid British censorship.

In the United States, the relationship between the press and the armed forces has changed over time. Generally, the military wants the press to report favorably on its efforts. From the Civil War to the Korean conflict, members of the press traveled with the troops and had unlimited access to them. Things went well in general. During the Vietnam War, however, the relationship became strained. Since then, the military has often held the press at arm's length. That was clearly the case during the invasions of Grenada and Panama and the Gulf War. (AP/Wide World Photos)

The government has also imposed censorship through codes, regulations, and guidelines. During World War I, the Espionage Act of 1917 stipulated fines and prison terms for anyone interfering with the war effort in any way. For example, criticism of arms manufacturers was said to be unpatriotic. This situation enraged newspaper publishers, and legal battles over the issue went all the way to the Supreme Court. Such censorship was later declared unconstitutional, but Congress passed new, even stricter laws to control information. The Sedition Act of 1918 made it a crime to publish anything that abused, scorned, or showed contempt for the government of the United States, its flag, or even the uniforms of its armed forces. As a way to enforce the law, such publications could be banned from the mails.

On December 19, 1941, only a few days after Japanese forces attacked Pearl Harbor, President Roosevelt created the U.S. Office of Censorship and charged it with reviewing all communications entering or leaving the United States for the duration of the war. At the peak of its activity, the office employed more than 10,000 people. Its main objective was to review all mail, cables, and radiograms. A Code of Wartime Practices for the American Press was also issued to newspapers requesting voluntary cooperation from the nation's editors and publishers. Its purpose was to deny the Axis powers any information concerning military matters, production, supplies, armaments, weather, and so on. (The case of the scholarly spy occurred before the guidelines were in effect.) For the most part, those responsible for the content of the print media cooperated very well, and often exceeded the guidelines set by government. A related code was issued for broadcasters, and their cooperation was also excellent. The system of codes, regulations, and guidelines in World War II worked because the media cooperated voluntarily. The United States attempted to find a way to deny vital information to the enemy without using official censors, and by and large it succeeded.

Even during peacetime, the press has often censored itself to protect the national interest. In 1960, for example, the Soviet Union shot down an American U2 spy plane. The incident temporarily ended attempts to improve Soviet-American relations. For a year before the plane was shot down, however, James Reston of the *New York Times* had known that American spy planes were flying over the Soviet Union, but "the *New York Times* did not publish this fact until one of the planes was shot down in 1960."[20] Later, as a favor to President John Kennedy, Reston withheld information about the planned U.S. invasion of Cuba at the Bay of Pigs.

## Challenges to Government Secrecy

Although the press often engages in voluntary censorship, there are many examples of conflict, when the media dispute the government's right to censor the news. Because a shared belief in the need for freedom of the press became such a tradition very early in the life of the nation, any effort by the government to limit that freedom has always met with hostility. During the Civil War, for example, the 57th Article of War stipulated a court martial and possible death sentence for anyone, civilian and military alike, who gave military information to the enemy. However, newspapers were an indirect source of military information, and Confederate leaders went to great lengths to obtain copies of major Northern papers because they often revealed the whereabouts of military units and naval vessels. As a result, the U.S. War Department tried to prevent newspapers from publishing any stories that described the movements of troops or ships. Editors generally ignored these orders. Even after the war, General Sherman refused to shake hands with Horace Greeley, publisher of the *New York Tribune*, maintaining that Greeley's paper had caused a heavy loss of life by revealing troop movements to the enemy.[21]

Thus, even in wartime Americans have questioned censorship, asking what kind of controls should be imposed and by whom. Clearly, the government has the need to protect itself and a duty to protect the nation. However, the press claims a right to inform the public of what government is doing, and the news media maintain that the public has the right to know. Therefore, an inherent conflict exists between the right to a free press and the need to control information that would be damaging to the government.[22]

The conflict between government and the press has grown in recent decades, as the government itself has increased in size. Since World War II we have supported a giant defense establishment, a complex network of foreign relationships, and a uniquely powerful nuclear arsenal. Government secrecy grew with all of these developments. The majority of editors and publishers cooperate with the government in maintaining secrecy when national security is clearly at stake. However, as a host of government bureaucrats classify thousands and thousands of secret documents each year, the press—and the public—often wondered how many of these secrets protected national security and how many protected the government from embarrassment. It is often difficult to determine what is being protected, or at what point a secret becomes so damaging to the national interest that the constitutional guarantee of free speech should be overruled. The historic case of the Pentagon Papers illustrates these questions dramatically.

During the Johnson administration, the Defense Department put together a forty-seven-volume history of American involvement in Vietnam from 1945 to 1967, including secret cables, memos, and other documents. The history, which came to be known as the "Pentagon Papers," was classified as *top secret*. In 1971, Daniel Ellsberg, who had worked on the papers but later opposed the war, leaked them to the *New York Times*, hoping that their release would turn public opinion against the war and help bring about its end. Although the papers were both stolen and classified, the *Times* began publishing a series of articles summarizing the contents and some of the documents themselves.

The Nixon administration went to court to stop the *Times* (and later other newspapers) from printing additional articles on the papers, arguing that their publication would endanger national security. In response, the courts issued a temporary restraining order stopping the *Times* from continuing its planned series on the papers. In effect, the courts imposed prior restraint.

Eventually, the case went to the Supreme Court, which ruled against the government. The government had failed to convince the Court that publication of the Pentagon Papers constituted a danger severe enough to warrant suspending freedom of the press. Relieved and triumphant, the newspapers resumed their articles. (Ellsberg was later tried for stealing the documents.) Yet the Court's decision in the Pentagon Papers case is still regarded as controversial and it resolved little of the debate between government and the press. Conflict continues over the press's right to publish, the public's right to know, and the government's need to protect the secrecy of some activities.

During the 1980s, the Reagan administration engaged in a contentious tug of war with the press over access to government information. President Reagan proposed sweeping changes in the Freedom of Information Act, which provides public access to the various departments and agencies of government, and issued executive orders making access to information about agencies like the FBI and CIA more difficult. Professional groups like the Society of Professional Journalists and the American Society of Newspaper Editors campaigned vigorously against these restrictions. In this instance, there was profound disagreement between the government, which claimed it acted in the best interest of the people by limiting access, and the press, which said the public was better served by the free flow of information.

The most divisive of the debates between press and government during the Reagan administration centered around what came to be called "Irangate" (borrowing from "Watergate"). It occurred in 1986 and 1987, when the press revealed covert arms negotiations between Washington and the Iranian government in an effort to free hostages. The government at first argued that the secret negotiations not be disclosed, for doing so might jeopardize the lives of the Americans held in the Middle East at the time. However, critics in the press and government argued that laws may have been violated and that full information about the matter should be reported. One of many such conflicts between the media and the government over the years, the incident illustrates the adversarial role of the press and the controversy over governmental secrecy versus freedom of information.

# ▼ *Protection for Reporters' Sources*

The government claims that some secrets are necessary for its survival, and the press makes a similar claim. For example, in 1966, Annette Buchanan, the editor of the student newspaper at the University of Oregon, published a story about marijuana smoking on the campus. A local court asked Buchanan to reveal the names of the people from whom she had obtained much of her information. She refused and was later fined $300.

Although this seemingly trivial incident involved neither serious crimes nor harsh punishments, it illustrates the elements of an important controversy regarding freedom of the press. Had Buchanan given the names of her informants to the police, her credibility with her sources would certainly have been destroyed. Similarly, news personnel claim that maintaining the confidentiality of sources is an important part of the machinery of reporting. If reporters are not allowed to keep their sources secret, they will not be able to obtain information that the public should have.

A case with more serious consequences involved Earl Caldwell, a reporter for the *New York Times*. In the 1960s, Caldwell gained the confidence of the Black Panthers, a radical black power organization considered by many people to be militant and dangerous. Caldwell wrote several stories about the Panthers but in a way that did not cost him the group's trust. Later, after David Hilliard, a member of the group, was charged by a grand jury with threatening to kill the president, Caldwell was asked to appear before the grand jury and testify. He refused. In fact, he refused to go anywhere near the grand jury on the grounds that once he entered the closed session, he would then lose the confidence of his informants, who would never be certain of what he had said behind closed doors. Because of his refusal to testify, Caldwell was held in contempt of court—a decision later upheld by the U.S. Supreme Court.

The case caused an uproar among journalists. During the Supreme Court's hearing on it, the Author's League of America argued that compelling a reporter to identify his sources imposes restraints on the freedom of the press to gather information. The threat of such interrogation would cause many reporters to steer clear of controversial issues, thus inducing the "self-censorship" that is repugnant to the First Amendment.[23]

The Caldwell decision appeared to provide a clear basis for legal action against reporters who refused to divulge such information. A few years later, Peter Bridges was the first reporter actually jailed as a result of the decision. In 1972, he remained in jail for twenty-one days because he refused to identify the sources for an article he had written on alleged illegal practices involving the Newark, N.J., housing authority.

Since that time, a number of legal measures have been adopted to protect news media and reporters who do not wish to divulge sources. Many states have passed so-called **shield laws,** which specifically exempt journalists from having to reveal their sources.[24] Some journalists and lawyers argue against such laws, saying that they imply acceptance of the Court's interpretation of the First Amendment. Many lawyers also oppose shield laws on the grounds that the courts need all the information they can get to protect citizens from wrongdoing and to provide fair trials.

The issue of confidentiality of sources is by no means resolved. In 1978, a New Jersey court jailed Myron Farber, a reporter for the *New York Times,* for refusing to turn over his notes in a murder trial. The defendant's lawyers claimed that they had a right to see the notes. Despite a New Jersey shield law that supposedly protected reporters' confidential sources, the court convicted Farber of civil and criminal offenses, and the *Times* was forced to pay a fine. The N.J. Supreme Court and the U.S. Supreme Court both said that in this case the Sixth Amendment, which guarantees a fair trial, took precedence over the claims of the press.

# ▼ *Political Constraints: The Agents of Control*

We have discussed several specific areas in which freedom of the press as guaranteed by the Constitution is limited, not absolute. In practice, however, freedom of the press depends not only on this abstract constitutional framework but also on the daily decisions of courts, bureaucrats, and politicians.[25] The constitutional framework itself continues to evolve as specific problems and conflicts arise. Moreover, in particular cases the actual freedom of the press may differ from its theoretical freedom. Therefore, we look next at the various agents of political control of the media, including the courts, legislatures, White House, bureaucrats, and even private citizens. These groups may exert both formal controls on the media and informal influence on the flow of information.

## The Courts

We have seen that the courts often act as referees in conflicts between the rights of the press, the rights of individuals, and the rights of the government at large. This role is nothing new—as early as 1835 the French writer Alexis de Tocqueville observed, "Scarcely any political question arises in the United States that is not resolved sooner or later into a judicial question." Today, we are even more litigious and conflicts involving the media often lead to lawsuits in local courts. Some of these resulting verdicts are appealed and occasionally wind up in the Supreme Court.

Often, the Supreme Court's interpretations of prevailing laws or the Constitution itself have broken new ground and established new policies. In recent years the Court has ruled on a long list of issues affecting the media, including newsroom searches, libel, confidentiality of journalists' sources, regulation of advertising, and laws regarding copyright and cable television. These rulings have often been the center of immense controversy. The prevailing view in the press is that, for many years, the Supreme Court under Chief Justice Warren E. Burger was generally, though not always, hostile to the press and its claims. Dan Rather of CBS News went so far as to claim that the Supreme Court has been "repealing the First Amendment" by its decisions. Many legal scholars, however, disagree.

What we see in the courts when the press is on trial is a legal battle involving private citizens, the media, and the government. It is all a matter of "rights in conflict." As journalist Anthony Lewis said in a 1983 speech:

We have libel suits because we think a civilized society should take account of an interest besides freedom to criticize. In other words, individuals have rights too; sometimes they conflict with the rights of the press. It is not uncommon to find rights in conflict; that's why we have judges. But sometimes the press sounds as though the Constitution considers only its interests. If a network or a newspaper loses a case, "That's it, the Constitution is gone; Big Brother has taken over." Well, I don't think life is so simple. The interest of the press may not be the only one of constitutional dimension when there are conflicts.[26]

As a social institution, the media pay more than passing attention to personnel changes at the Supreme Court. In 1986, when William Rehnquist became Chief Justice and Antonin Scalia became an Associate Justice, their "press records" were examined carefully by media leaders who predicted rough times for the press in an increasingly conservative and presumably antipress Supreme Court.

Just what the Rehnquist court will do in the years ahead, however, is anybody's guess. Some media lawyers say they are not eager to take press cases before the U.S. Supreme Court unless there is no other recourse. However, such fears may be unfounded. In a 1987 case, involving evangelist Jerry Falwell and *Screw* magazine publisher Larry Flynt, the court found for Flynt, who had written scurrilously about Falwell. Chief Justice Rehnquist himself wrote the majority opinion, proving that it is often difficult to predict what the Supreme Court will do. According to media scholar David Anderson, however, press defendants appearing before the Court, from its beginning two hundred years ago to the present, have generally fared worse than other defendants.[27]

## The Legislatures

Although the Supreme Court is the final staging ground for many media battles, the first rounds of these battles are fought in state legislatures. These bodies promulgate laws that have considerable impact on the mass media. They may amend or rewrite statutes dealing with libel, misrepresentation, business taxation, newspaper advertising, cable television, and many other subjects. Most major lobbying groups for the media, such as state broadcast and newspaper associations, have representatives at their state capitals continuously looking out for their interests.

Congress's influence on the media is greater than that of the state legislatures. Postal rates for books and magazines, for example, loom large on publishers' balance sheets. Like other businesses, the media can be hurt or helped by congressional decisions regarding taxes, antitrust policy, protection of copyrights, affirmative action, and so on. In addition, both houses of Congress have subcommittees that deal specifically with communications issues and policies. In the past, Congress has investigated the financial structure of the communications industry, tried to determine whether television networks pressured producers not to release films to pay-cable systems, written new copyright laws, passed laws on campaign spending in the media, and considered regulation of television advertising and a federal shield law. In the late

1960s, Congress authorized the Department of Health, Education and Welfare to fund studies of the effects of television, especially televised violence's effects on children.[28] Congress was also responsible for passing both censorship laws, as during World War I, and the Freedom of Information Act of 1966, which has opened the government to greater scrutiny by the media and the general public than ever before. Finally, Congress established and oversees agencies that regulate advertising and broadcasting.

In its regulation of broadcasting, Congress is sometimes accused of meddling with freedom of the press. On occasion, congressional committees call upon network heads, other media executives, and journalists to testify. Some refuse to do so, arguing that having to "report" to the government on their internal operations is an intrusion on freedom of the press. To date, however, Congress has taken no draconian measures to force compliance.

## The Executive Branch

The web of government influence gets more tangled when we consider the executive branch, which includes the White House and a host of other government departments and agencies. Many bureaucrats in federal departments and agencies exercise formal control over information through the government's classification system. Others exercise informal controls over the flow of information to the press and the public. Both federal and state governments are composed mainly of large bureaucracies that manage their own public relations, anxiously trying to maintain a favorable public image. At the federal level, agencies such as the FBI, the Department of Agriculture, and the Pentagon spend millions each year on domestic public relations. In fact, every division of government has its own information officers and staff, and reporters depend heavily on these official spokespersons for information about the daily workings of government. Reporters often have no way of assessing the validity of this information. Much of the news that is reported about the government is, therefore, what public relations people hand out to the press. Thus, through press releases, news conferences, and interviews, the bureaucrats control most of the news that appears about their agency or group. Obviously, this kind of control limits the ability of the press to gain access to factual information that they need to inform the public.

The White House also exercises informal influence on the flow of information. For example, it is a tradition for the president's press secretary to select a limited number of reporters from the pool of the more than two hundred assigned to the White House beat to cover an important political briefing or social event. The remainder of the pool must then obtain information from those selected. Whether the White House regards a member of the pool favorably or not has a significant influence on that reporter's prospects for firsthand access as he or she attempts to provide coverage.

There are a number of roundabout ways for the executive branch to influence the press. Former Vice President Spiro T. Agnew demonstrated one of them in 1969. When the media were debating the war in Vietnam, Agnew claimed (in essence) that the news media were dominated by the liberal eastern elite that did not adequately represent or care about the views of more conservative citizens. He implied that this constituted a "controlled press" and that it was time to "do something about" the situation. Agnew's speech sent shock waves through the media—a "chilling effect"—especially in the television industry, whose licenses are revocable by government. In fact, there is some evidence that the networks changed their policies after Agnew's remarks. For example, in 1971, when a half-million people flooded into Washington, D.C. to protest the war in Vietnam, the network news media gave the event only minimal coverage. A short time later, they gave thorough coverage to Bob Hope's "Honor America Day," which took a conservative view of the war.[29]

The executive branch also has more formal sources of influence on the media. The president appoints members to the two agencies that have power to regulate parts of the media: the Federal Trade Commission and the Federal Communications Commission. More importantly, the White House can propose new legislation to Congress, as well as lobby for or against any proposals that Congress considers. For example, during the early 1980s the Reagan administration, in an effort to tighten security, proposed changes in the federal Freedom of Information Act. It also issued a series of *executive orders*—which do not require the approval of Congress—intended to prevent leaks and curtail other activities by government employees. In one order alone, more than 100,000 former and current government employees were required to submit all articles, speeches, and even letters to the editor of their agencies for prepublication review. Although some commentators defended this practice for "national security" reasons, the American Society of Newspaper Editors called the new policy "peacetime censorship of a scope unparalleled in this country since the adoption of the Bill of Rights in 1791."[30]

Without a doubt, the Reagan administration news and information policies were the least popular with the press of any presidency since the Nixon-Agnew years—partly due to Reagan's infrequent press conferences and general avoidance of the press. In contrast, President George Bush during the early days of his administration seemed eager to court the press. President Bill Clinton's relationships with the press have been mixed. In his first campaign for President he was subjected to considerable sensational coverage involving his sex life. In his first term, Clinton rarely held news conferences, but was still

Although the executive branch cannot control the press, as is the case in countries run by dictators, there are many ways in which a president or other high official can influence journalists and what they report. President Bush used a very friendly style to achieve harmonious relationships with reporters. Some claim that this resulted in a more favorable press and softened criticism. (Reuters/Bettmann)

highly visible in the media as his administration proposed new policies both domestically and in foreign affairs. At the same time, coverage of the Whitewater controversy in Congress brought much negative coverage of the President and First Lady, as did the sexual harassment suit of Paula Corbin Jones. In the 1996 campaign, Clinton most often scored publicity coups over his seemingly hapless Republican challenger Bob Dole. However, almost as soon as the President was reelected, his campaign financing practices were under fire. Clinton is regarded, though, as an effective manager of his image and reputation in the media.[31] By summer 1990, Bush complained when reporters asked him questions about serious matters while he was vacationing in Maine. And by the time of his unsuccessful 1992 reelection campaign, he was openly at war with the media, claiming that it treated him unfairly.

## Regulation and Other Controls

The Federal Communications Commission (FCC) makes and enforces rules and policies that govern all kinds of communication industries, from telephone companies to television networks. The FCC's rulings have the status of law and can be overturned only by the federal courts or by congressional action. Its rules govern advertising, ownership of broadcasting stations, obscenity, and a number of special circumstances. For example, the FCC and the courts legislated a personal attack law, which gives individuals who are attacked by a broadcast station airtime to respond. The FCC also enforces the equal time rule for political candidates, which states: "If a licensee shall permit any person who is a legally qualified candidate for any public office to use a broadcasting station, he shall afford equal opportunities to all other such candidates for that office in the use of such broadcasting station." Based on the equal time rule, the commission later formed the *fairness doctrine*, which grants equal time to people representing issues and causes. Subsequently in the 1980s, the FCC dropped the fairness doctrine ruling, stating that it penalized the media and had outlived its usefulness in an era when abundance replaced scarcity of broadcast signals. Some members of Congress maintained that the fairness doctrine inhibited speech on the part of the media and the public, whereas most disagreed and reinstated the doctrine, only to have it vetoed by then President Reagan. This convoluted series of changes, and other aspects of broadcast regulation, are still being debated by media people, legal scholars, and legislatures.

Much of the FCC's attention is given to interpreting its own rules as it resolves disputes between various interests. In some instances these rules are very specific, as is the equal time rule. However, in other instances they are vague, and the commission frequently wrangles over terms like "the public interest," trying to determine just what it is in each circumstance.

The FCC also handles the issuance and renewal of broadcast licenses granted to radio and television stations. It has the power to revoke licenses, but it rarely does so. In recent years the government has greatly simplified procedures for license renewal and diminished its demands for detailed information from broadcasters. Still, the FCC is charged with seeing whether and how well a broadcast station is serving the public's interest, convenience, and needs. Although broadcasters often complain of the heavy hand of government, the FCC has been remarkably lenient in renewing licenses. In fact, one critic compared the relationship between the FCC and the industry to a wrestling match wherein "the grunts and groans resound through the land, but no permanent injury seems to result."[32]

A case in point is the FCC's handling of obscenity. The Federal Communications Act of 1934 gives the commission the power to revoke the licenses of stations broadcasting obscene or indecent material over the airways. Although there have been numerous instances of stations running pornographic films and comedy routines in the past, the maximum penalty usually imposed by the FCC is a small fine.

The deregulation of broadcasting, discussed in earlier chapters, has altered the role of the FCC in recent years. Although the commission has had a major economic impact, its rules on media content, children's programming, advertising, and even obscenity have relaxed considerably. Still, the very existence of a government agency regulating the entire communications industry is widely viewed as a constraint on broadcasting. Even with much less rigorous rules today, compared to earlier years, many broadcasters still grumble about the FCC, which they regard as a bureaucratic nuisance. However, the notion that broadcasters are obliged to fulfill the public trust by accepting a government license makes them markedly different from the print media. Former Chief Justice Warren Burger as a federal appeals court judge once stated:

> A broadcaster seeks and is granted the free and exclusive use of a limited and valued part of the public domain; when he accepts that franchise it is burdened by enforceable public obligations. A newspaper can be operated by the whim or caprice of its owners; a broadcast station cannot. [33]

## Controls by the Federal Trade Commission

In December 1978, the FTC began a series of hearings to determine whether the growing concentration of ownership in the media influenced the flow of information. Although the hearings generated no definitive answers, media owners denounced the FTC for its potential interference. Those hearings reflect only a small part of the FTC's interest in mass communication and other industries. Like the FCC, the FTC is an independent regulatory agency of the federal government that exists for the purpose of preventing unfair competition. In relation to the media, this task generally translates into the regulation of advertising.

Since its inception in 1914, the FTC has viewed deceptive advertising as unfair competition. Both the FTC and the FCC have brought suits against manufacturers and the media for false claims or misrepresentations. A classic illustration is the Rapid Shave case. Rapid Shave aired a television commercial in which a voice-over claimed that shaving with Rapid Shave was especially easy because it had a "deep wetting" ingredient. A demonstration showed a piece of sandpaper being shaved clean with Rapid Shave. Yet the commercial failed to mention that the sandpaper had been soaked in water for nearly an hour and a half prior to the demonstration. In another version, a Plexiglas surface sprinkled with sand was used in lieu of real sandpaper. The case was in the courts for six years while the commercial continued to be shown. Finally, the Supreme Court banned such trickery.

Another example of deceptive advertising banned by the FTC promoted Profile Bread. Its makers claimed that Profile Bread contained special ingredients helpful for dieters and that each slice had one-third fewer calories. Actually, the manufacturer was simply slicing the bread one-third thinner than a standard slice.

The most famous consumer protection case, however, came not from the FCC or the FTC but from Congress, which banned cigarette advertising from television and required manufacturers to label each package with a warning to users that cigarette smoking could endanger their health.

Although the FTC directs its actions mainly against individual advertisers, it has a strong indirect effect on the mass media, which are the channels for advertising. For example, the FTC clearly influenced the content of all advertising when it ordered Profile Bread to stop implying that its product had special ingredients.

In recent times, the FTC has cracked down on a lengthy list of food distributors that have been using such terms as "lite" and "low fat." New regulations have been issued requiring that the consumer be provided with detailed information about such claims, and about other ingredients, in labels on the products.

The FTC issues warnings before moving to formal orders. Some of these orders have the effect of law, and the commission can and has levied punitive fines on manufacturers, sometimes for hundreds of thousands of dollars.

Decisions by the FTC have defined the scope of deception in advertising, discussed the concept of truth in advertising, and denounced puffery (exaggerated claims). The FTC also legislates rules, holds conferences on trade practices, issues guides for advertising and labeling practices, and hands down advisory opinions for advertisers requesting advance comments about advertisements. In recent years, the FTC has frequently called on communications researchers to help examine issues such as the effects of television commercials aimed at children.

## Deregulation of Communication

Underlying deregulation has been the assumption that competition in the marketplace is the best way to conduct business in America, and that government rules, even if intended to protect the public, are an intrusion. Recently, both the FCC and the FTC have been more lenient in regulating the communication industry. This leniency reflects the general trend toward deregulation of various industries, which we discussed in previous chapters with regard to newspaper and broadcast ownership.

This trend seemed to peak with the election of George Bush, with many supporters of deregulation believing that it had gone as far as it was likely to go, given the transitional enthusiasm in Congress for tighter rules. Compared with the dramatic deregulation experienced by airlines and banks, deregulation in the communication industries, whether in broadcasting or advertising, has been somewhat quiet. One consequence of this relative deregulation has been less scrutiny of advertising content by the FTC.

By the early 1990s, there was again a call for more government regulation of television. In 1991, former FCC chairman Newton Minow declared in a speech that revisited his famous "Vast Wasteland" speech thirty years earlier:

> I reject the view of an FCC chairman in the early 1980s who said that "a television set is merely a toaster with pictures." I reject this ideological view that the marketplace will regulate itself and give us perfection.[34]

Overall, regulation of the media by the FCC and FTC is a complex arena that is constantly evolving. Regulation policies and implementation are shaped by many views and the uneasy relationship between these government agencies and the media will continue to generate debate.

## Outside Pressures on the Media

Political influences and pressures on the media do not exist in isolation or in the narrow confines of a government agency. Private lobbyists and special interest groups attempt to influence the media for their own purposes. Congressional committees sometimes provide them with a forum and allow testimony in favor of or against a piece of legislation affecting broadcasting and the print media. Over the past few years, lobbies and other special interest groups have tried to influence such matters as the amount of violence on television, hiring policies in the media (especially with regard to women and minorities), election coverage before the polls close, the screening of sexually explicit movies in local theaters, and a variety of other issues. These issues change, but one thing is sure: major public concern about the media will often become a political issue, because public concerns shape government legislation and agendas.

The complexity of communication-related issues causes some scholars and critics to ponder whether the United States needs a more coherent communication policy. At present our policy, if there is one, is spread among various governmental branches and the private sector. As new issues arise, it is difficult to know whether they should be resolved by the FCC, Congress, the executive branch, or others. Some even argue that many policy issues are simply resolved by the private sector because the government does not take enough of an interest.

In the late 1980s, the issue of high-definition television (HDTV) emerged, as discussed in Chapter 7. Amid global competition from Japan and Europe, U.S. manufacturers had difficulty in the race to be competitive partly because they lacked an overall policy with which to standardize their products. They sought guidance from the FCC, which outlined a policy that Congress is likely to challenge in the future. Without a communication policy per se, it may be difficult for U.S. communications industries to speak with clarity in their dealings with the rest of the world. This problem is likely to persist, and perhaps there will one day be a council of communications advisers, as media lawyer Stuart Brotman has proposed, or at least a presidential commission to make recommendations about how various technical, legal, and economic disputes can be handled and resolved.

The public can pressure the media in ways besides directly petitioning elected officials or testifying before Congress. For example, dozens of groups united in opposition to ABC's airing of "Amerika" in February 1987, presenting their disapproval in the media itself. The fourteen-and-a-half-hour miniseries portrayed America in 1997 controlled by a United Nations peace-keeping force manipulated by the Russians. Protesters felt the program's intent was to glorify conservative positions and to criticize the Kremlin. ABC did air the program, but only after some advertisers pulled out and boycotts were organized amid much negative publicity.

# CHAPTER REVIEW

▼ Although most Americans approve of a free press and believe we have one, the mass media in the United States operate in a complex web of limitations arising from politics and government.

▼ The First Amendment forbids Congress to make laws restricting the freedom of the press, but that freedom often conflicts with other rights, such as the right to privacy and the right to a fair trial.

▼ Libel laws are intended to protect people from false and damaging statements made about them, and libel suits today can result in awards of millions of dollars.

▼ The courts have sometimes placed restrictions on the press to try to limit publicity that might prejudice juries, but generally efforts in this area have centered on voluntary cooperation from the press.

▼ Obscene material is not clearly under the protection of the First Amendment. Although the courts take action to prevent the publication or broadcast of material deemed obscene, debate continues over what exactly constitutes obscenity and how far it should be controlled.

▼ During wartime, restrictions on the press have ranged from outright government censorship via codes and guidelines to voluntary self-regulation by the media. In peacetime, the federal government may attempt to keep information secret for national security reasons, but the media frequently disagree with the government about this policy.

▼ Reporters claim a right to keep their sources confidential. Some have been willing to go to jail rather than identify their sources when ordered to do so by the courts.

▼ The courts are frequently referees when the right to a free press and other rights conflict. Legislatures and the executive branch also influence the press, both through formal powers and informal influence over the flow of information. Both bureaucrats and politicians through informal influence can introduce bias in what is reported.

▼ The FCC has the power to regulate many aspects of broadcasting but is sometimes less than vigorous in doing so. Groups of private citizens as well as public opinion exert other pressures on the press.

▼ Overall, although the American media are generally free from direct government control or outright censorship, they are greatly influenced by economic and political conditions. As economic conditions, legal interpretations, and political pressures constantly change, so too will the media.

# Ethics

## Assessing the Behavior of the Media

*A*ccuracy, and therefore *credibility,* are very important to journalists. Indeed they are important to most of the communications industry. As our previous chapters have shown, those who present the news, public relations campaigns, advertising, and other media content want the public to believe that they tell the truth and that they transmit their messages within ethical bounds. After all, professional communicators know only too well that if the information, opinion, and even entertainment they present to the public lacks believability, public confidence will quickly erode and they will lose their audience. Communications in a civilized society must be not only competent but also credible to be valuable to people. Thus, ethics is more than an arcane topic debated by religious authorities, do-gooders, and philosophers. It is a deeply practical concern across all of the communications industries. When ethical norms are violated it upsets most professional communicators because it threatens their livelihood.

The issue of ethics affects not only mass communicators but also everyone in public life. In 1997, as a new Congress arrived in Washington and as President Bill Clinton began his second term, concern with ethics was clearly on the public agenda. A House of Representatives ethics committee ruled against Speaker Newt Gingrich for ethical violations in connection with political use of tax-exempt foundations and fined him $300,000. At the same time, the ethics of campaign finance in the Clinton administration were under scrutiny: Gifts from foreign contributors came under fire, as did the use of the White House (including the Lincoln bedroom) by people who gave money to the Clinton reelection campaign.

Concern over ethics is a lively one in American society. It is not uncommon for charges of breaches of ethics to be front-page news, whether the charge involves government, business, or other institutions or individuals in our society. In the 1990s, critics worried about Wall Street greed, government corruption, and hypocrisy in the lives of politicians, televangelists, and other public people.

It seems that no institution or individual is exempt from public concern about ethical breaches. Take the ethics of college presidents, for example. In 1997, after a lengthy investigation of Adelphi University's president and board of trustees, the New York Board of Regents fired the board and appointed a new one, which in turn fired the president, Peter Diamondopoulos, who was accused of lavish spending and greed—as were some members of the board. The Adelphi story began in an unlikely place, the *Chronicle of Higher Education*, which simply noted that the Adelphi president was one of the nation's highest paid college presidents at a time when his university suffered budget cuts and faculty were being dismissed. Earlier, the head of the charity United Way was also driven from office for unethical (and also illegal) breaches.

Of course, scandals and other incidents that are spurred by ethics issues are rarely simple. It is not just a matter of right and wrong, but also discovery of the questionable act and public exposure. Exposure is sometimes the work of "whistleblowers," people inside an organization who make revelations, often at great risk. They might have a noble cause, such as serving the public interest; at other times they are angry and disgruntled employees who want to get back at their bosses. In other instances, ethics violations are made public by political enemies of the people under fire.

It has been suggested that for some reason interest in the moral behavior of people is exceptionally high in the 1990s, especially in the face of such great social problems as AIDS and homelessness. It seems, in fact, that no field is exempt from ethical concerns, as various conferences and seminars have pointed out. Ethical conduct is on the docket in businesses, churches, schools, and other institutions. It is not unusual for a news magazine, like *Time*, *U.S. News & World Report*, or *Newsweek* to cover ethics as a beat and even to feature ethics as a cover story.

Although public preoccupation with ethical issues across so many fields is rare, media ethics have long been a subject of public discussion. Some critics ridicule the idea that competitive and profit-driven media can operate within an ethical framework. Most people disagree, however, and say that no media system can exist very long without public confidence—and that requires accurate, honest, and believable communication. As we have made clear in previous chapters, this does not mean that the media industries are always reliable or that all of them share the same values or ethical standards.

# ▼ What Is Unethical Is Not Always Illegal

Some people wonder why ethical breaches are not illegal and therefore punishable by censure, fines, or prison sentences. The answer is that many questionable practices and apparent deceptions are not necessarily illegal. There are whole categories of criminal acts prohibited by law including murder, robbery, theft, and many others. There are also various civil offenses and torts (or hurtful acts) that are also unlawful because legislation was enacted so defining them and courts (including juries and judges) make determinations in cases involving individuals who are sued by someone claiming damages. A moral code evolves based on social custom, but does not necessarily cross the legal line where blame can be assessed. For example, it may be unpleasant if your neighbor repeatedly shuns you and is rude and inconsiderate. This may hurt your feelings, but in most instances that is your problem and you have no legal course of action to say otherwise. If, on the other hand, your neighbor posts a large sign denouncing you and accusing you of a crime you did not commit, you can sue and, if you win your case, collect damages.

For the media, there are some acts that are clearly illegal, such as breaking into an office to steal papers, claiming to be someone else, engaging in insider trading in the stock market, and other acts that are usually thought unnecessary by courts in gathering the news. Sometimes such instances lead to ethical disputes, too. For example, a few years ago, the *Chicago Sun-Times* bought a bar called "The Mirage" and operated it, to have a window on the conduct of various city inspectors, who received payoffs and committed other criminal acts. The newspaper, in fact, misrepresented itself to gather news.

In another case involving unethical methods (lying on a job application and use of hidden cameras), ABC News' "Primetime Live" program exposed the food-handling practices of the Food Lion grocery chain. But a North Carolina court fined ABC News a whopping $5.5 million in early 1997 when the case was decided. Even though ABC News found unhealthy and improper practices in the food stores, the jury was offended that the reporters misrepresented themselves in getting the story by pretending to be ordinary employees rather than reporters.

About the same time, a news organization in New York City considered buying a race horse to get a window on the role of organized crime in horse racing and even presented the idea to law enforcement officials. The idea was eventually dropped.

Another perplexing case that led to spirited debates about media ethics was that of Richard Jewell, a security guard accused in the 1996 Olympic bombing in Atlanta. Jewell was a suspect fingered by the FBI and other law enforcement officials who also tipped off the press. Although never formally accused of the crime, he was hounded by the media and law enforcement officials and subject to a flood of negative publicity. Eventually, charges against him were dropped and he sorrowfully asked, "How can I recover my reputation?" Constitutional lawyers doubted that Jewell had much of a case against the press, which based their reports on police and FBI tips, but nevertheless most people in various surveys believed that Jewell was wronged. Eventually, NBC News and CNN settled out of court with Jewell. Other litigation involving the *Atlanta Constitution and Journal* was still pending as this is written.

In the Jewell case, wide publicity given to apparently wrong accusations was the issue and whether the press acted too zealously and recklessly in emphasizing the suspicion against the security guard without also balancing such claims against his rights—and consistent denials. The media, according to Lawrence Grossman, a former president of NBC News, has trouble "saying it is sorry for much of anything. Reporters just don't like to admit that they are wrong—even when they are shown to be so after the fact."[1] The Jewell case was

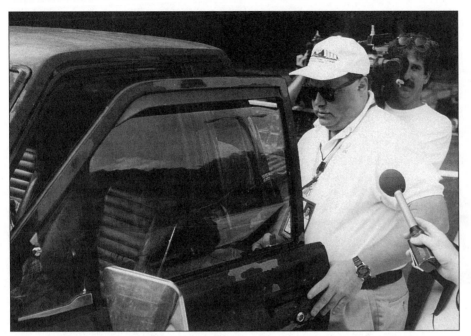

A classic case of ethical violation is that of Richard Jewell, a security guard investigated by the FBI in connection with a bombing during the Olympic Games in Atlanta. Although he was later cleared by the FBI, both newspapers and television networks ran numerous stories emphasizing that he was the chief suspect in the case. His reputation was seriously damaged.

especially illustrative because, initially, Jewell was thought to be a hero whose bravery was trumpeted in news stories and interviews. Then, when he was suspected of the bombing, press coverage emphasized the accusation and "hounded him like an animal," in his words. Jewell and his mother could not leave their Atlanta home without encountering a sea of cameras and microphones and shouting reporters. Whether the Jewell case represented a breach of ethics has been the subject of many seminars, articles, and television debates. No clear answers have emerged.

## ▼ Growing Concern Over Media Ethics

As a general field, ethics is a branch of philosophy that tries to promote good values and good will as opposed to mean-spirited or venal behavior. Some critics feel that the issue of media ethics is too broad and illusive to have much meaning. For example, no unified field of media ethics offers rules or standards that apply to all media fields. What is taboo for a newspaper reporter may be business as usual for an advertising salesperson from the same organization. Ethics, say critics, is simply a matter of personal integrity. This view ties the question of ethics for the media and media organizations to personal standards of forthright, honest, and competent behavior.

▲

In the spring of 1993, many U.S. news-papers ran a wire service story about a $200 haircut given to President Clinton by Beverly Hills stylist Cristophe aboard Air Force One while it sat on the runway at Los Angeles International Airport. An unnamed FAA spokesman was quoted as saying that other planes were forced to circle the airport while waiting and departures were delayed for up to twenty-five minutes. This was not true. Investigative analysts at *Newsday* ob-tained FAA records under the Freedom of Information Act and found that there were no circling planes and no backed-up runways. One plane was delayed—by two minutes. (Reuters/Bettmann)

Others say that ethics is a collective concept, and that corpo-rations, networks, and newspaper publishing chains have a re-sponsibility to see that they are honest and competent. The value of this may seem obvious, but in a society where business is often described as "dog eat dog," the idea that the media industry should be socially responsible and a good corporate citizen to the public might be dismissed as platitudinous. Indeed, some argue that the phrase "media ethics" is an oxymoron—a contradiction in terms. The reason it should not be is that media organizations and their people clearly have a self-interest in being ethical, espe-cially in the sense of being moral and credible.

Ethical behavior in a general sense is not hard to define. It simply means that people should not lie, steal, cheat, or commit other antisocial acts. Ethics is doing what is "right," but the prob-lem is that "right" is defined differently by different people. Thus, the need exists for serious attention to media ethics in a society in-creasingly concerned about the ethics of all occupational groups and professionals, whether they are lawyers, doctors, architects, or journalists. A commitment to basic ethical standards is what binds us together as a society, distinguishing us as socially respon-sible as opposed to self-serving individuals.

All of the media and their supporting systems—including the news, book publishing, movies, cable, newsletters, advertis-ing, public relations, and other enterprises—are governed by general business ethics. Moreover, most of them also have codes of ethics, standards of conduct, and good ethical practices for their employees. Most people who work in the media, ranging from financial writers to videographers, agree to abide by certain standards or rules that embody ethical values. Most, however, in-clude few explicit ethical values beyond those taught generally in the family, churches, or schools.[2]

At one time, some areas of communication were virtually exempt from ethics. For example, people did not apply the same standards of fact and verification to advertising and public rela-tions that they did to newspapers and magazines, arguing that advocates should have license to make the case for their clients to the point of exaggeration. Whether justified or not, people tended to discount a "public relations approach" or self-serving political or ideological appeals. Similarly, religious observers proclaiming their faith were not necessarily expected to be fair and impartial.

Now that is changing, partly because of the blurring and merging of the various functions of the media. For example, it is no longer possible to distin-guish easily between informational news and entertainment, for example. News programs increasingly use entertainment devices, dramatic language, and simulations of probable events, even if they did not occur that way. A good story sometimes carries the day, even if it is not true. Thus, ethics are some-times a casualty in the competitive struggle for a good story.

A recent example of competitiveness pushing aside ethics occurred in 1991. It was widely reported that when President George Bush visited a supermarket he was "utterly amazed" by an electronic scanner he supposedly saw for the first time. The truth of the story was less dramatic. Actually, the President was visiting a mock supermarket counter at a grocers' convention in Florida. Reporters present said that Bush saw the technology demonstrated but did not appear to be impressed. Later, a news story claimed that Bush had "a look of wonder" on his face. This exaggerated interpretation fit into a then-prevalent stereotype of a rich president out of touch with the recession and unfamiliar with supermarket lines most people know only too well. Then, in a paraphrase of Admiral Dewey at Manila Bay, it was "Damn the ethics, full speed ahead (to create a good story)." Given the fact that few presidents have ever done their own shopping, the story stuck that President Bush was amazed at the device, and it is widely believed to this day.[3] This minor ethical transgression may be forgotten, but it illustrates the same principle that was at work when Parson Weems created the story about George Washington and the cherry tree— another fiction that was "clearer than truth."

Sometimes, careless attention to ethics brings confusion as to just what constitutes news. Through the late 1980s, electronic media executives and critics worried about the injection of entertainment values into the news, especially as tabloid TV shows won viewer allegiance. At the same time, a Times Mirror survey indicated that many Americans had trouble distinguishing news and entertainment fare on television. And no wonder, for in the 1992 presidential campaign when Vice President Dan Quayle attacked the fictional TV character Murphy Brown for undermining family values by having a baby out of wedlock, Quayle's criticism quickly became news. When the producers of the series responded to Quayle in a pointed and critical episode, the press covered both the show and the Vice President's response as news. (Quayle spent the evening watching with a group of unwed mothers). One critic called the incident an example of "the entertainment of news."

Similarly, it is difficult to sort out when a particular article or program is news, entertainment, opinion, or even advertising. The blurring of lines between the traditional functions of the media creates an ethical dilemma. Under conventional "rules" there are clear ethical definitions of what news is supposed to be. It is clearly to be separated from opinion. Opinion has great latitude to do and say what it will, though there is typically a standard of "intellectual honesty" applied. Entertainment fare also has wide latitude and may engage in almost any kind of fiction. As these forms merge, the role and function of ethics appears to get lost in the confusion.

Comic artists and editorial cartoonists have often faced the problem of crossing the line between information and entertainment. Comic strips like "Doonesbury" have so enraged some people such as Frank Sinatra that lawsuits have been filed to protest humorous commentary. Such fare has increasingly been subject to libel suits, although ridicule is the basis for even offensive humor.

As new media industries evolve, ranging from business information services to pay-per-view TV fare and home shopping services, the question of what is ethical often arises. In 1992, CNN financial commentator Lou Dobbs was criticized for appearing in a promotional tape for a brokerage house. Some critics believed that Dobbs violated the public trust he had as a financial commentator and newscaster on the cable network. This was the tip of the iceberg about the extent to which reporters should mix their roles. Donna Hanover, a New York television anchor and commentator who is also married to New York Mayor Rudolph Giuliani, appeared in the film *The People vs. Larry Flynt* which was said by some to undermine family values by glorifying Flynt, the controversial publisher of *Hustler* magazine. Other questions about reporters' ethics and independence rose in articles in the *New Yorker* by media critic Ken Auletta and in a celebrated book by author and editor James Fallows. The issue was that of celebrity reporters taking large speaking fees from businesses, trade associations, colleges and universities, and others. To Auletta and Fallows, the practice is clearly wrong and needs public exposure. Others say that as long as the reporter's employer knows, there is no problem. The question, as we will see later in this chapter, has to do with conflicts of interest. Does a reporter breach his or her credibility by taking fees on the side as a celebrity and public speaker while still maintaining a position of independence in covering the news? Some say yes, others say no, not unless there is a clear conflict of interest. An example of this is a reporter speaking for a fee at a trade association meeting and then covering news about that same group later. Some highly compensated reporters who are on the lecture circuit maintain that they never cover the organizations they speak for, but others are not so sure, arguing that many issues these days are commingled and hard to separate out.

Ethical expectations and demands are crossing national boundaries as a result of the international concern about honesty, ethics, and accurate information. For example, although China's political news remains highly suspect, its financial information is now more accurate, for the international market expects and demands it and no market economy can function on unreliable information. This being the case, the issue of ethics is not only here to stay, but will probably play a greater role in all kinds of media—and not only in conventional news media, but also in new media that under earlier standards might not have been held accountable.

To many commentators, media ethics really refers to journalistic ethics, or the moral conduct and behavior of journalists doing their work as news gatherers, editors, and disseminators of information for the larger society. Journalists are expected to produce reliable and believable information gathered under scrupulously honest conditions and checked along the way for accuracy. On occasion, an ethical breach in journalism receives publicity. For example, in 1989, *TV Guide* deliberately printed a misleading photograph of Oprah Winfrey's head on actress Ann Margret's body. Realizing that misrepresentation and deception are almost universally regarded as unethical behavior and that the photo might jeopardize *TV Guide*'s credibility as a serious and respected publication, the magazine later recanted.

In 1994, at the outset of the O.J. Simpson case, *Time* magazine doctored a photo of Simpson by darkening his skin color to make him look more sinister.

The result was a debate over whether this visual alteration was an act of racism, something always unethical, if not illegal. Journalism professor Paul Lester calls this "images that injure," pictorial stereotypes in the media. In a book by the same name, Lester and several contributors decry racial, gender, age, physical, and sexual orientation stereotypes that cause psychological pain, ridicule, or embarrassment to individuals and groups.[4] Often, allegations of racism or sexism are at the root of many ethical dilemmas for the media. Here perception is often deemed more important than the motivation of the communicator. Thoughtlessness is more often a greater culprit than recklessness or deliberate efforts to denigrate others through images: still photos, moving images, cartoons, line drawings, and others. This ethical concern often runs head on into satire and humor, however. Some depictions—visual and verbal—by cartoonists, humorists, and others are meant to be funny or ironic, but still have the potential of offending someone at some time.

Closely connected to this debate is the complex and continuing controversy over what is called "political correctness," an idea that suggests there are appropriate ideas acceptable to most of society. Political correctness suggests that attacks on people for their race, gender, sexual orientation, disability, or other characteristics are out of line. Some argue that carried to the extreme this view thwarts free speech, however hurtful or inappropriate that speech may be. Another view suggests that political correctness carried to an extreme is counterproductive for a free society. Richard Bernstein, a *New York Times* reporter, in his book, *Dictatorship of Virtue*, argues that multiculturalism often insists on adherence to one view "with truth or fairness often falling victim to the demands of ethnic or racial self-esteem."[5]

As the foregoing examples illustrate and as we have shown elsewhere in this book, certain controls influence what the media do and how they do it. These controls include economic, political, and legal factors, but they also include cultural and philosophical forces. Media ethics is one such force.[6] The manner and method the various media of communication use to conduct their business and carry on discourse with the rest of society are often under scrutiny.

Here the media do not stand alone, but are seen in the context of social responsibility in general. Concern with ethics and ethical behavior has focused on business, government, religion, news media, and other institutions. Generally, then, some of the growing concern over media ethics has come from outside critics. However, some has also come from internal sources who want to elevate and advance the work of newspapers, magazines, radio, television and cable, databases, advertising agencies, public relations firms, and other media organizations or support services.

As our discussion has shown, media ethics is not an obscure or irrelevant topic, but one that arises daily as citizens observe the way media institutions relate to their communities as participants, observers, and critics. Ethical dilemmas also arise over the content of the media—whether it is entertainment, news, opinion, or advertising—as well as over the behavior of media people. In a simple sense, ethical choices are between right and wrong, good and bad, matters that are genuinely in the public interest or harmful to the common good.

Complicating the problem of examining and understanding media ethics is the fact that as simple as choices may seem at first, they typically are not. Ethical decisions involve complex human relationships and often pit values cherished by the media against those preferred by other people. The media are concerned with communicating to the rest of society, whether in news stories that emphasize conflict, in opinion journals that feature debates, or on entertainment programs that often promote consensus and reinforce values. Different media obviously have different purposes, yet most want to be considered ethical. Sometimes though, public exposure involves information about a person or organization that has heretofore been protected from outside scrutiny. In such instances a person's right to privacy conflicts with the media's interest in public disclosure. There is often no legal issue here, but there is an ethical issue—a matter of personal choice between doing what is good for society versus what is good for an individual.

# ▼ Special Privileges, Special Responsibilities

Are we being unreasonable when we demand that our press be fair and act ethically? The answer to that question is less clear than many might suppose. By consulting legal authorities, one may learn a good deal about the range and scope of the *rights* of news organizations and the people who work for them. First, there is the general franchise for press freedom laid out in the Bill of Rights, specifically the First Amendment. Then, there are rights set out in state constitutions, statutes, and various court decisions that have been described and celebrated in various books. Far less common is the discussion of the *duties* and *responsibilities* of our protected press and mass media. In fact, in 1947, when the famed Hutchins Commission on Freedom of the Press suggested that the press has such obligations, the press protested strongly and denounced the commission's report.

The Hutchins Commission was a privately financed effort to look carefully at freedom of the press in America, especially in the years immediately following World War II. The commission, made up of philosophers, legal scholars, and other intellectual and cultural leaders, wanted to publicly encourage a system of expression that was responsible to society at large yet free to practice without constraints. It made recommendations for the government, the press, and the public, none of them binding but all intriguing as statements of social criticism and as a plea for ethically sensitive media. Among other things, the commission proposed **press councils** made up of responsible citizens that would monitor the press and provide for feedback to the media and other mass communication agencies. Over the years, the Hutchins Commission's report

Another general concern about media ethics is that accuracy is sometimes sacrificed in the effort to get the story. That is, the media sometimes deliberately engage in fakery. For example, in 1993, NBC News produced a segment that showed a GM pickup truck bursting into flames when struck by another vehicle. It came out later that devices had been placed in the truck in order to start a fire upon impact. This faking of footage for a news report created a considerable controversy. (AP/Wide World Photos)

has gained respect and is now regarded as one of the most important documents in the history of American media. At the same time, it has no official standing.

Under the First Amendment to the Constitution of the United States, there is no requirement that the media be fair, responsible, or accurate. The courts have stated this quite explicitly, yet increasingly there is a higher standard for media performance evident in libel cases and other legal action against the mass and specialized media. It is not uncommon these days for those suing the press to bring expert witnesses into court to testify that a particular story or program did or did not meet "normal professional standards." Although there is no accepted norm for such standards, courts have looked to witnesses for guidance. In fact, some feel that they may write an ethical code for media institutions, perhaps without constitutional authority.

## Beyond the First Amendment

If the mass media derive their legal authority from the First Amendment, they derive their moral authority from holding the public trust. From the beginning, the media have claimed to play two roles: that of the *social conscience* of society or a representative of the people in a nonlegalistic sense, and that of a *profit-making business* that needs to survive to fulfill its first obligation. Newspapers have long cultivated this kind of self-image. In contrast, because of government

Many critics of the press protested the amount of publicity given to veteran newsman Pierre Salinger when he claimed that he had documentary evidence that TWA Flight 800, which exploded over Long Island Sound in 1996, had been brought down by a missile. His claims were seen as bizarre and unfounded by experts, who found no evidence whatever that any missile was involved in the crash. (AP Photo/Patrick Gardin)

regulation, broadcasting and other electronic media have been regarded as less free than the print media and therefore required to serve the public "interest, convenience and necessity" as stated in the Federal Communications Act. However, just where legal requirements end and ethical ones begin is not clear.

Other media institutions, such as advertising and public relations, have also laid claim to moral authority and assert that they pursue ethical ends in their work, although this claim may rest on shaky ground and is often disputed. Media support services like wire services and syndicates have generally been guided by the standards of the news media. Their value is in the quality of the work they produce, whether it is accurate news reports or entertainment matter such as comics, columns, and puzzles. Some media institutions, such as newspapers and newsmagazines, regard themselves as having more elevated ethical standards and concerns than their advertising agencies or political public relations consultants.

## The Long Struggle for Professionalism

Institutional media ethics have evolved considerably since the press of the nation's early years—a time sometimes called the dark ages of American journalism. In Chapter 3 we saw that the early press was often scurrilous, making unwarranted partisan attacks on political figures with little regard for truth or accuracy. Later, a sensational press played on the public's morbid curiosity to stir up the audience and attract readers. The press was known to run hoaxes and engage in deliberate deception. For example, even Benjamin Franklin, sometimes with tongue in cheek, made up interesting characters to illuminate the columns of his newspaper. We mentioned the famous "moon hoax" of 1835, in which the New York Sun claimed that a Scottish astronomer had observed lifelike creatures on the moon through his telescope.

Hoaxes continue to the present day and are sometimes transmitted on the Internet where instant communication is not always checked carefully. In 1996, journalist Pierre Salinger accused federal agents of covering up details of a major airline crash; the accusation was based on an Internet report that later proved to be false.

As the press became more responsible in the late nineteenth century, editors urged a dedication to the public interest and proclaimed statements of noble purpose. Although some of these statements were platitudes that would have been hard to enforce, they did establish the tradition of a public-spirited rather than a self-serving press. Eventually it was generally believed that the newspaper and magazine press had obligations of fairness and impartiality that went far beyond those of typical businesses. Although there was no enforcement clause for such assumptions, they were later supported by codes of ethics and books extolling the idea of a virtuous press crusading to rectify wrongs in a world where corruption and foul play were rampant. Journalism organizations ranging from publishers' and editors' societies to education groups also proclaimed concern for ethics and public accountability.

## ▼ Media Criticism and Media Ethics

If there has been a consistent thread promoting media ethics over the years, it is media *criticism*, which dates back to the nineteenth century. Critics typically charged the press with violating common decency and obscuring the truth. Many American presidents have criticized the press for what they regarded as irresponsible reporting. For example, during the period of muckraking (Chapter 3) magazine journalists just after the turn of the century crusaded to clean up sweatshops and reform corrupt businesses and governments. Soon afterward, the press confronted considerable criticism led by President Theodore Roosevelt, who thought muckraking journalism was far too negative and bad for the nation. Press critics such as Upton Sinclair began to censure the press for its internal inconsistencies and conflicts of interest, and even went so far as to claim that the press itself was corrupt and deliberately poisoning information. Much of this reproach concerned ethics, for rarely was it suggested that the transgressions of the press were illegal.

Journalism schools established in the years before World War I often had professional practice courses that promoted ideal or ethical behavior. The public outcry over ethics also led to a variety of codes and voluntary guidelines for the media. (The *Printer's Ink* statute aimed at deceptive advertising mentioned in Chapter 11 was one set.) The American Society of Newspaper Editors issued the "Canons of Journalism" in 1923. This code was followed by similar ones promulgated by the American Newspaper Publishers Association, the Associated Press Managing Editors, various broadcast organizations and stations including the CBS network, and public relations organizations. Over the fifty-year period from the 1920s to the 1970s, then, the bulk of American media developed ethical codes. Most were strictly voluntary but some were part of the work rules of media organizations. Employees who violate the codes of their organization today may be disciplined or even fired.

# SOCIETY OF PROFESSIONAL JOURNALISTS
# Code of Ethics

## Preamble

Members of the Society of Professional Journalists believe that public enlightenment is the forerunner of justice and the foundation of democracy. The duty of the journalist is to further those ends by seeking truth and providing a fair and comprehensive account of events and issues. Conscientious journalists from all media and specialties strive to serve the public with thoroughness and honesty. Professional integrity is the cornerstone of a journalist's credibility.

Members of the Society share a dedication to ethical behavior and adopt this code to declare the Society's principles and standards of practice.

## Seek Truth and Report It

Journalists should be honest, fair and courageous in gathering, reporting and interpreting information. Journalists should:

▶ Test the accuracy of information from all sources and exercise care to avoid inadvertent error. Deliberate distortion is never permissible.

▶ Diligently seek out subjects of news stories to give them the opportunity to respond to allegations of wrongdoing.

▶ Identify sources whenever feasible. The public is entitled to as much information as possible on sources' reliability.

▶ Always question sources' motives before promising anonymity. Clarify conditions attached to any promise made in exchange for information. Keep promises.

▶ Make certain that headlines, news teases and promotional material, photos, video, audio, graphics, sound bites and quotations do not misrepresent. They should not oversimplify or highlight incidents out of context.

▶ Never distort the content of news photos or video. Image enhancement for technical clarity is always permissible. Label montages and photo illustrations.

▶ Avoid misleading re-enactments or staged news events. If re-enactment is necessary to tell a story, label it.

▶ Avoid undercover or other surreptitious methods of gathering information except when traditional open methods will not yield information vital to the public. Use of such methods should be explained as part of the story.

▶ Never plagiarize.

▶ Tell the story of the diversity and magnitude of the human experience boldly, even when it is unpopular to do so.

▶ Examine their own cultural values and avoid imposing those values on others.

▶ Avoid stereotyping by race, gender, age, religion, ethnicity, geography, sexual orientation, disability, physical appearance or social status.

▶ Support the open exchange of views, even views they find repugnant.

▶ Give voice to the voiceless; official and unofficial sources of information can be equally valid.

- Distinguish between advocacy and news reporting. Analysis and commentary should be labeled and not misrepresent fact or context.
- Distinguish news from advertising and shun hybrids that blur the lines between the two.
- Recognize a special obligation to ensure that the public's business is conducted in the open and that government records are open to inspection.

## Minimize Harm

Ethical journalists treat sources, subjects and colleagues as human beings deserving of respect. Journalists should:

- Show compassion for those who may be affected adversely by news coverage. Use special sensitivity when dealing with children and inexperienced sources or subjects.
- Be sensitive when seeking or using interviews or photographs of those affected by tragedy or grief.
- Recognize that gathering and reporting information may cause harm or discomfort. Pursuit of the news is not a license for arrogance.
- Recognize that private people have a greater right to control information about themselves than do public officials and others who seek power, influence or attention. Only an overriding public need can justify intrusion into anyone's privacy.
- Show good taste. Avoid pandering to lurid curiosity.
- Be cautious about identifying juvenile suspects or victims of sex crimes.
- Be judicious about naming criminal suspects before the formal filing of charges.
- Balance a criminal suspect's fair trial rights with the public's right to be informed.

## Act Independently

Journalists should be free of obligation to any interest other than the public's right to know. Journalists should:

- Avoid conflicts of interest, real or perceived.
- Remain free of associations and activities that may compromise integrity or damage credibility.
- Refuse gifts, favors, fees, free travel and special treatment, and shun secondary employment, political involvement, public office and service in community organizations if they compromise journalistic integrity.
- Disclose unavoidable conflicts.
- Be vigilant and courageous about holding those with power accountable.
- Deny favored treatment to advertisers and special interests and resist their pressure to influence news coverage.
- Be wary of sources offering information for favors or money; avoid bidding for news.

## Be Accountable

Journalists are accountable to their readers, listeners, viewers and each other. Journalists should:

- Clarify and explain news coverage and invite dialogue with the public over journalistic conduct.
- Encourage the public to voice grievances against the news media.
- Admit mistakes and correct them promptly.
- Expose unethical practices of journalists and the news media.
- Abide by the same high standards to which they hold others.

## A Double Standard

Media criticism that centers on institutional, individual, or content-related ethics generally distinguishes between the editorial and business functions of the media. Editorial employees were once expected to avoid conflicts of interest, check their work for accuracy, and act as professionals at all times. Typically, this meant keeping distance from such newsmakers as politicians and not mixing one's personal views with the news. On the other hand, publishers and other business-side personnel faced no such prohibitions. They could seek public office and otherwise participate in community affairs without being considered guilty of conflict of interest or unprofessional behavior.

This situation would later be challenged, largely unsuccessfully, by such scholar-critics as Philip Meyer, who wrote a book titled *Ethical Journalism* that urged an institutional model for media ethics wherein all employees would have the same high standards. To Meyer, it was unthinkable that reporters and editors should be held to one standard for conflict of interest, while advertising managers, publishers, and others were not.[7]

Most of what is written about media ethics has to do with the behavior of media people or the content they produce. On occasion, the owners of the media also come under fire; that was the basis of much of the criticism of media critic George Seldes, who from the 1920s to the 1990s railed against corrupt ownerships. The ethics of a media baron were at issue when a controversy arose over a $5 million book advance offered House Speaker Newt Gingrich by a publishing company owned by Rupert Murdoch, who was lobbying Congress in connection with reform of the Communications Act. Gingrich eventually turned town the advance as criticism mounted. The 1947 Hutchins Commission Report, whose fiftieth anniversary was commemorated at conferences at the University of Illinois and Southern Methodist University in 1997, specifically pointed to the transgressions of owners like Hearst and Gannett. Other critics have critiqued the Congress in its supervision of communication legislation, foundations that try to influence the media, and others outside the behavior-content circle of media people.

At times virtually all media functions are scrutinized for ethical breaches whether this involves a movie that misrepresents or overstates (for example, Oliver Stone's *JFK* and *Nixon* films); a radio talk show host who is accused of lying; a rock video that panders to sexual misbehavior; a novelist who appropriates the work of others; or an Internet hacker who perpetrates a cruel hoax.

Clearly there is talk of ethics in entertainment media, opinion media, and in advertising and public relations. No aspect of the media industries are exempt from ethical considerations, though some seem to take the subject more seriously than others.

## The Link to Individuals and Content

Media ethics is rarely concerned with abstract institutional behavior, but is instead tied to the "blood and guts" of daily decision making and various disputes that later come to the attention of the public. Although journalistic inventions and fakery are not unknown in our history, the public was shocked in 1980 when it learned that *Washington Post* reporter Janet Cooke had faked a gripping story about "little Jimmy," an eight-year-old heroin addict in Washington's African American community. No such person existed. Cooke claimed that it was a "composite." To its considerable embarrassment, the *Post* (which had won a Pulitzer Prize for the story) had to admit the deception. The prize was returned, and the newspaper, to its credit, launched a major internal investigation of the ruse and released its findings to the public.

Later, the now-defunct National News Council, with a grant from the Twentieth Century Fund, produced a book about the "little Jimmy" controversy and its impact on American journalism and journalistic ethics in general. The deception shook the roots of American journalism as people worried about the accuracy of stories in the press and the ethical standards of reporters. Commentators scrutinized the press's institutional responsibility to prevent this kind of behavior in the future, calling for routine personnel procedures and checking of resumes (which had also sometimes been faked.)

The same issue of public deception rose in 1989, when ABC News aired a piece of news footage allegedly showing a U.S. diplomat passing secrets to the Soviets. The grainy and authentic-looking footage was actually staged and featured actors as reporters! The story was based on allegations in news reports, but anchor Peter Jennings later apologized to the American people for the newscast, which was a deliberate deception. By the 1990s, simulations on network news were a thing of the past, although they are still common on other TV shows, especially in tabloid fare such as "America's Most Wanted."

Of course, the fakery of Benjamin Franklin differs greatly from that of ABC News because news standards and social values have changed since the age of the printing press. The press was a primitive instrument in Franklin's day; now it is a large and powerful enterprise that has considerable influence over all of society's information, opinion, and entertainment.

# ▼ *Dimensions of Ethics for the Media*

Typically, media ethics have centered on three major issues: (1) *accuracy* and *fairness* in reporting and other activities; (2) the *behavior of reporters,* especially in relation to their sources; and (3) avoidance of *conflicts of interest.*

## Accuracy and Fairness

It is often said that the first rule of journalism is "accuracy, accuracy, accuracy." Burton Benjamin, a longtime producer at CBS News, got caught up

▶ The issue of television's preoccupation with violence has been debated since the medium first entered American households. Thousands of research studies have suggested that viewing violence can lead some children to behave more aggressively. Whether this is true or not, the majority of Americans believe that violence on television is excessive. In 1993, network proposals to provide warning labels for programs with obscene language, violence, or explicit sex were welcomed by some, but seemed like a half-hearted compromise to many critics. (By Dana Summers; © 1993, Washington Post Writers Group. Reprinted with permission.)

in an accuracy and fair-play conflict in the 1980s, when CBS was accused of deliberately distorting information about the Vietnam War and General William Westmoreland in a news documentary. Criticism from outside circles as well as from media people themselves was so fierce that CBS executives commissioned Benjamin to investigate the charges and deliver a report. He found his network colleagues guilty of violating their own stated (and written) news standards and later wrote a book about the incident titled *Fair Play*.[8]

Reports like Benjamin's (which are rare) and other critiques of media performance, good and bad, constitute a kind of common law of ethics. For almost every ethical dilemma in the press there is a history and context, but unfortunately the press has little "institutional memory" and often ignores the past or reinvents the wheel.

## The Behavior of Reporters

The second area of ethical concern, the behavior of reporters, has to do with an important aspect of professionalism—whether reporters and other media personnel conduct themselves honestly and with integrity, which usually means being honest and aboveboard to *sources* about the purposes of gathering information. For many years, it was thought to be unethical to misrepresent oneself deliberately to obtain information—for example, by claiming to be someone else, such as a lawyer or police officer. Yet, the precise relationship that should exist between journalists and sources has never been fully understood or established. In a 1989 article in The *New Yorker,* Janet Malcolm scored her fellow journalist Joe McGinniss for misleading a famous news source, Dr. Jeffrey MacDonald, who was convicted of murdering his wife and children. As Malcolm wrote:

> Every journalist who is not too stupid or too full of himself to notice what is going on knows that what he does is morally indefensible. He is a kind of confidence man, preying on people's vanity, ignorance, or loneliness, gaining their trust and betraying them without remorse. Like the credulous widow who wakes up one day to find the charming young man and all her savings gone, so the consenting subject of a piece of nonfiction writing learns—when the article or book appears—his hard lesson. Journalists justify their treachery in various ways according to their temperaments. The more pompous talk about freedom of speech and "the public's right to know"; the least talented talk about Art; the seemliest murmur about earning a living.[9]

The cause for Malcolm's criticism was that she felt McGinniss had convinced Dr. MacDonald that he was his friend and would actually do a book that was beneficial for his case. The issue of whether a journalist seeking full cooperation from a news source is prone to deceiving the source was widely discussed at the time. People joined from both sides, some condemning McGinniss and others accusing Malcolm of having committed similar breaches herself in the past. Malcolm's observations led to a lively nationwide debate in the journalistic community wherein the obligations, if any, of reporters to sources were thoroughly discussed. However, there was no clear resolution.

## Conflict of Interest

Conflict of interest is a third area of ethical concern. The term typically refers to engaging in activity that compromises one's integrity in the performance of one's professional or public duties. It is, for example, difficult to be engaged in partisan politics while writing impartially about politics. By the same token, media people have been urged to avoid cronyism, nepotism, and other conflicts that can compromise their integrity or give the appearance of such compromise. A closely related area has been **checkbook journalism,** wherein news organizations pay sources to give interviews. This practice is a violation of journalistic norms, although there are times when media people use it and defend its use. In the case of news people, conflict of interest usually involves a reporter or editor covering a topic in which he or she has a personal stake—a family member may be involved, the reporter may do work on the side for a company being scrutinized, and so forth. This sort of thing is strongly discouraged, even to the point where some reporters are fired for conflict of interest.

# ▼ *Alternative Approaches to Ethics*

Standardized codes of media ethics are difficult to establish because there are few ethical imperatives that work in all situations. Also, most codes of ethics and guidelines are so general that they are not always applicable to specific circumstances. For these reasons and others, a system of *situational ethics* has long been advocated for the media.

## Situational Ethics

In a situation covered by **situational ethics,** each decision is made not with respect to a universal or "one-size-fits-all" code, but within the context of a specific situation. In other words, it is argued, a decision about ethics "depends" on many time- and place-specific situations. Within this perspective, media ethics, like all other ethical considerations, is linked to human choices that involve doing the right thing at the right time. For example, in following up a report on a political candidate's secret sex life, a reporter may invoke "the people's right to know" (about the character of their public servants) as an ethical reason for violating privacy and digging deeply into the individual's private affairs. In the case of a private citizen with similar secrets, however, that standard may not make sense. Publicizing details about such a person's private life may simply be unethical snooping.

## The Continuing Search

The search for alternative answers has been a topic of lively debate among journalists for a long time. One thing is certain: the issue of media ethics remains on the agenda and is often discussed both within and outside the communications industry. Many industry seminars probe ethical issues and dilemmas. Fred W. Friendly has produced a PBS series on ethics with several programs devoted to the media. Journalism schools have taught journalistic ethics intermittently since the 1920s and have established scores of new courses. There are at least ten relatively new texts on the topic. Various study centers and think tanks are working on media ethics issues, and some are single-mindedly devoted to this topic. There is even a *Journal of Media Ethics*, which takes up important issues and seeks resolution.

Most of the efforts to encourage media ethics have been less intellectual and more action-oriented. Earlier we mentioned press councils—small groups of responsible citizens organized at the local, state, and national levels as feedback mechanisms. Although only partially successful, these efforts nonetheless represent models for accountability and ethical pursuit.

In one form or another, various codes of ethics have spread to virtually every part of the communications industry. Once mainly in the purview of journalism, there are now formalized ethical standards in advertising, public relations, opinion polling, market research, sports writing and other areas. The fact that they exist, however, does not mean that they will be followed. These documents are generalized and not usually enforceable, but they still represent a serious concern for ethics.

## Credibility Studies and Market Research

Perhaps the most important efforts to promote media ethics have been **credibility studies,** which probe public attitudes about the news media and dredge up concerns and problems ranging from sensationalism to reporter rudeness. A media credibility movement emerged in the 1980s because it was felt that news organizations in particular were losing ground as believable and trustworthy agencies. This belief probably stemmed from worry that a loss of credibility would both impair the media's moral authority and undermine its economic might. At a time of feverish competition among print and broadcast media for audiences and advertising, there was real reason to deal with matters of credibility and ethics.

Market research (Chapter 3) is also a force that perhaps unwittingly promotes media ethics. Market and audience research provides media organizations and others in the communications industry with certain kinds of feedback about public tastes, preferences, and concerns. Often this feedback centers on matters that have an ethical connection and are therefore appropriate for discussion.

As we suggested, a concern with ethics now stretches across all media fields. Opinion makers—whether talk show hosts, media consultants, advertising executives, or entertainment producers—have standards and codes of conduct. Authors have ethical concerns and so do those who produce and manufacture their work. It is still most common to tie ethics to professional rather than to technical functions, but even that distinction has broken down. Television camera operators must have ethical standards, or the work they direct will be tainted. The same is true with printers, operators of desktop-publishing systems, cartoonists, and others. It is true that the ethics of each of these categories of people may differ, reflecting varied concerns and values but, to be sure, they are all connected in some way with the current media ethics debate.

## ▼ Ethics, Technology, and the Future

New technologies of communication, especially in the last ten years, have raised a variety of ethical questions and controversies. In 1989, following the U.S. invasion of Panama, a split-screen device allowed viewers to see President

Bush's news conference on one part of the screen while featuring the unloading of soldiers' bodies in caskets on the other. The result was an ethical fiasco. The news conference was jocular and amusing, and the smiling president did not know that viewers were at the same time seeing a somber and tragic scene. It was little wonder that the broadcast was much criticized as a thoughtless use of technology. It embarrassed both the President and the media and brought unnecessary grief to those mourning for the fallen soldiers.

Other ethical breaches using technology are linked to privacy, including hidden cameras and microphones and the use of databases to mine personal information about individuals. For example, through distant sensing cameras it is easy to "spy" on news sources. Various audio and video recorders make this even easier.

Satellite communication allows for easy movement over national boundaries and into the midst of world crises and conflicts, which can result in ethical chaos. In December 1992, a circus-like atmosphere occurred when U.S. Marines waded ashore in an amphibious landing at Mogadishu, Somalia, to begin their campaign of moving food to the starving. While the Marines were following their carefully rehearsed procedures for large-scale assault landings, they were met on the beach by one hundred or more journalists with bright TV lights and a forest of microphones that were shoved into the faces of the landing party. The whole event was ridiculed by elements of the press, even though both the journalists and the Marines were carrying on their normal activities.

Because it is now relatively simple to capture news events on video cameras, many people have footage for sale. They range from amateur local "news hounds," who tape news events and try to hawk their footage to TV stations, to more professional freelancers who are nonetheless not under the control of an established news organization. Determining the veracity of this material and the qualifications and proficiency of the person who presents it is not easy.

Various deliberate or inadvertent problems for television have resulted. Just after the nuclear accident at Chernobyl, for example, American networks bought taped reports purportedly showing the crippled Ukrainian plant. Actually, it was a nuclear power plant in Italy. It was alleged in 1989 that CBS anchor Dan Rather had broadcast freelance footage from Afghanistan that was faked and done in another country. Such examples in both print and electronic media abound, and technology enhances the deceiver's ability. Sophisticated computer software makes it possible to create authentic-looking pictures of individuals embracing, although they have never met each other.

These are only a few examples of ethical problems raised by new communications technologies. The speed of these new tools and their reach makes them both liberating and dangerous devices that warrant discussion. Again, they affect virtually all aspects of the media industries and much of society.

As the twentieth century draws to a close, much of the discussion of media ethics is still locked firmly in the matrix of the past. However, it is also clear that much of the debate charts new ground and moves beyond established rules. Considerable thought, therefore, must go into determining (1) what should be codified as a lasting part of institutional and individual rules carried over from the past; (2) what should be left to the imagination of situational decision making in order to maximize freedom of expression; and (3) how ethical considerations need to be reevaluated to take into account the technologies of the future. Whatever those decisions, any system of accountability, no matter how modest, always impinges on freedom of choice. Of course, sometimes that infringement is warranted and even desirable.[10]

An important principle for the future is that voluntary methods of resolving ethical dilemmas are typically preferable to those that eventually end up in the courts. Although many ethical matters are not immediately legal concerns, in our litigious society one might guess that if they are not they soon might be. To date most of the impetus for media ethics has come internally from the media industries themselves and from communications education, but this might not always be the case. It is easy to imagine courts or legislative bodies mandating a system of ethics that would be onerous, especially during a period of unpopularity for the media. In fact, the idea of licensing journalists and giving them a required code of ethics was actually proposed. It was quickly dismissed, however, because of the seeming violation of the First Amendment.

Today, media ethics is something of a cottage industry and the subject of scores of professional seminars held for journalists, broadcasters, public relations people, and others. Many universities now offer courses in media ethics and have a rich literature on which to draw—not only many treatises, books, and articles, but also case studies that point to the dilemmas and decisions that people must make in a modern society, many of them coping directly with ethics.

That cottage industry may be leading to significant changes in media ethics. Communications law scholar Donald Gillmor has written that such changes come in cycles. In the 1920s, there was an ethics movement in the media that waned and later resurfaced. Perhaps with a continually improving system of information storage and retrieval, that will not happen again. Ethical dilemmas abound, and they seem to compel enough human attention both from media professionals and from the consumers of communication that we can likely look forward to a period of development and maturation for this new and still uncharted territory.

# CHAPTER REVIEW

▼ Some critics ridicule the idea that competitive and profit-driven media can operate within an ethical framework. Most people disagree, however, saying that no media system can exist very long without public confidence, which requires accurate, honest, and believable communication.

▼ Ethical behavior in a general sense simply means that people should not lie, steal, cheat, or commit other antisocial acts. Ethics is doing what is "right," but the problem is that "right" is defined differently by different people. Thus, the need exists for serious attention to media ethics in a society increasingly concerned about the ethics of all occupational groups and professionals.

▼ Media ethics is not an obscure or irrelevant topic, but something that arises daily as citizens observe the way media institutions relate to their communities as participants, observers, and critics. Ethical dilemmas also arise over the content of the media—whether it is entertainment, news, opinion, or advertising—as well as over the behavior of media people.

▼ Under the First Amendment to the Constitution of the United States, there is no requirement that the media be fair, responsible, or accurate. The courts have stated this quite explicitly, yet increasingly there is a higher standard of media performance evident in libel cases and other legal action against the mass and specialized media.

▼ Institutional media ethics have evolved considerably since the press of the early years of American journalism. During that time the press was often scurrilous, making unwarranted partisan attacks on political figures with little regard for truth or accuracy. Later, a sensational press played on the public's morbid curiosity to stir up the audience and attract readers.

▼ A consistent thread promoting media ethics over the years has been *media criticism*, which dates back to the nineteenth century. Critics typically charged the press with violating common decency and obscuring the truth. This criticism has kept public attention focused on the need for ethical standards.

▼ Typically, media ethics have centered on three major issues: (1) accuracy and fairness in reporting and other activities; (2) the behavior of reporters, especially in relation to their sources; and (3) avoidance of conflicts of interest.

▼ Standardized codes of media ethics are difficult to establish because there are few ethical imperatives that work in all situations. Also, most codes of ethics and guidelines are so general that they are not always applicable to specific circumstances. For these reasons and others, a system of *situational ethics* has long been advocated for the media.

▼ In one form or another, various codes of ethics have spread to virtually every part of the communications industry. Once mainly in the purview of journalism, there are now formalized ethical standards in advertising, public relations, opinion polling, market research, sports writing, and other areas. The fact that they exist, however, does not mean that they will be followed.

▼ New technologies of communication, especially in the last ten years, have raised a variety of ethical questions and controversies. The speed of these new tools and their reach makes them both liberating and dangerous devices that warrant discussion. They affect virtually all aspects of the media industries and much of society.

▼ An important principle for the future is that voluntary methods of resolving ethical dilemmas are typically preferable to those that eventually end up in the courts. To date most of the impetus for media ethics has come internally from the media industries themselves and from communications education, but this might not always be the case.

# Notes and References

## Chapter 1 Introduction

1. For a discussion of the broad implications of such dependency, see Dallas W. Smyth, *Dependency Road: Communication, Capitalism, Consciousness, and Canada* (Norwood, N.J.: Ablex, 1981). For a discussion of the origins of this basic dependency theory, see Melvin L. DeFleur and Sandra Ball Rokeach, *Theories of Mass Communication,* 4th ed. (New York: Longman, 1982), pp. 297–327.

2. An earlier version of this theory and its implications appeared in Melvin L. DeFleur and Sandra Ball Rokeach, *Theories of Mass Communication,* 4th ed. (New York: Longman, 1984), pp. 240–250. The theory in its form of five basic propositions shown in this chapter was developed by Margaret H. DeFleur and will appear in her forthcoming book, *Introduction to Mass Communication Theory: Explaining Media Processes and Effects.*

3. For an extended discussion of the basic nature of human face-to-face communication, see "Verbal Communication," Chapter 2 in Melvin L. DeFleur, Patricia Kearney, and Timothy G. Plax, *Fundamentals of Human Communication* (Mountain View, Calif.: Mayfield Publishing Company, 1993), pp. 33–62.

4. Phillip Lieberman, "The Evolution of Human Speech: The Fossil Record," Chapter 12 in *The Biology and Evolution of Language* (Cambridge, Mass.: Harvard University Press, 1984), pp. 287–329.

5. The full range of the incredibly flexible human voice comes through especially in opera. Anyone listening to the pronunciation required by Gilbert and Sullivan's *Mikado* or the range of sounds produced by Luciano Pavarotti singing the major role in *I Pagliacci* can appreciate how different our voice box, larynx, tongue, and lip structures are from those of the greater apes, who can make only a limited range of sounds.

6. For a more detailed explanation of these and other changes in human communication, see Melvin L. DeFleur and Sandra Ball Rokeach, "A Theory of Transitions," Chapter 1 in *Theories of Mass Communication,* 5th ed. (White Plains, N.Y.: Longman, 1989), pp. 7–26.

7. For a discussion of a simultaneous transactional model of human communication, see Melvin L. DeFleur, Patricia Kearney, and Timothy G. Plax, *Fundamentals,* pp. 21–25.

8. A frequently cited analysis of the "mass" concept can be found in Herbert Blumer, "Collective Behavior," in *Principles of Sociology,* ed. Alfred M. Lee (New York: Barnes and Noble, 1953), pp. 208–210.

9. See David Reisman, *The Lonely Crowd: A Study of the Changing American Character* (New Haven, Conn.: Yale University Press, 1950).

10. Marshall McLuhan and Fred McLuhan, *Law of the Media* (Toronto: University of Toronto Press, 1989).

## Chapter 2 Books

1. Miguel Angel Garcia Guinea, *Altamira and Other Cantabrian Caves* (Madrid: Silex, 1979), p. 4.

2. The sections on writing, the alphabet, early books, and the invention of printing are based on the following sources: Albertine Gaur, *A History of Writing* (London: Scribner's, 1984); Joseph Naveh, *Early History of the Alphabet* (Jerusalem: Magnes, 1982); Donald Jackson, *The Story of Writing* (New York: Taplinger, 1981); and Douglas McMurtrie, *The Book: A History of Printing and Book-Making* (New York: Oxford University Press, 1943).

3. Hendrik D. L. Vervliet, ed., *Through Five Thousand Years* (London: Phaidon, 1972), p. 18.

4. The Egyptians, who were very powerful during the same period, worked out a similar idea. However, they did not want to give up the beautiful pictograms that made up their earlier hieroglyphics, so they tried to mix an ideographic system with phonograms. It was not an effective solution. Furthermore, a serious shortcoming of their system was that they had no symbols to represent vowels. For example, the Egyptians would write (the equivalent of) the word *foot* as *ft,* or *beetle* as *btl.* Occasionally, we do this today with such words as *boulevard* and other "contractions." Unfortunately for the Egyptians, the pronunciation of missing sounds was lost over the centuries and their language died out.

5. McMurtrie, *The Book,* pp. 76–77.

6. Francis Falconer Madan, *Books in Manuscript: A Short Introduction to Their Study and Use,* 2nd ed. (Oxford: Oxford University Press, 1920).

7. Robert Hamilton Clapper, *Paper, An Historical Account of Its Making by Hand from the Earliest Times Down to the Present Day* (Oxford: Oxford University Press, 1934).

8. James Moran, *Printing Presses: History and Development from the Fifteenth Century to Modern Times* (Berkeley and Los Angeles: University of California Press, 1973), p. 17.

9. Moran, *Printing Presses,* p. 18.

10. David Stebenne, Seth Rachlin, and Martha Fitz-Simon, *Coverage of the Media in College Textbooks* (New York: Freedom Forum Media Studies Center, 1992).

11. The actual number will forever remain elusive. But it was clearly a great communication revolution, rivaling that which has occurred in the twentieth century. For a detailed analysis of the implications of that revolution, see Elizabeth Eisenstein, *The Printing Press as an Agent of Change,* vols. 1 and 2 (Cambridge: Cambridge University Press, 1979).

12. Frederick Seibert, *Freedom of the Press in England, 1476–1622* (Urbana: University of Illinois Press, 1952), Chapters 1–3.

13. See John E. Ponfret, *Founding the American Colonies: 1583–1660* (New York: Harper and Row, 1970).

14. John Tebbel, *The Media in America* (New York: Crowell, 1974).

15. Veronis, Suhler & Associates, *Communications Industry Forecasts* (annual). See also "Books by the Number" (compiled by Charles Barber), *Media Studies Journal* (New York: Freedom Forum Media Studies Center, Summer 1992), p. 15.

16. Charles A. Madison, *Book Publishing in America* (New York: McGraw-Hill, 1966), p. 402. See also Benjamin A. Campaigne, *The Book Industry in Transition* (White Plains, N.Y.: Knowledge Industry, 1978).

17. There is a considerable lag in the process of gathering and reporting such figures because publishers are often reluctant to disclose current sales trends. Therefore, completely current unit and dollar sales are not always available. The figures for trade and college text publishing in this chapter were obtained from the 1989 *Communications Industry Forecast,* an annual industry information publication by Veronis, Suhler & Associates.

18. Dan Lacy, "The Economics of Publishing, or Adam Smith and Literature," in *The American Reading Public* (New York: Bowker, 1965), based on an issue of *Daedalus.*

19. Lacy, "Economics of Publishing."

20. See *Books in Print* (New York: R. R. Bowker, Inc., 1991).

21. Everette E. Dennis, Craig Lamay, and Edward C. Pease, eds., *Publishing Books* (New Brunswick, N.J.: Transaction, 1997), p. xiv.

22. See "8 Publishers Charge Copyright Violation, Sue Copying Chain," *Chronicle of Higher Education,* May 3, 1989, p. A1.

23. David Berreby, "The Growing Battle of the Big Bookstores," *New York Times,* Business Section, November 8, 1992, p. F5.

### Chapter 3 Newspapers

1. C. A. Giffard, "Ancient Rome's Daily Gazette," *Journalism History* 2 (Winter 1975–76), pp. 107–108.

2. Edwin Emery, *The Press in America,* 5th ed. (Englewood Cliffs, N.J.: Prentice-Hall, 1972), p. 3.

3. Marvin Rosenberg, "The Rise of England's First Daily Newspaper," *Journalism Quarterly* 30 (Winter 1953), pp. 3–14.

4. Emery, *The Press in America,* p. 31.

5. For an especially insightful history of the newspaper and other media, see: Hilary H. Ward, *Mainstreams of American Media History* (Boston: Allyn and Bacon, 1997).

6. For an excellent discussion of the development of early press technology, see John W. Moore, *Historical Notes on Printers and Printing, 1420–1886* (1886; reprint, New York: Burt Franklin, 1968).

7. An excellent selection of Brady's photographs is reproduced in Phillip B. Kunhart, Jr., *Mathew Brady and His World* (New York: Time-Life, 1977).

8. For a thorough analysis of patterns in the adoption of innovation, see Everett M. Rogers and F. Floyd Shoemaker, *Communication of Innovations: A Cross-Cultural Approach* (New York: The Free Press, 1971).

9. For an explanation of the origins of the theory of the adoption of innovation and its current status, see Everett Rogers, *Diffusion of Innovations,* 3rd ed. (New York: Free Press, 1983). The five basic propositions of the theory as listed in this chapter will appear in Margaret H. DeFleur, *Introduction to Mass Communication Theory: Explaining Media Processes and Effects* (forthcoming).

10. See U. S. Bureau of the Census, *Statistical Abstract of the United States* (U.S. Government Printing Office: Washington, D.C., 1991–1996).

11. For an account of the history of wire services, see Victor Rosewater, *History of Co-Operative News-Gathering in the United States* (New York: Appleton-Century-Crofts, 1930).

12. A thorough history of the development of auxiliaries can be found in Richard A. Schwartzlose, *The Nation's Newsbrokers,* 2 vols. (Chicago: Northwestern University Press, 1989).

13. At present writing the financial status of UPI is uncertain at best. By mid-1992 it seemed that it

would go bankrupt if current trends persisted and if no buyer could be found for the service.

14. Michael W. Singletary, "Newspaper Use of Supplemental Services," *Journalism Quarterly* 52 (Winter 1975), pp. 750–751.

15. Milt Rockmore, "Do Syndicates Exert Undue Influence?" *Editor and Publisher*, February 3, 1990, p. 18.

16. David Astor, "A Features Controversy Erupts in Dallas," *Editor and Publisher*, August 12, 1989, pp. 42–43. See also "A High-Priced Feature Switch in Dallas," *Editor and Publisher*, September 23, 1988, p. 43.

17. This situation has prevailed for decades. For example, see Arnold H. Ismach, "The Economic Connection: Mass Media Profits, Ownership and Performance," in *Enduring Issues in Mass Communication*, ed. E. E. Dennis, D. M. Gilmore, and A. Ismach (St. Paul: West, 1978), pp. 143–259. For a more recent discussion that comes to the same basic conclusions, see Robert Picard, *Media Economics* (Newbury Park, Calif.: Sage Publications, 1990).

18. John C. Busterna, "Trends in Daily Newspaper Ownership," *Journalism Quarterly* 65 (Winter 1988), pp. 831–38.

19. The sources for these various figures on trends in ownership are Lynch, Jones and Ryan, Inc. and John Morton Research, Inc.

20. Richard McCord, *The Chain Gang: One Newspaper versus the Gannett Empire* (Columbia, Mo.: The University of Missouri Press, 1996).

21. William H. Henry III, "Learning to Love the Chains," *Washington Journalism Review* (September 1986), pp. 15–17.

22. Brent Baker, "Changing Technologies: New Challenges and New Opportunities in a Digital World," Chapter 17 in William David Sloan, Shirley Staples Carter, William J. Gozenbach, and Glen Stovall, *Mass Communication in the Information Age* (Northport, Ala.: Vision Press, 1996), pp. 387–422.

23. Margaret H. DeFleur, *Computer-Assisted Investigative Reporting: Its Development and Methodology* (Mahwah, N.J.: Lawrence Earlbaum Associates, 1997).

24. Antonio N. Fins, "Alien Beancounters Invade the *Enquirer*," *Business Week*, September 11, 1989, p. 35.

25. Robert E. Park, "The Natural History of the Newspaper," *American Sociological Review* 29 (1923), pp. 273–289.

26. Ernest H. Hynds, *American Newspapers in the 1980's* (New York: Hastings House, 1980), p.11.

27. Guido H. Stempel III, "Where People *Really* Get Most of Their News," *Newspaper Research Journal* 12 (Fall 1991), pp. 2–9.

28. Deborah Merskin and Mara Huberlie, "Companionship in the Classifieds: The Adoption of Personal Advertisements by Daily Newspapers," *Journalism and Mass Communication Quarterly* 73 (1996), pp. 219–229.

29. David H. Weaver and G. Cleveland Wilhoit, *The American Journalist in the 1990s: U.S. News People at the End of an Era* (Mahwah, N.J.: Lawrence Erlbaum Associates, 1996), p. 2.

30. Andrew Hearst, "Old Journalism, New Technology," *E-News* (on-line) http://www.enews.com/need/archive/1030.html, October 30, 1996.

31. Andrew Hearst, "Future Gazing," *E-News* (on-line) http://www.enews.com/need/archive/1003.html, October 3, 1996.

32. Andrew Hearst, "The Web's Election Night Coverage: Pointless?" *E-News* (on-line) http://www.enews.com/need/internet.html, November 7, 1996.

## Chapter 4 Magazines

1. Many of the details in this section concerning the first magazines were drawn from James P. Wood, *Magazines in the United States* (New York: Ronald, 1949), pp. 3–9.

2. Wood, *Magazines in the United States*, p. 10.

3. The details of these early American attempts to produce magazines are drawn from Frank Luther Mott, *A History of American Magazines, 1741–1850* (Cambridge, Mass.: Harvard University Press, 1930), vol. 1, pp. 13–72.

4. Melvin L. DeFleur, William V. D'Antonio, and Lois DeFleur, *Sociology* (Glenview, Ill.: Scott, Foresman, 1972), p. 279.

5. Frank Luther Mott, *A History of American Magazines*, vols. 3 and 4 (Cambridge, Mass.: The Belknap Press of Harvard University Press, 1957).

6. Paul S. Boyer, *Purity in Print: The Vice Society Movement and Book Censorship in America* (New York: Scribner's, 1968).

7. Theodore Peterson, *Magazines in the Twentieth Century* (Urbana: University of Illinois Press, 1964).

8. These various figures were painstakingly assembled from historical accounts and various early government documents by Mott in his five-volume

*History of American Magazines.* As he notes, many are approximations. The present section is a compilation of figures from several of his volumes.

9. Mott, *History of American Magazines,* vol. 4, p. 10.

10. Wood, *Magazines in the United States,* p. 131.

11. Fleming Meeks, "God Is Not Providing," *Forbes,* October 30, 1989, pp. 151–158.

12. *Prison Life* is aimed at the one million folks in the United States who call state and federal prisons home. Regular columns include "In-Cell Cooking" and "Ask the Law Professor." Advertising focuses on such products as body-building supplements. See *Newsweek,* October 26, 1992.

13. Theodore Peterson, *Magazines in the Twentieth Century,* 2nd ed. (Urbana: University of Illinois Press, 1964), p. 442.

14. Philip Dougherty, "Saturday Review's New Drive," *New York Times,* April 2, 1979.

15. Hendrick Hertzberg, "Journals of Opinion, An Historical Sketch," *Gannett Center Journal* (Spring 1989), p. 61.

16. Charles P. Daly, Patrick Henry, and Ellen Ryder, *The Magazine Publishing Industry* (Boston: Allyn and Bacon, 1997), p. xii.

**Chapter 5 Film**

1. Martin Quigley, Jr., *Magic Shadows: The Story of the Origin of Motion Pictures* (Washington, D.C.: Georgetown University Press, 1948), pp. 9–10.

2. Josef M. Eder, *History of Photography* (New York: Columbia University Press, 1948), pp. 209–45, 263–64, 316–21.

3. There were several claimants to the invention of celluloid roll film in the late 1880s. Eventually the courts decided a case on the matter in favor of the Reverend Hannibal Goodwin. However, George Eastman produced the film in his factory and marketed it to the public. See Frederick A. Talbot, *Moving Pictures: How They Are Made and Work* (London: Heinemann, 1923).

4. Talbot, *Moving Pictures,* p. 2.

5. Tino Balio, ed., *The American Film Industry* (Madison: University of Wisconsin Press, 1976), p. 63.

6. In 1988, the work of Theodore Case of Auburn, New York came to light. Very early sound films (1923) were discovered in a coal bin in his home, along with documents and equipment. It now appears that Case, rather than Lee DeForest, may have first developed the critical elements in the sound movie. At this point, however, it remains an open question.

7. Richard Schickel, "The Crisis in Movie Narrative," in the *Gannett Center Journal* (New York: Gannett Center for Media Studies, Summer 1989), pp. 17–28.

8. Robert Stanley, *The Celluloid Empire: A History of the American Motion Picture Industry* (New York: Hastings House, 1978).

9. Ephraim Katz, *The Film Encyclopedia* (New York: Putnam, 1996). Also see Robert Brent Toplin, *History by Hollywood, The Use and Abuse of the American Past* (Urbana: University of Illinois Press, 1997).

10. Edgar Dale, *The Content of Motion Pictures* (New York: Macmillan, 1935).

11. Dale, *The Contents of Motion Pictures,* p. 208. See also an excellent summary history of the major studios, in Cobbett Feinberg, *Reel Facts: The Movie Book of Records* (New York: Vintage, 1978), pp. 376–389.

12. Motion Picture Association of America, 1996.

13. James Monaco, *How to Read a Film,* rev. ed. (New York: Oxford University Press, 1977), p. 246.

14. Feinberg, *Reel Facts,* p. xiii.

15. For an excellent abbreviated analysis of the movies, see Garth Jowett and James M. Linton, *Movies as Mass Communication* (Beverly Hills, Calif.: Sage, 1990).

16. See Thomas Guback, "Theatrical Film," in *Who Owns the Media?* Benjamin M. Compaign, ed. (White Plains, N.Y.: Knowledge Industry, 1982), pp. 199–286. See also *Variety,* January 1 and January 8, 1986.

17. John L. Fell, *An Introduction to Film* (New York: Praeger, 1975), p. 127.

18. These estimates were obtained by one of the authors in an interview with the National Association of Theater Owners, 1992. We wish to thank the organization for its assistance.

19. These data were obtained from the National Association of Theater Owners in 1991.

20. All data here come from the Motion Picture Association of America, Inc., "Incidence of Motion Picture Attendance, July 1986," a study conducted by Opinion Research Corporation, Princeton, N.J.

21. See Christopher Sterling, ed., *The Mass Media: Aspen Guide to Industry Trends* (New York: Praeger, 1978), pp. 184–185.

22. The creeping cycle of desensitization theory was developed by Margaret H. DeFleur and will be included in her forthcoming book, *Introduction to Mass Communication Theory: Explaining Processes and Effects.* It is included here with her permission.

23. Andrew Sarris, "The Night They Left Garbo Alone," *Village Voice,* December 12, 1977, p. 51.

## Chapter 6  Radio

1. John Baptista Porta (or Giovanni Battista della Porta), *Natural Magik* (New York: Smithsonian Institute for Basic Books, 1957). This is a modern reprint of a book first printed in the late 1500s, just after the invention of the press.
2. The details of the history of radio presented in these sections are a summary of several chapters devoted to a more extended treatment of the subject in Melvin L. DeFleur, *Theories of Mass Communication,* 1st ed. (New York: McKay, 1966), pp. 44–69.
3. Gleason L. Archer, *History of Radio to 1926* (New York: American Historical Society, 1938), pp. 112–113.
4. For an excellent discussion of these early developments (from which the authors have drawn many insights), see Sydney W. Head and Christopher H. Sterling, *Broadcasting in America,* 5th ed. (Boston: Houghton Mifflin, 1987), pp. 62–65, 435–99.
5. For the most thorough and contemporary discussion currently available of the entire broadcasting industry and the details of its development, see Head and Sterling, *Broadcasting in America.* The present chapter incorporates many insights from this classic work.
6. Alfred G. Goldsmith and Austin C. Lescarboura, *This Thing Called Broadcasting* (New York: Holt, 1930), p. 279.
7. *U.S. Industry Outlook for Advertising.*
8. Provided by the Federal Communications Commission, Washington, D.C., this number is for December 31, 1992.
9. Radio Advertising Bureau, 1992.
10. *Five-Year Communications Industry Forecast, 1988–1992* (New York: Veronis, Suhler & Associates, July 1988).
11. This account is based on a report in the *Boston Globe* by David Arnold, "Racy Radio Jolts Parents," November 12, 1996, pp. A1 and A12.
12. Leon Panetta, Keynote speech, "Is American Journalism in Crisis?" conference, National Press Club, Washington, D.C., February 20, 1997; and in response to a question from one of the authors.
13. Andrew Kohut and Carol Bowman, "The Vocal Minority in U.S. Politics," in Edward C. Pease and Everette E. Dennis, *Radio, The Forgotten Medium* (New Brunswick, N.J.: Rutgers University Press, 1995), pp. 45–57.
14. The lyrics are from "Stroke You Up," by Changing Faces, Big Beat Records, Inc.
15. See "Triumph of the Idol—Rush Limbaugh and a Hot Medium," and "Talking over America's Electronic Backyard Fence," both in Pease and Dennis, *Radio,* pp. 59, 69. Also see Neal Gabler, *Winchell, Power Gossip and the Culture of Celebrity* (New York: Knopf, 1994).

## Chapter 7  Television

1. See "The Development of the Television Industry," Melvin L. DeFleur and Sandra Ball Rokeach, *Theories of Mass Communication,* 5th ed. (White Plains, N.Y.: Longman, 1989), pp. 110–122.
2. Randall Rothenberg, "Change in Consumer Markets Hurting Advertising Industry," *New York Times,* October 3, 1989, pp. A-1, D-23.
3. For a thorough history of television up to the mid-1970s, see Eric Barnouw, *Tube of Plenty: The Evolution of American Television* (New York: Oxford University Press, 1975).
4. "Trends in Television," A Research Trend Report of the Television Advertising Bureau, 477 Madison Avenue, New York, N.Y. 10022, April 1989.
5. Nielsen Media Research, Inc., 1996.
6. Ray E. Hiebert, Donald F. Ungurait, and Thomas W. Bohn, *Mass Media IV* (New York: Longman, 1985), pp. 419–425.
7. *Newsweek,* July 10, 1970, p. 42.

## Chapter 8  The New Media

1. Everette E. Dennis and John V. Pavlik, "The Coming of Convergence and Its Consequences," in Pavlik and Dennis, *Demystifying Media Technology* (Mountain View, Calif.: Mayfield, 1993), p. 14; also see Pavlik, *New Media Technology, Cultural and Commercial Perspectives* (Needham Heights, Mass.: Allyn and Bacon, 1996) and Dan Lacy, *From Grunts to Gigabytes, Communications and Society* (Urbana: University of Illinois Press, 1996).
2. Nicholas Negroponte, *Being Digital* (New York: Alfred A. Knopf, 1995), passim. Another useful book with elegant essays about cyberspace is Derrick De Kerckhove, *The Skin of Culture, Investigating the New Electronic Reality* (Toronto: Somerville House, 1995).
3. Martin Irvine, *Web Works* (New York: W.W. Norton, 1997), pp. 1–6.

4. Bruce L. Egan, *Information Superhighway Revisited, The Economics of Multimedia* (Boston, Mass.: Artech, 1996), pp. 40–46.

5. Wilson Dizard, Jr., *Old Media New Media, Mass Communications in the Information Age,* 2nd ed. (New York: Longman, 1997), p. 5.

6. Alfred C. Sikes in Roger Fidler, *Mediamorphosis, Understanding New Media* (Thousand Oaks, Calif.: Pine Forge Press, 1997), p. xiii.

7. Egan, *Information Superhighway Revisited,* pp. 43–44.

8. Fidler, *Mediamorphosis,* pp. 31–44.

9. Bill Gates, *The Road Ahead* (New York: Viking, 1995), pp. 225–27.

10. E. M. Forster, "The Machine Stops," *The Eternal Moment and Other Stories* (New York: Harcourt, Brace, 1928).

11. Forster, "The Machine Stops," p. 78.

12. Fidler, *Mediamorphosis.*

13. "Paul Saffo and the 30-Year Rule," *Design World* 24 (1992), p. 18; John Carey, "Looking Back into the Future: How Communication Technologies Enter American Households," in Pavlik and Dennis, *Demystifying Media Technology,* pp. 32–39; Margaret H. DeFleur, "The Development and Adoption of Computers in American Society," forthcoming; and E. E. Dennis, *Of Media and People* (Newbury Park, Calif.: 1992), pp. 113–18 for a discussion of convergence and communication education, and John Carey quotations.

14. Lawrence K. Grossman, *The Electronic Republic.*

15. Richard Saul Wurman, *Information Anxiety* (New York, Doubleday, 1989).

16. David Shenk, *Data Smog, Surviving in the Information Glut* (New York: HarperEdge, 1997).

17. Jodi B. Cohen, "Web Audits: A Complex Art," *Editor and Publisher,* February 8, 1997, p. 24I–26I.

18. A. Michael Noll, *Highway of Dreams—A Critical View Along the Information Superhighway* (Mahwah, N.J.: Lawrence Ehrlbaum Associates, 1997), p. 17.

19. Randall Rothenberg, "Strangers in a Strange Land," *Esquire,* June 1996, pp. 58–61.

20. Michael Dertouzos, "El Mercado de la Informacion," in E. Dennis, M. Dertouzos, B. Nosty, R. Nozick, and A. Smith, *La Sociedad de la Información, Amenazas y Opportunidades* (Madrid: Editorial Complutense, 1996), pp. 31–43.

21. Lawrence K. Grossman, *The Electronic Republic, Reshaping Democracy in the Information Age* (New York: Viking, 1995).

## Chapter 9 News

1. The *Iliad* describes how Paris, the son of King Menelaus of Sparta, brought his father's wife Helen—"the face that launched a thousand ships"—back to Troy with him. To get her back, a coalition of Greek cities sent an expedition (the thousand ships) under Agamemnon (brother of Menelaus) to lay siege to Troy. Finally, the Greeks used a clever strategy, hiding soldiers inside a large wooden horse offered as a gift to the Trojans. As the Greeks sailed away, the Trojans took the horse inside the city. Late at night the Greeks came out and opened the gates of the city for their forces, who had returned. From this episode we get the saying, "Beware of Greeks bearing gifts."

2. For the original statement of the two-step flow theory, see Paul F. Lazarsfeld, Bernard Berelson, and Hazel Gaudet, *The People's Choice* (New York: Columbia University Press, 1948). The two-step flow theory in the propositional form given here was developed by Margaret H. DeFleur and will appear in her book *Introduction to Mass Communication Theory: Explaining Media Processes and Effects* (forthcoming). It is used here with her permission.

3. These classifications are based on a similar discussion in Gaye Tuchman, *Making News: A Study in the Construction of Reality* (New York: Free Press, 1978), pp. 23–31.

4. The significance of this distinction between locals and cosmopolitans, and their roles in the formation of media-related opinion in a community, can be found in the classic study by Robert K. Merton, "Types of Influentials: The Local and the Cosmopolitan," in his *Social Theory and Social Structure* (Glencoe, Ill.: Free Press, 1949), pp. 387–420.

5. Commission on Freedom of the Press, *A Free and Responsible Press* (Chicago: University of Chicago Press, 1947).

6. Hanna Fenichel Pitkin, *The Concept of Representation* (Berkeley: University of California Press, 1972). See also Hanna Pitkin, *Representation* (New York: Atherton Press, 1969); Everette E. Dennis, "Rhetoric and the Reality of Representation," in Bernard Rubin, ed., *Small Voices and Great Trumpets* (New York: Prager, 1980), pp. 67–88; and Everette E. Dennis and John Merrill, *Media Debates: Issues in Mass Communication* (New York: Longman, 1991).

7. William Blackstone, *Commentaries on the Laws of England, of Public Wrongs*, vol. 4 (Boston: Beacon Press, 1962), p. 161.

8. *Saxbe v. Washington Post Co.*, 417 U.S. 843, 864 (1974), Justice Powell dissenting.

9. Walter Lippmann, *Public Opinion* (New York: Harcourt, Brace, 1922), pp. 354 and 358.

10. Walter Lippman, *Public Opinion* (New York: Macmillan, 1922). The gatekeeping theory in the propositional form shown here was developed by Margaret H. DeFleur and will appear in her book *Introduction to Mass Communication Theory: Explaining Media Processes and Effects* (forthcoming). It is used here with her permission.

11. Alan Barth, quoted in Herbert Brucker, "What's Wrong with Objectivity," *Saturday Review*, October 11, 1969, p. 77.

12. For various views on civic journalism, see the following: Carl Sessions Stepp, "Public Journalism: Balancing the Scales," *American Journalism Review* (May 1996), pp. 38–40; Davis Merritt, *Public Journalism and Public Life: Why Telling the News Is Not Enough* (Mahwah, N.J.: Lawrence Erlbaum Associates, 1995); Jay Rosen, *Getting the Connections Right: Public Journalism and the Troubles in the Press* (New York: Twentieth Century Fund, 1996); "The New Communitarianism and Public Journalism," in Everette Dennis and John C. Merrill, *Media Debates*, 2nd ed. (White Plains, N.Y.: Longman, 1996), pp. 156–65; Everette Dennis, "Questions about Public Journalism," *Editor and Publisher*, July 29, 1995, pp. 48.

13. Although the basic concept of "gatekeeper" originated in social psychology as a means of describing decision processes, the use of the term as an important part of the news process stems from an early study by David White of "Mr. Gates," a wire editor who had the task of selecting stories from the associated press to include in a local newspaper. See David Manning White, "The Gatekeeper: A Case Study in the Selection of News," *Journalism Quarterly* (Fall 1950), pp. 383–390. Later studies are Phillip Moffat, "The Editorial Process," *Esquire*, April 1980; Murray Schumach, *The Face on the Cutting Room Floor* (New York: Morrow, 1964) pp. 142–43; Stephan Zito, "Inside Sixty Minutes," *American Film 2* (December-January 1977), pp. 31–36, 55–57.

14. Kurt Lewin, "Channels of Group Life," *Human Relations*, vol. 1, no. 2, p. 145. See also David Man-

ning White, "The 'Gatekeeper': A Case Study in the Selection of News," *Journalism Quarterly*, vol. 27 (1950), pp. 383–390. The gatekeeping theory in propositional form was developed by Margaret DeFleur and will appear in *Introduction to Mass Communication Theory: Explaining Media Processes and Effects* (forthcoming). It is used here with her permission.

15. Philip Meyer, "In Defense of the Marketing Approach," *Columbia Journalism Review* (January-February 1978), pp. 60–62. See also Everette E. Dennis, "Can Ethics Survive Business-Editorial Harmony?" in *Readings in Mass Communication*, 6th ed., ed. M. Emory and T. Smythe (Dubuque, Iowa: W. C. Brown, 1986), pp. 45–50.

16. The authors wish to thank Margaret H. DeFleur of the College of Communication of Boston University for bringing together many of the ideas and citations used in this section.

17. John Ullmann and Steve Honeyman, eds., *The Reporter's Handbook: An Investigator's Guide to Documents and Techniques* (New York: St. Martin's, 1983), p. vii.

18. Iris Noble, *Nellie Bly: First Woman Reporter* (New York: Julian Messner, 1956).

19. See "The History of the Standard Oil Company," in Mary E. Tomkins, *Ida M. Tarbell* (New York: Twayne Publishers, 1974), pp. 59–92.

20. See Margaret D. DeFleur, *Computer-Assisted Investigative Reporting: Its Development and Methodology* (Mahwah, N.J.: Lawrence Erlbaum Associates, 1997).

21. See Margaret H. DeFleur, "Supporting the Watchdog: Aiding the Press through Computer-Assisted Investigative Reporting," in Keith R. Billingsley, Hilton Brown III, and Ed Dohanes, eds., *Computer-Assisted Analysis and Modeling on the IBM 3090* (Athens: The Baldwin Press, University of Georgia, 1992), pp. 847–63; also, David Burnham and Margaret DeFleur, *The Prosecutors: Criminal and Civil Cases Brought in Federal Court by the Offices of Eleven U.S. Attorneys from 1980 to 1987* (Syracuse, N.Y.: Transactional Records Access Clearinghouse, October 21, 1989).

22. The original study was: Maxwell E. McCombs and Donald Shaw, "The Agenda-Setting Function of the Mass Media," *Public Opinion Quarterly*, 1972, pp. 176–87. The agenda-setting theory in the propositional form shown here was developed by

Margaret DeFleur and will appear in her book *Introduction to Mass Communication Theory: Explaining Media Processes and Effects* (forthcoming). It is used here with her permission.

23. Melvin L. DeFleur, Lucinda Davenport, Mary Cronin, and Margaret DeFleur, "Audience Recall of News Stories Presented by Newspapers, Computer, Television and Radio," *Journalism Quarterly,* vol. 69, no. 4 (Winter, 1992).

24. Leo Bogart, *Press and Public: Who Reads What, Where and Why in American Newspapers* (Hillsdale, N.J.: Erlbaum, 1981), p. 115.

25. Barry Gunter, *Poor Reception: Misunderstanding and Forgetting Broadcast News* (Hillsdale, N.J.: Erlbaum, 1987), pp. 83–109. For a summary of how people of different categories attend to the news in one state, see Pamela J. Shoemaker, "Predicting Media Uses," in Frederick Williams, ed., *Measuring the Information Society* (Newbury Park, Calif.: Sage Publications, 1988) pp. 229–42.

26. Melvin L. DeFleur and Luis Buceta Facorro, "A Cross-Cultural Experiment on How Well Audiences Remember News Stories from Newspaper, Computer, Television and Radio Sources," *Journalism Quarterly,* vol. 70, no. 3 (Autumn 1993), pp. 585–601.

27. Barry Gunter, "News Sources and News Awareness: A British Survey," *Journal of Broadcasting and Electronic Media,* vol. 29, no. 4 (1985), pp. 339–406.

28. J. P. Robinson, "World Affairs Information and Mass Media Exposure," *Journalism Quarterly,* vol. 44 (1967), pp. 23–40.

29. John P. Robinson and Mark R. Levy, *The Main Source: Learning from Television News* (Beverly Hills, Calif.: Sage, 1986) pp. 81–83.

## Chapter 10  Popular Culture

1. Asa Briggs and Daniel Snowman, *Fins de Siècle: How Centuries End, 1400–2000* (New Haven: Yale University Press, 1997).

2. Richard Maltby, *Passing Parade: A History of Popular Culture in the Twentieth Century* (New York: Oxford, 1989), p. 8.

3. Maltby, *Passing Parade,* p. 8.

4. William Morris, *Morris Dictionary of Word and Phrase Origins* (New York: Harper and Row, 1977), p. 101.

5. Ray B. Browne, "Popular Culture: Notes toward a Definition," in Ray B. Browne and David Madden, eds., *The Popular Culture Explosion* (Dubuque, Iowa: William C. Brown, 1973), p. 207.

6. David Madden, "Why Study Popular Culture," in Ray B. Browne and David Madden, eds., *The Popular Culture Explosion* (Dubuque, Iowa: William C. Brown, 1973), p. 4.

7. Asa Briggs, *Victorian Things* (Chicago: University of Chicago Press, 1988).

8. Herbert J. Gans, "Bodies as Billboards," *New York,* November 11, 1985, p. 29.

9. Bill Carter, "Amy Fisher Story, A Surprise Smash in Three TV Movies," *New York Times,* January 5, 1993, p. C11.

10. Carter, "Amy Fisher Story," p. C18. Also see "Joey, Mary Jo Rip 'Donahue,'" *Newsday,* January 6, 1993, p. 1. For a useful discussion of sensationalization and its origins, see John D. Stevens, *Sensationalisms in the New York Press* (New York: Columbia University Press, 1990).

11. Hidetoshi Kato, *Essays in Comparative Popular Culture, Coffee, Comics and Communication,* no. 13 (Honolulu, Hawaii: Papers of the East-West Communication Institute, 1976).

12. See Michael R. Real, "The Significance of Mass-Mediated Culture," in Michael R. Real, *Mass-Mediated Culture* (Englewood Cliffs, N.J.: Prentice-Hall, 1977).

13. Tad Friend, "The Case for Middlebrow," *The New Republic,* March 2, 1992, p. 24.

14. The word "culture" is being used here in an aesthetic sense rather than in the way anthropologists and sociologists use it (and as it is used elsewhere in this book). The reason is that in the literature on popular culture, the term is used consistently to refer to art, music, drama, and other aesthetic products.

15. Michael Real, *Mass-Mediated Culture* (Englewood Cliffs, N.J.: Prentice-Hall, 1977), pp. 6–7.

16. Dwight MacDonald, "The Theory of Mass Culture," *Diogenes,* Summer 1953, p. 2

17. Clement Greenberg, "Avant Garde and Kitsch," *Partisan Review* (Fall, 1939), p. 23.

18. MacDonald, "The Theory of Mass Culture," p. 14.

19. This theory was developed in this form by Melvin L. DeFleur and Everette E. Dennis for their text *Understanding Mass Communication,* 5th ed. (Boston: Houghton Mifflin, 1994).

20. Leo Lowenthal, "Biographies in Popular Magazines," in Paul F. Lazarsfeld and Frank N. Stanton, *Radio Research, 1942–1943* (New York: Duell, Sloan and Pearce, 1944), pp. 507–548.

21. Paul F. Lazarsfeld and Robert K. Merton, "Mass Communication, Popular Taste, and Organized

Social Action," in Wilbur Schramm, ed., *Mass Communications* (Urbana: University of Illinois Press, 1974), pp. 69–94.

22. Herbert J. Gans, *Popular Culture and High Culture* (New York: Harper Collins/Basic Books, 1974), pp. 69–102.

23. W. H. Thomas, ed., *The Road to Syndication* (New York: Fleet, 1967), p. 12.

24. David Astor, "A Features Controversy Erupts in Dallas," *Editor and Publisher*, August 12, 1989, pp. 42–43. See also "A High Priced Feature Switch in Dallas," *Editor and Publisher*, September 23, 1989, p. 34.

25. Milt Rockmore, "Do Syndicates Exert Undue Influence?" *Editor and Publisher*, February 3, 1990, p. 18.

26. Rockmore, "Do Syndicates Exert Undue Influence?"

27. Rockmore, "Do Syndicates Exert Undue Influence?"

## Chapter 11 Advertising

1. David M. Potter, *People of Plenty*, 2nd ed. (Chicago: University of Chicago Press, 1969), p. 167.

2. *The American Heritage Dictionary of the English Language* (Boston: Houghton Mifflin, 1970), p. 19.

3. John S. Wright et al., *Advertising*, 5th ed. (New York: McGraw-Hill, 1982), p. 6.

4. Wright et al., *Advertising*, p. 9.

5. James W. Carey, "Advertising: An Institutional Approach," in C. H. Sandage and V. Fryburger, eds., *The Role of Advertising* (Homewood, Ill: Irwin, 1960), p. 16.

6. Carey, "Advertising."

7. Potter, *People of Plenty*, p. 172.

8. Stuart Elliott, "Awarding Case Prizes to Stamp Out Boredom in Billboards," *New York Times*, September 3, 1992, p. D6.

9. Norman Douglas, *South Wind* (1917), in *Bartlett's Familiar Quotations*, 13th ed., p. 840.

10. Daniel J. Boorstin, "Advertising and American Civilization," in Yale Brozen, ed., *Advertising and Society* (New York: New York University Press, 1972), p. 12.

11. Potter, *People of Plenty*, p. 172.

12. Potter, *People of Plenty*, p. 168.

13. Wright et al., *Advertising*, pp. 161–62.

14. *Media Private Market Value Estimates*, Paul Kagan Associates, Inc., 1992.

15. Russell H. Colley, *Defining Advertising Goals for Measured Advertising Results* (New York: Association of National Manufacturers, 1961), p. 35.

16. Colley, *Defining Advertising Goals*, p. 38.

17. Wright et al., *Advertising*, p. 392.

18. Otto Kleppner, *Advertising Procedure*, 7th ed. (Englewood Cliffs, N.J.: Prentice-Hall, 1985), pp. 301–302.

19. Sources are Karen Miller, "Smoking Up a Storm," *Journalism Monographs* 136, December 1992, pp. 1–35; John A. Meyer, "Cigarette Century," *American Heritage*, December 1992, pp. 72–80. A 1996 film titled "Tell the Truth and Run," depicting the life of a muckraking radical journalist, illustrates how even his hard-hitting antismoking crusade from the 1930s forward failed to deter advertising appeals.

20. Daniel Pope, *The Making of Advertising* (New York: Basic Books, 1983), pp. 289–90. See also Kim B. Rotzoll and James E. Haefner, *Advertising in Contemporary Society* (Cincinnati: South-Western, 1986).

21. John S. Wright and John E. Mertes, *Advertising's Role in Society* (St. Paul, Minn.: West, 1974), pp. vii–viii.

22. Wright and Mertes, *Advertising's Role.*

23. John Kenneth Galbraith, "Economics and Advertising: Exercise in Denial," *Advertising Age*, November 9, 1988, p. 81.

24. For an extended discussion of research evidence on television advertising and children, see Robert M. Liebert, Joyce N. Sprafkin, and Emily S. Davidson, *The Early Window: Effects of Television on Children and Youth*, 2nd ed. (New York: Pergamon Press, 1982), pp. 142–59.

25. Joanne Lipman, "Double Standard for Kids' TV Ads," *Wall Street Journal*, June 10, 1988, section 2, p. 1. See also Jeanne Saddler, "Congress Approves Limiting TV Ads Aimed at Children," *Wall Street Journal*, October 20, 1988, section 2, p. 6.

26. Katharine E. Heinz, "Smarter Than We Think—Kids, Passivity and the Media," in E. E. Dennis and E. C. Pease, eds., *Children and the Media* (New Brunswick, N.J.: Transaction Press, 1996), p. 171–72.

27. Ellen Seiter, *Sold Separately: Parents and Children in Consumer Culture* (New Brunswick, N.J.: Rutgers University Press, 1993).

28. *Stereotyping in Advertising* (Lexington, Mass.: Heath/Lexington, 1983), p. 195.

29. "Advertising Stereotypes," *Washington Post*, December 13, 1983, section B, p. 5.

30. "Advertising Stereotypes."

31. Dottie Enrico, "The Big Ad Rush," *USA Today*, January 21, 1997, p. B1.

32. Michael Schudson, *Advertising, The Uneasy Persuasion: Its Dubious Impact on American Society* (New York: Basic Books, 1984), pp. 239–41.

**Chapter 12 Public Relations**

1. Frank Cobb, *The New Republic,* December 31, 1919, p. 44.
2. Walter Lippmann, *Public Opinion* (New York: Harcourt, Brace, 1922), p. 345.
3. Lippmann, *Public Opinion,* p. 64. See also James E. Grunig and Todd Hunt, *Managing Public Relations* (New York: Holt, 1984), Chapter 5.
4. Sources are Susan B. Trento, "Lord of the Lies, How Hill and Knowlton's Robert Gray Pulls Washington's Strings," *Washington Monthly,* September 1992, pp. 12–21; Gary Lee, "Kuwaitis Pay $5.6 Million to Publicity Firm," *Washington Post,* December 19, 1990, p. 21A; John R. MacArthur, *Second Front: Censorship and Propaganda in the Gulf War* (New York: Hill and Wang, 1992), pp. 46–58. For a general treatment of the role of the media in the Persian Gulf War, see Everette E. Dennis et al., *The Media at War: The Press and the Persian Gulf Conflict* (New York: Gannett Foundation Media Center, 1991). An important work in this field is Philip M. Taylor, *Munitions of the Mind: War Propaganda from the Ancient World to the Nuclear Age* (London: Patrick Stephens, 1990); also, Stephen Hess, *International News and Foreign Correspondents* (Washington: Brookings, 1996).
5. S.M. Cutlip, A.H. Center, and G.M. Broom, *Effective Public Relations,* 6th ed. (Englewood Cliffs, N.J.: Prentice-Hall, 1985), pp. 138–230.
6. *American Heritage Dictionary of the English Language* (Boston: Houghton Mifflin, 1970).
7. The nation was saddened when Ron Brown was killed in an airplane crash in 1996.
8. John V. Pavlik, *Public Relations: What Research Tells Us* (Beverly Hills: Sage Publications, 1987).
9. Michel Elasmar, Philip Napoli, and Melvin DeFleur, "The Effect of Political Television Advertising on Voting Intentions During the 1996 New Hampshire Primaries," paper presented at Broadcast Education Assoc., Las Vegas, 1997.

**Chapter 13 The Audience**

1. For detailed summaries of the Payne Fund research, Erie County study, Army film project, and Hovland experiments, see Shearon Lowery and Melvin L. DeFleur, *Milestones in Mass Communication Research,* 3rd ed. (White Plains, N.Y.: Long-man, 1995). The selective and limited influences theory in the propositional form shown here was developed by Margaret H. DeFleur and is reproduced here with her permission.
2. The first Homestead Act was signed by President Lincoln in 1862. In 1909, the amount of free land was increased to 320 acres. Then, in 1916, it was expanded again to 640 acres (reflecting the fact that only less desirable land remained to be awarded). By the end of the nineteenth century, over a quarter billion acres of land had been distributed under the Homestead Act.
3. U.S. Bureau of the Census, *Population Projections of the United States by Age, Sex, Race and Hispanic Origin, 1992–2050.* (Washington, D.C.: Government Printing Office, December 1992).
4. This means that if one were born in 1900, one could expect to live 47.3 years on average, providing that the death rates prevailing that year remained constant throughout one's lifetime. Of course, they do not, and the older one becomes, the greater the chance of living on for additional years. This is a reflection of the improvements in public health measures and medicine that constantly take place.
5. U.S. Bureau of the Census, *Vital Statistic Rates in the United States, 1900–1940* (Washington, D.C.: Government Printing Office, 1943).
6. John Carey, "Looking Back to the Future: How Communication Technologies Enter American Households," in John V. Pavlik and Everette E. Dennis, *Demystifying Media Technology* (Mountain View, Calif.: Mayfield, 1993), pp. 32–39.
7. David Poltrack, "The Big Three Networks," *Gannett Center Journal* (now the Media Studies Journal) (Summer 1988), p. 53. See also W. Brian Arthur, "Positive Feedbacks in the Economy," *Scientific American* (February 1990), pp. 92–99. Also see Roger Fidler, *Mediamorphosis* (Thousand Oaks, Calif.: Pine Forge Press, 1997) for discussion of factors in success and failure of new technologies.
8. Sydney Head and Christopher Sterling, *Broadcasting in America,* 5th ed. (Boston: Houghton Mifflin, 1986), p. 227.
9. For a detailed discussion of the history of broadcast audience measurement, see Hugh Malcolm Beville, Jr., *Audience Ratings: Radio, Television and Cable* (Hillsdale, N.J.: Lawrence Erlbaum Associates, 1988).
10. Head and Sterling, *Broadcasting in America,* pp. 373–403.

11. Head and Sterling, *Broadcasting*, p. 228. See, generally, Head and Sterling's excellent discussion of audience measurement, pp. 373–403.

12. Julius K. Hunter and Lynn S. Gross, *Broadcast News: The Inside Out* (St. Louis: Mosby, 1980), p. 280.

13. From a confidential report prepared by a market research firm for a large metropolitan daily newspaper.

## Chapter 14 International Media

1. Matie Molinaro, Corinne McLuhan and William Toye, eds.; *Letters of Marshall McLuhan* (Toronto: Oxford University Press, 1987), pp. 253–4.

2. Ed Turner, "Instant Decision Making in the Global Village," address at "Freedom and Responsibility in a New Media Age," Southern Methodist University, February 18, 1997.

3. Jon Vanden Heuvel and Everette E. Dennis, *The Unfolding Lotus: East Asia's Changing Media* (New York: Media Studies Center, 1993, pp. 1–3; 134–35. Also see Leonard Sussman and Kristen Guida, "Democracy, yes; Press Freedom, maybe," *Freedom Review: Freedom around the World* (New York: Freedom House, 1997).

4. Everette E. Dennis, George Gerbner, and Yassen Zassoursky, eds., *Beyond the Cold War* (Newbury Park, Calif.: Sage Publications, 1991) passim.; also see Dennis and Vanden Heuvel, *Emerging Voices, East European Media in Transition* (New York: Gannett Foundation, 1990).

5. Jeremy Tunstall, *The Media Are American: Anglo-American Media in the World* (London: Constable, 1977); also see Tunstall, "Are the Media Still American?" *Media Studies Journal*, Fall 1995, pp. 7–16.

6. Vanden Heuvel, *Unfolding Lotus*, p. 23.

7. See discussion of "Global Media Dominance," in Everette E. Dennis and John C. Merrill, *Media Debates, Issues in Mass Communication* (New York: Longman, 1991), pp. 211–222.

8. Herbert Altschull, *Agents of Power* (White Plains N.Y.: Longman, 1995). See also Jon Vanden Heuvel and Everette E. Dennis, *Changing Patterns, Latin America's Vital Media* (New York: Media Studies Center, 1995).

9. Altshull, *Agents of Power*. See also Vanden Heuvel and Dennis, *Changing Patterns*.

10. These five propositions were developed by Margaret H. DeFleur and will appear in her forthcoming book *Introduction to Mass Communication Theory: Explaining Media Processes and Effects*. It is used here with her permission. For an excellent summary of research related to the theory and similar propositions, see Michael Elasmar and Kathleen Sim, "Unmasking the Myopic Effect: Questioning the Adequacy of Media Imperialism Theory in Explaining the Impact of Foreign TV," paper presented at the annual meetings of the Broadcast Education Association, Las Vegas, 1997.

11. Everette E. Dennis and John C. Merrill, *Media Debates, Issues in Mass Communication*, 2nd. ed. (White Plains, N.Y.: 1996), pp. 218–27.

12. Michael Salwin and Bruce Garrison, *Latin American Journalism* (Hillsdale, N.J.: Lawrence Erlbaum Associates, 1991), and Vanden Heuvel and Dennis, *Changing Patterns*.

13. John C. Merrill, "Global Media: A Newspaper Community of Reason," *Media Studies Journal*, Fall 1990, pp. 91–102.

14. James F. Hoge, Jr., "The End of Predictability," *Media Studies Journal*, Fall 1990, pp. 1–11.

15. Mort Rosenblum, *Coups and Earthquakes: Reporting the World for America* (New York: Harper, 1979); also see Rosenblum, *Who Stole the News* (New York: Wiley, 1993) and Everette E. Dennis, "Watching the Whole World," Charles Francis Adams Lecture, Tufts University, March 5, 1992.

16. Michael Emery, "An Endangered Species, The International Newshole," *Media Studies Journal*, Fall 1989, pp. 151–64; also see the best recent study of this topic in Stephen Hess, *International News and Foreign Correspondents* (Washington: Brookings Institution, 1996).

17. John Maxwell Hamilton, *Main Street America and the Third World*, 2nd ed. (Cabin John, Md., and Washington, D.C.: Seven Locks Press, 1987).

## Chapter 15 Limited Effects

1. Gustav Le Bon, *The Crowd: A Study of the Popular Mind* (New York: The Viking Press, 1960), first published in Paris in 1895.

2. The magic bullet theory in the propositional form shown here was developed by Margaret H. DeFleur and will appear in her book *Introduction to Mass Communication Theory: Explaining Media Processes and Effects* (forthcoming). It is used here with her permission.

3. Edgar Dale, *Children's Attendance at Motion Pictures* (New York: Arno Press, 1970), p. 73; originally published in 1935.

4. Herbert Blumer, *The Movies and Conduct* (New York: MacMillan, 1933).

5. Hadley Cantril, *The Invasion from Mars: A Study in the Psychology of Panic* (Princeton, N.J.: Princeton University Press, 1940), p. 96.

6. Cantril, *The Invasion from Mars*.

7. Howard Koch, *The Panic Broadcast: Portrait of an Event* (Boston: Little, Brown, 1970).

8. The full account of the study and its findings can be found in Cantril, *The Invasion from Mars*.

9. C. J. Hovland, A. A. Lumsdaine, and F. D. Sheffield, *Experiments on Mass Communication, Vol. III of Studies of Social Psychology in World War II* (New York: John Wiley and Sons, 1965).

10. C. J. Hovland, I. L. Janis, and H. H. Kelley, *Communication and Persuasion* (New Haven, N.J.: Yale University Press, 1953).

11. Paul Lazarsfeld, Bernard Berelson, and Hazel Gaudet, *The People's Choice* (New York: Columbia University Press, 1948).

12. Joseph Klapper, *The Effects of Mass Communication* (Glencoe, Ill.: The Free Press of Glencoe, 1960), p. 5.

13. A detailed discussion of this theory and its implications can be found in Jay Blumler and Elihu Katz, eds., *The Uses and Gratifications Approach to Communications Research*, Sage Annual Review of Communication Research (Beverly Hills, Calif.: Sage Publications, 1975). The uses and gratifications theory in the propositional form shown here was developed by Margaret H. DeFleur. It will appear in her forthcoming book *Introduction to Mass Communication Theory: Explaining Media Processes and Effects* and is used here with her permission.

14. Herta Herzog, "What Do We really Know about Daytime Serial Listeners," in Paul F. Lazarsfeld and Frank N. Stanton, *Radio Research, 1942–1943* (New York: Duell, Sloan and Pierce, 1944), pp. 3–33.

15. Bernard Berelson, "What Missing the Newspaper Means," in Paul F. Lazarsfeld and Frank N. Stanton, *Communications Research, 1948–1949* (New York: Harper and Brothers, 1949), pp. 111–29.

16. Berelson, "What Missing the Newspaper Means," p. 116.

17. Katherine M. Wolfe and Margery Fiske, "Children Talk about the Comics," in Lazarsfeld and Stanton, *Communications Research*, pp. 3–50.

18. Douglas Waples, Bernard Berelson, and Franklin R. Bradshaw, *What Reading Does to People* (Chicago: University of Chicago Press, 1940).

19. Eleanor E. Maccoby, "Television: Its Impact on School Children," *Public Opinion Quarterly* (1951), pp. 421–44; also Paul I. Lyness, "The Place of Mass Media in the Lives of Boys and Girls," *Journalism Quarterly* 29 (1952), pp. 43–54.

20. Wilbur Schramm, Jack Lyle, and Edwin Parker, *Television in the Lives of Our Children* (Palo Alto, Calif.: Stanford University Press, 1961).

21. Each volume has this title with a different subtitle; the subtitles are *Media Content and Control* (Volume 1), *Television and Social Learning* (Volume 2), *Television and Adolescent Aggression* (Volume 3), *Television in Day-to-Day Life: Patterns of Use* (Volume 4), and *Television's Effects: Further Explorations* (Volume 5). The various reports were prepared by George A. Comstock, John P. Murray, and Eli A. Rubenstein. They were published by the Government Printing Office, Washington, D.C., in 1971. The summary volume, *Television and Growing Up*, appeared in 1972.

22. A. Bandura and S. A. Ross, "Transmission of Aggression through Imitation of Aggressive Models," *Journal of Abnormal and Social Psychology* 63 (1961), pp. 575–582.

23. *Television and Growing Up*, p. 11.

24. Surgeon General's Scientific Advisory Committee on Television and Social Behavior, *Television and Growing Up: The Impact of Televised Violence*. Report to the Surgeon General, United States Public Health Service (Washington D.C.: U.S. Government Printing Office, 1971), p. 11.

25. J. L. Steinfield, "TV Violence Is Harmful," *Reader's Digest*, April 1973, pp. 34–40.

26. *Television and Behavior: Ten Years of Scientific Progress and Implications for the Eighties* (Rockville, Md.: National Institute of Mental Health, 1982).

**Chapter 16　Powerful Effects**

1. This particular theory has been developed for the purposes of this text, and it does not appear by this name in the theory literature.

2. John McCormick, *Reclaiming Paradise: The Global Environmental Movement* (Bloomington: Indiana University Press, 1989), pp. 49–56. See also Star A. Muir and Thomas L. Veenerdall, eds., *Earthtalk: Communication Empowerment for Environmental Action* (Westport, Conn.: Praeger, 1996).

3. Geoffrey Norman, "The Flight of Rachel Carson," *Esquire,* December 1983, pp. 472–478.

4. Allen Schnalberg, "Politics, Participation and Pollution: The Environmental Movement," in John Walton and Donald E. Carns, eds., *Cities in Change: Studies in the Urban Condition* (Boston: Allyn and Bacon, 1977), p. 466.

5. "Environmental Reporting: Now It's an International Affair," *SIPI Scope* (New York: Scientist's Institute for Public Information, Spring 1990). Also see Craig L. LaMay and Everette E. Dennis, eds., *Media and the Environment* (Washington, D.C.: Island Press, 1991).

6. This theory was originally formulated by Melvin L. DeFleur and Everette E. Dennis. It first appeared in the fourth edition of *Understanding Mass Communication* (Boston: Houghton Mifflin, 1991), pp. 560–65. The theory in the propositional form shown here was developed by Margaret H. DeFleur and will appear in her book *Introduction to Mass Communication Theory: Explaining Media Processes and Effects* (forthcoming), and is used here with her permission.

7. Gabriel Tarde, *The Laws of Imitation,* trans. E. C. Parsons (New York: Holt, 1903).

8. Everest M. Rogers and F. Floyd Shoemaker, *Communication of Innovations: A Cross-Cultural Approach* (New York: Free Press, 1971), pp. 52–70.

9. For a discussion of the general learning theory from which modeling theory has been drawn, see Albert Bandura, *Social Learning Theory* (Englewood Cliffs, N. J.: Prentice-Hall, 1977).

10. For a discussion of social learning theory and the modeling process, see Alfred Bandura, *Aggression: A Social Learning Analysis* (Englewood Cliffs, N.J.: Prentice-Hall, 1973). Modeling theory in the propositional form shown here was developed by Margaret H. DeFleur. It will appear in her forthcoming book *Introduction to Mass Communication Theory: Explaining Media Processes and Effects* and is used here with her permission.

11. For an extended treatment of these features of social organization and how they shape behavior for the members of human groups, see "Social Organization," in Melvin L. DeFleur, et al., *Sociology: Human Society* (New York: Random House, 1984), pp. 72–104.

12. Social expectations theory originally appeared in Melvin L. DeFleur and Sandra Ball Rokeach, *Theories of Mass Communication,* 5th ed. (White Plains, N.Y.: Longman, 1989), pp. 219–26. The theory in the propositional form shown here was developed by Margaret H. DeFleur. It will appear in her forthcoming book *Introduction to Mass Communication Theory: Explaining Media Processes and Effects* and is used here with her permission.

13. For a detailed discussion of several meaning theories, see Melvin L. DeFleur and Sandra Ball Rokeach, *Theories of Mass Communication,* 5th ed. (White Plains, N.Y.: Longman, 1989), pp. 228–269.

14. For a summary of the literature on the diffusion of the news, see Melvin L. DeFleur, "The Growth and Decline of Research on the Diffusion of the News," *Communication Research,* vol. 14, no. 1, pp. 109–130.

15. This theory of the functions of media portrayals was first developed in Melvin L. DeFleur and Timothy G. Plax, "Human Communication as a Bio-Social Process," paper presented to the International Communication Association, Acapulco, Mexico, 1980.

16. Walter Lippmann, *Public Opinion* (New York: Macmillan, 1922). See Chapter 1, "The World Outside and the Pictures in Our Heads," pp. 1–19.

17. Robert M. Entman, "Blacks in the News: Television, Modern Racism and Cultural Change," paper presented at the annual conference of the International Communication Association, Chicago, 1991.

18. A theory of the influence of mass communication on our meanings and actions was first developed in Melvin L. DeFleur and Timothy G. Plax, "Human Communication as a Bio-Social Process," paper presented to the International Communication Association, Acapulco, Mexico, 1980. The theory in the propositional form shown here was developed by Margaret H. DeFleur. It will appear in her forthcoming book *Introduction to Mass Communication Theory: Explaining Media Processes and Effects* and is used here with her permission.

19. Although the study of stereotypes began many decades ago in social psychology and a large literature has accumulated concerning their nature and functions, the term "stereotype theory" in the context of a meaning theory of media effects was developed for present purposes.

20. Stereotype theory in the context of mass communication, a well-established concept in social science, was included in Melvin L. DeFleur and Everette E. Dennis, *Understanding Mass Communication,* 5th ed. (Boston: Houghton Mifflin, 1994). The theory

UNIVERSITY OF NEW HAVEN LIBRARY

in the propositional form shown here was developed by Margaret H. DeFleur. It will appear in her forthcoming book *Introduction to Mass Communication Theory: Explaining Media Processes and Effects* and is used here with her permission.

21. Michel Foucault, *Madness and Civilization* (New York: Random House, 1965), p.11.

22. See Briggitte Goldstein, "Television's Portrayals of the Mentally Ill," master's thesis, University of New Mexico, 1980. See also: Donald L. Diefenbach, "The Creation of a Reality: The Portrayal of Mental Illness and Violent Crime on Television," doctoral dissertation, Syracuse University, 1995.

## Chapter 17  Controls

1. Everette E. Dennis, "Liberal reporters, yes; liberal slant, no," *American Editor,* January/February 1997, pp. 4–10. See also speeches by Dennis entitled, "How 'Liberal' Are the Media, Anyway?" and "How 'Liberal' Are the Liberal Media?" (given at the University of Minnesota and the University of Texas in 1996). An excellent source on the politics and ideology of journalists is David Weaver and G. Cleveland Wilhoit, *The American Journalist* (Bloomington: Indiana University Press, 1996).

2. This was a complex case that was tried, reversed, and taken to the U.S. Supreme Court, which sent it back to the Minesota court. The newspaper appealed twice, but the final verdict went to Cohen. See 479 N.W.2d 387 (1992) and 481 N.W. 2d 840 (1992), Supreme Court of Minnesota.

3. John L. Hulting and Roy P. Nelson, *The Fourth Estate,* 2nd ed. (New York: Harper and Row, 1983), p. 9.

4. "Government Enjoined from Enforcing Indecency Law," in *The News Media and the Law,* Summer 1996, p. 19.

5. William S. Holdsworth, "Defamation in the Sixteenth and Seventeenth Centuries," *Law Quarterly Review* 40 (1924), pp. 302–304.

6. "The Cost of Libel: Economic and Policy Implications," conference report by The Gannett Center for Media Studies, New York, 1986.

7. David Anderson, "The Legal Model: Finding the Right Mix," in *Media Freedom and Accountability,* Everette E. Dennis, Donald M. Gillmor, and Theodore Glasser, eds. (Westport, Conn.: Greenwood Press, 1989).

8. Everette E. Dennis and Eli M. Noam, eds., *The Cost of Libel: Economic and Policy Considerations* (New York: Columbia University Press, 1989).

9. Donald M. Gillmor, *Power, Publicity, and the Abuse of Libel Law* (New York: Oxford University Press, 1992).

10. Robert W. Chandler, "Controlling Conflict: Working Proposal for Settling Disputes between Newspapers and Those Who Feel Harmed by Them," working paper from The Gannett Center for Media Studies, New York, 1989.

11. Evan Jenkins, "News Councils: The Case for . . . and Against," *Columbia Journalism Review* (March/April 1997), pp. 38–39.

12. John D. Stevens, *Wretched Excess* (New York: Columbia University Press, 1990).

13. Richard Findlater, *Comic Cuts* (London: Andre Deutsch, 1970), pp. 21–22.

14. "A Fine for Radio's Trouble Maker," *New York Times,* October 1992.

15. John C. Merrill, *The Dialectic in Journalism: Toward a Responsible Use of Press Freedom* (Baton Rouge: Louisiana State University Press, 1989). See also Everette E. Dennis and John Merrill, *Media Debates: Enduring Issues in Communication* (White Plains, N.Y.: Longman, 1990).

16. Douglas Cater, *The Fourth Branch of Government* (Boston: Houghton Mifflin, 1959), p. 119.

17. "The Media at War: The Press and the Persian Gulf Conflict," a Gannett Foundation Report, New York, 1991.

18. Nicholas Hopkinson, *War and the Media,* Wilton Park Paper 55 (London: Her Majesty's Printing Office, 1992), p. 1.

19. Howard Kurtz and Barton Gellman, "Press and Pentagon Set Reporting Rules." *International Herald Tribune,* May 23–24, 1992, p. 3.

20. James Reston, *The Artillery of the Press* (New York: Harper and Row, 1966), p. 20.

21. Frank Luther Mott, *American Journalism,* 3rd ed. (New York: Macmillan, 1962), pp. 336–338.

22. Hulting and Nelson, *Fourth Estate,* p.9.

23. "Freedoms to Read and Write and Be Informed," *Publishers Weekly,* December 13, 1971, p. 29.

24. A good example is New York's 1970 law. Essentially, it protects journalists and newscasters from charges of contempt in any proceeding brought under state law for refusing or failing to disclose the sources of information obtained while gathering news for publication. See *Editor and Publisher,* May 6, 1972, p. 32.

25. J. Herbert Altschull, *From Milton to McLuhan: Ideas and American Journalism* (White Plains N.Y.: Longman, 1989).

26. Anthony Lewis, "Life Isn't So Simple as the Press Would Have It," *ASNE Bulletin*. September 1983, p. 34.
27. David A. Anderson, "Media Success in the Supreme Court," working paper from The Gannett Center for Media Studies, New York, 1987.
28. *Television and Growing Up: The Impact of Televised Violence* (Washington, D.C.: United States Department of Health, Education and Welfare, December 31, 1971).
29. Fred Powledge, *The Engineering of Restraint* (Washington, D.C.: Public Affairs Press, 1971), p. 46.
30. Tony Mauro, "Reagan Imposes Ironclad Grip on Words by Government Employees," in 1983–1984 Freedom of Information Report (Chicago: Society of Professional Journalists, 1984).
31. "The Press, the Presidency and the First Hundred Days," conference report by The Gannett Center for Media Studies, New York, 1989.
32. R. H. Coase, "Economics of Broadcasting and Government," *American Economic Review, Papers and Proceedings* (May 1966), p. 442.
33. *United Church of Christ v. the Federal Communications Commission*, 349 F.2d 994 (D.C. Cir. 1966).
34. Newton H. Minow, "How Vast the Wasteland Now?" Gannett Foundation Media Center public lecture, New York, May 1991.

## Chapter 18 Ethics

1. Lawrence K. Grossman, "To Err Is Human, to *Admit* It Divine," *Columbia Journalism Review* (March/April 1997), p. 16.
2. Everette E. Dennis, Donald M. Gillmor, and Theodore Glasser, eds., *Media Freedom and Accountability* (Westport, Conn.: Greenwood, 1990).
3. "Dear Reader—Facts Must Not Give Way Even When Fiction Is 'Clearer Than Truth,'" *The Post Standard*, Syracuse, New York, March 4, 1992, p. A6.
4. Paul K. Lester, ed., *Images that Injure: Pictorial Stereotypes in the Media* (Westport, Conn.: Praeger, 1996).
5. Richard Bernstein, *Dictatorship of Virtue: Multiculturalism and the Battle for America's Future* (New York: Knopf, 1994).
6. Edmund B. Lambeth, *Committed Journalism: An Ethic for the Profession* (Bloomington: Indiana University Press, 1986).
7. Philip Meyer, *Ethical Journalism* (White Plains, N.Y.: Longman, 1987).
8. Burton Benjamin, *Fair Play* (New York: Harper and Row, 1988).
9. Janet Malcolm's work appeared in *The New Yorker*, March 13 and March 20, 1989. It was later published as *The Journalist and the Murderer* (New York: Knopf, 1990).
10. John C. Merrill, *The Dialectic in Journalism: Toward a Responsible Use for Press Freedom* (Baton Rouge: Louisiana State University Press, 1989). Also see Merrill, *Journalism Ethics: Philosophical Foundations for News Media* (New York: St. Martin's Press, 1997).

# Glossary

**Account executive** Advertising agency executive who arranges meetings between a client's executives and the account management director and other agency personnel to discuss potential advertising objectives.

**Account management director** Advertising agency executive who is responsible for relations between the agency and a client.

**Accumulation of minimal effects theory** The view that the impact of any one message on any specific person may be minimal, but consistent, persistent, and corroborated (between media) messages result in minor changes among audiences that gradually add up over time to produce significant changes in a society or culture.

**Accuracy principle** The principle that the lower the level of fidelity between the intended meanings of the sender and the interpreted meanings of the receiver is, the less effective the act of communication will be.

**Activation** The process of getting people to do what they are predisposed to do by their social category memberships. For example, one effect of a mass media voting campaign is to persuade (activate) voters who are predisposed to support a political candidate to go to the polls and vote.

**Adoption of innovation theory** The view that the media influence social change by bringing innovations, whether borrowed or invented, to the attention of potential adopters, who often, in turn, take up and begin to use new cultural items on the basis of information that is supplied.

**Adversarial approach (in journalism)** A style of reporting that sees news as information needed by the public and that emphasizes the watchdog role of the press—even at the expense of profits. Contrast with *marketing approach.*

**Advertising** A form of controlled communication that attempts to persuade consumers, through the use of a variety of appeals and strategies, to buy or use a particular product or service. Advertising messages are often presented via mass media.

**Advertising agency** An organization that provides, for a fee, creative and research assistance and advertising strategies to clients.

**Advertising department** In a newspaper organization, the part of the staff that handles both display advertising from merchants and businesses and the classified section containing such announcements as apartments for rent, used autos, and help wanted. In a store or business, the part of the staff that produces advertising for the firm's products.

**Advocacy style** An alternative journalistic approach in which the journalist openly advocates or promotes a cause or position.

**Advocate** Media's role of taking a stand on issues and representing the people when other institutions need an independent evaluation.

**Affiliate** Local TV station that distributes network and other programming to people in a given market.

**Agenda-setting theory of the press** A set of statements showing why audiences for news come to think some stories are more important than others. This theory predicts that if a particular issue is presented prominently in terms of time and space by the press, the public will come to believe it is important.

**America Online (AOL)** One of the largest subscriber data services and Internet access points for consumers.

**Audience-assessment information** Data about readers, listeners, or viewers in terms of size, composition, interests, tastes, and purchasing power. The data are gathered by various agencies and services using such means as circulation audits, ratings, and polls.

**Audience research** A study of the audience to be reached, including the numbers of people in various demographic groups who see and respond to a medium or to advertising.

**Audiometer** Device attached to a television that records how long a television set is on and what channel the set is tuned to. Data from the device are delivered to a central computer for analysis.

**Audion** A type of vacuum tube, said to have been invented by Lee De Forest in 1906, based on a three-element circuit, allowing more sophisticated circuits and applications and the amplification of radio signals.

**Auteurs** Movie directors who have created films with a distinctive style.

**Authorized newspaper** A newspaper whose content is controlled and screened prior to publication by a governmental authority.

**Baby Bells** Regional Bell operating companies created after a court-ordered divestiture of AT&T in 1984. Opened the way for the use of phone lines for entertainment and information services to the home.

**Barter syndication** The process by which television program syndicators sell their wares to independent, non-network stations.

**Beat reporters** Journalists assigned to particular areas of societal activity, such as courts, police, schools, or centers of government.

**Blacklisting** The practice of listing people for being involved in some activity, such as being Communists, and threatening to boycott advertisers that sponsor shows or any other media from hiring those on the list.

**Block booking** Outlawed studio practice that required theater owners to take and show a set of studio films (both bad and good)—or receive none at all.

**Blues** A form of folk music, originating among poor blacks, that expressed feelings about the difficult experiences of everyday life. During the early twentieth century, blues became a form of popular music.

**Boutique agency** A small advertising agency that has more limited goals and fewer services than a full-service agency. This type of agency has a creative department and may hire other agencies or groups to provide other kinds of advertising services to clients.

**Business advertising** Special advertising directed to an industry or business, as in trade magazines and trade shows.

**Business department (newspaper)** The portion of a newspaper organization that handles such things as accounting, personnel, and building maintenance.

**Business magazines** Magazines that cover particular industries, trades, or professions and go mainly to people in those fields.

**CAIR** Acronym for Computer-Assisted Investigative Reporting. The use of systematic strategies for computer analysis of the electronic records of government agencies at all levels to develop news stories about their activities.

**Change of venue** The movement of a court trial to another location under the assumption that jurors in the chosen location will not have been influenced by prejudicial pretrial publicity.

**Checkbook journalism** The practice, in violation of journalistic ethics, of paying individuals who are sources of news for interviews.

**Cinema vérité** A style of film making, most often associated with documentaries, that uses spontaneous, direct filming of events.

**Compunications** A concept originated by Anthony Oettinger of Harvard's Information Resources Policy Program that describes the merger of computers and communications.

**CompuServe** A large subscriber data service offered to personal computer users and also an Internet access point.

**Consumer magazine** Type of magazine that is readily available to the public by subscription or through direct purchase at newsstands.

**Continuing news** News events that have no clear beginning or end, but are an ongoing series of related events. For example, the disposal of nuclear waste issue provides continuing news of protests, counterprotests, court cases, and political debates.

**Control variable** Factor, condition, or situation that must be identified and measured or controlled in such a way that it does not affect the cause-and-effect sequence being studied in a research project.

**Convention** A well-established rule agreed upon by those involved.

**Convergence** The coming together of all forms of communications—text, audio, video, graphics—in one electronically based computer system.

**Conversion** The process of changing a person's beliefs from one position to another. For example, a study of an election campaign found that the mass media had limited ability to convert a person's support from one candidate or political party to another.

**Copy editor** The print media employee responsible for editing a manuscript. Some work in the newspaper industry; others edit copy for magazines and books.

**Correlation function (of mass communication)** A medium's role of interpreting society and its parts, projecting trends, and explaining news by bringing together fragmented facts.

**Creative department** The part of an advertising agency that develops ideas for an advertising campaign and designs the advertisements.

**Credibility studies** Research that probes public attitudes and concerns about the news media, such as concerns about completeness, accuracy, sensationalism, or reporters' rudeness.

**Critics** People who judge a film by artistic and theoretical criteria and try to ascertain its social importance.

**Crystal sets** Early, very basic, radio receivers that could be put together at home from simple parts.

**Cuneiform writing** A system of writing developed by the ancient Sumerians. The characters were made by jabbing a wedge-shaped stick into a pad of soft clay to form little drawings (or later) stylized symbols.

**Curve of adoption** Patterns of adoption and use of inventions introduced into society or borrowed from other societies. Typically, the accumulation of adoptions over time forms an s-shaped curve. See also *adoption of innovation theory*.

**Cyberspace** An artificial environment and communication system generated by computers and characterized by interactivity. The term was first introduced in William Gibson's futuristic novel, *Neuromancer*.

**Daguerreotype** The first practical form of photographs that came into wide use. Produced first by Louis Daguerre in 1839, the process imprinted an image on a polished copper plate coated in silver iodide. The pictures were clear and sharp but no copies could be made as there was no negative.

**Damage control** Diverting public attention from (or explaining away) a difficult or embarrassing situation after its occurrence.

**DBS** Direct broadcast satellite. A system that communicates signals transmitted to a satellite to be sent back to earth stations or dishes bringing television channels to the home without wires or rebroadcasting on the ground.

**Delayed feedback** Reverse communication that has a time lag, such as letters to the editor or phone calls to a studio following a broadcast.

**Demographic characteristics and trends** Characteristics of the population such as age, gender, income, education, race and ethnicity, family composition and place of residence, and the changes in relative percentages of individuals identifiable by certain characteristics.

**Desktop publishing** The use of small computers for electronic composition and editing of documents such as newsletters, magazines, and other media. It makes use of special software that allows for integration of text, photos and other visual material.

**Detailed coverage and analytic function** Newspaper's function to provide detailed information about news events, such as relevant background details, explanations of related events, and analyses of their importance and implications.

**Developing news** News events that occur in stages, like the acts of a play, and that are covered by a series of news stories. Developing news will eventually come to an end and no longer be newsworthy. An example is a series on a crime. The stages might be the arrest of a suspect, that person's arraignment, the trial, and sentencing.

**Diffusion** The increasing use of an innovation in a society as larger and larger numbers of members adopt the item.

**Diffusion of the news** The transmission of news through word-of-mouth networks.

**Digest** A collection of excerpts from other publications.

**Digital** A system for transmitting, receiving, or recording electronic information as a series of bits, which can be thought of as ones and zeros.

**Direct broadcast satellite** A technology that uses a small disk, about the size of a large dinner plate, to receive transmissions directly from networks via a satellite transmission, rather than from local stations.

**Direct mail** Advertising medium using letters, brochures, electronic mail, automatic telephone messages, and fax and video appeals.

**Dual identity of newspapers** The two, sometimes conflicting, functions of a newspaper: (1) to serve as a quasi-public institution charged with being the watchdog of the public interest and often an antagonist of government or other powerful forces, and (2) to make a profit while functioning as a member of the business community.

**Editor-in-chief (editor, executive editor)** The head of the editorial department of a newspaper, who is responsible for all the paper's content, except advertising.

**Editorial operations** The portion of the newspaper business that includes those who acquire and process the information going into the paper's news stories and other editorial (nonadvertising) content.

**Editorial page editor (associate editor)** The newspaper employee responsible for the editorial page and the "op ed" page; reports directly to the editor-in chief.

**Electronic advertising** Advertising displayed in online services used by personal computer owners.

**Elite art** Artistic products that are technically and thematically complex, highly individualistic, and inventive. These products represent high culture.

**E-mail** Electronic messages sent via computer from one person to one or more others. The messages are stored at the receiving end until the receiving person calls them onto the screen.

**Encode (encoding)** To formulate and produce intended meanings in media messages by the use of words, visual images, sounds, and other means.

**Entertainment function** Providing diversion to an audience as opposed to explanation or interpretation. For example, newspapers amuse and gratify readers with human interest stories and such content as crossword puzzles, recipes, gardening hints, sports scores, and advice.

**Establishment** The process by which new words and new meanings become part of the language system through audience exposure to media portrayals of the meanings of words.

**Ethnic press** Both foreign-language papers and papers written in English but aimed at a particular national, racial, cultural, or ethnic group. Such newspapers have a long history among immigrants to the United States.

**Executive order** An order issued by the President that does not have to be approved by Congress. For example, President Reagan issued a series of such orders intended to prevent leaks of information by government employees.

**Extension** The expansion of meanings that are attached to familiar symbols, which can occur as an outcome of media portrayals. For example, the word "crack" used to mean "a physical defect in a surface," but now it also refers to a dangerous drug.

**External communication** Communication via the mass media to an audience or to particular segments of the population outside an organization.

**Feature syndicates** Commercial groups that contract with publishers to provide a great many of the features used in today's newspapers, such as national and international news, editorial cartoons, comic strips, columns, and crossword puzzles. Syndication is common in broadcasting as well.

**Feedback** A reverse communication by the receiver back to the sender that indicates to the sender whether the message is getting through or needs to be modified for clarification.

**Feedback principle** The principle that if adequate feedback (reverse communication) is provided by the receiver, fidelity will be increased.

**Folk art** Artistic products and styles developed spontaneously as part of the traditions of ordinary people; these products are unsophisticated, localized, and natural.

**Format** Organization or sequence in which facts are presented in a news story or other type of media message.

**Full-service agency** An advertising agency that performs virtually every aspect of the advertising process for its clients—including planning and researching advertising, creating advertising and contacting the appropriate media to present the advertising, and coordinating the work of salespeople, distributors, and retailers.

**Gatekeepers** Those who select which news items, music, or other content for a medium will be presented to the public.

**Gatekeeping** Process of selection of items for release in a medium (such as newspapers and television news broadcasts).

**General American culture** The overall pattern of living in the United States that has resulted from the mixing of diverse ethnic groups in ways that reduce their differences.

**General assignment reporters** Journalists who cover a wide range of news as it happens, regardless of the topic.

**Genre** A category of films with the same basic story type, including typical characters, settings, and plots. Examples include the gangster film, war film, musical, and Western genres.

**Group norms** Generalized rules that all members of a particular group are expected to follow.

**Hard news** News about events that occur at a particular point in time and must be reported in a timely manner, so as not to diminish their value. Examples include murders, robberies, and disasters. Contrast with *soft news.*

**HDTV** High-definition television. A broadcasting and receiving system that provides for a much sharper image and wider picture than that of standard contemporary television sets.

**High culture taste public** Those who like the products of serious writers, artists, and composers and value innovation and experimentation with form, substance, method, overt content, and covert symbolism.

**HUT** Households using television. The number of households in an area with the television on, divided by the total number of televisions, multiplied by 100.

**Identification** (in modeling theory) Circumstance in which an observer approves of the portrayal of behavior and either wants to be like the model or believes that he or she is already like the model.

**Ideographic writing (pictographic writing)** A form of writing that uses simple graphic representations.

**Information superhighway** A global information network that theoretically allows all people everywhere to be connected to everyone else. Based on cyberspace, E-mail technologies, the Internet, and cable television.

**Institutional advertising** Advertising that focuses on the corporation rather than on a specific product.

**Interactive media** Media in which the user has the capacity to send messages back immediately to the transmitting person or agency. Also a system in which the user can intervene with the transmitting system to control the flow of information.

**Internet** A huge computer network consisting of many thousands of smaller networks connected via high-speed telephone lines throughout the world.

**Invention** Process by which an individual or group brings together elements that already exist in the culture, putting them together into some new pattern (innovation).

**Inverted pyramid style** Format for news stories, originally developed for wire transmittal. The reporter explains who, what, where, why, and when and gives the most important elements first, then the next important, and so on.

**Investigative reporters** Journalists whose probes help the press fulfill its vital watchdog role.

**Investigative reporting** News-gathering style, begun in the nineteenth century, in which reporters probe deeply into a situation and assemble evidence to expose unusual, unethical, or illegal activities.

**Journalistic style** The way in which a particular set of facts is combined into a news story. For example, stories can be written in a sensational, objective, or advocacy style.

**Juke box** A coin-operated electronic record player that offered a variety of the latest songs and allowed patrons to see the discs being changed. By the late 1930s, the juke box was found in restaurants, drugstores, taverns, and beer halls, where it helped pump new energy into the popular music industry.

**Kinetoscope** One-viewer-only peep-show device developed by Thomas Edison to exhibit his moving pictures.

**Kitsch** Art forms that are low-quality, unsophisticated, simplistic, trivial, and in bad taste. Many media critics charge that the demands for entertainment have resulted in a constant flow of kitsch in the form of popular culture.

**Laboratory simulation** Experimental research in which small groups are exposed to various independent variables under highly controlled conditions in a laboratory-like setting. The research aims to reproduce (simulate) some real-life social process or condition.

**Law of large numbers** The view that the greater the size of an audience for a medium, the greater is the profit that the medium can make for advertisers and thus for the owners of the medium.

**Libel** The act of deliberately and maliciously publicizing untruths that tend to damage someone's reputation.

**Lifestyle research** Studies of trends in living patterns and buying behavior. These studies inform advertisers about changing attitudes and lifestyles of potential consumers at different ages.

**Linear communication model** A model of the process of communicating that divides the process into six stages: deciding what to communicate, encoding intended meanings, transmitting the message, perceiving the incoming message, decoding and interpreting the message, and influencing the receiver.

**Lobbying** Attempting to influence legislators to introduce or vote for measures favorable to the lobbyist's organization.

**Low culture taste public** Those who prefer unsophisticated art and media content with action (often violent) and slapstick-type humor.

**Lower-middle taste public** Those who prefer artistic products in which old-fashioned virtue is rewarded and that do not have complex personalities nor philosophical conflicts. The majority of the public falls into this category.

**Magazine** Originally, a storehouse of different items, usually military supplies, explosives, etc. In reference to the printed medium, a collection of writings about various topics. Magazines are published periodically, but less frequently than newspapers, and are usually manufactured in a different format with better paper and binding.

**Magic bullet theory** Theory that predicted immediate, direct, and uniform effects on everyone who received a media message. Thus, communications were seen as "magic bullets" penetrating every eye and ear in the same way. This theory is no longer considered valid by scholars, but many segments of the public still believe it to be true.

**Majuscule letters** Capital letters that we continue to use today. They were developed by the Romans and were kept in the upper case of type by early printers.

**Managing editor** The newspaper employee responsible for the day-to-day operation of the newsroom, including hiring, firing, and supervising specialized editors. The managing editor reports directly to the editor-in-chief.

**Market** The people who live in a given geographical area or city and who can be reached by a medium, such as television or radio.

**Marketing approach (to journalism)** Approach to journalism that pursues the goal of maximizing profits by selling news as a product, devoting considerable resources to audience research, and sharply limiting public service. Contrast with *adversarial approach.*

**Mass communication** An essentially linear, multistage process in which professional communicators design and use media to disseminate messages widely, rapidly, and continuously in attempts to influence large and diverse audiences in a variety of ways.

**Mass media** Devices used to accomplish mass communication. The major mass media in modern society are print (including books, magazines, and newspapers), film (motion pictures), and broadcasting (radio, television, cable, and videocassettes).

**Meaning** A sender's intended understanding of an outgoing message and a receiver's interpretation of that message. A communicator assigns meanings to symbols by searching his or her memory for a specific trace configuration of experience appropriate to the perceived symbol.

**Media** Plural of "medium." Often used as a singular term (in grammatically incorrect way) by professional communicators as a label for all systems over which their messages are delivered.

**Media department** The part of an advertising agency that selects specific media to be used for particular ads.

**Media influence** Changes in people's beliefs, attitudes, or behavior brought about by messages received from the media. These changes can range from trivial to profound.

**Media information dependency theory** An explanation of the relationship between the content of the mass media, the nature of society, and the communication behavior of audiences. It states that people in urban-industrial societies are dependent on mass communication for the information they need to make many kinds of decisions.

**Media service organizations** Specialized organizations that buy space in the media at reasonable rates and then sell the use of the space to advertising agencies. These organizations may have expertise in choosing the best times to display advertising for particular kinds of products.

**Medical model** The assumption that a problem behavior (such as alcoholism, drug addiction, or crime) is a manifestation of a "sickness" that was acquired by the individual (and can be cured by treatment), rather than a deliberate moral choice or a manifestation of other causes, such as a curse indicating possession by demons or inherited bad blood.

**Medium** (plural, *media*) Any object or device used for communicating a message by moving physical information over distance or preserving it through time. The medium links the sender to the receiver. A medium may be as simple as a carved stone or as complex as a satellite-linked television system.

**Medium of public record** Special function of newspapers to publish a legislative body's acts, resolves, advertisements, and notices.

**Memory** A function based in the central nervous system that allows humans to recover prior experience, meanings, and rules and that is essential to communication.

**Microsoft Network** A consumer-oriented data service offered by subscription in a manner similar to CompuServe and AOL.

**Migration** Population movement from one area to another.

**Minuscule letters** Non-capital, or lower-case, letters developed by the Romans and refined under the influence of Charlemagne in the eighth century.

**Modeling theory** The view that one way in which people acquire new modes of acting is by observing behavior portrayed by other people or in the mass media. Such behavior is adopted if the individual identifies with those portraying the behavior and receives positive reinforcement for trying out the behavior. Modeling theory is an application of more general social learning theory.

**MSNBC** A news and information service that connects a TV network to the Internet in order to deliver more timely and detailed content via the Internet.

**MSOs** Multi system operators. That is, cable entrepreneurs such as TCI that own more than one system.

**Muckraking** A term applied by President Theodore Roosevelt to characterize journalists whose reporting aimed at exposing the dark and seamy side of political, social, and economic conditions in the United States.

**Multimedia** Communication systems (generally computer-based) that allow for information storage and delivery of a blend of text, graphics, sound, video, and other types of messages.

**National advertising** Advertising in a medium used across the country and aimed at a national audience.

**National Information Infrastructure** A strategic plan and administrative effort to facilitate the information superhighway and provide for its infrastructure and protocols.

**New journalism** Alternative reporting format, begun in the 1960s, that used fiction-writing techniques, such as scene setting, extended dialogue, personal point of view, interior monologues (the thoughts of news sources), and composite characters, rather than actual ones.

**News** Current or fresh knowledge about an event or subject that is gathered, processed, and disseminated via a medium to a significant number of interested people.

**News distortion theory of the press** The view that the meanings constructed by news audiences often have limited correspondence to the facts of reality because news reports are often characterized by selectivity, omissions, and distortions due to limits on the press. As a result, people may behave in ways unrelated to the original events and situations.

**News editor** The newspaper employee responsible for supervising copy editors, preparing copy for insertion into the newspaper, designing pages, and deciding placement of stories.

**News hole** The portion of the newspaper that is actually devoted to the news of the day; generally about 20 percent of the paper.

**News process** A series of steps or stages by which accounts of events flow from reporters through news organizations and media to the public.

**News release** A prepared handout provided to reporters by an organization to summarize the issuer's version of some event or situation.

**News values** The criteria used by news personnel to judge the newsworthiness of a story. Criteria include potential impact of the event on the audience, timeliness, prominence of those involved, proximity of the event to the audience, bizarreness, amount of conflict, and currency (of public concern).

**Newsboys** Youngsters who bought newspapers in lots of a hundred and sold them for a profit.

**Newsmagazine** A term coined by Henry Luce and Briton Haddon when they founded *Time;* refers to a national magazine that provides weekly summaries of news and interpretation.

**Newspaper** A publication produced regularly on a mechanical printing press that provides news of general or specialized interest, is available to people of all walks of life and is readable by them, and is stable over time.

**Newsworthiness** The potential interest level of a news story.

**Nipkow disk** An early technology in the transmission of images. Developed by Paul Nipkow in 1884, the rotating disk had small holes arranged in a spiral pattern. Aiming a strong light at the disk, so that light passed through the holes, produced a very rapid scanning effect. The disk could produce electrical impulses that could be sent along a wire so as to transmit pictures.

**Objective journalism** Reporting format that generally separates fact from opinion, presents an emotionally detached view of the news, and strives for fairness and balance.

**Observational learning** The acquisition of ideas, behavior, knowledge, attitudes, or values by watching the actions of someone else. See *modeling theory.*

**Observational study** Qualitative research design, also called field research, in which an investigator lives or works with subjects or is a participant observer.

**One-reelers** Early motion pictures that lasted ten to twelve minutes and told a story; they were produced on a variety of topics ranging from prize fights to religious plays.

**Opinion leaders** People who pay particular attention to the media, thus becoming more knowledgeable about news events, and who influence others through their interpretation of the news as they pass it on.

**Option** An agreement giving a producer the right to purchase a story at a later date.

**Overgeneralizing** Extending a conclusion too broadly, such as assuming that a generalization that applies to teenagers also applies to the entire society.

**Paperback** A less expensive and smaller paperbound version of a book.

**Papyrus** A large reed that was pounded, pressed, and dried into a paper-like surface by the ancient Egyptians. The surface could be written on with brush or reed pen, and the sheets could be joined together and rolled up on a stick to produce a scroll.

**Parchment** An early writing surface made of the tanned skin of a sheep or goat.

**Partisan paper** A newspaper that consistently argues one point of view or is controlled by a political party.

**Pay per view** Mainly refers to entertainment programming such as movies and sports delivered via cable TV systems, ordered individually by customers.

**Penetration (saturation)** The number of television or radio receivers in working order in relation to the total number of households in a particular area.

**Penny press** The first mass newspapers. Originating in the early 1830s in New York, they sold for a penny in the streets, made a profit from advertising, and were oriented toward less-educated citizens. Early penny papers were often vulgar and sensational, but later ones carried basic economic and political views, financial information, and editorial comment.

**People meter** A device used to monitor people's television watching. The users press buttons to record times and stations of the shows they say they are viewing. The device consists of a small box on top of the television and a hand-held gadget; the information recorded is immediately sent to a central computer.

**Perception** The mental activity by which sensory input (from eyes, ears, touch, etc.) is classified into recognizable categories and meanings. In other words, interpreting sensory stimuli in meaningful ways. For example, when perceiving a spoken sound, humans must identify the incoming pattern of physical events as a known language symbol. Its meaning can then be established via a rapid memory search.

**Personal influence** Changes in people's beliefs, attitudes, or behavior brought about by messages received by personal, face-to-face communications.

**Persuasion function** A medium's function of altering or reinforcing the beliefs and opinions of its audience by supporting political candidates, promoting public policies, endorsing programs, and taking positions in their editorial content. As part of the persuasion function, a medium may provide favorable or unfavorable coverage of institutions, candidates, and issues.

**Persuasive appeal** A theme or meaning incorporated into a message intended to convince people to buy or use a particular product or to behave or believe in some other way desired by the sender.

**Phonogram** A graphic symbol linked to a specified sound by a convention or rule that prevails among those who speak a particular language. A good example is the letters in the alphabet.

**Pirating** The illegal copying of any mediated message, such as movies for film and videocassette distribution abroad.

**Pocket people meter** Small device, worn by an individual in an audience sample, which is used to monitor automatically what the person is listening to on radio or viewing on television, at home or elsewhere.

**Policy consultants** Public relations consultants who suggest courses of action to public and private institutions that want to develop a policy for the use of information resources.

**Popular culture** A broad term implying anything produced for wide use by the public. This includes mass-communicated messages that make limited intellectual and aesthetic demands—their content is designed to amuse and entertain media audiences, rather than to educate or uplift them. Examples include soap operas, movies, or popular music.

**Precision journalism** Reporting and writing form that makes use of some social science methods to gather and analyze quantitative information for news stories. Precision journalism may be *active*, in which reporters conduct their own surveys or research, or *reactive*, in which reporters use information (such as census data) already assembled by government agencies, universities, or private firms.

**Premium** Advertising method in which a company attempts to lure customers by offering something in exchange for a specified number of a product's labels or product codes.

**Press council** A group of responsible citizens brought together formally to monitor the press and provide feedback to the media and other mass communication agencies. The Hutchins Commission recommended that such councils be formed to ensure the media met ethical standards.

**Prior restraint** Legal restriction that allowed government to engage in censorship by examining proposed news stories before publication.

**Prodigy** A consumer information service and data network originally set up by Sears Roebuck and IBM. Offers text, graphics, and video on-line.

**Production department** The part of a newspaper organization responsible for typesetting and printing.

**Product-oriented advertising** Advertising whose content is a persuasive message about the attributes of a product.

**Profession** Currently, almost any specialized occupational group. Traditionally, a vocational pursuit based on commanding an extensive body of sophisticated knowledge which requires long periods of formal study to master. Its practitioners use the body of knowledge on behalf of the public within a set of ethical norms and monitor each other to ensure compliance with their norms.

**Program rating** The number of households receiving a program divided by total TV households in the market area, multiplied by 100.

**Pronunciation** Socially accepted ways to make the sounds of words.

**Propaganda** Communications designed to gain people's approval concerning some policy or program.

**Public accountability** Idea that a responsible corporation should make a positive contribution to local communities or the nation as a whole.

**Public figure** A legal term designating a person who is well known, such as a media personality, politician, or scientist.

**Public relations** A planned and organized communication process, conducted by communicators hired by a client, in which messages are transmitted via a variety of channels to relevant and targeted audiences in an attempt to influence the audiences' beliefs, attitudes, or even actions regarding that client, whether a person or a group.

**Public relations agency** A firm that helps clients communicate with the public and develop a positive public image.

**Public relations campaign** Organized series of carefully designed messages with specific meanings to targeted audiences. The campaign is intended to resolve a problem or provide an image change.

**Public relations department** A department within an agency, organization, or firm that acts as part of the overall management team and attempts to interpret the group to public and internal constituents and to provide channels for feedback from the public to management. The department helps the group achieve its overall goals.

**Publicity** Messages intended to expand the number of people who are aware of some policy, program, or person.

**Quasi-folk taste public** Those who like simple, unsophisticated media content and other items of popular culture. Such items often preserve elements of their ethnic culture.

**Ranking (of group members)** The relative level of authority, status, and reward of a member of a group.

**Ratings** Surveys and polling techniques used to determine the size of audiences and/or their preferences for particular types of media content.

**Readability** How easy or hard a given passage of print is to read and comprehend.

**Reinforcement** Process of strengthening tendencies, preferences, or intentions already held. For example, one effect of a mass media election campaign is to increase the commitment of voters who attended to the political messages of their favored party or candidate.

**Research department** The part of an organization, such as an advertising agency, that conducts studies or assembles information to answer questions of potential clients or customers.

**Role-taking** A sender's assessment of which symbols and nonverbal cues will work best to arouse the intended meanings in a receiver; that is, the sender evaluates how the message looks from the receiver's point of view.

**Role-taking principle** Principle that the fidelity (accuracy) will increase in communication situations in which the sender can engage in sensitive role-taking.

**Royalties** An agreed-upon small percentage of a publisher's earnings from selling books that is given to the author of the book.

**Sanctions** Rewards and punishments used by a group to prevent excessive deviation from, or to reward conformity to, its social expectations. Sanctions range in nature from mild, such as words or gestures of approval or disapproval, to significant, such as awarding of medals for outstanding performance or execution for intolerable deviation.

**Scriptoria** Commercial establishments that manufactured and sold hand-copied books following the Dark Ages.

**Scroll** A sheet of paper, papyrus, or parchment rolled up on a stick; an early, but cumbersome book.

**Sedition** Publishing or speaking so as to promote disaffection with government; inciting people to revolt against constituted authority.

**Selective and limited influences theory** The view that the effects of any particular mass-communicated message on individuals are minimal and that the messages to which people attend are influenced strongly by their individual differences, social relationships, and social categories.

**Selectivity** (in perception) The principle that what a person observes, understands, and recalls is a product of that individual's unique sets of needs, beliefs, attitudes, values, and other cognitive factors.

**Sensational journalism** Style of newswriting, characteristic of a number of major newspapers from the late 1800s to about 1920, that emphasized shocking details, bizarre events, and (sometimes) appalling transgressions of social norms.

**Sex ratio** The number of males divided by the number of females in the population times 100.

**Share** The percentage of audience presumed to be viewing the programming offered by a particular station at a particular time. It is calculated as the number of households tuned to a particular station divided by the number of households in the area with the television on, multiplied by 100.

**Shield law** A law that exempts journalists from having to reveal their sources, even to courts or the police.

These laws are opposed by some on the grounds that the courts may need such information to protect citizens from wrongdoing and to provide fair trials. Yet without such laws, many reporters fear that being compelled to reveal their sources will inhibit their ability to get confidential information.

**Shoppers** Free-distribution newspapers that contain advertisements and may have news and entertainment material, calendars of local events, and various features.

**Simultaneous feedback** Immediate reverse communication, which takes place in face-to-face or interpersonal communication.

**Situational ethics** A code of behavior that is based on the context of a specific situation. For example, reporting on a political candidate's secret sex life may be considered within "the people's right to know" and thus ethical, but reporting on a private citizen's sex life would not be ethical.

**Social categories** The organization of society into groupings of similar people defined by such factors as economic level, age, gender, education, and racial and ethnic identities.

**Social controls** See *sanctions.*

**Social expectations theory** The view that knowledge of norms, roles, ranks, and controls can be acquired through a process of incidental learning. This learning takes place through exposure to media portrayals of many aspects of social life and kinds of human groups.

**Social organization** The rules and expectations (norms, roles, ranks, and controls or sanctions) that coordinate behavior in a group and govern the activities of each of its members so that the group's goals can be accomplished.

**Social relationships** People's ties to family, friends, and acquaintances that have truly significant influences on their interpretations and actions toward the world in which they live.

**Socialization** The extended learning process in families, among friends, in school, and in the community at large by which the rules of behavior of a society, and all of the demands of its culture, are incorporated into the psychological organization of the individual participating in its social order.

**Soft news** News stories that focus on human interest situations, people or events and do not need to be reported in a timely manner. Contrast with *hard news.*

**Specialist reporters** Journalists who cover well-defined fields such as fashion, business, or science.

**Specialized consultants** Public relation specialists who work in a specific area, such as political consultants during campaigns or experts in communications in a specific field, such as health, transportation, or insurance.

**Specialized roles** Particular rules for behavior that apply to persons playing well-defined parts or positions in a group.

**Specialty advertising** Advertising using items such as pencils or calendars.

**Spin control** Interpreting or re-interpreting situations that arise in connection with a candidate or issue to reflect a more favorable image. The term "spin control" is taken from billiards, where a left or right spin can be put on a ball to make it curve one way or the other as it moves across the table.

**Spot news** News stories that are one-time events, such as a house burning down. The event has no history behind it—it does not occur in stages.

**Stabilization** The standardization of meanings. By repeatedly showing accepted meanings for symbols, the media reinforce the conventions regarding their denotative and connotative interpretations.

**Stand-up** Television newscast format in which the anchor switches to a tape of a reporter in the field who makes comments at the scene of an event.

**Stand-up with package** Television newscast format in which the anchor switches to a tape of a reporter interviewing someone at the scene of an event.

**Stars** A term originating in early motion pictures, in which movie actors and actresses were publicized by producers as important artists and personalities.

**Stereotype** A term that described the type used in early roller printing presses. Today, a set of rigidly formed ideas or generalizations, often negative, about a minority group or other category of people that is used as justification for treating all members of the group in the same way.

**Stereotype theory** The view that the mass media reinforce the dominant segment of society's existing patterns of attitudes and behavior toward minorities by perpetuating rigid and usually negative portrayals, which can have the result of keeping minorities in subordinate positions.

**Story board** A series of drawings on a panel indicating each step of a commercial or story.

**Substitution** The displacement of older meanings for a word in favor of newer ones as a result of media portrayals. For example, "gay" once meant light-hearted and jovial rather than a sexual orientation.

**Surveillance function** The news media's function of keeping track of events in society and, through the news process, giving the public reliable reports about what appears to be important.

**Symbol** A word, action, or object that stands for and arouses a standardized internal meaning in people who are members of a given language community.

**Syndicates** See *feature syndicates.*

**Syntax** Rules for ordering symbols in combination so as to make their meanings clear.

**Tabloid** A newspaper printed on paper of a special size (usually twelve by sixteen inches or five columns wide). Originally, tabloids were of low quality and had sensational or bizarre content, but today tabloids include papers that mix sensationalism with professionalism.

**Talkies** Motion picture with a full sound track, developed in the late 1920s.

**Teletext** A digital data system featuring news, information, and advertising. Originally available on the vertical blanking interval of television receivers.

**Testimonial** An advertising strategy in which a famous or beautiful person endorses or promotes a product.

**Theory** A set of propositions that, taken together, provide an explanation of how antecedent conditions or events lead to specific consequences. Theories vary in the degree to which they have been supported by factual evidence from research.

**Total fidelity** A perfect match between the meanings of communicating parties.

**Trace** Some aspect or element of experience that is stored in the brain in such a way that it can be recalled.

**Transit advertising** Advertising that is displayed on buses, subway cars, and other vehicles.

**Tuning inertia** The degree of viewer loyalty to a particular program.

**Two-step flow of communication (diffusion) theory** The view that mass communication is attended to directly by opinion leaders, who then tell others and interpret the news topics they have selected.

**Upper-middle taste public** Those who are consumers of literature, music, theater, and other art that is accepted as "good"; these people are usually well-educated and relatively affluent.

**Used-book trade** System in which college bookstores buy back textbooks from students to be resold at high profit levels to other students the following semester.

**User-oriented advertising** Advertising with content aimed at the specific needs, interests, and desires of particular groups of consumers.

**Uses and gratifications theory** The view that each individual in the media audience is active, freely choosing and selectively using message content, rather than passive and acted upon by the media. Each audience member chooses and uses media messages based on his or her own structure of interests, needs, attitudes, and values.

**Vellum** An early writing surface that resembled parchment but was made from the skin of a young calf, rather than a sheep or goat.

**Victrola** A commercial brand of early wind-up phonograph; the term became a generic name for record players.

**Video news release (VNR)** A self-serving promotion of a person or organization, presented on videotape and distributed either on videocassette or by satellite transmission. A VNR seeks to communicate a certain point of view or argue a case. Media organizations that receive VNRs from candidates or organizations may use them verbatim without comment, edit them heavily, or identify them as a statement from those appearing therein.

**Videotext** An information transmission system in which data are made available over television sets. It is sometimes interactive.

**Visual persistence (visual lag)** A process, discovered by Dr. Peter Mark Roget, that results in a series of still pictures that capture a moving object in progressively different motions being perceived as smooth motion. The viewer "sees" an image for a fraction of a second after the thing itself has changed or disappeared. When two images are presented in a row, the first image fills in the time lag between the two, so they seem to be continuous.

**Vitascope** Early motion picture projection system developed by Thomas Edison and Thomas Armat.

**VOT** Voice-over tape. Television newscast format that first shows the anchorperson but then switches to a videotape with the anchor's voice heard as the viewer sees the ongoing picture.

**Wire service** Associations formed to transmit stories to newspapers throughout the country via the telegraph line.

**Wire service editor (news service editor)** The newspaper employee responsible for selecting, editing, and coordinating the national and international news from the wire services.

**Word-meaning relationship theory of media portrayals** The view that the meanings people hold for various words are strongly influenced by their exposure to the content of mass communications. These meanings, in turn, shape people's understandings of, and actions in, situations with which they must cope in the real world.

**Word story** The simplest format for a television newscast story, in which the anchorperson tells what happened while sitting behind a desk (rather than being on the scene).

**World Wide Web** A system for delivering hypertext and multimedia files on the Internet.

**Yellow journalism** A late nineteenth-century type of newspaper publishing that placed profit above truthfulness, emphasizing sensationalism, human interest and reader appeal at the expense of public responsibility.

# Index

# Credits

*Photo:*
**1:** © Ted Soqui, Impact Visuals; **29** (also **30, 60, 97**): Courtesy of NASA; **127** (also **128, 162, 190, 217**): Reproduced from the Collections of the Library of Congress; **235** (also **236, 279, 307, 340, 371, 409**): PhotoEdit; **425** (also **426, 458, 490, 525**): Copyright © B. Daemmrich / The Image Works.

*Text:*
**50,** Table 2.1: From Datus Smith, *A Guide to Book Publishing,* Revised Edition, pp. 128–129. Used by permission. **51,** Figure 2.2: From *Communications Industry Forecast.* Used by permission of Veronis, Suhler & Associates, Communications Industry Forecast, New York, NY, Tel (212) 935-4990. **55,** Tables 2.2 and 2.3: From *Communications Industry Forecast.* Used by permission of Veronis, Suhler & Associates, Communications Industry Forecast, New York, NY, Tel (212) 935-4990. **197, 198, 202, 204,** Figures 7.1, 7.2, 7.3, 7.4: Nielsen Media Research. **284,** lyrics from "Ballad of a Thin Man" by Bob Dylan: Copyright © 1965 by Warner Bros. Music, copyright renewed 1993 by Special Rider Music. All rights reserved. International copyright secured. Reprinted by permission. **358,** definition of "lobbyist": Copyright © 1981 by Houghton Mifflin Company. Reprinted by permission from *The American Heritage Dictionary of the English Language.* **510–511,** list: From Howard Kurtz and Barton Gellman, "Press and Pentagon Set Reporting Rules," *International Herald Tribune,* May 23–24, 1992, p. 3. Copyright © 1992 The Washington Post. Reprinted with permission. **538–539,** Society of Professional Journalists Code of Ethics: Reprinted by permission of the Society of Professional Journalists.

The following theories developed by Margaret N. DeFleur, *Fundamentals of Mass Communication Theory: Processes and Effects.* Reprinted by permission of the author: **3,** Media Information Dependency; **75,** Adoption of Innovation; **156,** Creeping Cycle of Desensitization; **178, 446–447,** Uses and Gratifications; **240–241,** Two-Step Flow of Communication; **251,** Lippman's News Distortion Theory of the Press; **261,** Gatekeeping; **272** Agenda-Setting Theory of the Press; **374–375,** Selected and Limited Influences; **420,** Cultural Imperialism; **430–431,** "Magic Bullet"; **466,** Accumulation of Minimal Effects; **471,** Modeling; **475,** Social Expectations; **481,** Word-Meaning Theory of Media Portrayals; **482–483,** Stereotype.